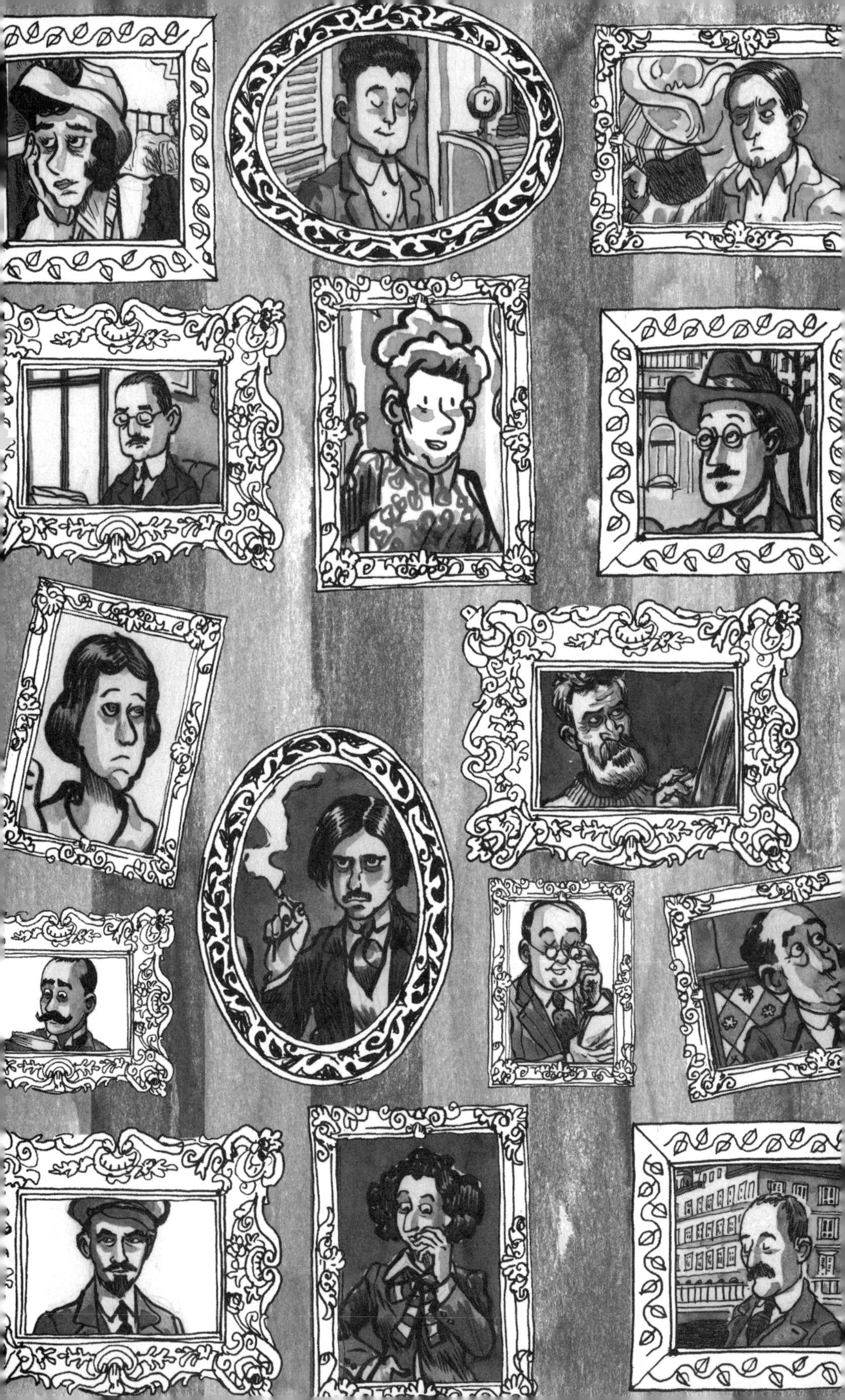

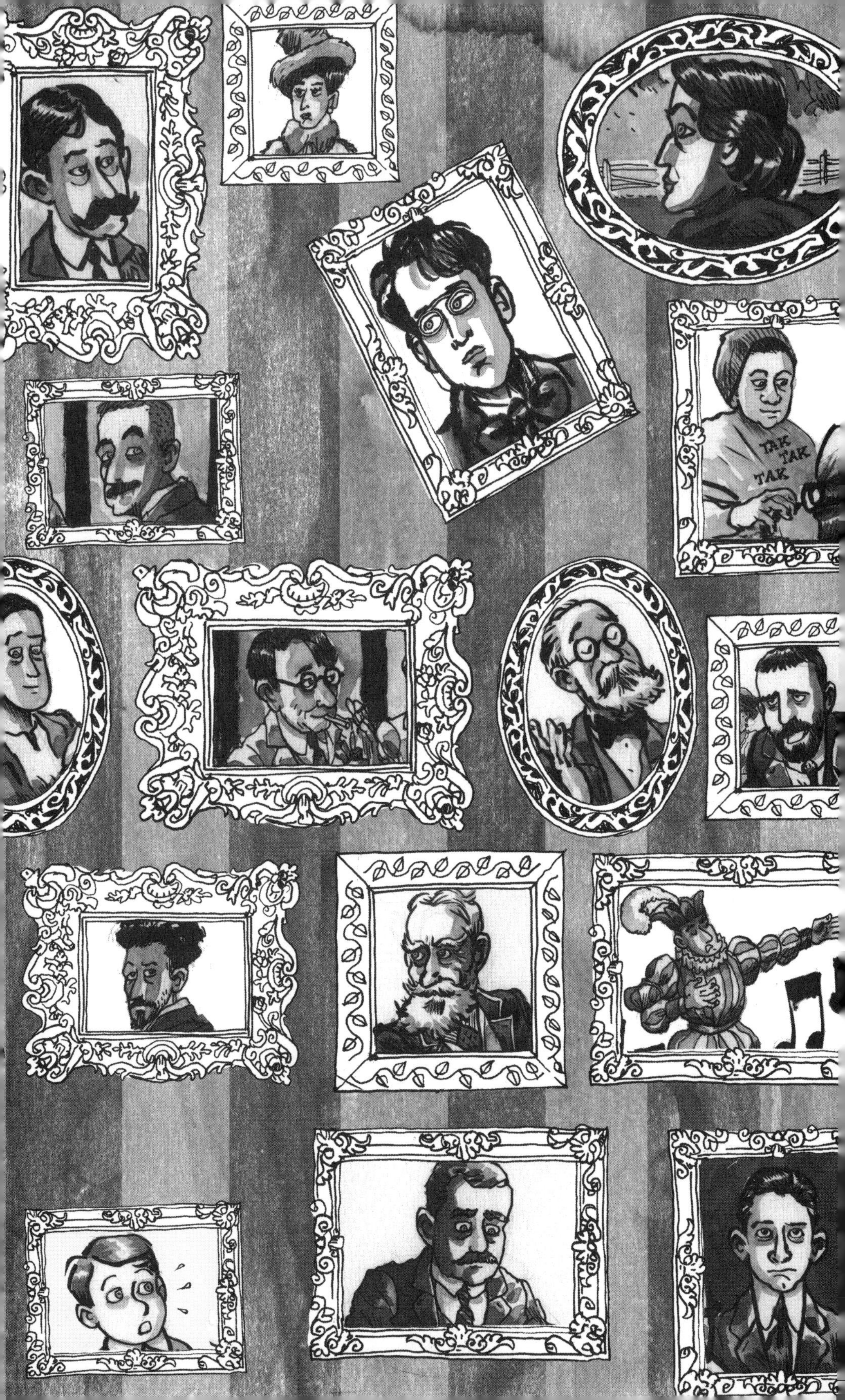
TAK
TAK
TAK

JAMES JOYCE

Portrait of a Dubliner

JAMES JOYCE

Portrait of a Dubliner

Alfonso Zapico

Arcade Publishing • New York

First North American Edition 2016

First published in 2011 in Spanish by Astiberri Ediciones as *Dubliné*
This edition first published in 2013 by The O'Brien Press Ltd., Dublin
Translation by David Prendergast

Arcade Publishing books may be purchased in bulk at special discounts for sales promotion, corporate gifts, fund-raising, or educational purposes. Special editions can also be created to specifications. For details, contact the Special Sales Department, Arcade Publishing, 307 West 36th Street, 11th Floor, New York, NY 10018 or arcade@skyhorsepublishing.com.

Arcade Publishing® is a registered trademark of Skyhorse Publishing, Inc.®, a Delaware corporation.

Visit our website at www.arcadepub.com.
Visit the author's website at www.alfonsozapico.com.

10 9 8 7 6 5 4 3 2

Library of Congress Cataloging-in-Publication Data is available on file.
LCCN number: 2016005080

Hardcover ISBN: 978-1-62872-655-8
Ebook ISBN: 978-1-62872-658-9

Printed in the United States of America

JAMES JOYCE

Portrait of a Dubliner

Chapter I

The Joyce Family

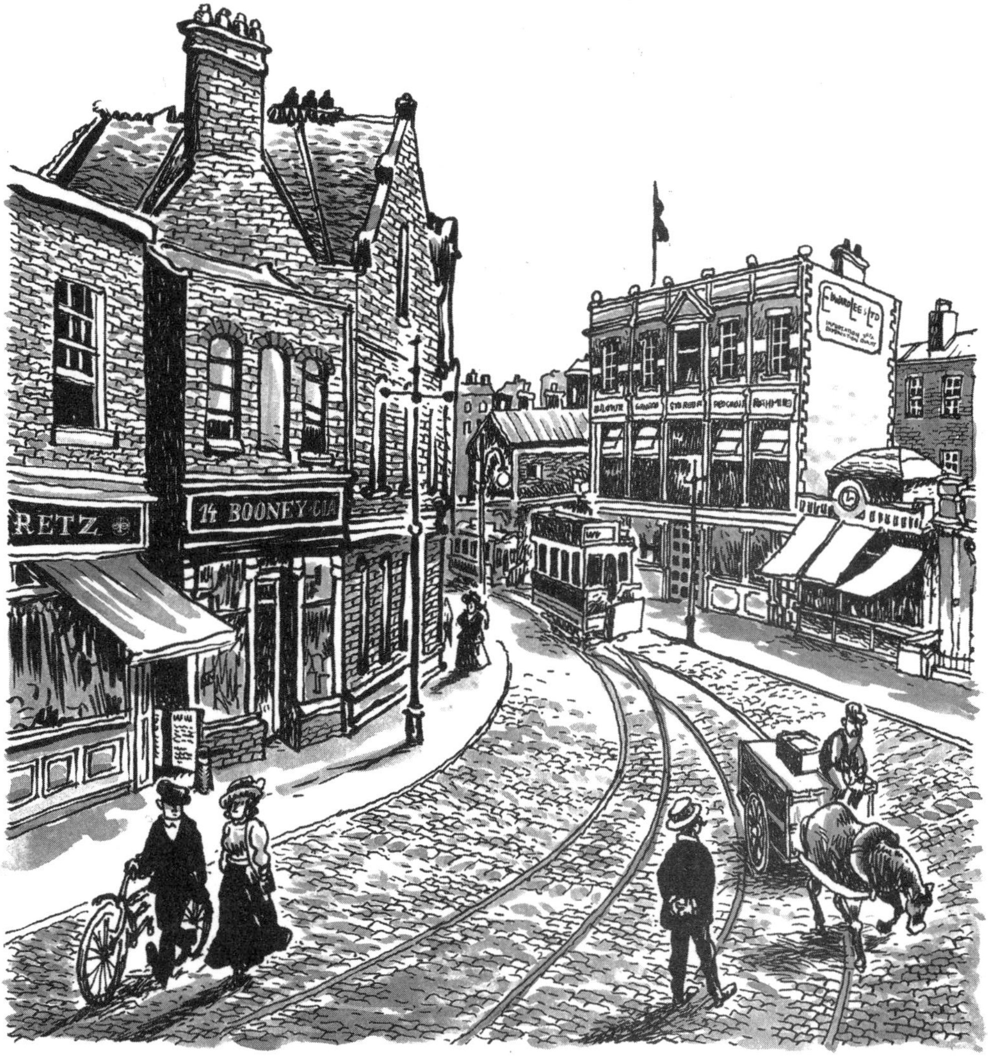
RETZ
14 BOONEY

James Joyce I

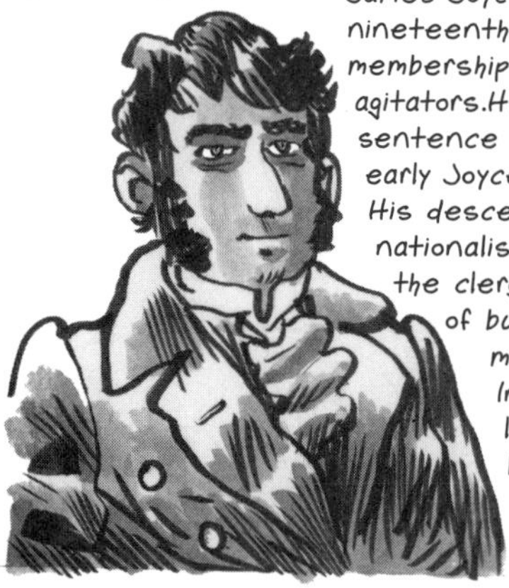

James Joyce's great grandfather was born in Cork in the early nineteenth century. His turbulent life was marked by his membership of the Whiteboys, a group of anti-landlord, Catholic agitators.He was sentenced to death for this, though the sentence was later annulled.A lucky man, this early Joyce.

His descendants inherited his passionate nationalism, along with a deep contempt for the clergy and an inability to run any kind of business. This last trait was clearly manifested by all the later Joyces.

In 1835,Joyce obtained the licence to exploit a salt and lime mine near Cork. This was a profitable, prosperous business, but by 1852 he was completely bankrupt.

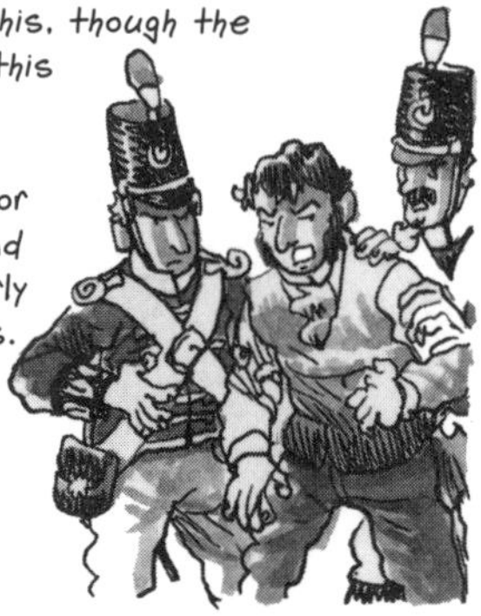

James Joyce II

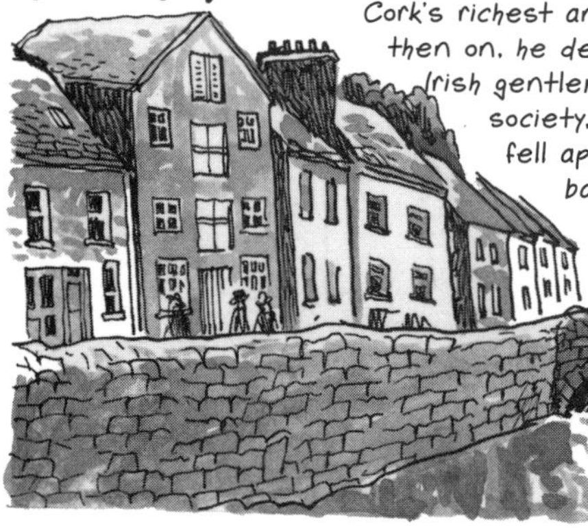

Joyce's son was a know-it-all. When he was twenty-one, he married Ellen O'Connell, from Cork's richest and most powerful family. From then on, he devoted himself to playing the Irish gentleman and hobnobbing with high society, until his business affairs fell apart and he declared himself bankrupt. His in-laws helped him to get a modest job as an inspector for Hackney Coaches, a position he held till his death in 1866.

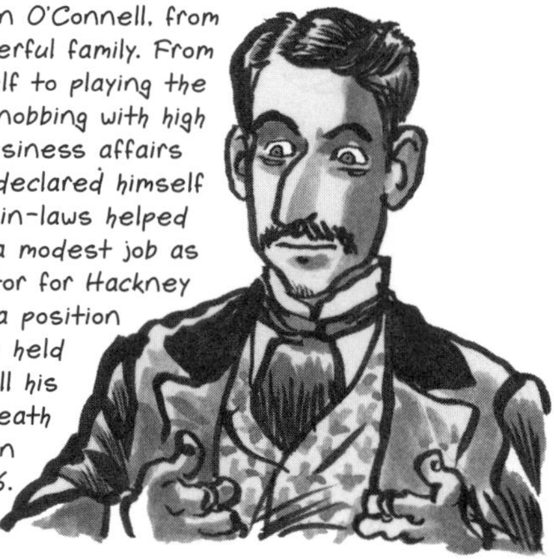

John Joyce

James' father hada complex personality, and the same kind of genius for which his son would become famous. He was a good student, a champion jumper, an excellent shot, a great cross-country runner and a marvellous singer and actor. John'shandicap was his wealth of talents, which ultimately led him to failure. His youthful recklessness forced his mother to move to Dublin, in the hope that her unusual son would settle down and find honest employment. Instead of this, John bought himself a sailing boat and spent his time sailing around Dalkey.

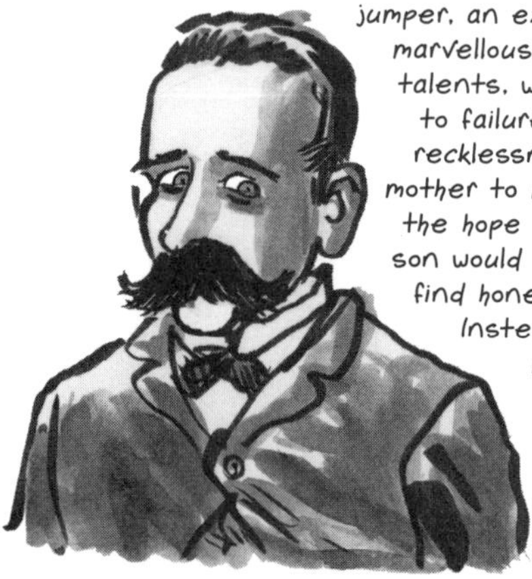

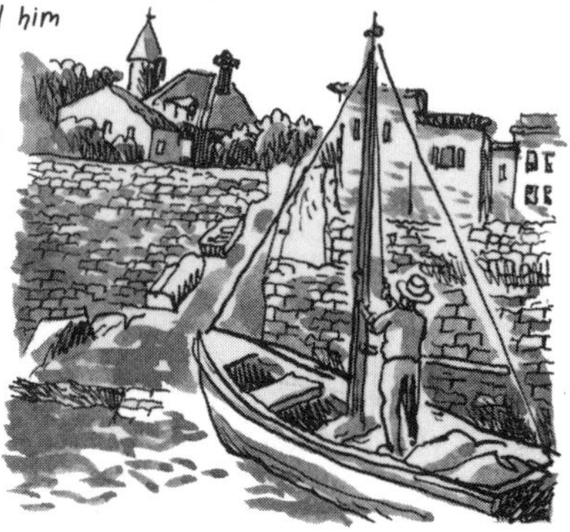

John Joyce allowed himself to be conned by a Cork man into buying a distillery with him on the outskirts of Dublin.

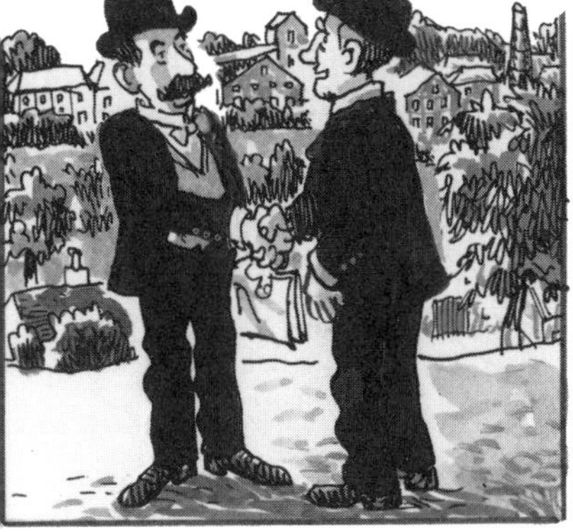

John was no genius when it came to business, and one day he discovered that his partner had swindled him out of all of their funds. The Chapelizod Distilling Company was ruined.

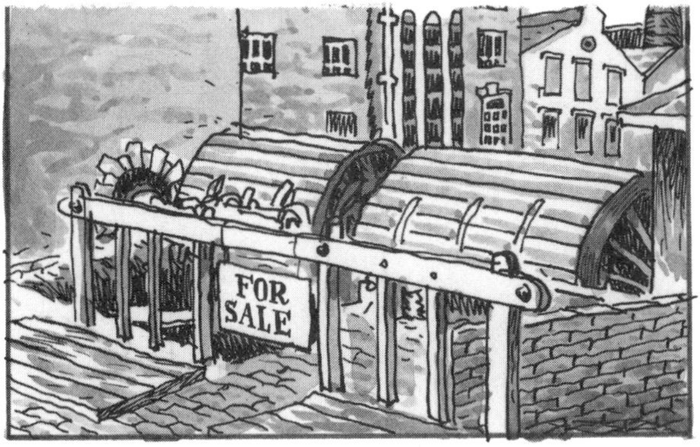
FOR SALE

But luck hadn't turned its back on the charismatic Joyce. John was a nationalist, andhe decided to devote himself to the politics of those turbulent years. In 1880 there was a general election.

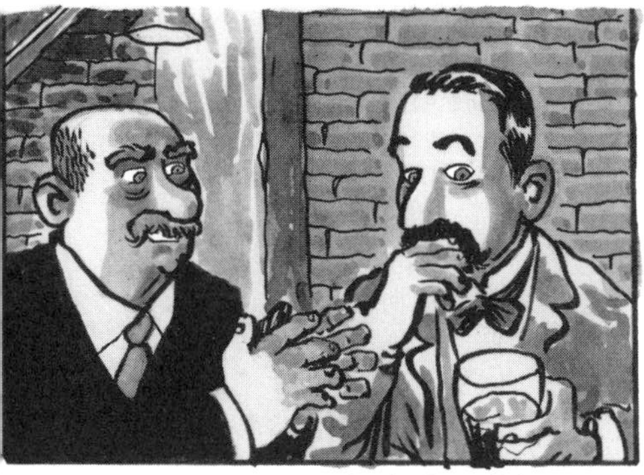

He became secretary of the United Liberal Club, and campaigned for Brooks and Lyons, the two liberal candidates for Dublin. They were running against two conservatives: Jim Sterling and Guinness, the powerful beer magnate.

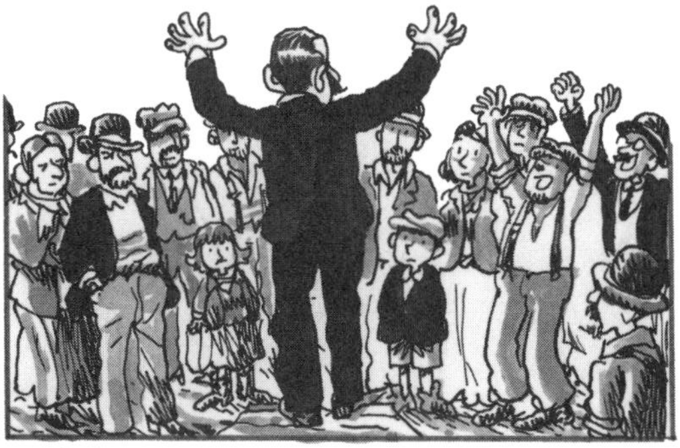

Brooks and Lyons were elected, and John was rewarded with a life-long post in the Dublin Tax Office.

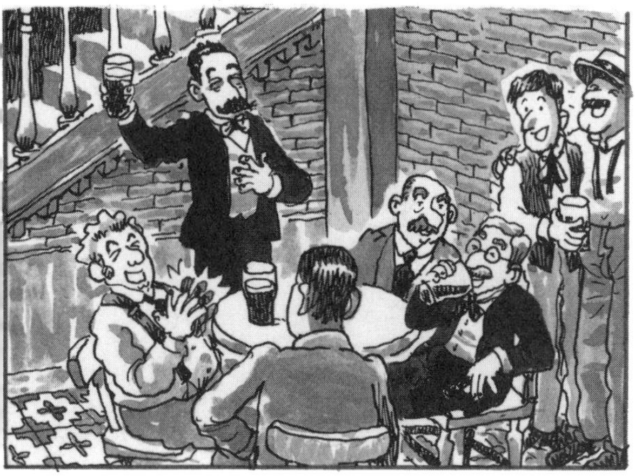

Well set up socially and financially, John Joyce was now ready for marriage. He set his eyes on a young lady who sang with him in the Rathgar Church Choir.

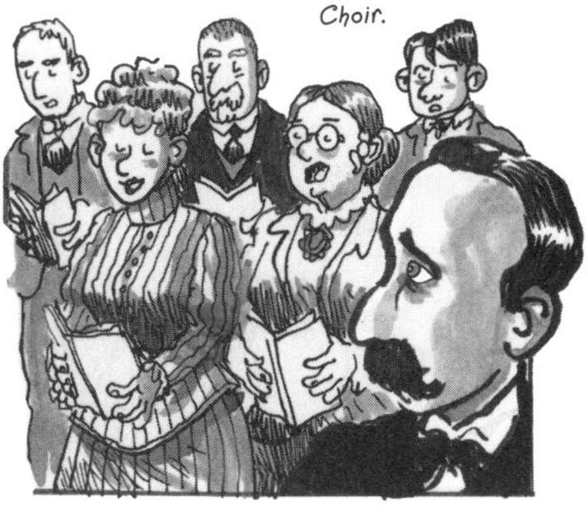

May Murray, a young lady with blonde hair and infinite patience, soon felt attracted to the cheerful young man with the refined tenor voice. They formed the kind of couple that people would say were 'made for each other'.

Of course, not everybody agreed. May's father and John's mother didn't approve of the relationship.

Stay away from my daughter, you drunkard.

'That Murray is beneath you!'

In the end the lovers did as they pleased. They were married in Rathmines Church on 5 May 1880.

John Joyce's mother never spoke to her son again.

Mr and Mrs Joyce were very happy together, even though they had no support from the Murray family. John detested his in-laws profoundly, and invented the most cruel and derogatory jokes and epithets to describe them.

He called John Murray, the patriarch, 'the old fornicator', because he had been married twice.

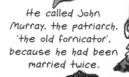

NGAAAA

May's brothers William and John became 'the highly respectable gondoliers' or, respectively, 'the little drunken pen pusher' and 'the cornet player'. An accurate description of William, an accountant with a love for the drink, and John, who led a generally unfortunate life.

Then there was May's cousin, a priest who went mad and lost his parish.

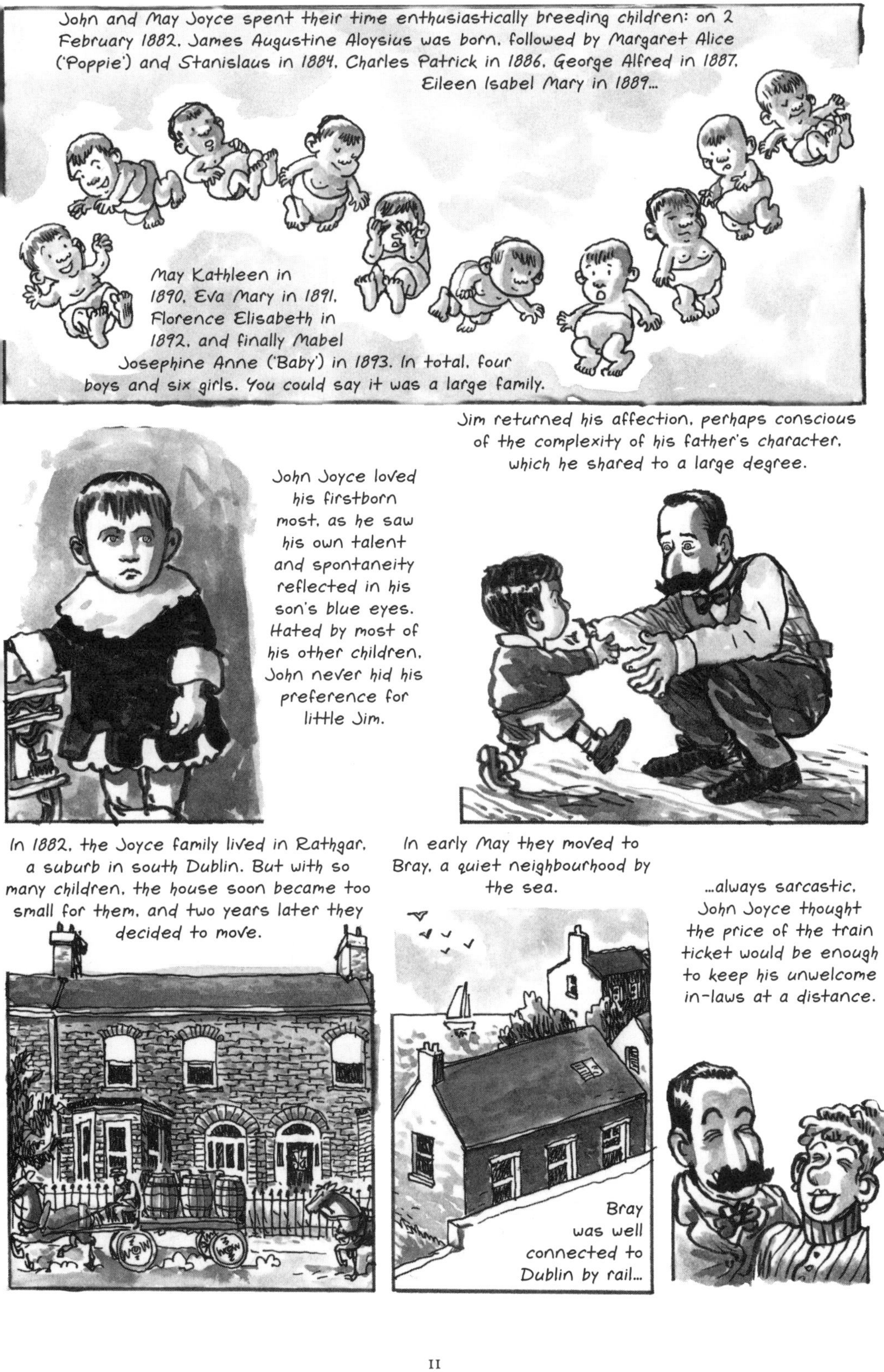
John and May Joyce spent their time enthusiastically breeding children: on 2 February 1882, James Augustine Aloysius was born, followed by Margaret Alice ('Poppie') and Stanislaus in 1884, Charles Patrick in 1886, George Alfred in 1887, Eileen Isabel Mary in 1889...
May Kathleen in 1890, Eva Mary in 1891, Florence Elisabeth in 1892, and finally Mabel Josephine Anne ('Baby') in 1893. In total, four boys and six girls. You could say it was a large family.
John Joyce loved his firstborn most, as he saw his own talent and spontaneity reflected in his son's blue eyes. Hated by most of his other children, John never hid his preference for little Jim.
Jim returned his affection, perhaps conscious of the complexity of his father's character, which he shared to a large degree.
In 1882, the Joyce family lived in Rathgar, a suburb in south Dublin. But with so many children, the house soon became too small for them, and two years later they decided to move.
In early May they moved to Bray, a quiet neighbourhood by the sea.
Bray was well connected to Dublin by rail...
...always sarcastic, John Joyce thought the price of the train ticket would be enough to keep his unwelcome in-laws at a distance.

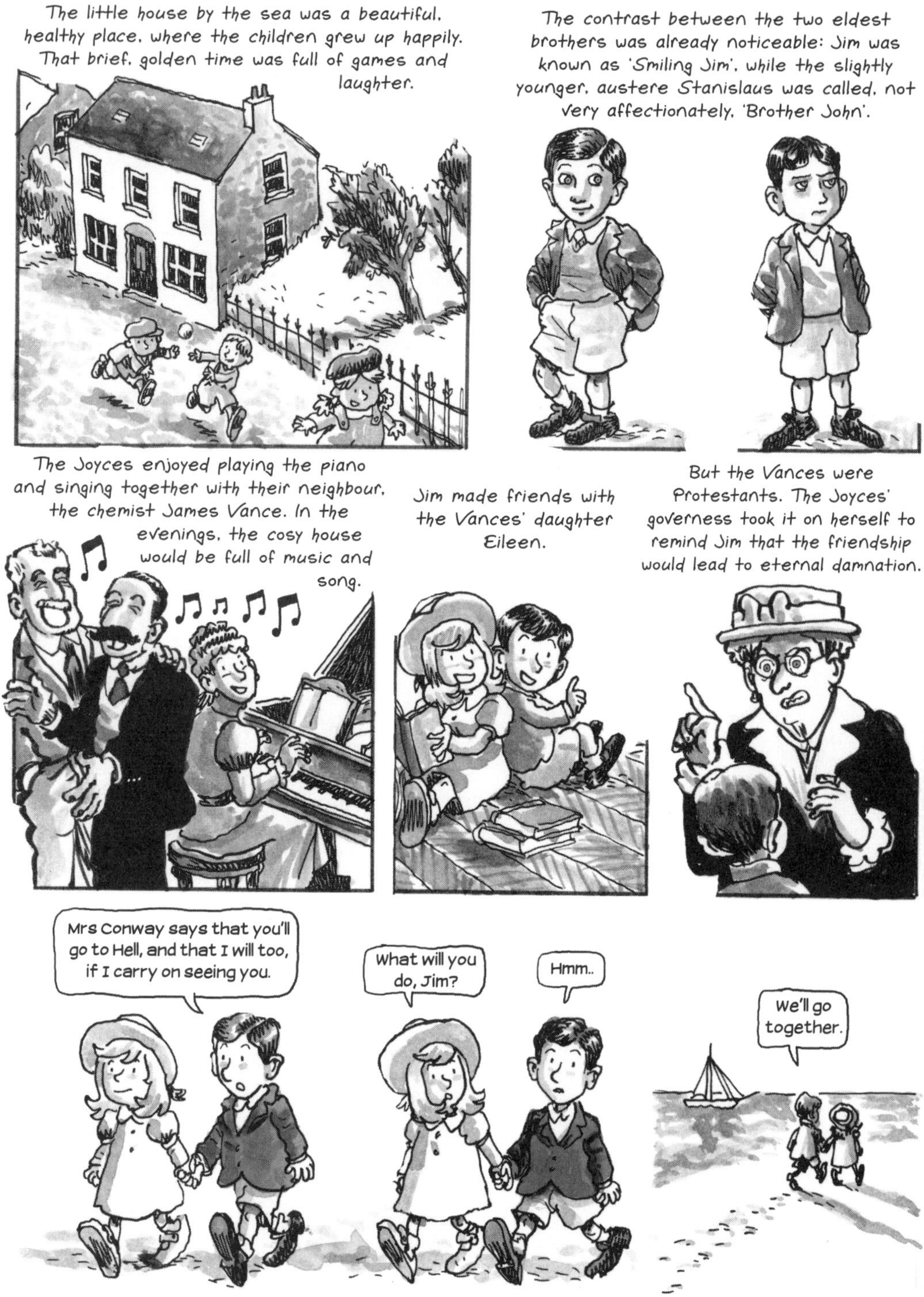
The little house by the sea was a beautiful, healthy place, where the children grew up happily. That brief, golden time was full of games and laughter.
The contrast between the two eldest brothers was already noticeable: Jim was known as 'Smiling Jim', while the slightly younger, austere Stanislaus was called, not very affectionately, 'Brother John'.
The Joyces enjoyed playing the piano and singing together with their neighbour, the chemist James Vance. In the evenings, the cosy house would be full of music and song.
Jim made friends with the Vances' daughter Eileen.
But the Vances were Protestants. The Joyces' governess took it on herself to remind Jim that the friendship would lead to eternal damnation.
Mrs Conway says that you'll go to Hell, and that I will too, if I carry on seeing you.
What will you do, Jim?
Hmm..
We'll go together.

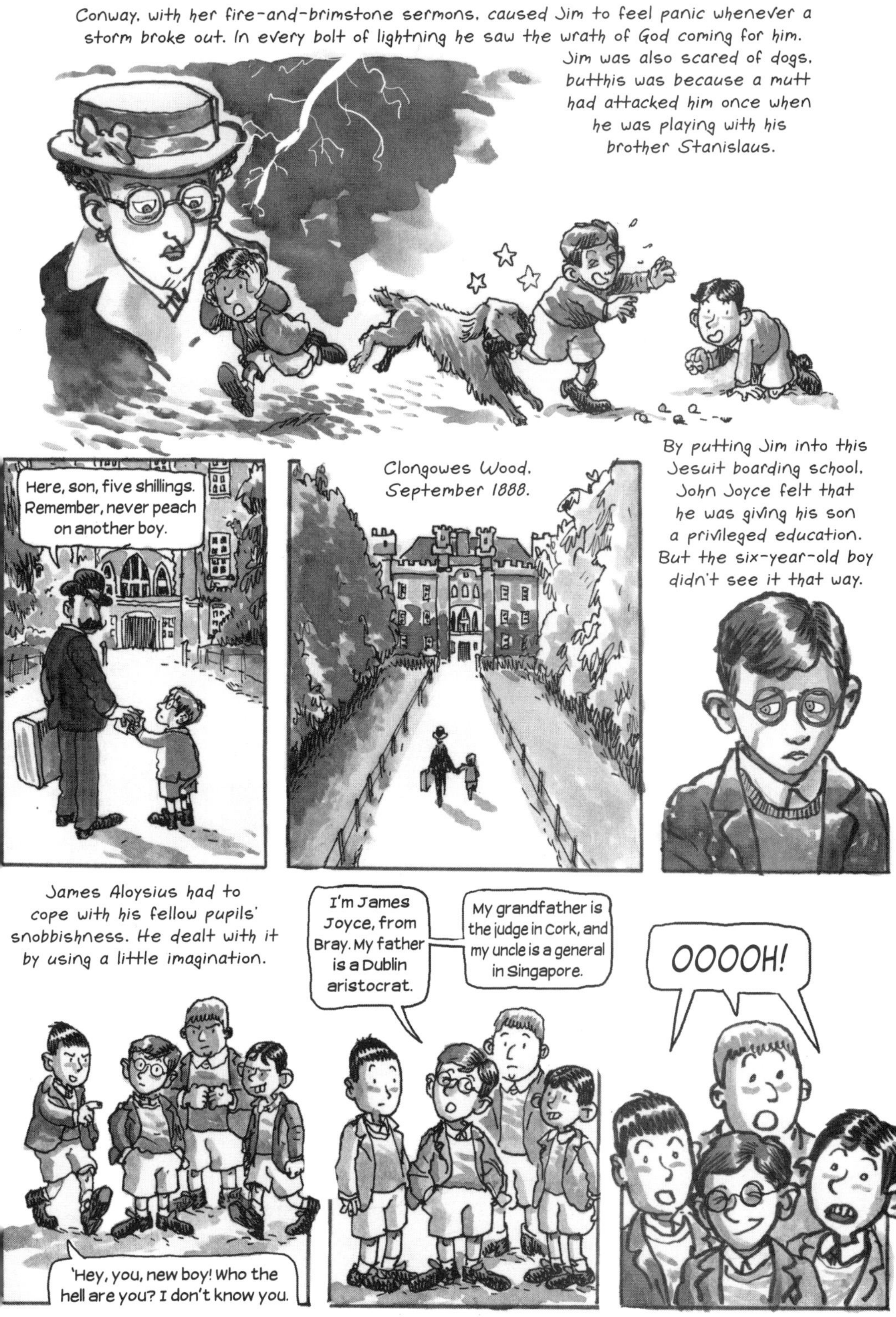
Conway, with her fire-and-brimstone sermons, caused Jim to feel panic whenever a storm broke out. In every bolt of lightning he saw the wrath of God coming for him.
Jim was also scared of dogs, butthis was because a mutt had attacked him once when he was playing with his brother Stanislaus.
Here, son, five shillings. Remember, never peach on another boy.
Clongowes Wood, September 1888.
By putting Jim into this Jesuit boarding school, John Joyce felt that he was giving his son a privileged education. But the six-year-old boy didn't see it that way.
James Aloysius had to cope with his fellow pupils' snobbishness. He dealt with it by using a little imagination.
'Hey, you, new boy! Who the hell are you? I don't know you.
I'm James Joyce, from Bray. My father is a Dublin aristocrat.
My grandfather is the judge in Cork, and my uncle is a general in Singapore.
OOOOH!

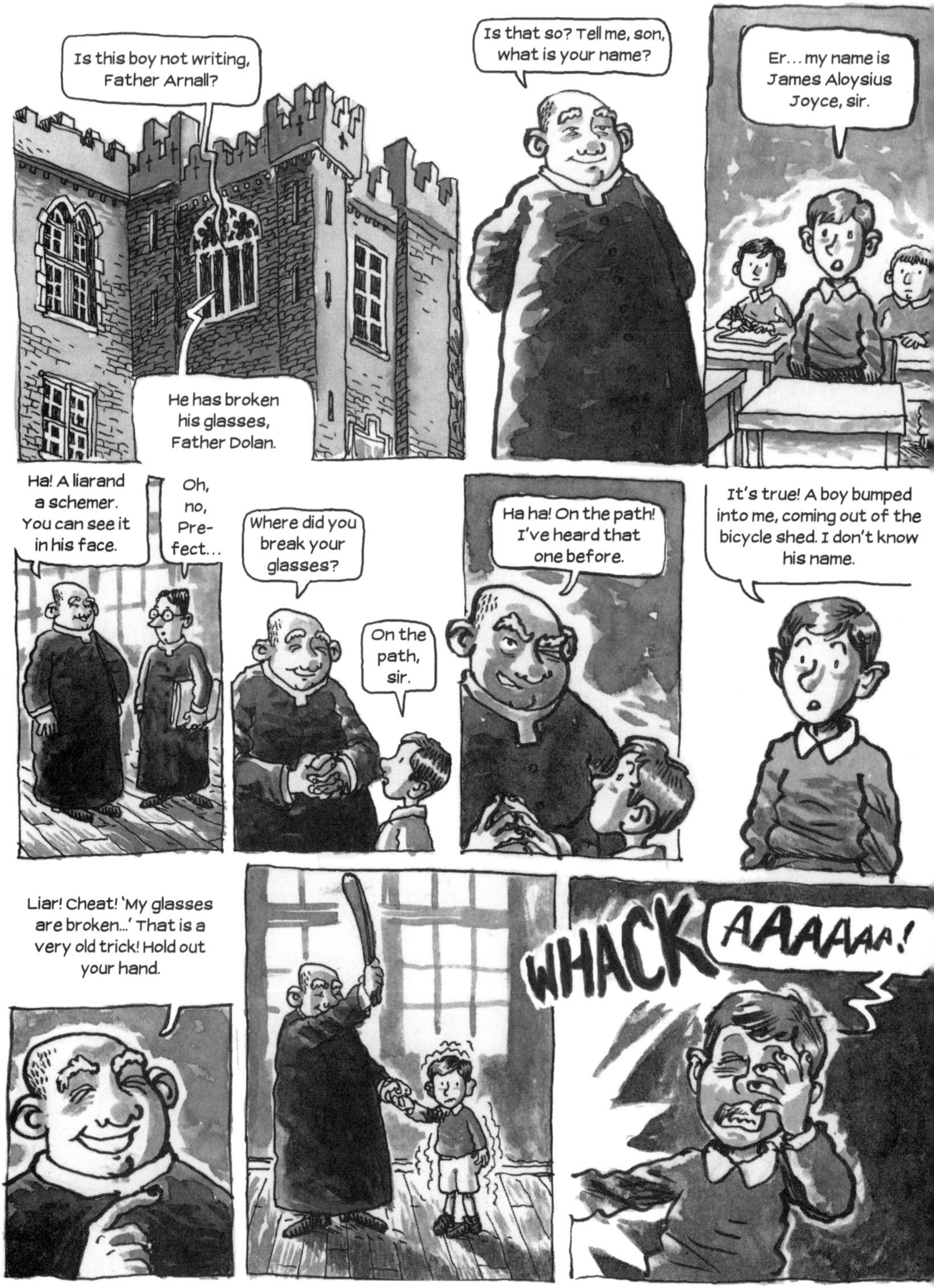
Is this boy not writing, Father Arnall?
He has broken his glasses, Father Dolan.
Is that so? Tell me, son, what is your name?
Er... my name is James Aloysius Joyce, sir.
Ha! A liar and a schemer. You can see it in his face.
Oh, no, Pre- fect...
Where did you break your glasses?
On the path, sir.
Ha ha! On the path! I've heard that one before.
It's true! A boy bumped into me, coming out of the bicycle shed. I don't know his name.
Liar! Cheat! 'My glasses are broken...' That is a very old trick! Hold out your hand.
WHACK
AAAAAA!

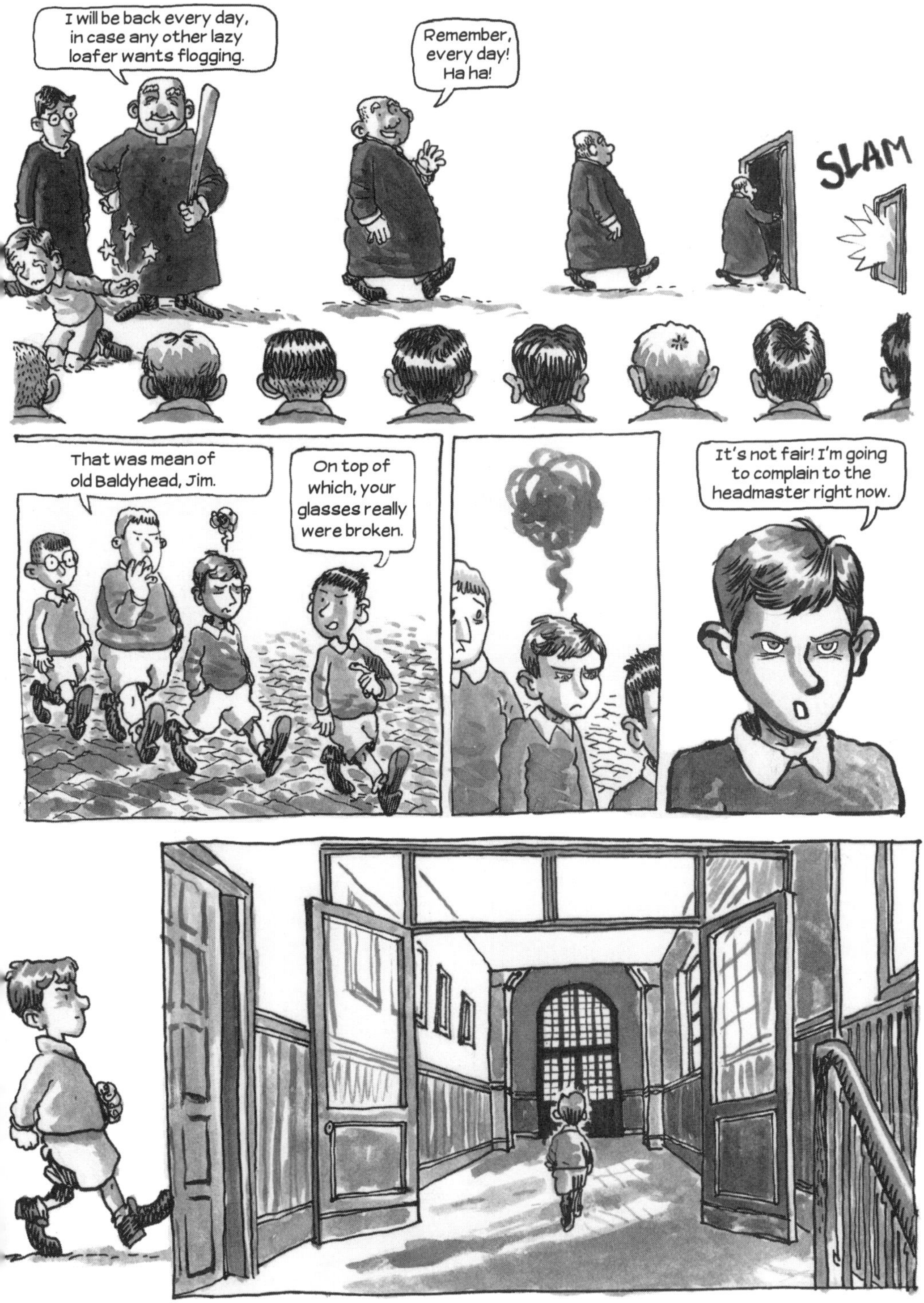
I will be back every day, in case any other lazy loafer wants flogging.
Remember, every day! Ha ha!
SLAM
That was mean of old Baldyhead, Jim.
On top of which, your glasses really were broken.
It's not fair! I'm going to complain to the headmaster right now.

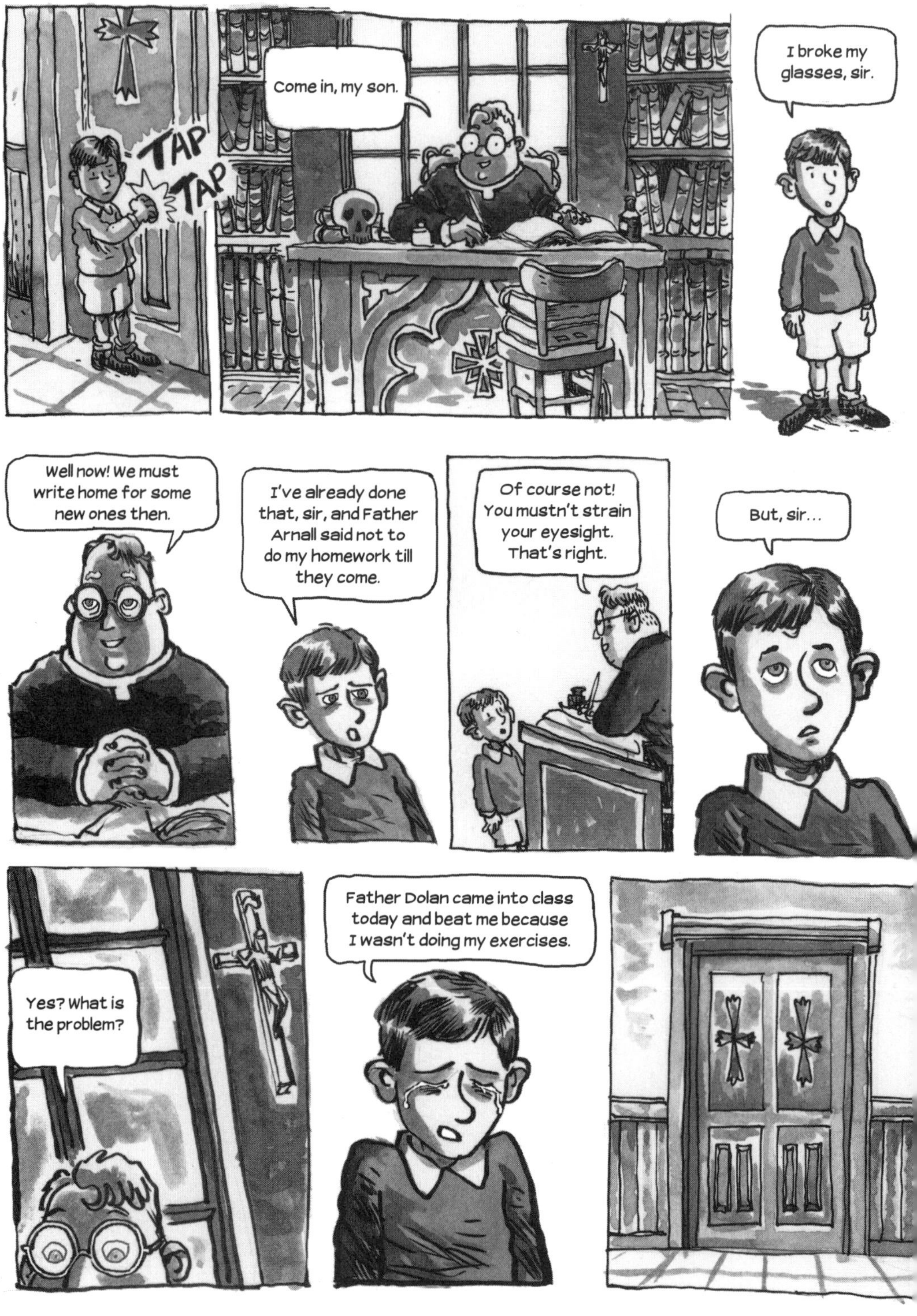
TAP TAP
Come in, my son.
I broke my glasses, sir.
Well now! We must write home for some new ones then.
I've already done that, sir, and Father Arnall said not to do my homework till they come.
Of course not! You mustn't strain your eyesight. That's right.
But, sir...
Yes? What is the problem?
Father Dolan came into class today and beat me because I wasn't doing my exercises.

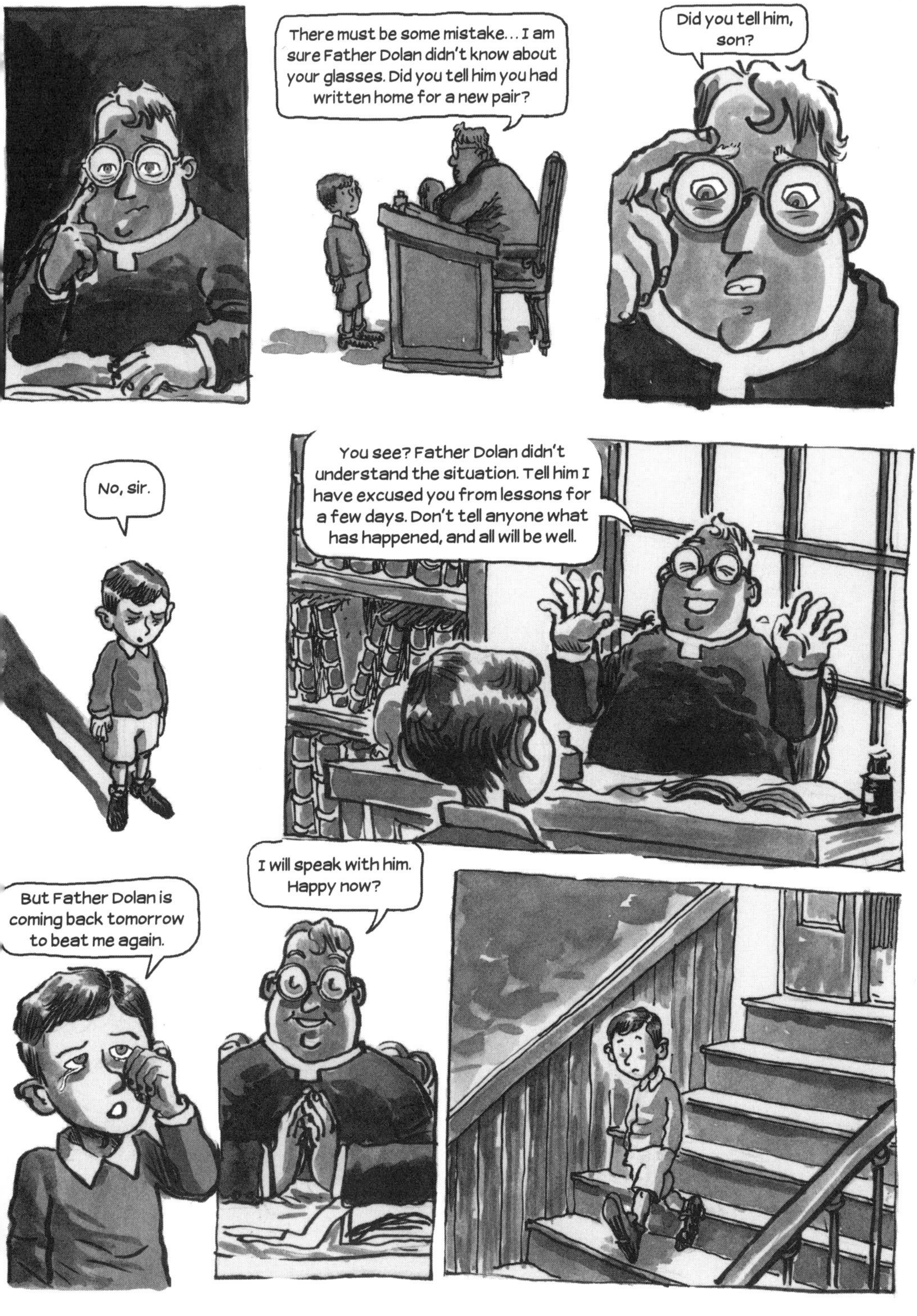
There must be some mistake... I am sure Father Dolan didn't know about your glasses. Did you tell him you had written home for a new pair?
Did you tell him, son?
No, sir.
You see? Father Dolan didn't understand the situation. Tell him I have excused you from lessons for a few days. Don't tell anyone what has happened, and all will be well.
But Father Dolan is coming back tomorrow to beat me again.
I will speak with him. Happy now?

In 1888, the British Crown exerted its power over Ireland through a policy of cultural, political and, of course, military repression.

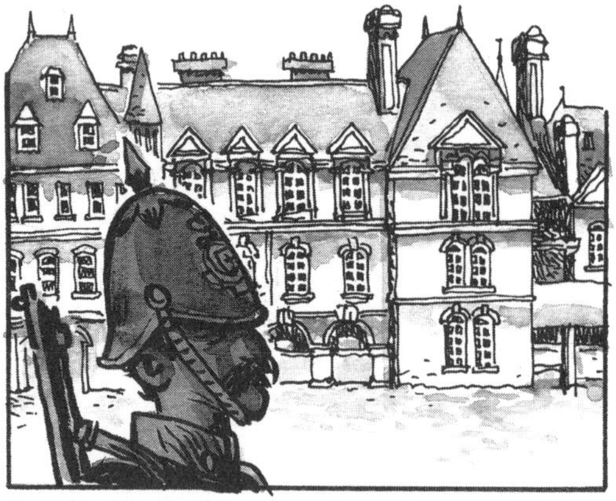

But the island had an 'uncrowned king': Charles Stewart Parnell, an Irish nationalist, leaderof the Irish Parliamentary Party in London. With his eighty-five MPs in the House of Commons, Parnell kept up a constant fight for self-governance for Ireland. However, 'Home Rule' did not flourish, and the fall of this great man would be a tragedy in two acts.

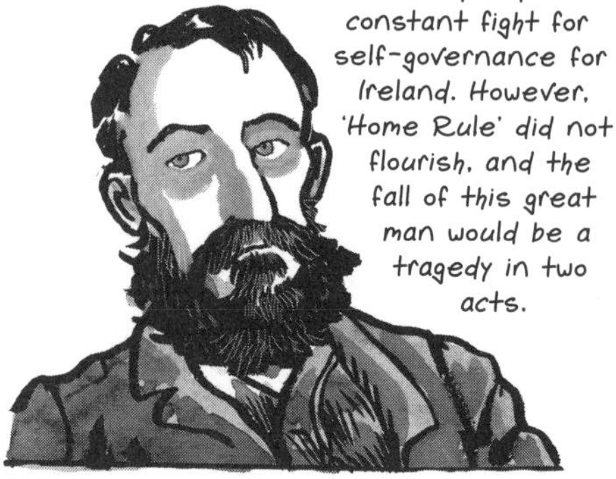

In 1892, the English Liberals and Conservatives, the Church, and even traitors within his own party were against Parnell.

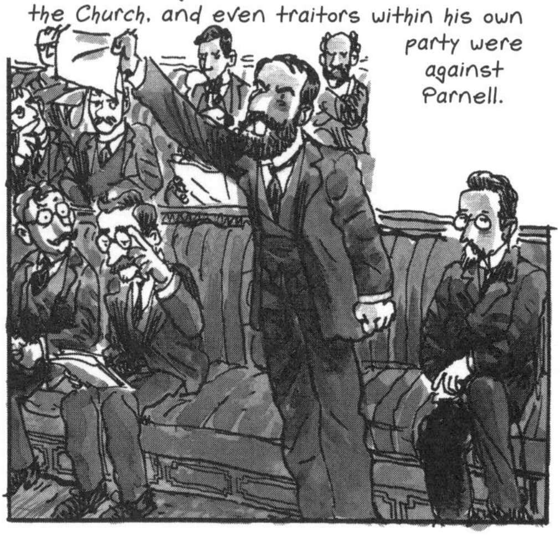

The first plot against him came from the conservative press, who tried to link him to some political murders perpetrated in Phoenix Park. But Parnell stood firm.

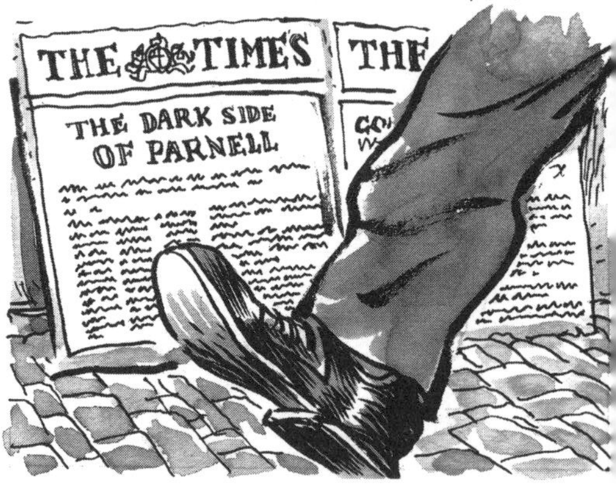
THE TIMES
THE DARK SIDE OF PARNELL

The second attack came shortly after. Parnell had been in a relationship with a married woman, Kitty O'Shea, for over ten years.

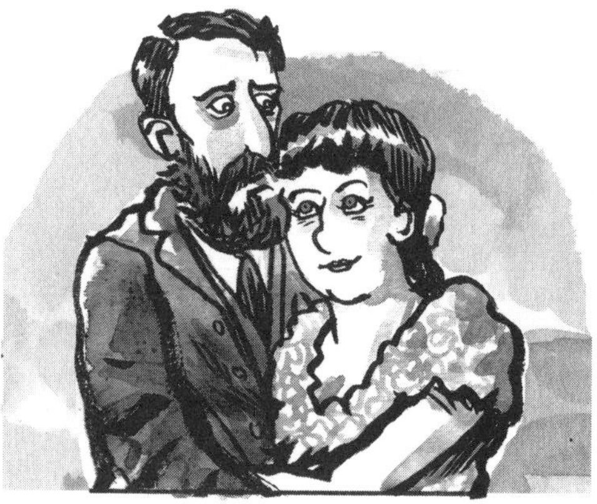

Her husband, Captain O'Shea, had accepted the situation in exchange for a place as a Member of Parliament. But now things were different.

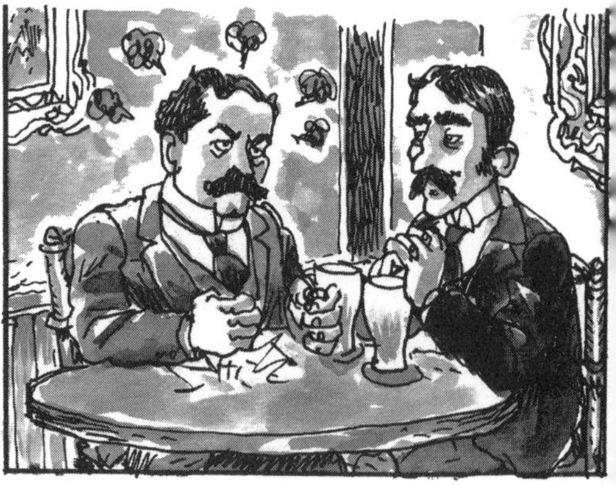

Ireland's Catholic Church, which loathed Parnell, took advantage of the situation to launch a fierce smear campaign against him.

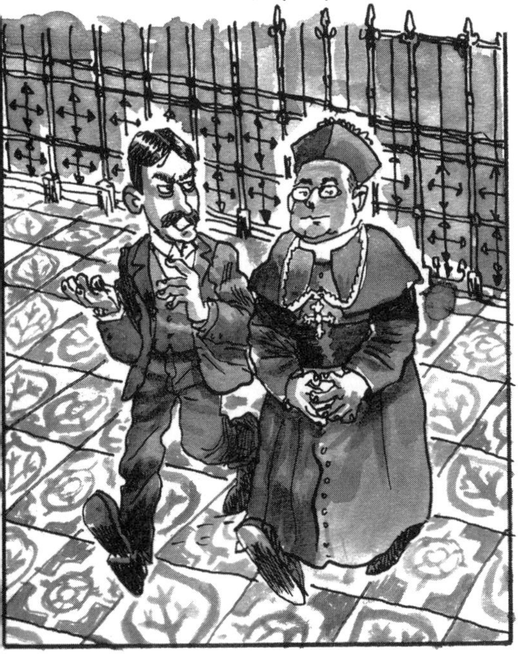

The bishops pressed Tim Healy, Parnell's right-hand man, to hasten his fall. Healy, who defended his chief in public, harboured few qualms about the idea of a change in the party's leadership.

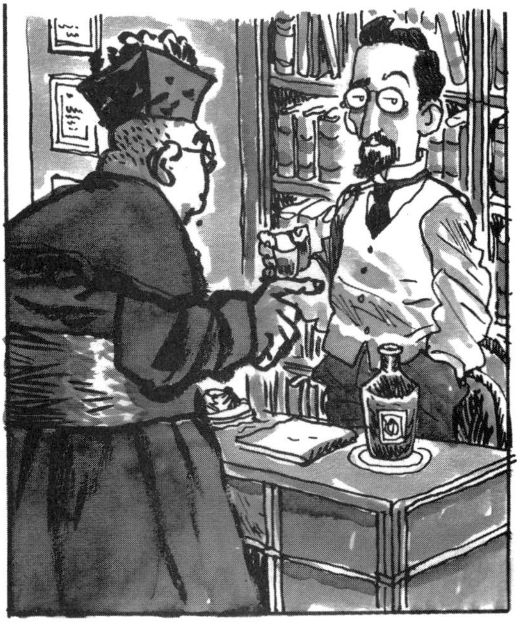

The British Prime Minister, William Gladstone, also pressed Healy to get rid of the 'adulterous sinner'. A pretty hypocritical stance, given that promiscuity and fox-hunting were the main hobbies of the British ruling class.

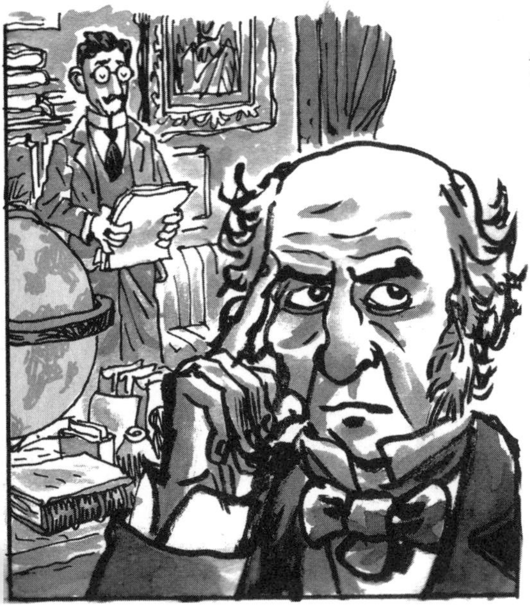

Finally the prey was brought down.

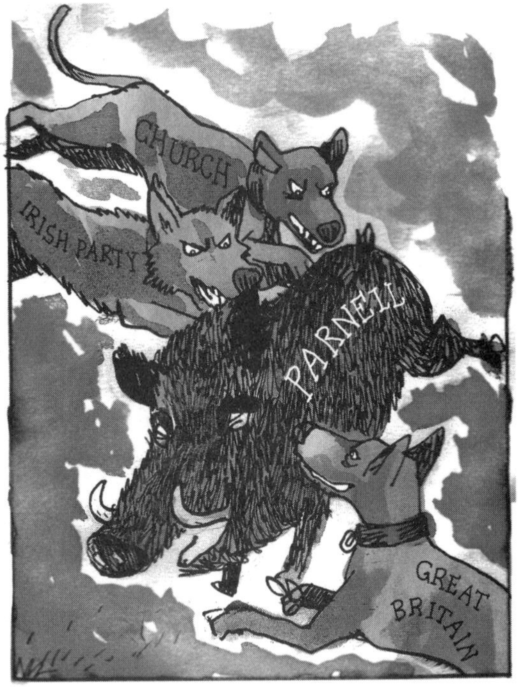
CHURCH
IRISH PARTY
PARNELL
GREAT BRITAIN

With all the infighting, the party fell apart three weeks later, and Parnell abandoned the political scene.

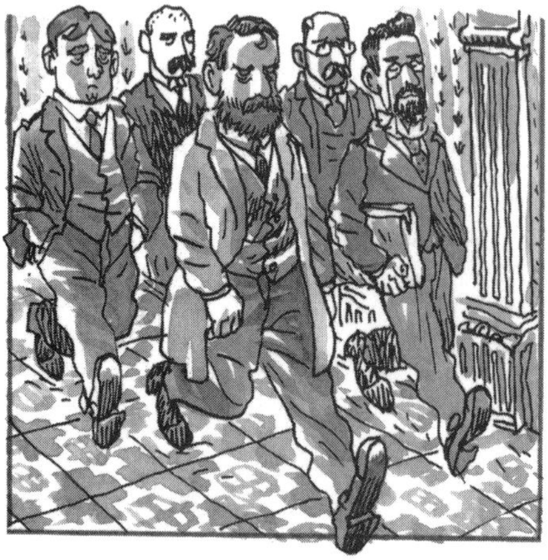

The 'uncrowned king' retired to his little kingdom of Avondale with his beloved Kitty. There he lived under a cloud of constant slander and defamation spewed out by the Catholic bishops.

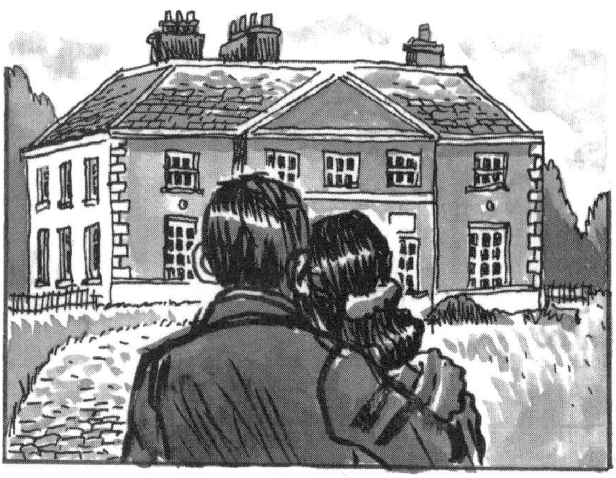

The tragedy ended a year later, when Parnell died after an intense and painful illness. His death closed a chapter of Ireland's history, and opened a wound that would take years to heal. Many citizens believed their leader had died, not from his ailments, but from the terrible betrayal he had suffered.

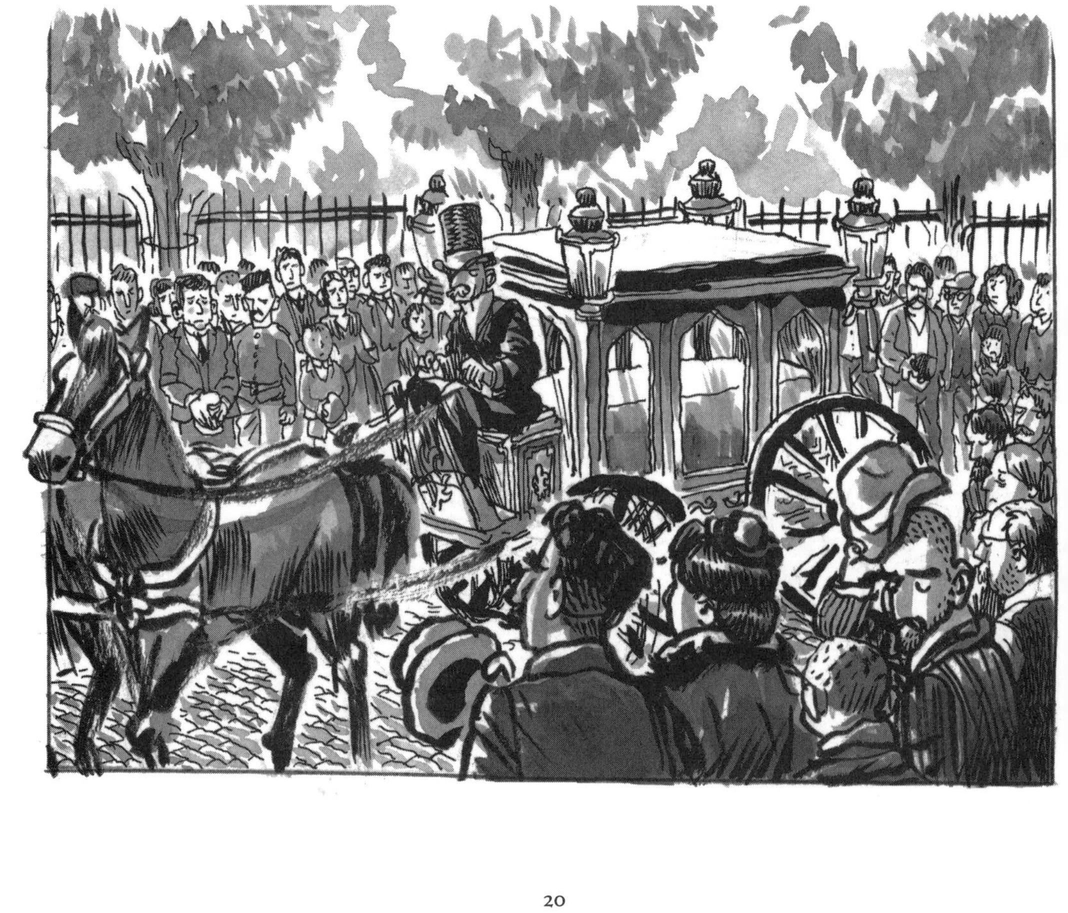

One of these disenchanted citizens was John Joyce. With Parnell were also buried his political hopes and ideals, and his romantic vision of the heroic Ireland of bygone times.

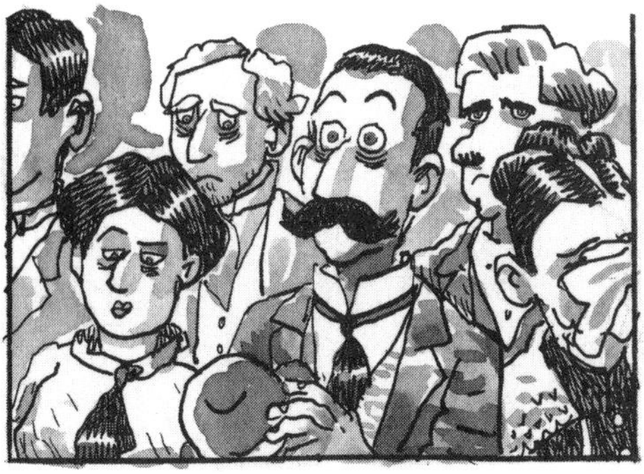

The great leader's fall was reflected in Joyce's own decadence. He spent the long nights wandering from pub to pub, given over to drinking.

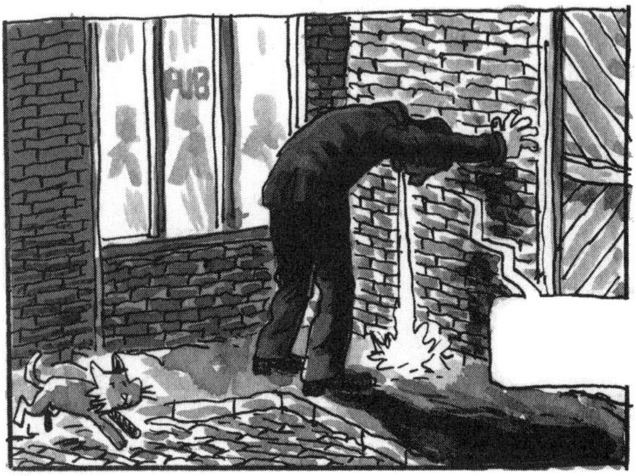

In order to meet his growing debts, Joyce had to sell his properties in Cork, thus blowing his inheritance.

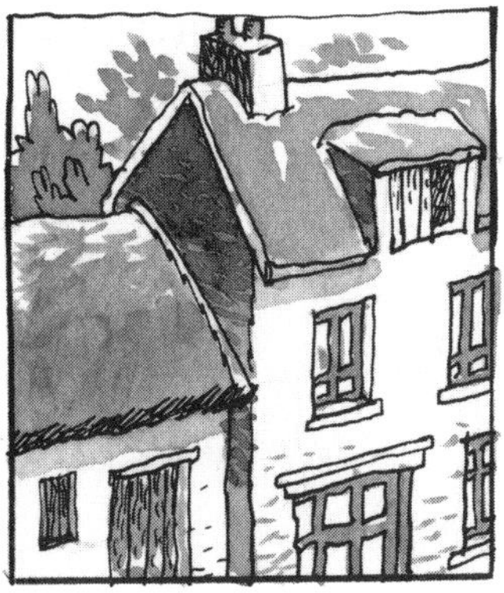

Later he took out a mortgage to raise money, considerably reducing his pension.

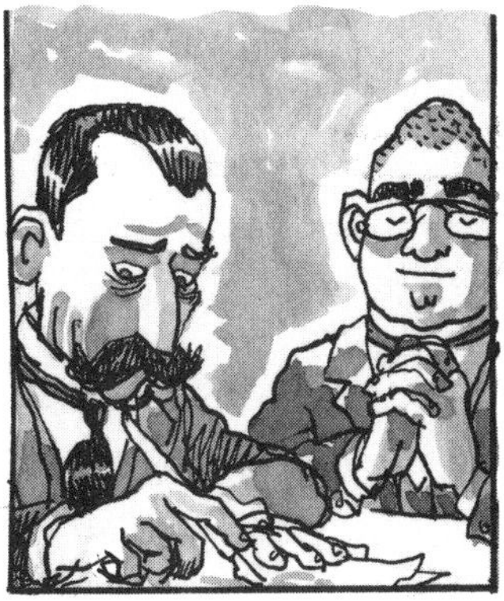

As things got ever worse, he took out another mortgage. This led to the financial ruin of the family.

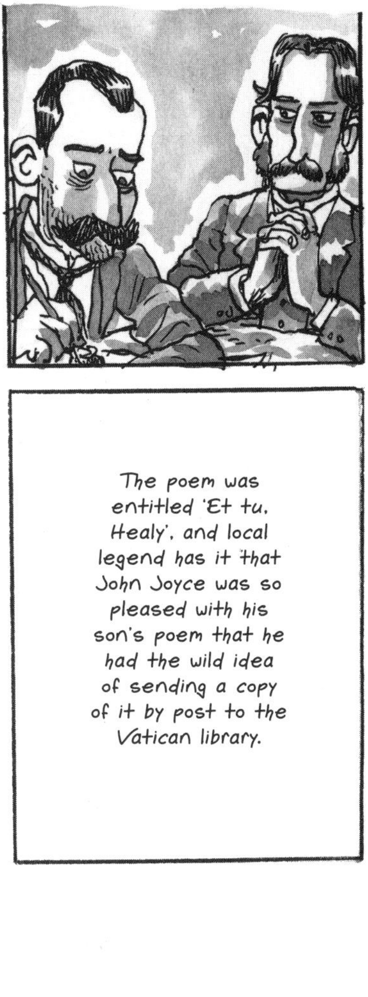

The Joyces all felt a deep connection between Parnell's catastrophe and their own misfortune.

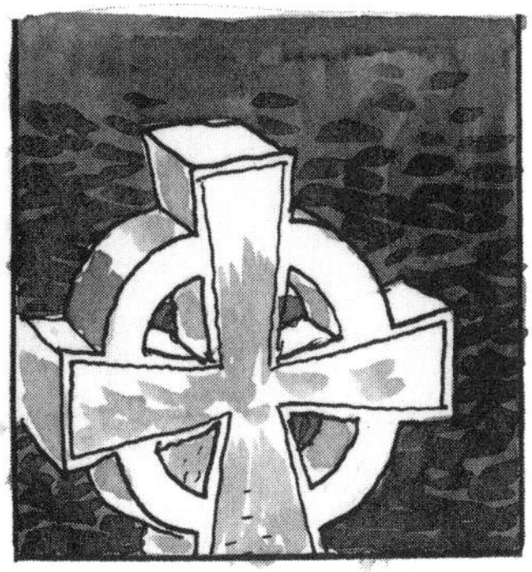

Even little nine-year-old James, who wrote a poem commemorating the event. It was aimed at Tim Healy and those who had betrayed their leader.

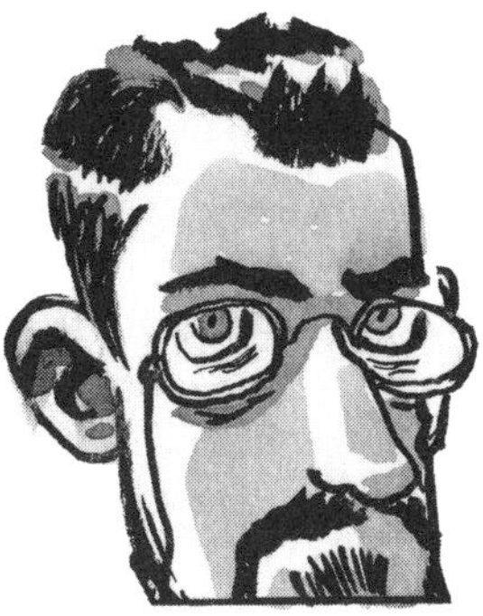

The poem was entitled 'Et tu, Healy', and local legend has it that John Joyce was so pleased with his son's poem that he had the wild idea of sending a copy of it by post to the Vatican library.

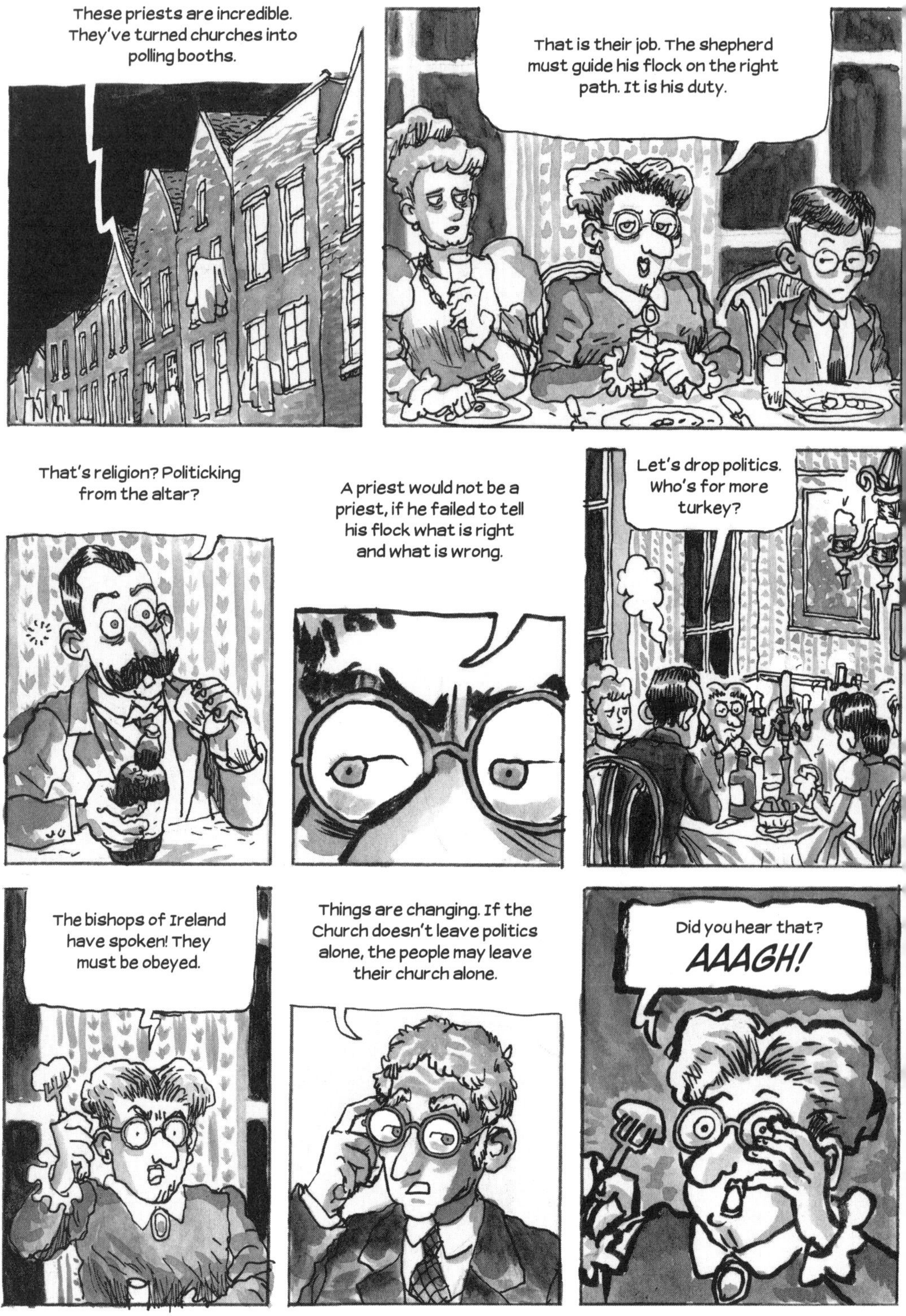

These priests are incredible. They've turned churches into polling booths.
That is their job. The shepherd must guide his flock on the right path. It is his duty.
That's religion? Politicking from the altar?
A priest would not be a priest, if he failed to tell his flock what is right and what is wrong.
Let's drop politics. Who's for more turkey?
The bishops of Ireland have spoken! They must be obeyed.
Things are changing. If the Church doesn't leave politics alone, the people may leave their church alone.
Did you hear that?
AAAGH!

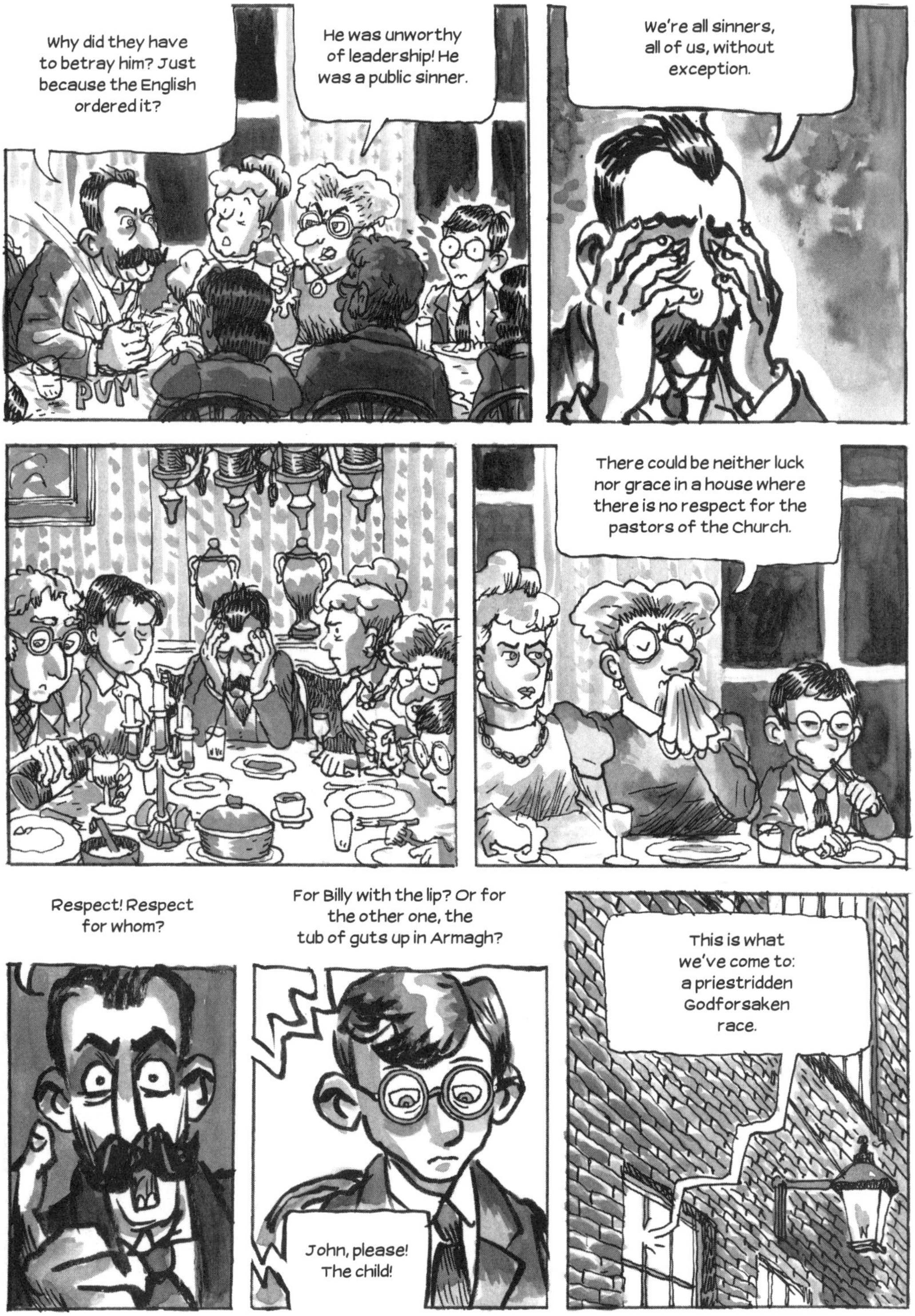
Why did they have to betray him? Just because the English ordered it?
He was unworthy of leadership! He was a public sinner.
PUM
We're all sinners, all of us, without exception.
There could be neither luck nor grace in a house where there is no respect for the pastors of the Church.
Respect! Respect for whom?
For Billy with the lip? Or for the other one, the tub of guts up in Armagh?
John, please! The child!
This is what we've come to: a priestridden Godforsaken race.

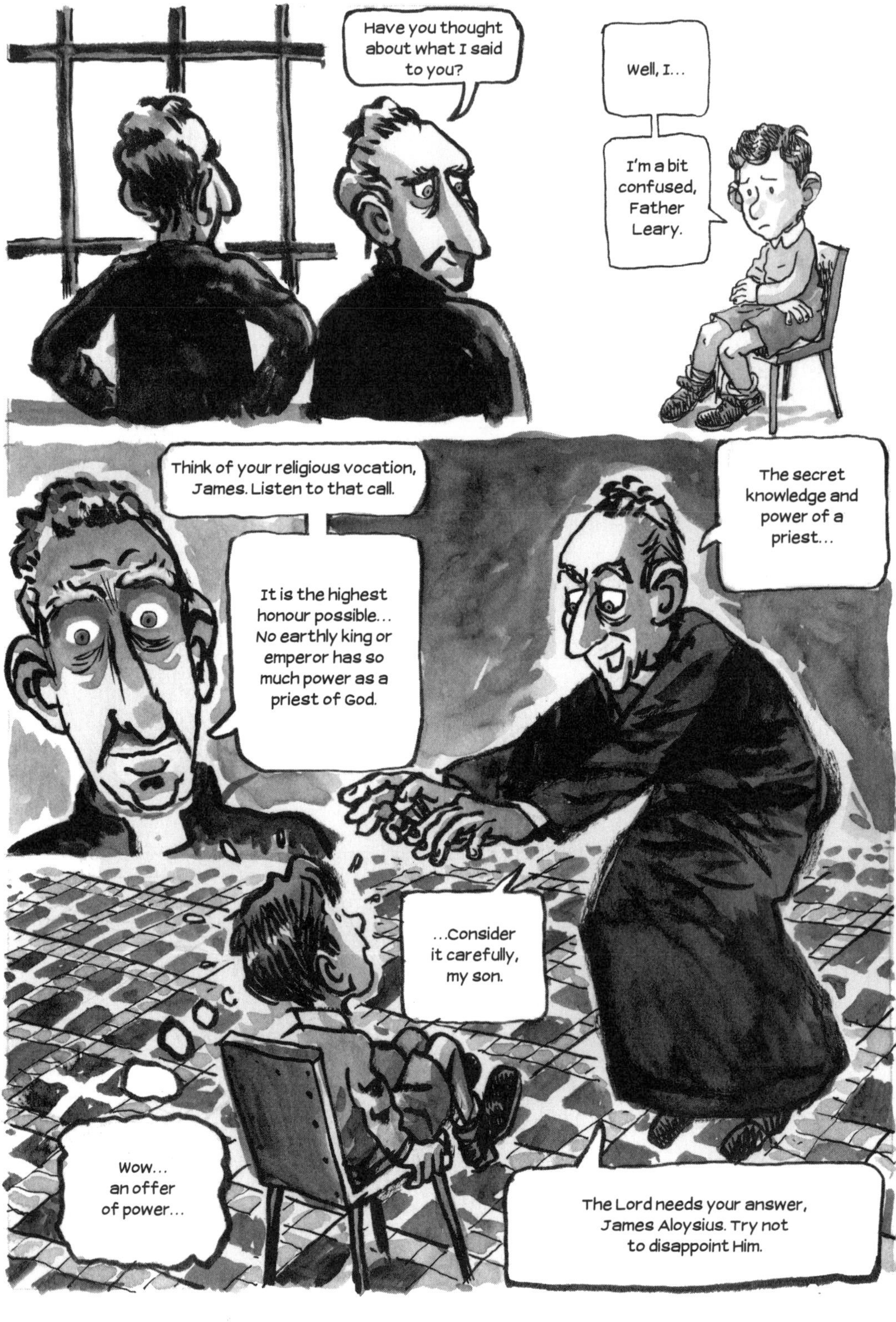
Have you thought about what I said to you?
Well, I...
I'm a bit confused, Father Leary.
Think of your religious vocation, James. Listen to that call.
It is the highest honour possible... No earthly king or emperor has so much power as a priest of God.
The secret knowledge and power of a priest...
...Consider it carefully, my son.
Wow... an offer of power...
The Lord needs your answer, James Aloysius. Try not to disappoint Him.

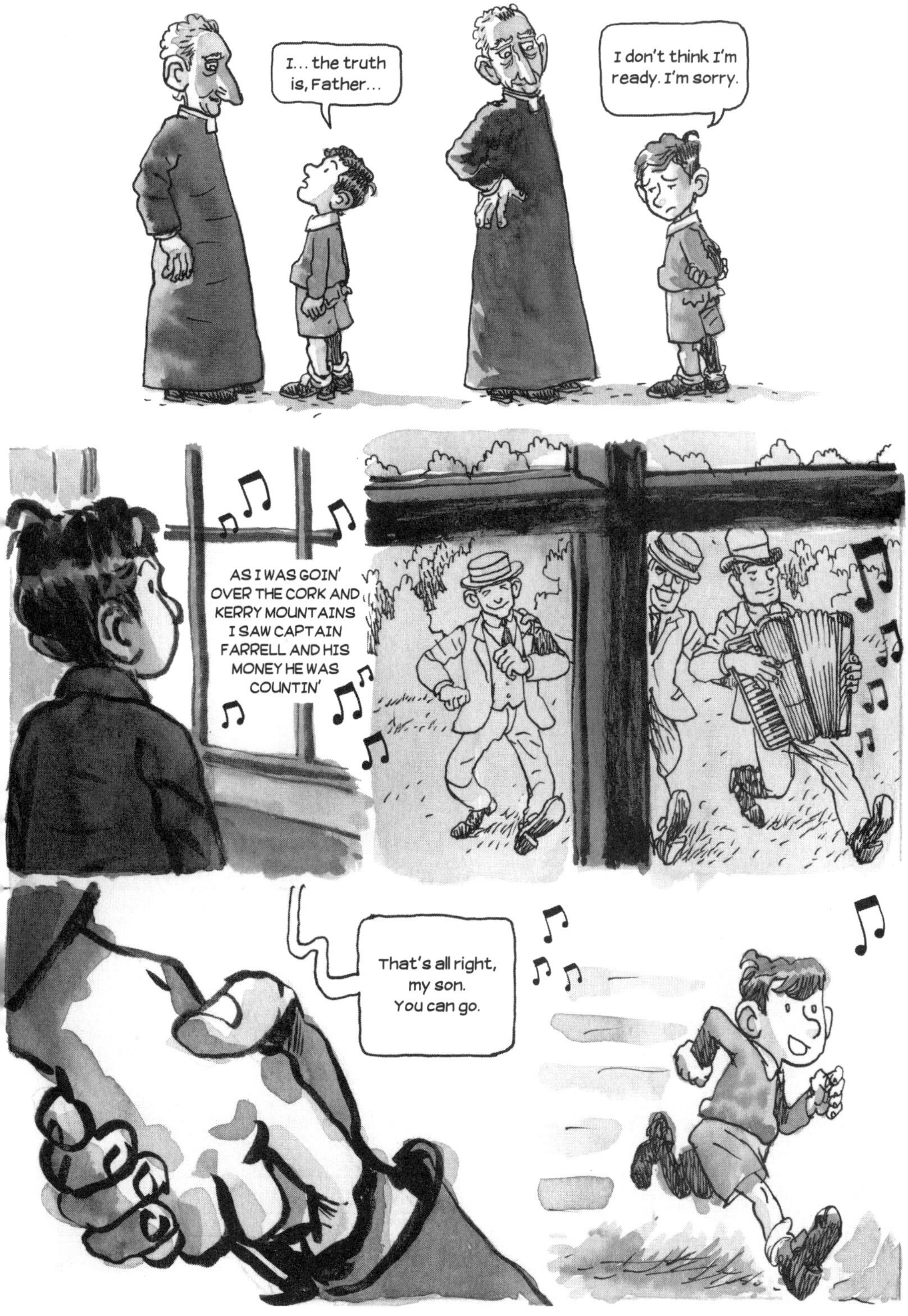
I... the truth is, Father...
I don't think I'm ready. I'm sorry.
AS I WAS GOIN' OVER THE CORK AND KERRY MOUNTAINS I SAW CAPTAIN FARRELL AND HIS MONEY HE WAS COUNTIN'
That's all right, my son. You can go.

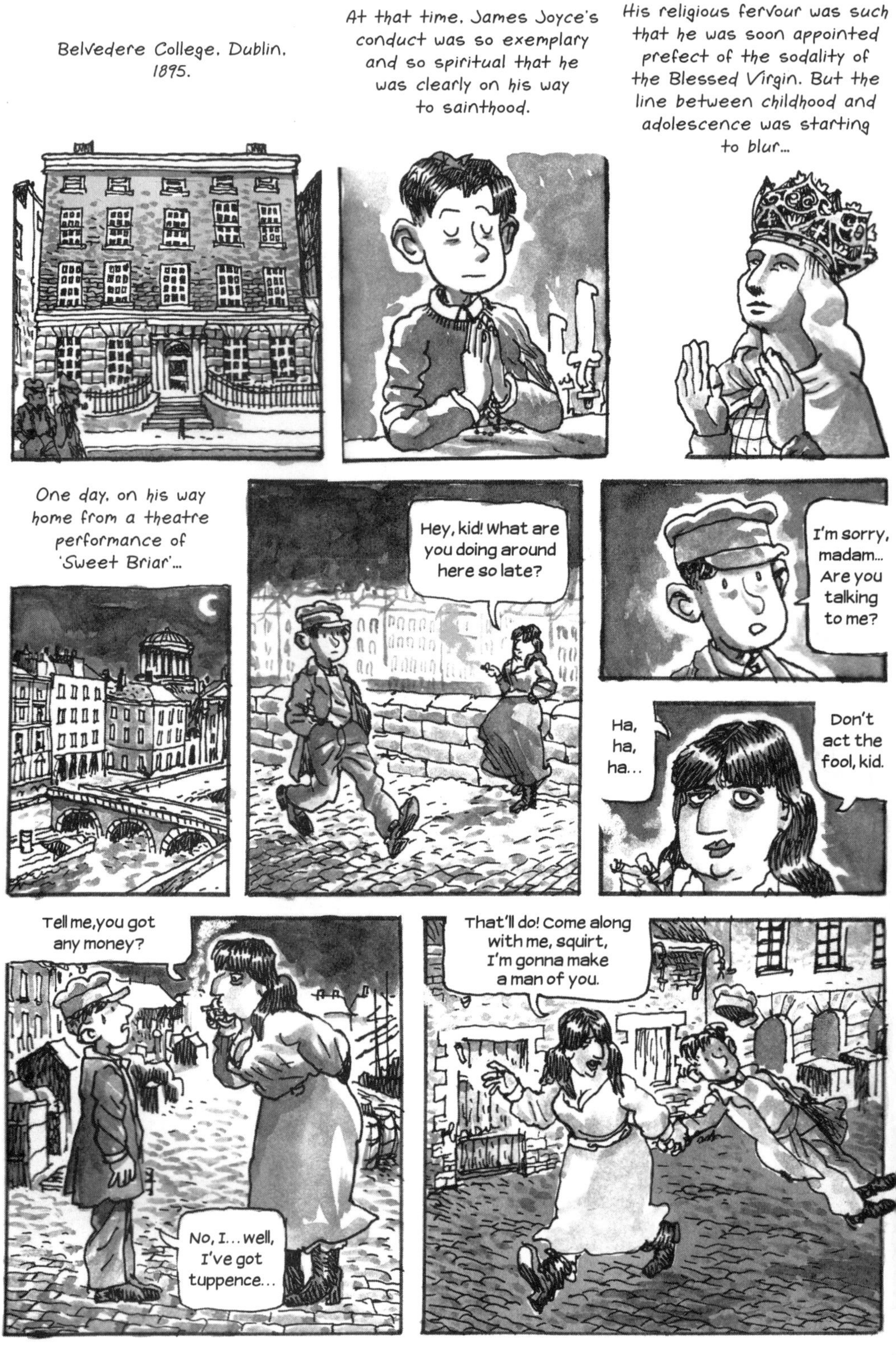

Belvedere College, Dublin. 1895.
At that time, James Joyce's conduct was so exemplary and so spiritual that he was clearly on his way to sainthood.
His religious fervour was such that he was soon appointed prefect of the sodality of the Blessed Virgin. But the line between childhood and adolescence was starting to blur...
One day, on his way home from a theatre performance of 'Sweet Briar'...
Hey, kid! What are you doing around here so late?
I'm sorry, madam... Are you talking to me?
Ha, ha, ha...
Don't act the fool, kid.
Tell me, you got any money?
No, I... well, I've got tuppence...
That'll do! Come along with me, squirt, I'm gonna make a man of you.

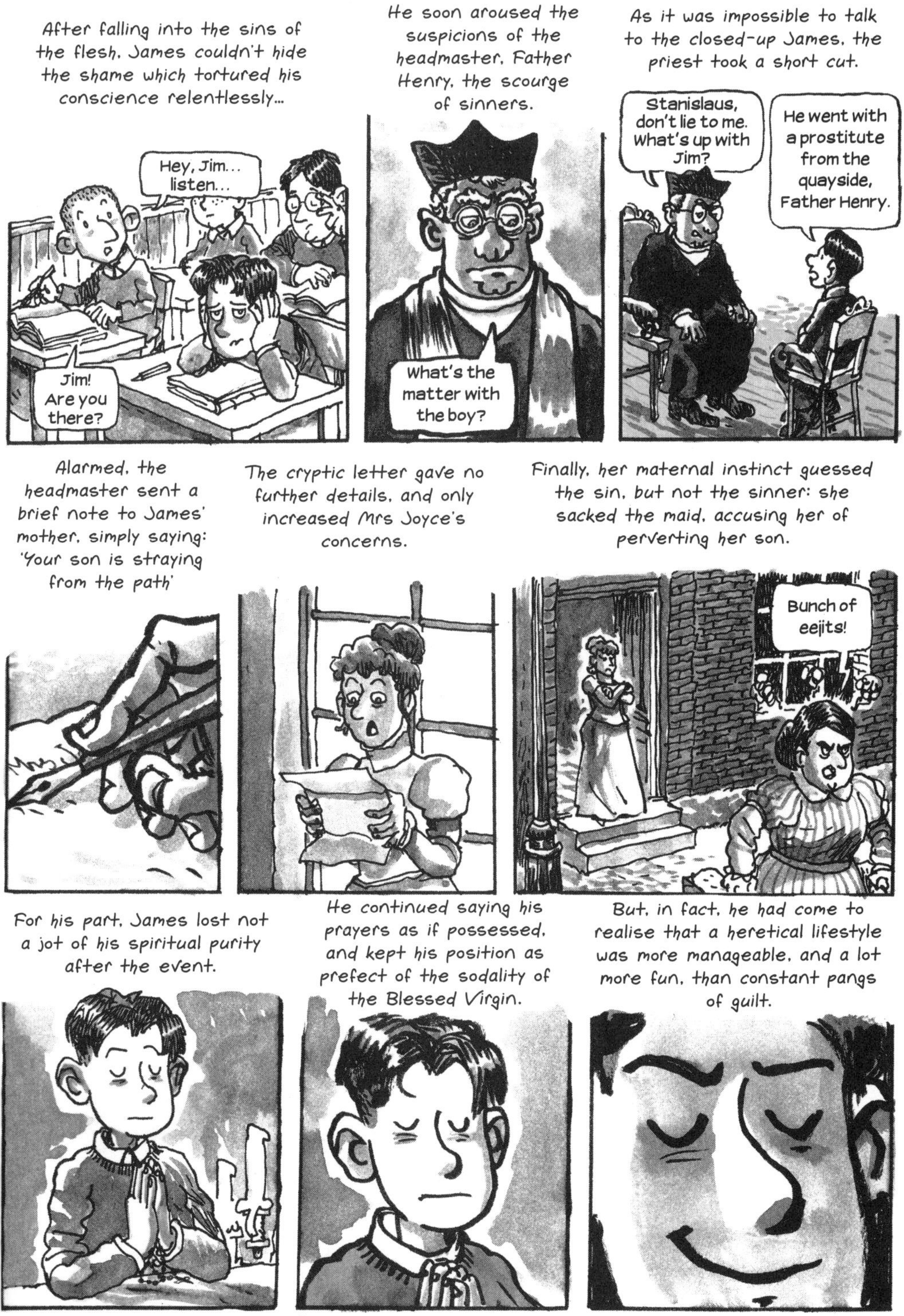
After falling into the sins of the flesh, James couldn't hide the shame which tortured his conscience relentlessly...
Hey, Jim... listen...
Jim! Are you there?
He soon aroused the suspicions of the headmaster, Father Henry, the scourge of sinners.
What's the matter with the boy?
As it was impossible to talk to the closed-up James, the priest took a short cut.
Stanislaus, don't lie to me. What's up with Jim?
He went with a prostitute from the quayside, Father Henry.
Alarmed, the headmaster sent a brief note to James' mother, simply saying: 'Your son is straying from the path'
Mrs J
The cryptic letter gave no further details, and only increased Mrs Joyce's concerns.
Finally, her maternal instinct guessed the sin, but not the sinner: she sacked the maid, accusing her of perverting her son.
Bunch of eejits!
For his part, James lost not a jot of his spiritual purity after the event.
He continued saying his prayers as if possessed, and kept his position as prefect of the sodality of the Blessed Virgin.
But, in fact, he had come to realise that a heretical lifestyle was more manageable, and a lot more fun, than constant pangs of guilt.

In 1898, University College Dublin was the poor relative of Trinity. This small Catholic university received no support from the British government.

James Joyce was sixteen when he enrolled in Languages. They were difficult times for the University.

Hi, lads!

Good morning, Jim.

George Clancy was one of Joyce's inner circle of friends. A fervent nationalist, he played hurling and was a member of the Gaelic League. He even convinced Jim to take Gaelic classes for a while (though Jim was not really interested in the Irish question).

Clancy later became mayor of Limerick, and was murdered in 1921 by the Black and Tans (the pro-British paramilitary militia).

Francis Skeffington, considered by Joyce the cleverest student in University College (after himself, of course). Cultured, vegetarian, a pacifist and a defender of equal rights between the sexes, he even adopted his wife's surname when they married.

Thomas Kettle was a Catholic nationalist intellectual, and though his views on Ireland differed from Joyce's, they were good friends.

Such a utopian character was doomed to come to a dramatic end, and it came during the 1916 Easter Rising.

When the Great War broke out in 1914, Kettle volunteered for the British Army, believing that the British would reward the Irish volunteers by granting independence. He fell in battle in France in 1916.

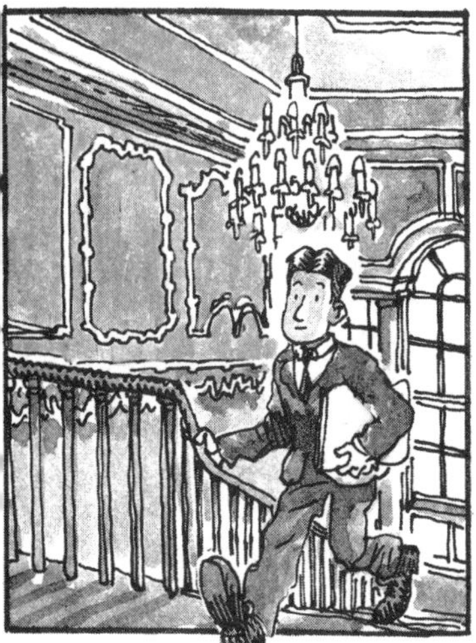

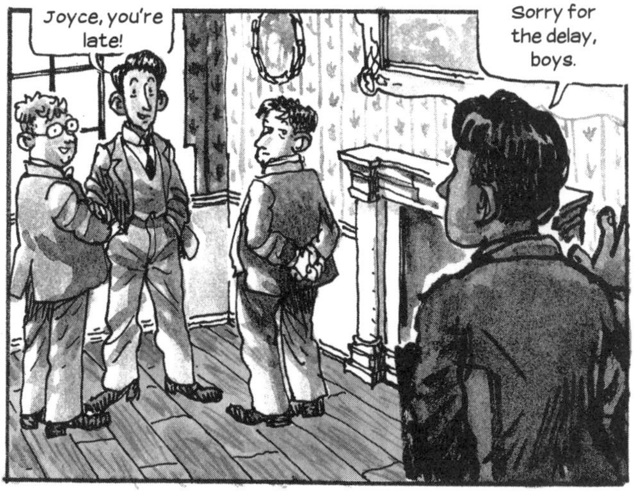
Joyce, you're late!
Sorry for the delay, boys.

Constantine Curran was a good-natured, moderate young man, much admired by Joyce. He had a great knowledge of literature and architecture, and later became a Supreme Court registrar.

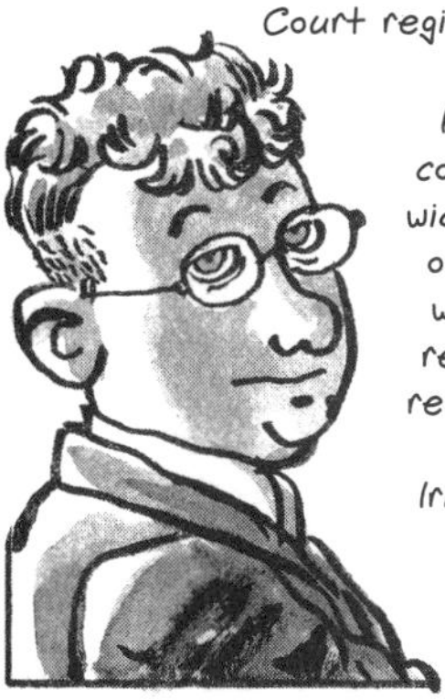

His travels to the continent gave him a wider, European vision of the world; but he was so devout that religion overcame his reason, and he ended up with a typical Irishman's prejudices and hang-ups.

John Francis Byrne was Joyce's best friend. Simple and quiet, he was a talented sportsman, clever, but a hopeless student. He spent summers on his Wicklow farm, which puzzled his city friends. Byrne and Joyce were fascinated by each other, and Byrne's distinguished silence was a perfect complement to Joyce's shameless chatter.

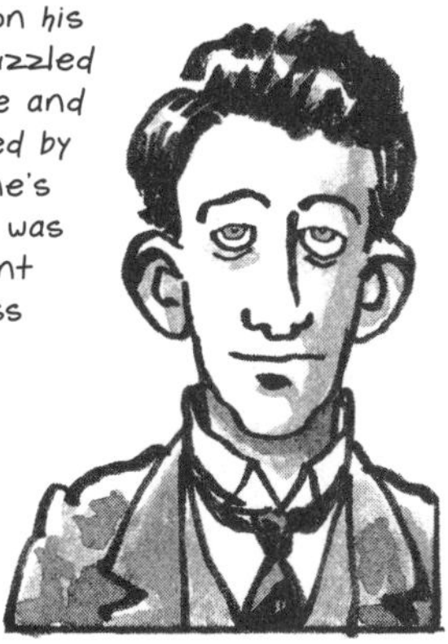

Vincent Cosgrave completed Joyce's circle of friends. He was proudly ignorant, vulgar and simple. Joyce wasn't particularly close to him, but he could always be counted on to go drinking or whoring at night. Cosgrave was destined to be a mediocre, resentful failure. As the years passed he became more and more bitter. He came to a sudden end in London: his body was found floating in the Thames. He had probably committed suicide.

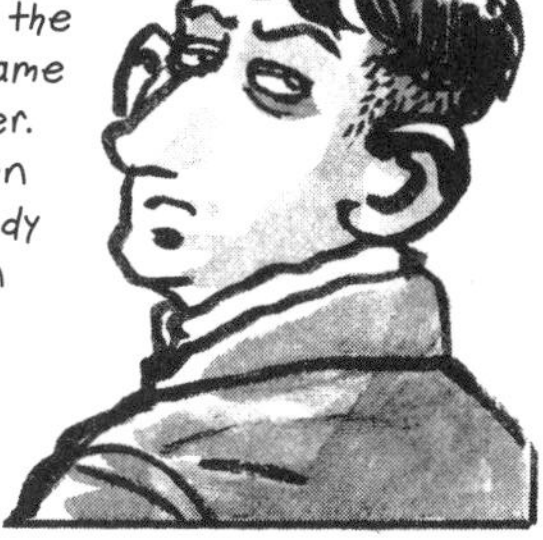

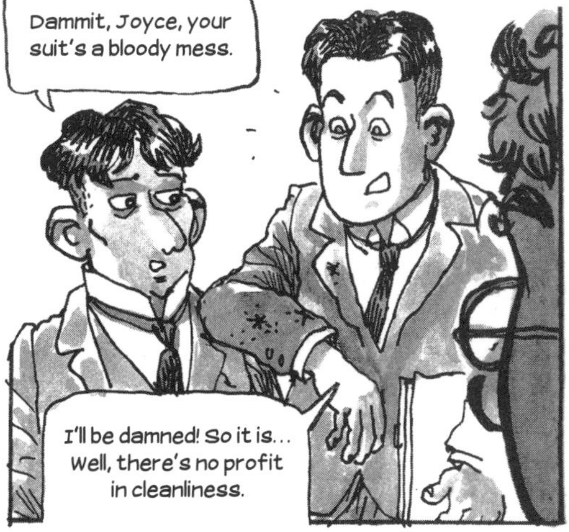
Dammit, Joyce, your suit's a bloody mess.
I'll be damned! So it is... Well, there's no profit in cleanliness.

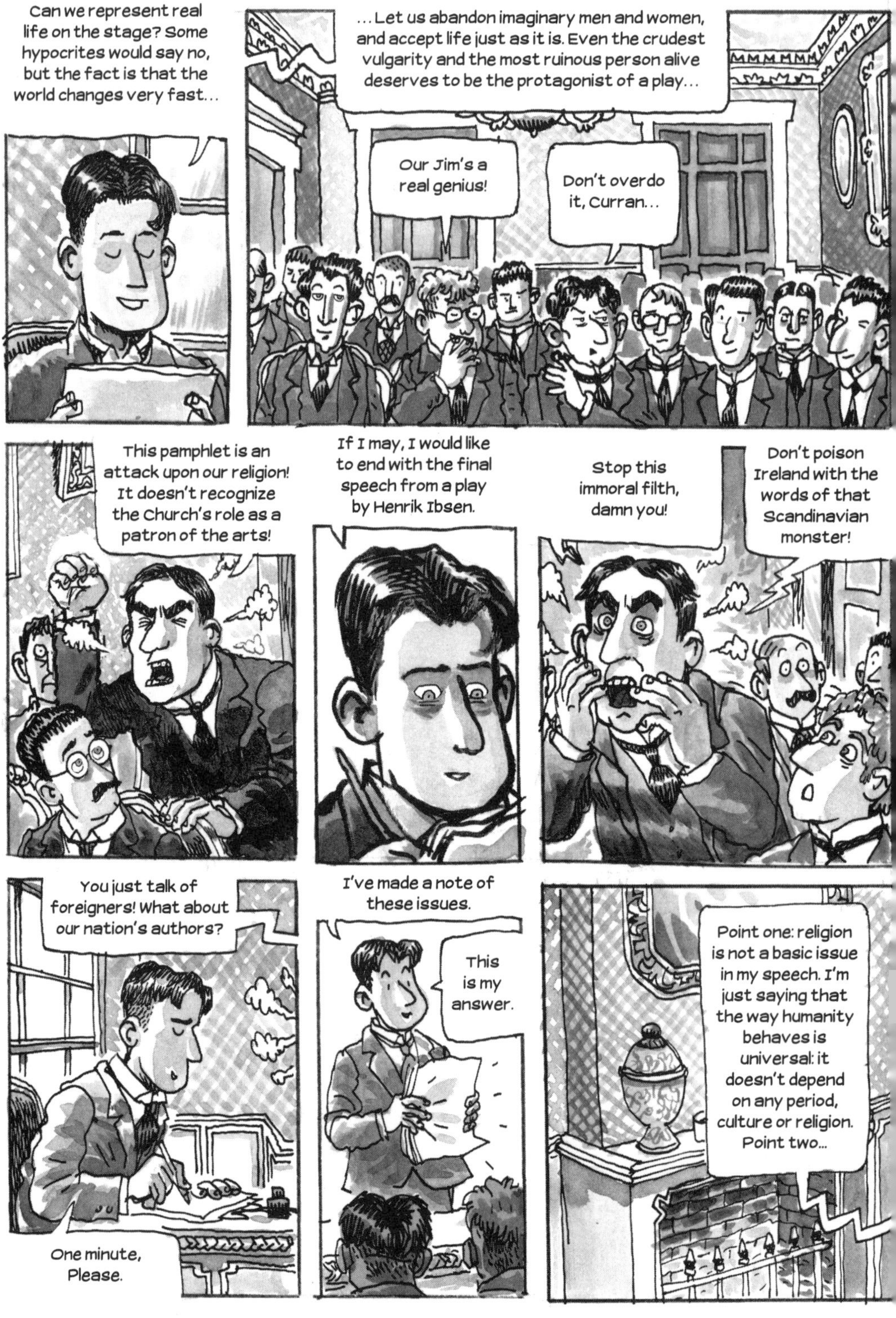
Can we represent real life on the stage? Some hypocrites would say no, but the fact is that the world changes very fast...
...Let us abandon imaginary men and women, and accept life just as it is. Even the crudest vulgarity and the most ruinous person alive deserves to be the protagonist of a play...
Our Jim's a real genius!
Don't overdo it, Curran...
This pamphlet is an attack upon our religion! It doesn't recognize the Church's role as a patron of the arts!
If I may, I would like to end with the final speech from a play by Henrik Ibsen.
Stop this immoral filth, damn you!
Don't poison Ireland with the words of that Scandinavian monster!
You just talk of foreigners! What about our nation's authors?
One minute, please.
I've made a note of these issues.
This is my answer.
Point one: religion is not a basic issue in my speech. I'm just saying that the way humanity behaves is universal: it doesn't depend on any period, culture or religion. Point two...

...The role of the Church as a patron of the arts is not the topic of this talk. And anyway, the Church is not the only patron of artists, nor are works of art a monopoly of the Church. Point three: Henrik Ibsen is a damned genius.

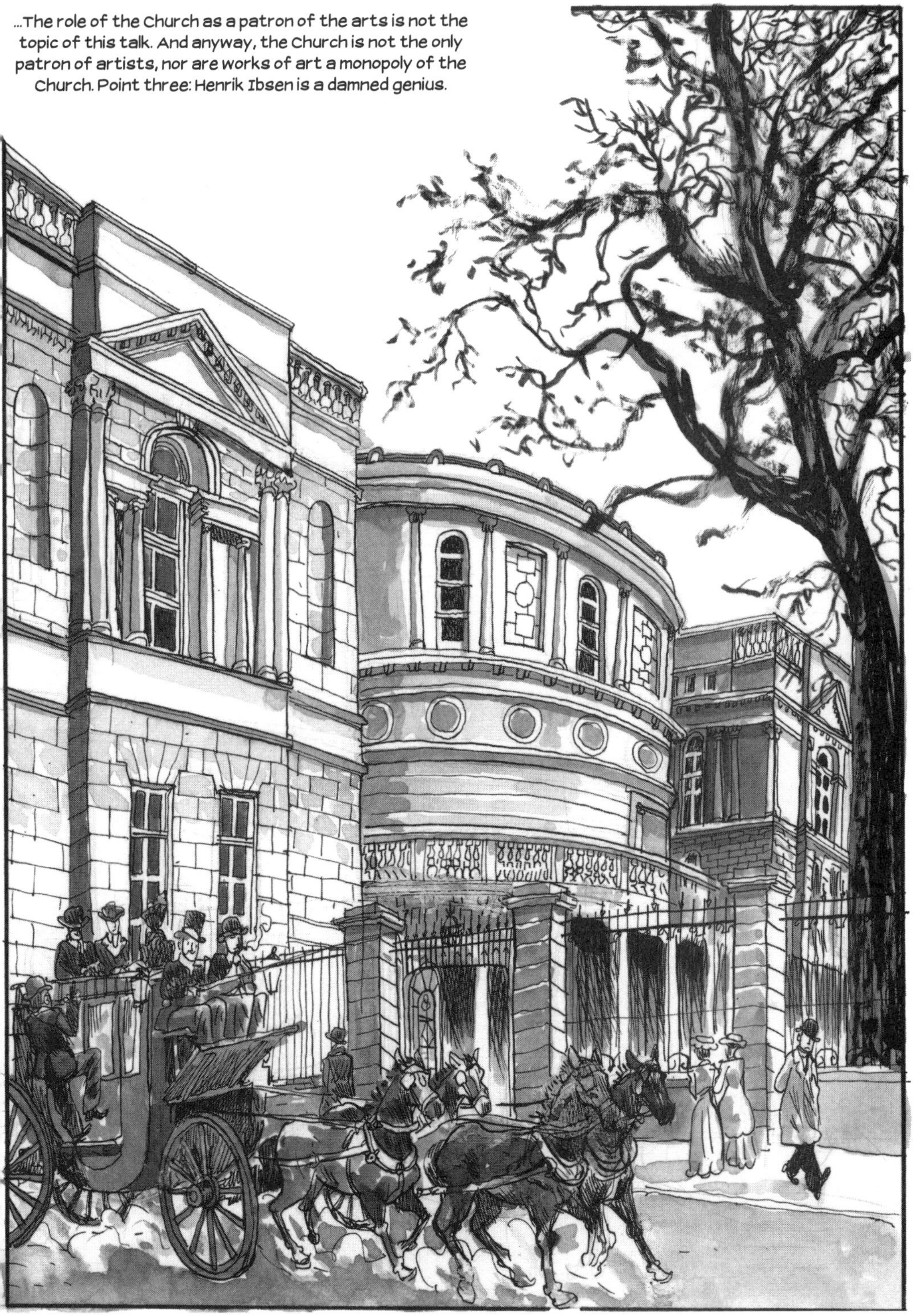

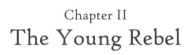

Chapter II

The Young Rebel

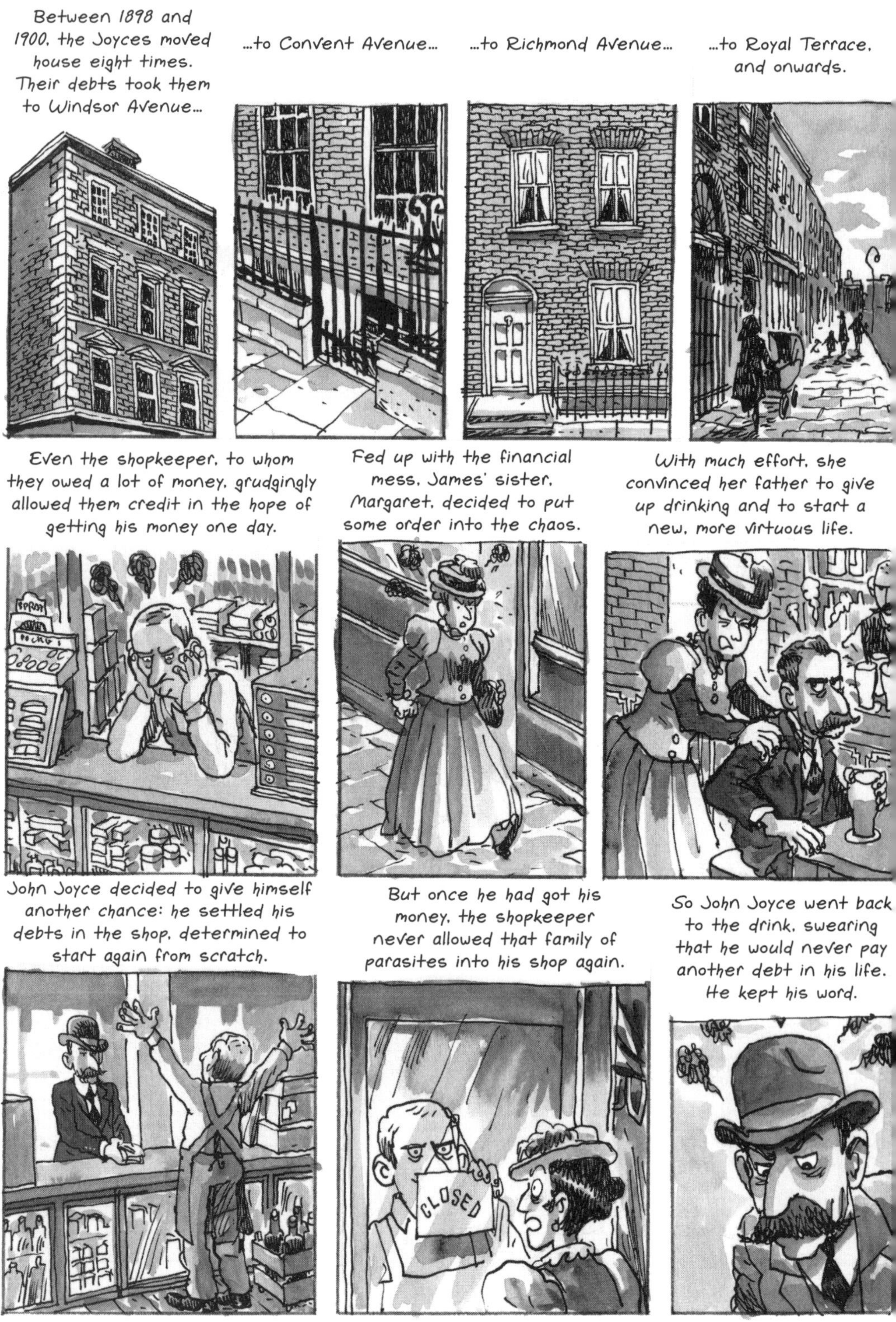

Between 1898 and 1900, the Joyces moved house eight times. Their debts took them to Windsor Avenue...
...to Convent Avenue...
...to Richmond Avenue...
...to Royal Terrace, and onwards.
Even the shopkeeper, to whom they owed a lot of money, grudgingly allowed them credit in the hope of getting his money one day.
Fed up with the financial mess, James' sister, Margaret, decided to put some order into the chaos.
With much effort, she convinced her father to give up drinking and to start a new, more virtuous life.
John Joyce decided to give himself another chance: he settled his debts in the shop, determined to start again from scratch.
But once he had got his money, the shopkeeper never allowed that family of parasites into his shop again.
CLOSED
So John Joyce went back to the drink, swearing that he would never pay another debt in his life. He kept his word.

Meanwhile, young James was leading a dissolute life in the company of the pernicious Cosgrave.

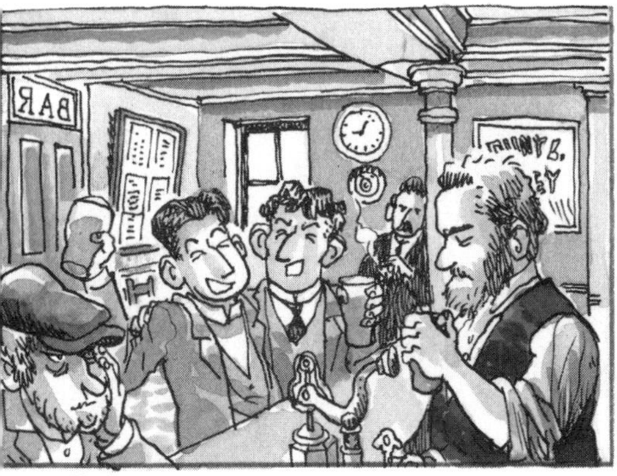

But his life was to change radically and unexpectedly, after writing an article in 1900 for a Dublin literary magazine called the 'Fortnightly Review'. It was a critique of a play by Ibsen.

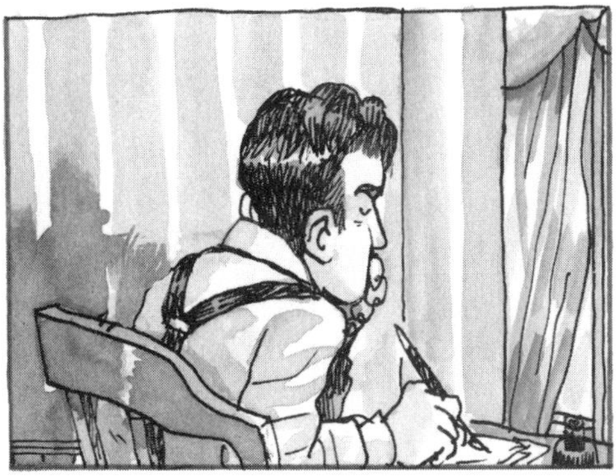

The magazine was published and distributed as usual.

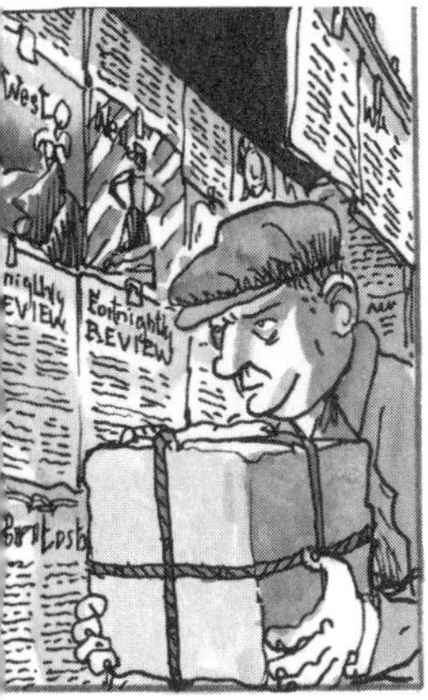
Fortnightly REVIEW

But a copy of it reached the Norwegian town of Kristiania, where it ended up in the hands of Henrik Ibsen himself.

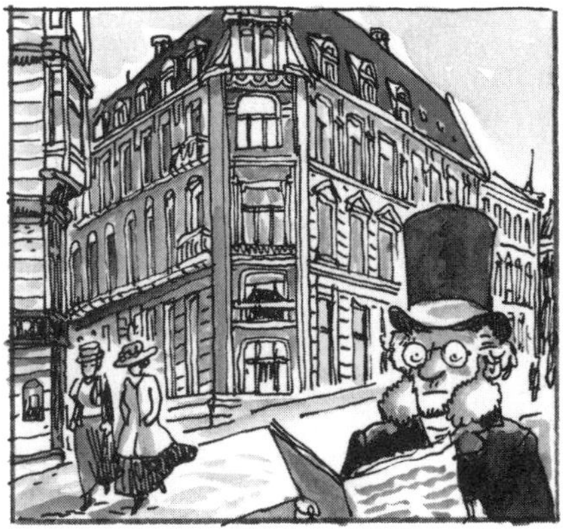

Pleased with the young Irishman's text, Ibsen wrote a letter to Archer, the publisher of the magazine.

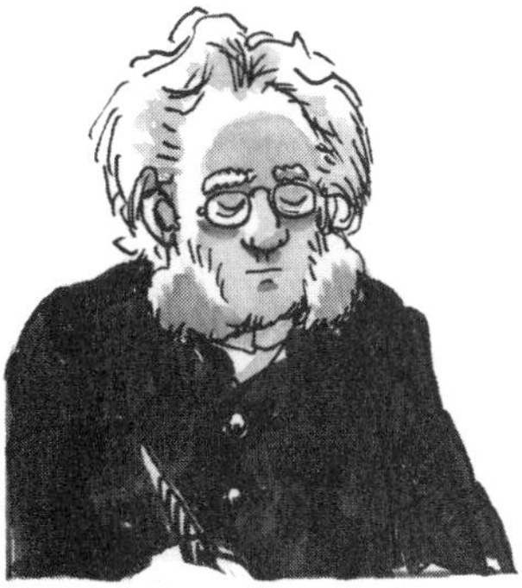

Archer contacted Joyce. It was a huge surprise!

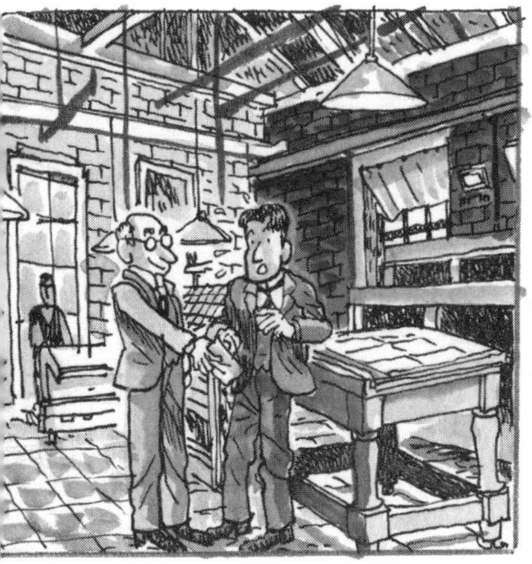

When Joyce read Ibsen's letter, he almost doubled in stature. Not in height, but in pride and self-confidence.

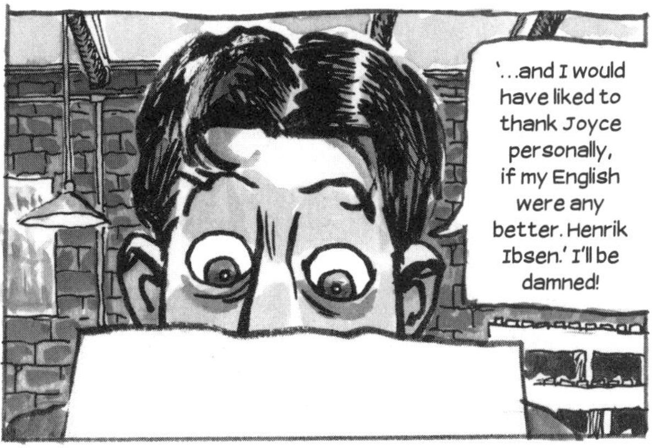
'...and I would have liked to thank Joyce personally, if my English were any better. Henrik Ibsen.' I'll be damned!

In contrast to the general apathy in Ireland, the literary scene in Dublin in 1902 was ambitious and vibrant. There was a new generation of lively young writers, such as Padraic Colum, Seamus O'Sullivan, Standish O'Grady and John O'Leary, along with the veteran Synge. James Joyce formed no part of the movement, but he would benefit from it in the future.

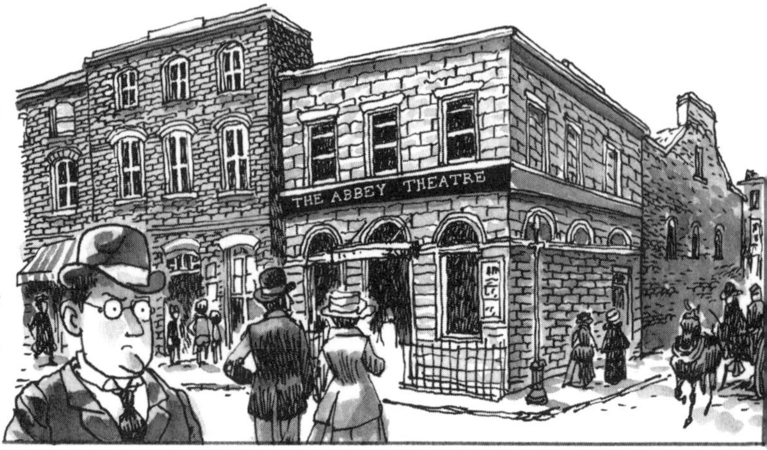
THE ABBEY THEATRE

The literary 'heavyweights' at that time were:

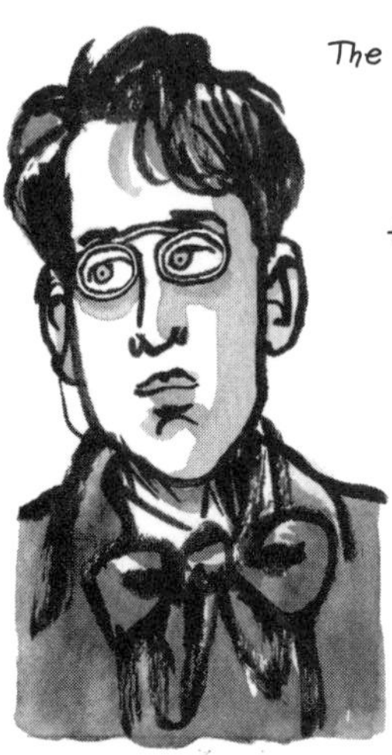

WB Yeats, who had just founded the Abbey Theatre and the Irish National Theatre Company. Yeats was the author of the acclaimed 'Countess Cathleen', and a champion of the Irish literary revival.

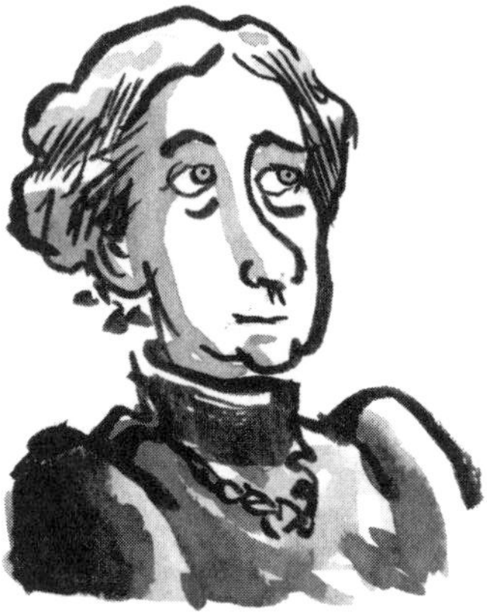

Isabella Augusta Gregory, known as 'Lady Gregory', was a brilliant playwright. Like Yeats, her works were devoted to themes of nationalism, folklore and Celtic culture (this was unusual, coming from an Anglo-Irish aristocrat).

George Moore was already an established novelist, poet, art critic and playwright. His plays contributed to the cultural movement led by Lady Gregory and Yeats.

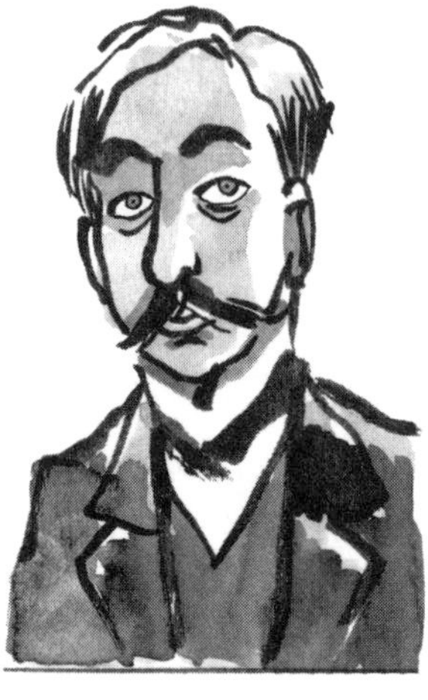

Finally, George Russell, writer, painter and art critic. Russell, despite his nationalism, was the writer who Joyce most admired at the time: he was also the most approachable. He was to be James' link to the cultural world of Dublin.

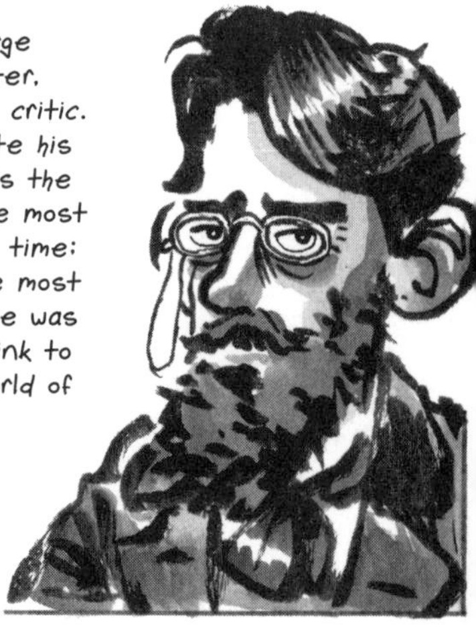

To gain access to this closed circle, Joyce decided to wait outside Russell's house one night.

When Russell finally appeared...

Is it too late, Mr Russell?

It is never too late.

After a long talk with Joyce (who spent his time tearing all the contemporary Irish writers to shreds), Russell was impressed both by his poems and his bad manners. He wrote to Yeats, asking him to 'suffer' Joyce.

The much awaited meeting took place on Yeats' return from London. It was certainly an evening to remember.

Please read me some of your poems.

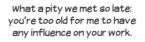

Well, if you like... But I want you to know that your opinion means no more to me than any stranger's in the street.

Young man, I must admit that your poetry is very interesting.

Please, don't waste your time flattering me. We'll both be forgotten one day.

What a pity we met so late: you're too old for me to have any influence on your work.

I've never seen such a mixture of colossal conceit and miniscule literary talent in one person!

37

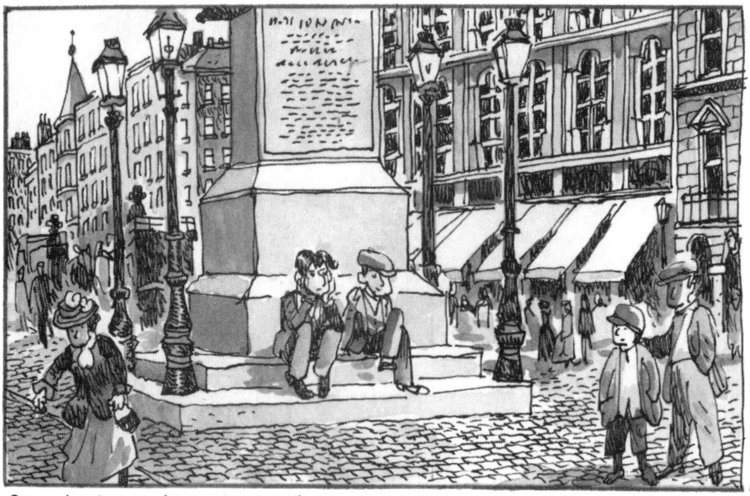

After graduation, Joyce showed no interest in any specific career. He didn't fancy going into the civil service, practising law or becoming as academic. He spent his days in the streets of Dublin, watching the grass grow.

One day he made up his mind, though without much conviction.

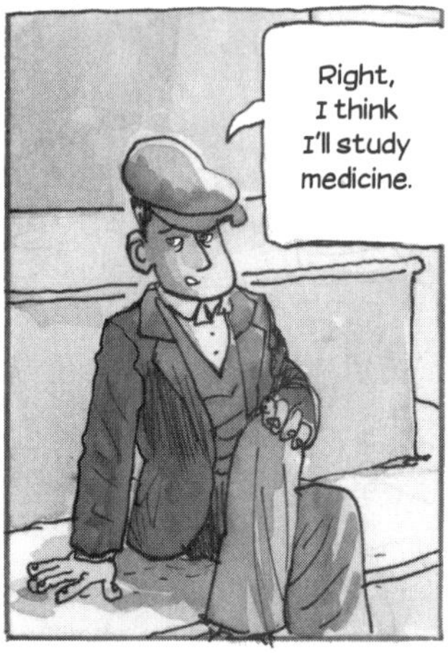
Right, I think I'll study medicine.

He wasn't keen on the Faculty of Medicine in Dublin, so Joyce decided to enroll in the one in Paris. As was his way, he didn't bother to find out if a French qualification would be valid in Ireland. He just packed his bag, and on 1 December 1902 he left Ireland for the first time.

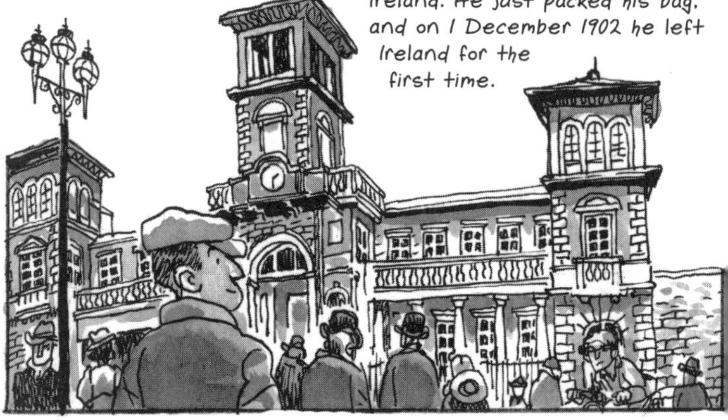

Paris was a terribly expensive city for an Irish student with no means. Giving English classes didn't seem a good idea to him, and he wasn't good at managing his money.

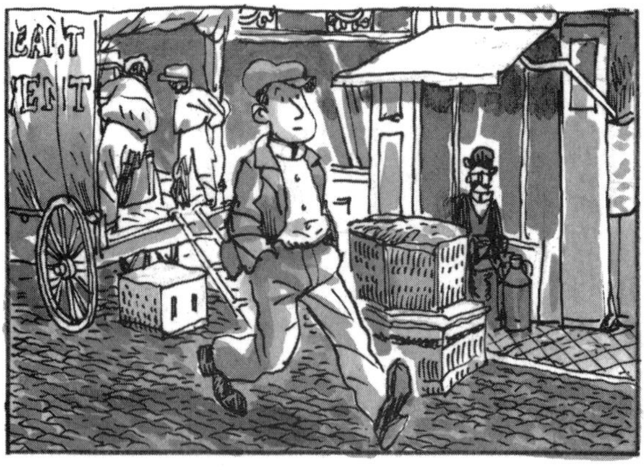

Whenever his father managed to scrape a few pounds together to send him, James quickly blew it on French wine, theatre and opera.

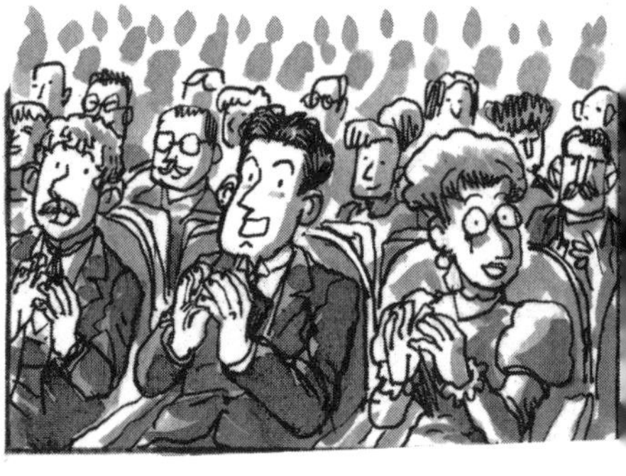

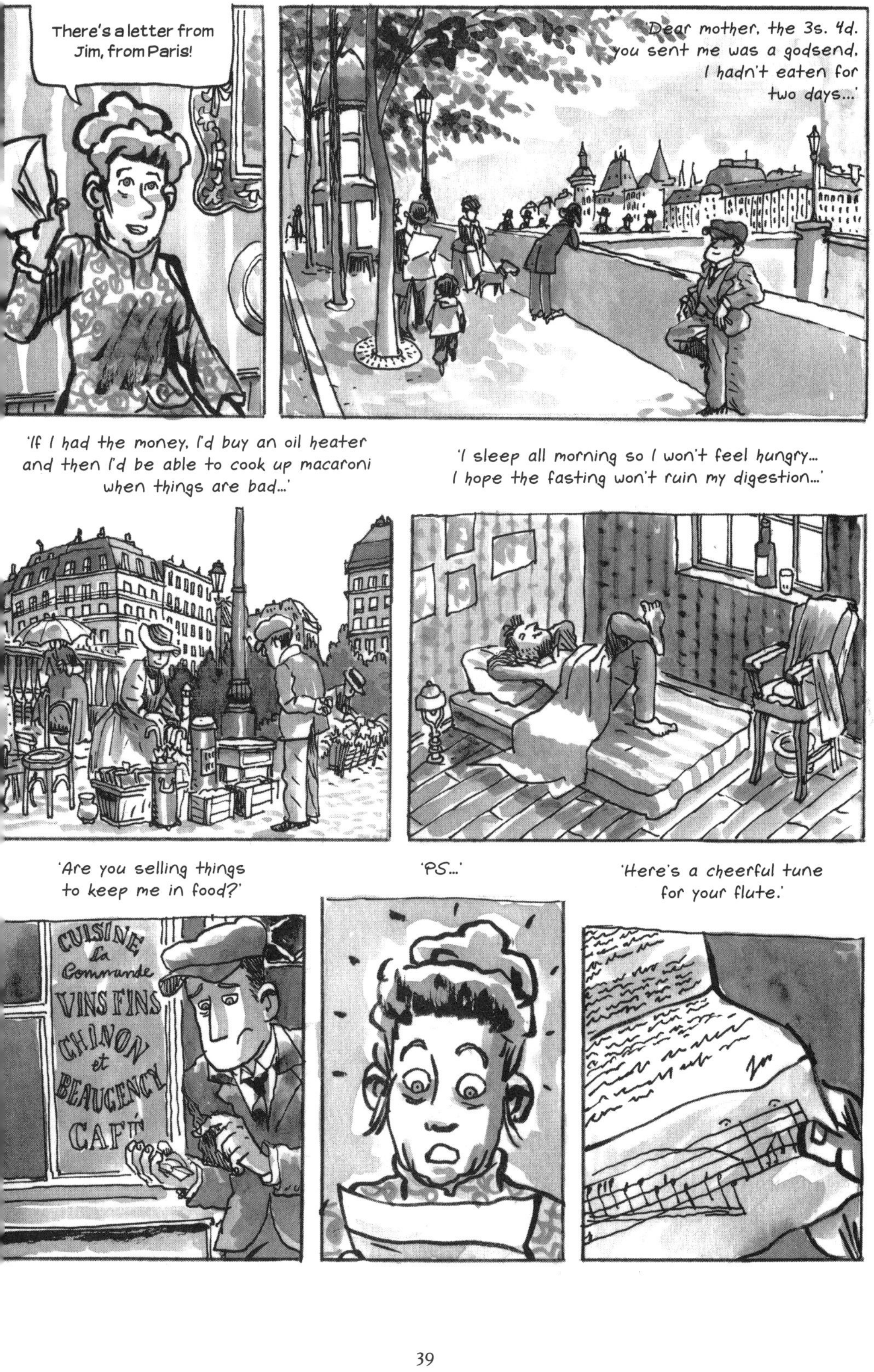
There's a letter from Jim, from Paris!
'Dear mother, the 3s. 4d. you sent me was a godsend. I hadn't eaten for two days...'
'If I had the money, I'd buy an oil heater and then I'd be able to cook up macaroni when things are bad...'
'I sleep all morning so I won't feel hungry... I hope the fasting won't ruin my digestion...'
'Are you selling things to keep me in food?'
CUISINE
la Commande
VINS FINS
CHINON
et
BEAUCENCY
'PS...'
'Here's a cheerful tune for your flute.'

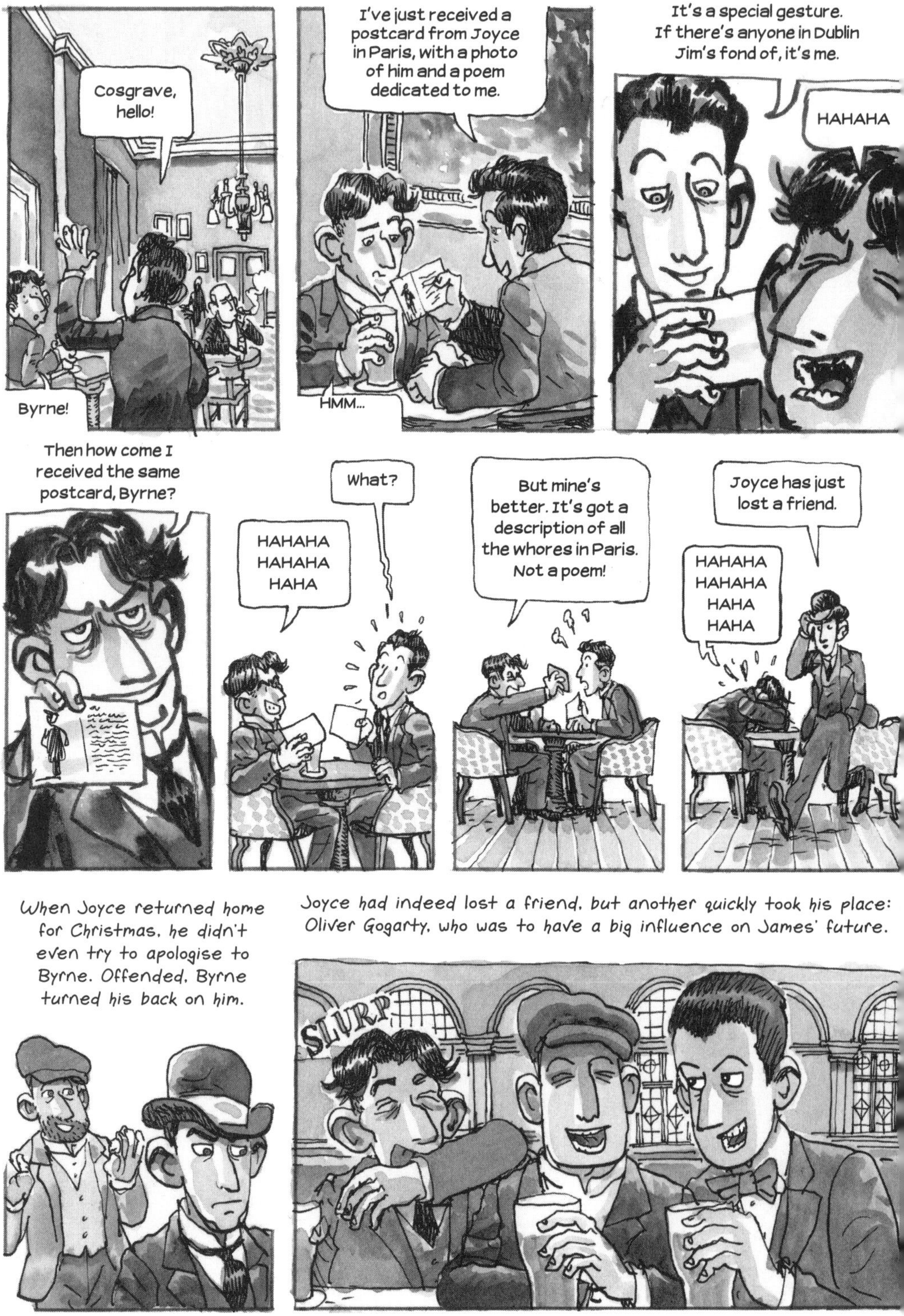
Cosgrave, hello!
Byrne!
I've just received a postcard from Joyce in Paris, with a photo of him and a poem dedicated to me.
HMM...
It's a special gesture. If there's anyone in Dublin Jim's fond of, it's me.
HAHAHA
Then how come I received the same postcard, Byrne?
HAHAHA HAHAHA HAHA
What?
But mine's better. It's got a description of all the whores in Paris. Not a poem!
Joyce has just lost a friend.
HAHAHA HAHAHA HAHA HAHA
When Joyce returned home for Christmas, he didn't even try to apologise to Byrne. Offended, Byrne turned his back on him.
Joyce had indeed lost a friend, but another quickly took his place: Oliver Gogarty, who was to have a big influence on James' future.
SLURP

1903. At the beginning of the year, Joyce returned to his medical studies in Paris.

He started to wear a large black cravat to hide his dirty shirt, since he couldn't afford to have his clothes cleaned. A moustache and a bohemian hat completed his look.

Between one absinthe and another, Joyce made friends with another Irish writer living in Paris: John Synge.

Synge had just written 'Riders to the Sea', a great play, universally praised by the critics.

Could I take a look at the manuscript, Synge?

Of course, Joyce.

Joyce envied his fellow countryman's success. He read the play and tore it to shreds.

Look, Synge, your play is a tragic poem, it's not drama. It has many faults, and the truth is, Ireland needs less useless blather and more true art.

What?

It's a one-act play!

It has a lot of quality in it!

One-act plays and puny dramas. I don't want to argue about it any more.

Good-bye, Synge.

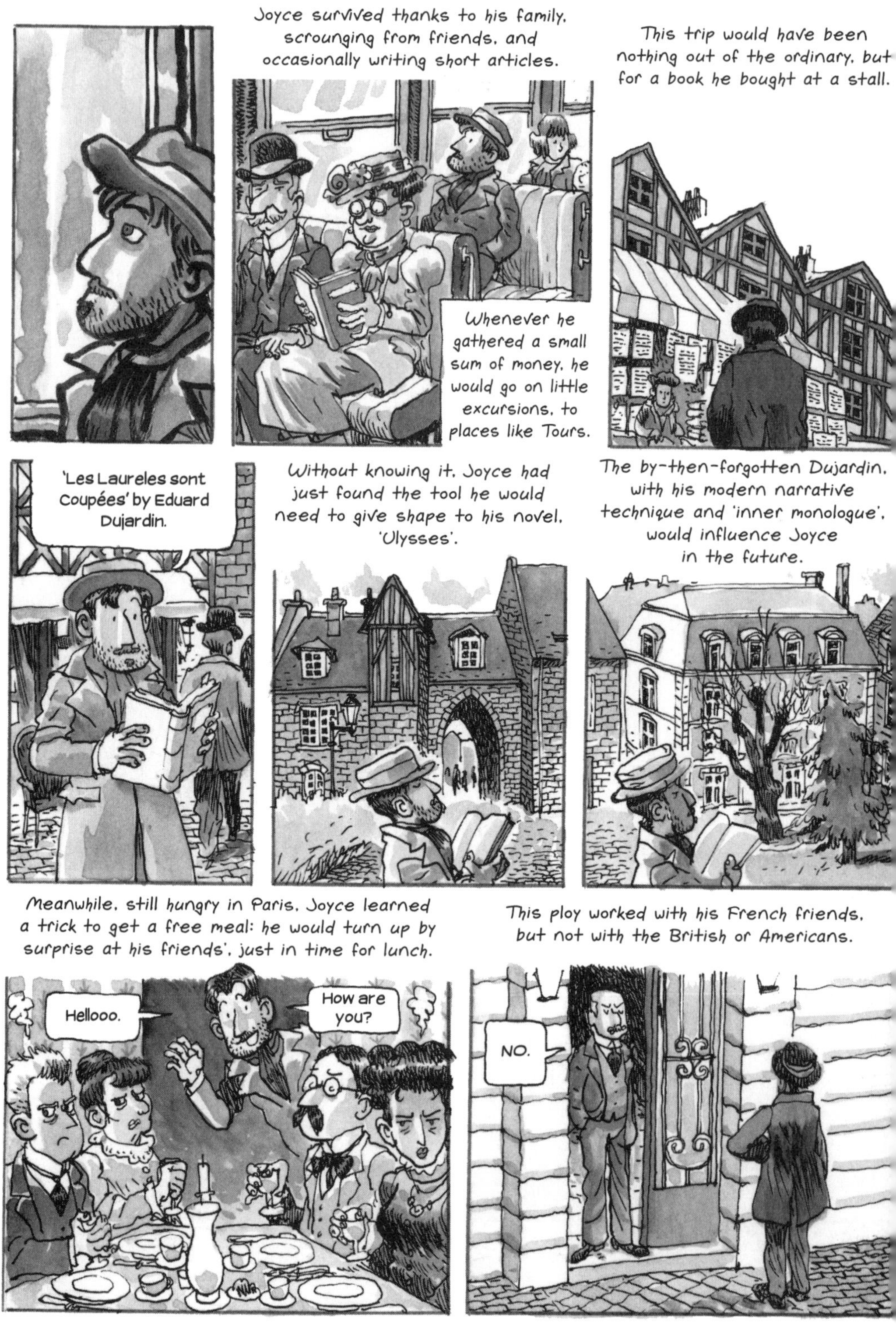
Joyce survived thanks to his family, scrounging from friends, and occasionally writing short articles.
Whenever he gathered a small sum of money, he would go on little excursions, to places like Tours.
This trip would have been nothing out of the ordinary, but for a book he bought at a stall.
'Les Laureles sont Coupées' by Eduard Dujardin.
Without knowing it, Joyce had just found the tool he would need to give shape to his novel, 'Ulysses'.
The by-then-forgotten Dujardin, with his modern narrative technique and 'inner monologue', would influence Joyce in the future.
Meanwhile, still hungry in Paris, Joyce learned a trick to get a free meal: he would turn up by surprise at his friends', just in time for lunch.
Hellooo.
How are you?
This ploy worked with his French friends, but not with the British or Americans.
NO.

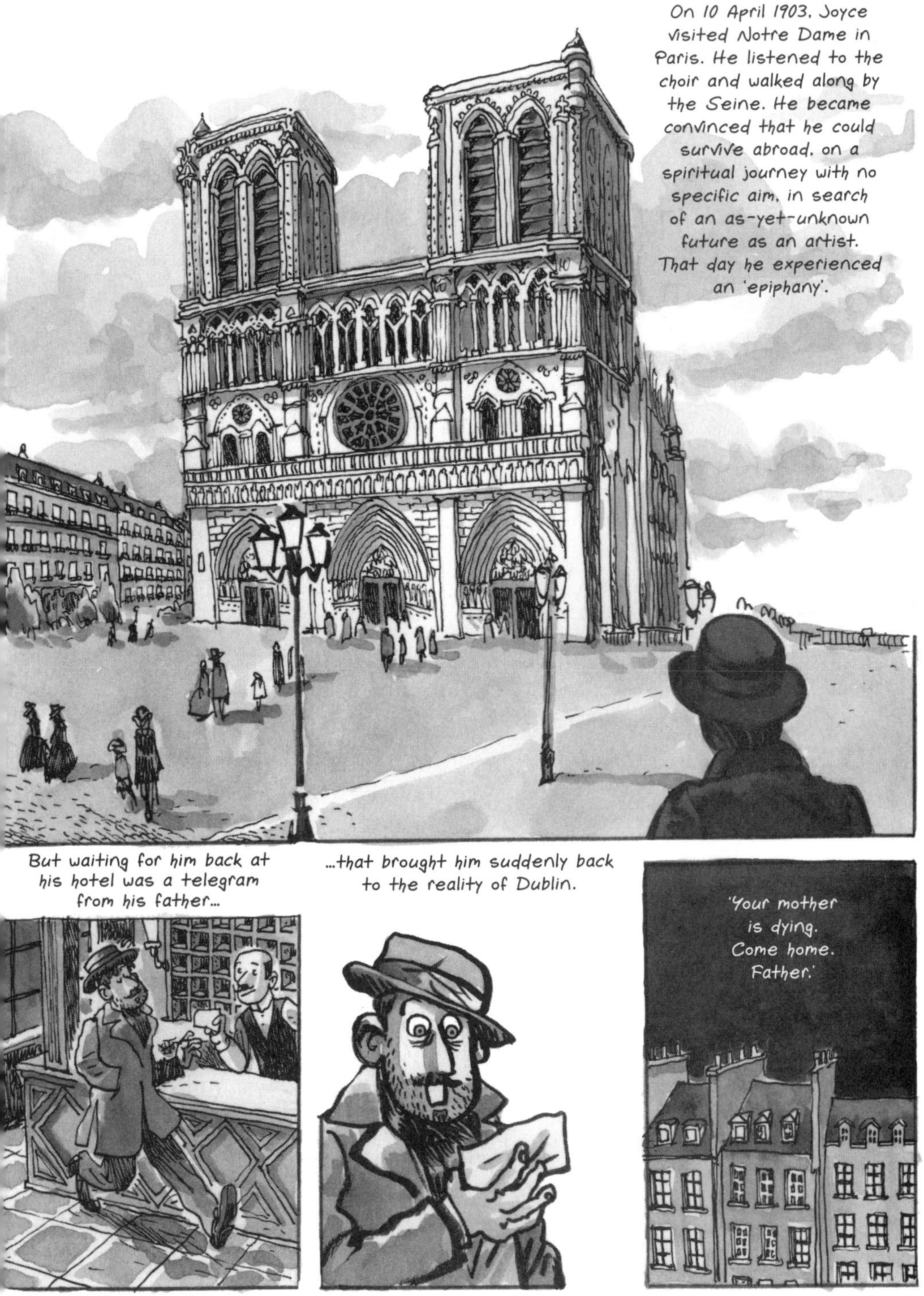
On 10 April 1903, Joyce visited Notre Dame in Paris. He listened to the choir and walked along by the Seine. He became convinced that he could survive abroad, on a spiritual journey with no specific aim, in search of an as-yet-unknown future as an artist. That day he experienced an 'epiphany'.
But waiting for him back at his hotel was a telegram from his father...
...that brought him suddenly back to the reality of Dublin.
'Your mother is dying. Come home. Father.'

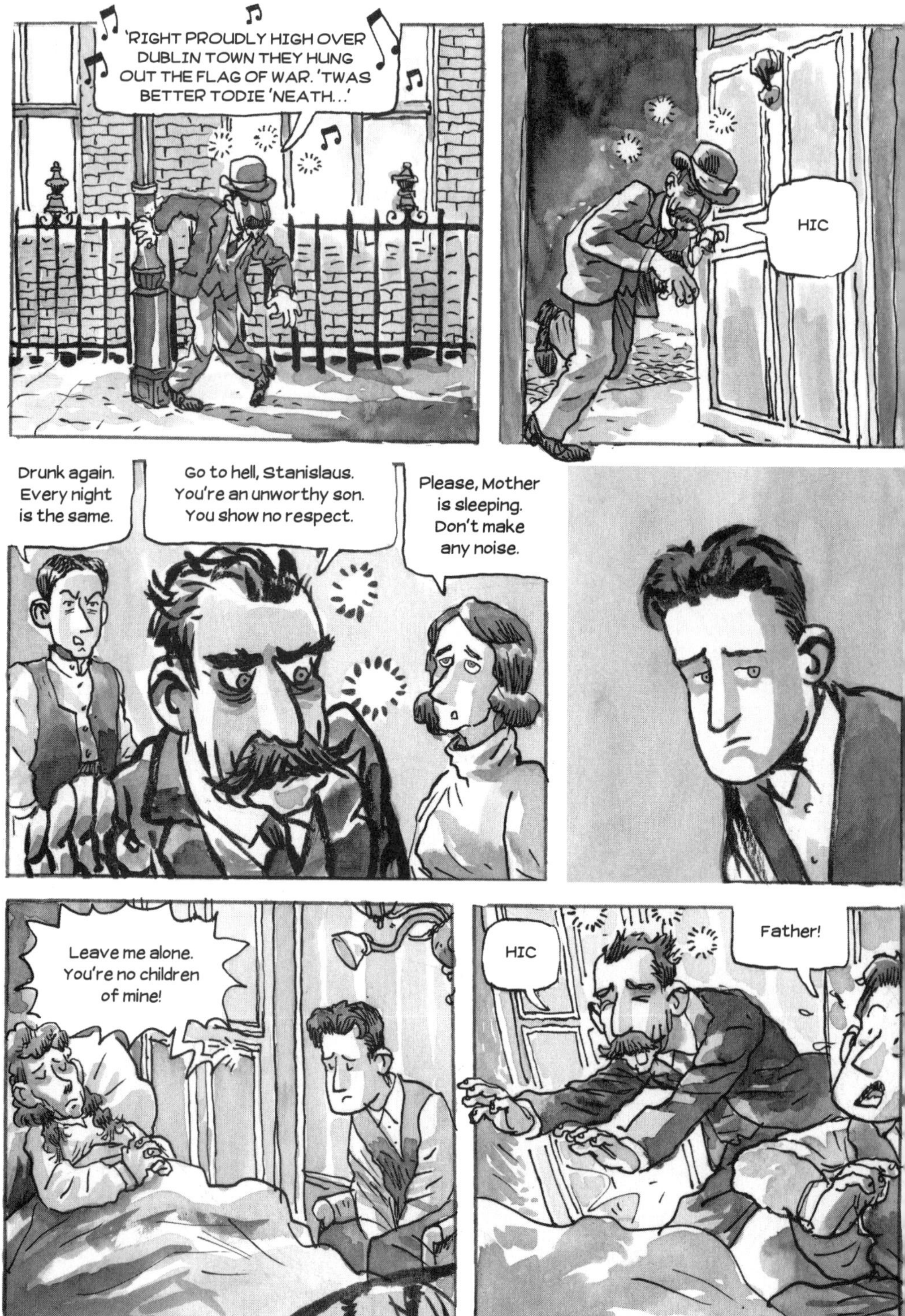
'RIGHT PROUDLY HIGH OVER DUBLIN TOWN THEY HUNG OUT THE FLAG OF WAR. 'TWAS BETTER TODIE 'NEATH...'
HIC
Drunk again. Every night is the same.
Go to hell, Stanislaus. You're an unworthy son. You show no respect.
Please, Mother is sleeping. Don't make any noise.
Leave me alone. You're no children of mine!
HIC
Father!

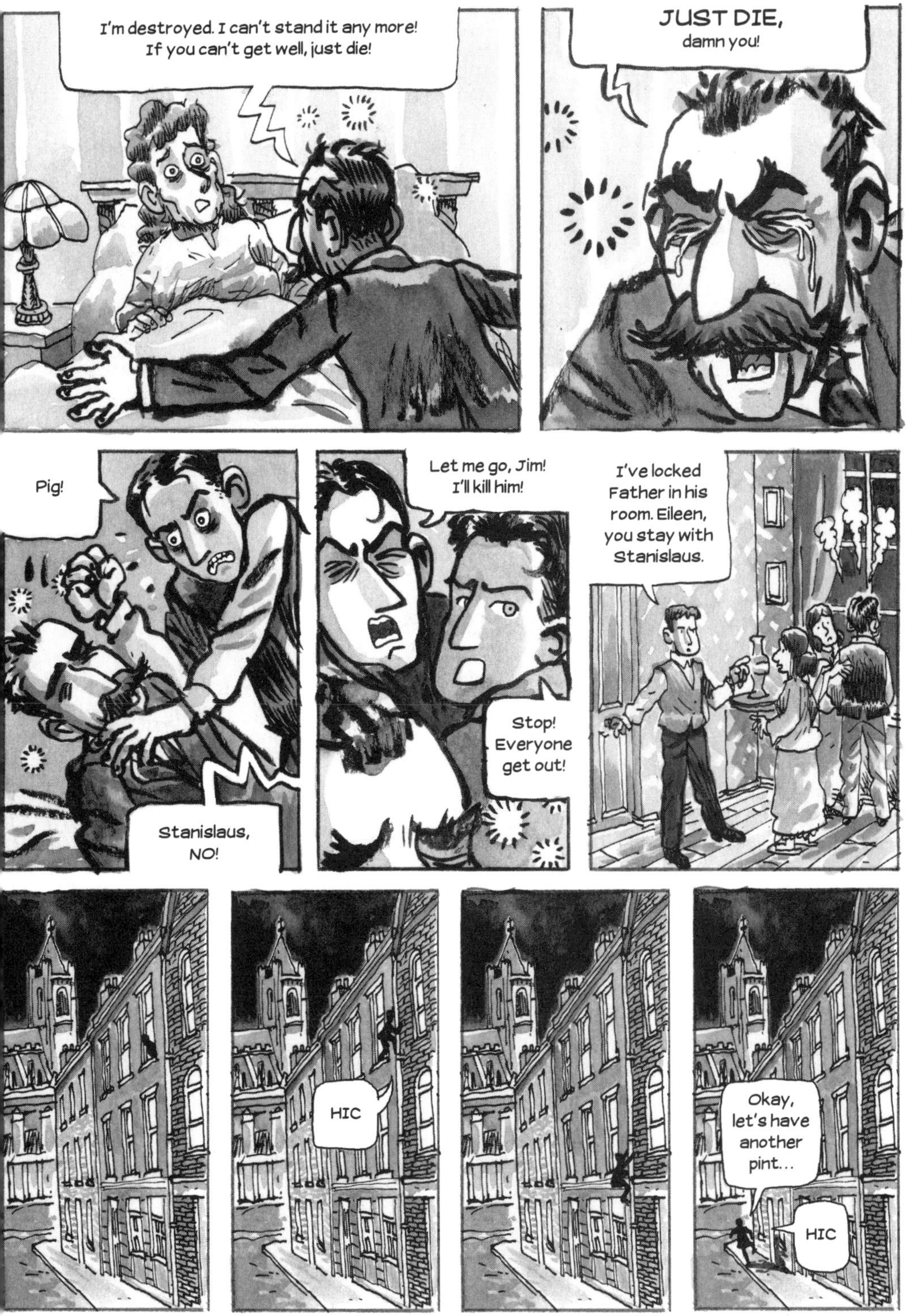
I'm destroyed. I can't stand it any more! If you can't get well, just die!
JUST DIE, damn you!
Pig!
Stanislaus, NO!
Let me go, Jim! I'll kill him!
Stop! Everyone get out!
I've locked Father in his room. Eileen, you stay with Stanislaus.
HIC
Okay, let's have another pint...
HIC

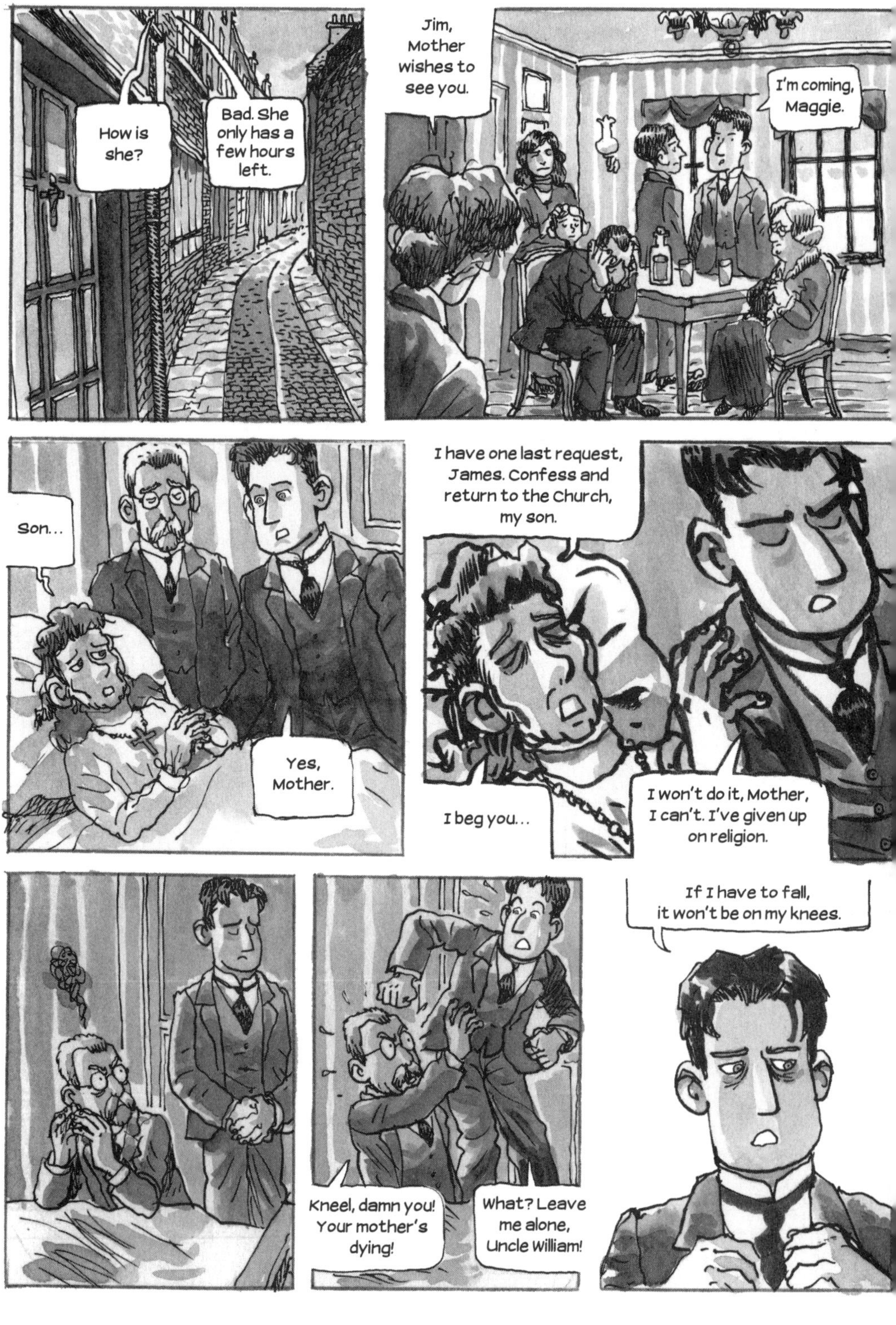
How is she?
Bad. She only has a few hours left.
Jim, Mother wishes to see you.
I'm coming, Maggie.
Son...
Yes, Mother.
I have one last request, James. Confess and return to the Church, my son.
I beg you...
I won't do it, Mother, I can't. I've given up on religion.
Kneel, damn you! Your mother's dying!
What? Leave me alone, Uncle William!
If I have to fall, it won't be on my knees.

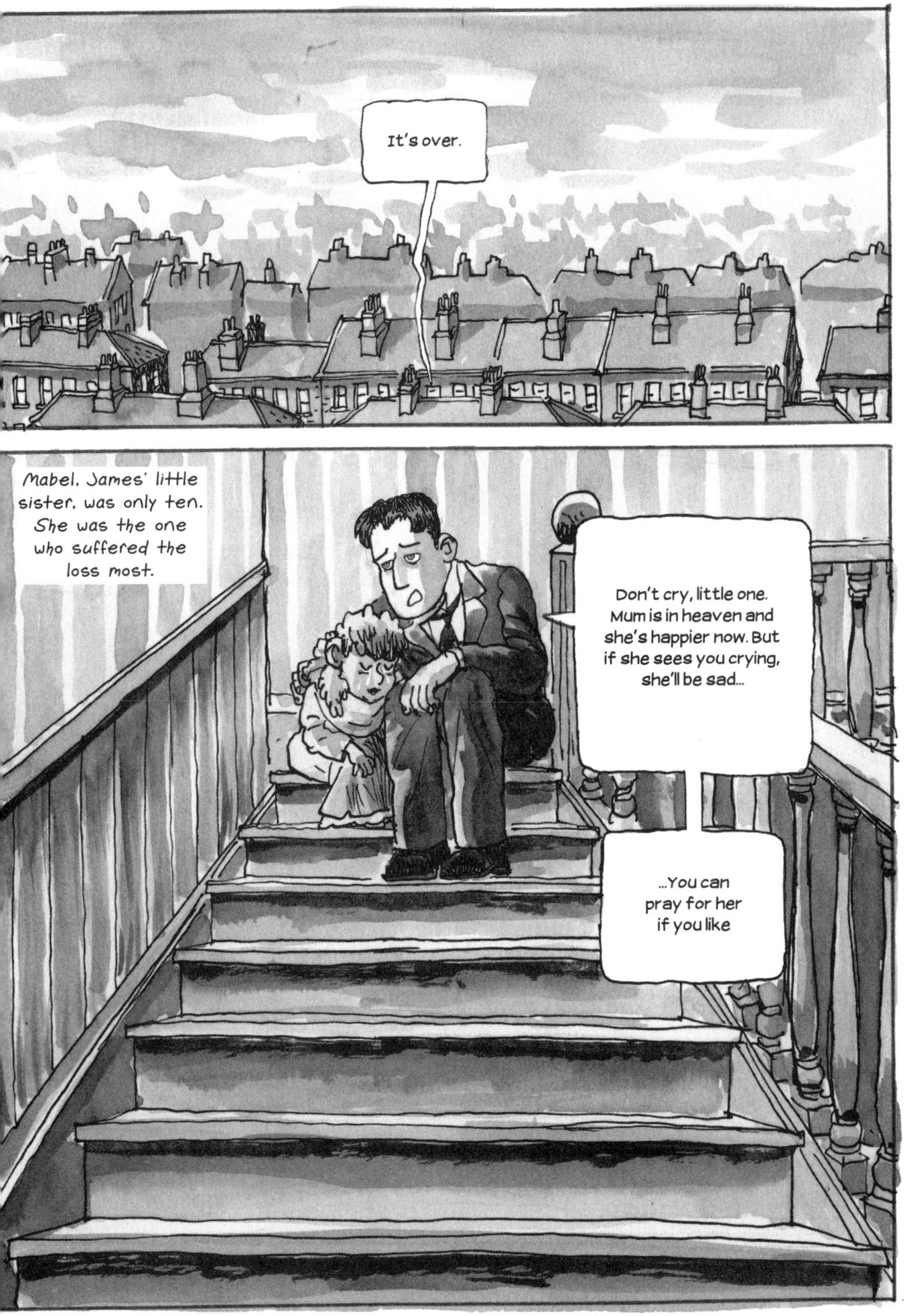
It's over.
Mabel, James' little sister, was only ten. She was the one who suffered the loss most.
Don't cry, little one. Mum is in heaven and she's happier now. But if she sees you crying, she'll be sad...
...You can pray for her if you like

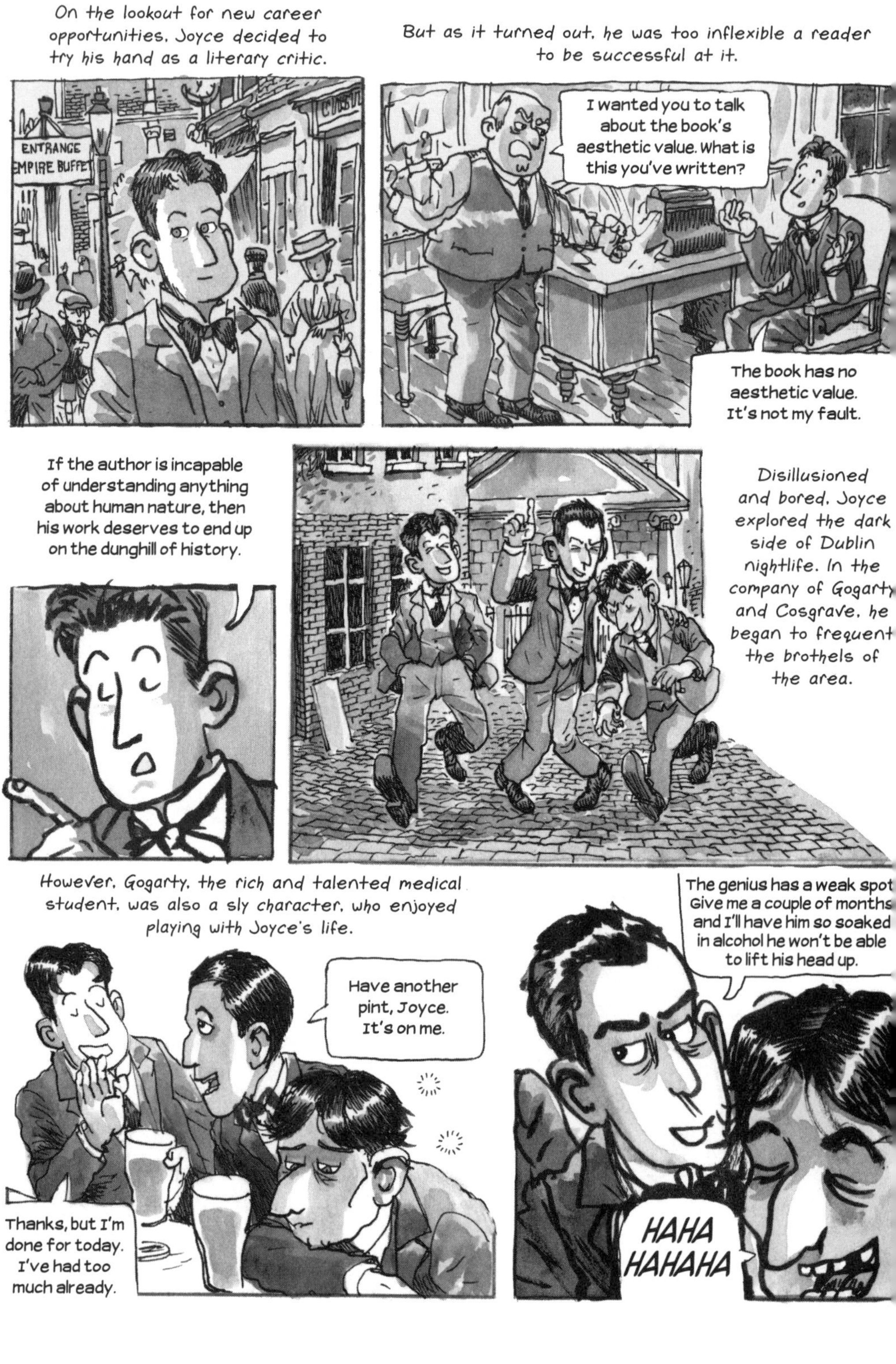
On the lookout for new career opportunities, Joyce decided to try his hand as a literary critic.
ENTRANCE
EMPIRE BUFFET
But as it turned out, he was too inflexible a reader to be successful at it.
I wanted you to talk about the book's aesthetic value. What is this you've written?
The book has no aesthetic value. It's not my fault.
If the author is incapable of understanding anything about human nature, then his work deserves to end up on the dunghill of history.
Disillusioned and bored, Joyce explored the dark side of Dublin nightlife. In the company of Gogarty and Cosgrave, he began to frequent the brothels of the area.
However, Gogarty, the rich and talented medical student, was also a sly character, who enjoyed playing with Joyce's life.
Have another pint, Joyce. It's on me.
Thanks, but I'm done for today. I've had too much already.
The genius has a weak spot Give me a couple of months and I'll have him so soaked in alcohol he won't be able to lift his head up.
HAHA HAHAHA

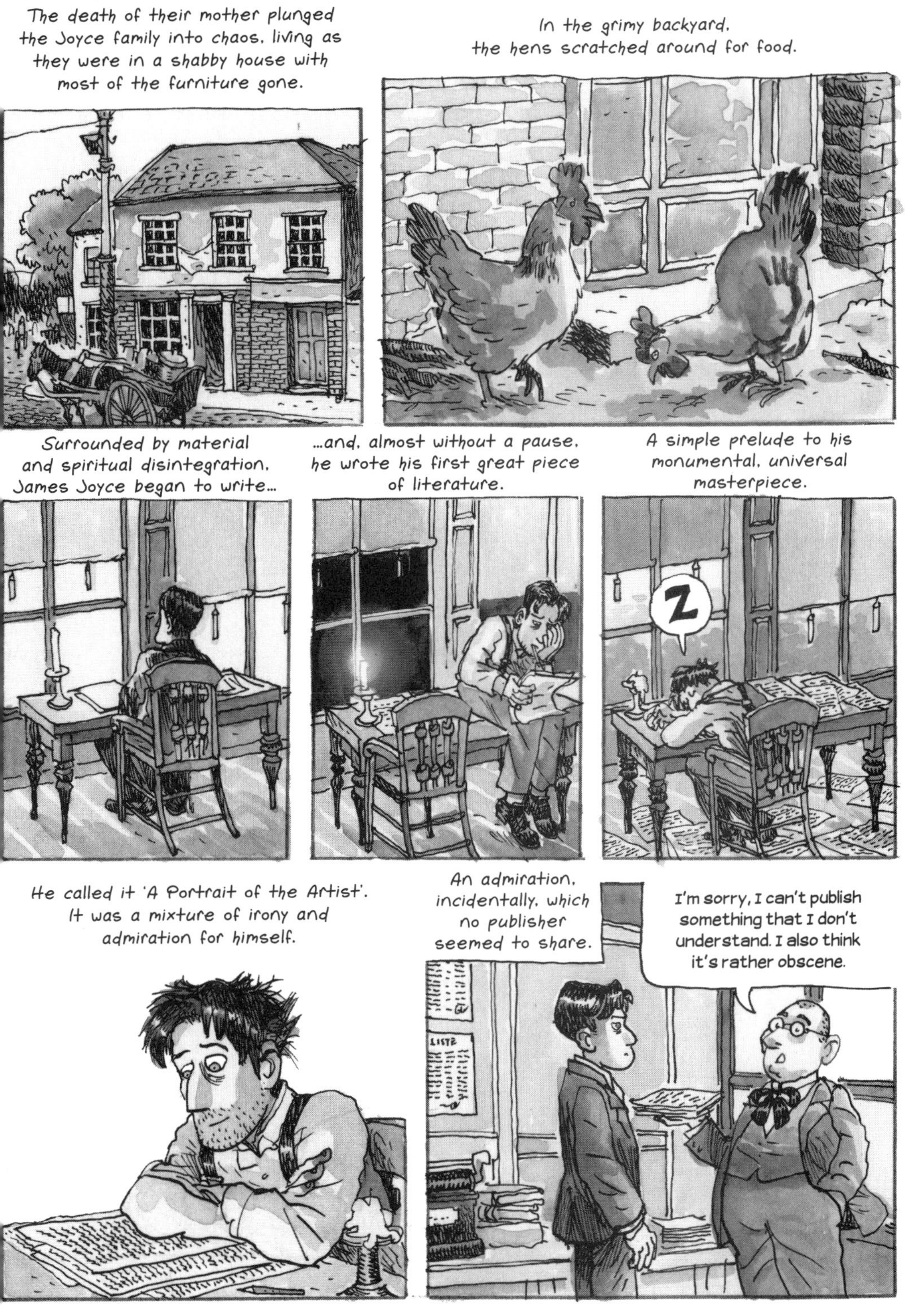

The death of their mother plunged the Joyce family into chaos, living as they were in a shabby house with most of the furniture gone.
In the grimy backyard, the hens scratched around for food.
Surrounded by material and spiritual disintegration, James Joyce began to write...
...and, almost without a pause, he wrote his first great piece of literature.
A simple prelude to his monumental, universal masterpiece.
Z
He called it 'A Portrait of the Artist'. It was a mixture of irony and admiration for himself.
An admiration, incidentally, which no publisher seemed to share.
I'm sorry, I can't publish something that I don't understand. I also think it's rather obscene.
LISTE

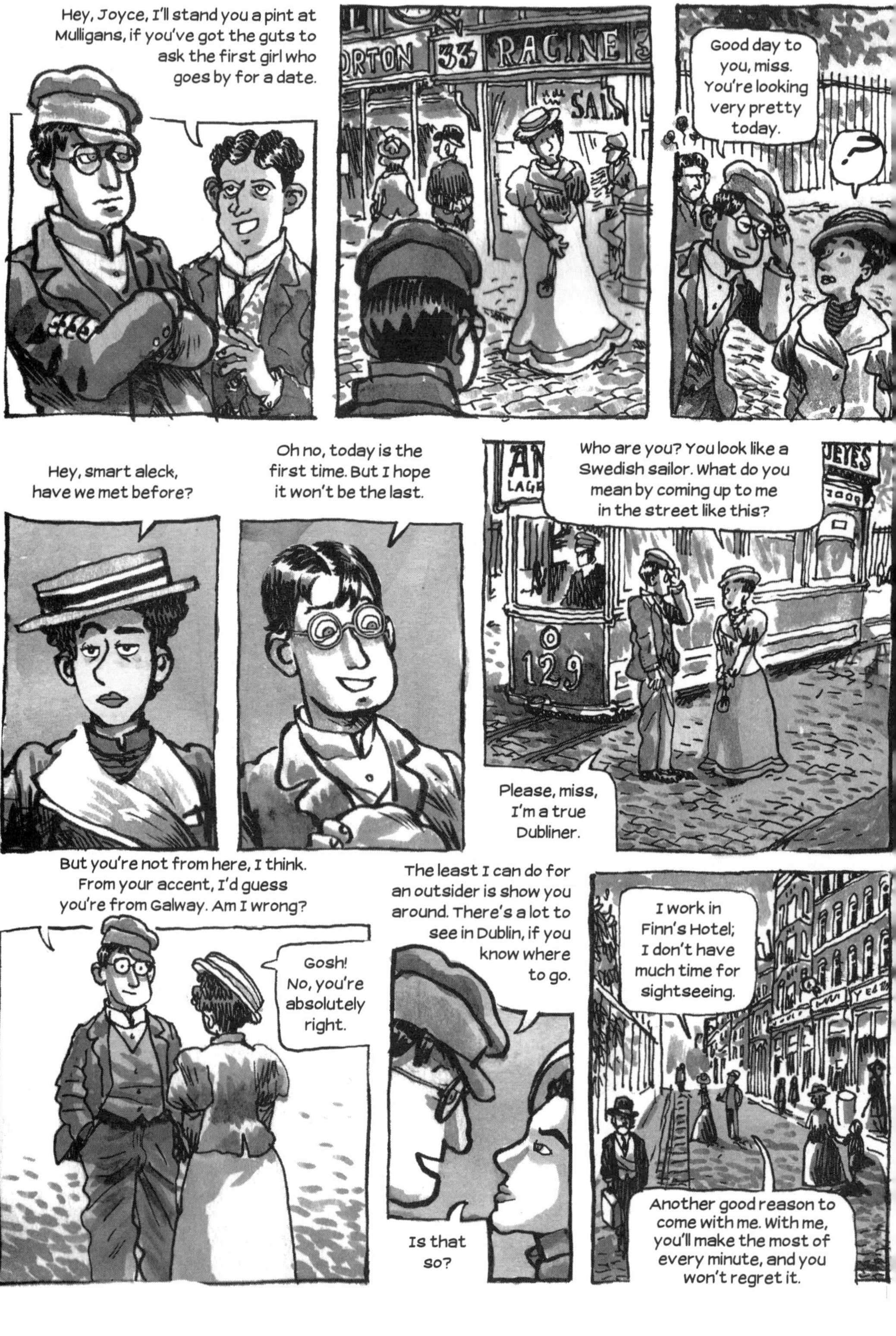
Hey, Joyce, I'll stand you a pint at Mulligans, if you've got the guts to ask the first girl who goes by for a date.
ORTON 33 RACINE
SALS
Good day to you, miss. You're looking very pretty today.
?
Hey, smart aleck, have we met before?
Oh no, today is the first time. But I hope it won't be the last.
Who are you? You look like a Swedish sailor. What do you mean by coming up to me in the street like this?
129
Please, miss, I'm a true Dubliner.
But you're not from here, I think. From your accent, I'd guess you're from Galway. Am I wrong?
Gosh! No, you're absolutely right.
The least I can do for an outsider is show you around. There's a lot to see in Dublin, if you know where to go.
Is that so?
I work in Finn's Hotel; I don't have much time for sightseeing.
Another good reason to come with me. With me, you'll make the most of every minute, and you won't regret it.

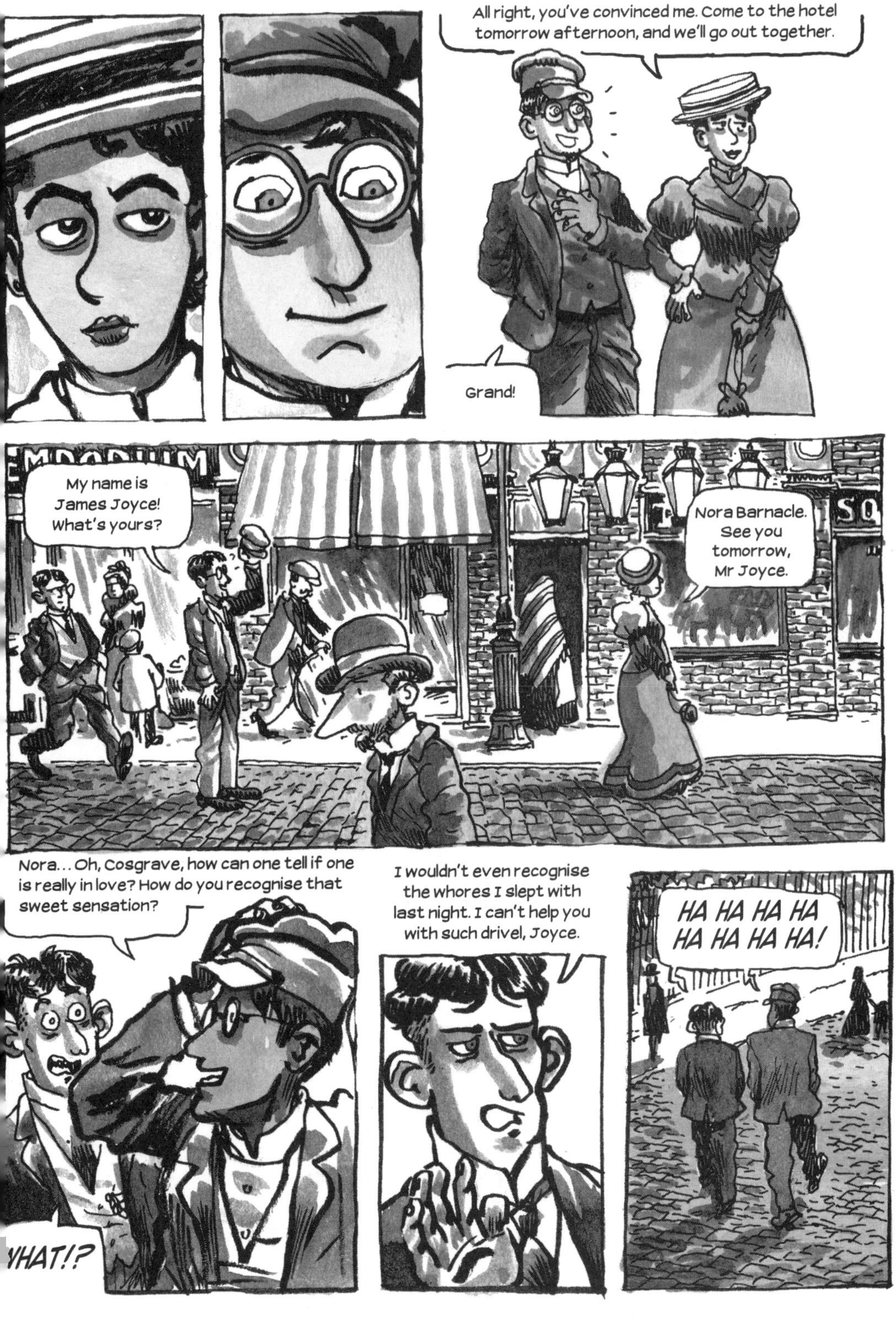
All right, you've convinced me. Come to the hotel tomorrow afternoon, and we'll go out together.
Grand!
My name is James Joyce! What's yours?
Nora Barnacle. See you tomorrow, Mr Joyce.
Nora... Oh, Cosgrave, how can one tell if one is really in love? How do you recognise that sweet sensation?
WHAT!?
I wouldn't even recognise the whores I slept with last night. I can't help you with such drivel, Joyce.
HA HA HA HA HA HA HA HA!

On 14 June, Joyce waited for Nora at the corner of Merrion Square.

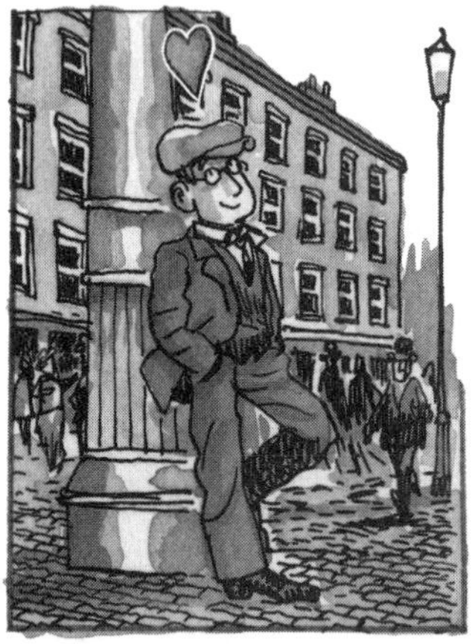

The hours went by...

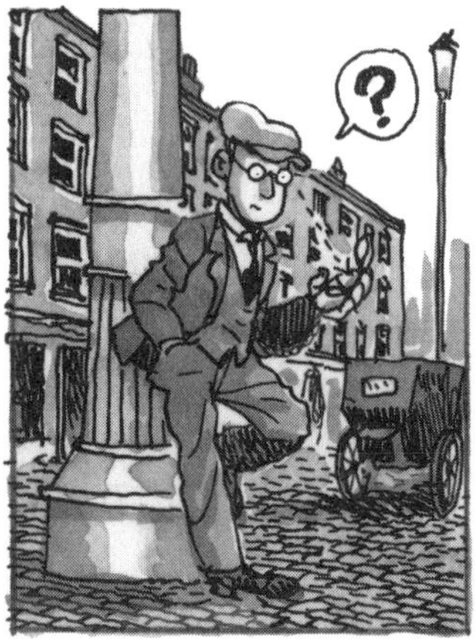
?

...but Nora didn't show up.

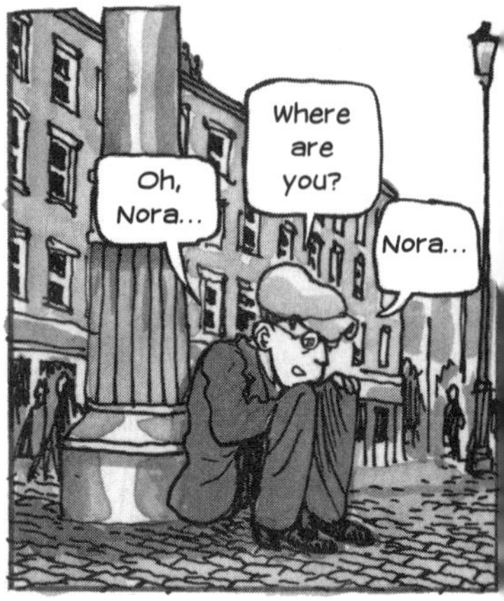
Oh, Nora...
Where are you?
Nora...

On 15 June, Joyce sent a letter to his beloved, begging her for another date.

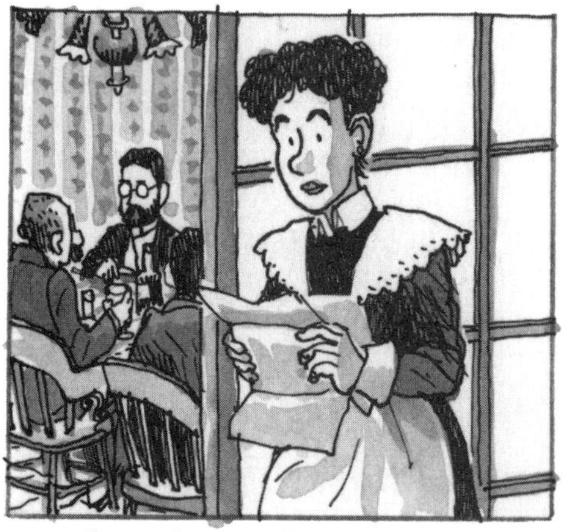

Finally, on 16 June, they went for a walk together.

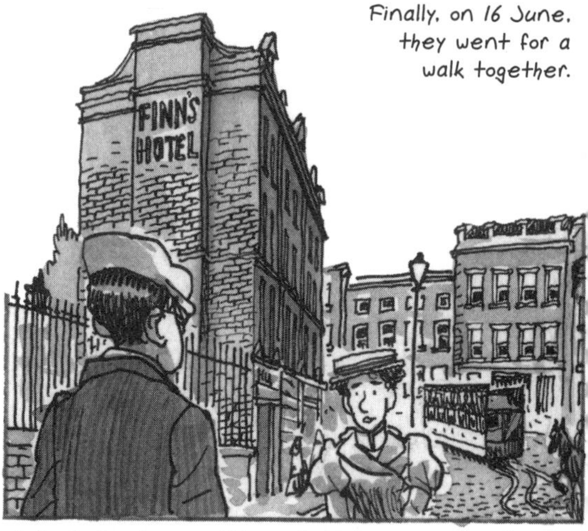
FINN'S HOTEL

Though they barely knew each other, they talked about many things, both happy and sad. About Galway, about Nora's uncle, Tom Healy, who gave her a beating once because of her friend Mary, who forgot to tell her one day that she was with her boyfriend, Willie Mulvey...

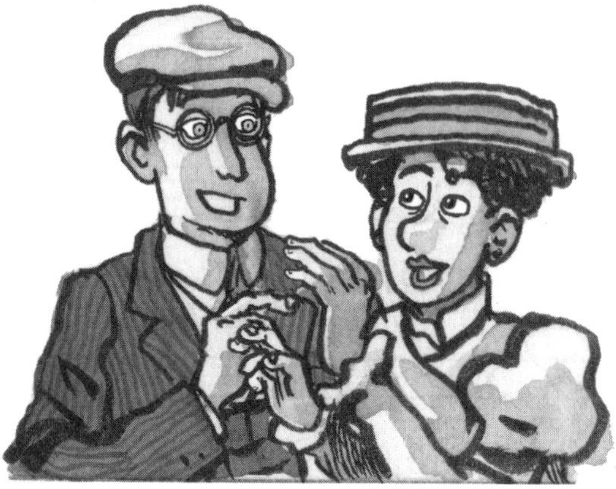

They talked about Will Bodkin, a Galway boy who was in love with Nora, who stood outside her house the day before she left for Dublin so she would see him from her window. Will was ill, and it was pouring with rain: as a result he died shortly after. That day in Ringsend, Joyce was captivated by Nora: the whimsical student turned into a genius in love.

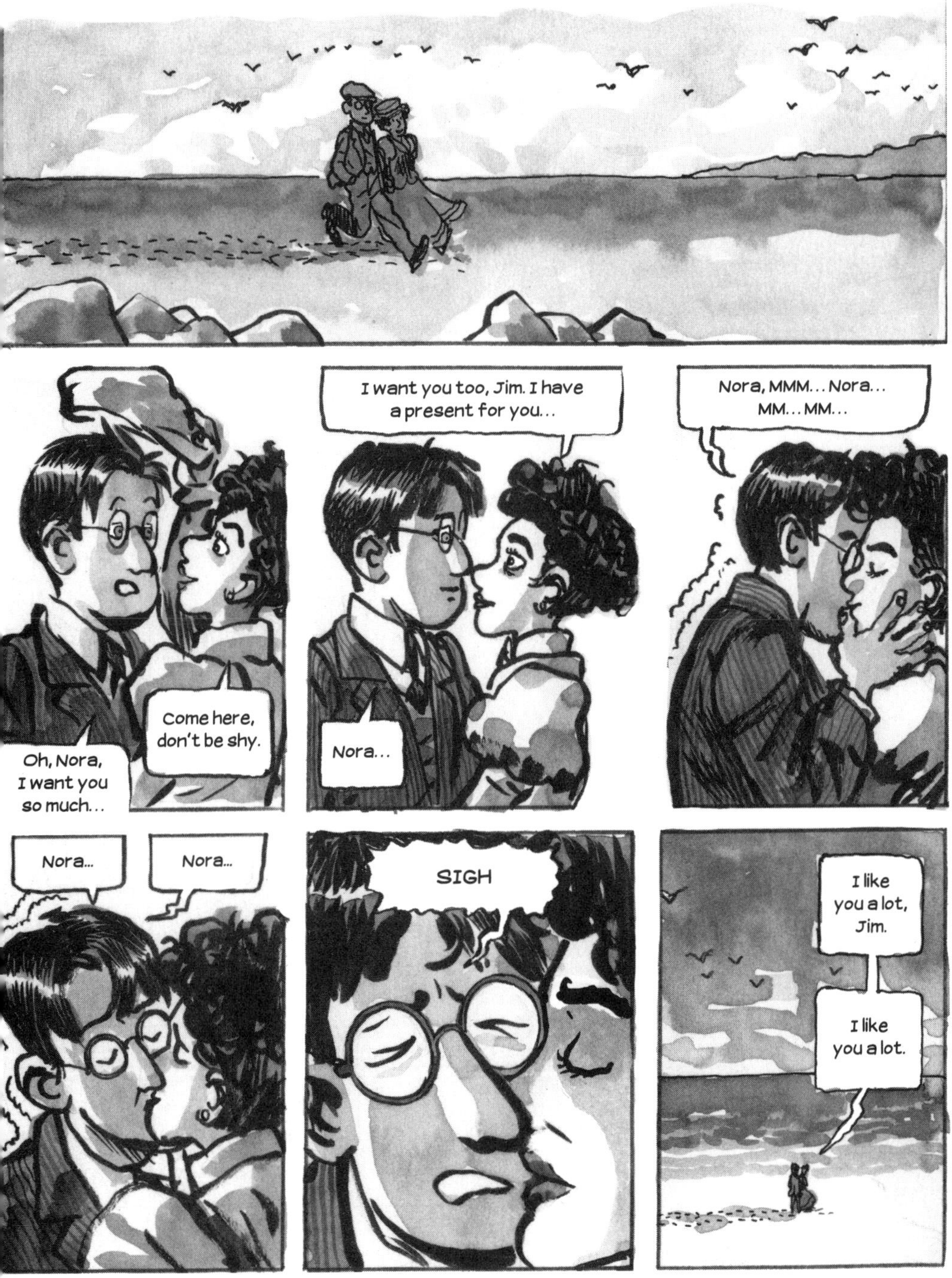

Oh, Nora, I want you so much...
Come here, don't be shy.
I want you too, Jim. I have a present for you...
Nora...
Nora, MMM... Nora... MM... MM...
Nora...
Nora...
SIGH
I like you a lot, Jim.
I like you a lot.

Joyce kept up his correspondence with Nora Barnacle.

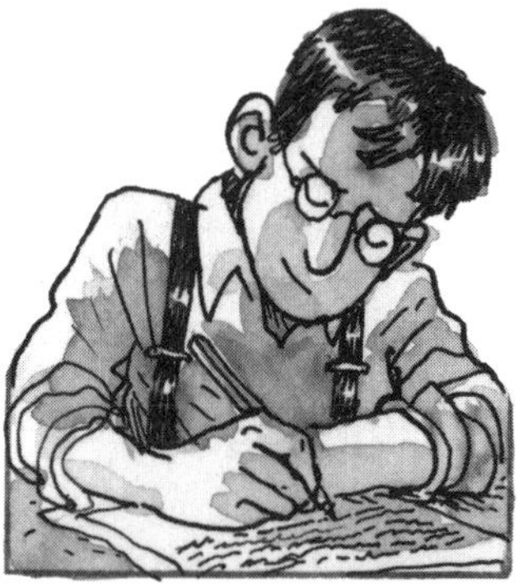

Still working at Finn's Hotel, she enjoyed having a poet-lover.

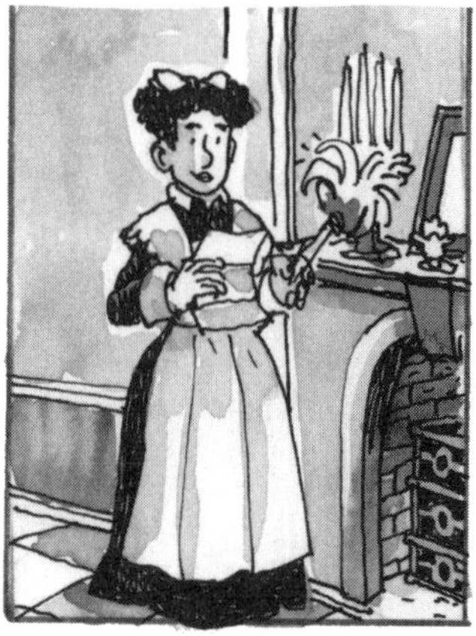

Joyce was deeply in love.

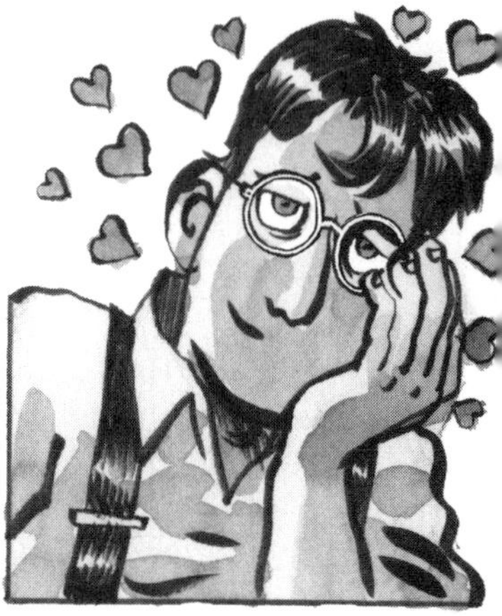

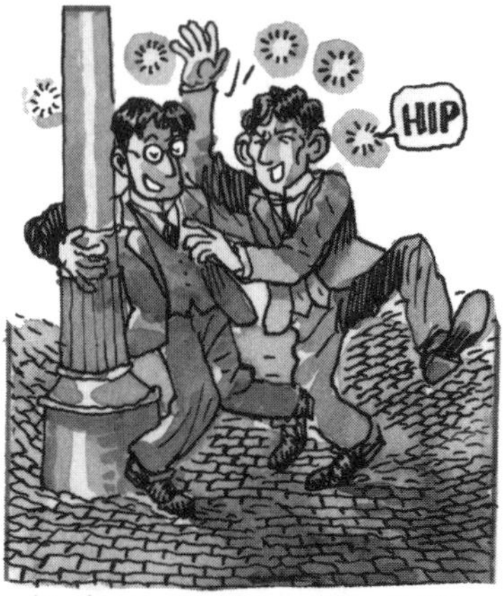
HIP

In other ways, his habits didn't change. He kept up his daily binges with Cosgrave...

Till one afternoon in St Stephen's Green, Joyce bothered a married woman, and got beaten up by her husband.

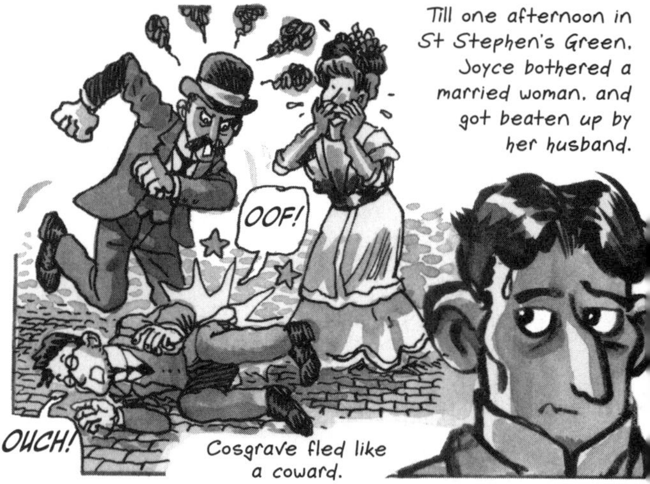
OOF!
OUCH!

Cosgrave fled like a coward.

Joyce hadn't a penny to his name, and continued to ask his friends for help.

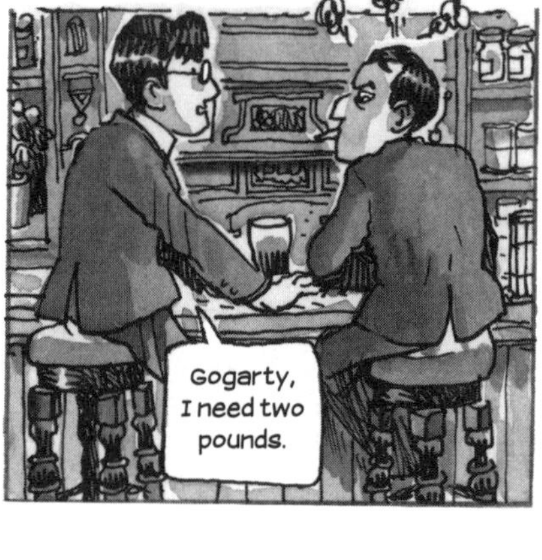
Gogarty, I need two pounds.

Joyce didn't consider himself a parasite. On the contrary, he thought it was a great honour for his friends to be given the opportunity to help out a future genius.

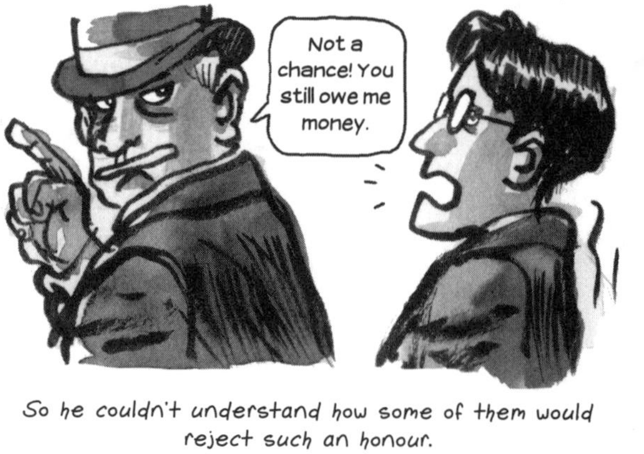
Not a chance! You still owe me money.

So he couldn't understand how some of them would reject such an honour.

Russell asked him to write something rural, lively, with a touch of pathos, for the 'Irish Homestead'. They would pay him a pound.

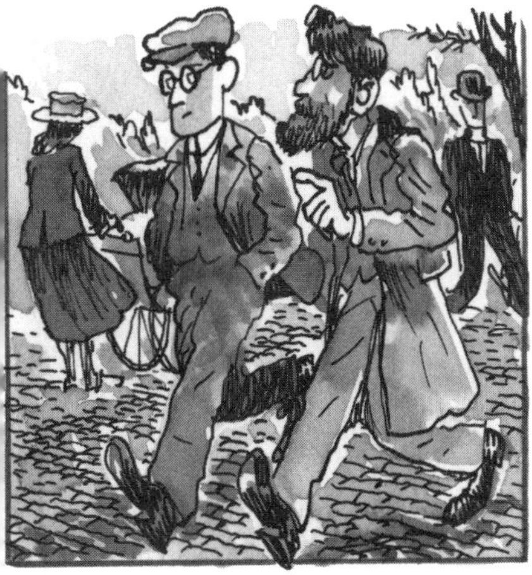

So James sat down, put pen to paper, and wrote 'The Sisters', a story based on the death of the old, mad priest who had been his mother's cousin.

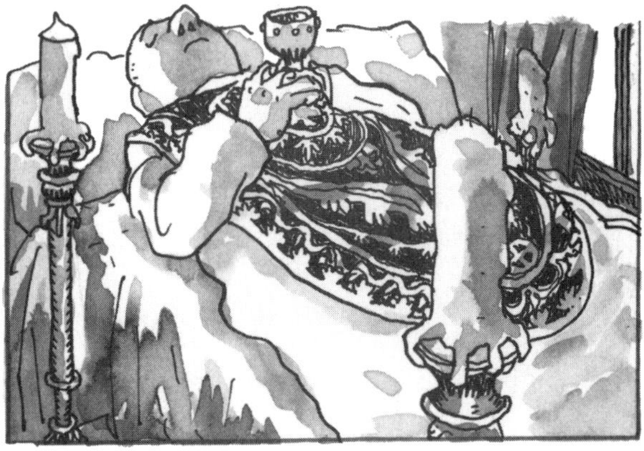

From then on, Joyce took a hostile approach to the world around him. He found strength in Nora and in art, while declaring war on a grey nation, a paralytic society, a reactionary Church, and even on the Irish literary revival itself for forming part of it all.

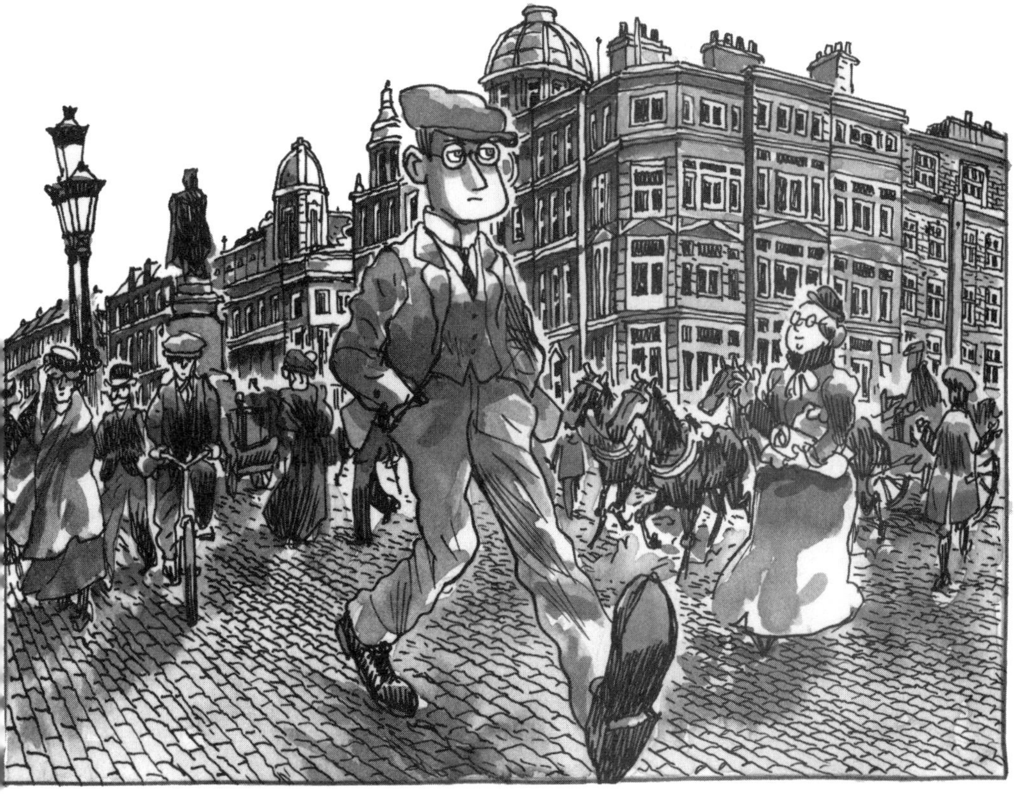

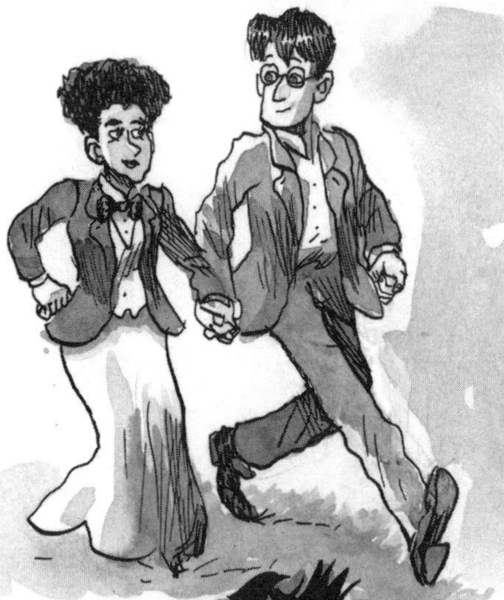

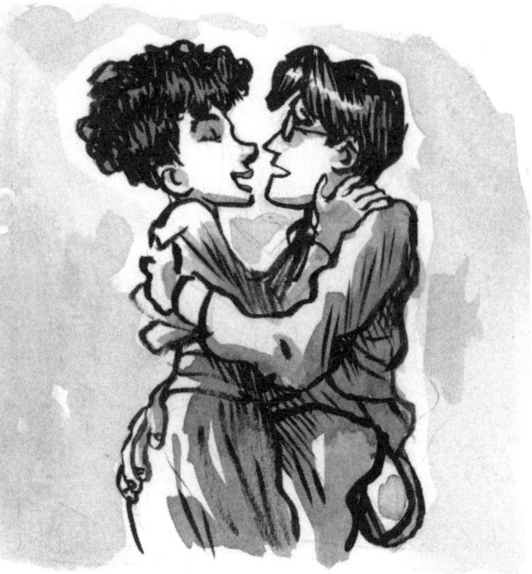

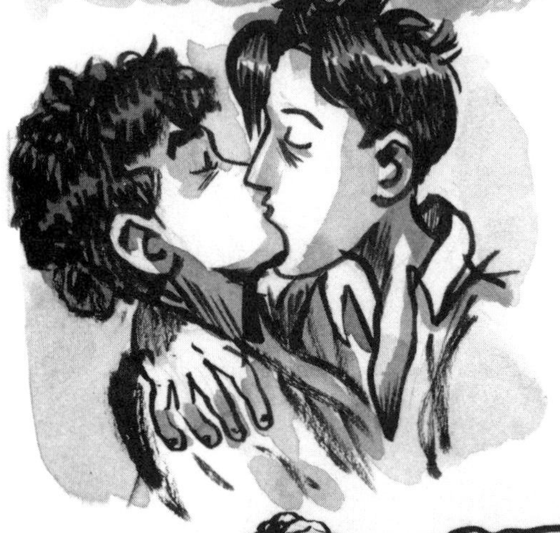

Joyce the poet had found a muse in Nora, in whom he could love an image of the beauty of the world. In her, he could uncover the mystery of beauty and life, and in her he could see the images of purity and spiritual compassion that he used to believe in as a child.

Nora's soul, her name, her eyes were like rare, lovely, wild blue flowers that grow in the tangled hedgerows, wet with rain.

Beside her soul, he felt his own soul tremble, and in the middle of the night he would utter her name softly: 'Nora, Nora', crying as he watched time pass by in front of his eyes.

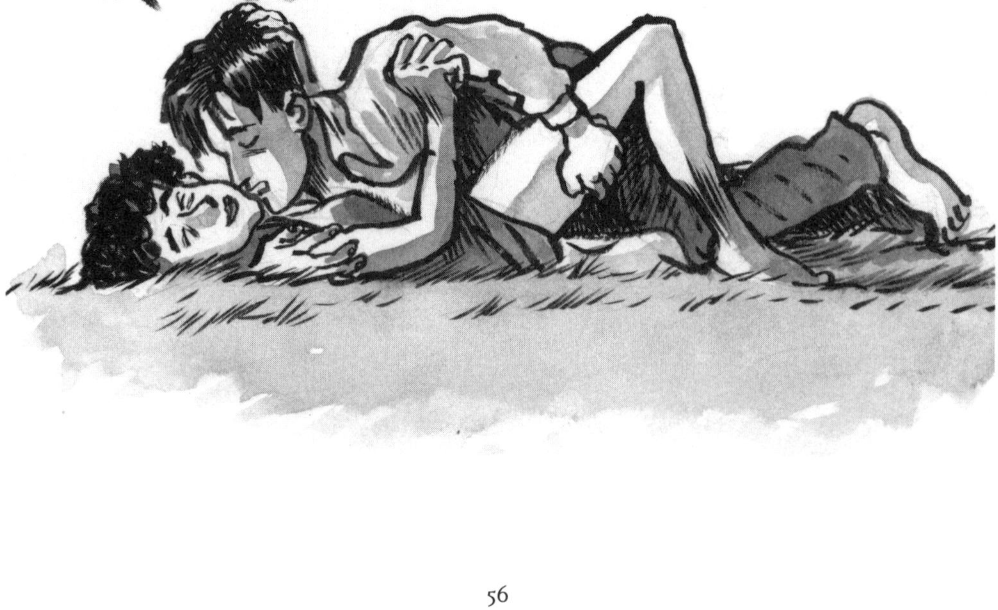

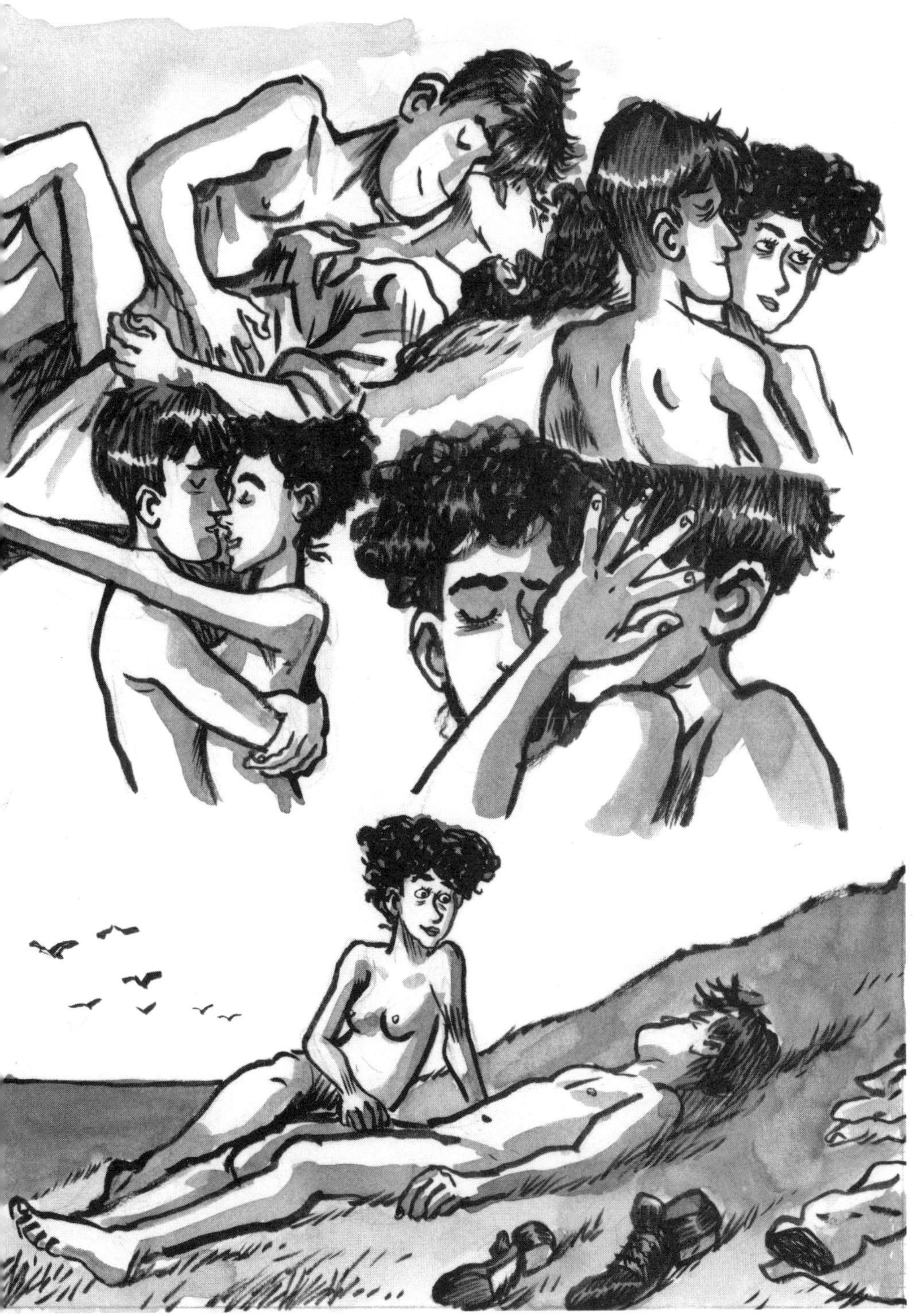

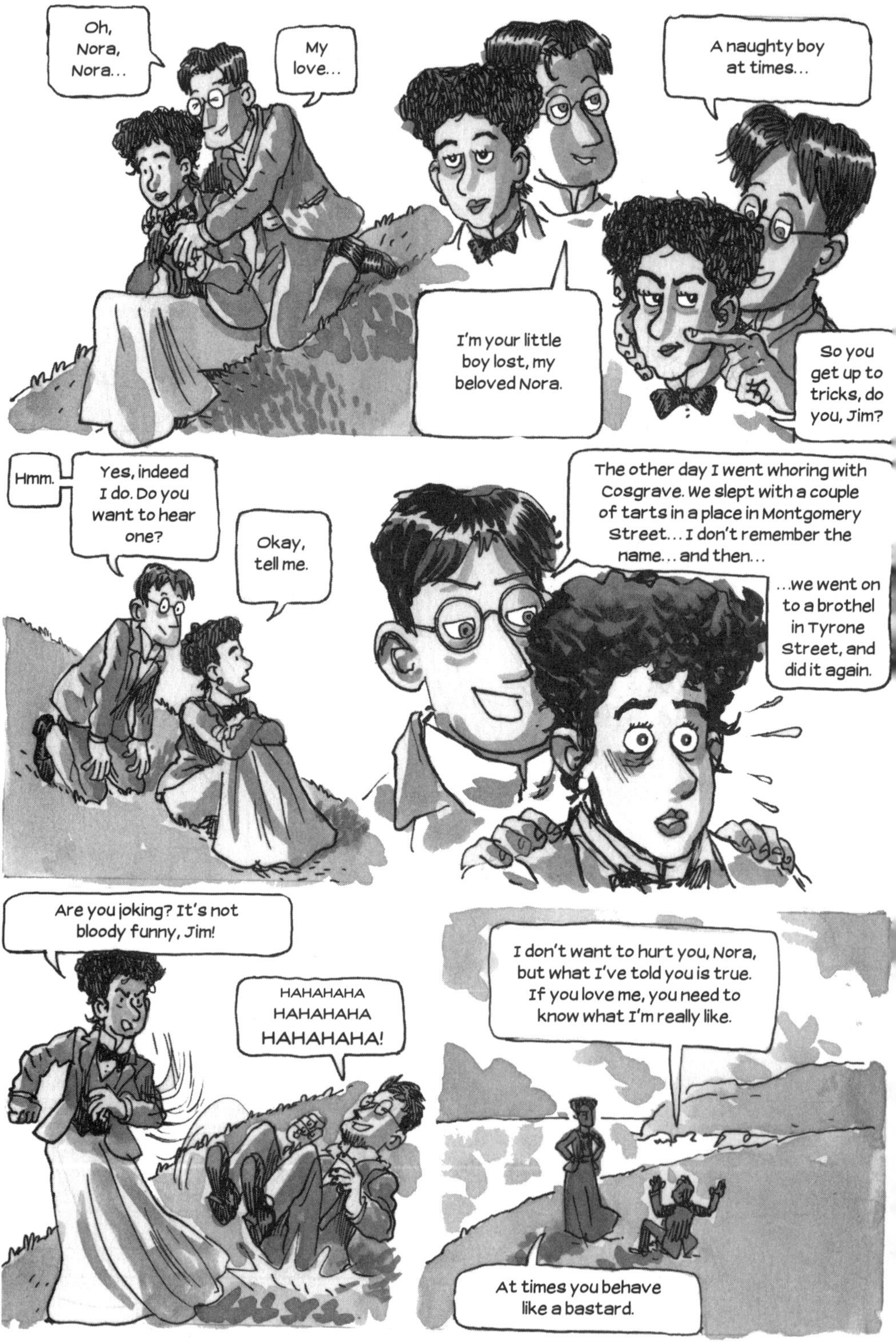
Oh, Nora, Nora…
My love…
A naughty boy at times…
I'm your little boy lost, my beloved Nora.
So you get up to tricks, do you, Jim?
Hmm.
Yes, indeed I do. Do you want to hear one?
Okay, tell me.
The other day I went whoring with Cosgrave. We slept with a couple of tarts in a place in Montgomery Street… I don't remember the name… and then…
…we went on to a brothel in Tyrone Street, and did it again.
Are you joking? It's not bloody funny, Jim!
HAHAHAHA HAHAHAHA HAHAHAHA!
I don't want to hurt you, Nora, but what I've told you is true. If you love me, you need to know what I'm really like.
At times you behave like a bastard.

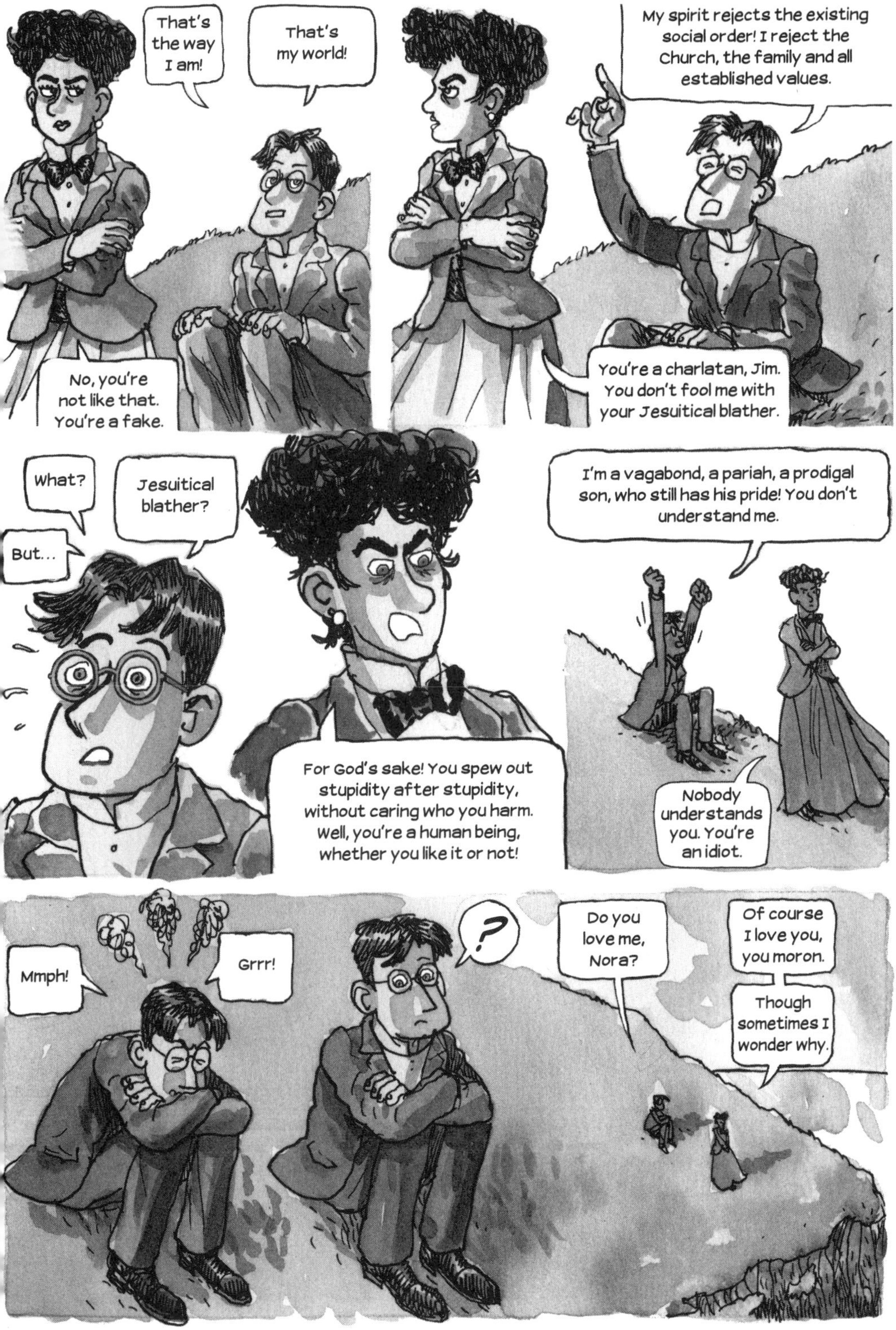
That's the way I am!
That's my world!
No, you're not like that. You're a fake.
My spirit rejects the existing social order! I reject the Church, the family and all established values.
You're a charlatan, Jim. You don't fool me with your Jesuitical blather.
What?
Jesuitical blather?
But...
For God's sake! You spew out stupidity after stupidity, without caring who you harm. Well, you're a human being, whether you like it or not!
I'm a vagabond, a pariah, a prodigal son, who still has his pride! You don't understand me.
Nobody understands you. You're an idiot.
Mmph!
Grrr!
?
Do you love me, Nora?
Of course I love you, you moron.
Though sometimes I wonder why.

In September 1904, Joyce moved into a strange, picturesque residence...

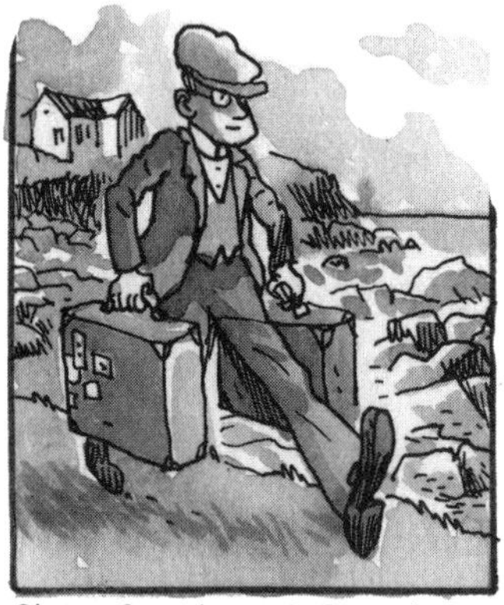

...the Martello Tower in Sandycove, one of the forts built around the Bay of Dublin during the Napoleonic wars.

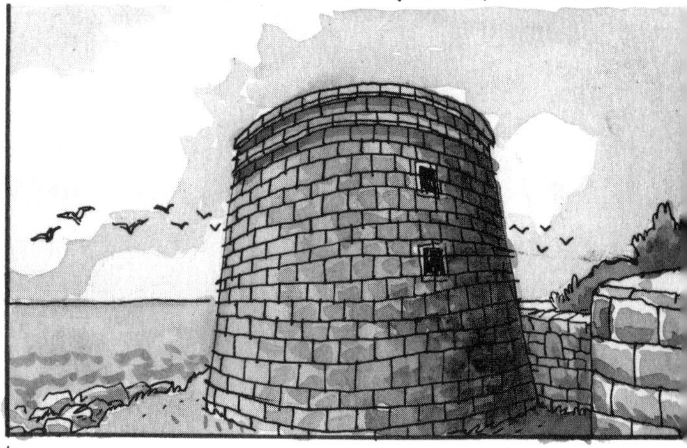

Oliver Gogarty and Samuel Trench, a unbalanced Anglo-Irish character, were the two other tenants who formed this bohemian community.

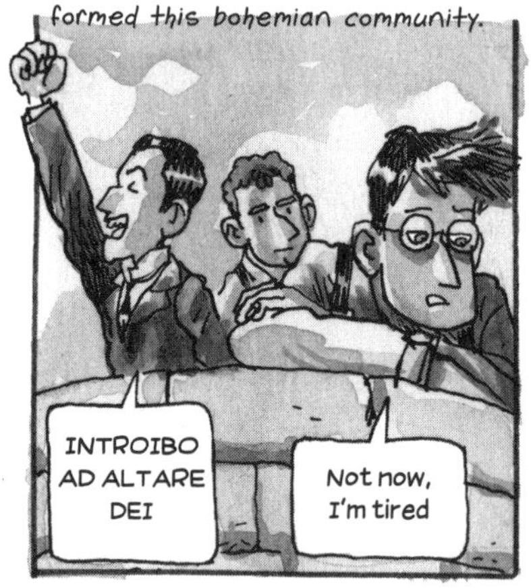
INTROIBO AD ALTARE DEI
Not now, I'm tired

Life in the tower was simple and pleasant.

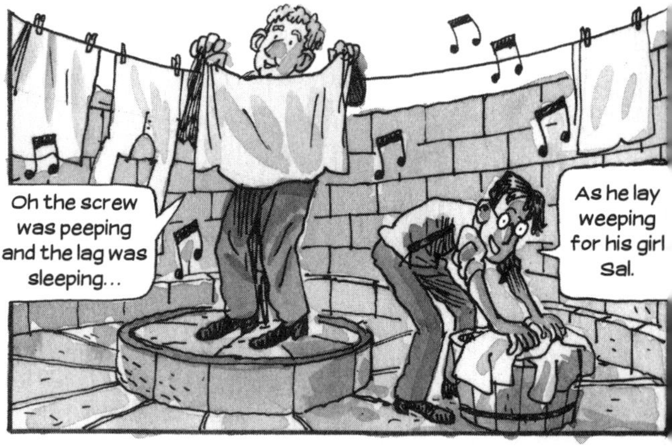
Oh the screw was peeping and the lag was sleeping...
As he lay weeping for his girl Sal.

Gogarty, however, spent his free time slandering Joyce...

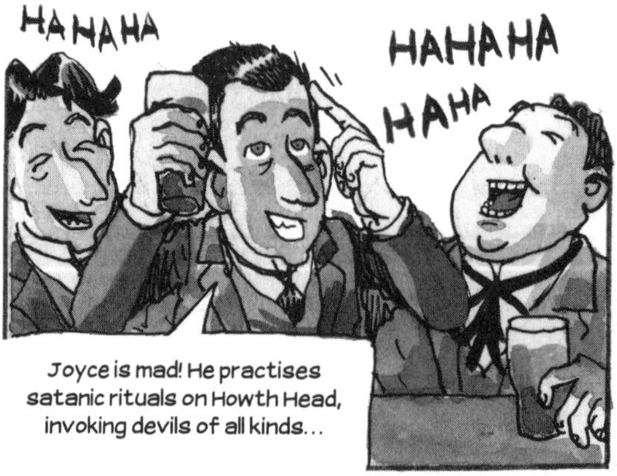
HAHAHA
HAHAHA
HAHA
Joyce is mad! He practises satanic rituals on Howth Head, invoking devils of all kinds...

...till the situation finally became unbearable.

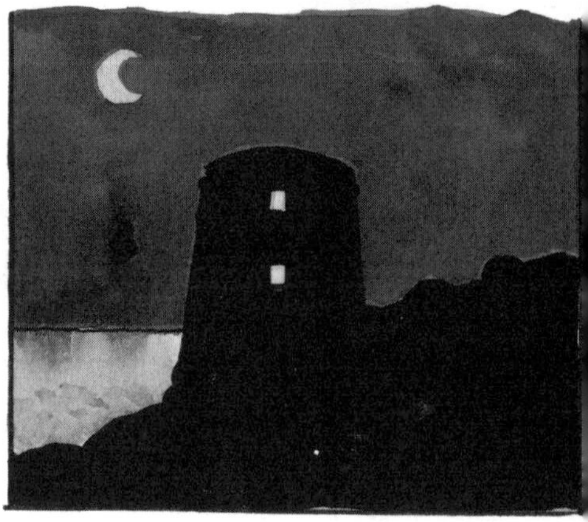

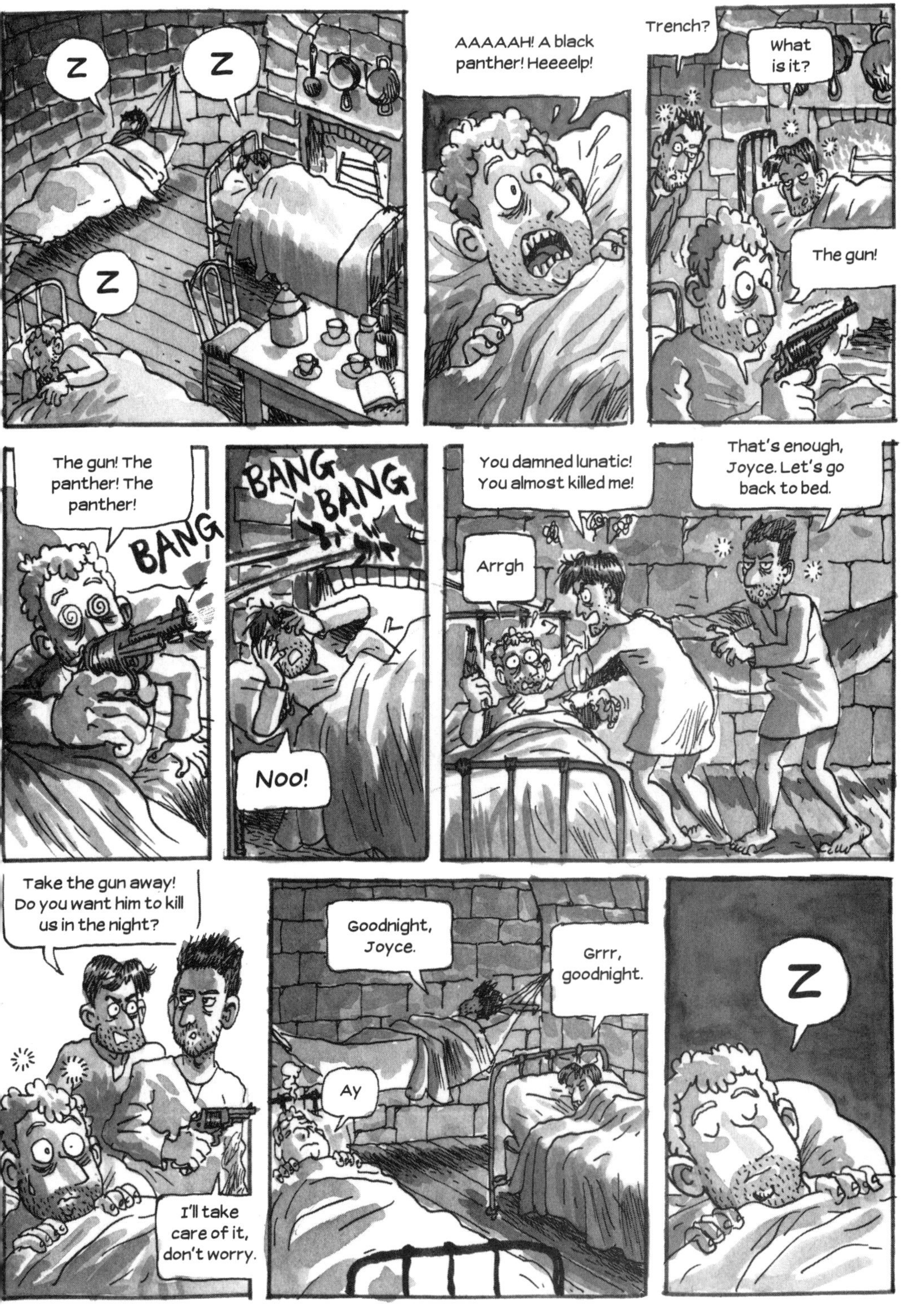
Z
Z
Z
AAAAAH! A black panther! Heeeelp!
Trench?
What is it?
The gun!
The gun! The panther! The panther!
BANG
BANG
BANG
Noo!
You damned lunatic! You almost killed me!
That's enough, Joyce. Let's go back to bed.
Arrgh
Take the gun away! Do you want him to kill us in the night?
I'll take care of it, don't worry.
Goodnight, Joyce.
Grrr, goodnight.
Ay
Z

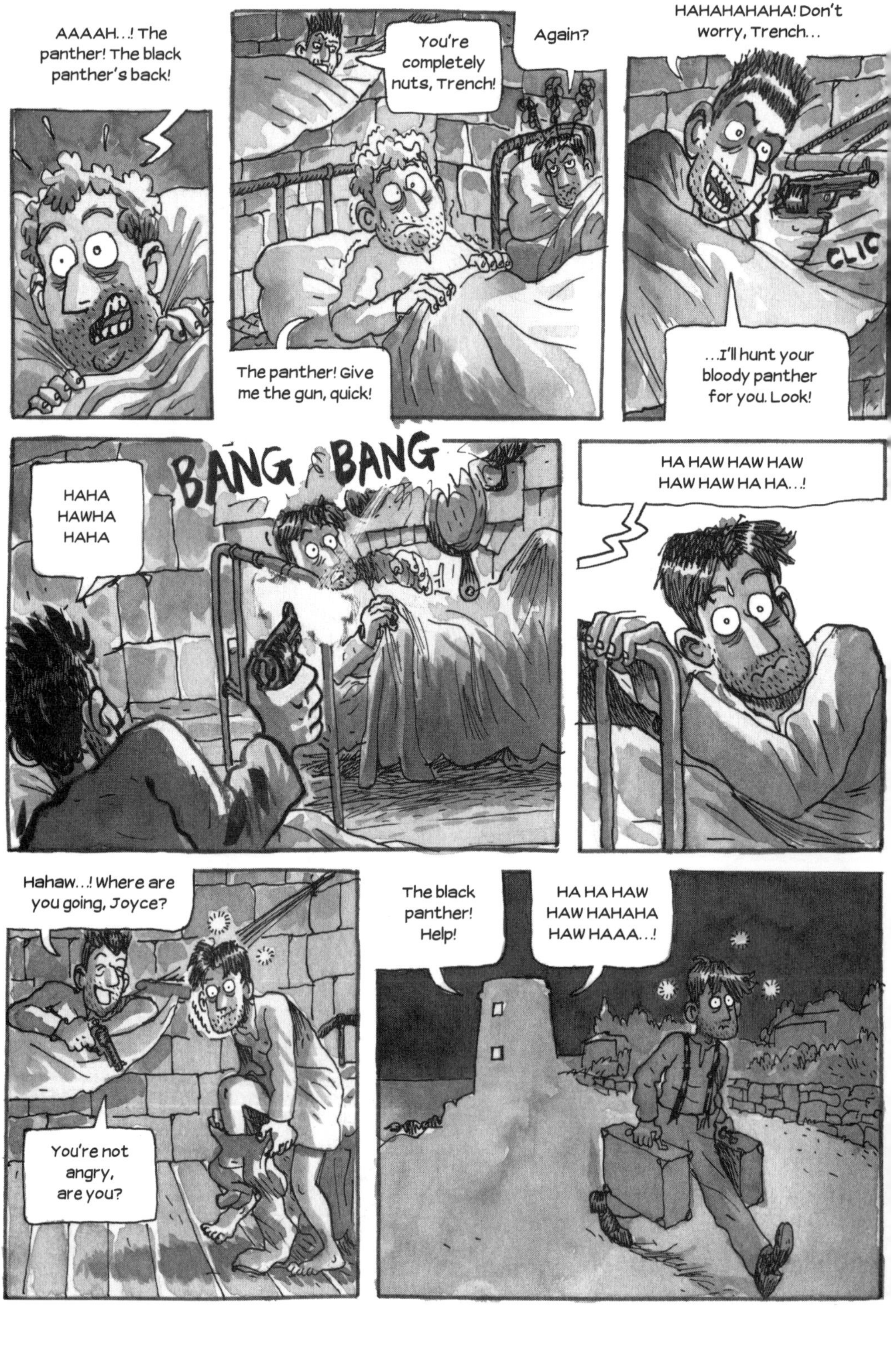

AAAAH...! The panther! The black panther's back!
You're completely nuts, Trench!
Again?
The panther! Give me the gun, quick!
HAHAHAHAHA! Don't worry, Trench...
CLIC
...I'll hunt your bloody panther for you. Look!
BANG BANG
HAHA HAWHA HAHA
HA HAW HAW HAW HAW HAW HA HA...!
Hahaw...! Where are you going, Joyce?
You're not angry, are you?
The black panther! Help!
HA HA HAW HAW HAHAHA HAW HAAA...!

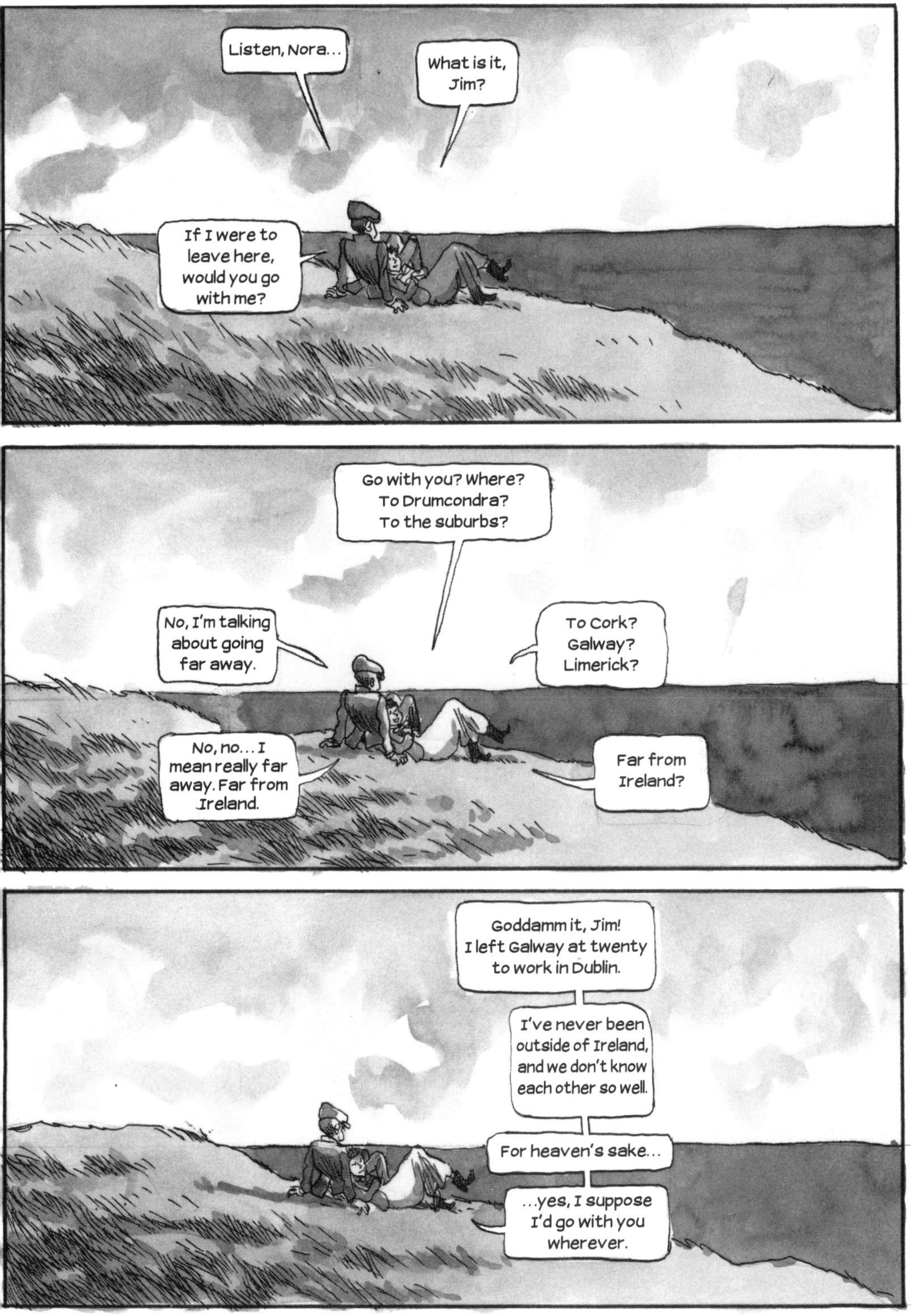

Listen, Nora...
What is it, Jim?
If I were to leave here, would you go with me?
Go with you? Where? To Drumcondra? To the suburbs?
No, I'm talking about going far away.
To Cork? Galway? Limerick?
No, no... I mean really far away. Far from Ireland.
Far from Ireland?
Goddamm it, Jim! I left Galway at twenty to work in Dublin.
I've never been outside of Ireland, and we don't know each other so well.
For heaven's sake...
...yes, I suppose I'd go with you wherever.

Chapter III

The New World

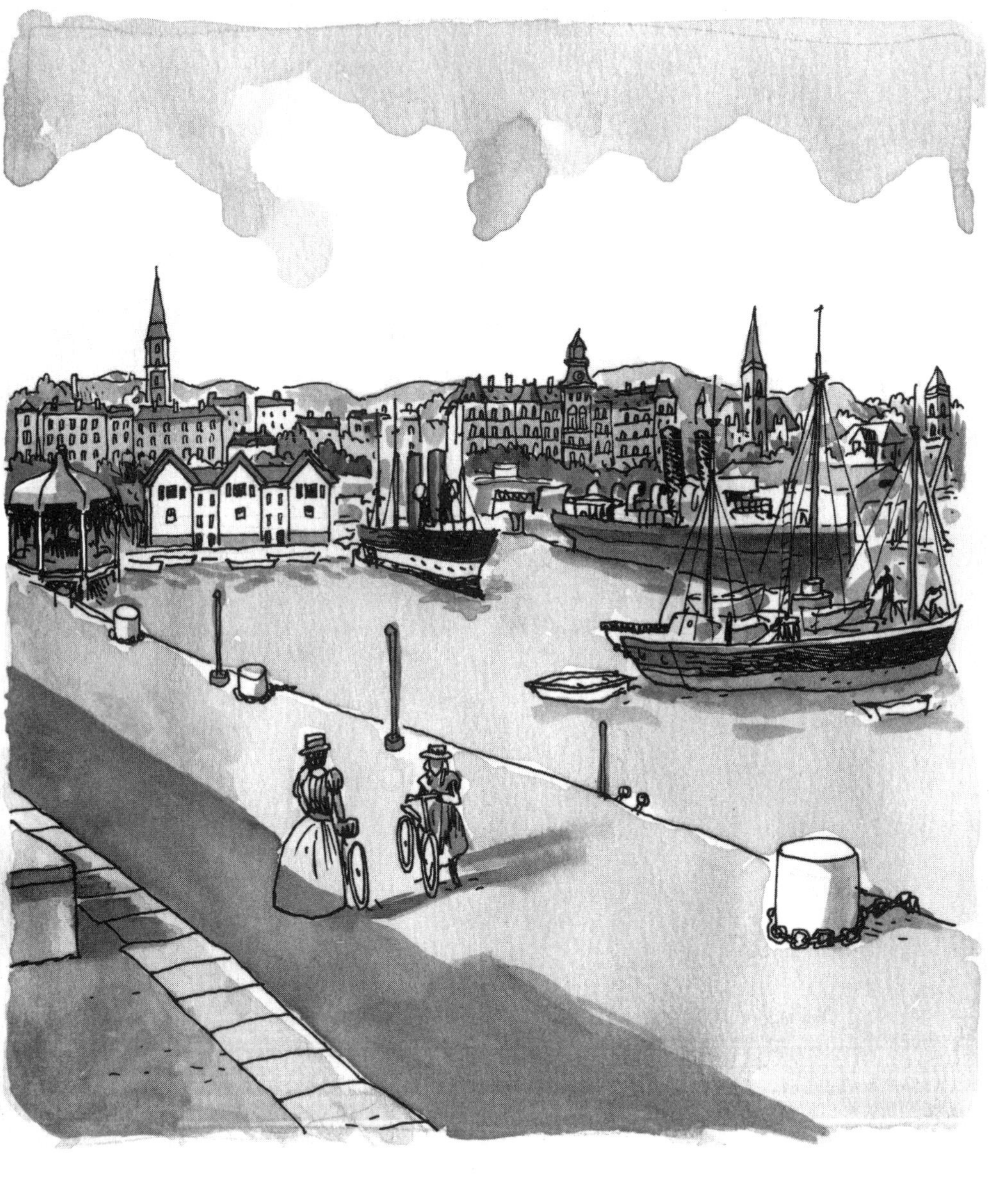

We're off on a great spiritual journey that will change our lives, Nora. And it hardly seems to matter to you!

These new boots hurt my feet.

On 6 October 1904, James and Nora set sail for London. James had reserved a post in Zurich as an English teacher, at the Berlitz School of Languages.

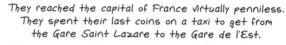

They travelled to Paris...

They reached the capital of France virtually penniless. They spent their last coins on a taxi to get from the Gare Saint Lazare to the Gare de l'Est.

Joyce went off to touch a couple of his friends in Paris for money...

...while Nora waited by herself in a park with the luggage.

Finally, on 8 October, they were able to take the train to Switzerland.

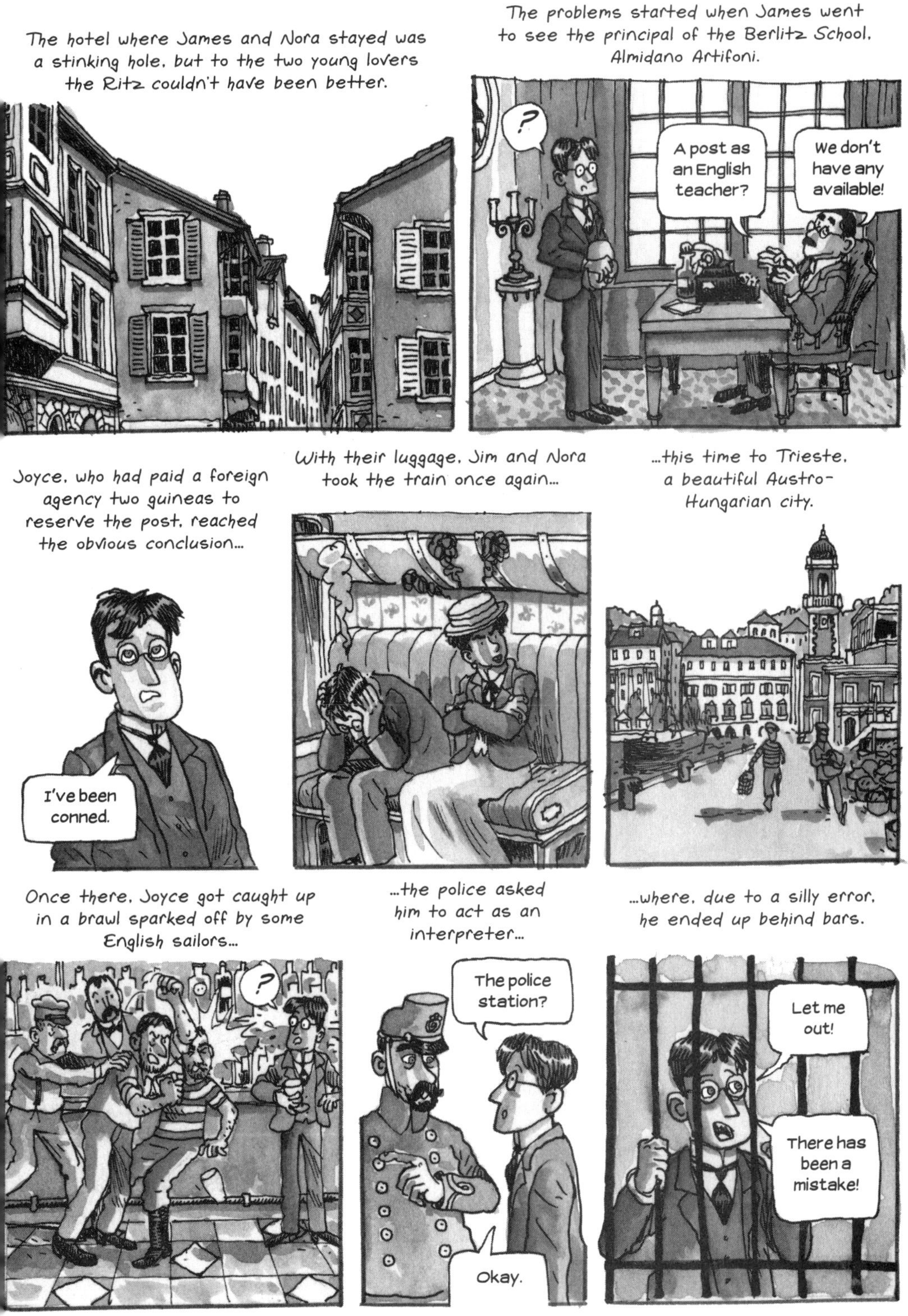
The hotel where James and Nora stayed was a stinking hole, but to the two young lovers the Ritz couldn't have been better.
The problems started when James went to see the principal of the Berlitz School, Almidano Artifoni.
?
A post as an English teacher?
We don't have any available!
Joyce, who had paid a foreign agency two guineas to reserve the post, reached the obvious conclusion...
I've been conned.
With their luggage, Jim and Nora took the train once again...
...this time to Trieste, a beautiful Austro-Hungarian city.
Once there, Joyce got caught up in a brawl sparked off by some English sailors...
?
...the police asked him to act as an interpreter...
The police station?
Okay.
...where, due to a silly error, he ended up behind bars.
Let me out!
There has been a mistake!

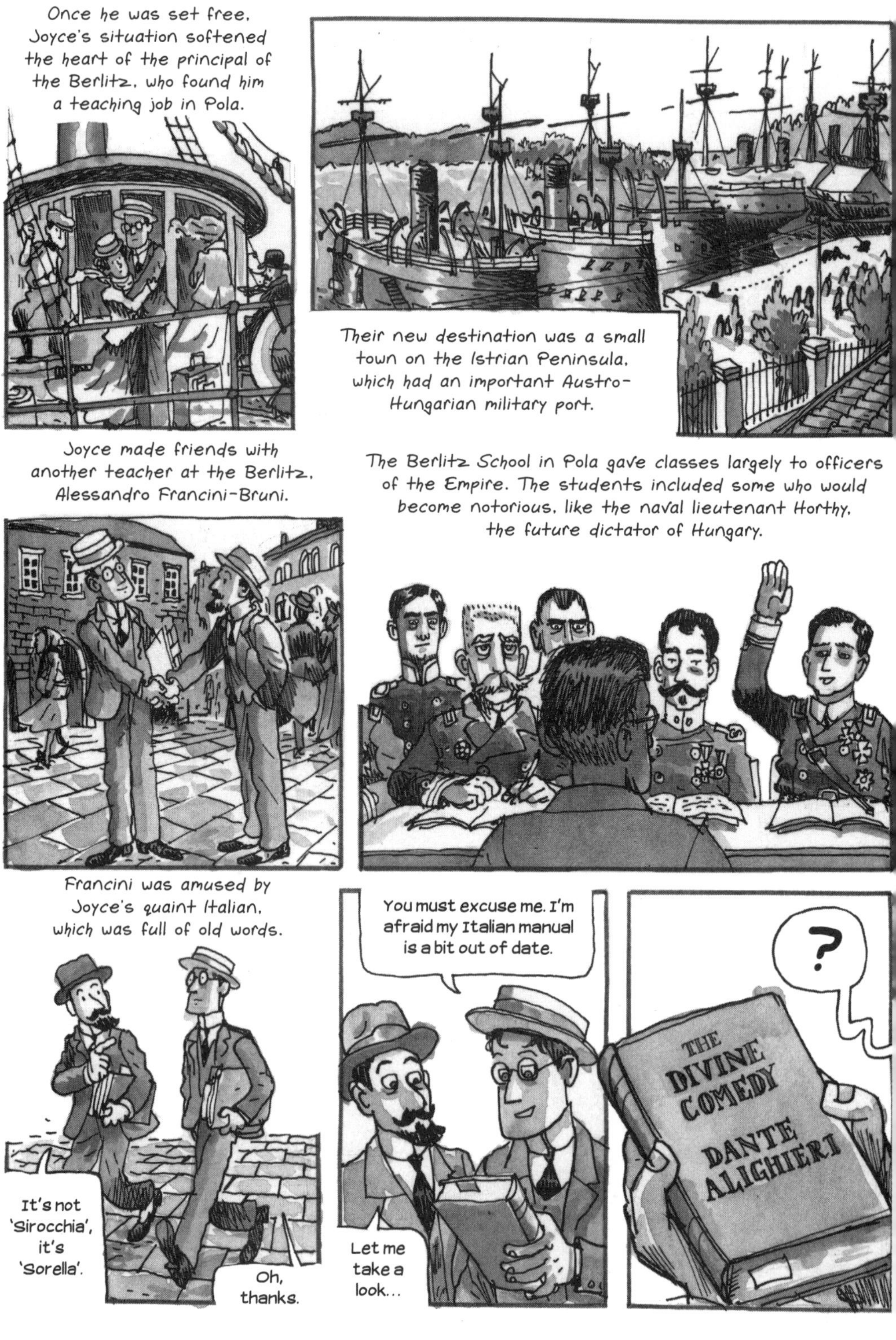

Once he was set free, Joyce's situation softened the heart of the principal of the Berlitz, who found him a teaching job in Pola.
Their new destination was a small town on the Istrian Peninsula, which had an important Austro-Hungarian military port.
Joyce made friends with another teacher at the Berlitz, Alessandro Francini-Bruni.
The Berlitz School in Pola gave classes largely to officers of the Empire. The students included some who would become notorious, like the naval lieutenant Horthy, the future dictator of Hungary.
Francini was amused by Joyce's quaint Italian, which was full of old words.
It's not 'Sirocchia', it's 'Sorella'.
Oh, thanks.
You must excuse me. I'm afraid my Italian manual is a bit out of date.
Let me take a look...
?
THE DIVINE COMEDY
DANTE ALIGHIERI

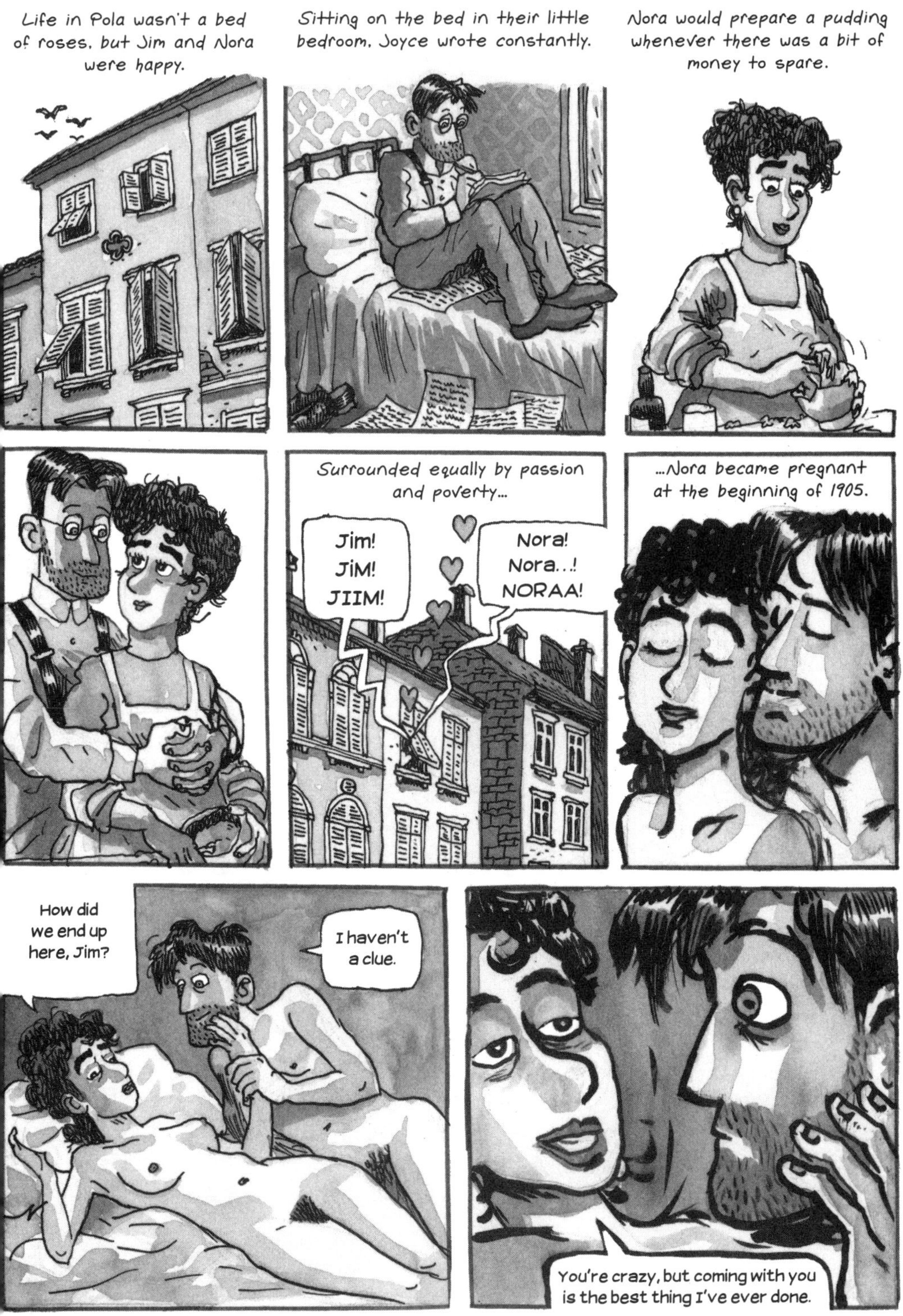
Life in Pola wasn't a bed of roses, but Jim and Nora were happy.
Sitting on the bed in their little bedroom, Joyce wrote constantly.
Nora would prepare a pudding whenever there was a bit of money to spare.
Surrounded equally by passion and poverty...
Jim! JiM! JIIM!
Nora! Nora...! NORAA!
...Nora became pregnant at the beginning of 1905.
How did we end up here, Jim?
I haven't a clue.
You're crazy, but coming with you is the best thing I've ever done.

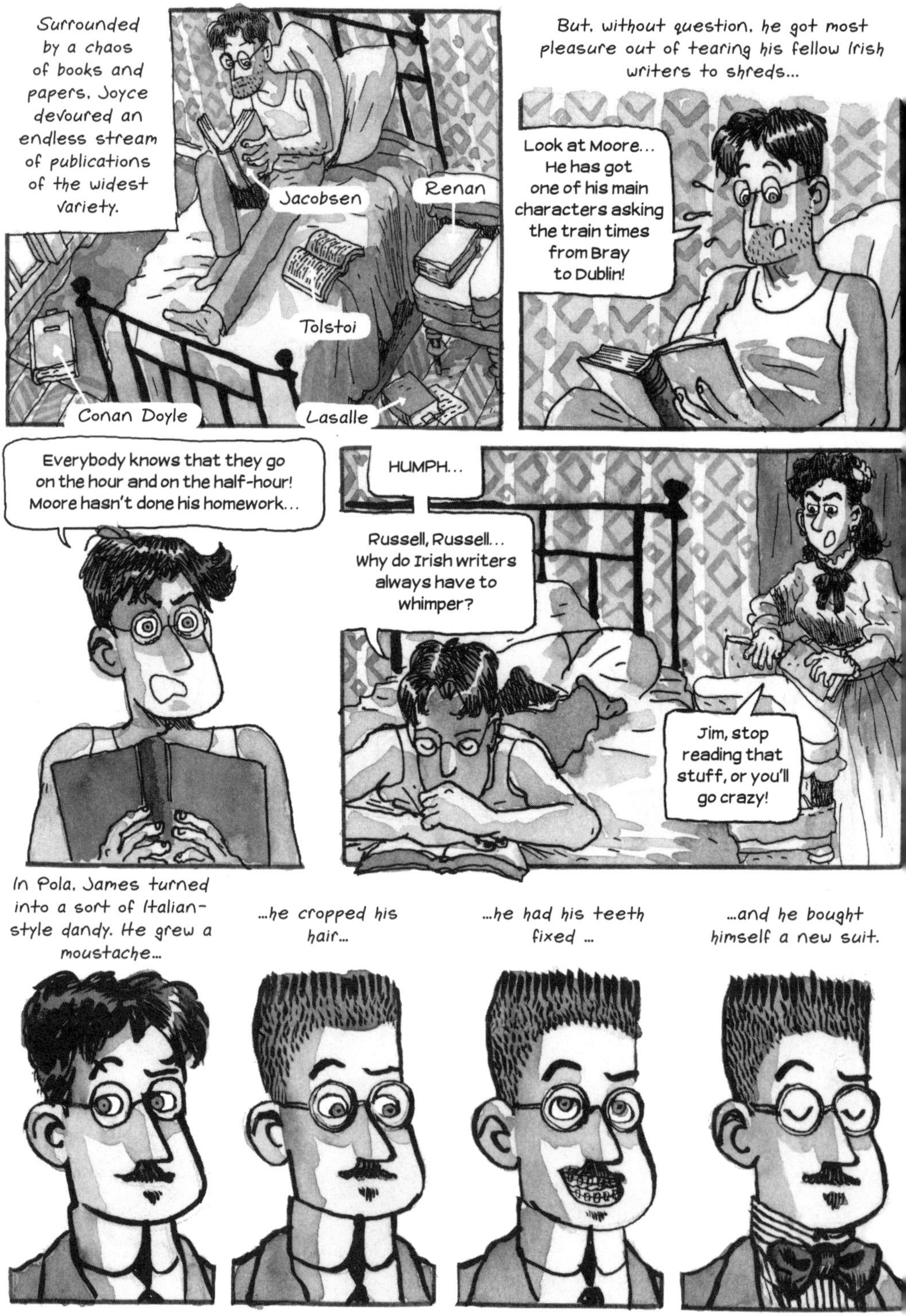
Surrounded by a chaos of books and papers, Joyce devoured an endless stream of publications of the widest variety.
Jacobsen
Renan
Tolstoi
Conan Doyle
Lasalle
But, without question, he got most pleasure out of tearing his fellow Irish writers to shreds...
Look at Moore... He has got one of his main characters asking the train times from Bray to Dublin!
Everybody knows that they go on the hour and on the half-hour! Moore hasn't done his homework...
HUMPH...
Russell, Russell... Why do Irish writers always have to whimper?
Jim, stop reading that stuff, or you'll go crazy!
In Pola, James turned into a sort of Italian-style dandy. He grew a moustache...
...he cropped his hair...
...he had his teeth fixed ...
...and he bought himself a new suit.

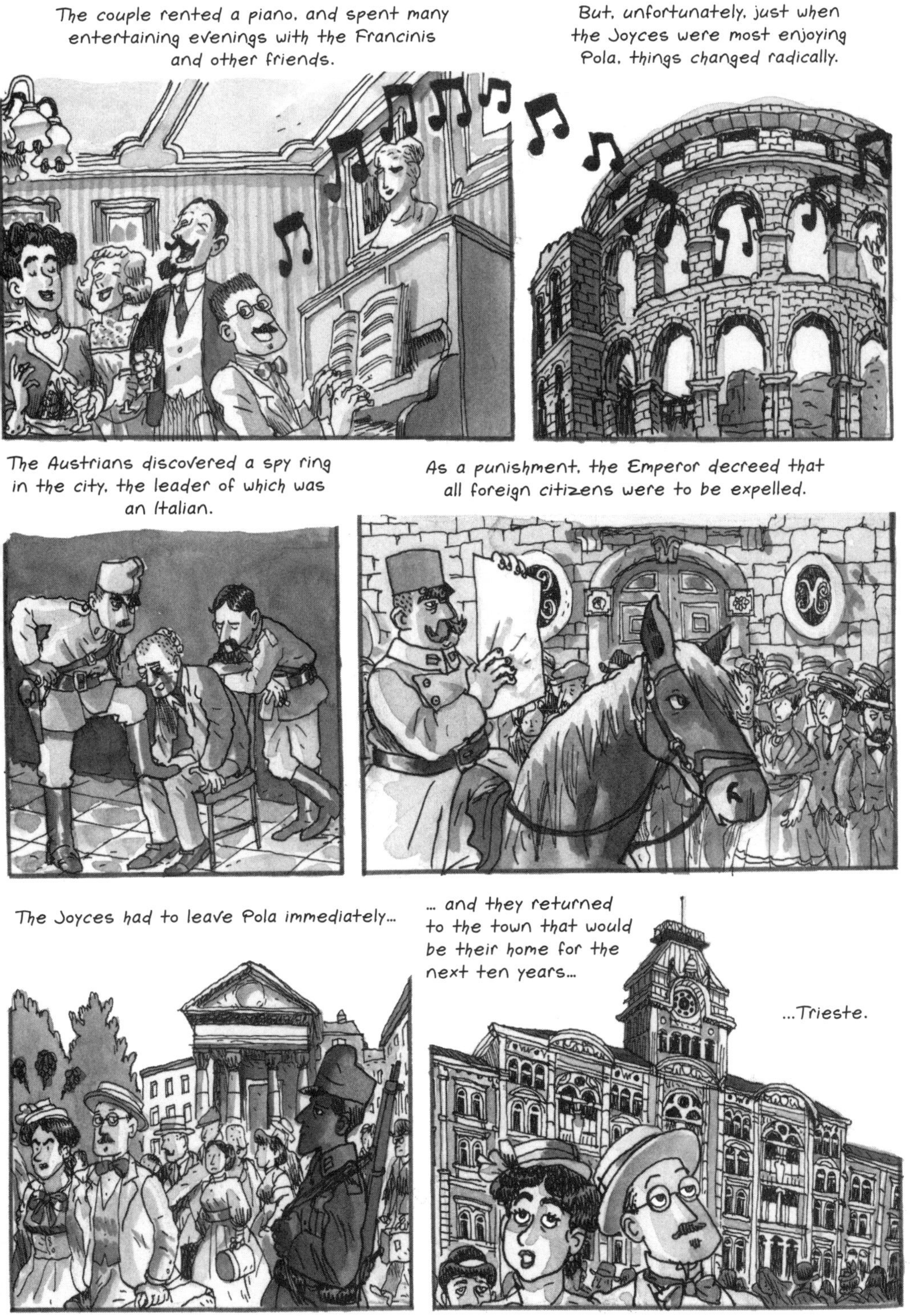

The couple rented a piano, and spent many entertaining evenings with the Francinis and other friends.
But, unfortunately, just when the Joyces were most enjoying Pola, things changed radically.
The Austrians discovered a spy ring in the city, the leader of which was an Italian.
As a punishment, the Emperor decreed that all foreign citizens were to be expelled.
The Joyces had to leave Pola immediately...
... and they returned to the town that would be their home for the next ten years...
...Trieste.

Trieste, 1905.

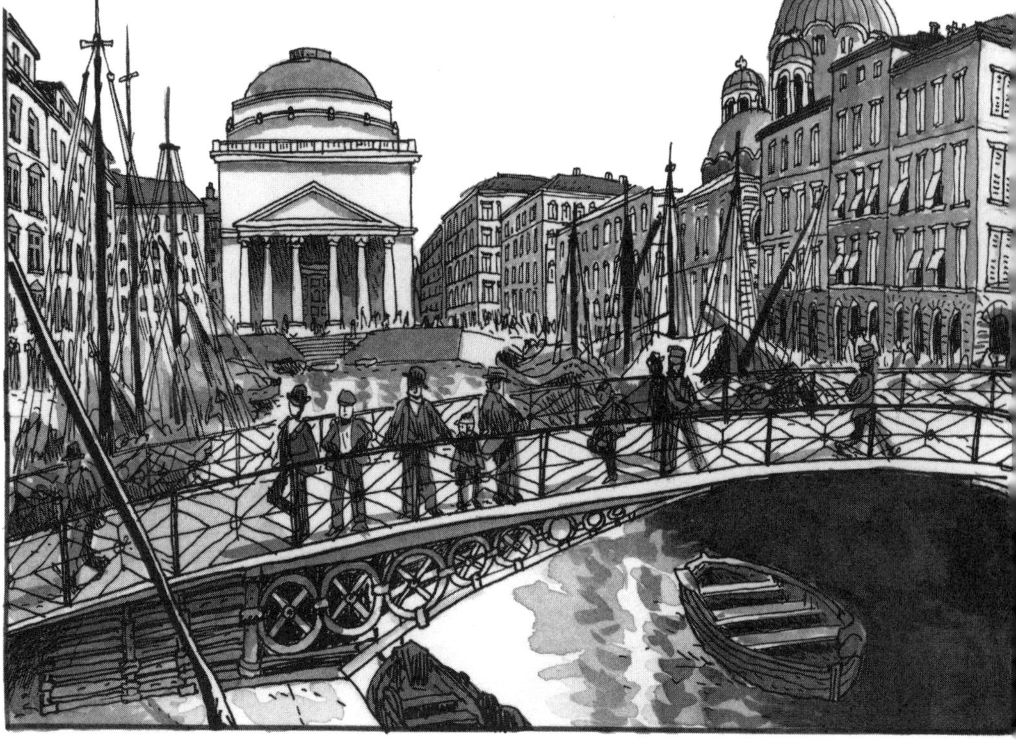

At that time, Trieste was one of the principal ports of Europe, the maritime jewel of the Austro-Hungarian Empire and its navy.

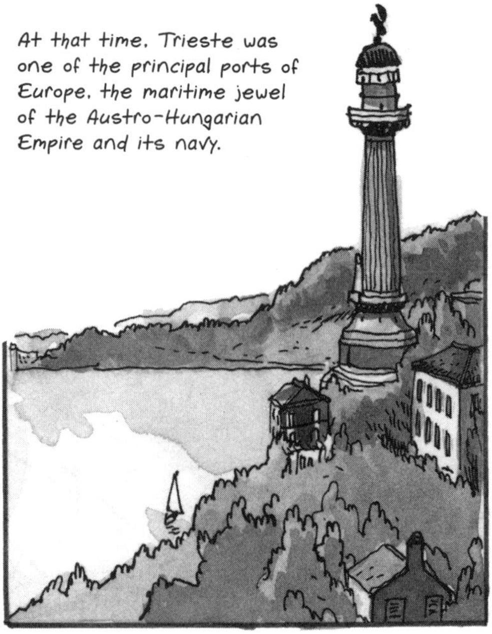

It was a cosmopolitan, multicultural city, and Joyce was enormously surprised by the variety of people there:

Central Europeans

Balkans

Russians

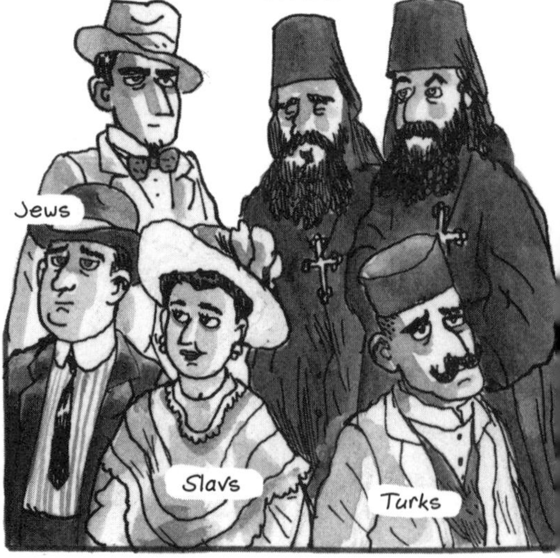
Jews
Slavs
Turks

Three-quarters of the population of Trieste was Italian, and the nationalist movement opposed to Imperial rule was growing stronger.

Germans, get out of Trieste!

Long live King Victor Emmanuel of Italy!

Joyce was a nationalist, but also a socialist. He frequented the workers' cafés in the old quarter, explaining his ideas.

I am a socialist, because only a socialist state protects artists.

With capitalism, I'm done for.

In the beginning, things were difficult at the Berlitz. Artifoni paid him a pittance, and also detested the idea of having an unmarried teacher with a pregnant lover about to give birth.

He only kept him on because rich students, like Count Sordini and Baron Ralli, adored the Irishman.

Man is born free, and everywhere in shackles.

J.J. Rousseau

As for Nora, she spent the suffocatingly hot summer lying in bed.

When she ventured out, the women looked at her and murmured in a language she didn't understand.

Bla bli bla

bla blu bla bli bla

Nora was hardly having a good time...

It's a nightmare!

Bla bli blu

bli blu bla

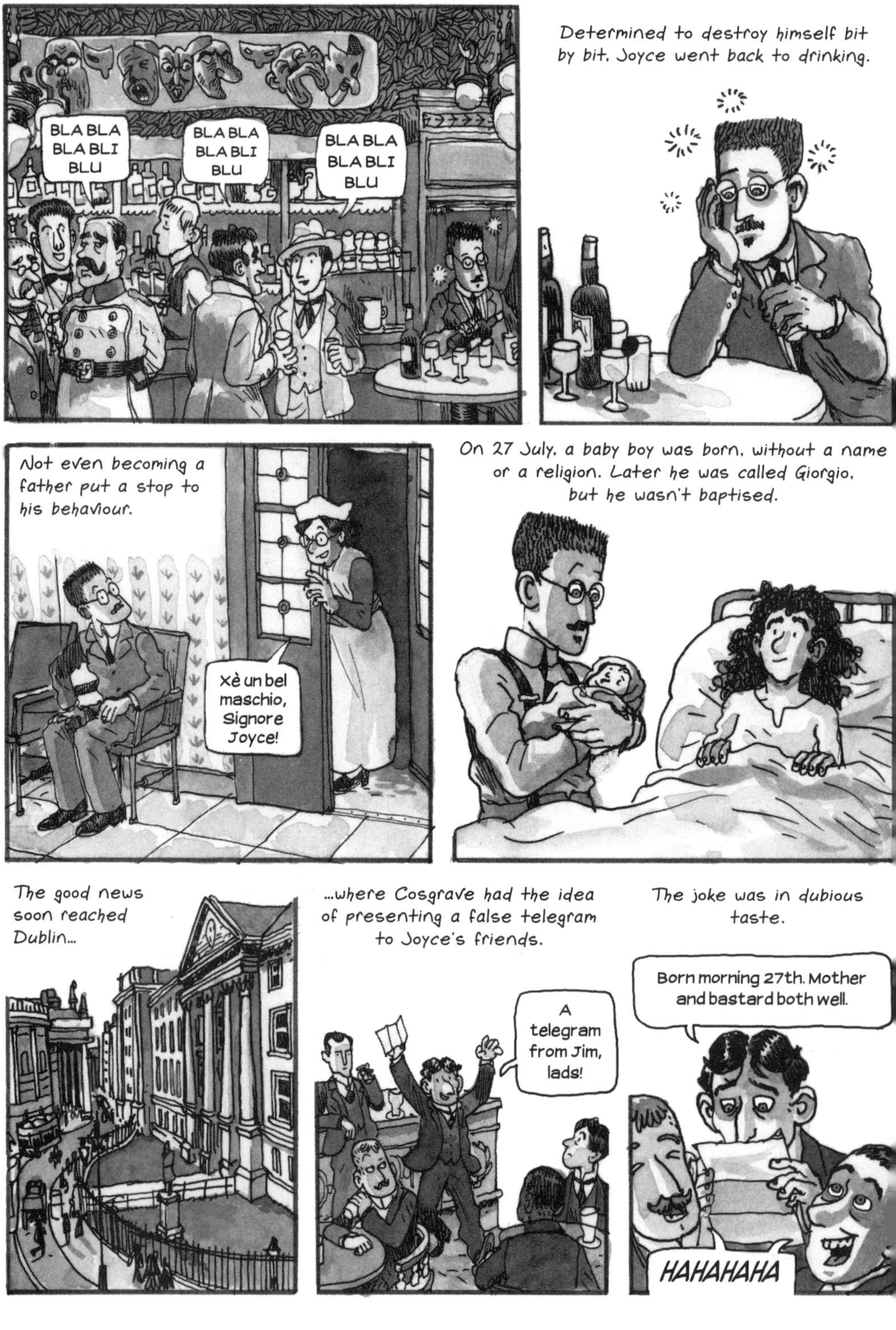

BLA BLA BLA BLI BLU
BLA BLA BLA BLI BLU
BLA BLA BLA BLI BLU
Determined to destroy himself bit by bit, Joyce went back to drinking.
Not even becoming a father put a stop to his behaviour.
Xè un bel maschio, Signore Joyce!
On 27 July, a baby boy was born, without a name or a religion. Later he was called Giorgio, but he wasn't baptised.
The good news soon reached Dublin...
...where Cosgrave had the idea of presenting a false telegram to Joyce's friends.
A telegram from Jim, lads!
The joke was in dubious taste.
Born morning 27th. Mother and bastard both well.
HAHAHAHA

Since the incident in the Martello Tower, Joyce was still angry with Gogarty. Cosgrave wrote to congratulate Joyce on the birth of Giorgio, and took the opportunity to ask him to forgive his old friend.

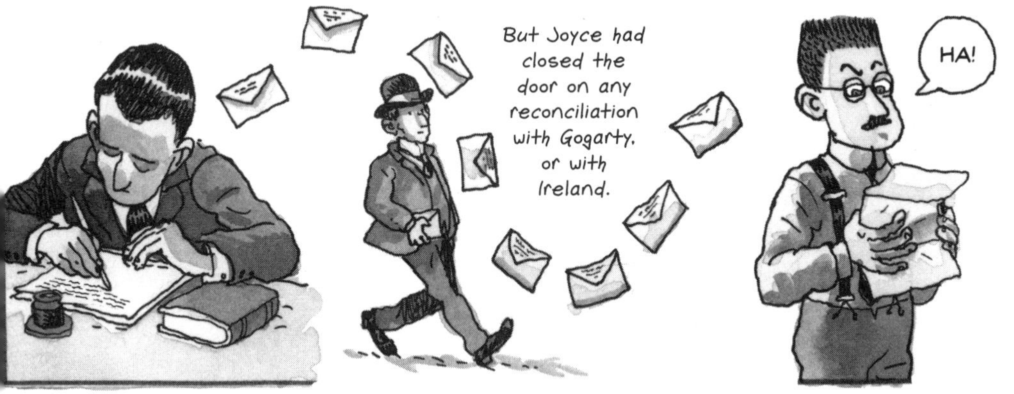
But Joyce had closed the door on any reconciliation with Gogarty, or with Ireland.
HA!

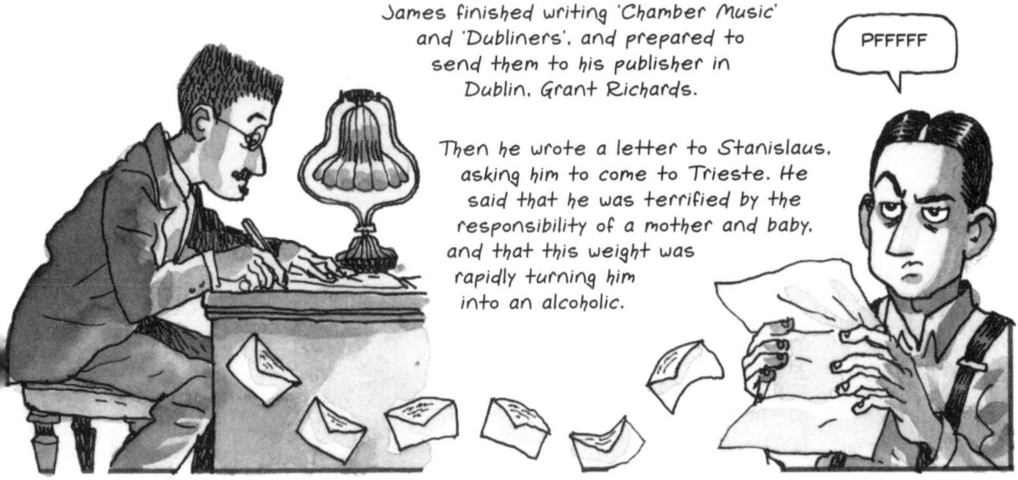
James finished writing 'Chamber Music' and 'Dubliners', and prepared to send them to his publisher in Dublin, Grant Richards.
PFFFFF
Then he wrote a letter to Stanislaus, asking him to come to Trieste. He said that he was terrified by the responsibility of a mother and baby, and that this weight was rapidly turning him into an alcoholic.

Stanislaus didn't hesitate for a minute. To save his brother, and to escape from the darkness of Dublin, he left the city on 20 October 1905.

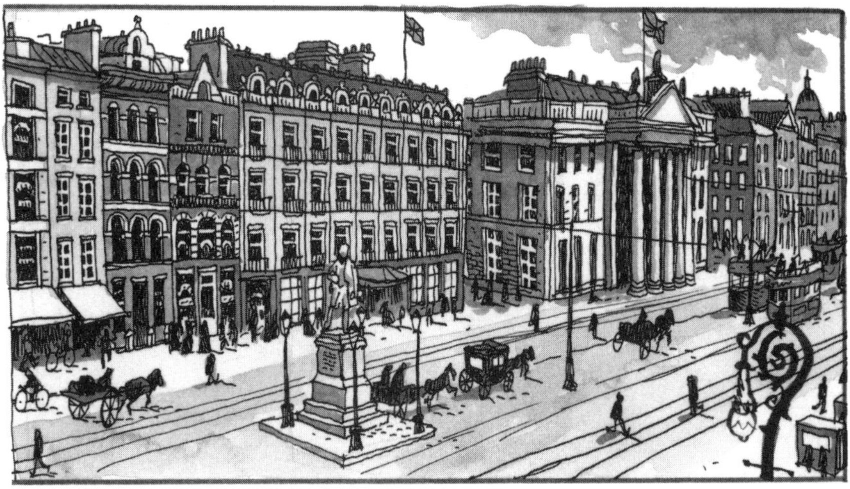

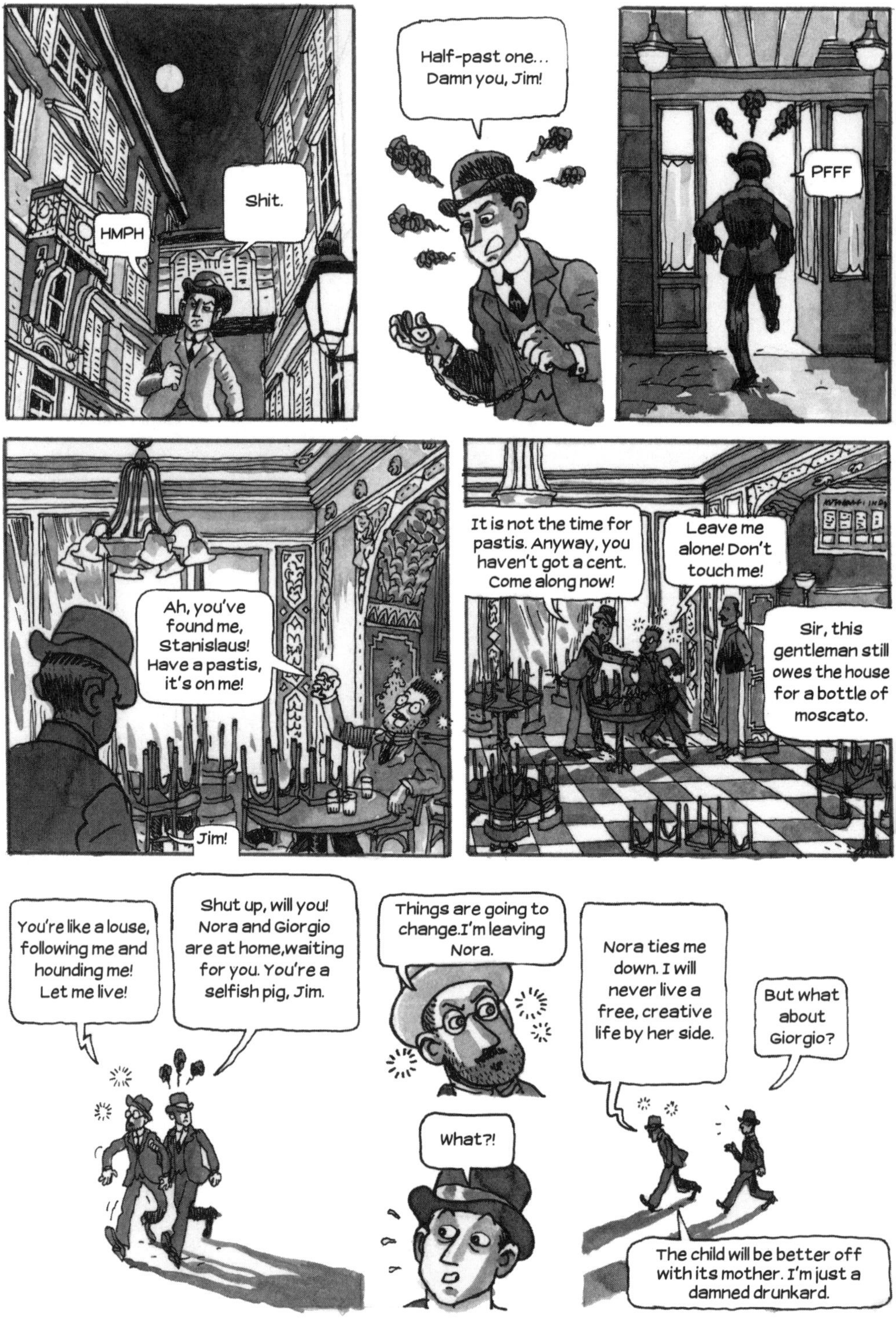
HMPH
Shit.
Half-past one... Damn you, Jim!
PFFF
Ah, you've found me, Stanislaus! Have a pastis, it's on me!
Jim!
It is not the time for pastis. Anyway, you haven't got a cent. Come along now!
Leave me alone! Don't touch me!
Sir, this gentleman still owes the house for a bottle of moscato.
You're like a louse, following me and hounding me! Let me live!
Shut up, will you! Nora and Giorgio are at home,waiting for you. You're a selfish pig, Jim.
Things are going to change.I'm leaving Nora.
What?!
Nora ties me down. I will never live a free, creative life by her side.
But what about Giorgio?
The child will be better off with its mother. I'm just a damned drunkard.

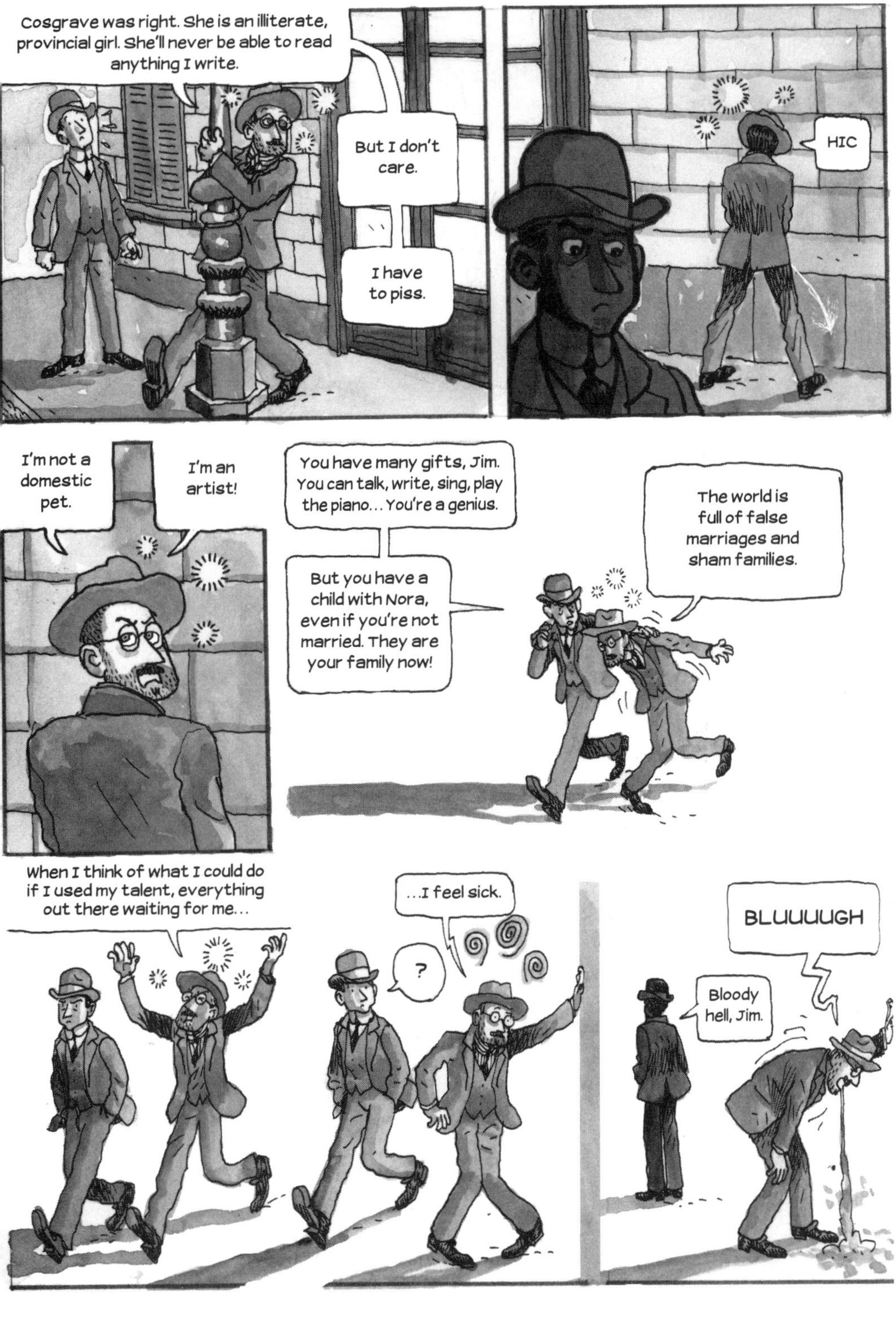

Cosgrave was right. She is an illiterate, provincial girl. She'll never be able to read anything I write.
But I don't care.
I have to piss.
HIC
I'm not a domestic pet.
I'm an artist!
You have many gifts, Jim. You can talk, write, sing, play the piano... You're a genius.
But you have a child with Nora, even if you're not married. They are your family now!
The world is full of false marriages and sham families.
When I think of what I could do if I used my talent, everything out there waiting for me...
...I feel sick.
?
BLUUUUGH
Bloody hell, Jim.

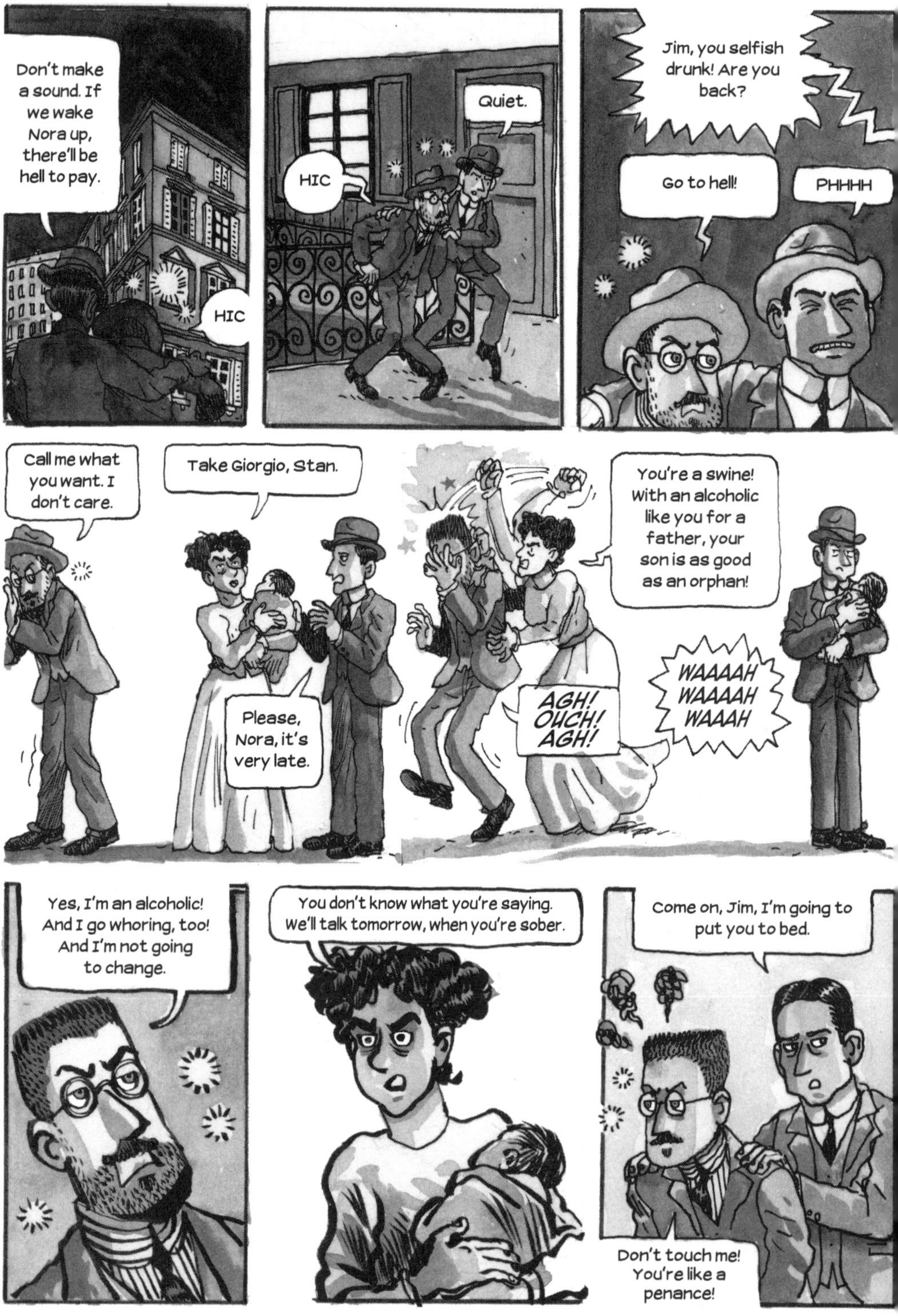
Don't make a sound. If we wake Nora up, there'll be hell to pay.
HIC
HIC
Quiet.
Jim, you selfish drunk! Are you back?
Go to hell!
PHHHH
Call me what you want. I don't care.
Take Giorgio, Stan.
Please, Nora, it's very late.
You're a swine! With an alcoholic like you for a father, your son is as good as an orphan!
AGH! OUCH! AGH!
WAAAAH WAAAAH WAAAH
Yes, I'm an alcoholic! And I go whoring, too! And I'm not going to change.
You don't know what you're saying. We'll talk tomorrow, when you're sober.
Come on, Jim, I'm going to put you to bed.
Don't touch me! You're like a penance!

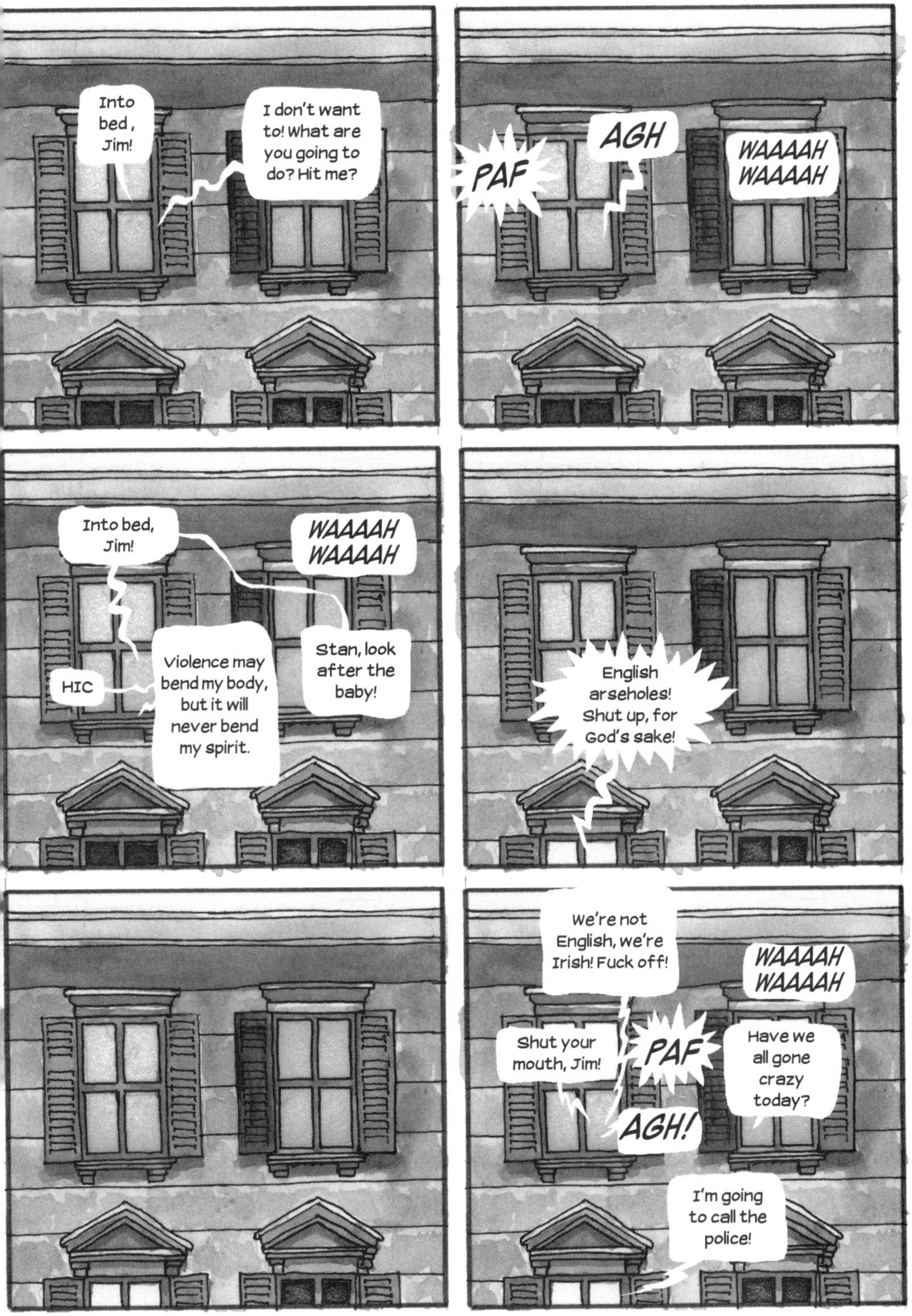
Into bed, Jim!
I don't want to! What are you going to do? Hit me?
PAF
AGH
WAAAAH WAAAAH
Into bed, Jim!
WAAAAH WAAAAH
HIC
Violence may bend my body, but it will never bend my spirit.
Stan, look after the baby!
English arseholes! Shut up, for God's sake!
We're not English, we're Irish! Fuck off!
WAAAAH WAAAAH
Shut your mouth, Jim!
PAF
AGH!
Have we all gone crazy today?
I'm going to call the police!

Writing from a distance, Joyce always dealt with the subject of Ireland. He was obsessed with the wasteland that the British had turned Ireland into. Now, in the earth where the British government had sowed misery, syphilis, superstition and alcoholism, puritans, jesuits and reactionaries sprouted up.

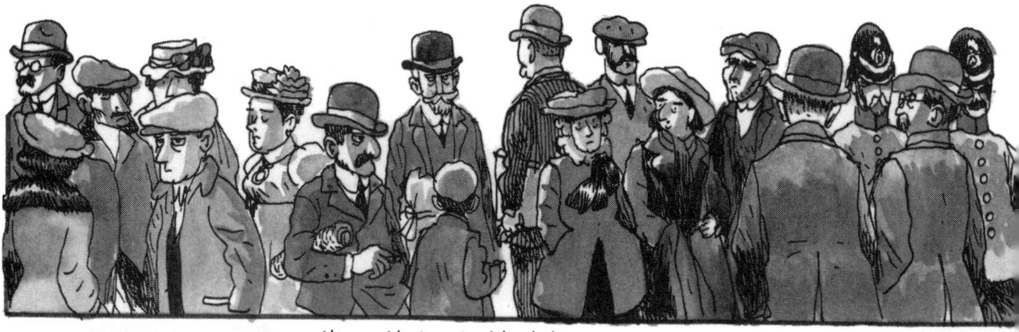

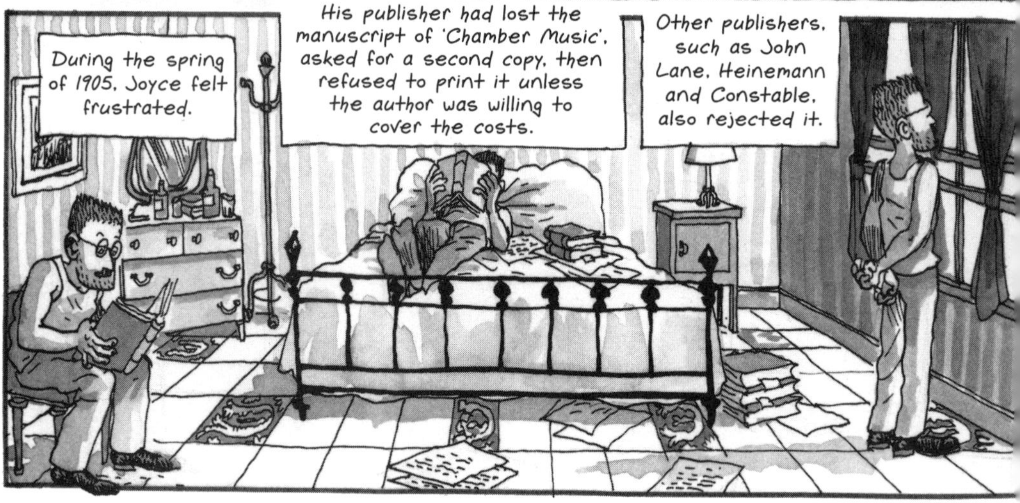
During the spring of 1905, Joyce felt frustrated.
His publisher had lost the manuscript of 'Chamber Music', asked for a second copy, then refused to print it unless the author was willing to cover the costs.
Other publishers, such as John Lane, Heinemann and Constable, also rejected it.

However, it was not all bad news. In December 1905, Richards discovered the manuscript of 'Dubliners', and in March 1906 he signed the contract for its publication.

Joyce had celebrated too soon. The printer had objections to some of the chapters, which he thought should be censored.

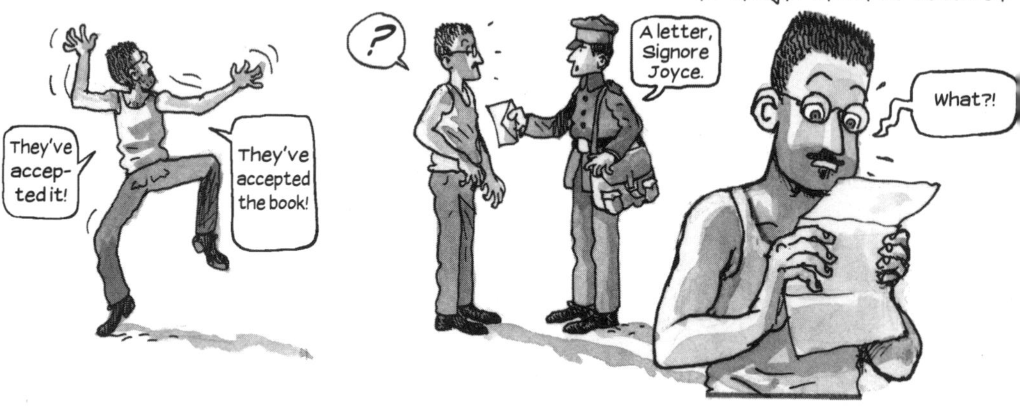
They've accepted it!
They've accepted the book!
?
A letter, Signore Joyce.
What?!

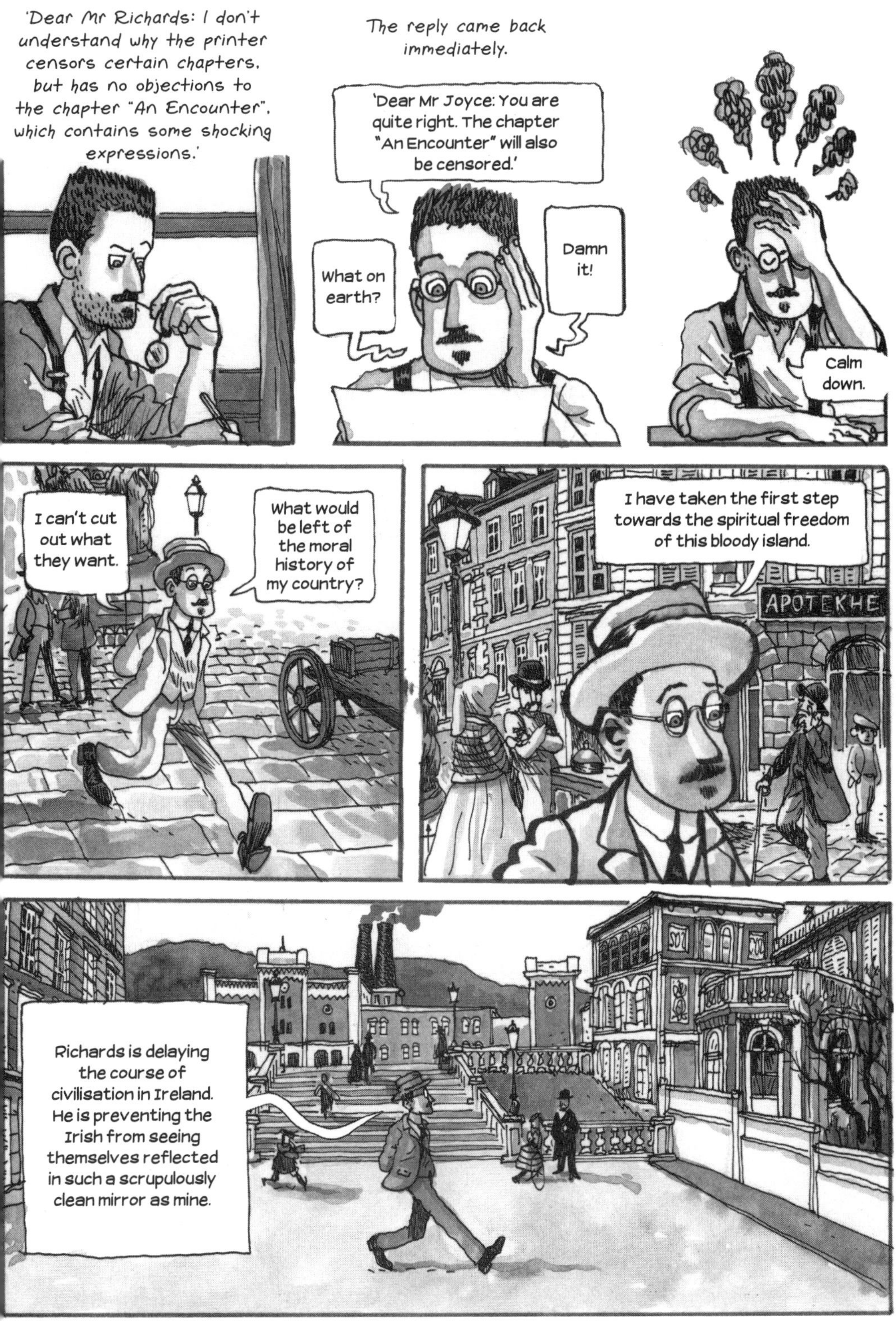
'Dear Mr Richards: I don't understand why the printer censors certain chapters, but has no objections to the chapter "An Encounter", which contains some shocking expressions.'
The reply came back immediately.
'Dear Mr Joyce: You are quite right. The chapter "An Encounter" will also be censored.'
What on earth?
Damn it!
Calm down.
I can't cut out what they want.
What would be left of the moral history of my country?
I have taken the first step towards the spiritual freedom of this bloody island.
APOTEKHE
Richards is delaying the course of civilisation in Ireland. He is preventing the Irish from seeing themselves reflected in such a scrupulously clean mirror as mine.

Joyce could stand Trieste no longer. By 31 July, he had finally had enough, and left with Nora and Giorgio for Rome.

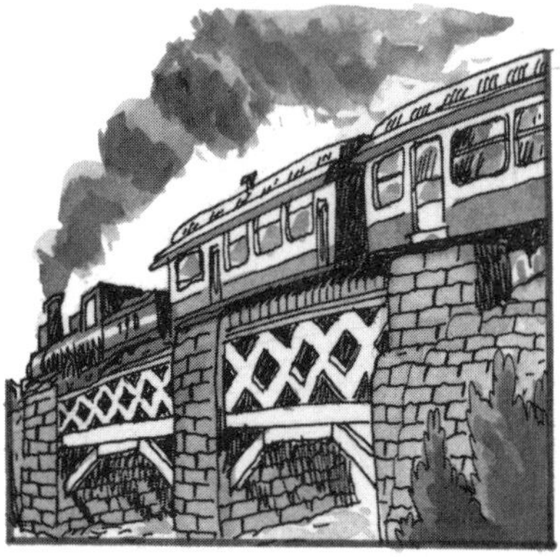

The Eternal city both moved and frightened Joyce

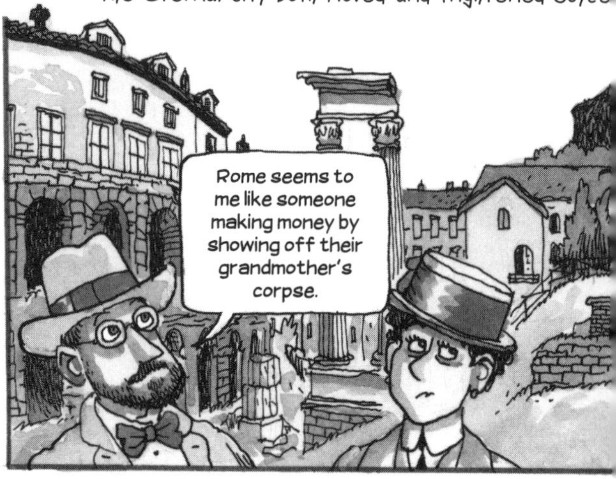
Rome seems to me like someone making money by showing off their grandmother's corpse.

Joyce found an office job in Nast-Kolb & Schumacher, an Austrian bank in the Piazza Calonna.

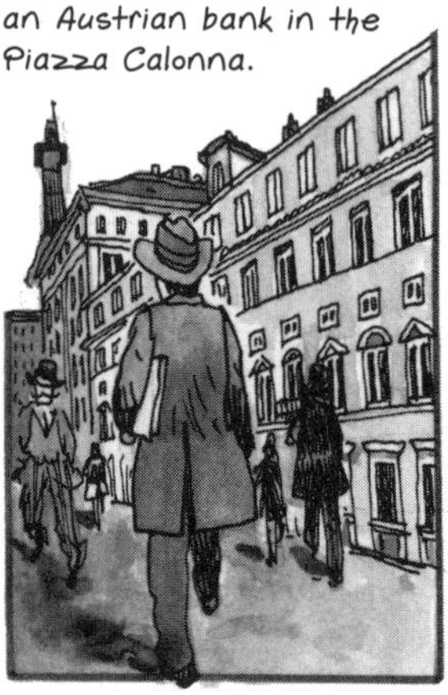

But it was very boring to sit all day surrounded by grey, anonymous people.

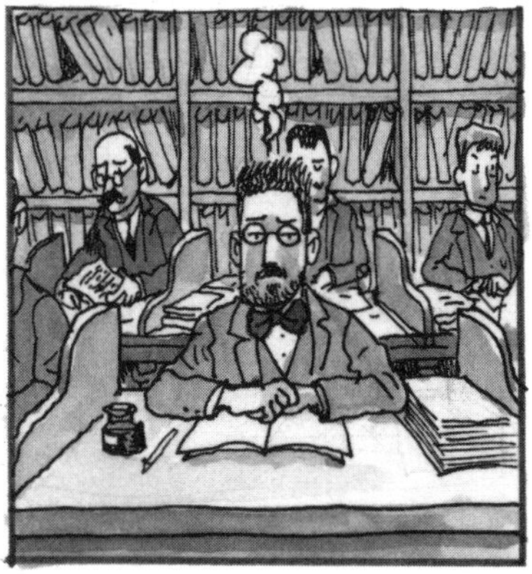

His trousers, of course, were the first to suffer...

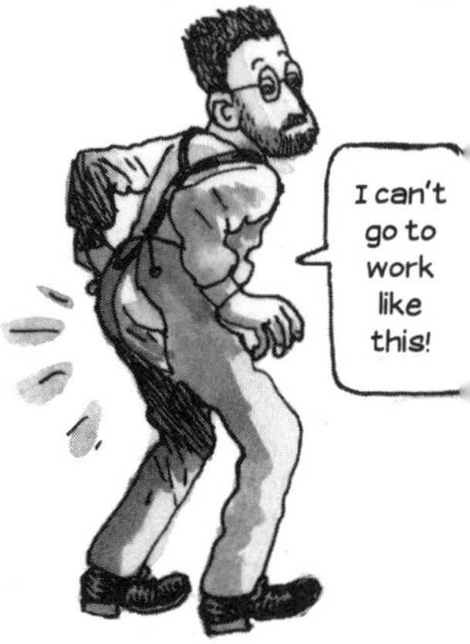
I can't go to work like this!

To hide his sewed-up trousers, Joyce never took off his coat... not even in August!

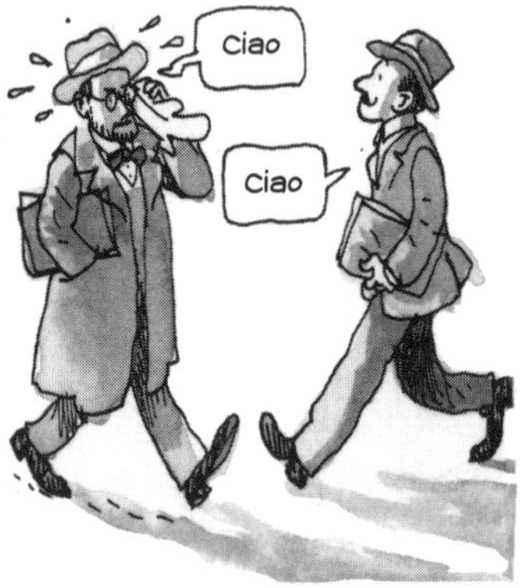
Ciao
Ciao

In Rome, Joyce went on spending. He spent his time in the Caffe Greco, and asked Stanislaus to send him money from Trieste.

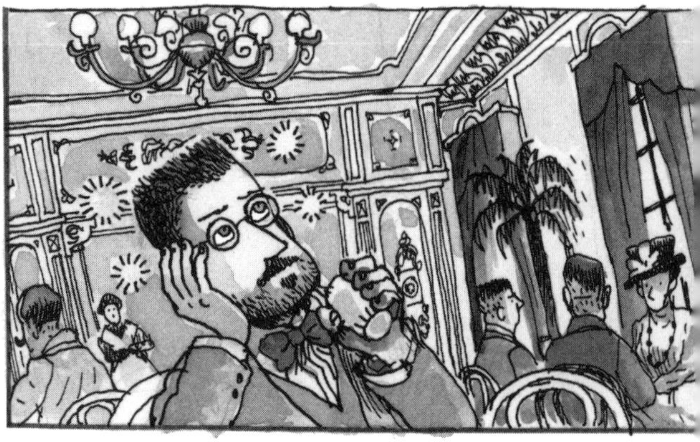

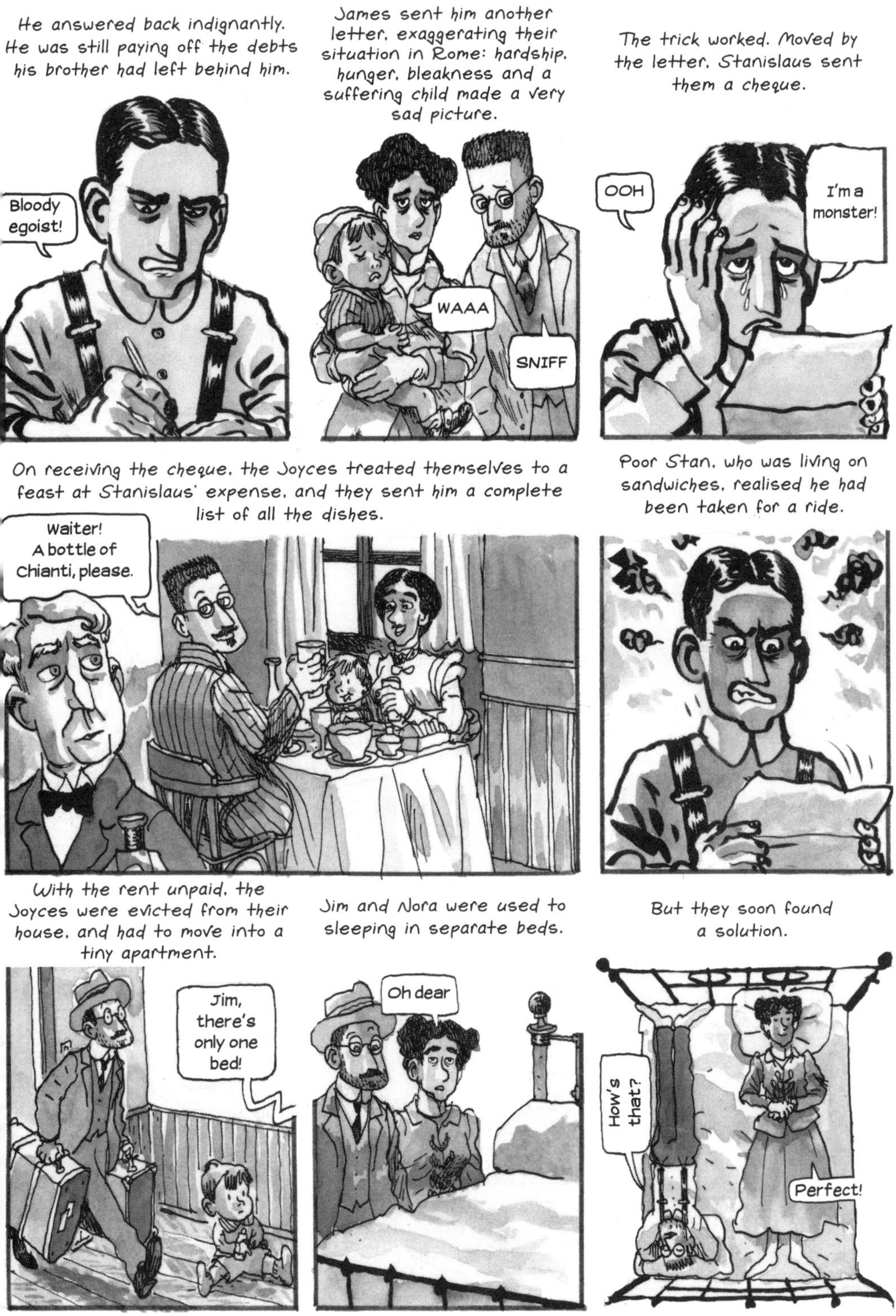
He answered back indignantly. He was still paying off the debts his brother had left behind him.
Bloody egoist!
James sent him another letter, exaggerating their situation in Rome: hardship, hunger, bleakness and a suffering child made a very sad picture.
WAAA
SNIFF
The trick worked. Moved by the letter, Stanislaus sent them a cheque.
OOH
I'm a monster!
On receiving the cheque, the Joyces treated themselves to a feast at Stanislaus' expense, and they sent him a complete list of all the dishes.
Waiter! A bottle of Chianti, please.
Poor Stan, who was living on sandwiches, realised he had been taken for a ride.
With the rent unpaid, the Joyces were evicted from their house, and had to move into a tiny apartment.
Jim, there's only one bed!
Jim and Nora were used to sleeping in separate beds.
Oh dear
But they soon found a solution.
How's that?
Perfect!

Joyce hated Rome because of their situation, and because he was unable to write a single line there.

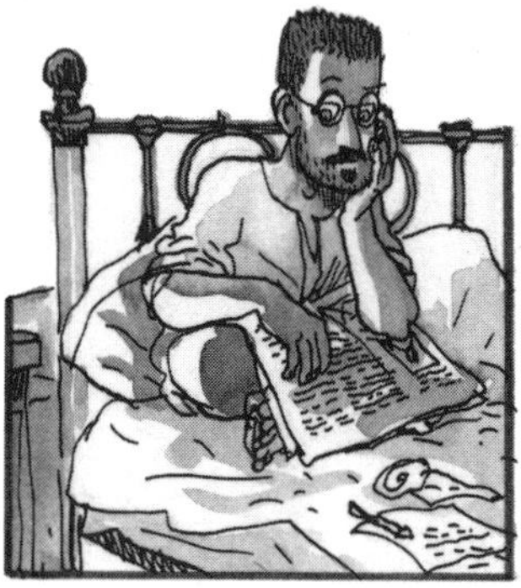

At the end of September, Richards, his publisher, told him that he wouldn't publish Dubliners, but that he would publish his first, autobiographical novel.

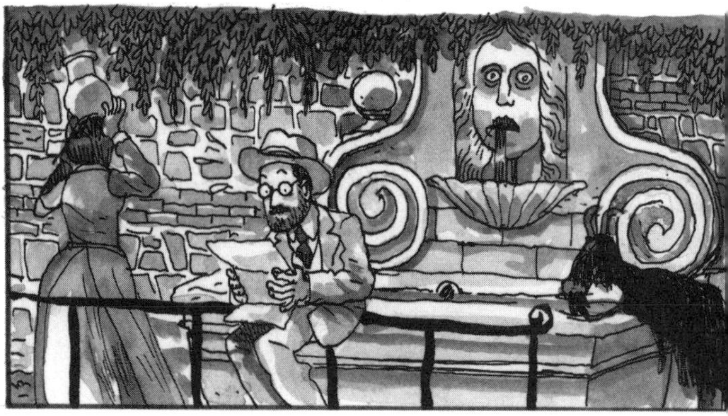

Joyce sent 'Dubliners' to Arthur Symons, another publisher, in the hope that he would be more accommodating.

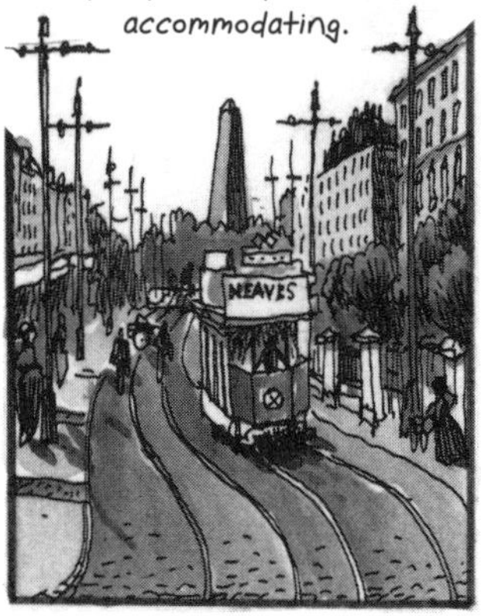

Symons sent him back good and bad news: he said no to 'Dubliners', but said that another publisher, Elkin Mathews, would publish his poems.

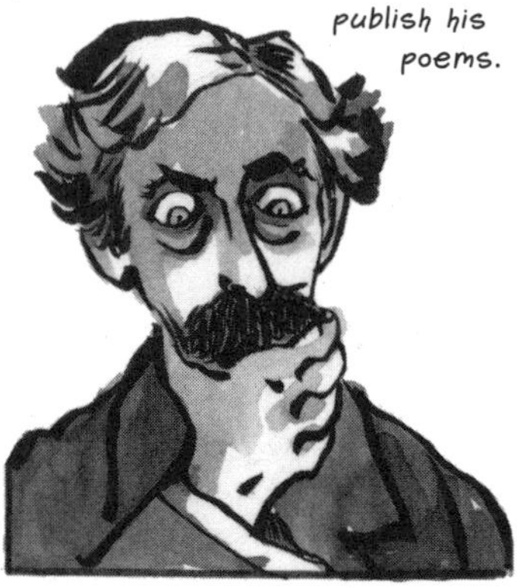

On 17 January , Mathews sent Joyce the contract for the publication of 'Chamber Music'.

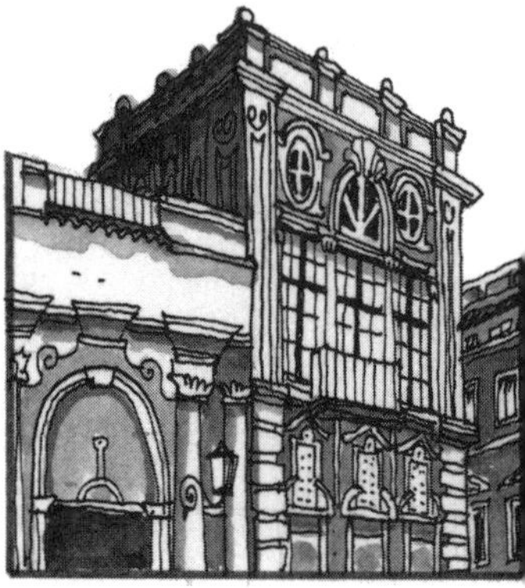

In spite of the distance, Joyce was up to date with events in Ireland.

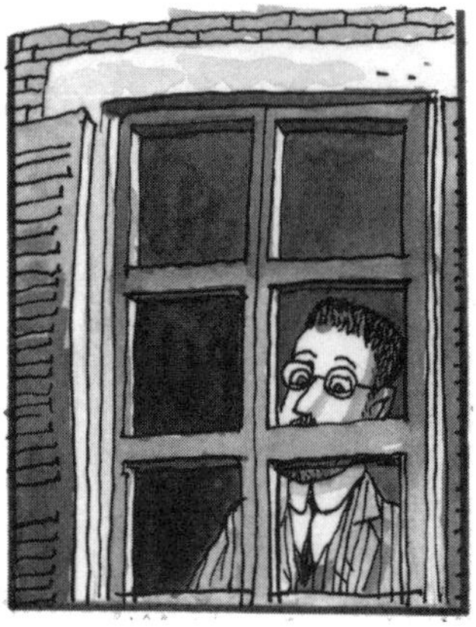

Gogarty was now a prominent citizen. He constantly asked James' family for news of him, attempting to renew their old friendship.

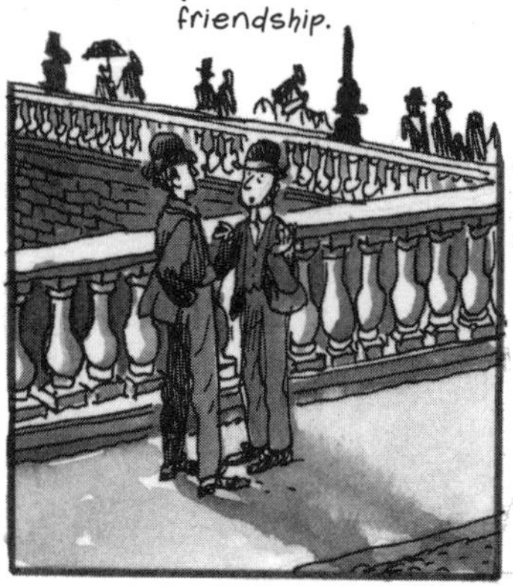

Kettle was now a Member of Parliament, advocating political dialogue on the 'Irish question'.

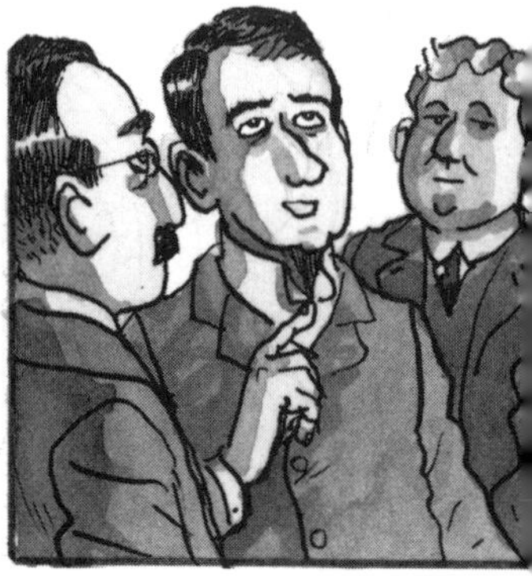

Joyce, who had always kept out of politics, decided to make known his own surprising views.

Instead of supporting his friend Kettle's parliamentary approach, Joyce defended the position of Arthur Griffith and Sinn Féin.

Griffith's 'United Irishman' was the only respectable newspaper in the country, and Griffith was a charismatic leader, detested equally by the English and the priests.

Joyce thought that parliamentarism had reached its limit with Parnell, and in Sinn Féin he saw great advantages for Ireland.

But Dublin was far away. In the small apartment in Rome, major events were taking place: Nora was pregnant again.

So, once more, the Joyces packed their bags and returned to Trieste. Stanislaus was not happy to have his bloodsucking relatives back.

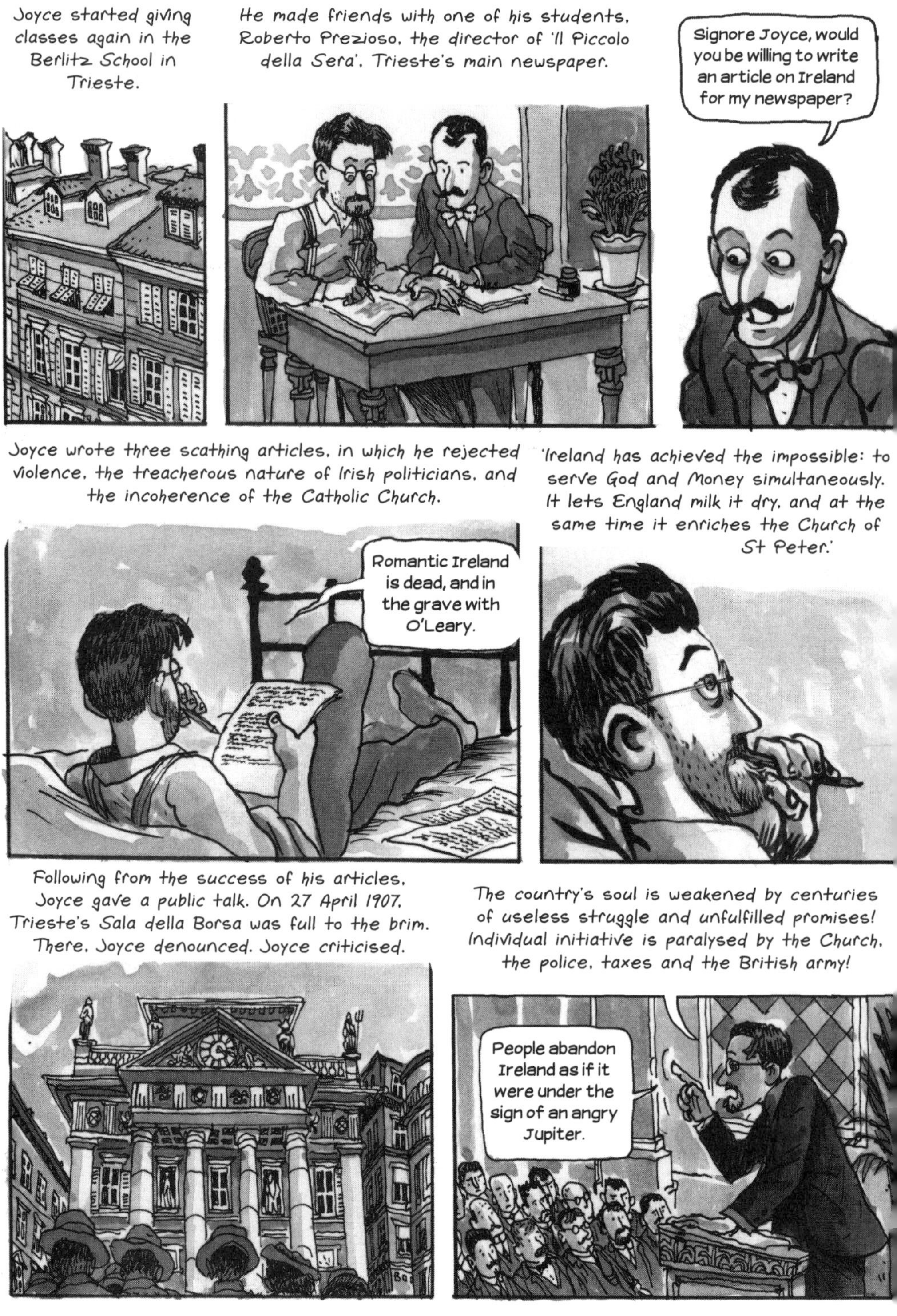
Joyce started giving classes again in the Berlitz School in Trieste.
He made friends with one of his students, Roberto Prezioso, the director of 'Il Piccolo della Sera', Trieste's main newspaper.
Signore Joyce, would you be willing to write an article on Ireland for my newspaper?
Joyce wrote three scathing articles, in which he rejected violence, the treacherous nature of Irish politicians, and the incoherence of the Catholic Church.
Romantic Ireland is dead, and in the grave with O'Leary.
'Ireland has achieved the impossible: to serve God and Money simultaneously. It lets England milk it dry, and at the same time it enriches the Church of St Peter.'
Following from the success of his articles, Joyce gave a public talk. On 27 April 1907, Trieste's Sala della Borsa was full to the brim. There, Joyce denounced. Joyce criticised.
The country's soul is weakened by centuries of useless struggle and unfulfilled promises! Individual initiative is paralysed by the Church, the police, taxes and the British army!
People abandon Ireland as if it were under the sign of an angry Jupiter.

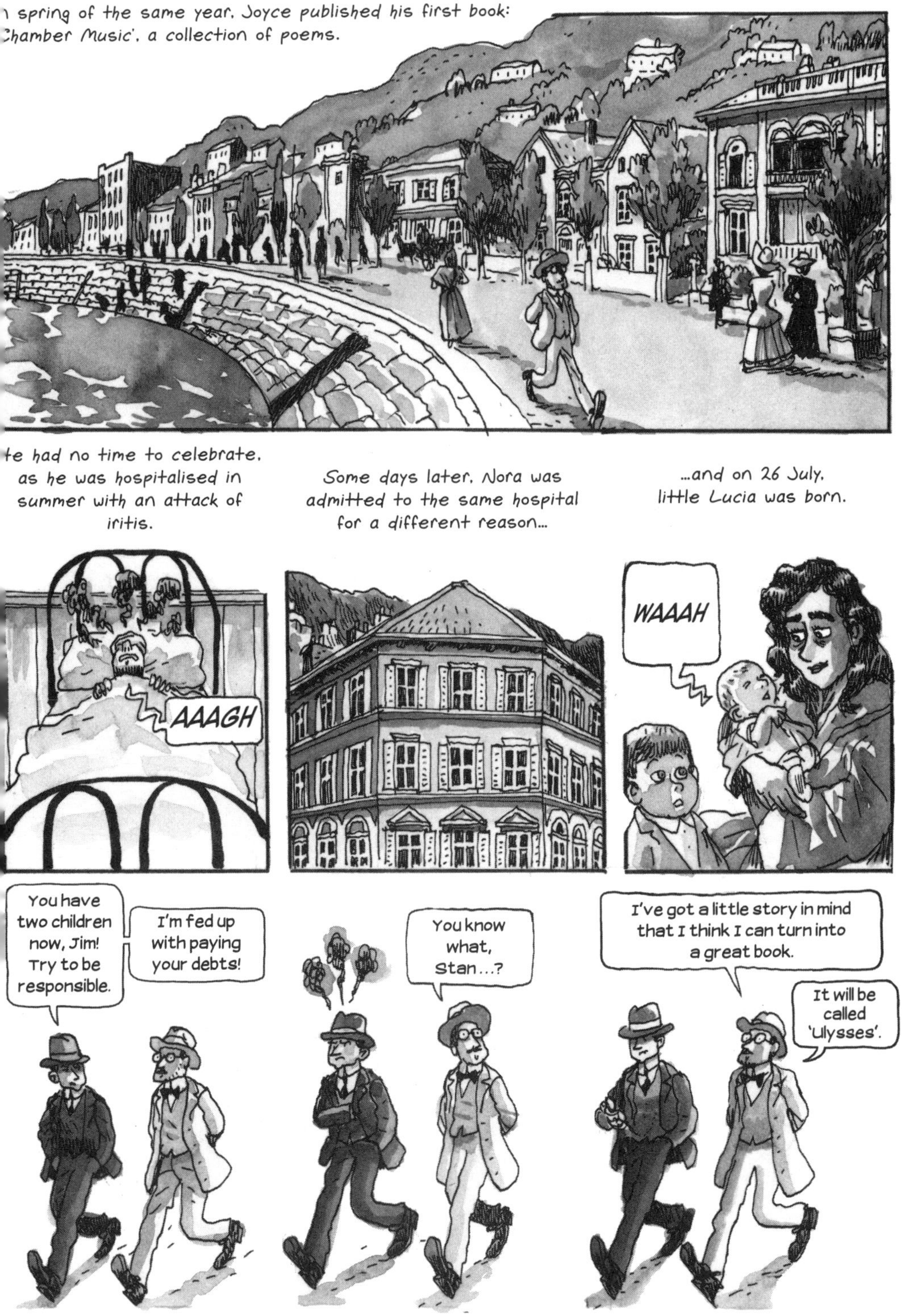
spring of the same year, Joyce published his first book:
Chamber Music', a collection of poems.
had no time to celebrate, as he was hospitalised in summer with an attack of iritis.
Some days later, Nora was admitted to the same hospital for a different reason...
...and on 26 July, little Lucia was born.
AAAGH
WAAAH
You have two children now, Jim! Try to be responsible.
I'm fed up with paying your debts!
You know what, Stan...?
I've got a little story in mind that I think I can turn into a great book.
It will be called 'Ulysses'.

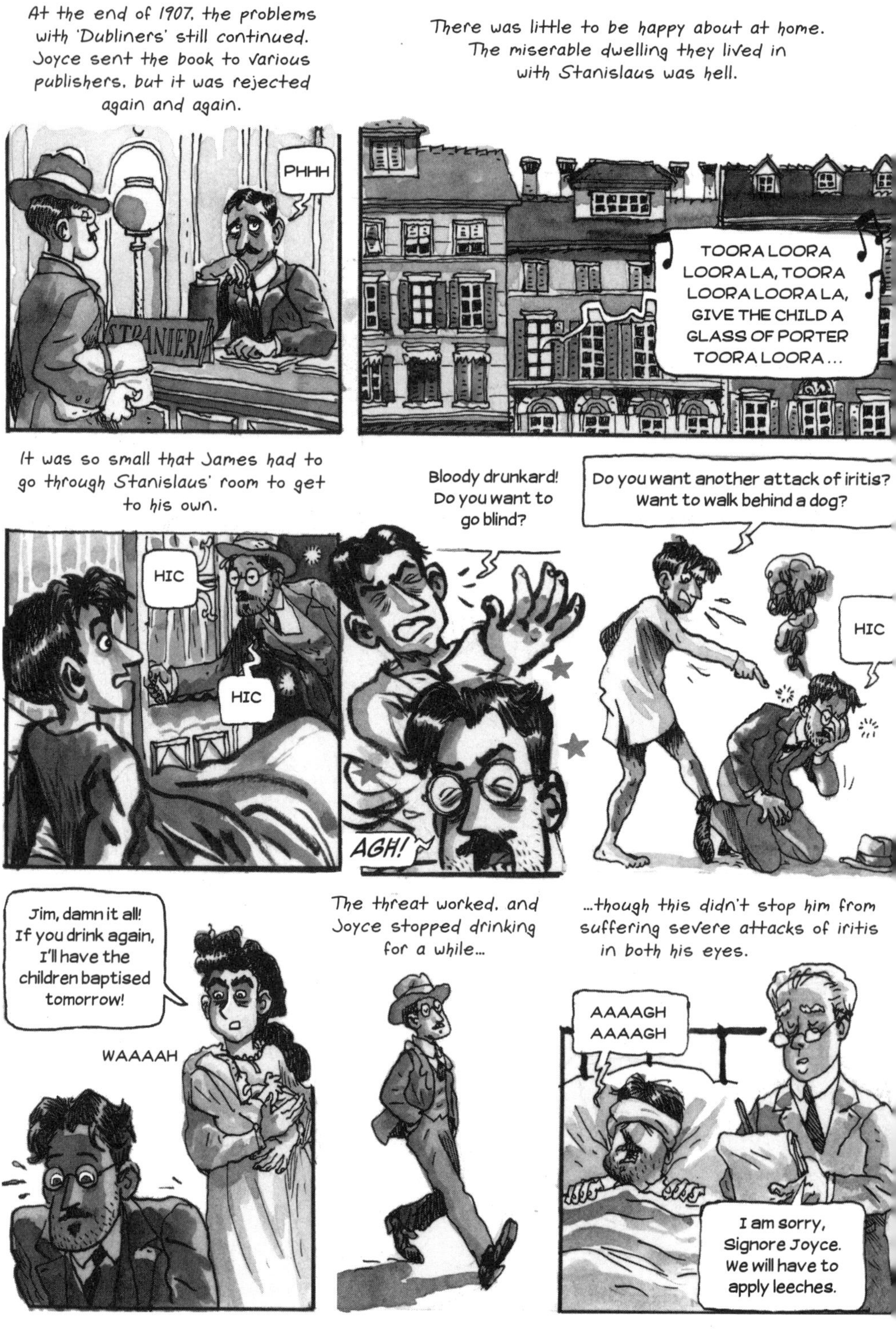

At the end of 1907, the problems with 'Dubliners' still continued. Joyce sent the book to various publishers, but it was rejected again and again.
STRANIERI
PHHH
There was little to be happy about at home. The miserable dwelling they lived in with Stanislaus was hell.
TOORA LOORA LOORA LA, TOORA LOORA LOORA LA, GIVE THE CHILD A GLASS OF PORTER TOORA LOORA...
It was so small that James had to go through Stanislaus' room to get to his own.
HIC
HIC
Bloody drunkard! Do you want to go blind?
AGH!
Do you want another attack of iritis? Want to walk behind a dog?
HIC
Jim, damn it all! If you drink again, I'll have the children baptised tomorrow!
WAAAAH
The threat worked, and Joyce stopped drinking for a while...
...though this didn't stop him from suffering severe attacks of iritis in both his eyes.
AAAAGH AAAAGH
I am sorry, Signore Joyce. We will have to apply leeches.

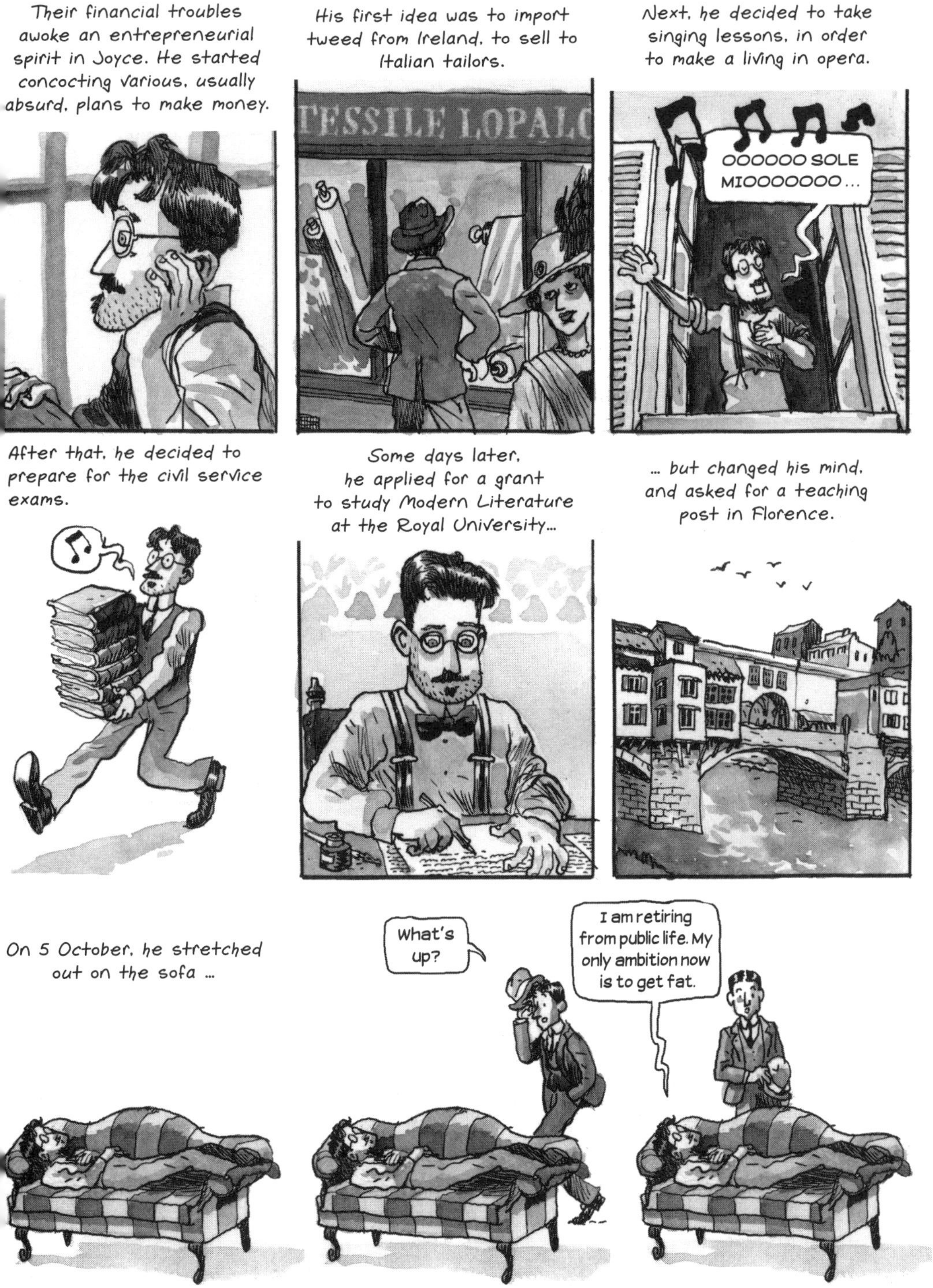
Their financial troubles awoke an entrepreneurial spirit in Joyce. He started concocting various, usually absurd, plans to make money.
His first idea was to import tweed from Ireland, to sell to Italian tailors.
TESSILE LOPALC
Next, he decided to take singing lessons, in order to make a living in opera.
OOOOOO SOLE MIOOOOOOO...
After that, he decided to prepare for the civil service exams.
Some days later, he applied for a grant to study Modern Literature at the Royal University...
... but changed his mind, and asked for a teaching post in Florence.
On 5 October, he stretched out on the sofa ...
What's up?
I am retiring from public life. My only ambition now is to get fat.

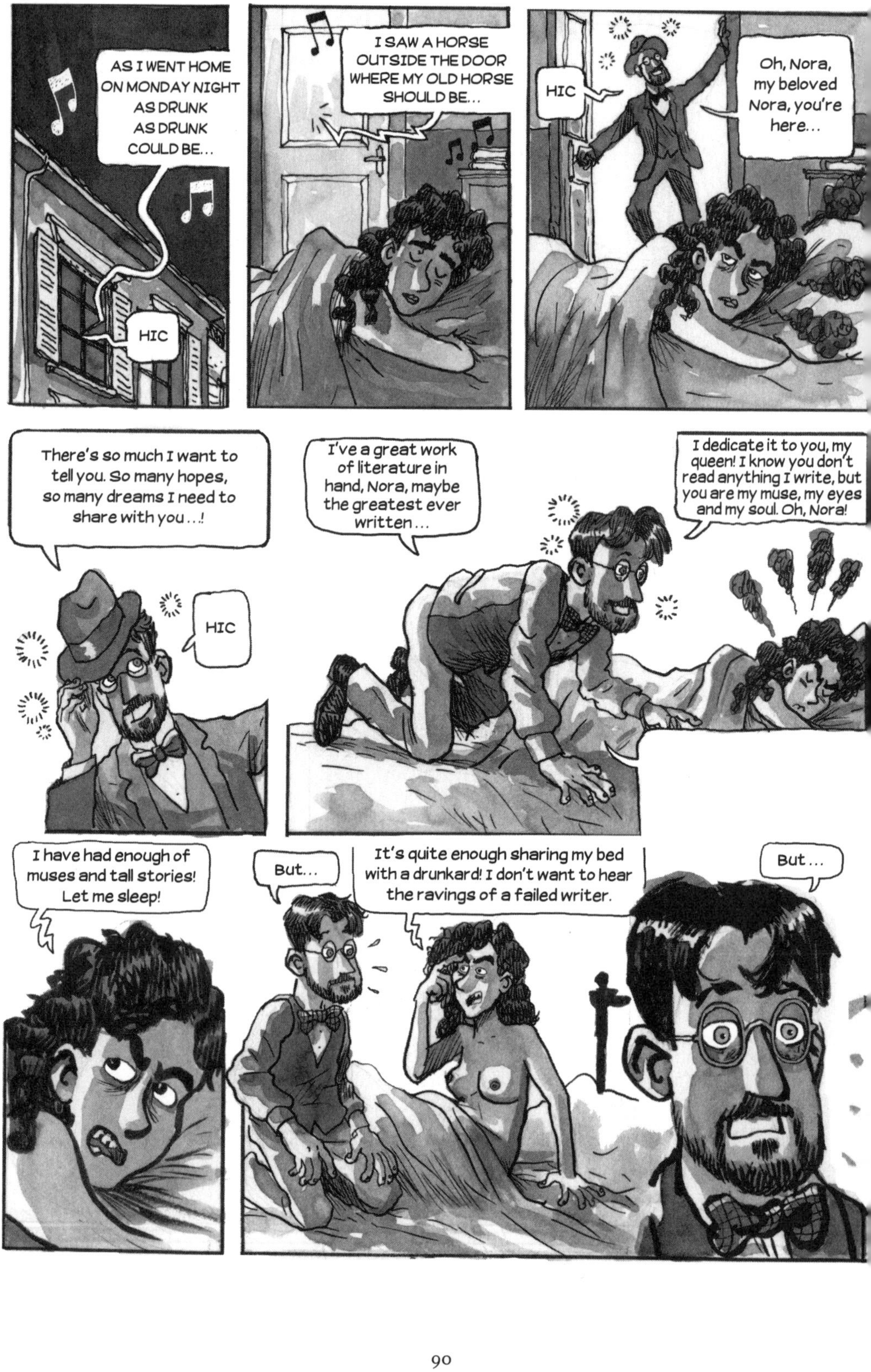
AS I WENT HOME ON MONDAY NIGHT AS DRUNK AS DRUNK COULD BE...
HIC
I SAW A HORSE OUTSIDE THE DOOR WHERE MY OLD HORSE SHOULD BE...
HIC
Oh, Nora, my beloved Nora, you're here...
There's so much I want to tell you. So many hopes, so many dreams I need to share with you...!
HIC
I've a great work of literature in hand, Nora, maybe the greatest ever written...
I dedicate it to you, my queen! I know you don't read anything I write, but you are my muse, my eyes and my soul. Oh, Nora!
I have had enough of muses and tall stories! Let me sleep!
But...
It's quite enough sharing my bed with a drunkard! I don't want to hear the ravings of a failed writer.
But...

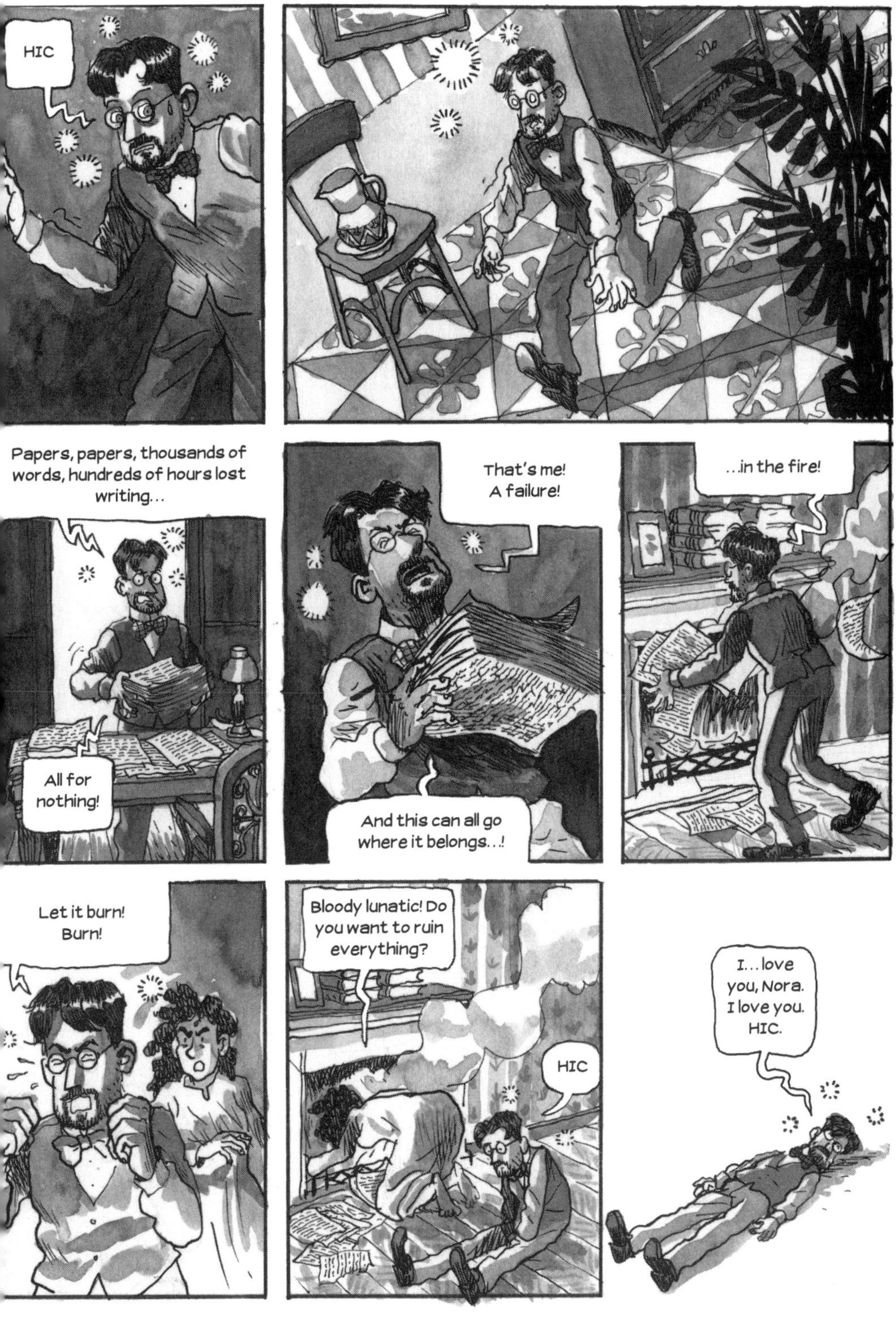
HIC
Papers, papers, thousands of words, hundreds of hours lost writing…
All for nothing!
That's me! A failure!
And this can all go where it belongs…!
…in the fire!
Let it burn! Burn!
Bloody lunatic! Do you want to ruin everything?
HIC
I… love you, Nora. I love you. HIC.

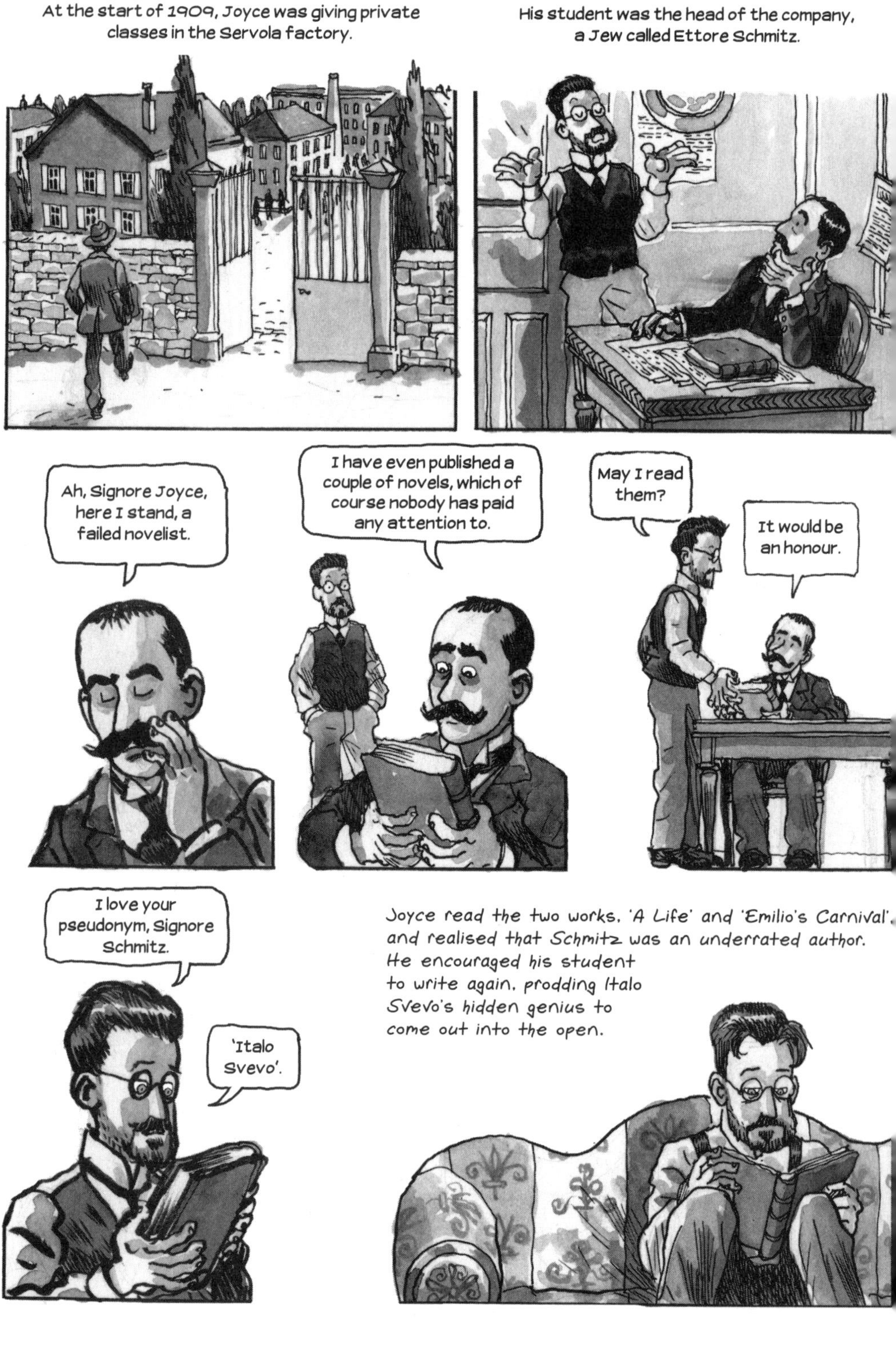
At the start of 1909, Joyce was giving private classes in the Servola factory.
His student was the head of the company, a Jew called Ettore Schmitz.
Ah, Signore Joyce, here I stand, a failed novelist.
I have even published a couple of novels, which of course nobody has paid any attention to.
May I read them?
It would be an honour.
I love your pseudonym, Signore Schmitz.
'Italo Svevo'.
Joyce read the two works, 'A Life' and 'Emilio's Carnival', and realised that Schmitz was an underrated author. He encouraged his student to write again, prodding Italo Svevo's hidden genius to come out into the open.

He also seized on Schmitz's Jewishness to question him on Hebraic matters, gaining information that he would include later in 'Ulysses'.

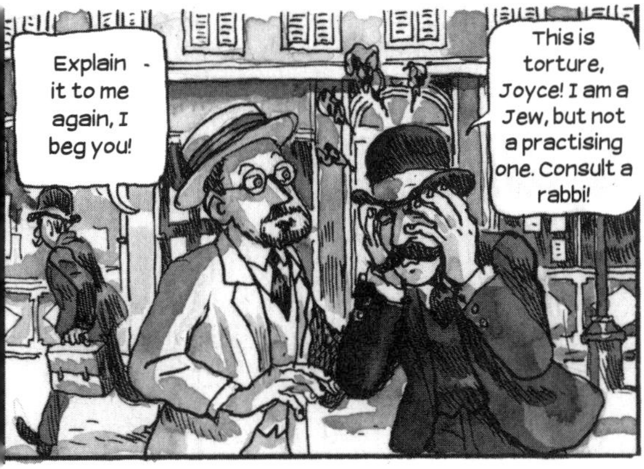
Explain it to me again, I beg you!
This is torture, Joyce! I am a Jew, but not a practising one. Consult a rabbi!

'The twelve tribes were grouped in two kingdoms: Judea (basically the tribes of Judah, of Benjamin, and that part of Levi's tribe which had no land) and Israel ...'

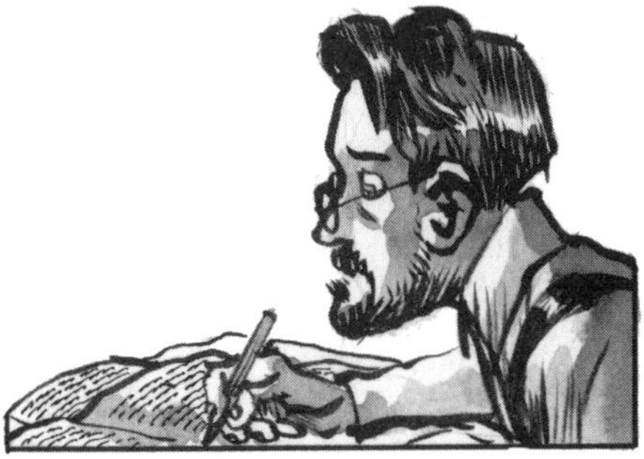

Joyce greatly enjoyed Schmitz's company. The student became his friend, and inspired part of his work.

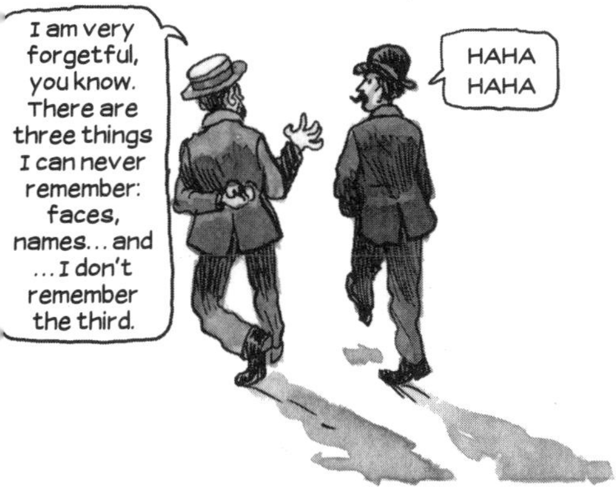
I am very forgetful, you know. There are three things I can never remember: faces, names... and ...I don't remember the third.
HAHA HAHA

In July, Joyce felt the urge to check out the situation in Ireland.

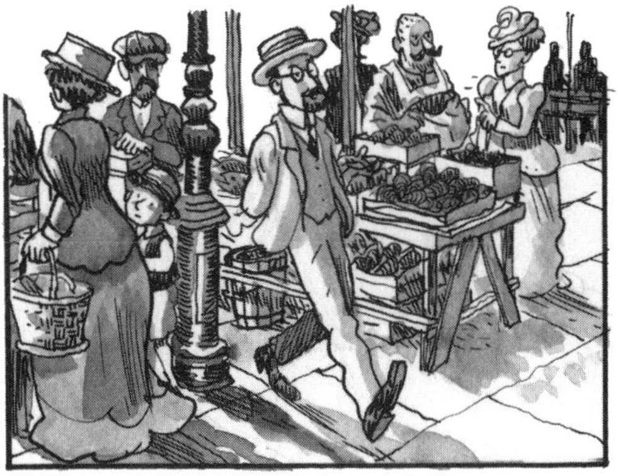

To find out what those who had betrayed him were doing.

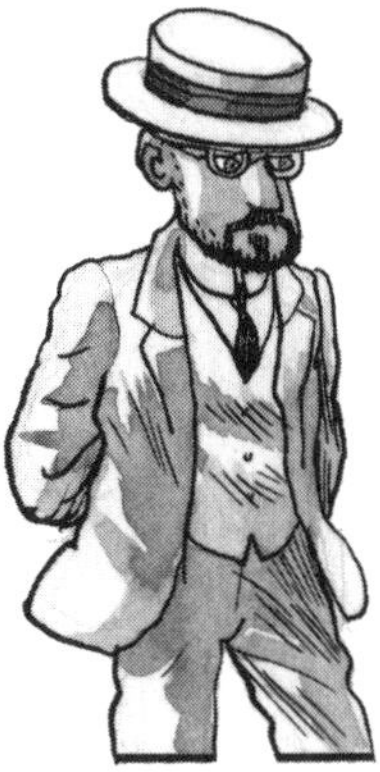

To find out what would happen if he went back to the scene of those betrayals.

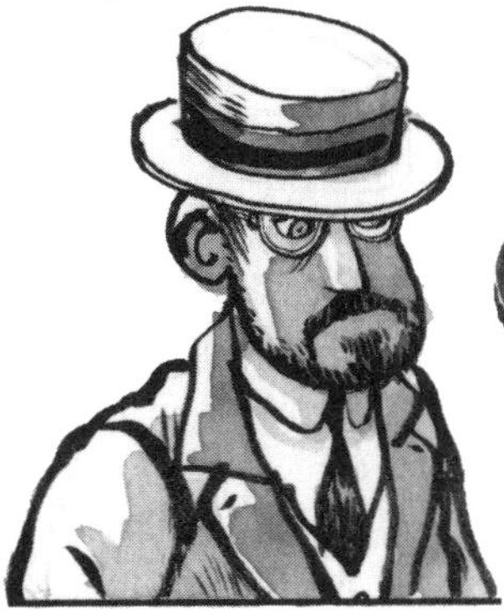

In July, Joyce decided to return to the black hole that was Dublin, to submerge himself in its detritus.

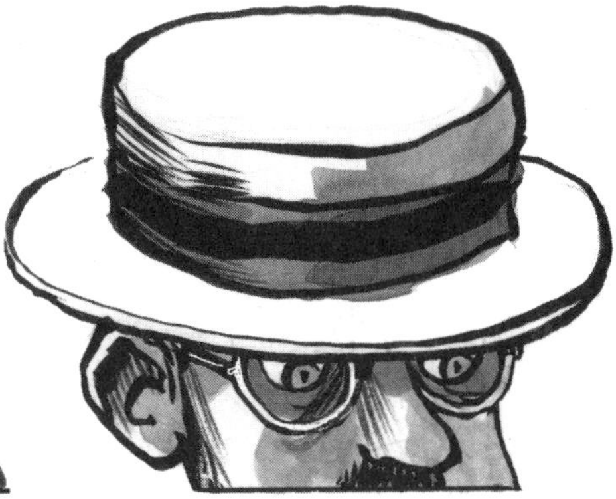

On 29 July, a mailboat arrived at Kingstown, Dublin.

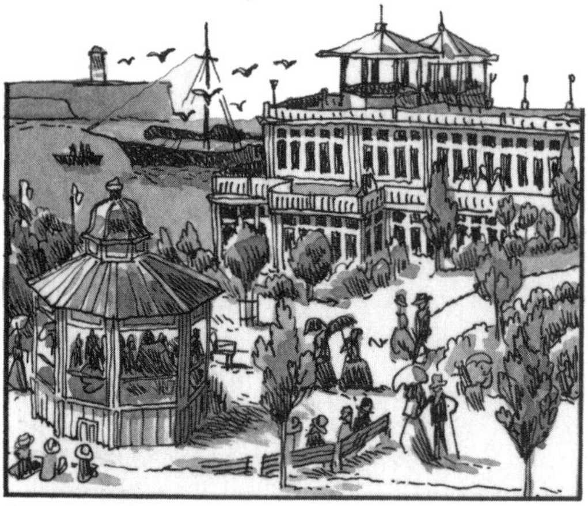

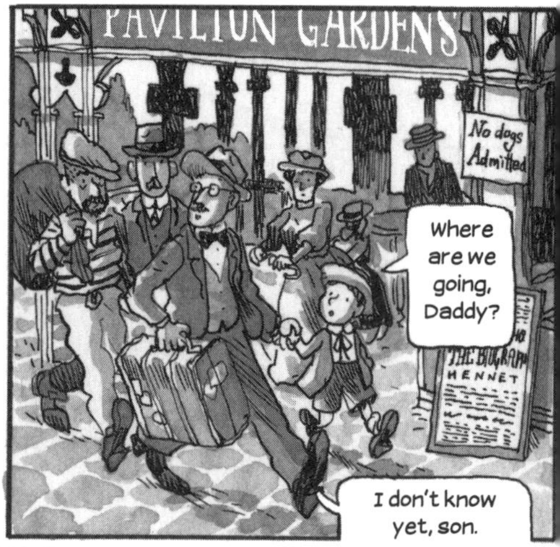
PAVILION GARDENS
No dogs Admitted
Where are we going, Daddy?
I don't know yet, son.

Joyce went in search of his ghosts, one by one. First, he went for a few drinks with his father, and ended up singing 'La Traviata' in an old pub.

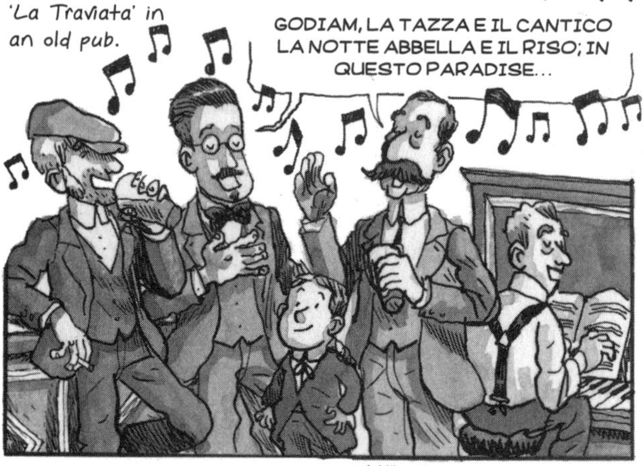
GODIAM, LA TAZZA E IL CANTICO LA NOTTE ABBELLA E IL RISO; IN QUESTO PARADISE...

One afternoon, he bumped into Gogarty in Merrion Square.

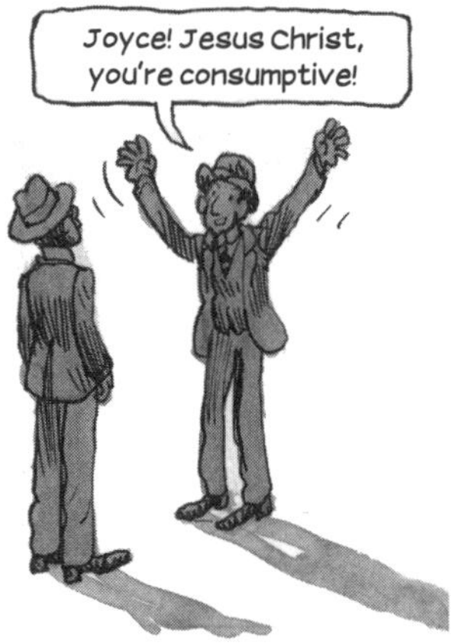
Joyce! Jesus Christ, you're consumptive!

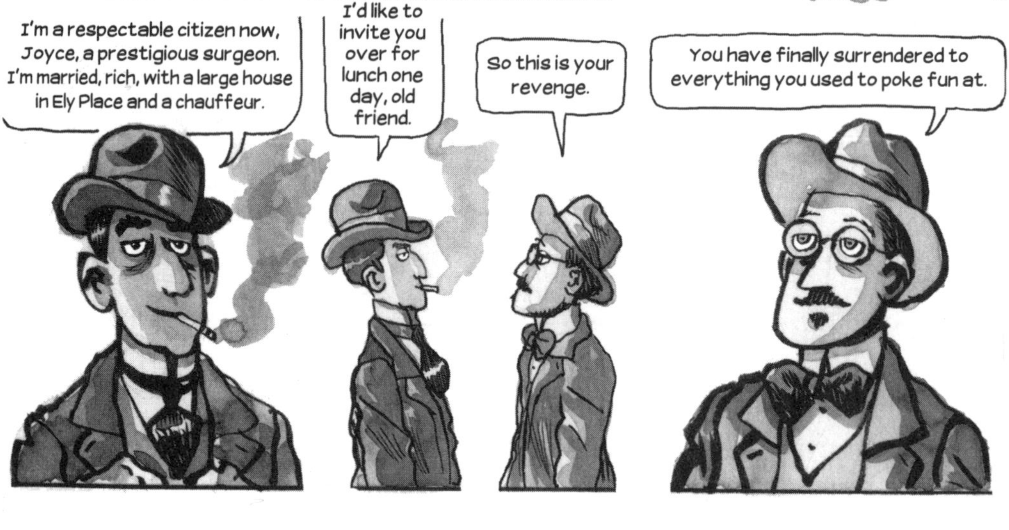
I'm a respectable citizen now, Joyce, a prestigious surgeon. I'm married, rich, with a large house in Ely Place and a chauffeur.
I'd like to invite you over for lunch one day, old friend.
So this is your revenge.
You have finally surrendered to everything you used to poke fun at.

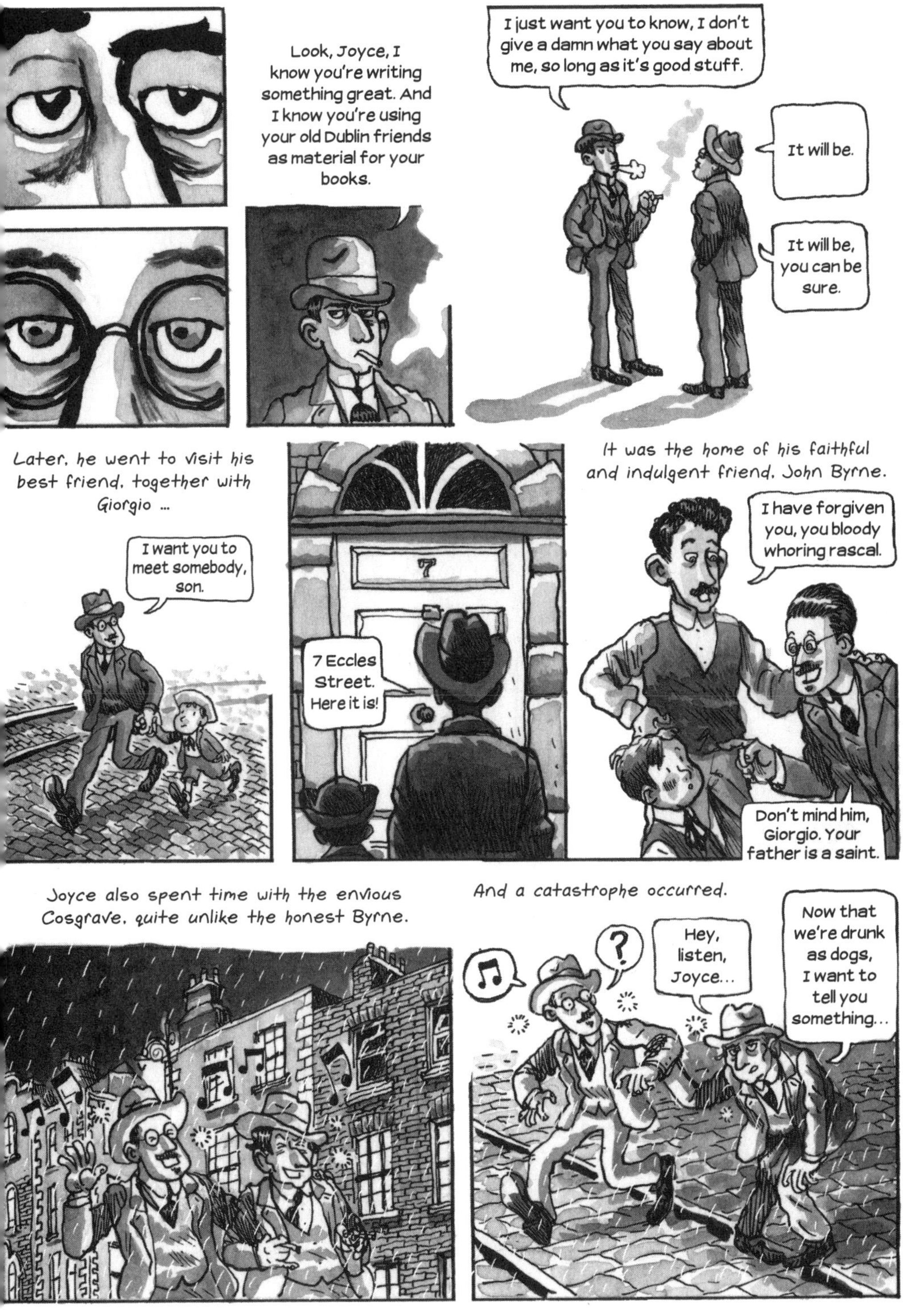
Look, Joyce, I know you're writing something great. And I know you're using your old Dublin friends as material for your books.
I just want you to know, I don't give a damn what you say about me, so long as it's good stuff.
It will be.
It will be, you can be sure.
Later, he went to visit his best friend, together with Giorgio ...
I want you to meet somebody, son.
7
7 Eccles Street. Here it is!
It was the home of his faithful and indulgent friend, John Byrne.
I have forgiven you, you bloody whoring rascal.
Don't mind him, Giorgio. Your father is a saint.
Joyce also spent time with the envious Cosgrave, quite unlike the honest Byrne.
And a catastrophe occurred.
?
Hey, listen, Joyce...
Now that we're drunk as dogs, I want to tell you something...

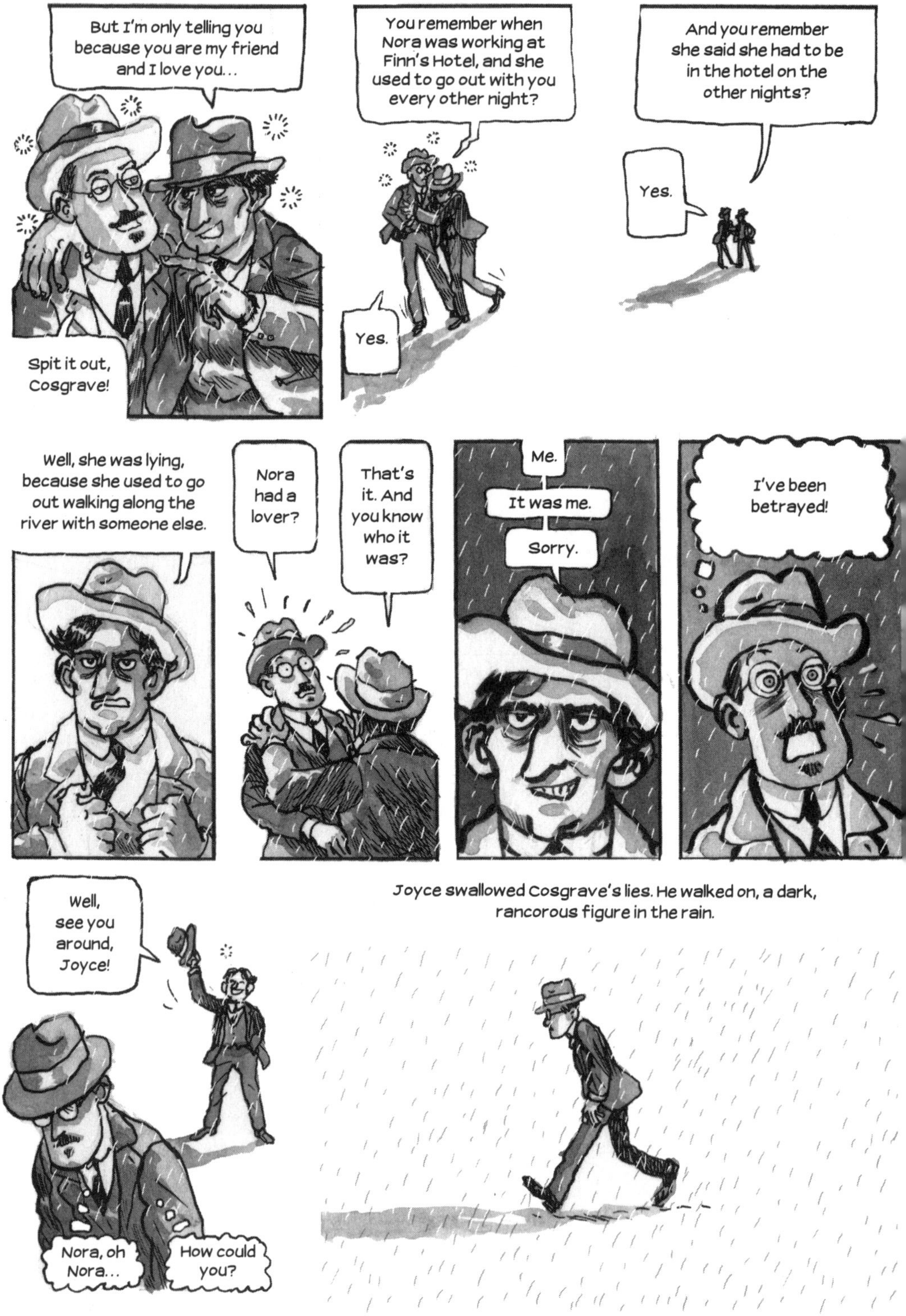
But I'm only telling you because you are my friend and I love you...
Spit it out, Cosgrave!
You remember when Nora was working at Finn's Hotel, and she used to go out with you every other night?
Yes.
And you remember she said she had to be in the hotel on the other nights?
Yes.
Well, she was lying, because she used to go out walking along the river with someone else.
Nora had a lover?
That's it. And you know who it was?
Me.
It was me.
Sorry.
I've been betrayed!
Well, see you around, Joyce!
Nora, oh Nora...
How could you?
Joyce swallowed Cosgrave's lies. He walked on, a dark, rancorous figure in the rain.

He wrote a letter to Nora, full of accusations and reproaches.

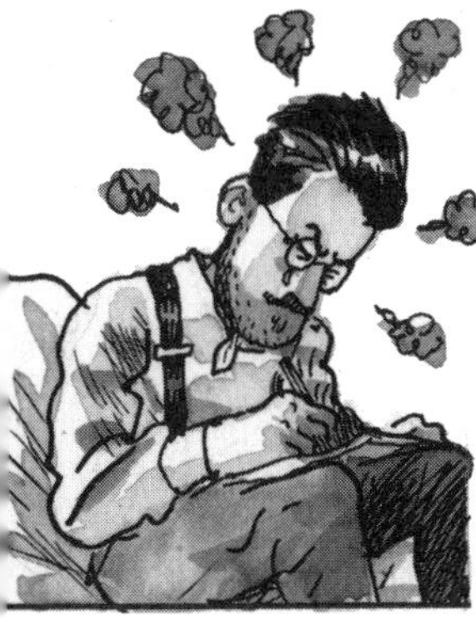

When Nora received it, she couldn't believe her eyes.

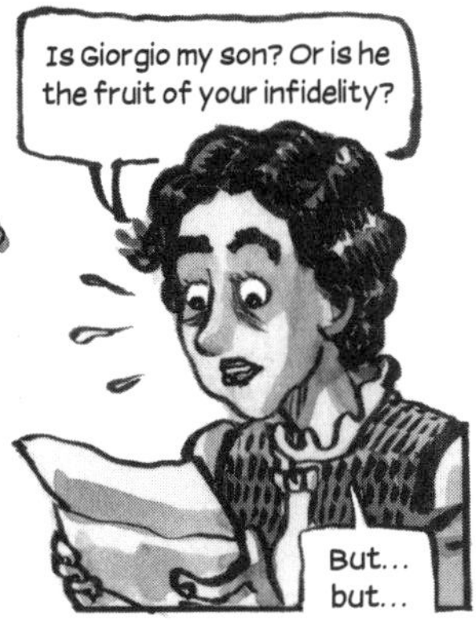
Is Giorgio my son? Or is he the fruit of your infidelity?
But... but...

Joyce was the victim of his own gullibility as well as Cosgrave's malevolence.

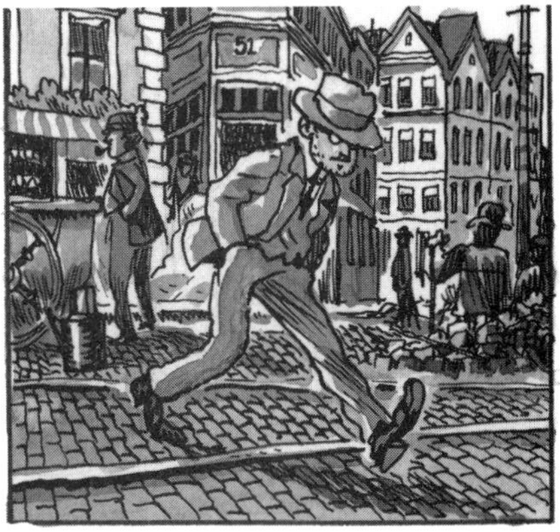

He turned for comfort to his only friend, in 7 Eccles Street.

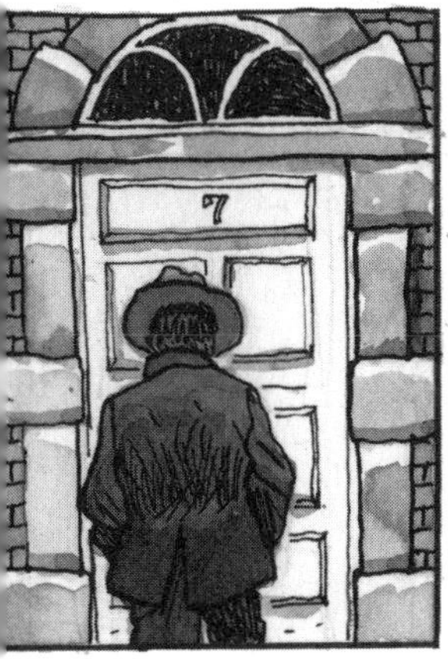

He wept and groaned in desperation, and received the only coherent, honest reply possible.

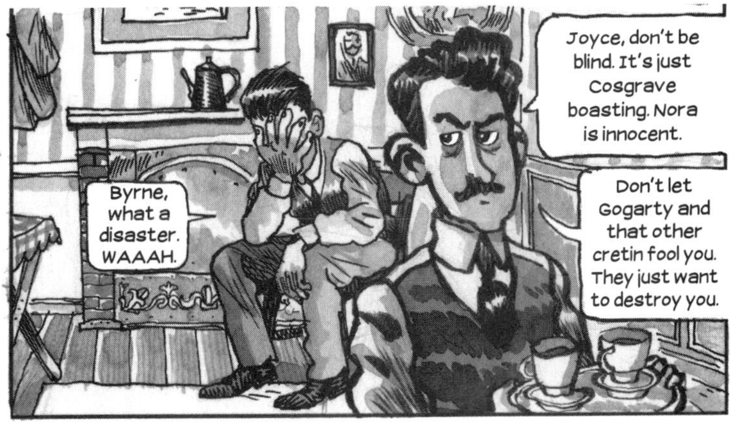
Byrne, what a disaster. WAAAH.
Joyce, don't be blind. It's just Cosgrave boasting. Nora is innocent.
Don't let Gogarty and that other cretin fool you. They just want to destroy you.

Thanks to Byrne, Joyce came to his senses. He wrote again to Nora, asking her forgiveness.

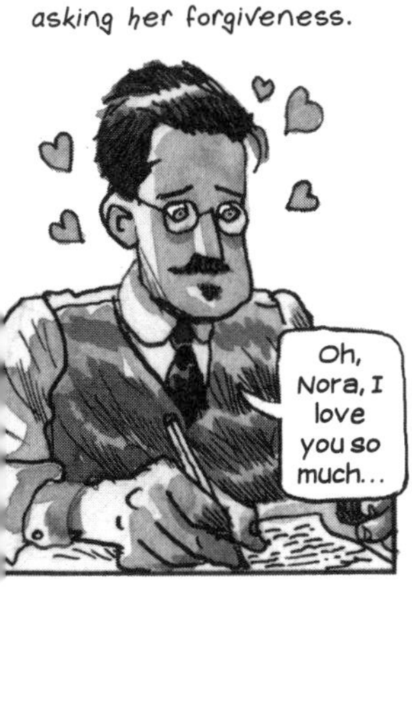
Oh, Nora, I love you so much...

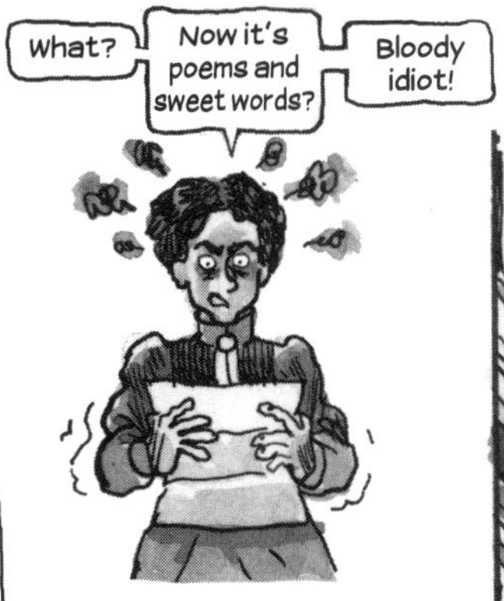
What?
Now it's poems and sweet words?
Bloody idiot!

Nora had suffered deeply as a result of Joyce's angry attack. Now she was furious.

But, as always, her incomprehensible and uncomprehended love for him overcame her logic.

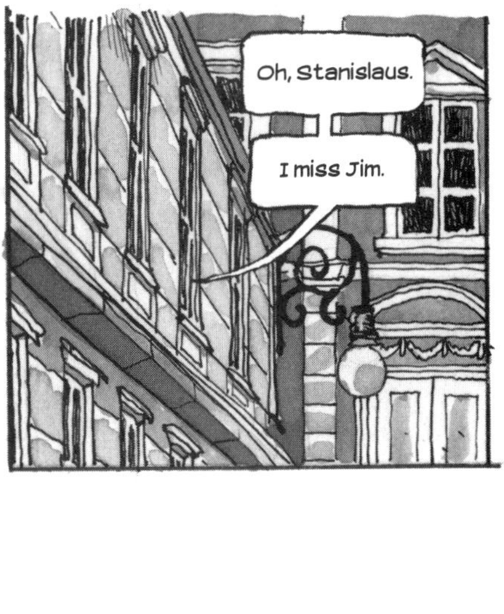
Oh, Stanislaus.
I miss Jim.

After these bad times, some good news came. On 19 August, Joyce signed a contract with Hone & Roberts to publish 'Dubliners'.

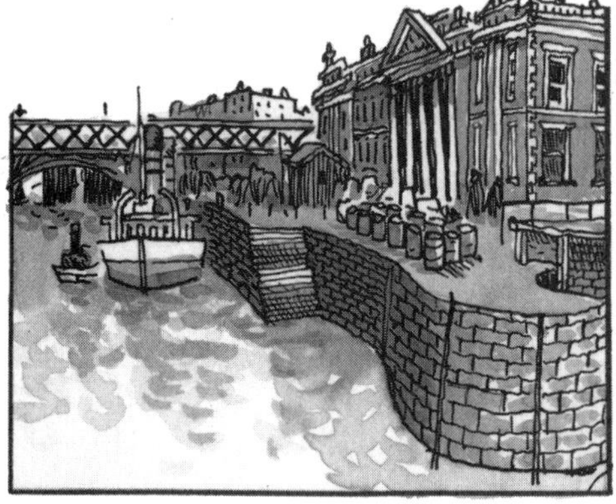

Meanwhile, the Joyces' home in Dublin was falling apart. Fed up with all the responsibility, Margaret, the eldest sister, became a nun and went off to a convent in New Zealand.

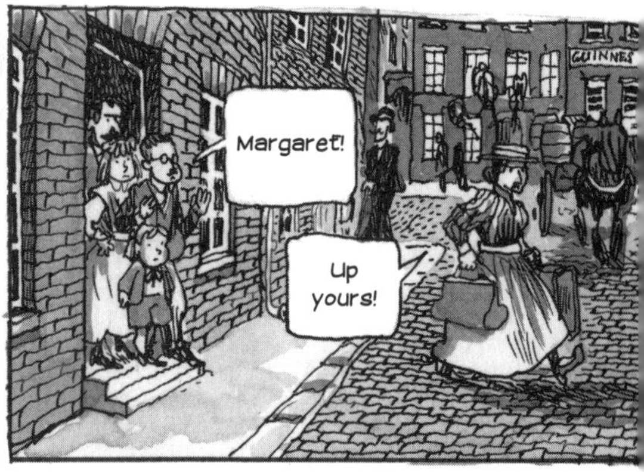
GUINNES
Margaret!
Up yours!

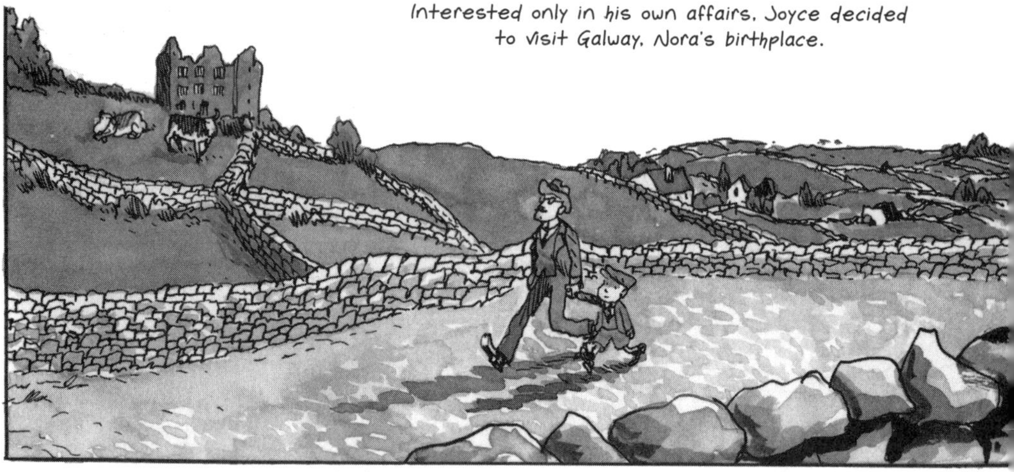
Interested only in his own affairs, Joyce decided to visit Galway, Nora's birthplace.

In the kitchen of Nora Barnacle's aunt and uncle, he sang traditional Connacht songs.

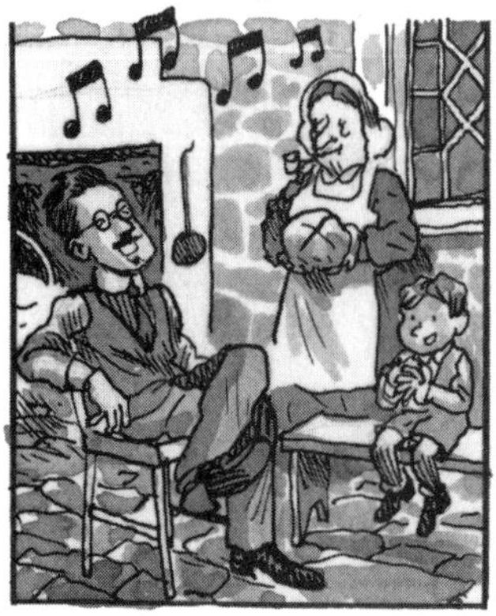

In the mornings he would walk along the estuary, watching the seagulls.

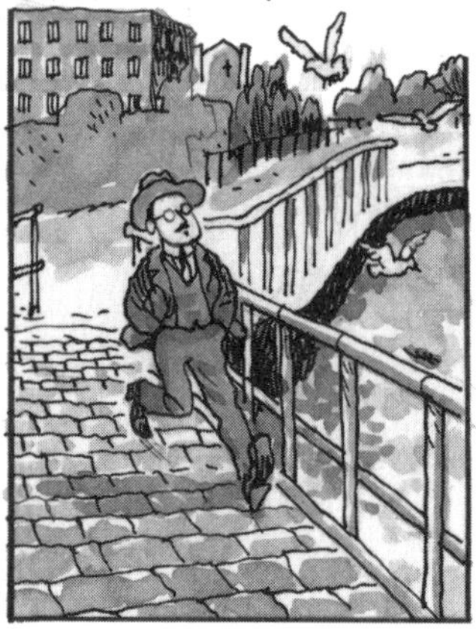

Joyce sighed, more in love than ever.

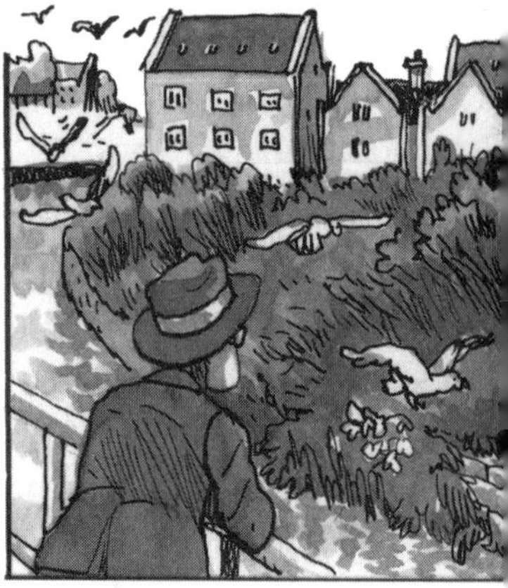

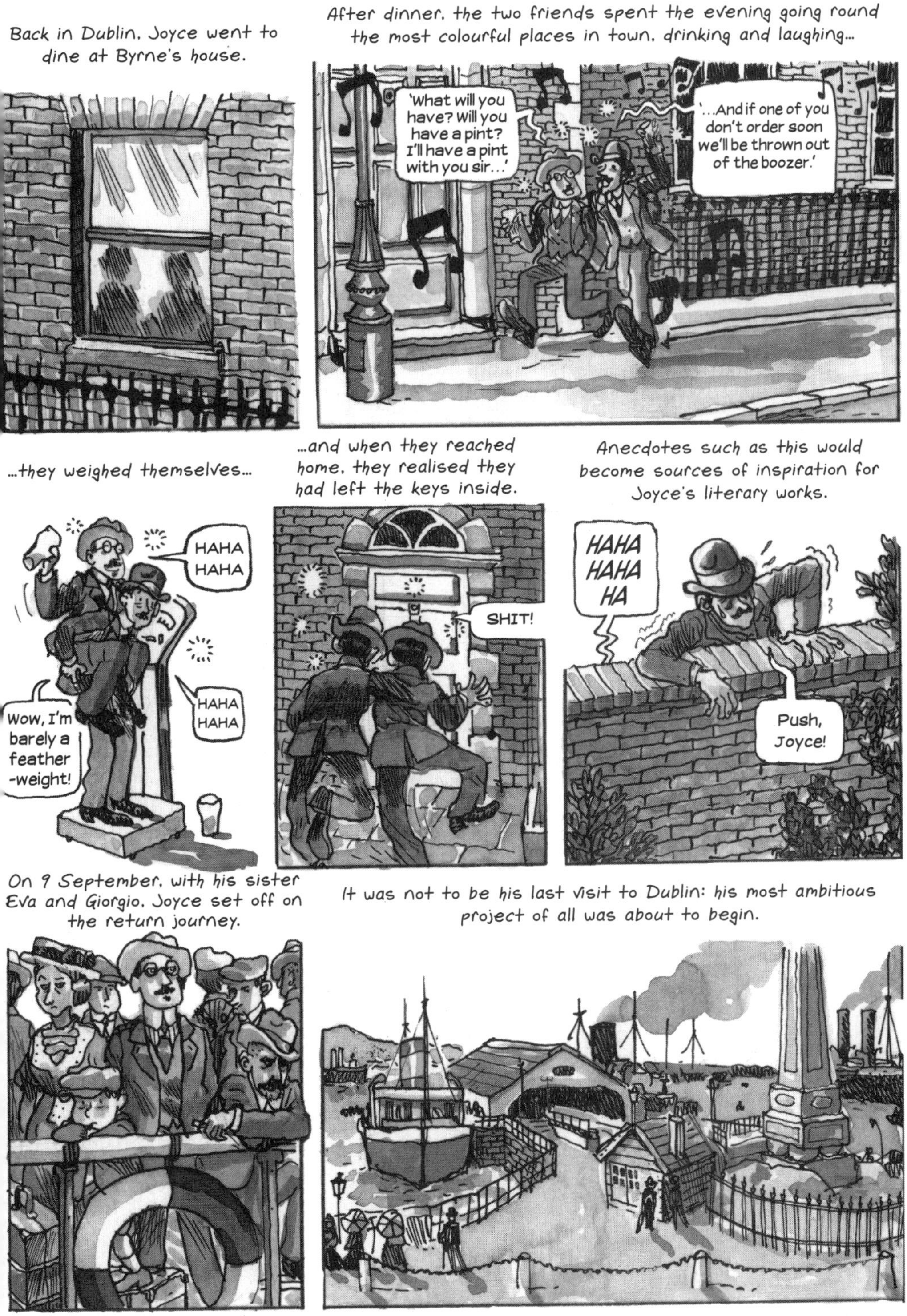
Back in Dublin, Joyce went to dine at Byrne's house.
After dinner, the two friends spent the evening going round the most colourful places in town, drinking and laughing...
'What will you have? Will you have a pint? I'll have a pint with you sir...'
'...And if one of you don't order soon we'll be thrown out of the boozer.'
...they weighed themselves...
HAHA HAHA
HAHA HAHA
Wow, I'm barely a feather-weight!
...and when they reached home, they realised they had left the keys inside.
SHIT!
Anecdotes such as this would become sources of inspiration for Joyce's literary works.
HAHA HAHA HA
Push, Joyce!
On 9 September, with his sister Eva and Giorgio, Joyce set off on the return journey.
It was not to be his last visit to Dublin: his most ambitious project of all was about to begin.

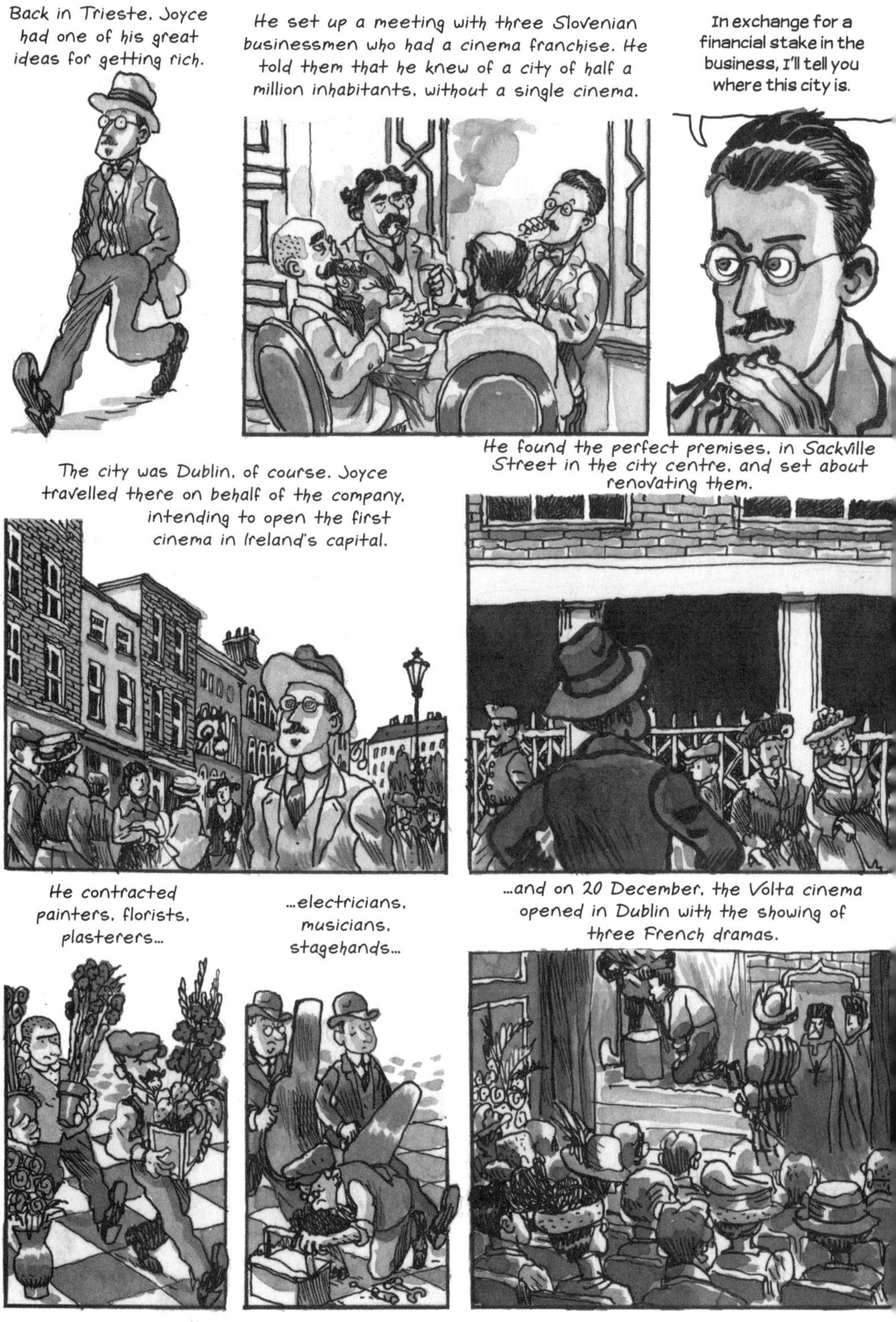
Back in Trieste, Joyce had one of his great ideas for getting rich.
He set up a meeting with three Slovenian businessmen who had a cinema franchise. He told them that he knew of a city of half a million inhabitants, without a single cinema.
In exchange for a financial stake in the business, I'll tell you where this city is.
The city was Dublin, of course. Joyce travelled there on behalf of the company, intending to open the first cinema in Ireland's capital.
He found the perfect premises, in Sackville Street in the city centre, and set about renovating them.
He contracted painters, florists, plasterers...
...electricians, musicians, stagehands...
...and on 20 December, the Volta cinema opened in Dublin with the showing of three French dramas.

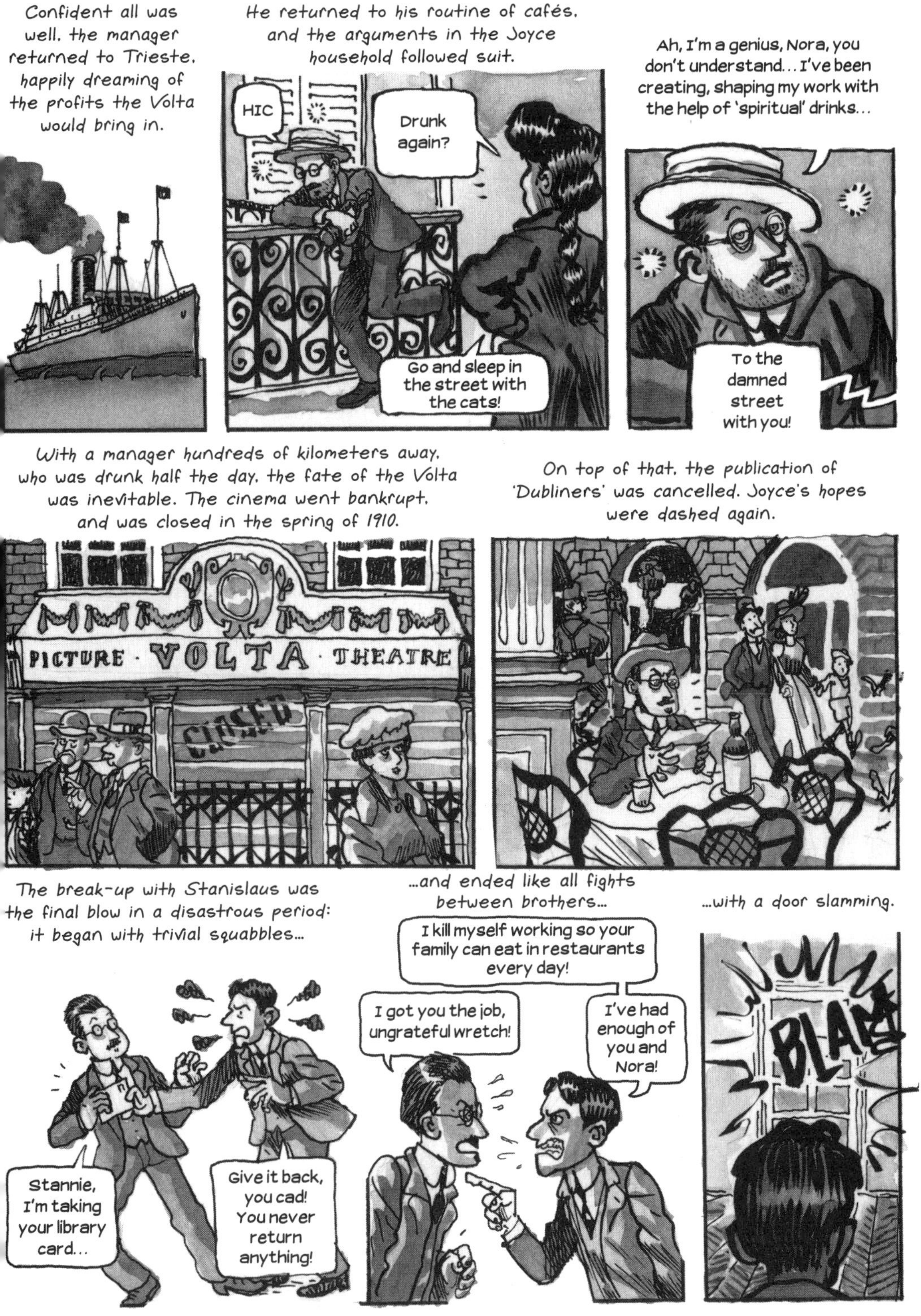
Confident all was well, the manager returned to Trieste, happily dreaming of the profits the Volta would bring in.
He returned to his routine of cafés, and the arguments in the Joyce household followed suit.
HIC
Drunk again?
Go and sleep in the street with the cats!
Ah, I'm a genius, Nora, you don't understand... I've been creating, shaping my work with the help of 'spiritual' drinks...
To the damned street with you!
With a manager hundreds of kilometers away, who was drunk half the day, the fate of the Volta was inevitable. The cinema went bankrupt, and was closed in the spring of 1910.
PICTURE · VOLTA · THEATRE
CLOSED
On top of that, the publication of 'Dubliners' was cancelled. Joyce's hopes were dashed again.
The break-up with Stanislaus was the final blow in a disastrous period: it began with trivial squabbles...
Stannie, I'm taking your library card...
Give it back, you cad! You never return anything!
...and ended like all fights between brothers...
I kill myself working so your family can eat in restaurants every day!
I got you the job, ungrateful wretch!
I've had enough of you and Nora!
...with a door slamming.
BLAM

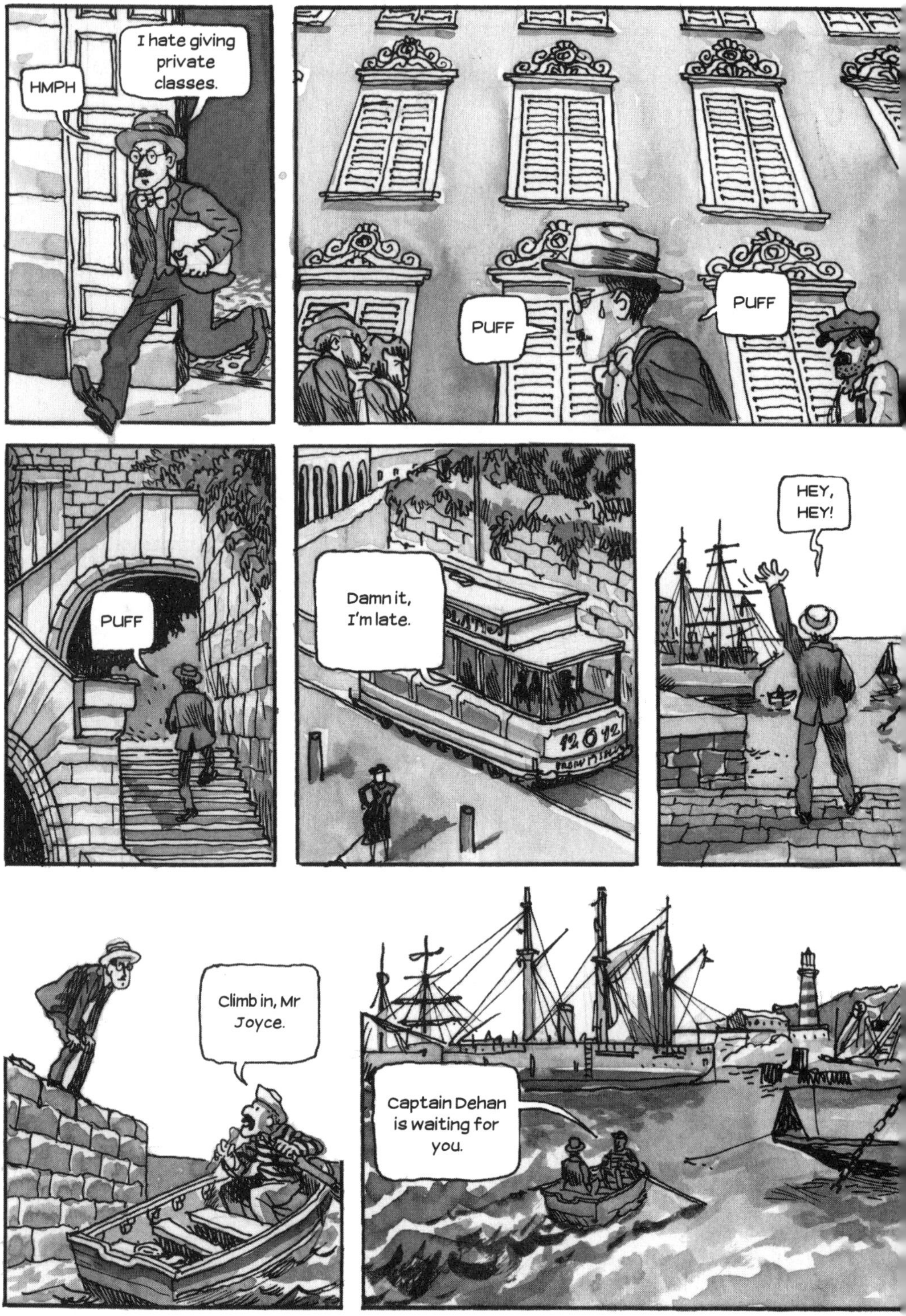
HMPH
I hate giving private classes.
PUFF
PUFF
PUFF
Damn it, I'm late.
HEY, HEY!
Climb in, Mr Joyce.
Captain Dehan is waiting for you.

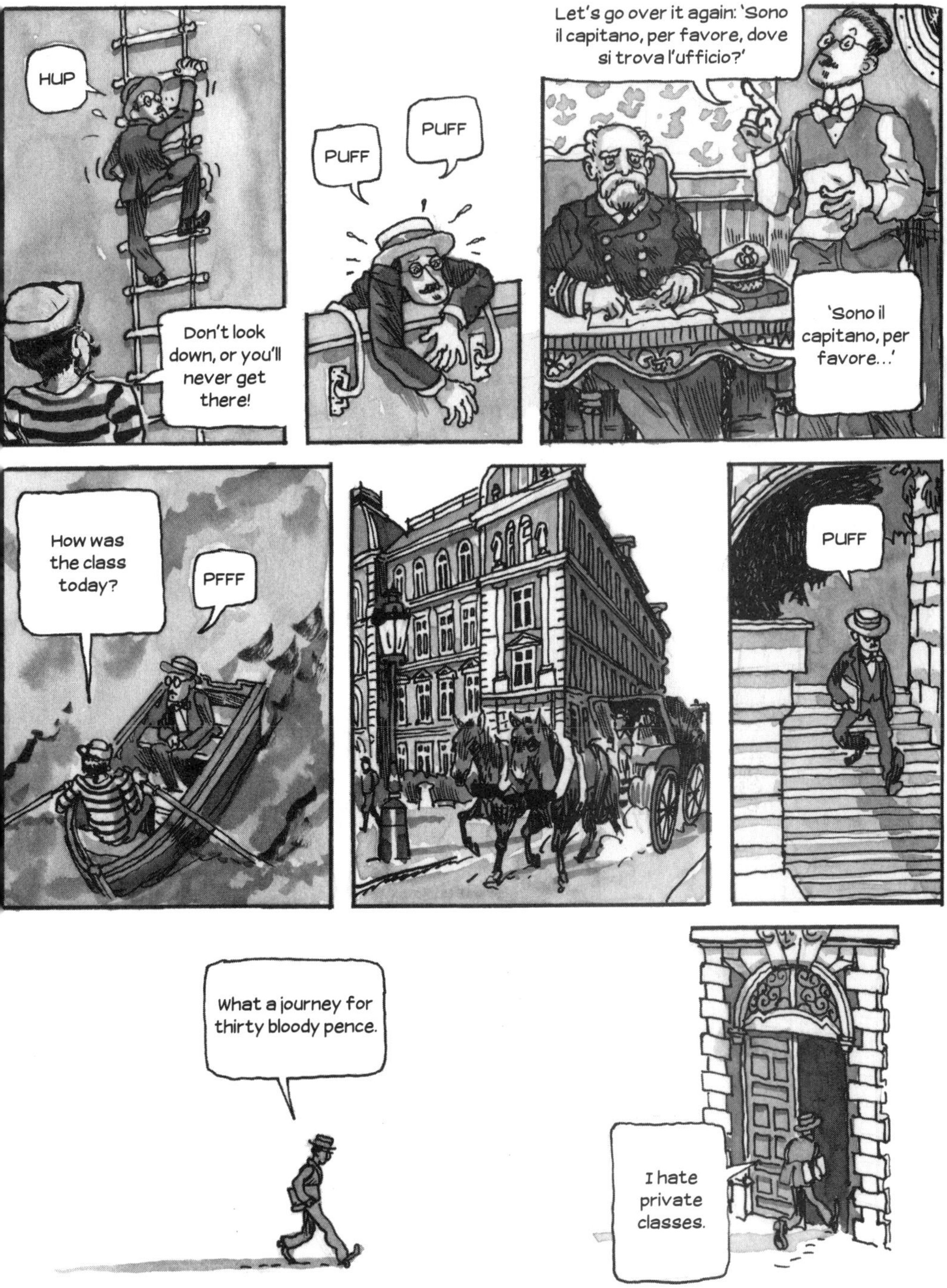
HUP
Don't look down, or you'll never get there!
PUFF
PUFF
Let's go over it again: 'Sono il capitano, per favore, dove si trova l'ufficio?'
'Sono il capitano, per favore…'
How was the class today?
PFFF
PUFF
What a journey for thirty bloody pence.
I hate private classes.

The never-ending story of 'Dubliners' continued. In December 1910, Roberts, the publisher, wrote to Joyce saying he hoped to publish it in January.

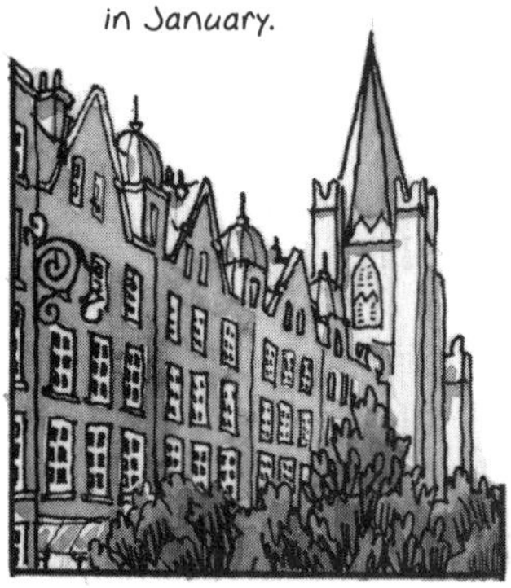

Joyce received the news, happy but exhausted...

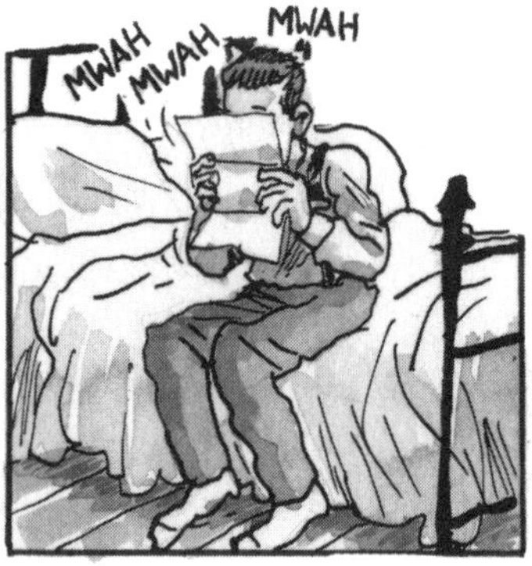
MWAH
MWAH
MWAH

...only to find in January that 'Dubliners' was postponed again, once more in the limbo of books pending publication.

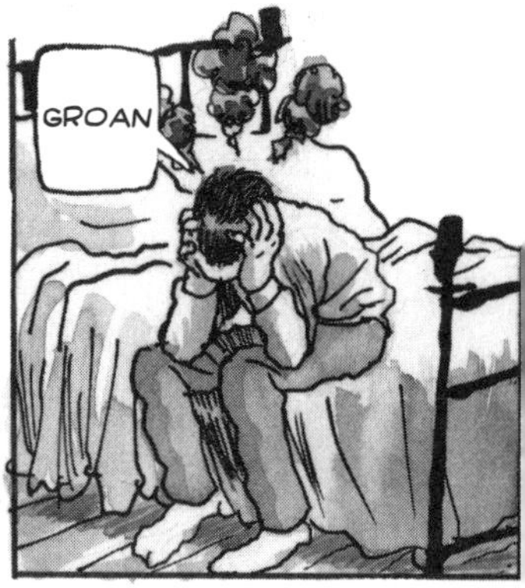
GROAN

The publisher asked him to cut out all references to Edward VII, the previous king. Joyce was furious, but he had an eccentric idea.

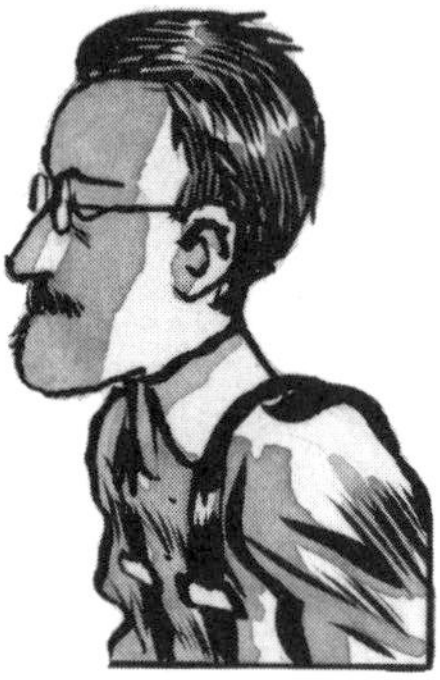

He wrote a letter to King George V of England, enclosing a copy of the chapter and asking him if the text was offensive to his father's memory.

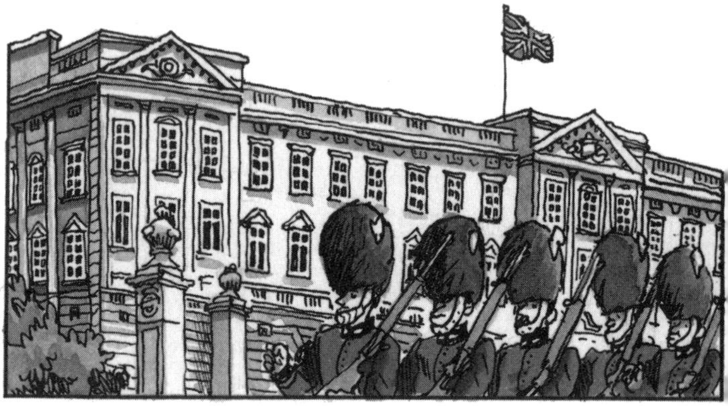

On 11 August, His Majesty's secretary replied, saying that the king could not give an opinion on such matters.

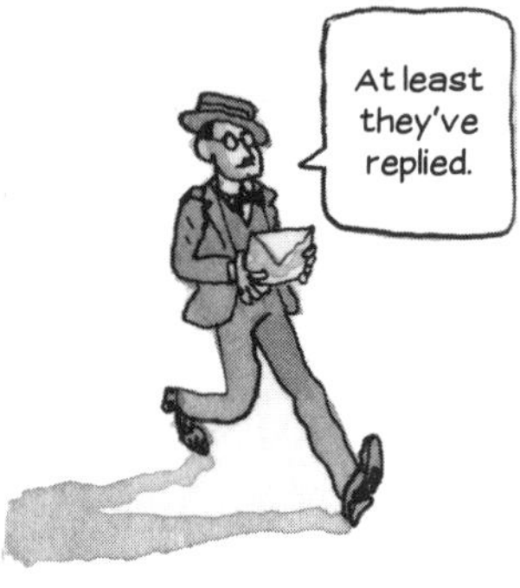
At least they've replied.

In the midst of these publishing problems, some emotional complications arose. The cause of them: Roberto Prezioso.

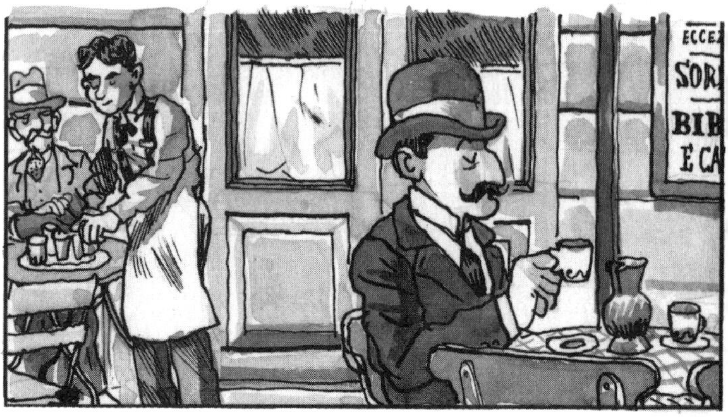

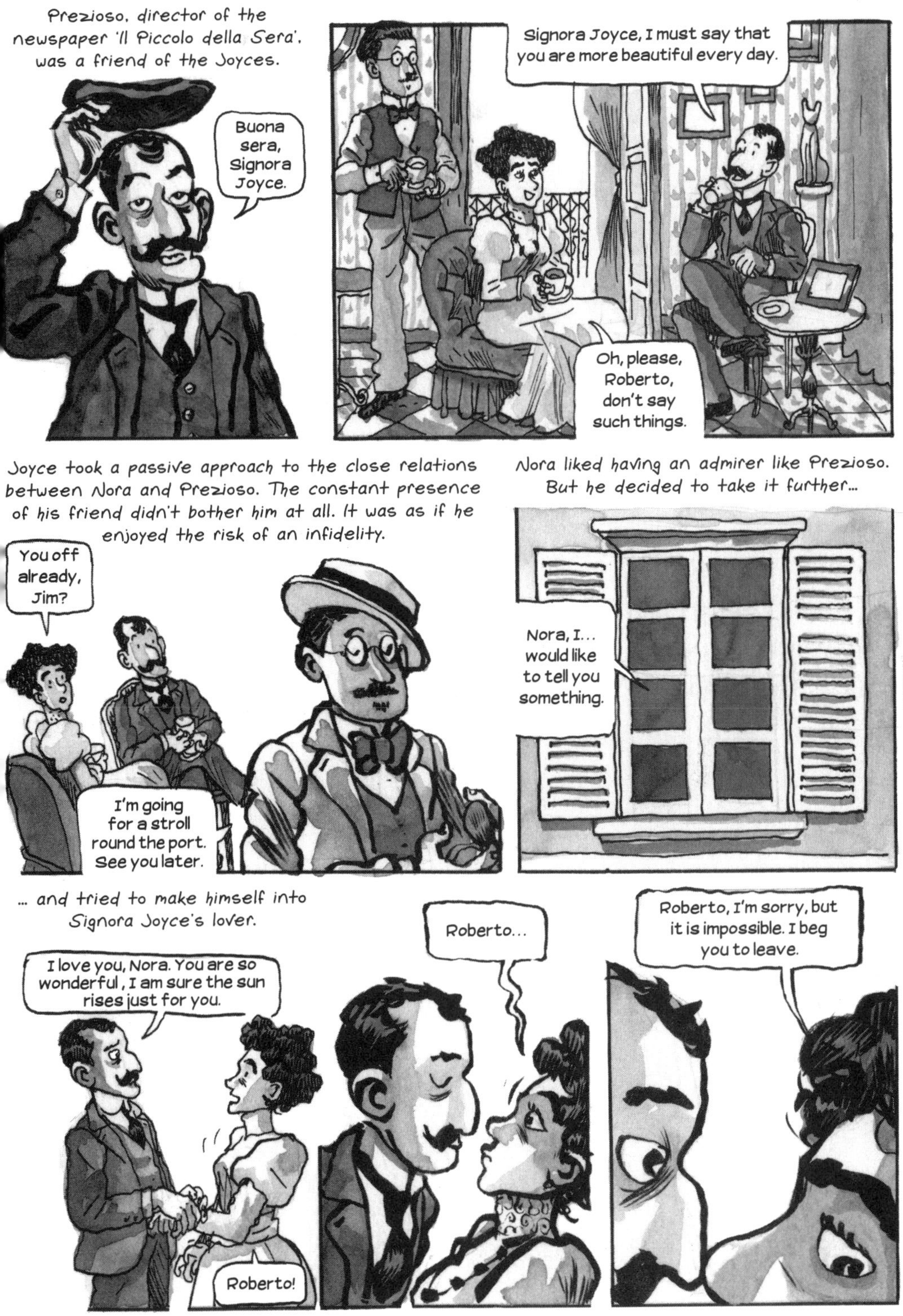
Prezioso, director of the newspaper 'Il Piccolo della Sera', was a friend of the Joyces.
Buona sera, Signora Joyce.
Signora Joyce, I must say that you are more beautiful every day.
Oh, please, Roberto, don't say such things.
Joyce took a passive approach to the close relations between Nora and Prezioso. The constant presence of his friend didn't bother him at all. It was as if he enjoyed the risk of an infidelity.
You off already, Jim?
I'm going for a stroll round the port. See you later.
Nora liked having an admirer like Prezioso. But he decided to take it further...
Nora, I... would like to tell you something.
... and tried to make himself into Signora Joyce's lover.
I love you, Nora. You are so wonderful, I am sure the sun rises just for you.
Roberto!
Roberto...
Roberto, I'm sorry, but it is impossible. I beg you to leave.

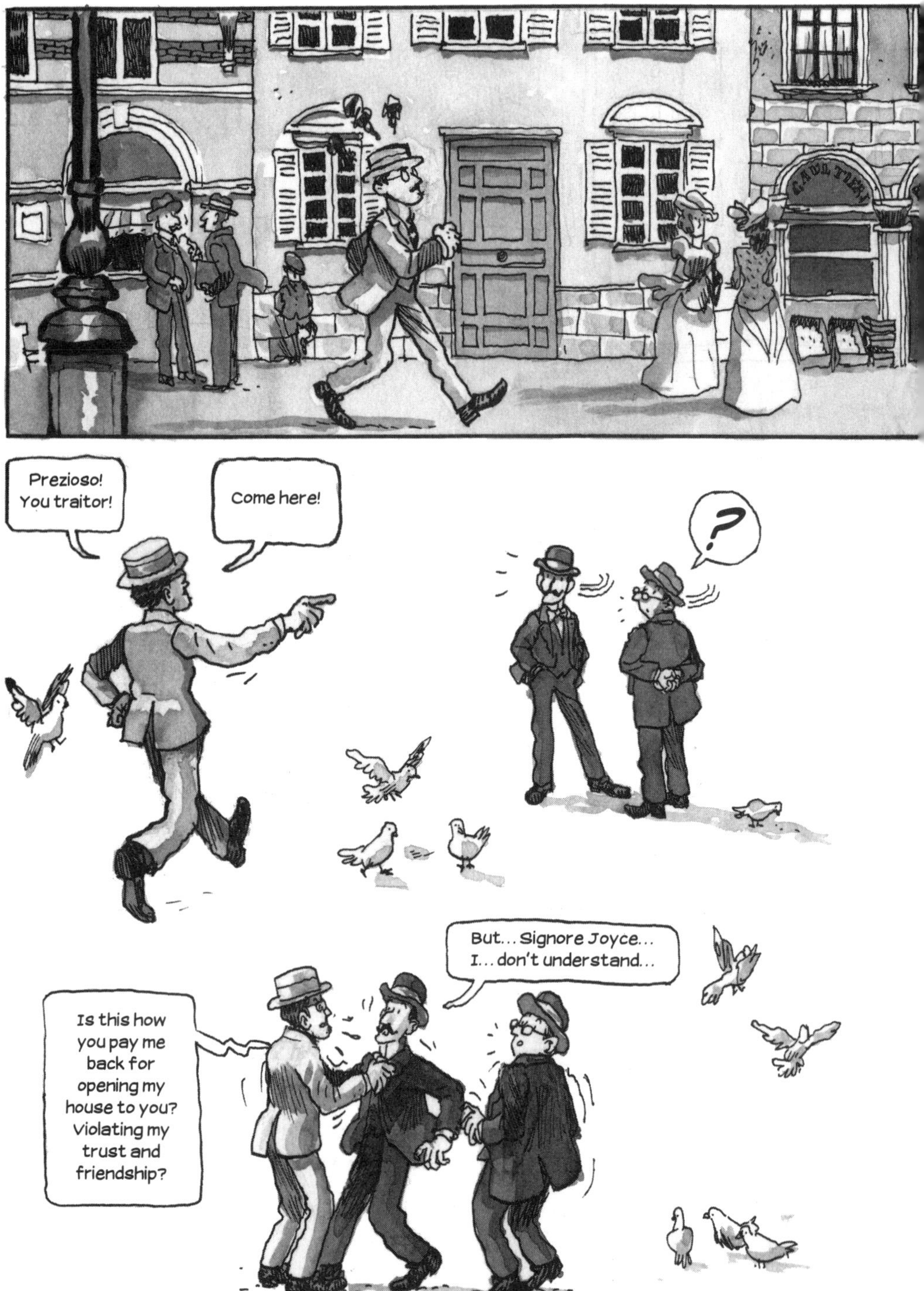
Prezioso! You traitor!
Come here!
?
Is this how you pay me back for opening my house to you? Violating my trust and friendship?
But... Signore Joyce... I... don't understand...

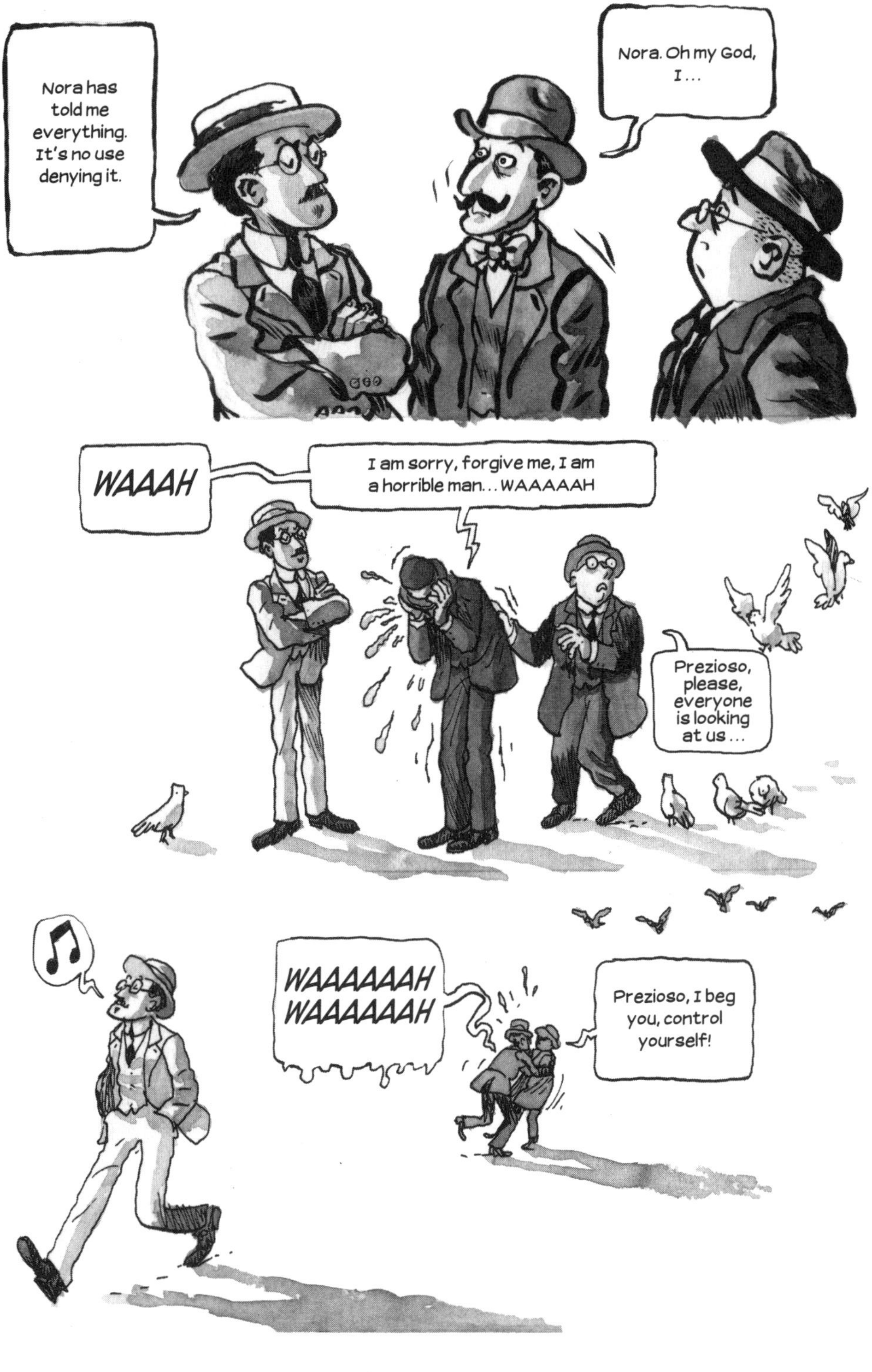
Nora has told me everything. It's no use denying it.
Nora. Oh my God, I...
WAAAH
I am sorry, forgive me, I am a horrible man... WAAAAAH
Prezioso, please, everyone is looking at us...
WAAAAAAH WAAAAAAH
Prezioso, I beg you, control yourself!

Towards the end of 1911, Joyce decided to make another effort at earning a living. He travelled to Padua to sit the exams for a teaching post in the Italian public school system.

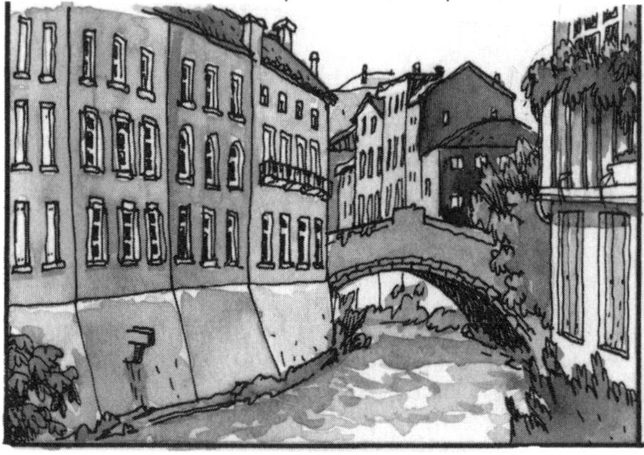

He wrote two essays in Italian for the exam, one of them on Dickens.

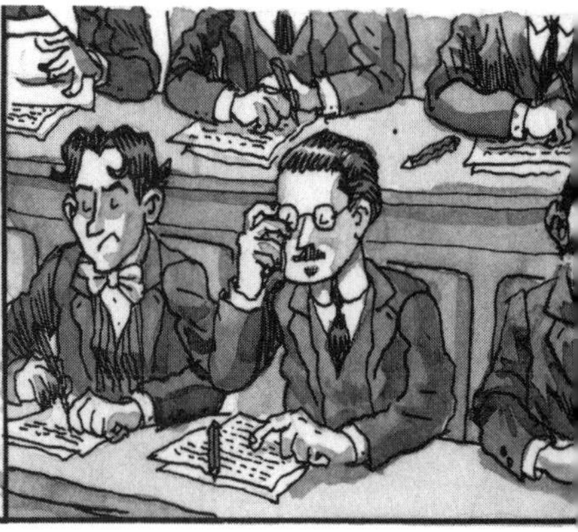

He got 421 points out of 450, perhaps not surprising if we bear in mind that he was the finest prose writer of the twentieth century.

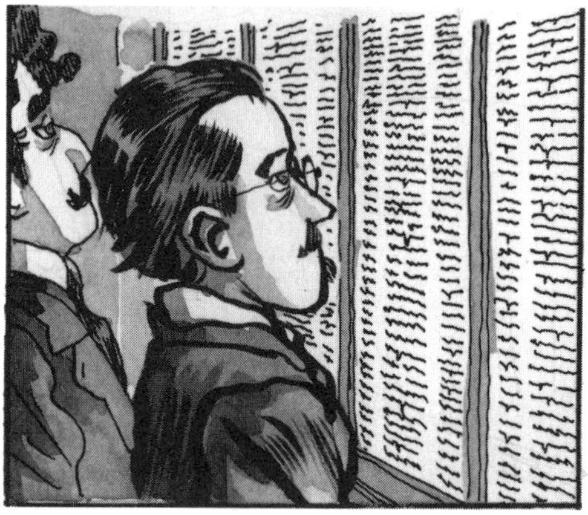

His joy was short-lived: the civil servants ruled that his title from Dublin University didn't meet requirements, and Joyce was pronounced NOT SUITABLE.

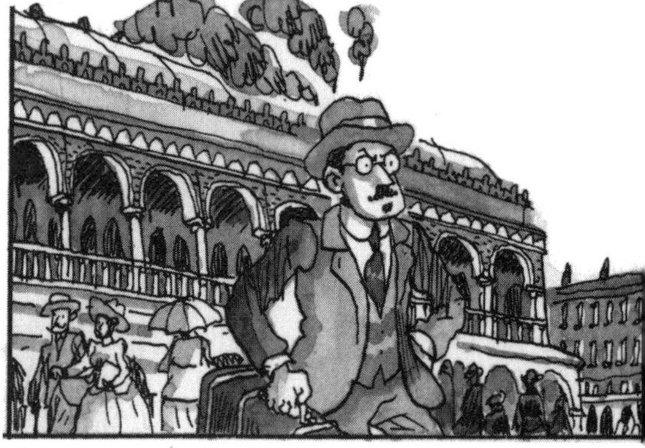

The creditors gave no quarter either. The family was evicted on 24 February.

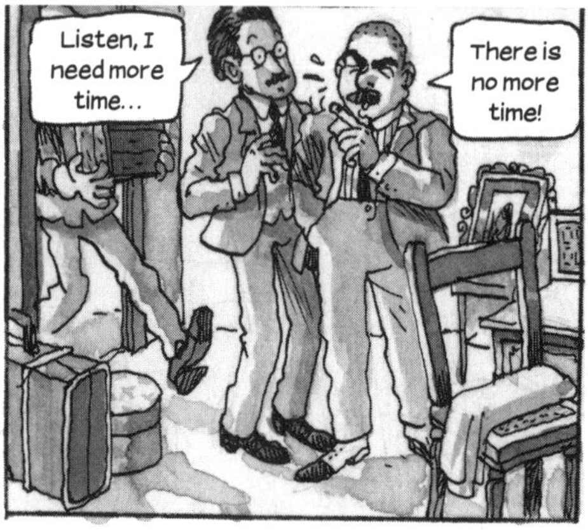
Listen, I need more time...
There is no more time!

Their furniture, on the move again, ended up in a small apartment on Via Donato Bramante.

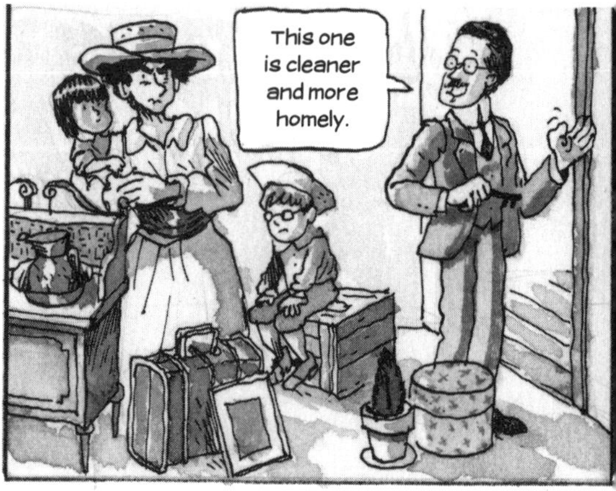
This one is cleaner and more homely.

Joyce focused his attention on 'Dubliners' again. In August he returned to Dublin, with Nora and the children, to counterattack.

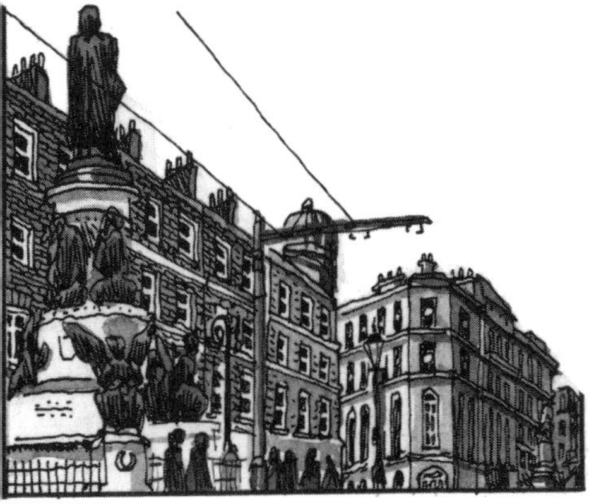

But the publication of the stories got more complicated.

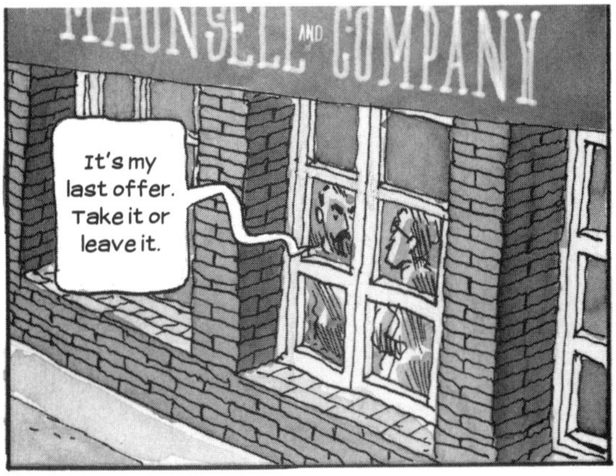
It's my last offer. Take it or leave it.

Roberts demanded that Joyce pay for the first edition, and leave a deposit of 4,000 pounds.

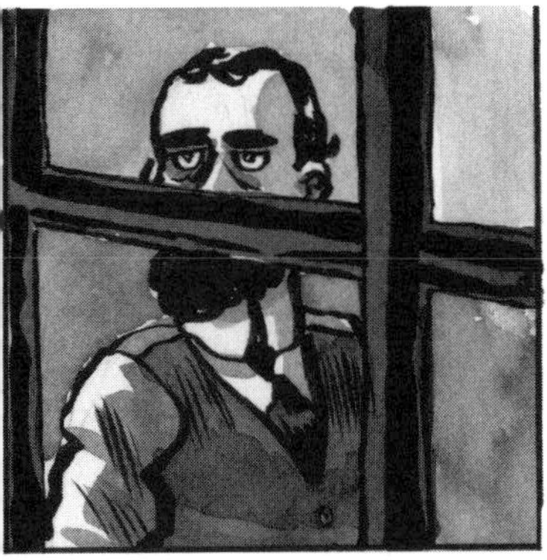

Joyce, in a state of extreme poverty, couldn't even dream of paying.

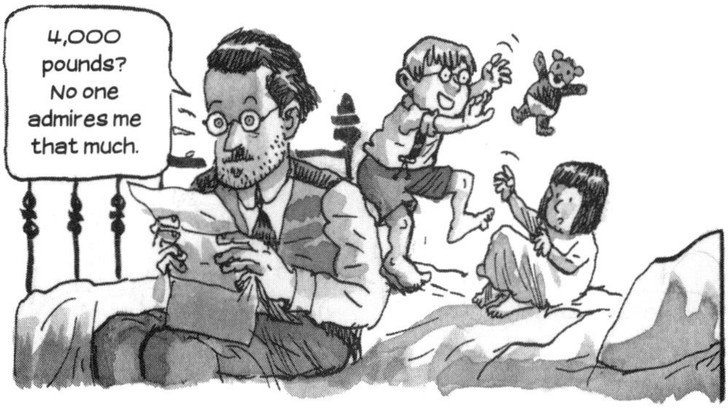
4,000 pounds? No one admires me that much.

Dispirited, Joyce walked sadly through Dublin. In Dawson Street he encountered someone very unusual.

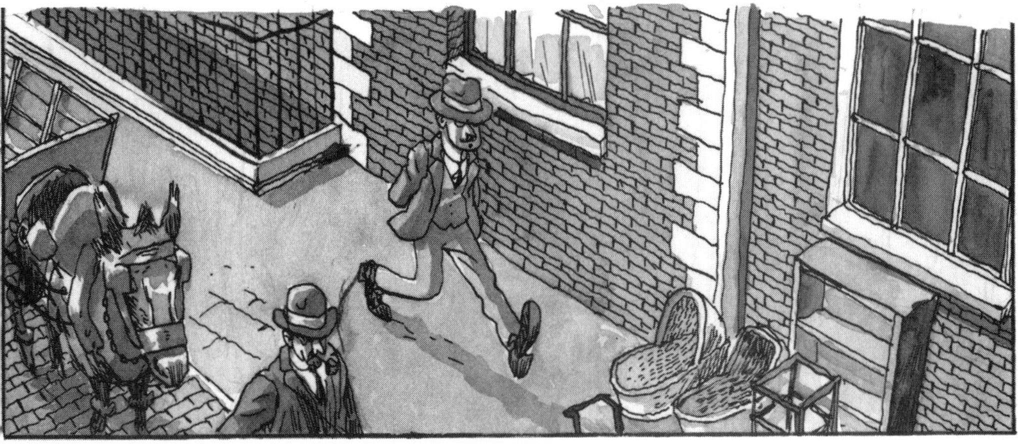

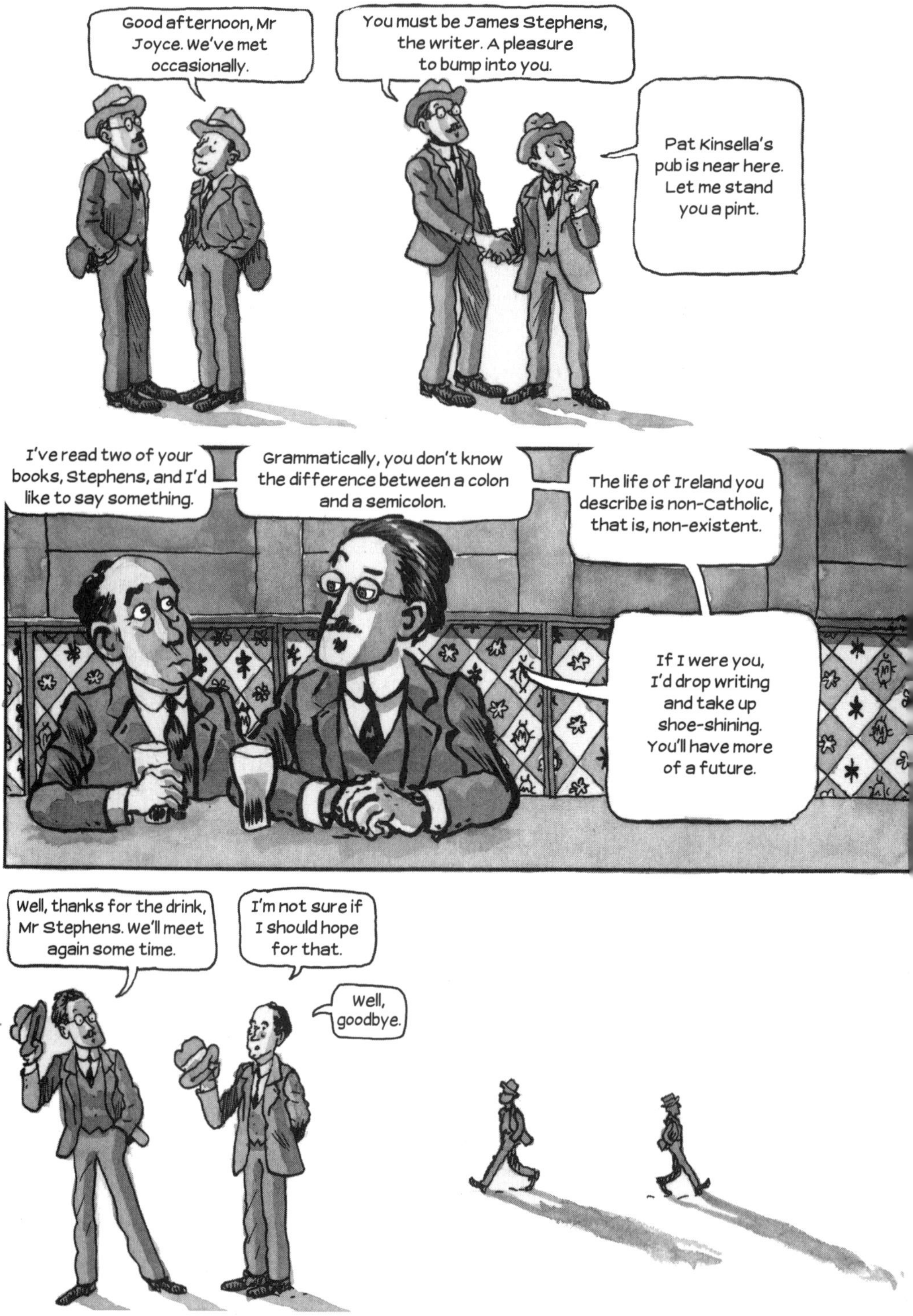
Good afternoon, Mr Joyce. We've met occasionally.
You must be James Stephens, the writer. A pleasure to bump into you.
Pat Kinsella's pub is near here. Let me stand you a pint.
I've read two of your books, Stephens, and I'd like to say something.
Grammatically, you don't know the difference between a colon and a semicolon.
The life of Ireland you describe is non-Catholic, that is, non-existent.
If I were you, I'd drop writing and take up shoe-shining. You'll have more of a future.
Well, thanks for the drink, Mr Stephens. We'll meet again some time.
I'm not sure if I should hope for that.
Well, goodbye.

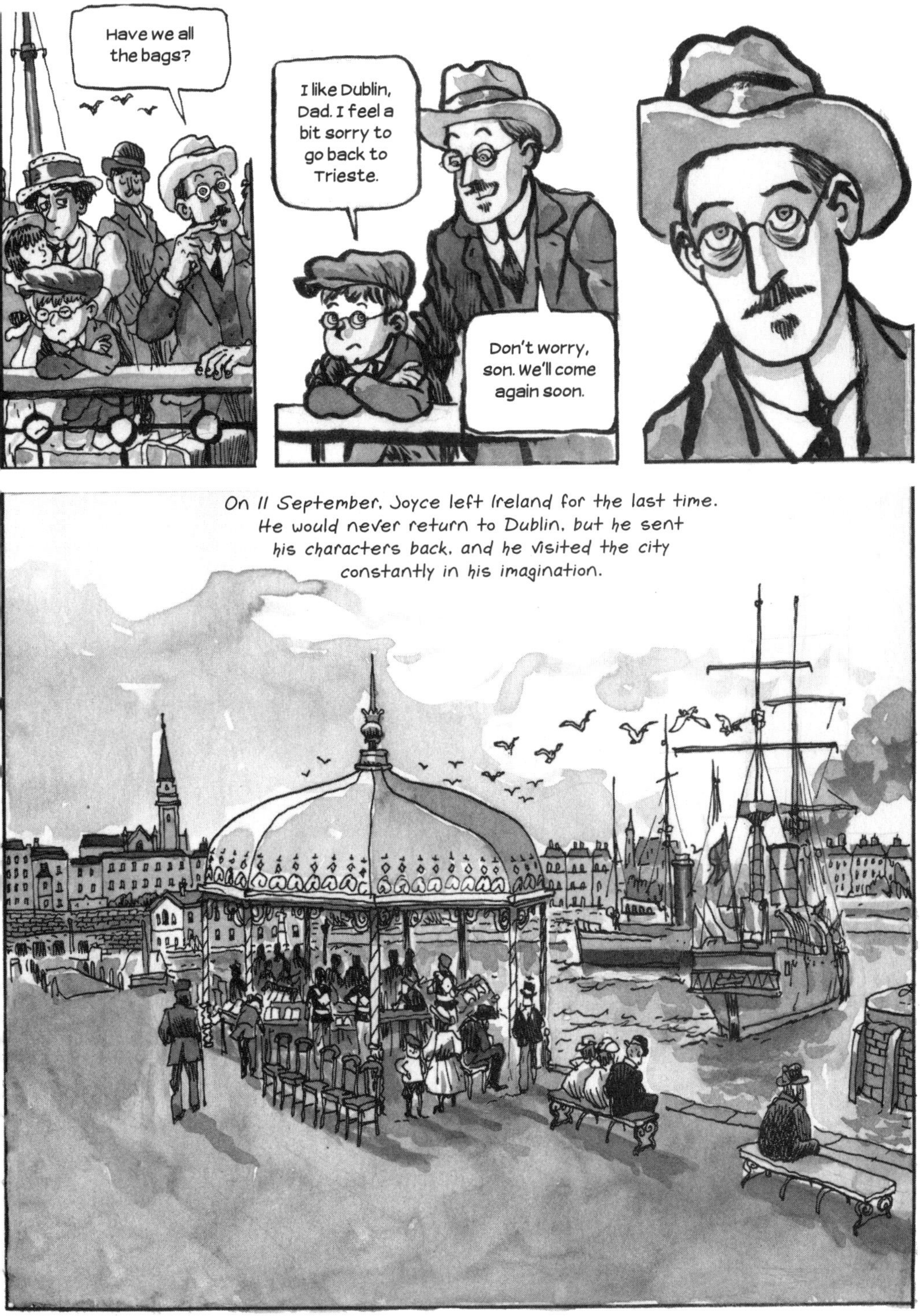
Have we all the bags?
I like Dublin, Dad. I feel a bit sorry to go back to Trieste.
Don't worry, son. We'll come again soon.
On 11 September, Joyce left Ireland for the last time. He would never return to Dublin, but he sent his characters back, and he visited the city constantly in his imagination.

Chapter IV
Exiled

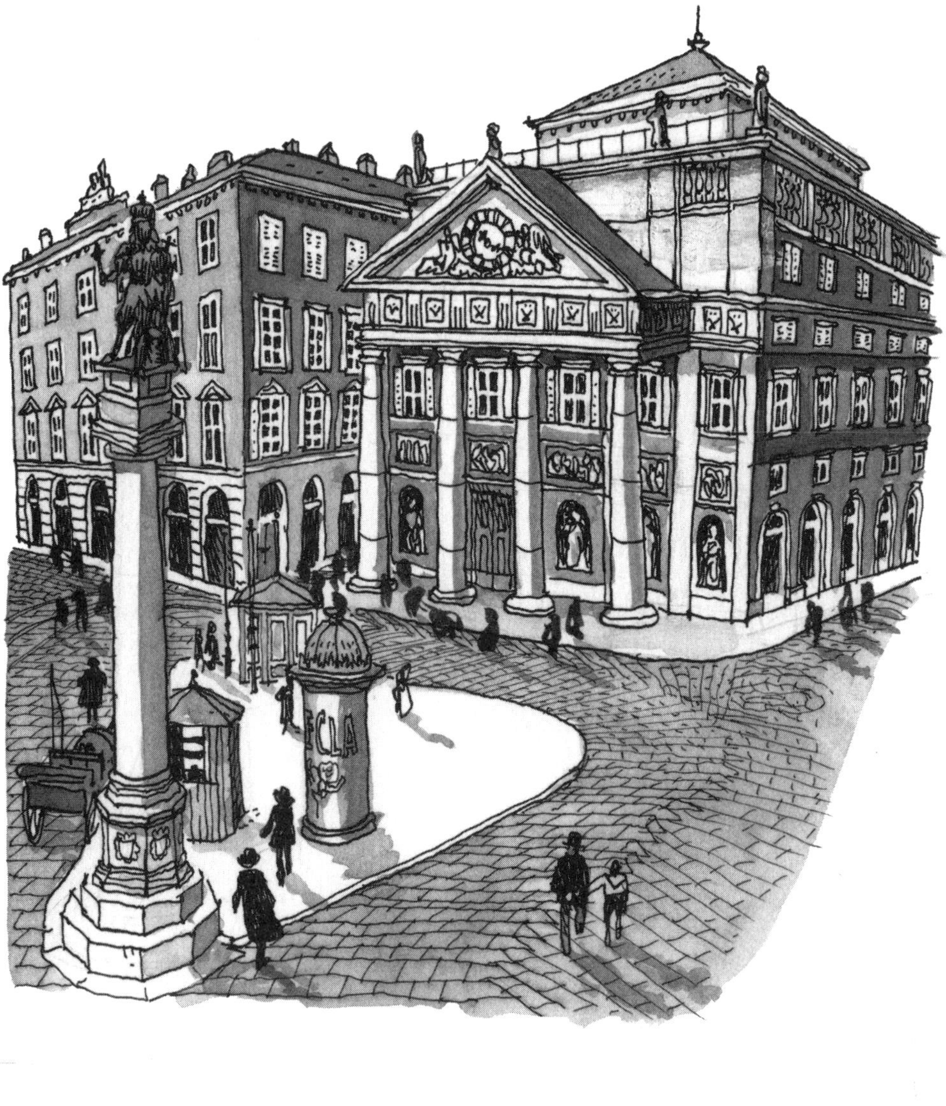

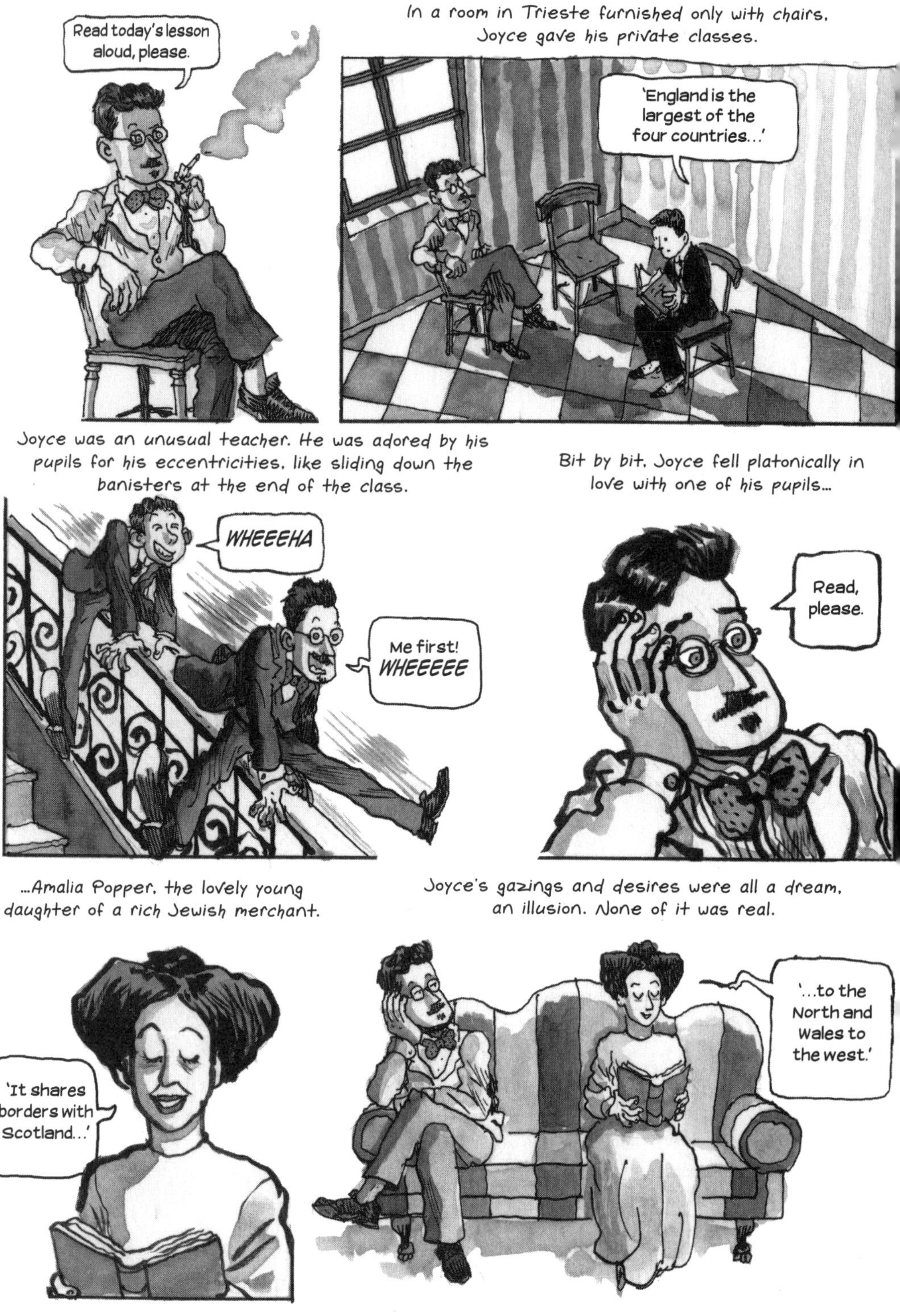
Read today's lesson aloud, please.
In a room in Trieste furnished only with chairs, Joyce gave his private classes.
'England is the largest of the four countries...'
Joyce was an unusual teacher. He was adored by his pupils for his eccentricities, like sliding down the banisters at the end of the class.
WHEEEHA
Me first! WHEEEEE
Bit by bit, Joyce fell platonically in love with one of his pupils...
Read, please.
...Amalia Popper, the lovely young daughter of a rich Jewish merchant.
'It shares borders with Scotland...'
Joyce's gazings and desires were all a dream, an illusion. None of it was real.
'...to the North and Wales to the west.'

Joyce wrote several poems and courted Amalia silently, with the melancholy of a lover doomed to failure.

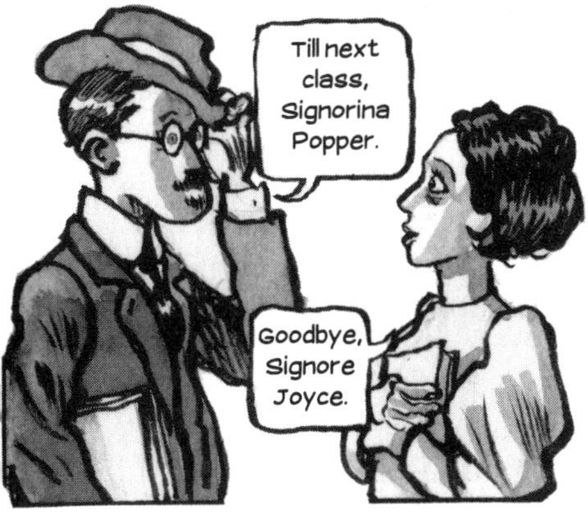
Till next class, Signorina Popper.
Goodbye, Signore Joyce.

One day, Amalia Popper married and went to live in Florence, and it was all over.

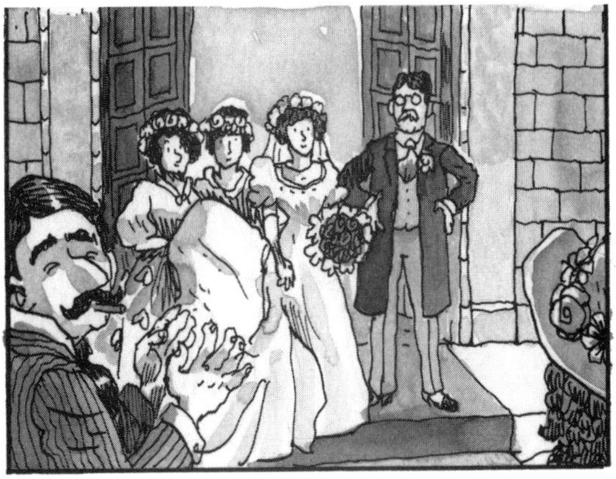

With the arrival of two letters in November 1913, Joyce's life was to undergo a radical change.

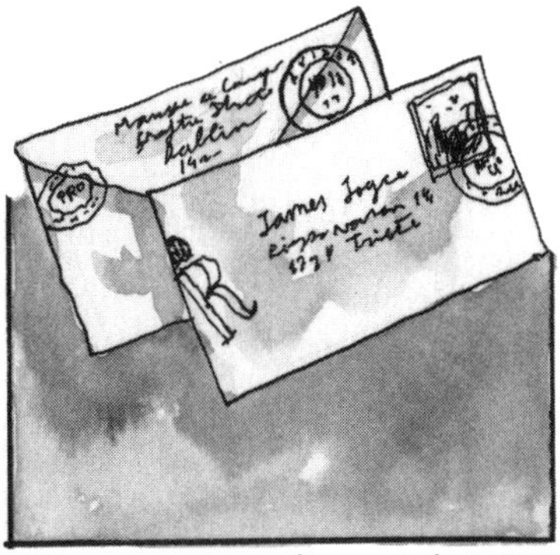
James Joyce

The first was from Dublin, from the publisher Grant Richards, who asked to see 'Dubliners' with a view to its publication.

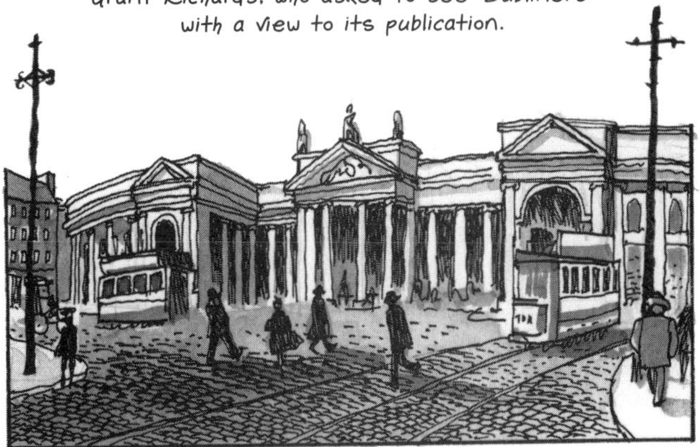

The second was from an American friend of Yeats, interested in publishing Joyce's work in literary magazines like 'The Egoist', 'The Smart Set' or 'Poetry'.

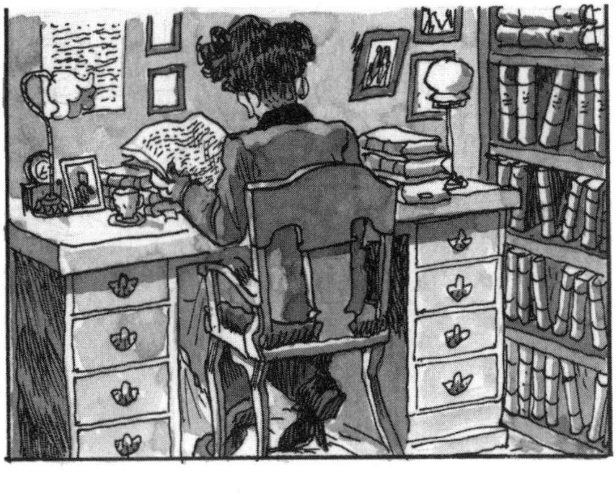

The appearance of Ezra Pound brought an unexpected ray of light into the dark panorama of Joyce's future.

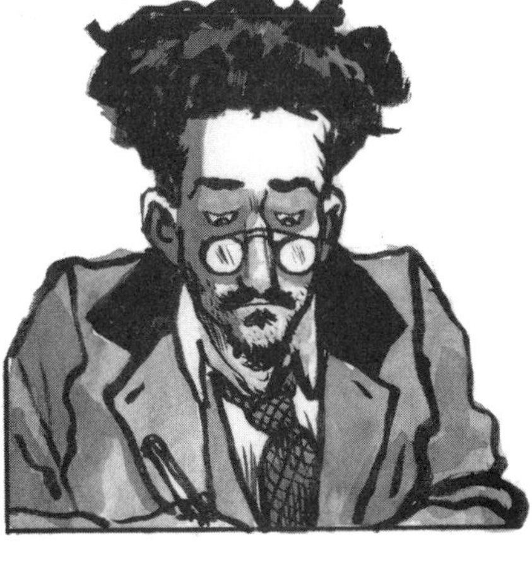

Pound rapidly saw that 'The Egoist' was the ideal setting for Joyce's genius. The magazine was run by Dora Marsden, a British feminist writer.

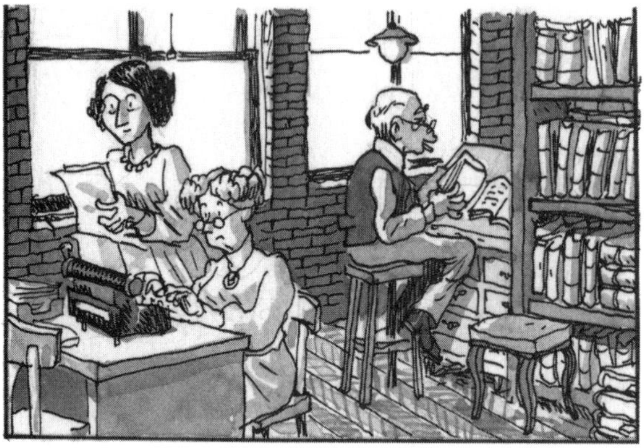

But it was the publisher, Harriet Shaw Weaver, who would be of invaluable help to Joyce.

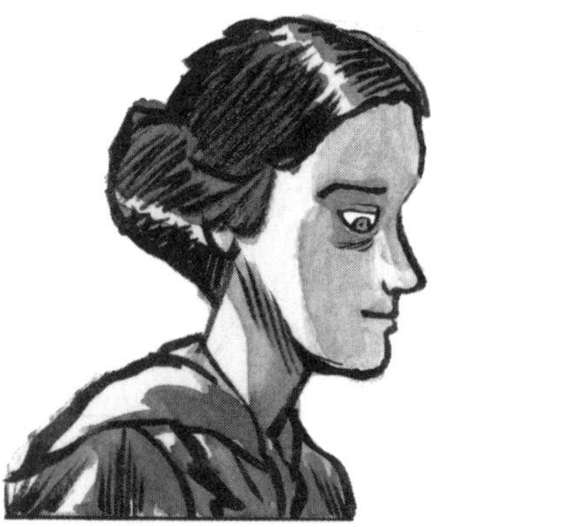

No one would have guessed that this timid Englishwoman, brought up in the strict Quaker religion, could have got on with the eccentric Irish writer.

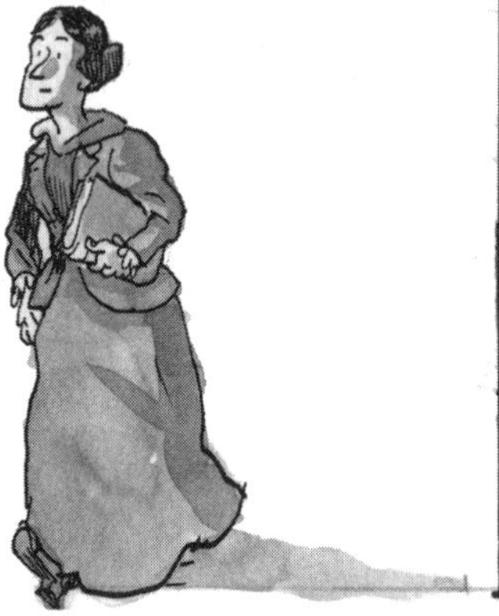

Nevertheless, Miss Weaver's generous, tolerant friendship with Joyce was to last throughout his life.

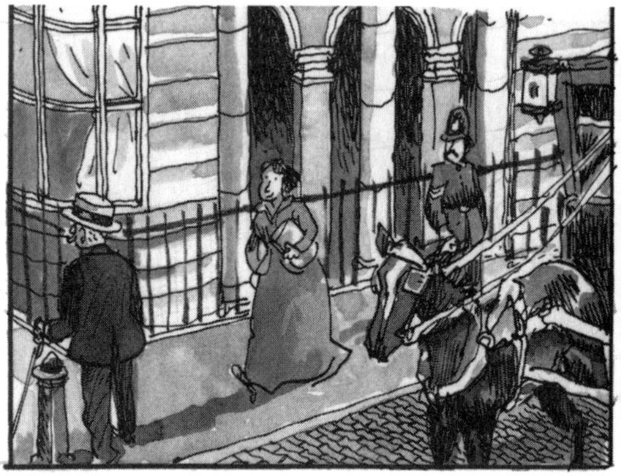

The wind was in Joyce's favour, and on 15 June 1914, the first edition of 1250 copies of 'Dubliners' appeared.

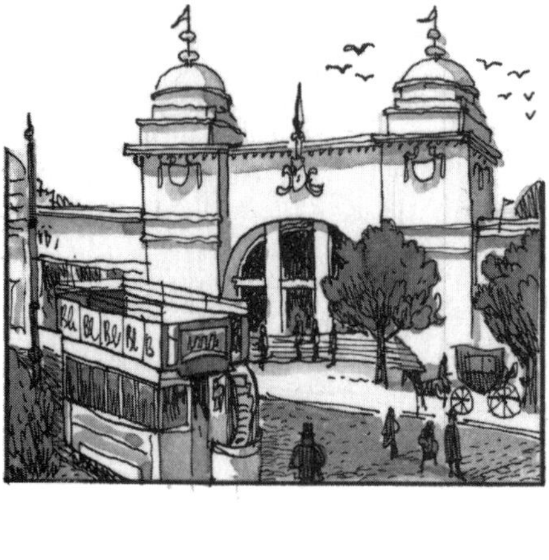

Filled with enthusiasm, Joyce worked incessantly to send installments of 'A Portrait of the Artist' to 'The Egoist' for periodic publication.

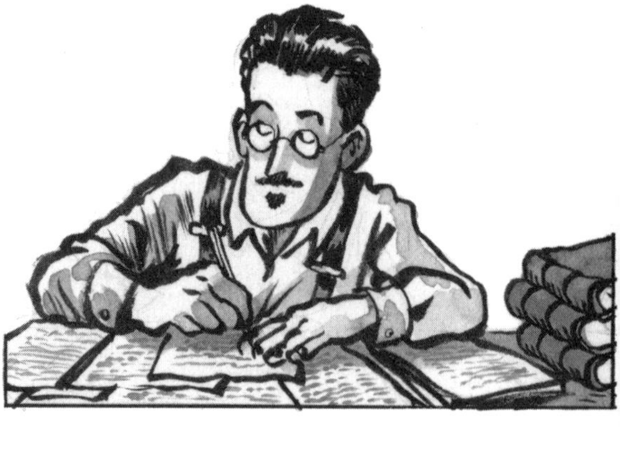

The Great War put a stop to the postal service between England and Austria, interrupting delivery of the book.

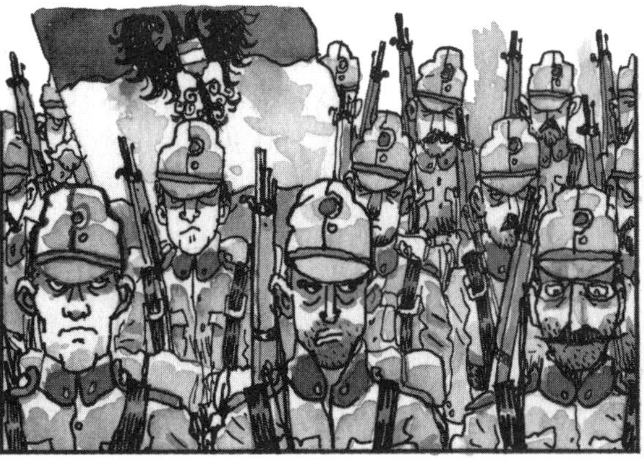

Fortunately, Ettore Schmitz's father-in-law had a factory in Murano. So the chapters of 'A Portrait' were sent via Italy, thus overcoming the obstacles of war.

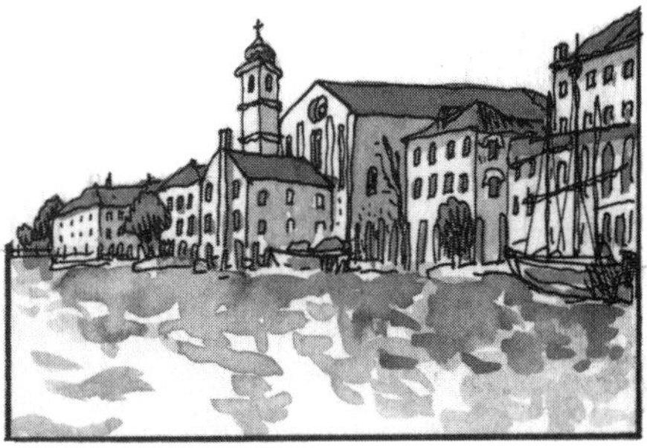

When Joyce was on the point of finishing the book, riots flared up in the city. The Italian consulate was attacked by a pro-Austro-Hungarian mob.

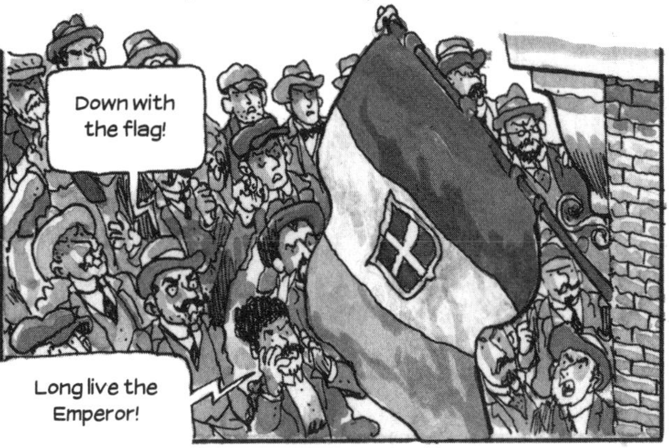
Down with the flag!
Long live the Emperor!

Joyce, who was passing by with Giorgio, fled in fright.

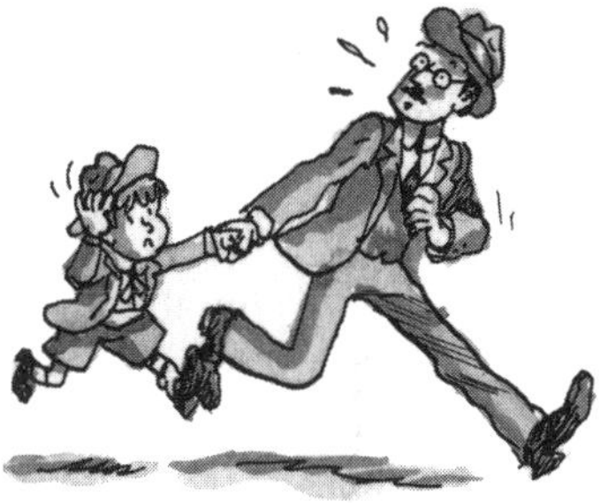

Stanislaus was more revolutionary than his brother, and he gave strong support to Garibaldi's anticlerical liberalism...

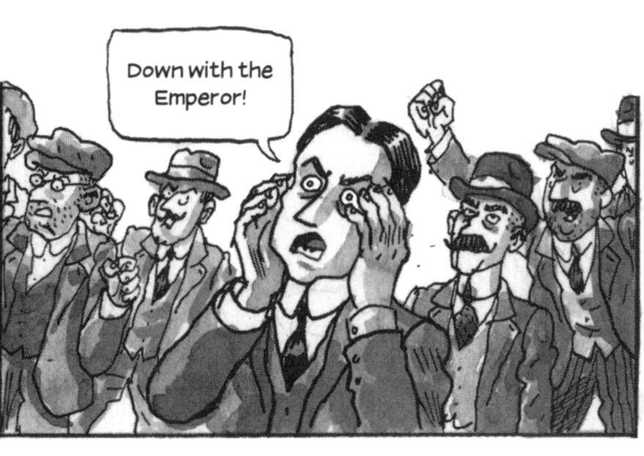
Down with the Emperor!

...for which he was arrested on 9 January, and put in an Austrian prisoner-of-war camp till the end of the war.

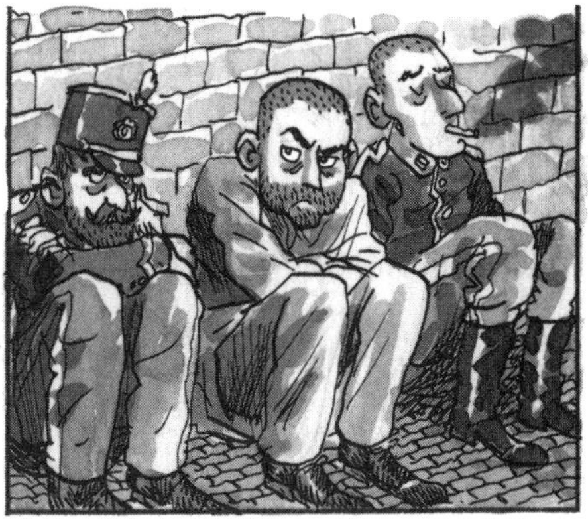

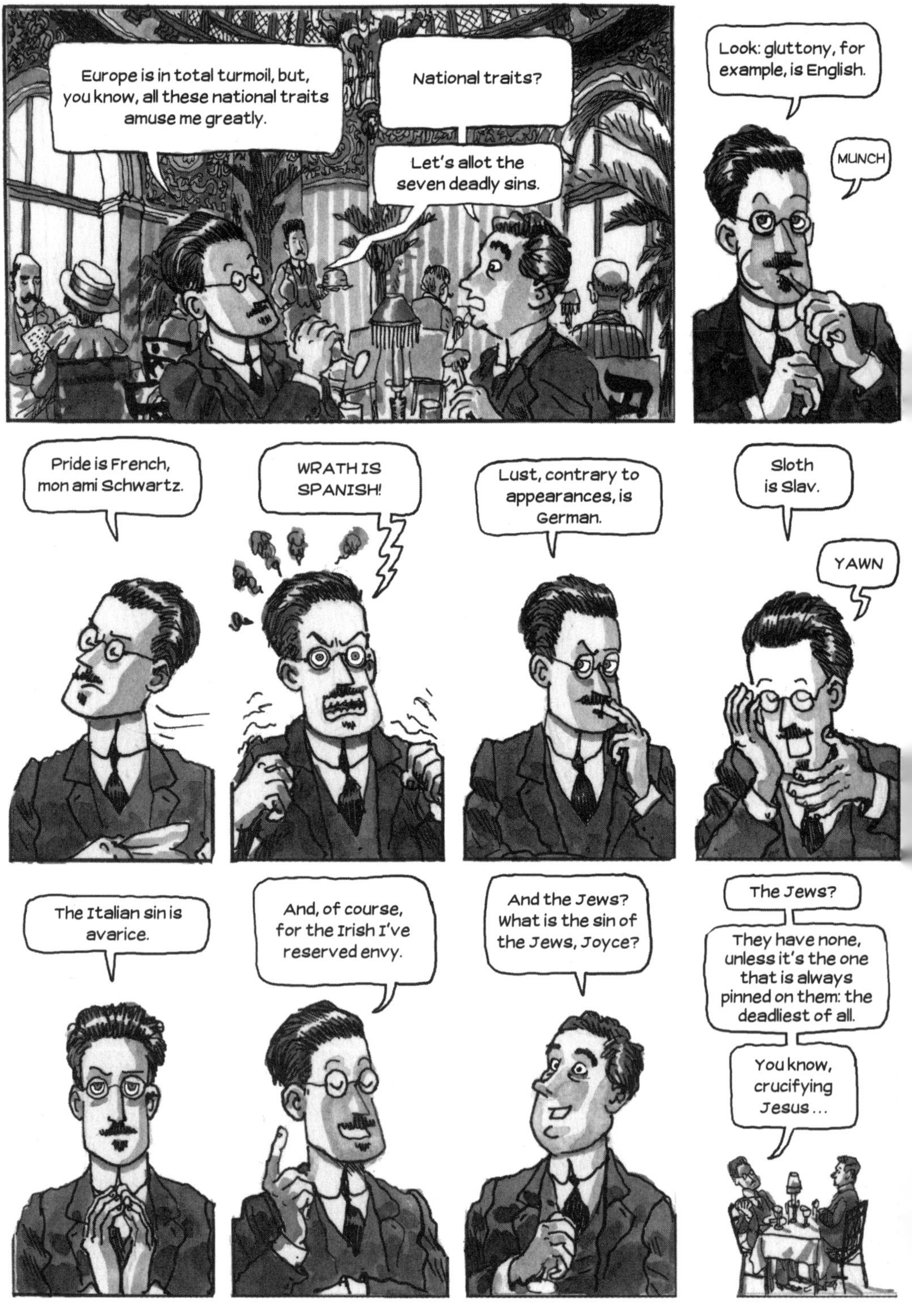
Europe is in total turmoil, but, you know, all these national traits amuse me greatly.
National traits?
Let's allot the seven deadly sins.
Look: gluttony, for example, is English.
MUNCH
Pride is French, mon ami Schwartz.
WRATH IS SPANISH!
Lust, contrary to appearances, is German.
Sloth is Slav.
YAWN
The Italian sin is avarice.
And, of course, for the Irish I've reserved envy.
And the Jews? What is the sin of the Jews, Joyce?
The Jews?
They have none, unless it's the one that is always pinned on them: the deadliest of all.
You know, crucifying Jesus . . .

In May, Italy declared war on Austria, and the situation in Trieste became untenable.

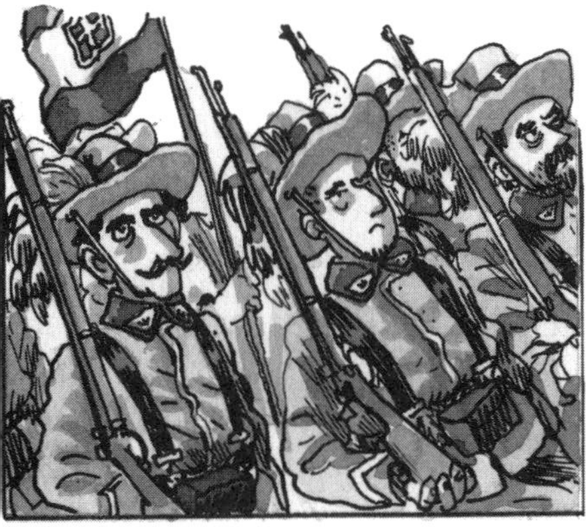

Of course, the geniuses tried to stay out of things.

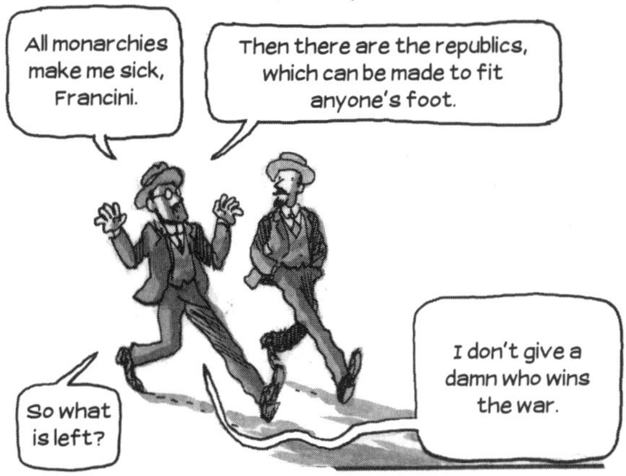
All monarchies make me sick, Francini.
Then there are the republics, which can be made to fit anyone's foot.
So what is left?
I don't give a damn who wins the war.

In his ivory tower, Joyce continued working on his play 'Exiles', and on 'Ulysses'.

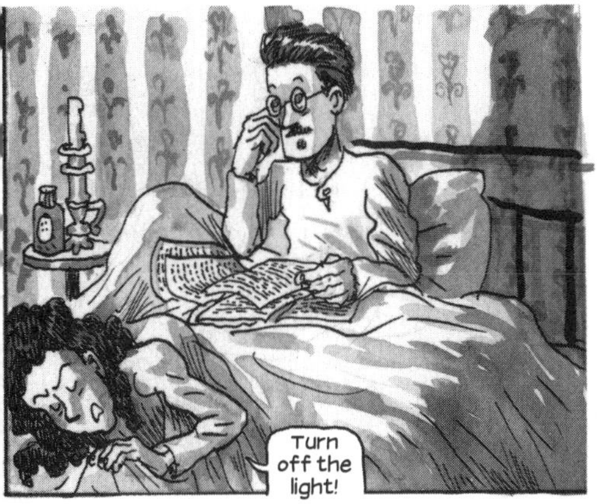
Turn off the light!

In April 1915, the American author HG Wells wrote to Joyce, to express his admiration for the work published in 'The Egoist'.

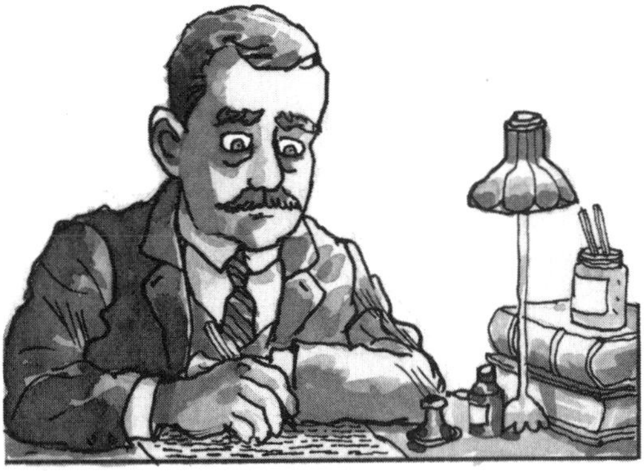

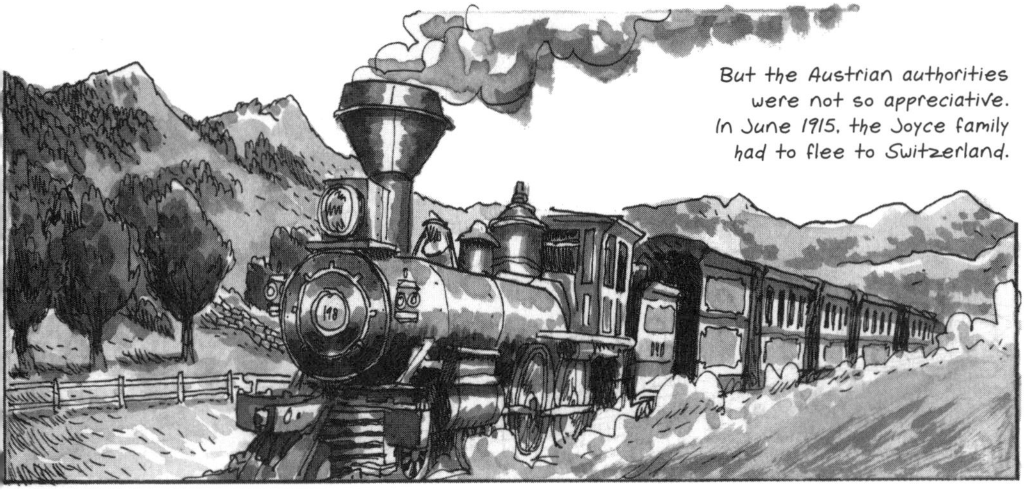
But the Austrian authorities were not so appreciative. In June 1915, the Joyce family had to flee to Switzerland.

Ezra Pound, Ford Madox Ford and HG Wells suggested that Joyce go to England, but the Irishman and his family stayed in Switzerland.

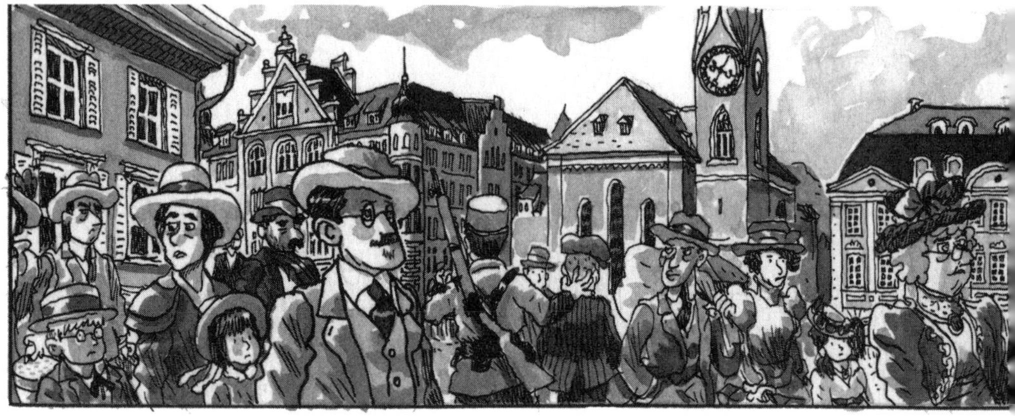

Joyce had escaped from war, but not from poverty. He was without a penny in the expensive city of Zürich.

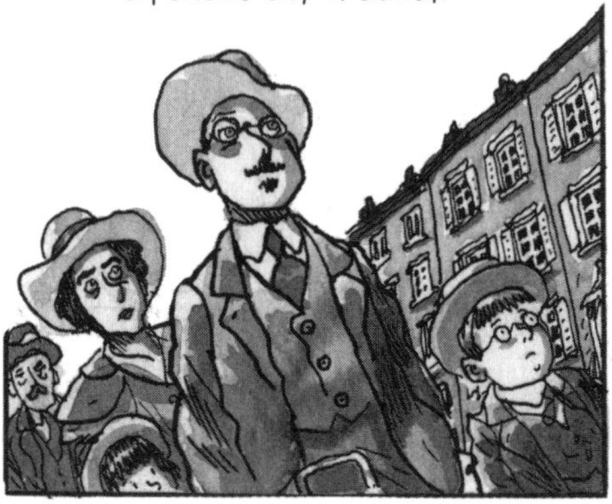

Ezra Pound pulled strings: he spoke to Miss Weaver and to Yeats, and the latter spoke on Joyce's behalf to the Royal Foundation for Literature. Joyce was a struggling writer and needed a grant.

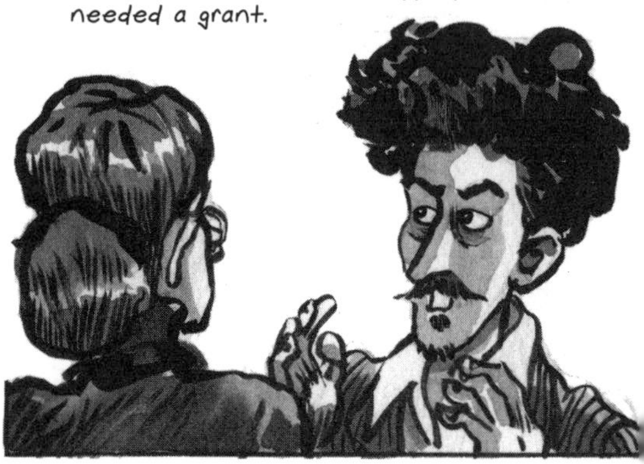

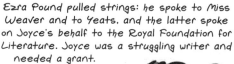

He was awarded a grant of seventy-five pounds, in recognition of his literary worth.

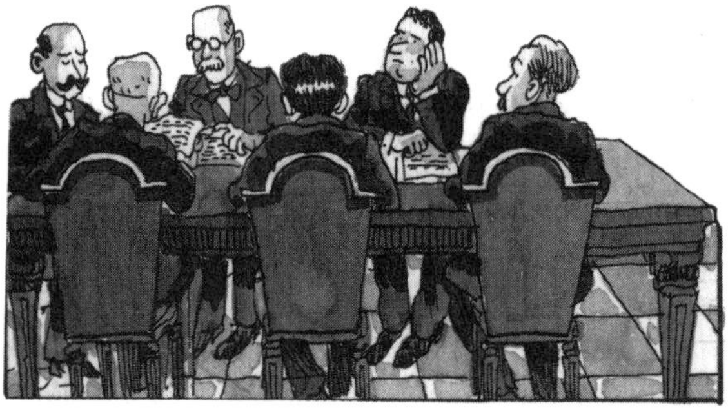

More relaxed, and out of the war, Joyce went on writing.

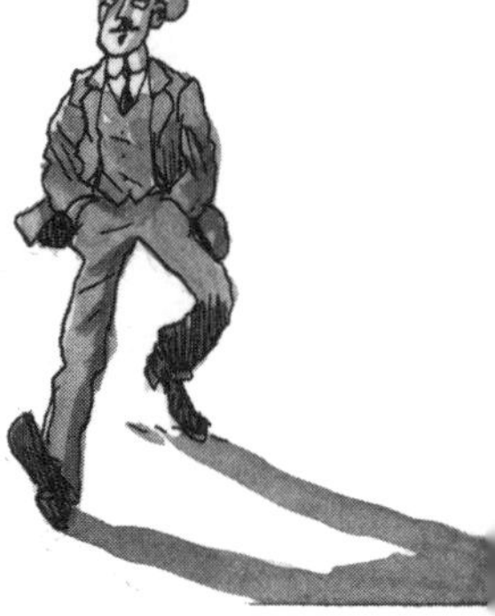

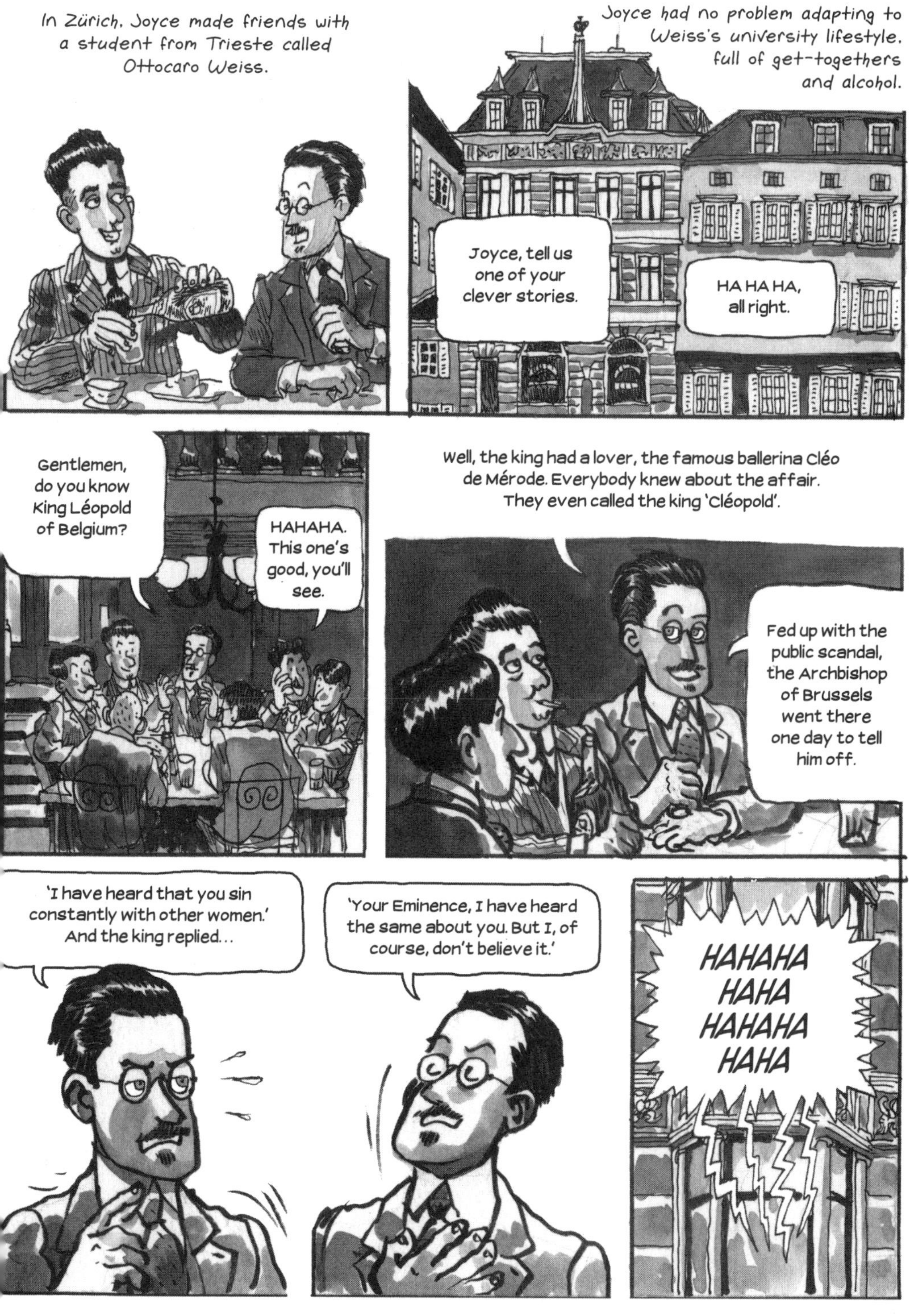
In Zürich, Joyce made friends with a student from Trieste called Ottocaro Weiss.
Joyce had no problem adapting to Weiss's university lifestyle, full of get-togethers and alcohol.
Joyce, tell us one of your clever stories.
HA HA HA, all right.
Gentlemen, do you know King Léopold of Belgium?
HAHAHA. This one's good, you'll see.
Well, the king had a lover, the famous ballerina Cléo de Mérode. Everybody knew about the affair. They even called the king 'Cléopold'.
Fed up with the public scandal, the Archbishop of Brussels went there one day to tell him off.
'I have heard that you sin constantly with other women.' And the king replied...
'Your Eminence, I have heard the same about you. But I, of course, don't believe it.'
HAHAHA
HAHA
HAHAHA
HAHA

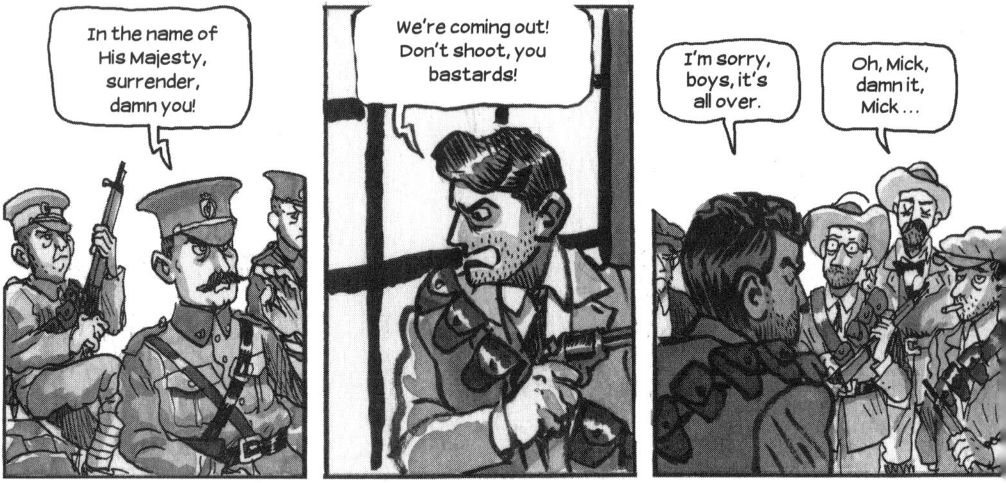
In the name of His Majesty, surrender, damn you!
We're coming out! Don't shoot, you bastards!
I'm sorry, boys, it's all over.
Oh, Mick, damn it, Mick...

Easter 1916 witnessed the Easter Rising in Dublin.
Besieged in the Post Office, the rebel leaders were defeated.

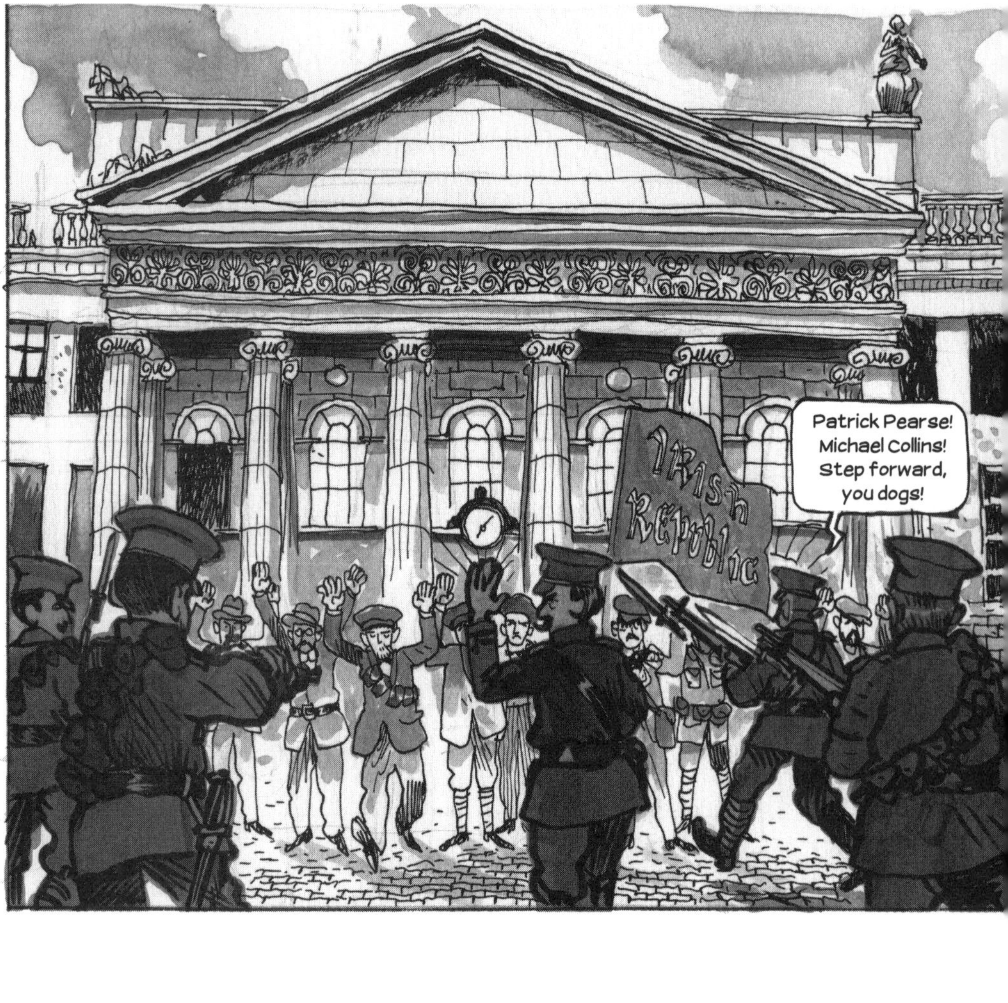
Patrick Pearse! Michael Collins! Step forward, you dogs!
Irish Republic

Eamon de Valera was imprisoned...

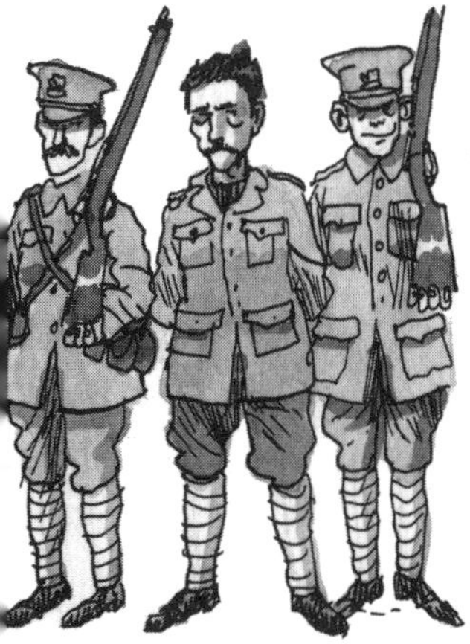

...while many other, less fortunate, leaders were executed.

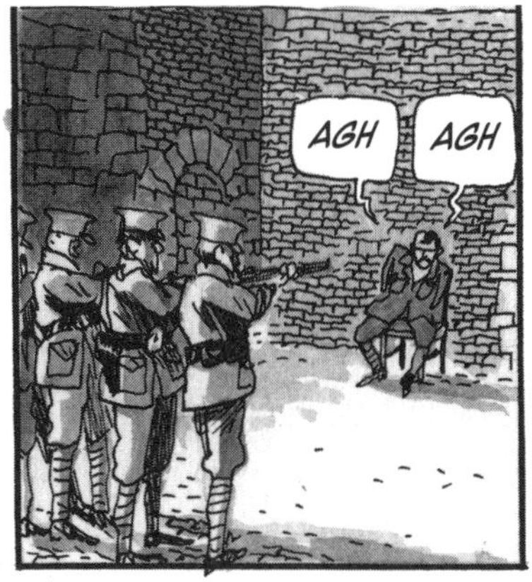
AGH
AGH

Including Patrick Pearse, Joyce's teacher of Gaelic, whom Joyce had never liked...

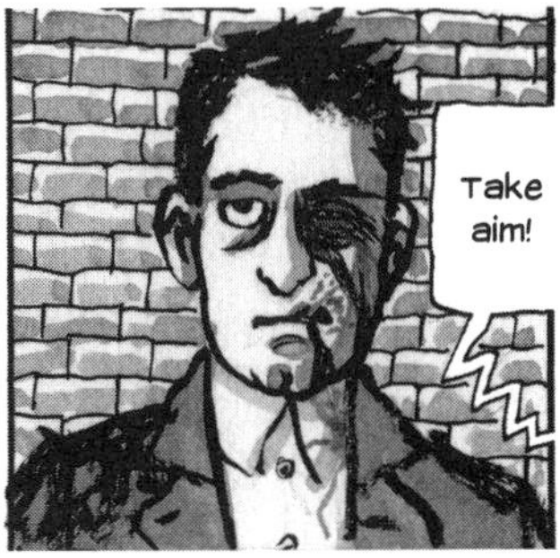
Take aim!

...but whose death saddened him deeply.

Francis Sheehy-Skeffington, a good friend of Joyce's, was also caught up in the rebellion.

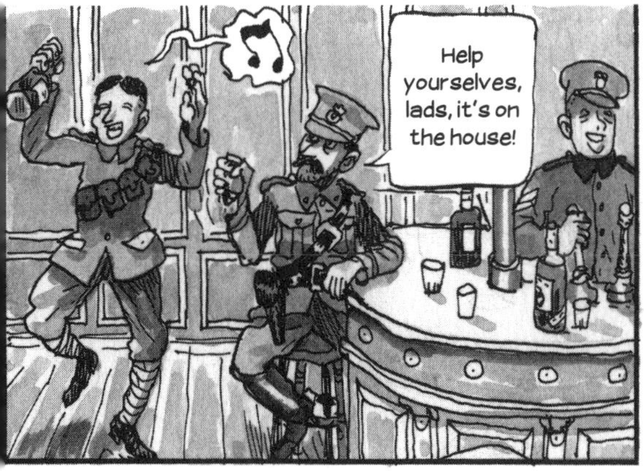
Help yourselves, lads, it's on the house!

Not from any attachment to Sinn Féin...

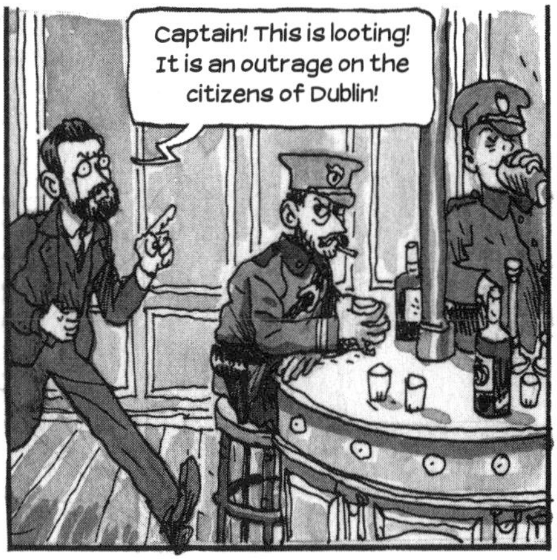
Captain! This is looting! It is an outrage on the citizens of Dublin!

...but out of idealism.

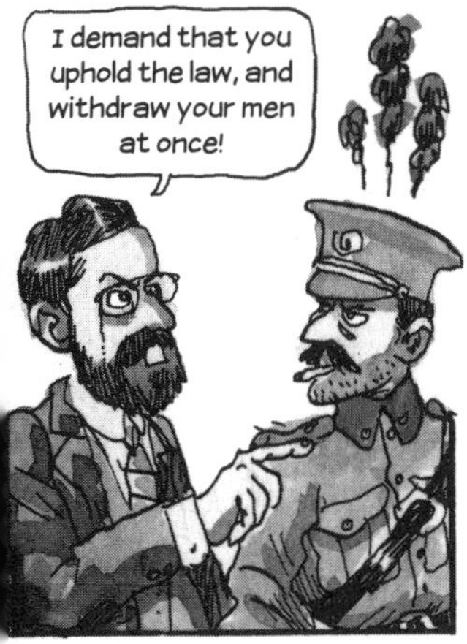
I demand that you uphold the law, and withdraw your men at once!

An idealism which cost him his life.

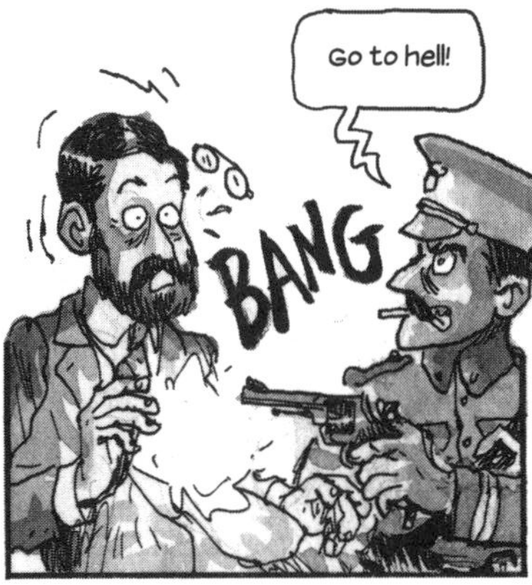
Go to hell!
BANG

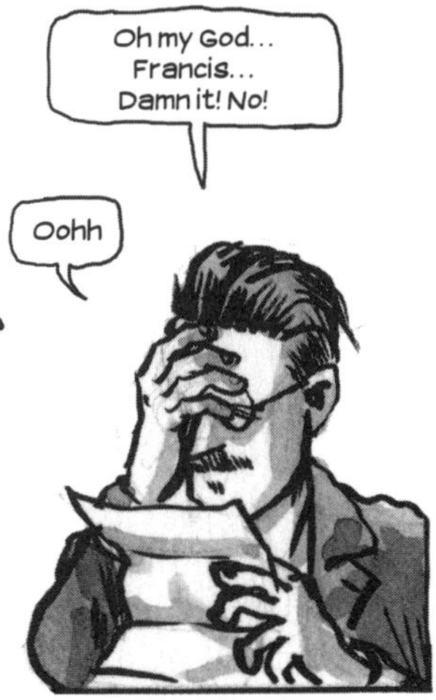
Oh my God... Francis... Damn it! No!
Oohh

At the beginning of 1916, Joyce was still running up against a brick wall with his projects. He sent his play Exiles to his friend Yeats.

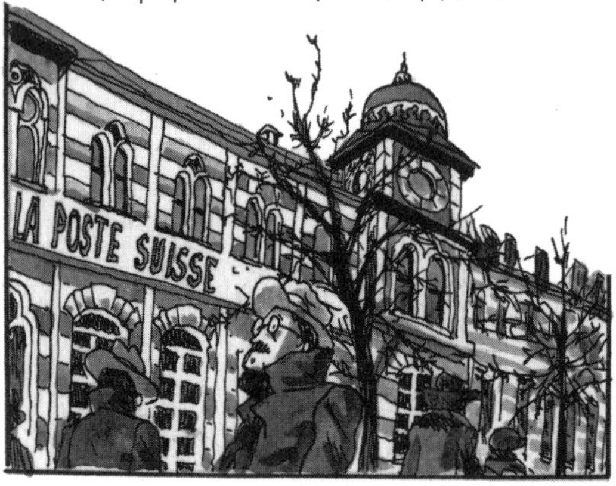
LA POSTE SUISSE

But Yeats rejected it, on the grounds that it wasn't appropriate for the Abbey Theatre.

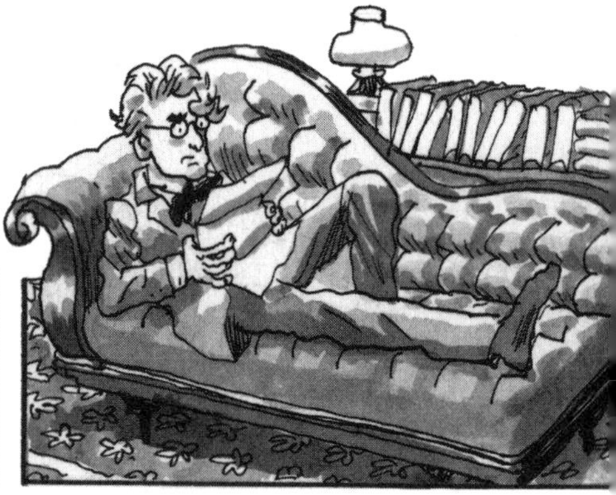

Shortly afterwards, Pinker, his publisher for 'A Portrait', rejected the play. He said that its sordidness and lack of originality were reasons enough for turning it down.

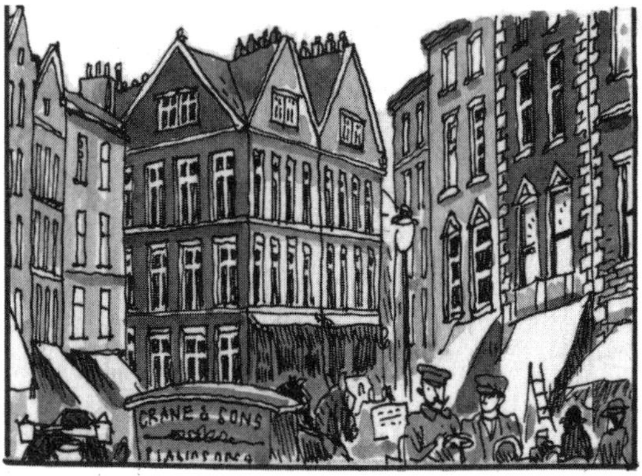
CRANE & SONS

Then the unquenchable Harriet Weaver appeared, bought the manuscript, advanced Joyce twenty-five pounds, and prepared to publish it.

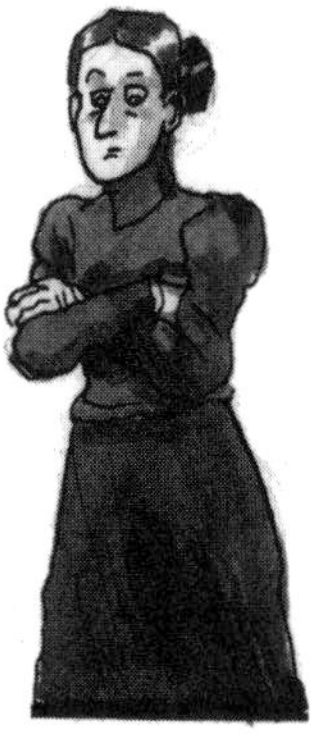

But the trouble was not over yet. In March, seven printers, one after another, refused to print the book for fear of future lawsuits.

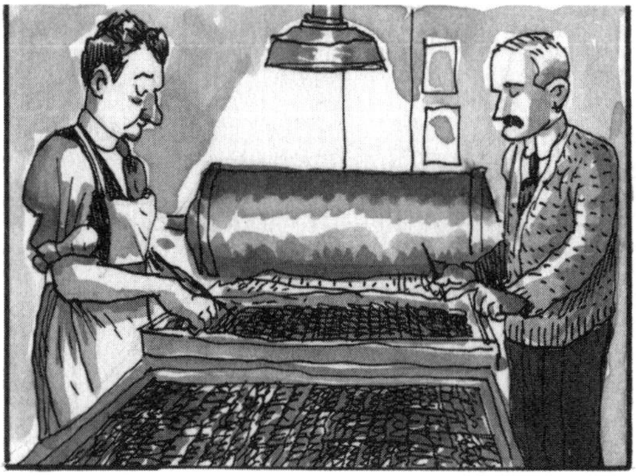

On 19 July, a solution was found. WB Huebsch of New York was willing to publish it.

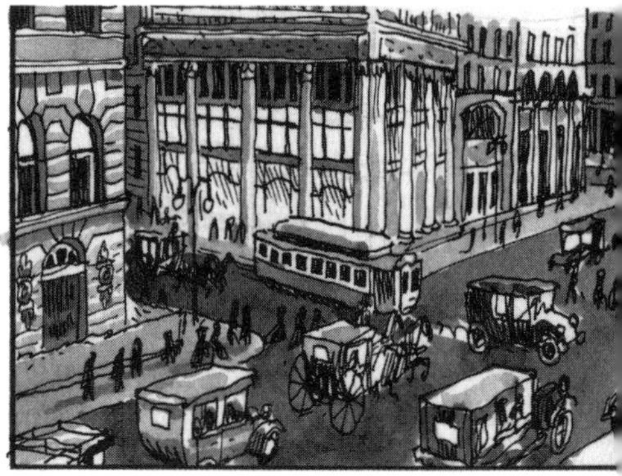

Apart from Miss Weaver, more help was on its way.

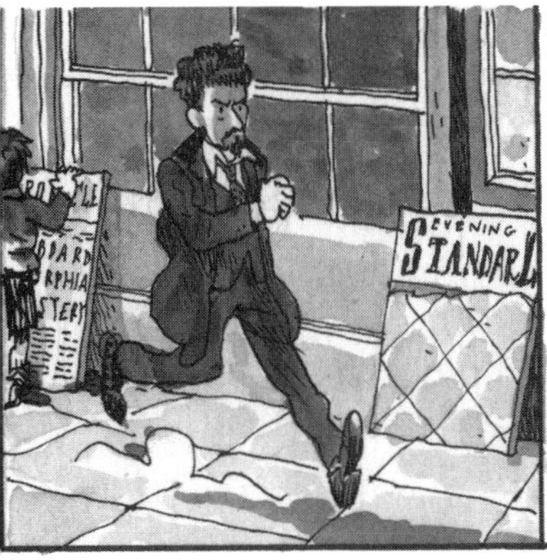
EVENING

Ezra Pound used all his heavy artillery to get institutional support for Joyce. He wrote to Yeats and George Moore, and approached Lady Cunard as a means to reach the Prime Minister.

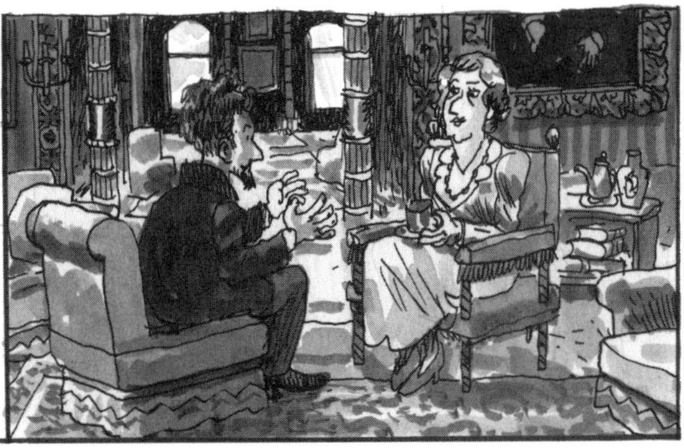

Prime Minister Asquith's secretary read Joyce's works and was favourably impressed.

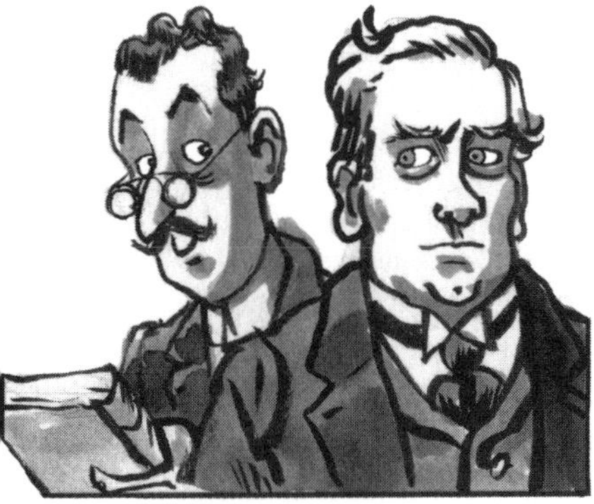

In August, the British Prime Minister awarded James Joyce 100 pounds to help him out.

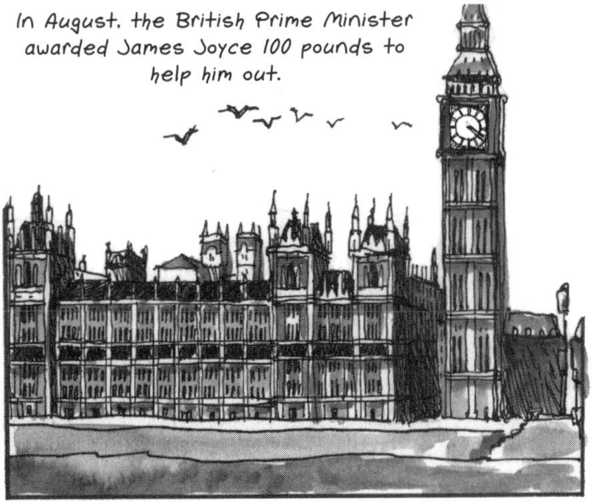

In December, Huebsch published the American edition of 'Dubliners', and the first edition of 'A Portrait of the Artist as a Young Man' in book form.

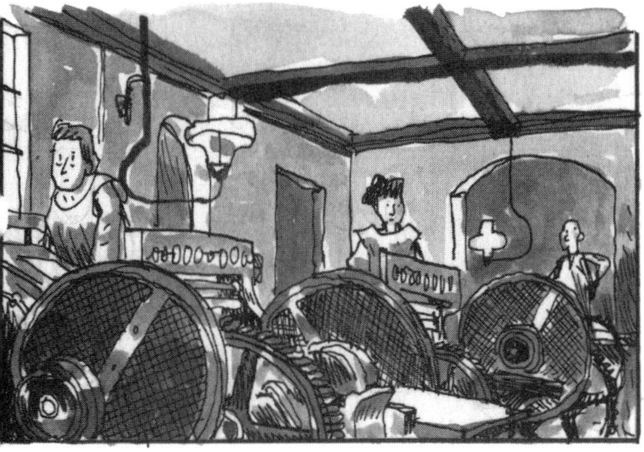

However, Joyce's difficulties were not over.

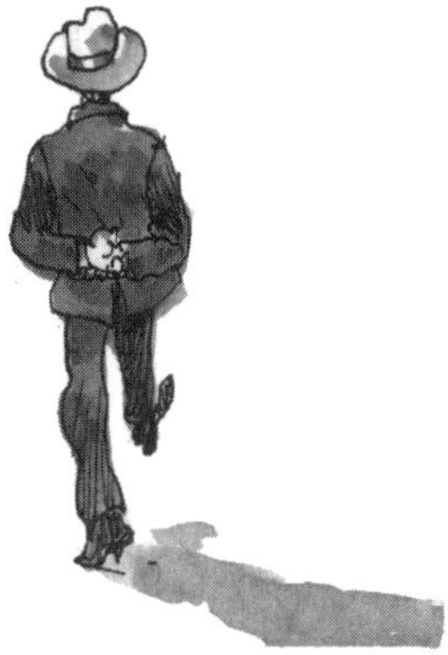

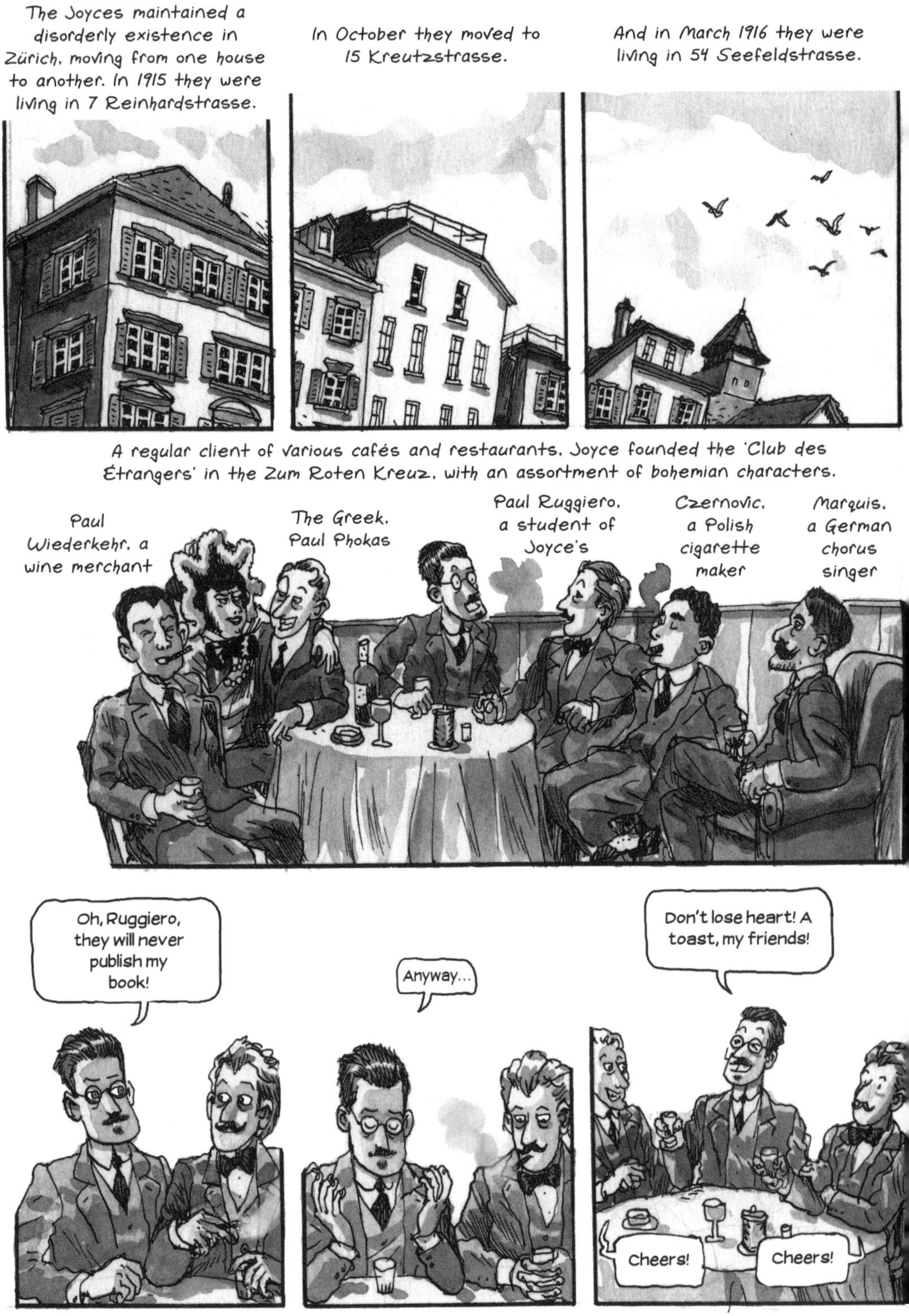
The Joyces maintained a disorderly existence in Zürich, moving from one house to another. In 1915 they were living in 7 Reinhardstrasse.
In October they moved to 15 Kreutzstrasse.
And in March 1916 they were living in 54 Seefeldstrasse.
A regular client of various cafés and restaurants, Joyce founded the 'Club des Étrangers' in the Zum Roten Kreuz, with an assortment of bohemian characters.
Paul Wiederkehr, a wine merchant
The Greek, Paul Phokas
Paul Ruggiero, a student of Joyce's
Czernovic, a Polish cigarette maker
Marquis, a German chorus singer
Oh, Ruggiero, they will never publish my book!
Anyway...
Don't lose heart! A toast, my friends!
Cheers!
Cheers!

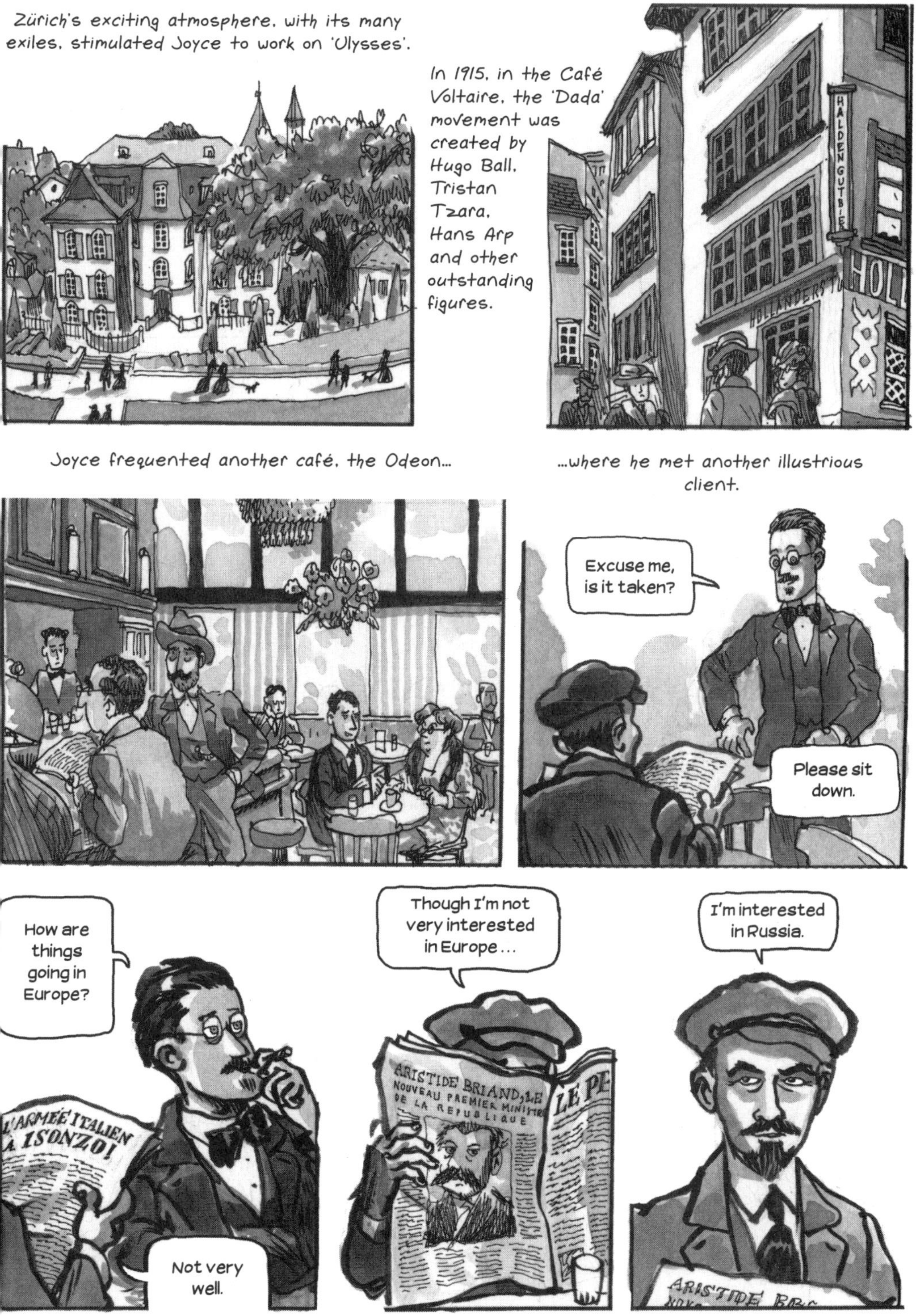

Zürich's exciting atmosphere, with its many exiles, stimulated Joyce to work on 'Ulysses'.
In 1915, in the Café Voltaire, the 'Dada' movement was created by Hugo Ball, Tristan Tzara, Hans Arp and other outstanding figures.
HALDENGUTBIE
HOLL
Joyce frequented another café, the Odeon...
...where he met another illustrious client.
Excuse me, is it taken?
Please sit down.
How are things going in Europe?
L'ARMÉE ITALIEN A ISONZO!
Not very well.
Though I'm not very interested in Europe...
ARISTIDE BRIAND, LE NOUVEAU PREMIER MINISTRE DE LA REPUBLIQUE
LE PE
I'm interested in Russia.
ARISTIDE BR

In 1917, thanks to the war, Zürich was the theatre centre of the world. All of the most important theatre companies came to the city.

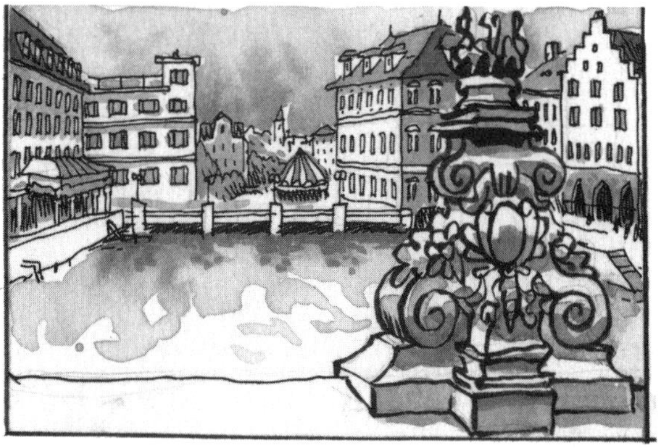

Joyce was anxious to get 'Exiles' on stage. He met an out-of-work actor who survived by giving English classes. His name was Claud W Sykes.

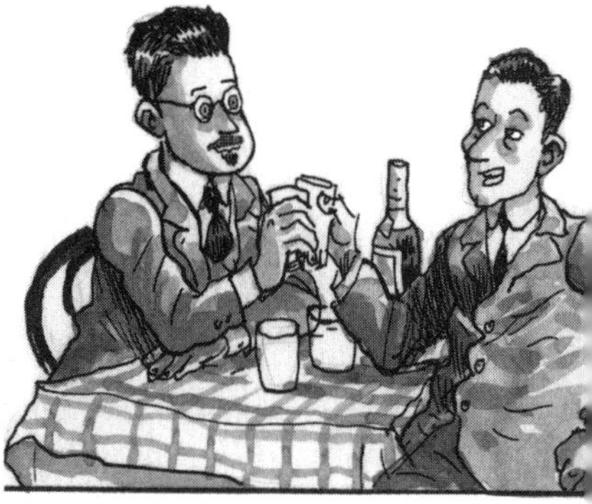

After a while, Joyce developed a friendship with Sykes and his beautiful, lively wife, the actress Daisy Race.

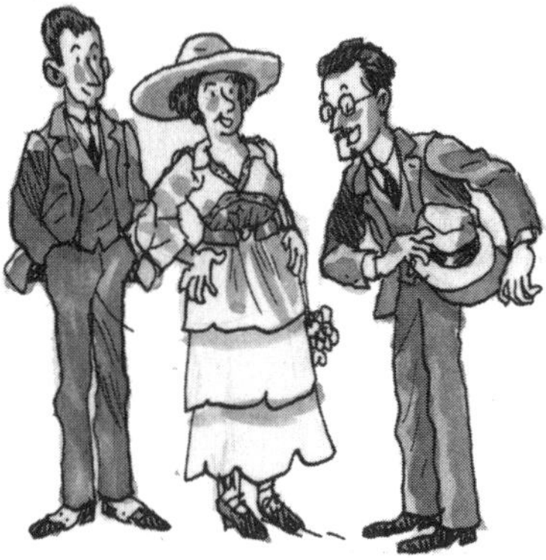

The Irish writer was now a part of the cultural kaleidoscope of the city. He knew figures such as the Austrian writer René Schickele and the German playwright Frank Wedekind.

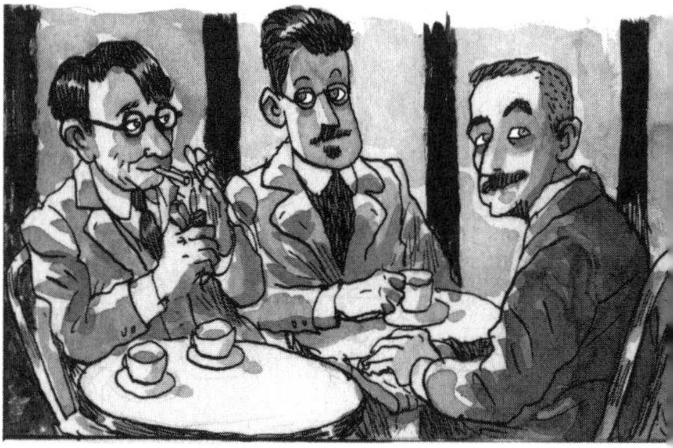

But the pain in his eyes returned, and was more and more unbearable.

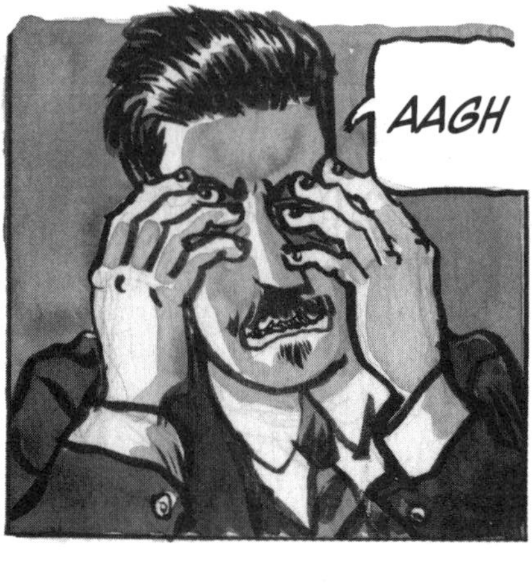
AAGH

One day, he had a severe attack of glaucoma. Bit by bit, Joyce was going blind.

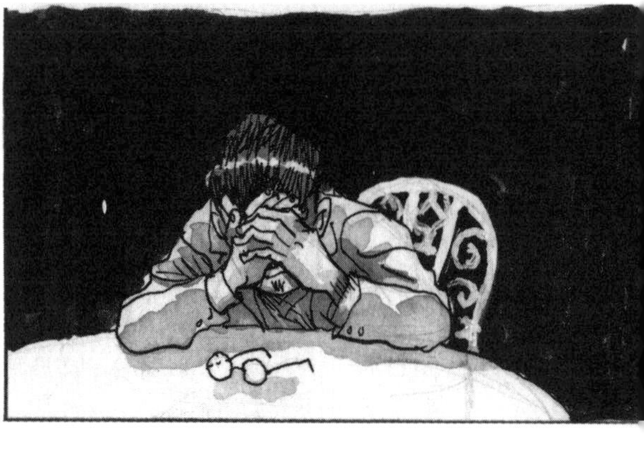

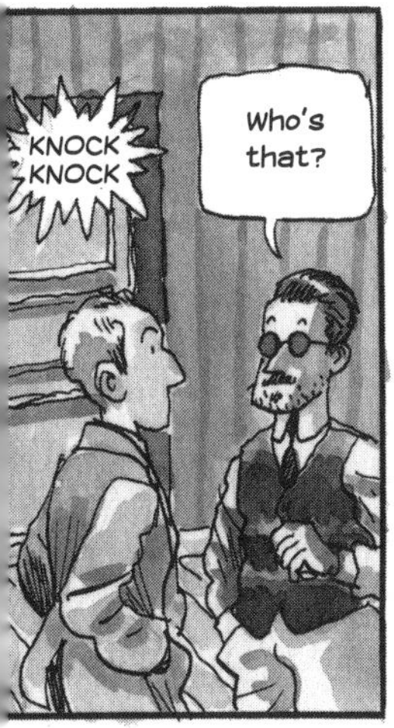
KNOCK KNOCK
Who's that?

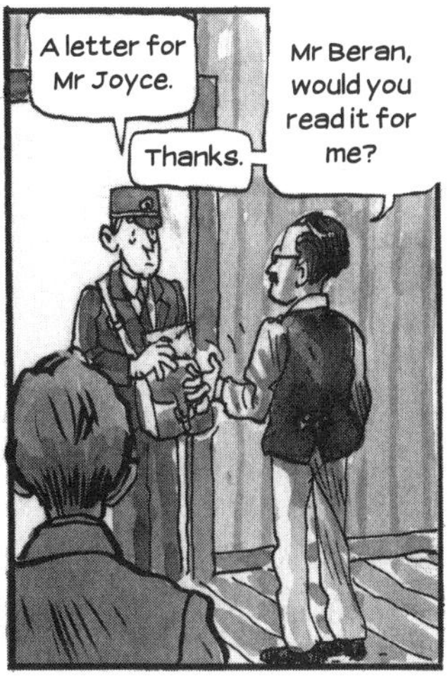
A letter for Mr Joyce.
Thanks.
Mr Beran, would you read it for me?

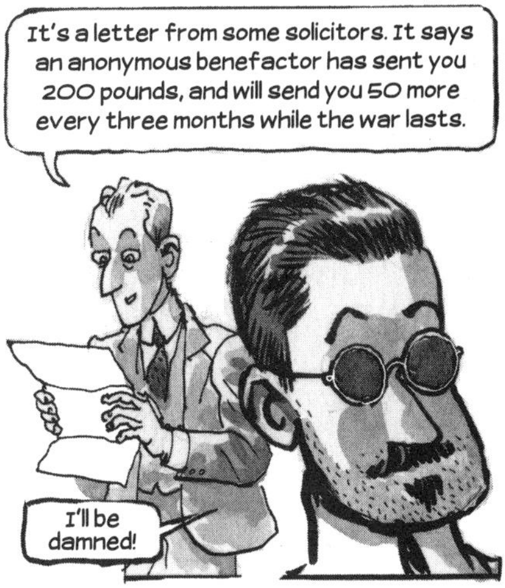
It's a letter from some solicitors. It says an anonymous benefactor has sent you 200 pounds, and will send you 50 more every three months while the war lasts.
I'll be damned!

His fame was growing. A famous New York lawyer, John Quinn, bought the manuscript of 'Exiles' from Joyce on Ezra Pound's recommendation.

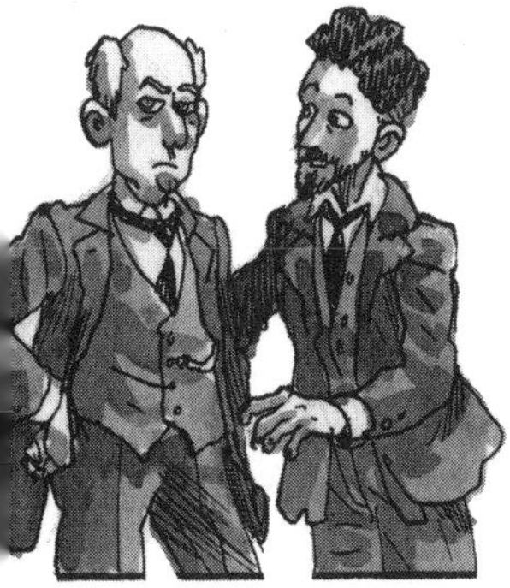

In May a critique of 'A Portrait' appeared in 'Vanity Fair', praising Joyce's work.

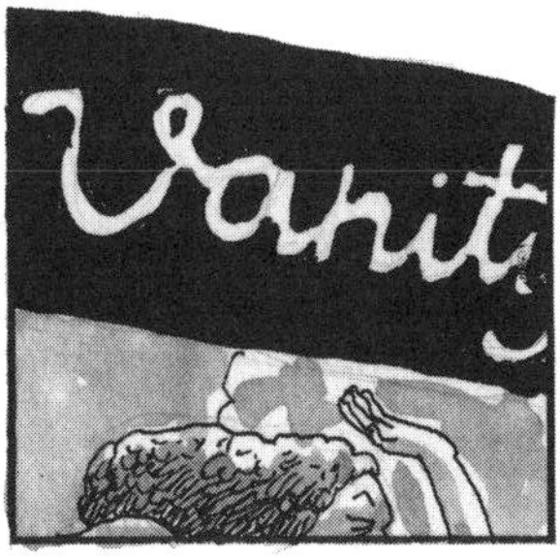

Later, Yeats, Lady Gregory, TS Elliot and HG Wells, amongst others, expressed their enthusiasm for the book.

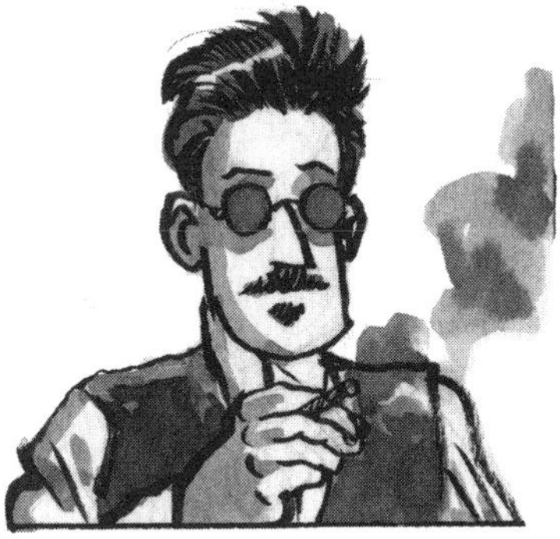

In August, Joyce signed a contract to publish 'Exiles'.

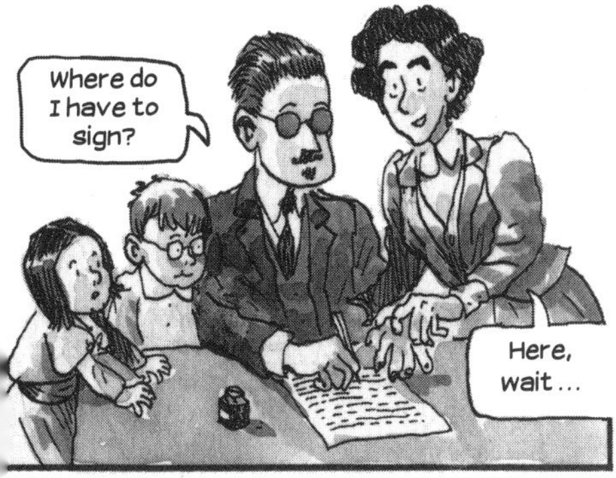
Where do I have to sign?
Here, wait...

In the same month, he suffered another terrible attack of glaucoma, which left him unconscious in the street.

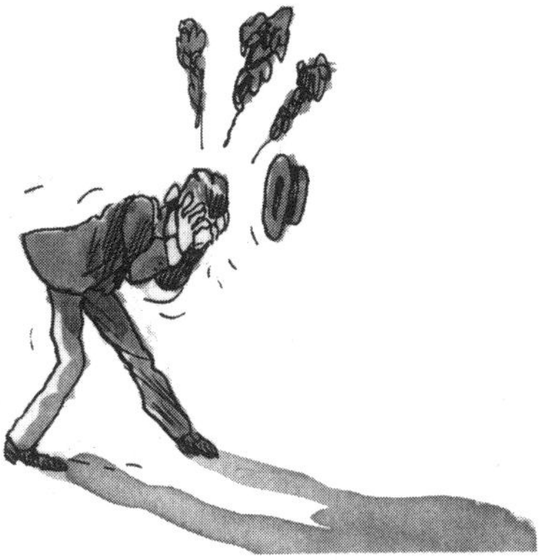

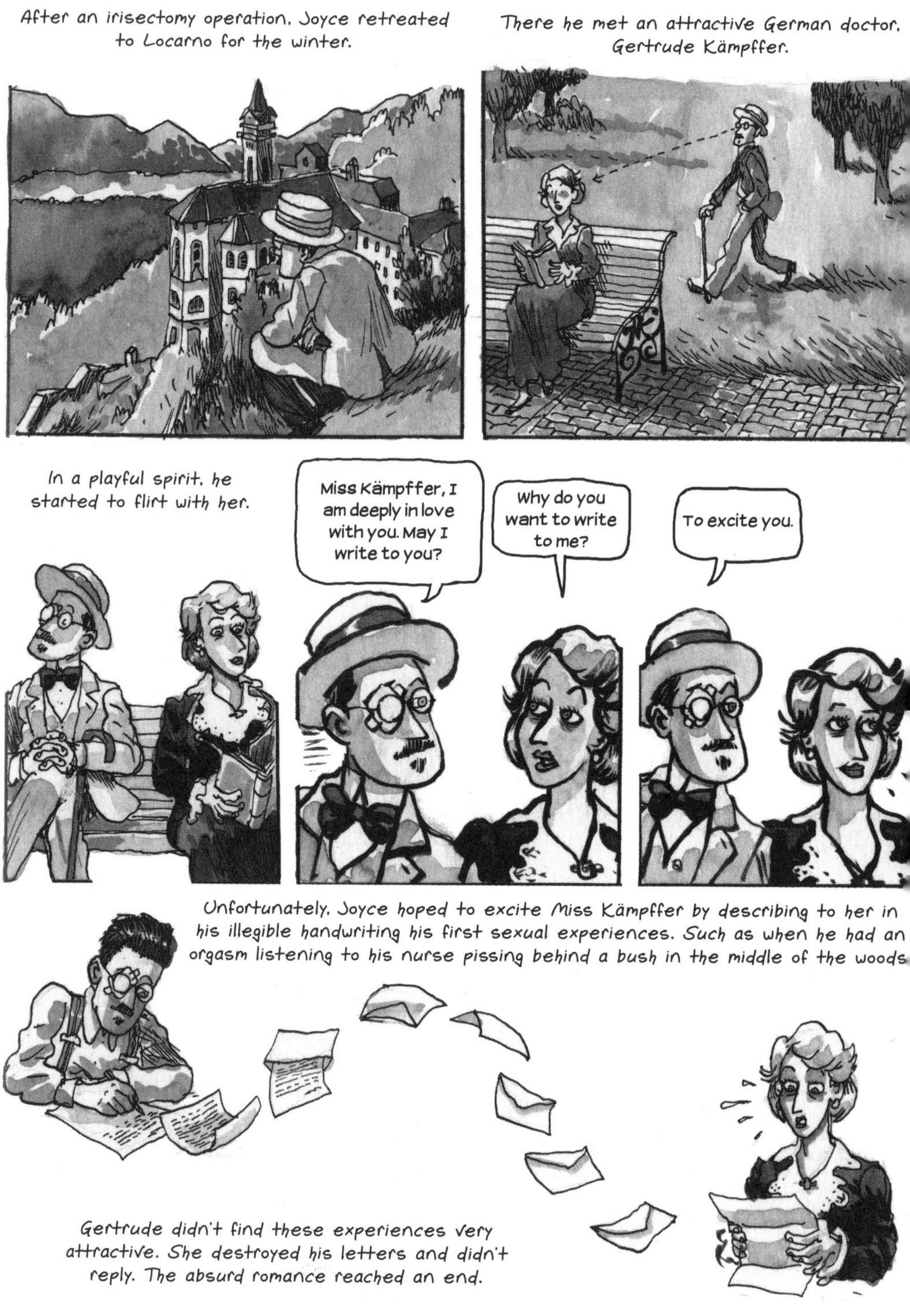
After an irisectomy operation, Joyce retreated to Locarno for the winter.
There he met an attractive German doctor, Gertrude Kämpffer.
In a playful spirit, he started to flirt with her.
Miss Kämpffer, I am deeply in love with you. May I write to you?
Why do you want to write to me?
To excite you.
Unfortunately, Joyce hoped to excite Miss Kämpffer by describing to her in his illegible handwriting his first sexual experiences. Such as when he had an orgasm listening to his nurse pissing behind a bush in the middle of the woods
Gertrude didn't find these experiences very attractive. She destroyed his letters and didn't reply. The absurd romance reached an end.

Returning to 'Ulysses', the first chapters were now ready for publication. Pound and Miss Weaver decided that the book should appear in instalments.

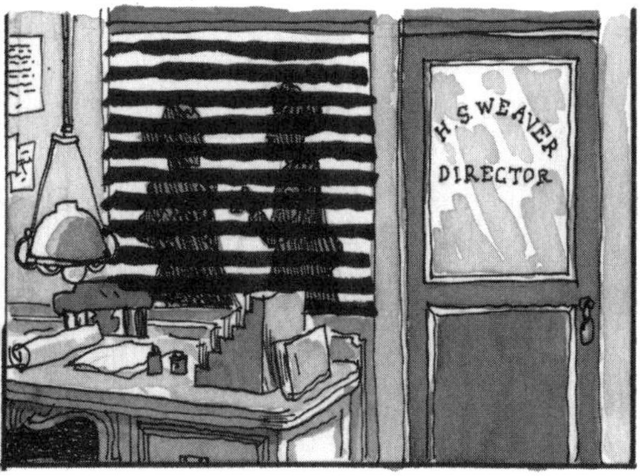
H.S. WEAVER
DIRECTOR

In March 1918, the first part appeared in 'Little Review'.

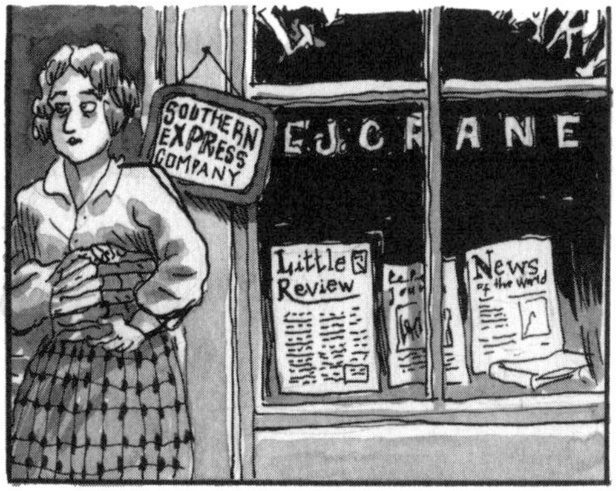
SOUTHERN EXPRESS COMPANY
E.J.C ANE
Little Review
News of the World

But his work was interrupted, when he received a letter from the director of Eidgenosissche Bank in Zürich.

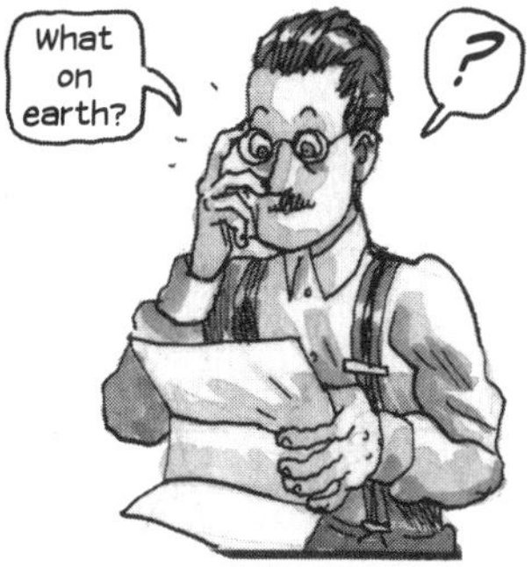
What on earth?
?

His presence was required at the bank. Joyce went to the appointment wearing a borrowed morning coat.

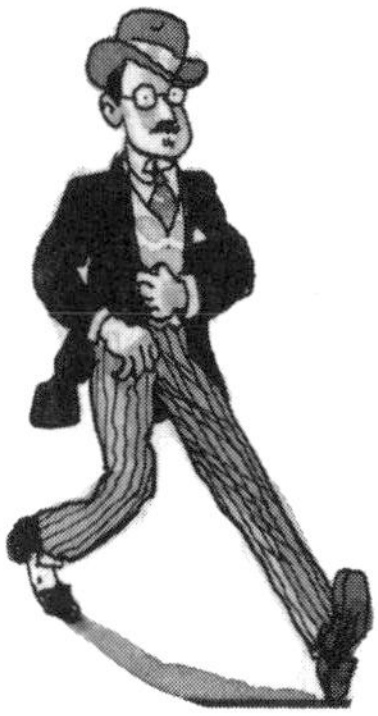

The director of the bank informed him that an anonymous client had given him a kind of grant, 1000 francs a month.

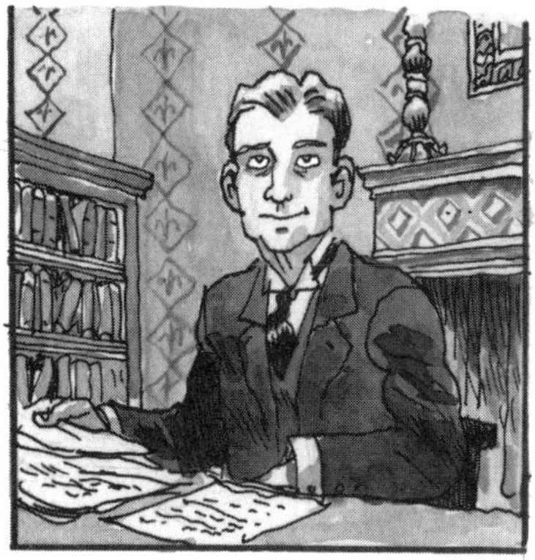

Without ever imagining it, Joyce had become a rich man. But ... thanks to whom? Who was this anonymous benefactor?

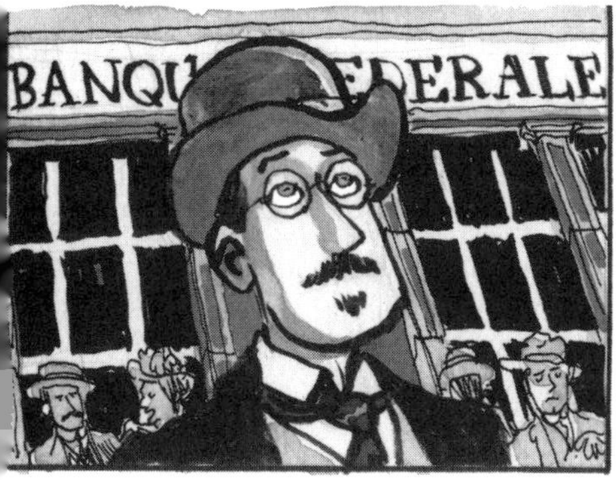
BANQU
EDERALE

His patron was none other than Mrs Rockerfeller-McCormick, the millionaire patron of famous psychoanalyst Carl Jung, and of other writers and artists.

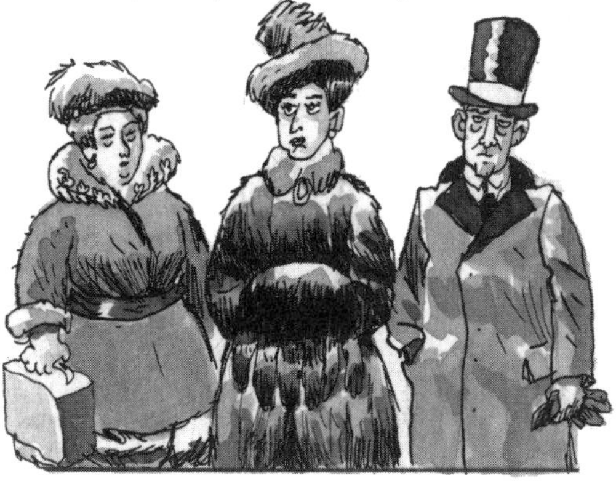

Claud Sykes came to see Joyce when he learned of his luck, and together they decided to found a theatre company in Zürich.

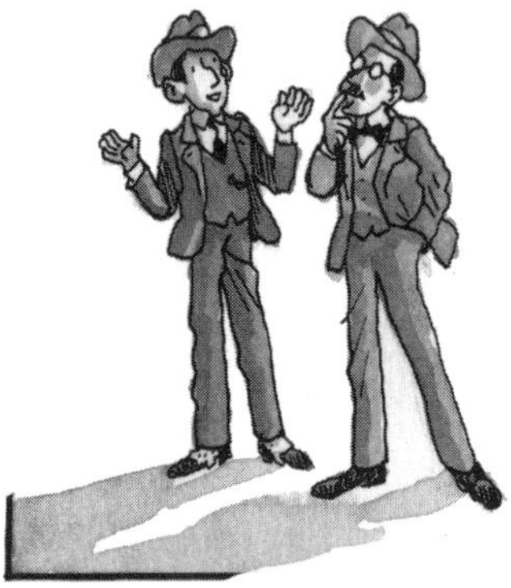

The new project of the two Irishmen had a curious name: 'ENGLISH PLAYERS'.

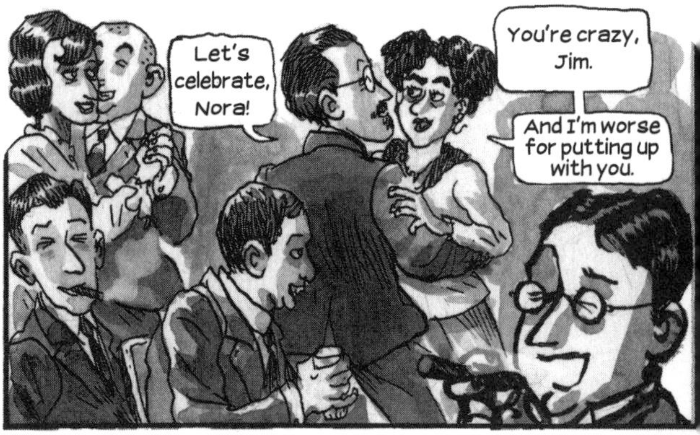

Let's celebrate, Nora!
You're crazy, Jim.
And I'm worse for putting up with you.

Though Joyce wanted to use the company to stage 'Exiles', it was decided that their first play would be Oscar Wilde's 'The Importance of Being Ernest'.

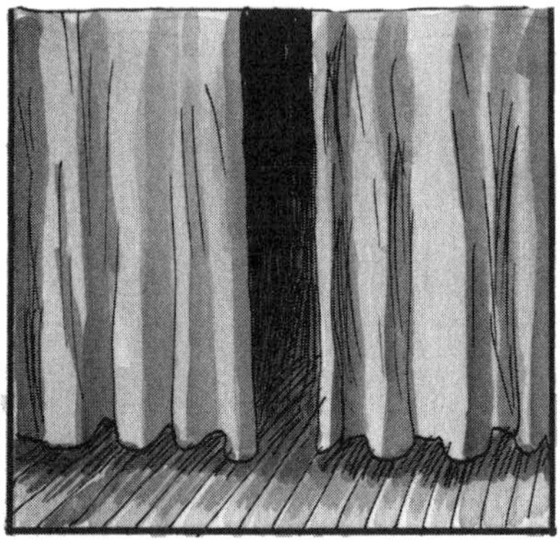

The night of 29 April, the Zur Kaufleuten Theatre in Zurich was packed.

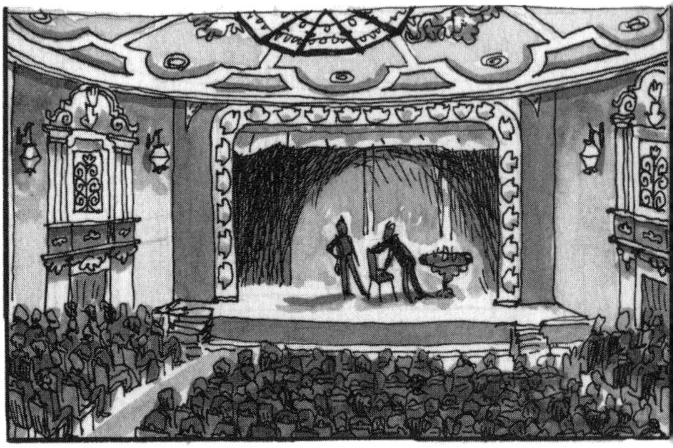

The play was a success.

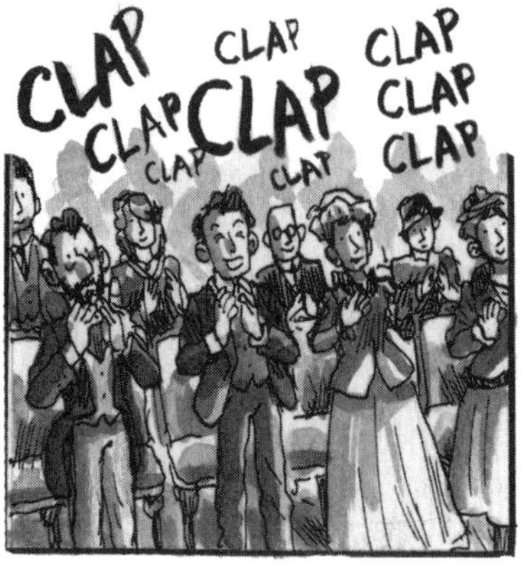

CLAP CLAP CLAP CLAP CLAP CLAP CLAP CLAP CLAP CLAP

And apart from the odd squabble with actors over money...

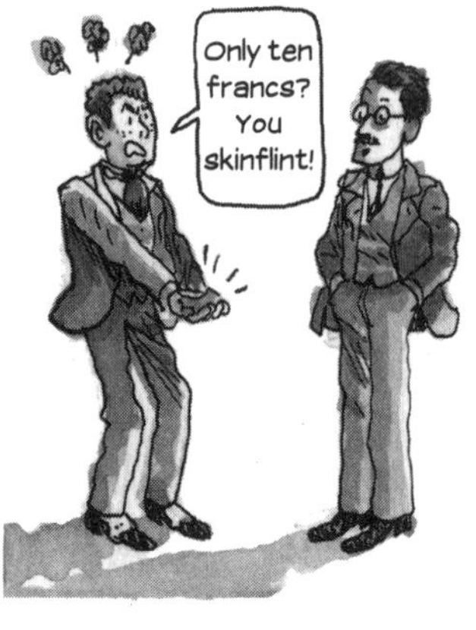

Only ten francs? You skinflint!

...Joyce could feel happy with his first experience as a theatre producer.

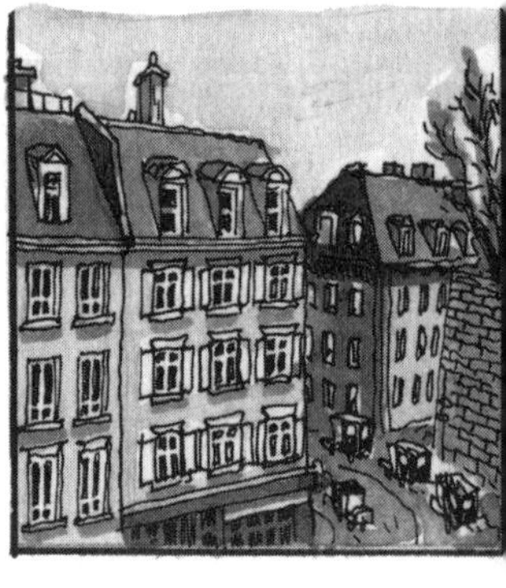

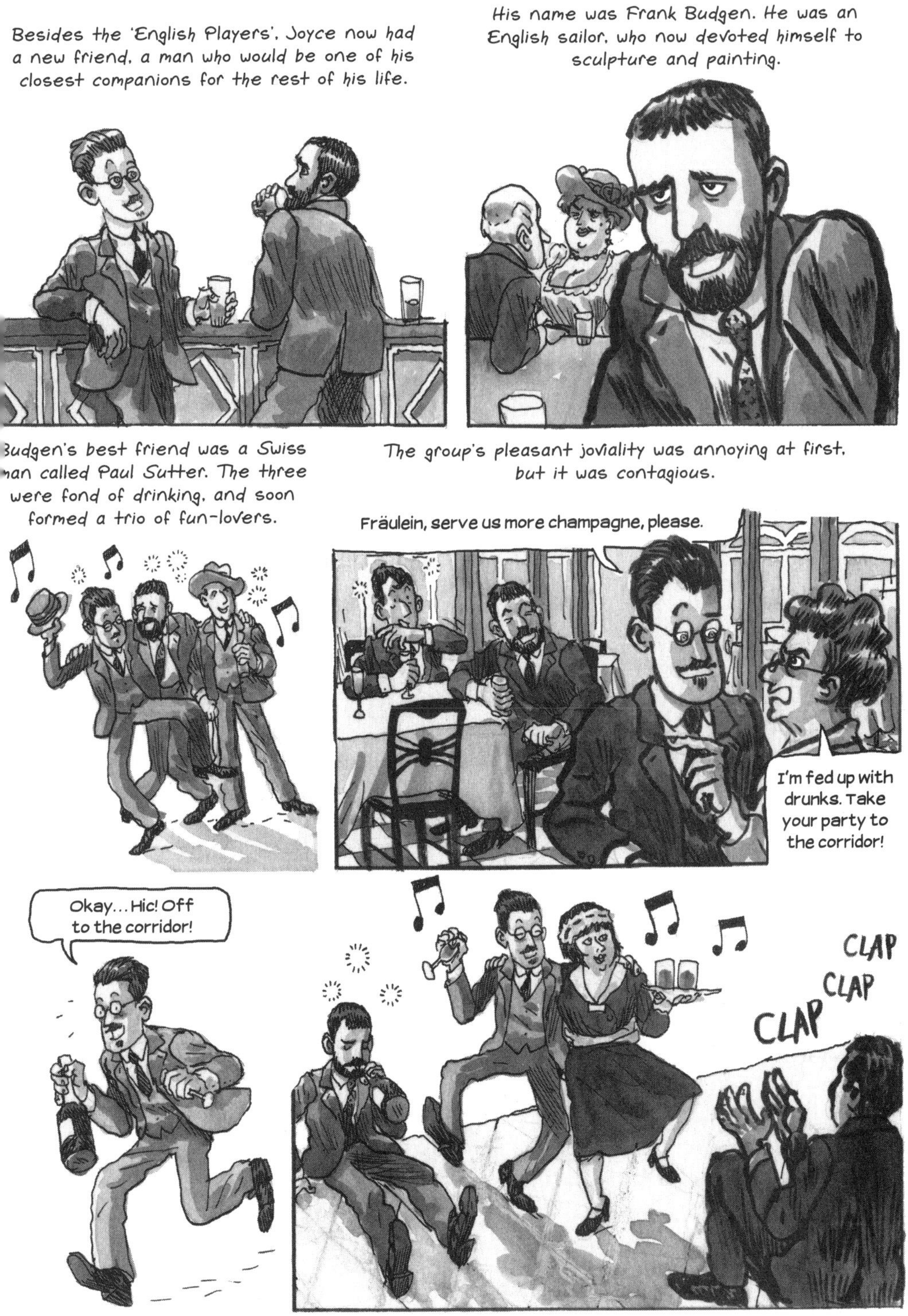
Besides the 'English Players', Joyce now had a new friend, a man who would be one of his closest companions for the rest of his life.
His name was Frank Budgen. He was an English sailor, who now devoted himself to sculpture and painting.
Budgen's best friend was a Swiss man called Paul Sutter. The three were fond of drinking, and soon formed a trio of fun-lovers.
The group's pleasant joviality was annoying at first, but it was contagious.
Fräulein, serve us more champagne, please.
I'm fed up with drunks. Take your party to the corridor!
Okay... Hic! Off to the corridor!
CLAP
CLAP
CLAP

Contrary to appearances, James and Nora got on well together. Her husband's craziness rarely upset her.

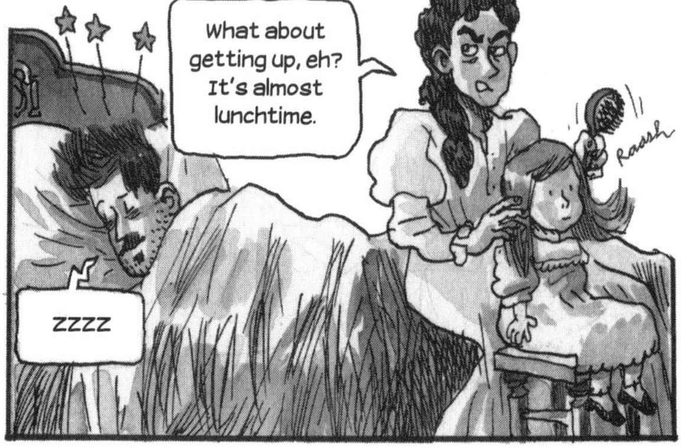
What about getting up, eh? It's almost lunchtime.
Raash
ZZZZ

Joyce adored his children, especially Lucia, though he was permissive and gave in to all their whims.

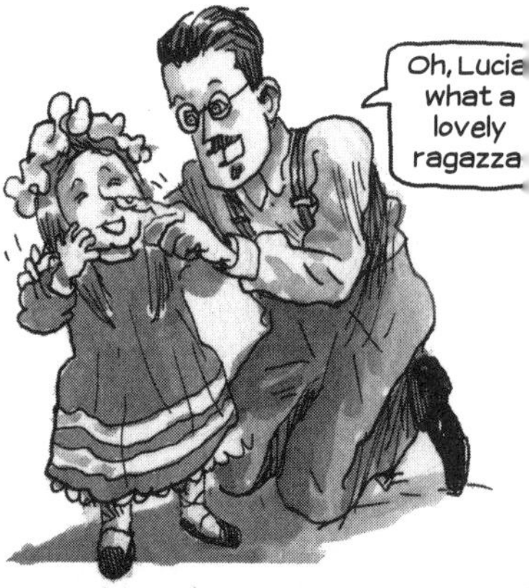
Oh, Lucia what a lovely ragazza

Giorgio, who boasted in school about his father being a writer, decided one day to satisfy his schoolfriends' curiosity.

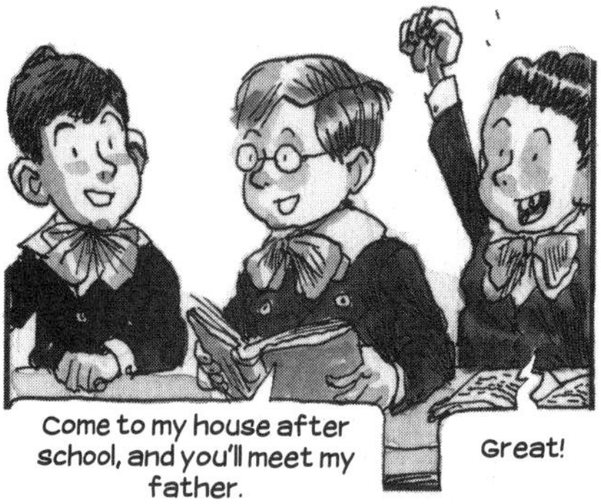
Come to my house after school, and you'll meet my father.
Great!

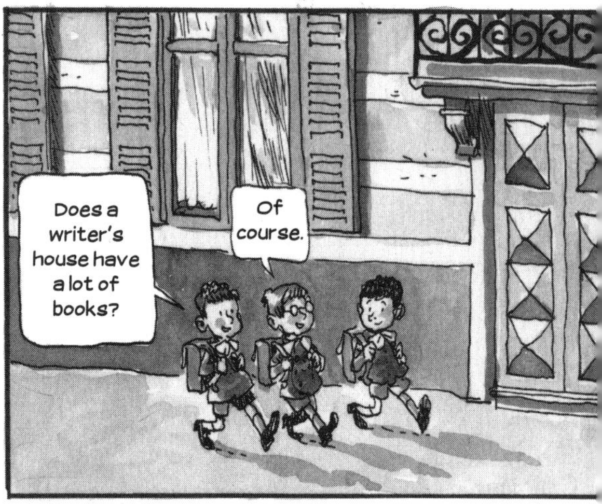
Does a writer's house have a lot of books?
Of course.

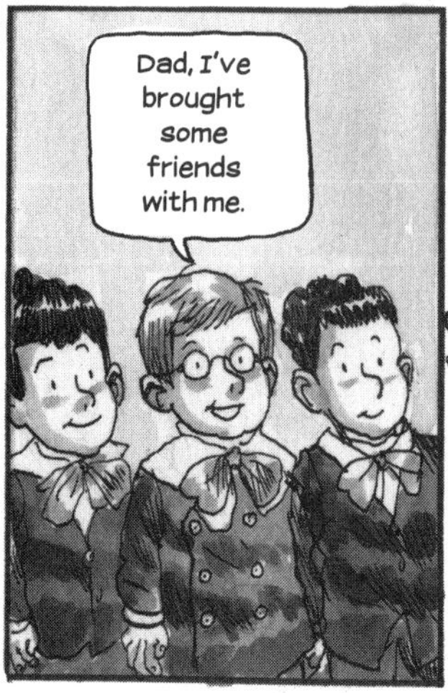
Dad, I've brought some friends with me.

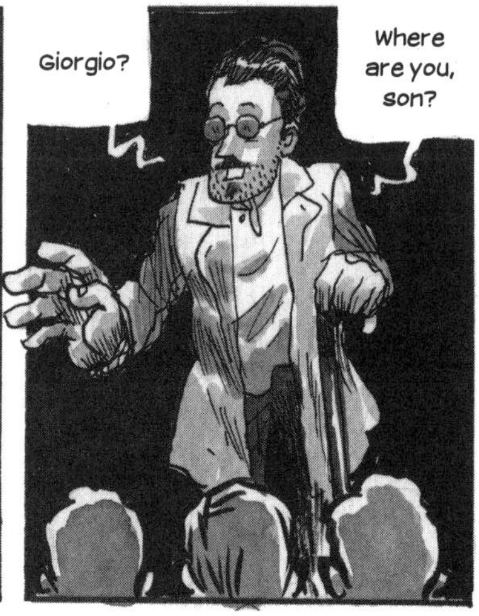
Giorgio?
Where are you, son?

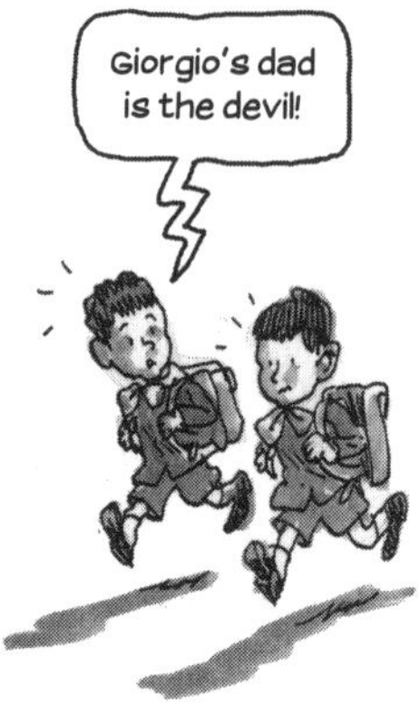
Giorgio's dad is the devil!

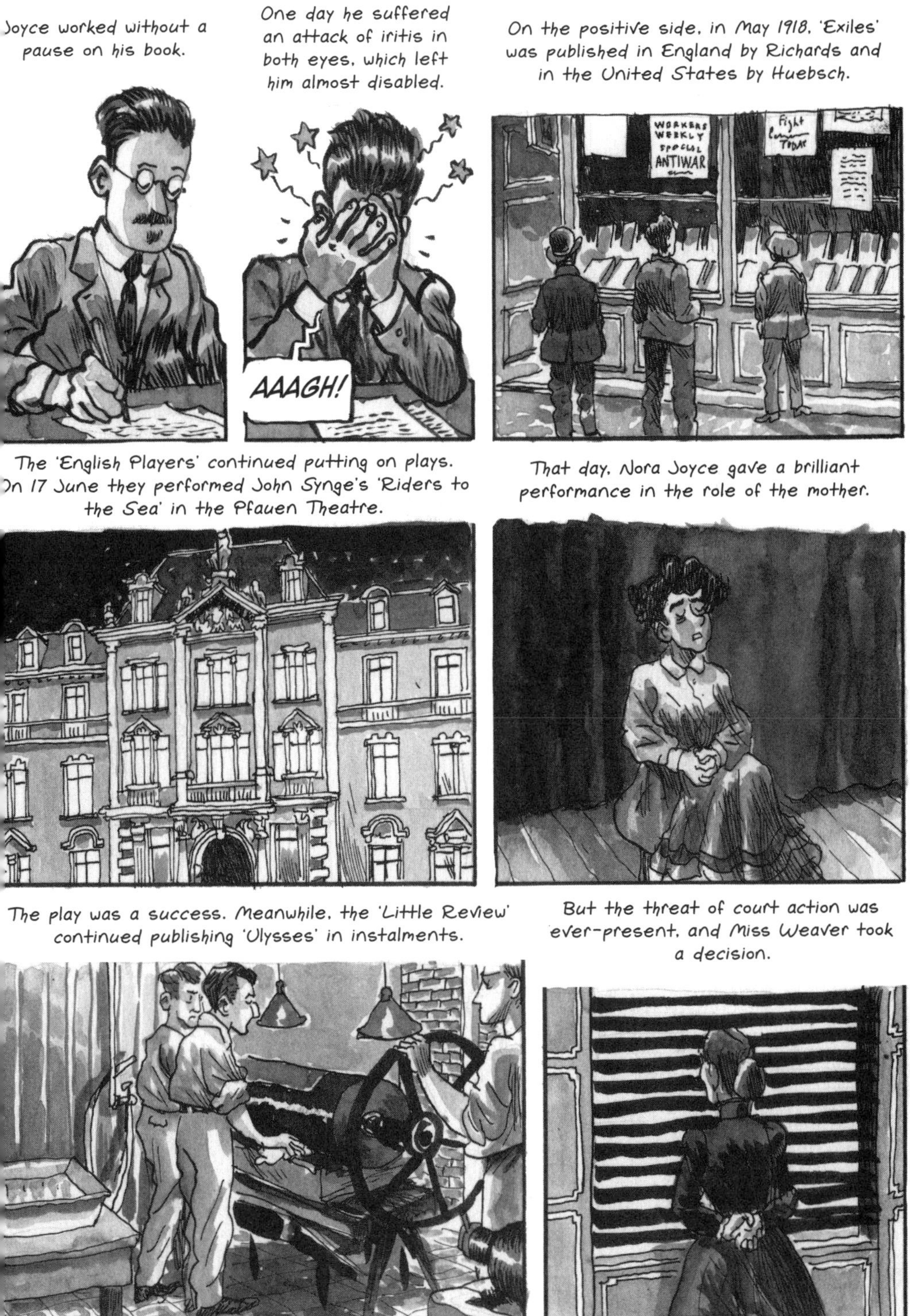
Joyce worked without a pause on his book.
One day he suffered an attack of iritis in both eyes, which left him almost disabled.
AAAGH!
On the positive side, in May 1918, 'Exiles' was published in England by Richards and in the United States by Huebsch.
WORKERS WEEKLY SPECIAL ANTIWAR
The 'English Players' continued putting on plays. On 17 June they performed John Synge's 'Riders to the Sea' in the Pfauen Theatre.
That day, Nora Joyce gave a brilliant performance in the role of the mother.
The play was a success. Meanwhile, the 'Little Review' continued publishing 'Ulysses' in instalments.
But the threat of court action was ever-present, and Miss Weaver took a decision.

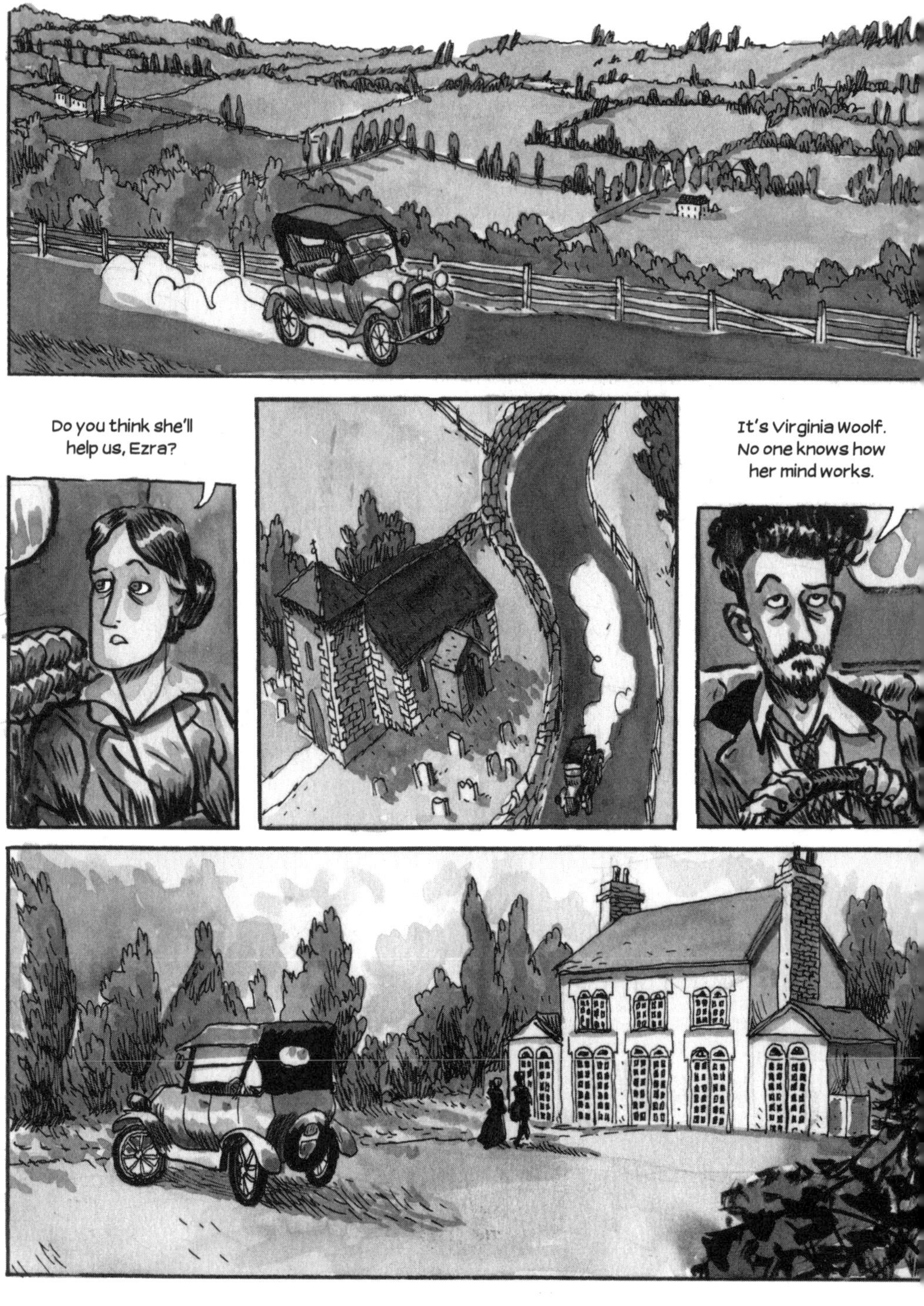

Do you think she'll help us, Ezra?
It's Virginia Woolf. No one knows how her mind works.

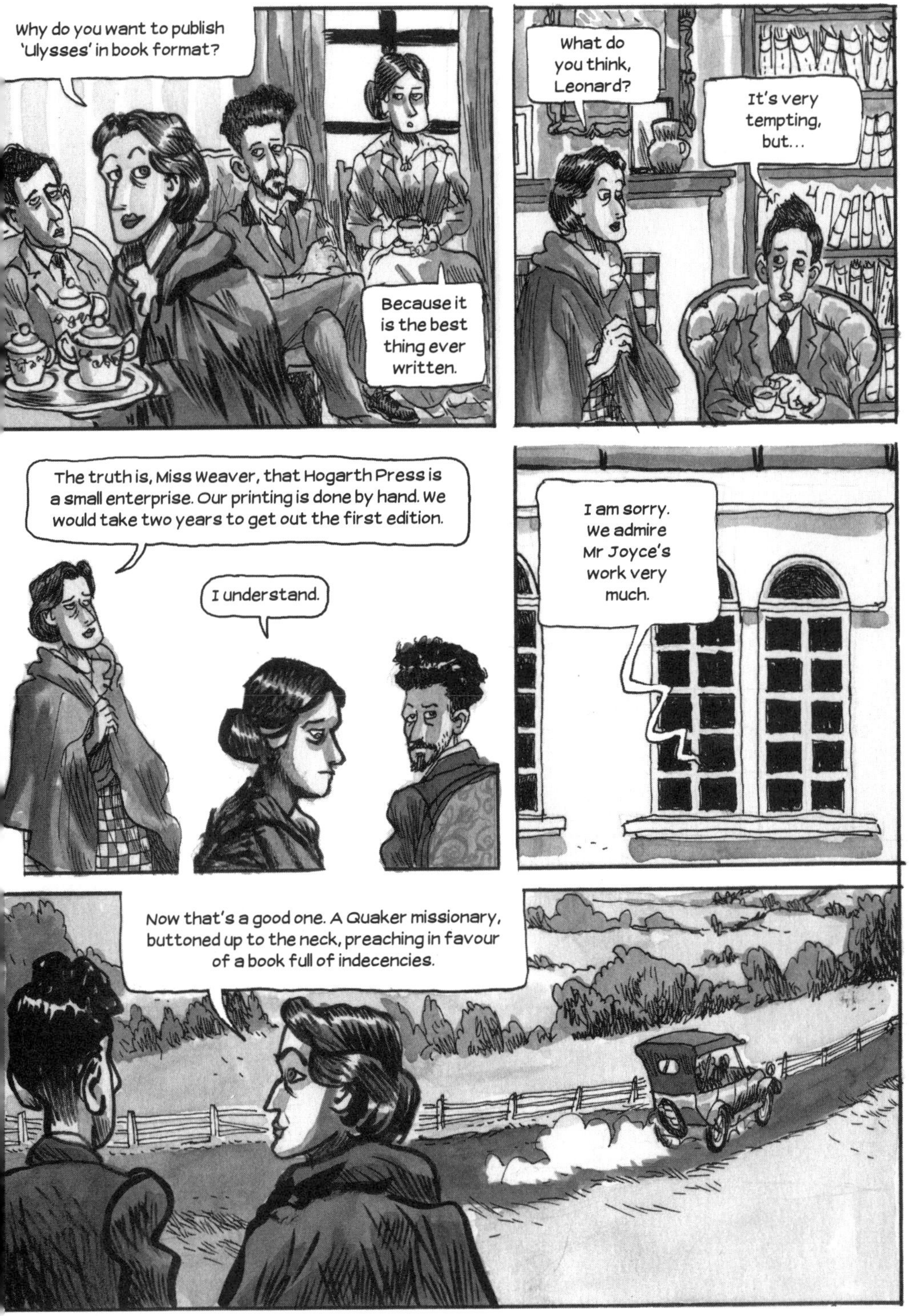
Why do you want to publish 'Ulysses' in book format?
Because it is the best thing ever written.
What do you think, Leonard?
It's very tempting, but...
The truth is, Miss Weaver, that Hogarth Press is a small enterprise. Our printing is done by hand. We would take two years to get out the first edition.
I understand.
I am sorry. We admire Mr Joyce's work very much.
Now that's a good one. A Quaker missionary, buttoned up to the neck, preaching in favour of a book full of indecencies.

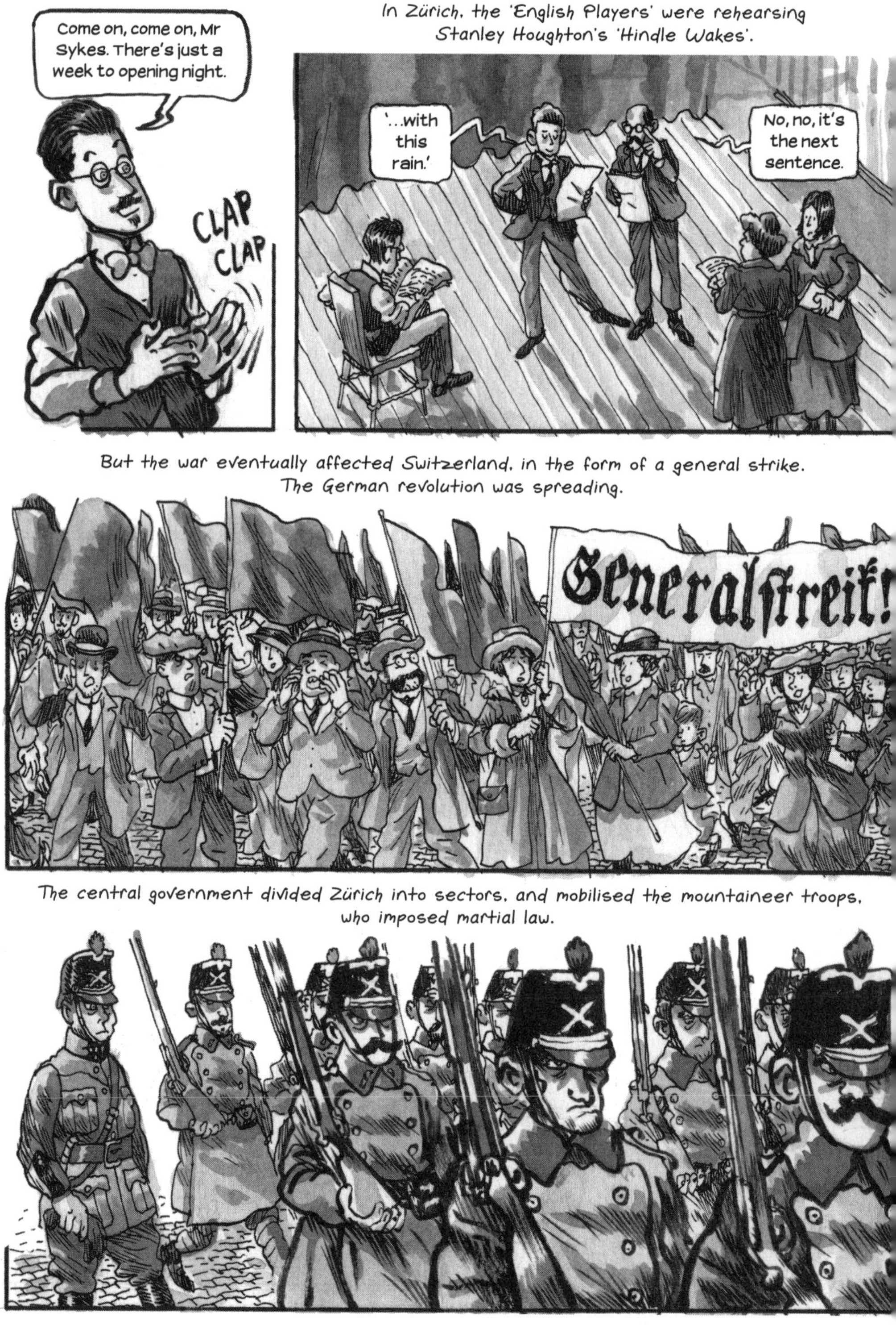
Come on, come on, Mr Sykes. There's just a week to opening night.
CLAP CLAP
In Zürich, the 'English Players' were rehearsing Stanley Houghton's 'Hindle Wakes'.
'...with this rain.'
No, no, it's the next sentence.
But the war eventually affected Switzerland, in the form of a general strike. The German revolution was spreading.
Generalstreik!
The central government divided Zürich into sectors, and mobilised the mountaineer troops, who imposed martial law.

The 'English Players' were affected: in order to ehearse, they had to avoid the guards' hostility. And one of their actors died from flu.

Joyce decided to renew their energy, by putting on plays in French, English and Italian. He started preparing his actors.

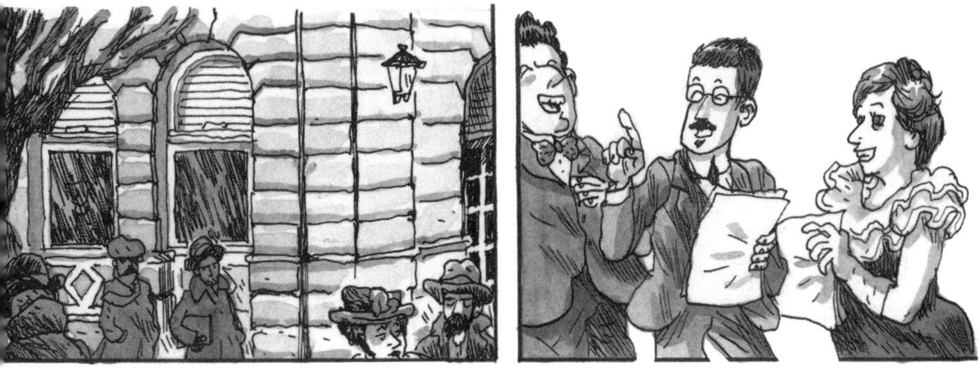

On 11 December 1917, they put on a triple show: Felice Cavallotti's 'Il cantico del cantici', Banville's 'Le Baiser' and Browning's 'In a Balcony'. Accompanied by Ruggiero on guitar, Joyce sang the opening song.

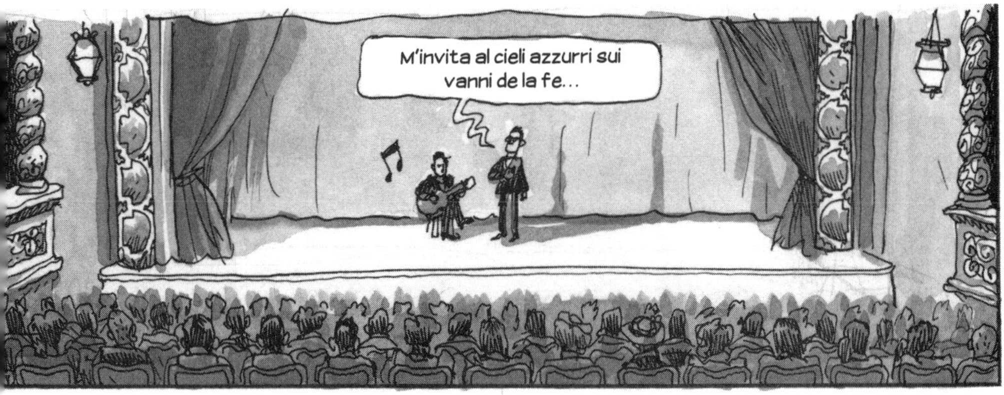
M'invita al cieli azzurri sui vanni de la fe...

With not enough support, the 'English Players' couldn't overcome their difficulties, and after their last show, the company closed down.

But Joyce's journey continued.

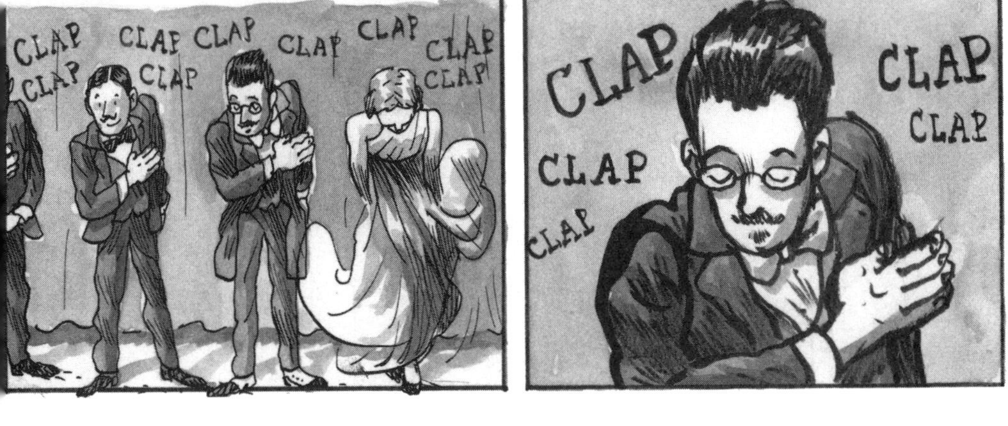
CLAP
CLAP
CLAP
CLAP
CLAP
CLAP
CLAP
CLAP
CLAP
CLAP
CLAP
CLAP
CLAP
CLAP

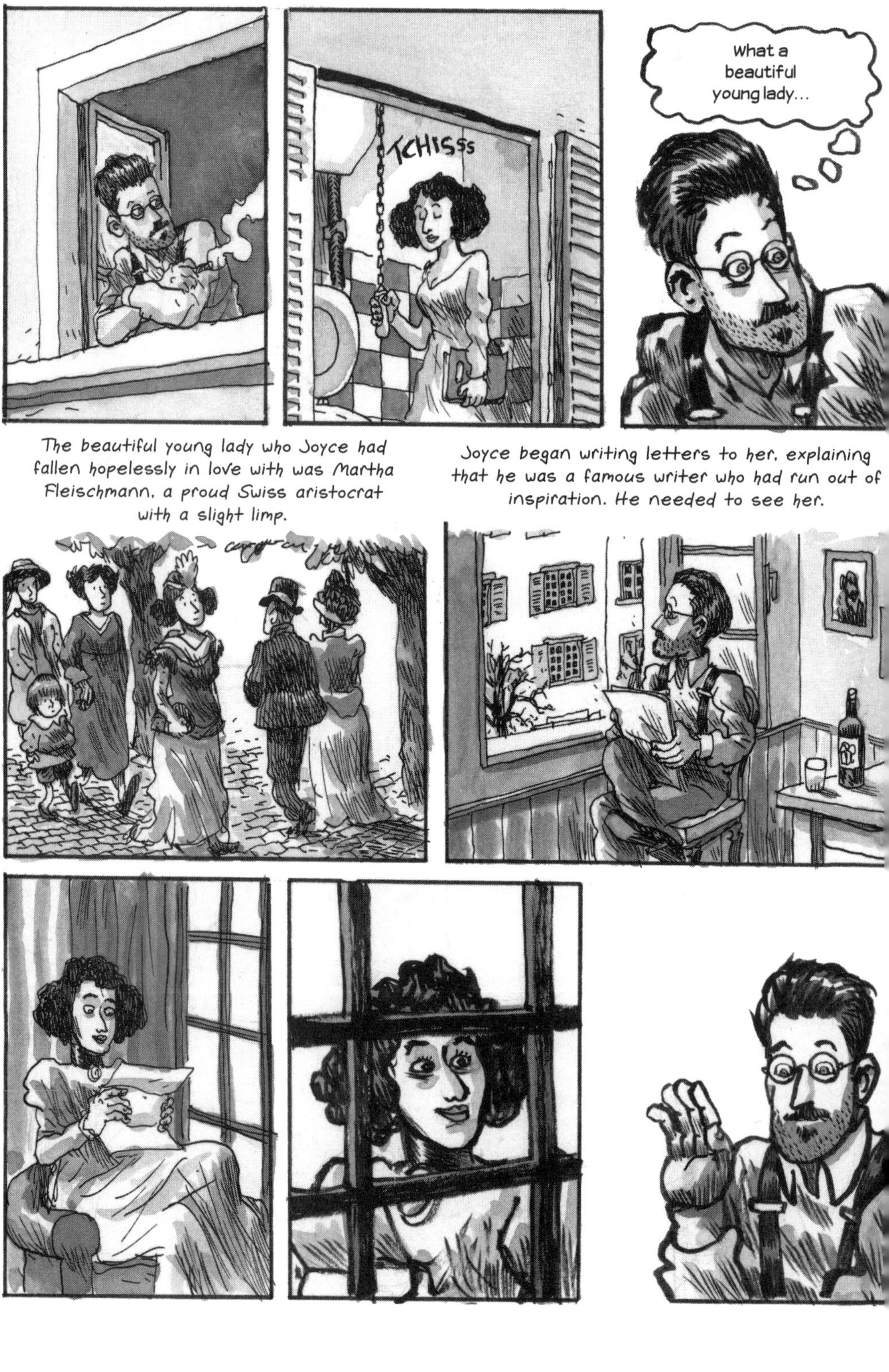
TCHISSS
What a beautiful young lady...
The beautiful young lady who Joyce had fallen hopelessly in love with was Martha Fleischmann, a proud Swiss aristocrat with a slight limp.
Joyce began writing letters to her, explaining that he was a famous writer who had run out of inspiration. He needed to see her.

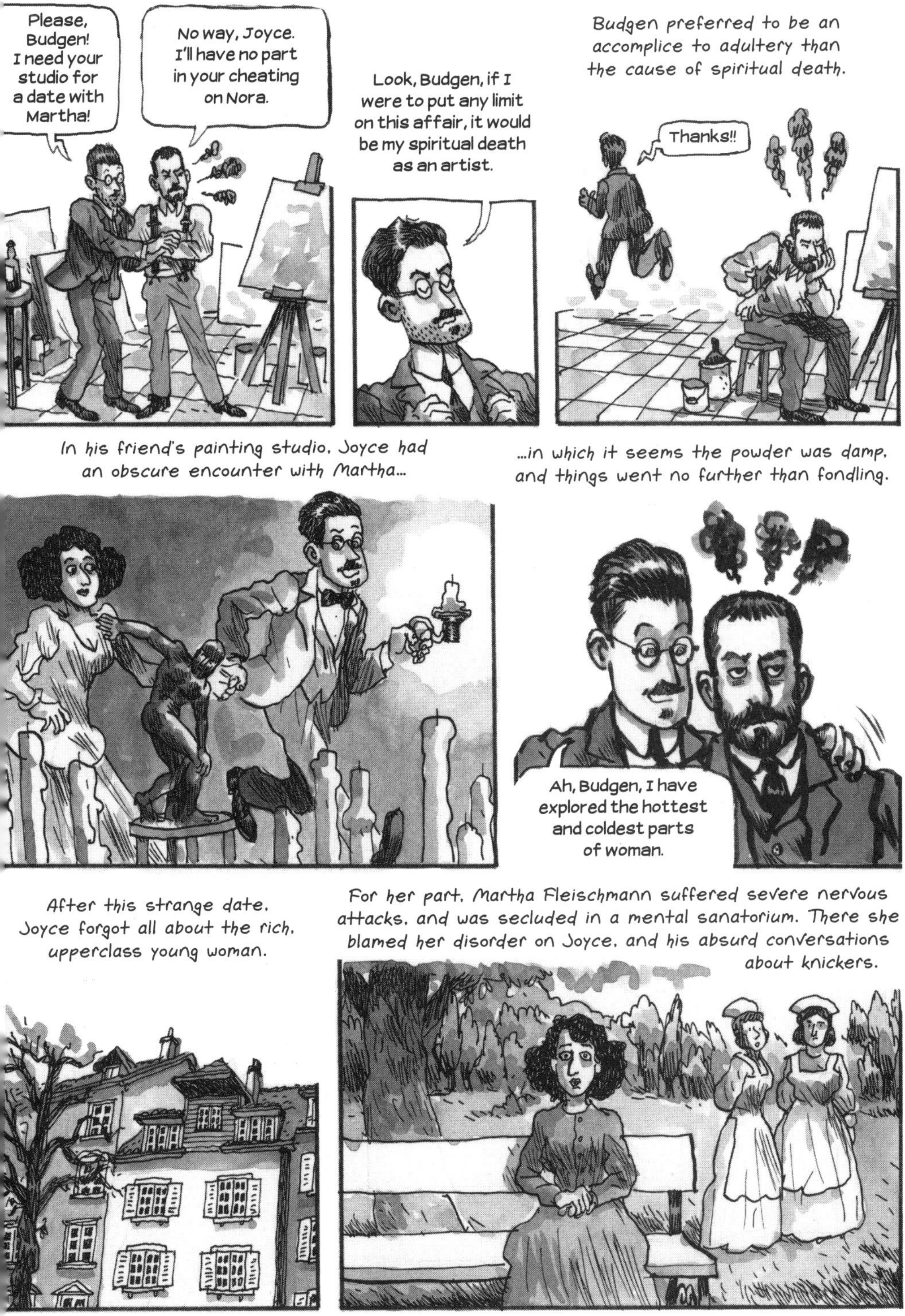
Please, Budgen! I need your studio for a date with Martha!
No way, Joyce. I'll have no part in your cheating on Nora.
Look, Budgen, if I were to put any limit on this affair, it would be my spiritual death as an artist.
Budgen preferred to be an accomplice to adultery than the cause of spiritual death.
Thanks!!
In his friend's painting studio, Joyce had an obscure encounter with Martha...
...in which it seems the powder was damp, and things went no further than fondling.
Ah, Budgen, I have explored the hottest and coldest parts of woman.
After this strange date, Joyce forgot all about the rich, upperclass young woman.
For her part, Martha Fleischmann suffered severe nervous attacks, and was secluded in a mental sanatorium. There she blamed her disorder on Joyce, and his absurd conversations about knickers.

The pain in Joyce's eyes persisted. Driven to distraction by his illness, he decided to give up absinthe for wine. In May, tired and irritable, he left with Budgen for Locarno.

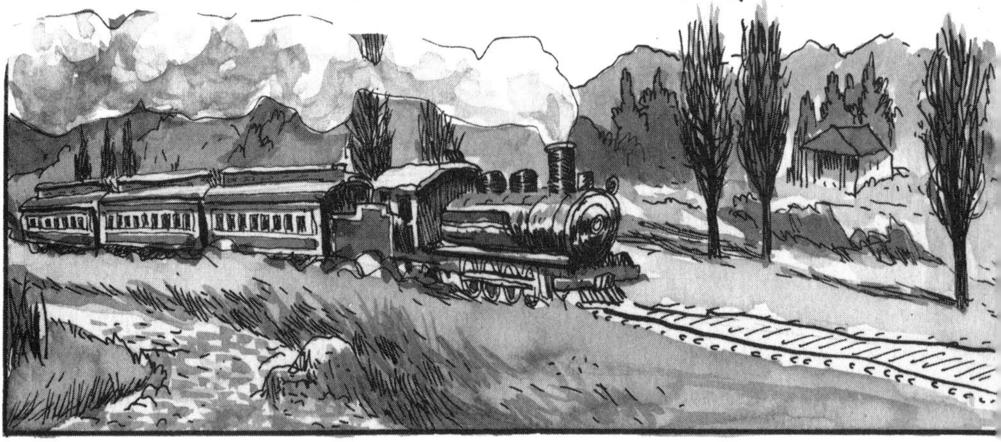

In the course of creating 'Ulysses', Joyce went to visit Baroness St Leger, the widow of seven husbands, who lived on the Isle of Brissago in Lake Maggiore.

Without a doubt, a story very like Greek mythology.

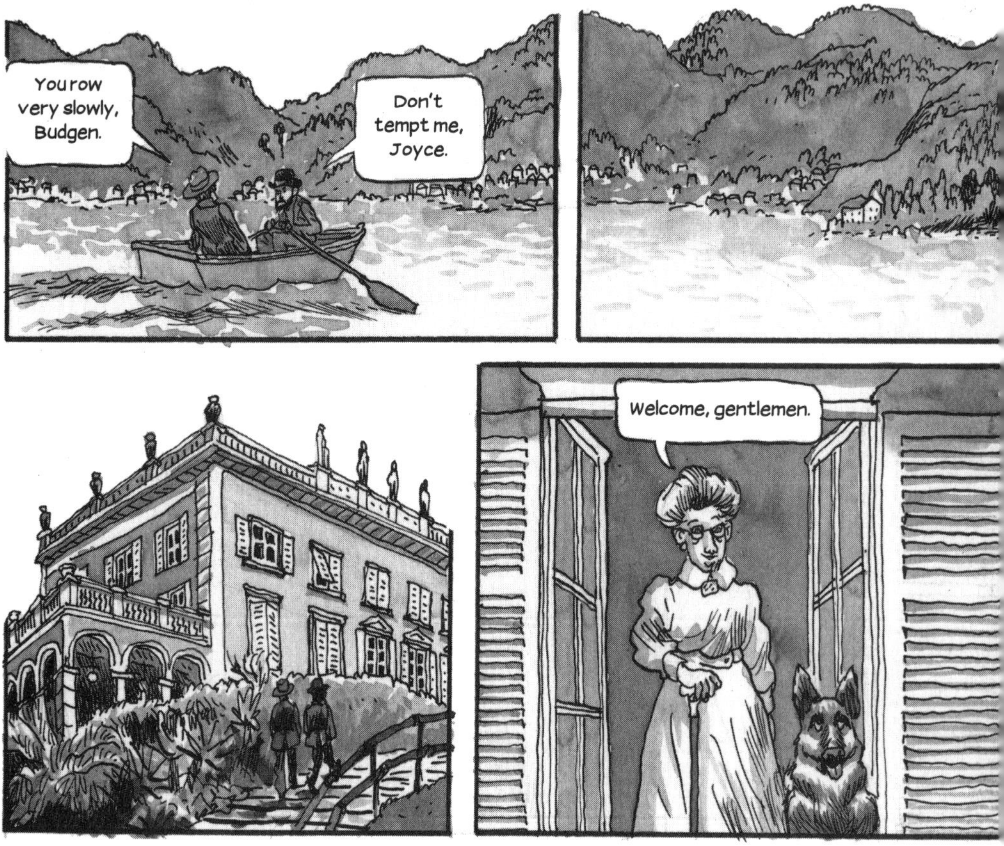
You row very slowly, Budgen.
Don't tempt me, Joyce.
Welcome, gentlemen.

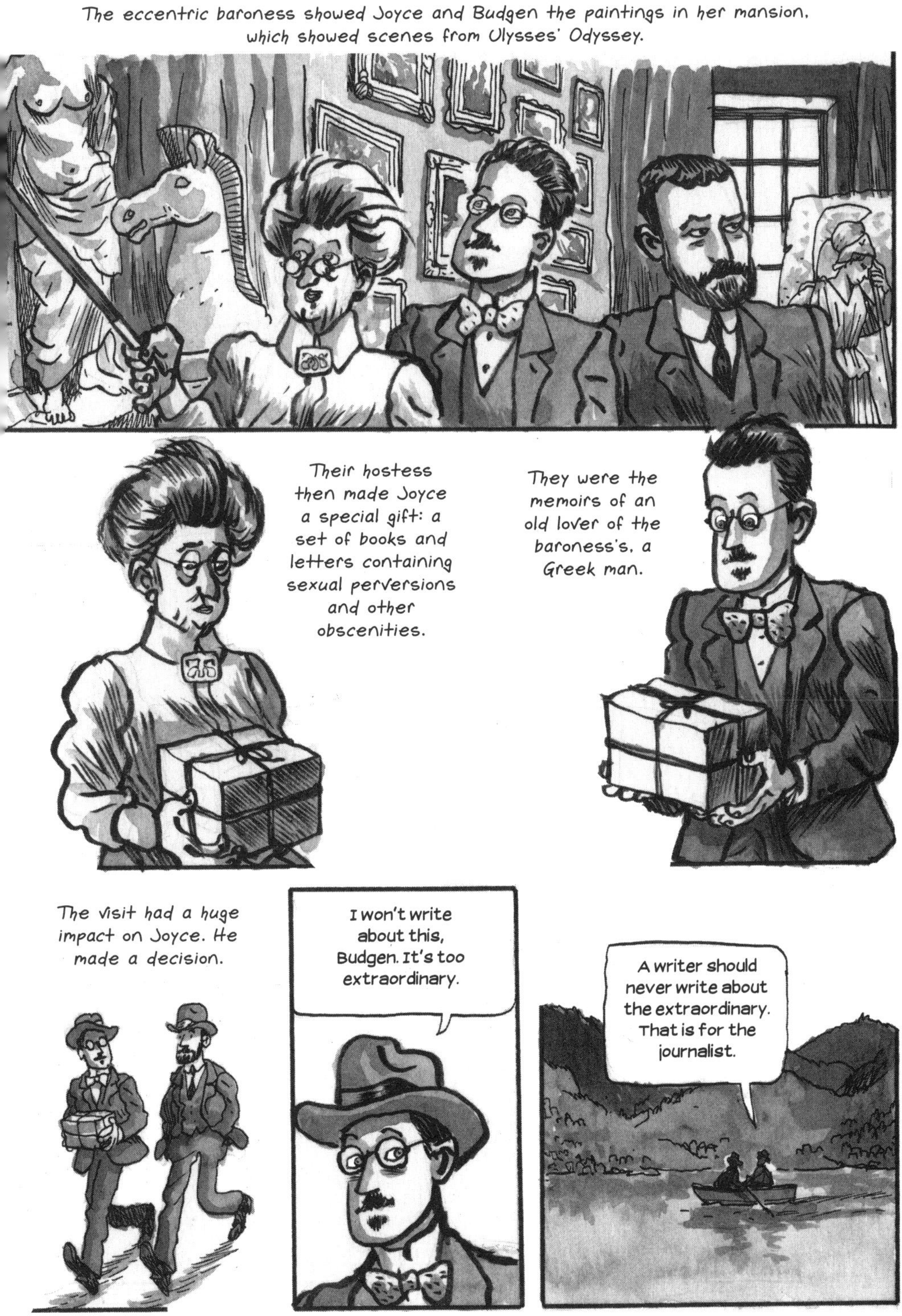
The eccentric baroness showed Joyce and Budgen the paintings in her mansion, which showed scenes from Ulysses' Odyssey.
Their hostess then made Joyce a special gift: a set of books and letters containing sexual perversions and other obscenities.
They were the memoirs of an old lover of the baroness's, a Greek man.
The visit had a huge impact on Joyce. He made a decision.
I won't write about this, Budgen. It's too extraordinary.
A writer should never write about the extraordinary. That is for the journalist.

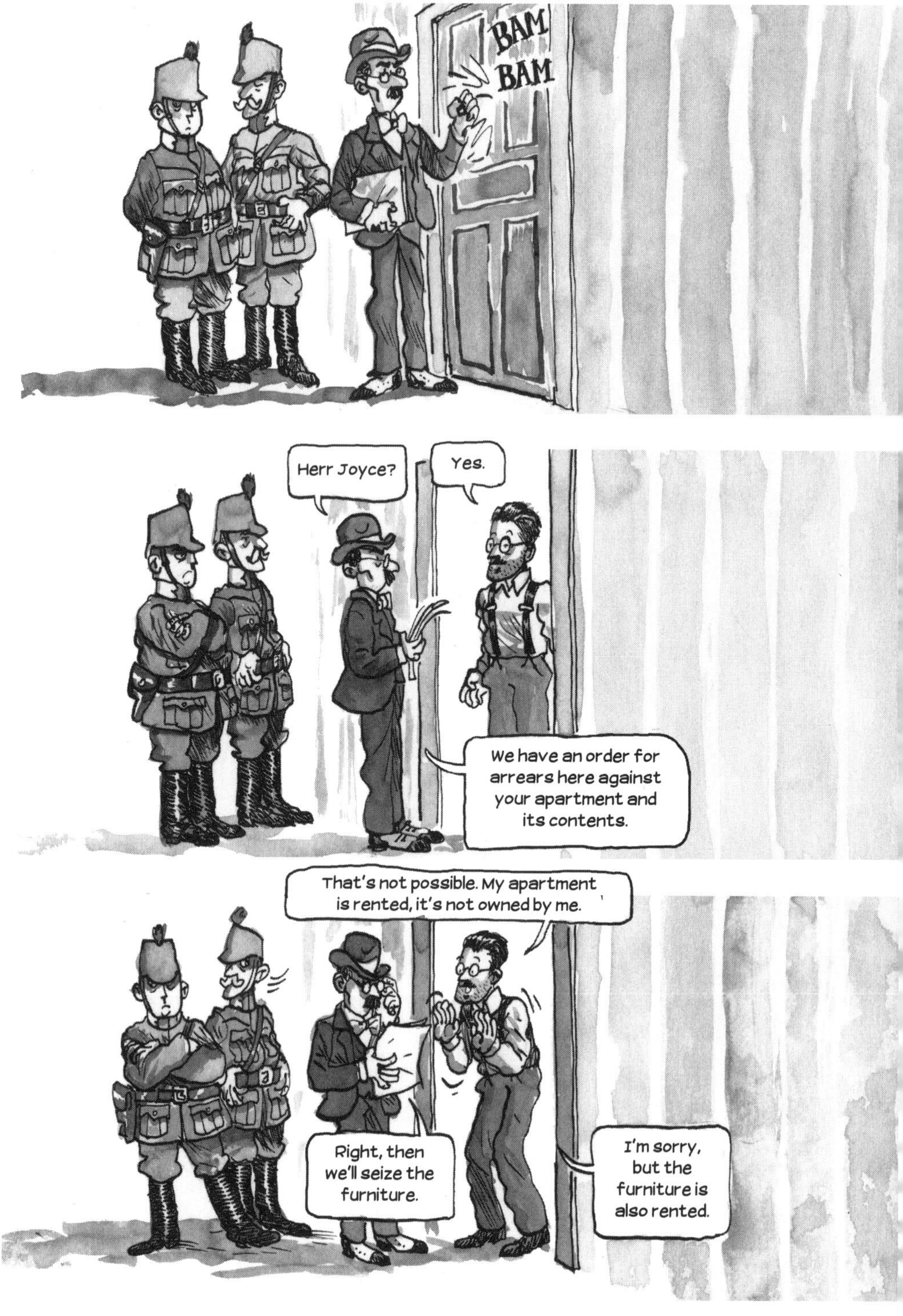
BAM
BAM
Herr Joyce?
Yes.
We have an order for arrears here against your apartment and its contents.
That's not possible. My apartment is rented, it's not owned by me.
Right, then we'll seize the furniture.
I'm sorry, but the furniture is also rented.

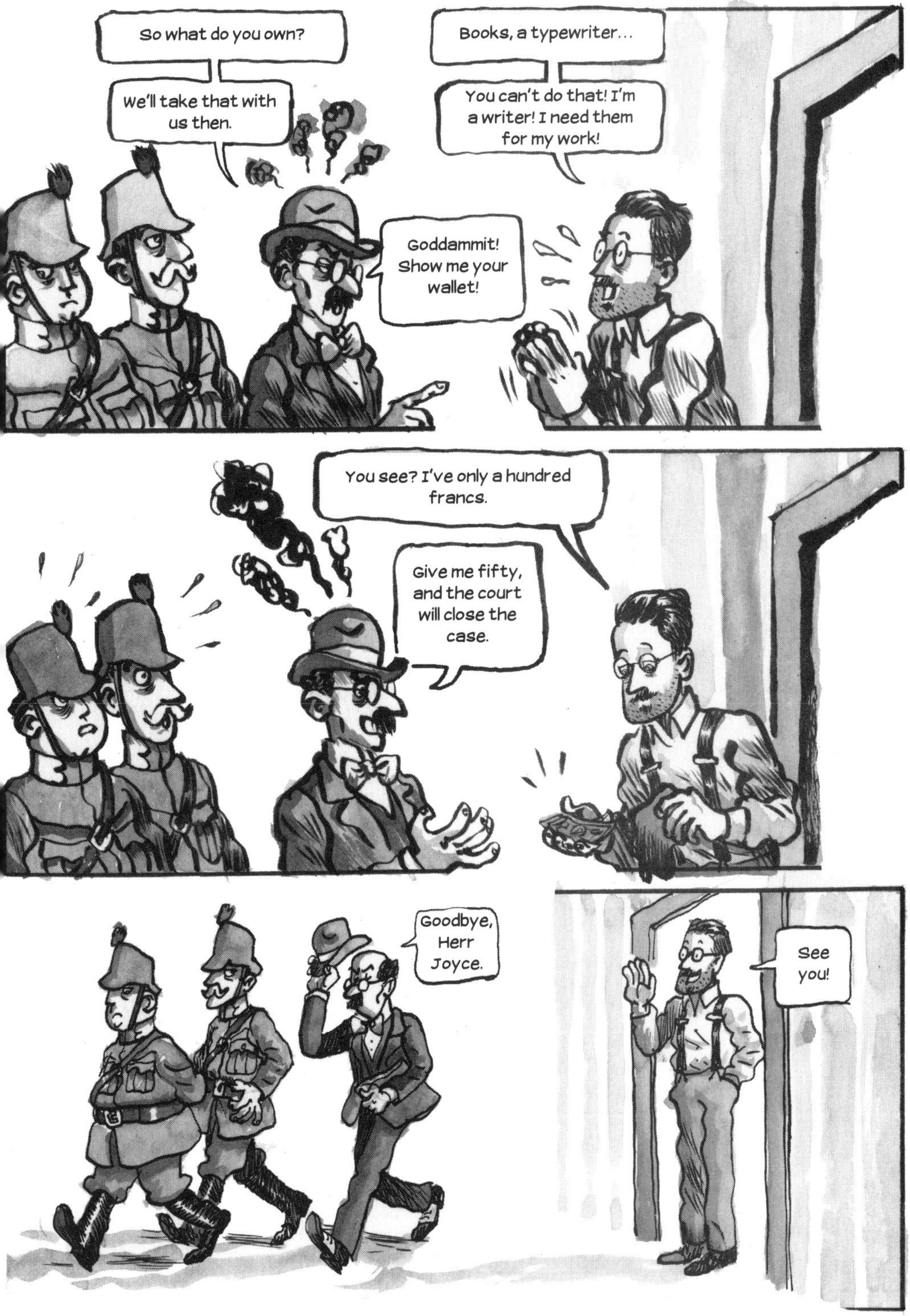
So what do you own?
We'll take that with us then.
Books, a typewriter...
You can't do that! I'm a writer! I need them for my work!
Goddammit! Show me your wallet!
You see? I've only a hundred francs.
Give me fifty, and the court will close the case.
Goodbye, Herr Joyce.
See you!

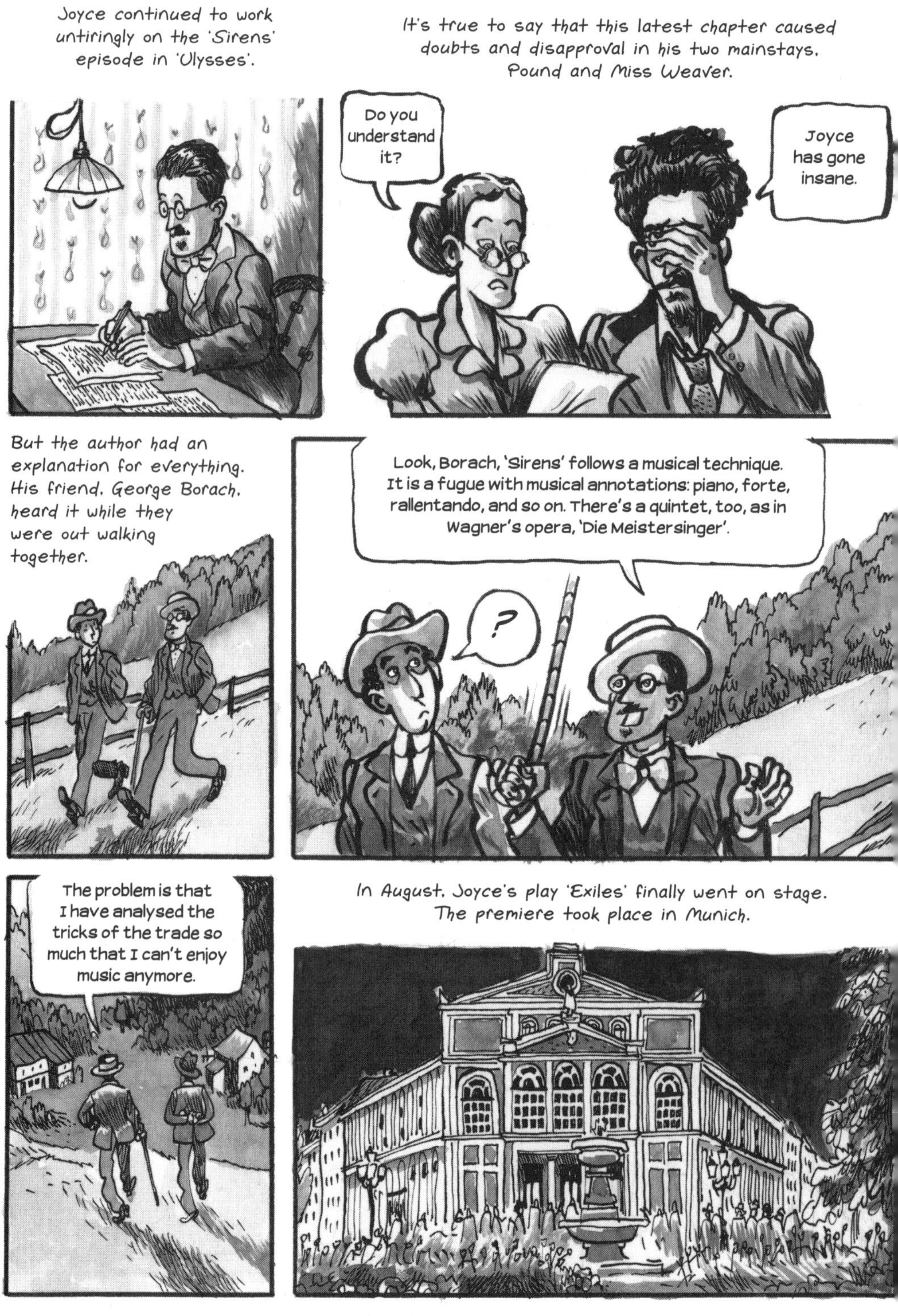
Joyce continued to work untiringly on the 'Sirens' episode in 'Ulysses'.
It's true to say that this latest chapter caused doubts and disapproval in his two mainstays, Pound and Miss Weaver.
Do you understand it?
Joyce has gone insane.
But the author had an explanation for everything. His friend, George Borach, heard it while they were out walking together.
Look, Borach, 'Sirens' follows a musical technique. It is a fugue with musical annotations: piano, forte, rallentando, and so on. There's a quintet, too, as in Wagner's opera, 'Die Meistersinger'.
?
The problem is that I have analysed the tricks of the trade so much that I can't enjoy music anymore.
In August, Joyce's play 'Exiles' finally went on stage. The premiere took place in Munich.

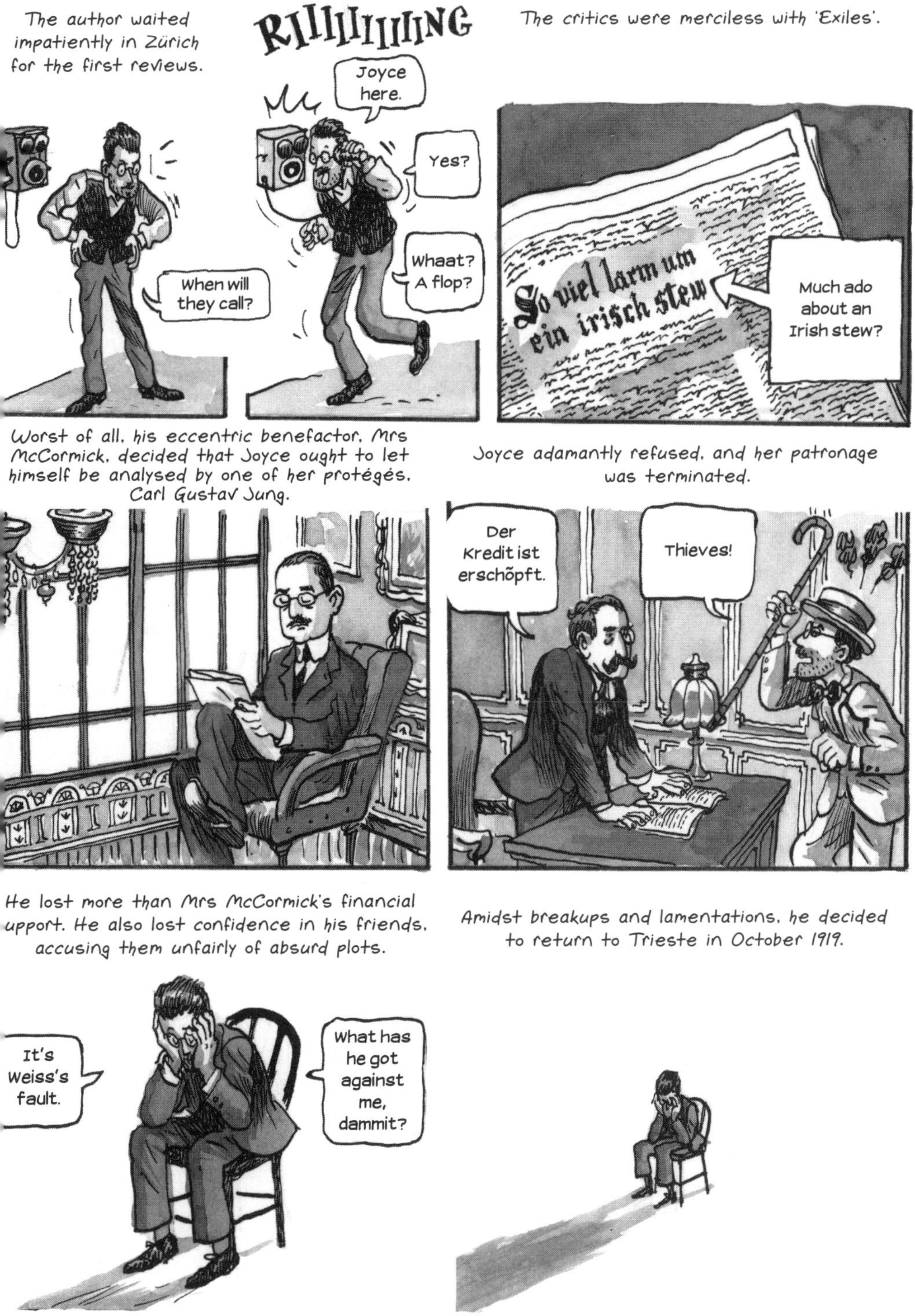
The author waited impatiently in Zürich for the first reviews.
RIIIIIIIIING
Joyce here.
When will they call?
Yes?
Whaat? A flop?
The critics were merciless with 'Exiles'.
So viel larm um ein irisch stew
Much ado about an Irish stew?
Worst of all, his eccentric benefactor, Mrs McCormick, decided that Joyce ought to let himself be analysed by one of her protégés, Carl Gustav Jung.
Joyce adamantly refused, and her patronage was terminated.
Der Kredit ist erschöpft.
Thieves!
He lost more than Mrs McCormick's financial upport. He also lost confidence in his friends, accusing them unfairly of absurd plots.
It's Weiss's fault.
What has he got against me, dammit?
Amidst breakups and lamentations, he decided to return to Trieste in October 1919.

Trieste had changed since Joyce had last seen it. It now belonged to the Kingdom of Italy, and had turned into a port of little importance.

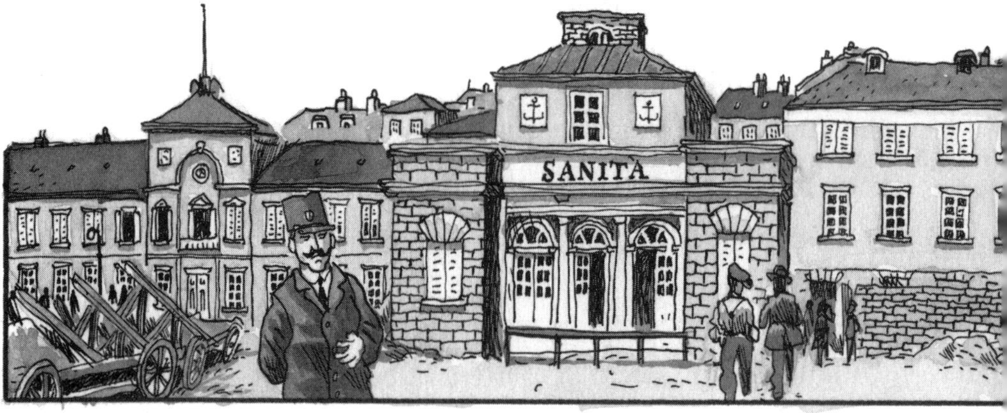
SANITA

Joyce too had changed: in the city of his happy earlier years, he now felt like a stranger.

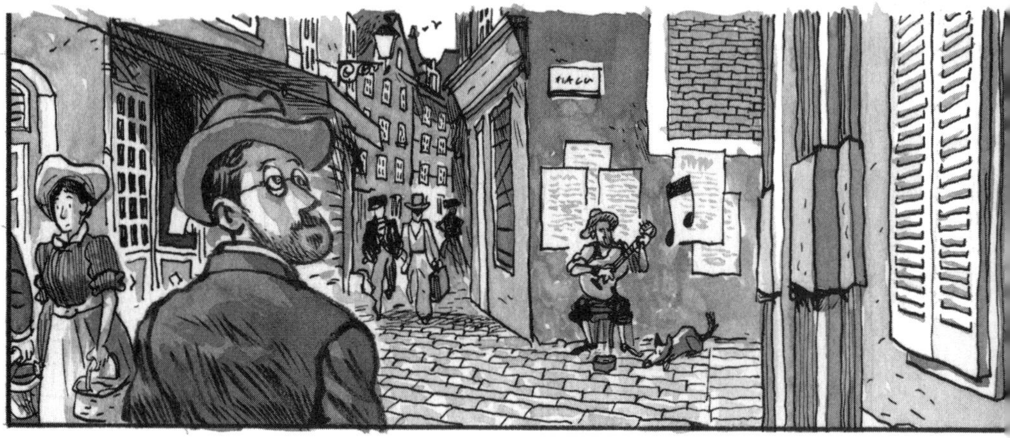

Crammed into a tiny apartment, together with his sister Eileen, her Czech husband, and ex-prisoner-of-war Stanislaus, the Joyces were hardly comfortable.

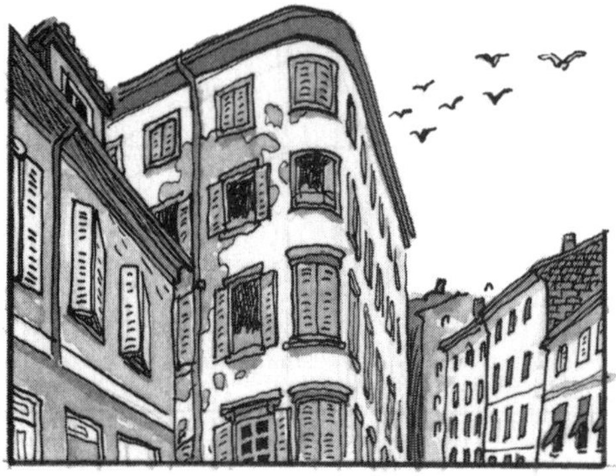

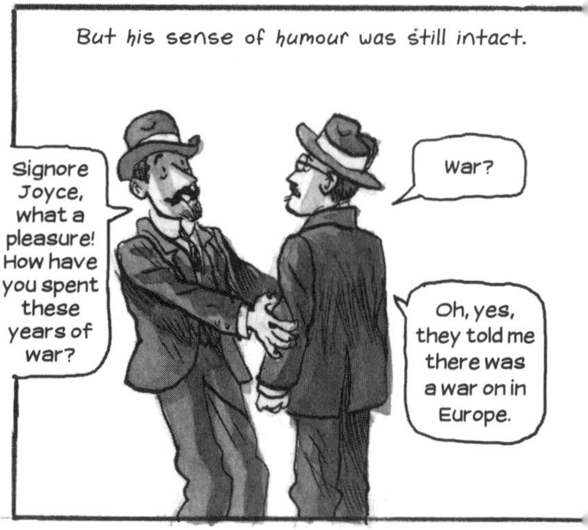
But his sense of humour was still intact.
Signore Joyce, what a pleasure! How have you spent these years of war?
War?
Oh, yes, they told me there was a war on in Europe.

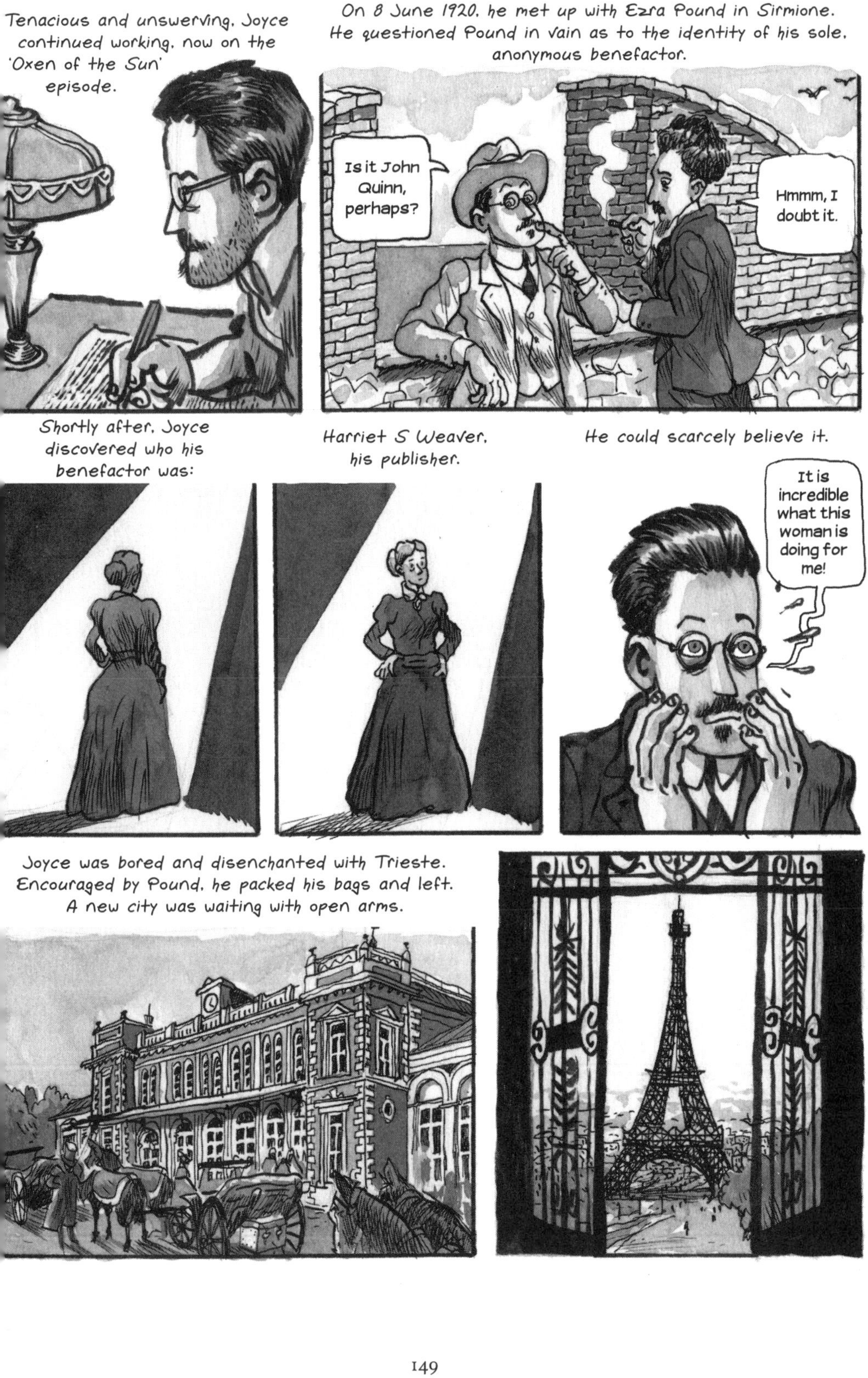
Tenacious and unswerving, Joyce continued working, now on the 'Oxen of the Sun' episode.
On 8 June 1920, he met up with Ezra Pound in Sirmione. He questioned Pound in vain as to the identity of his sole, anonymous benefactor.
Is it John Quinn, perhaps?
Hmmm, I doubt it.
Shortly after, Joyce discovered who his benefactor was:
Harriet S Weaver, his publisher.
He could scarcely believe it.
It is incredible what this woman is doing for me!
Joyce was bored and disenchanted with Trieste. Encouraged by Pound, he packed his bags and left. A new city was waiting with open arms.

Chapter V
Joyce and Company

In the Paris of 1920, James Joyce was a well-known writer.

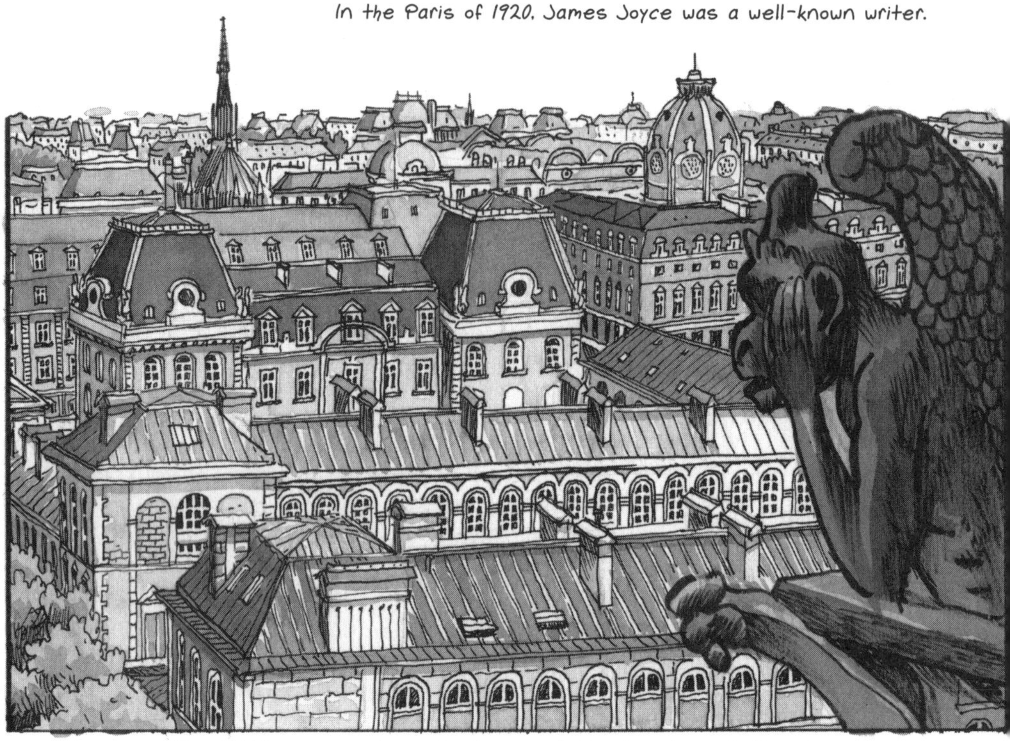

His arrival was eagerly awaited amongst the Parisian intelligentsia, and he soon made new friends.

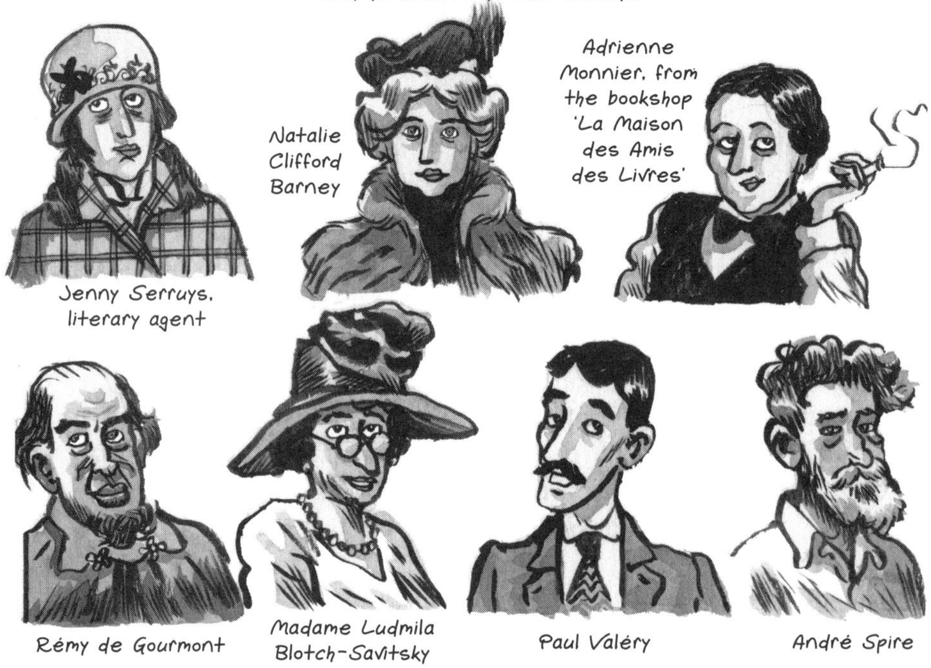

Jenny Serruys, literary agent
Natalie Clifford Barney
Adrienne Monnier, from the bookshop 'La Maison des Amis des Livres'
Rémy de Gourmont
Madame Ludmila Blotch-Savitsky
Paul Valéry
André Spire

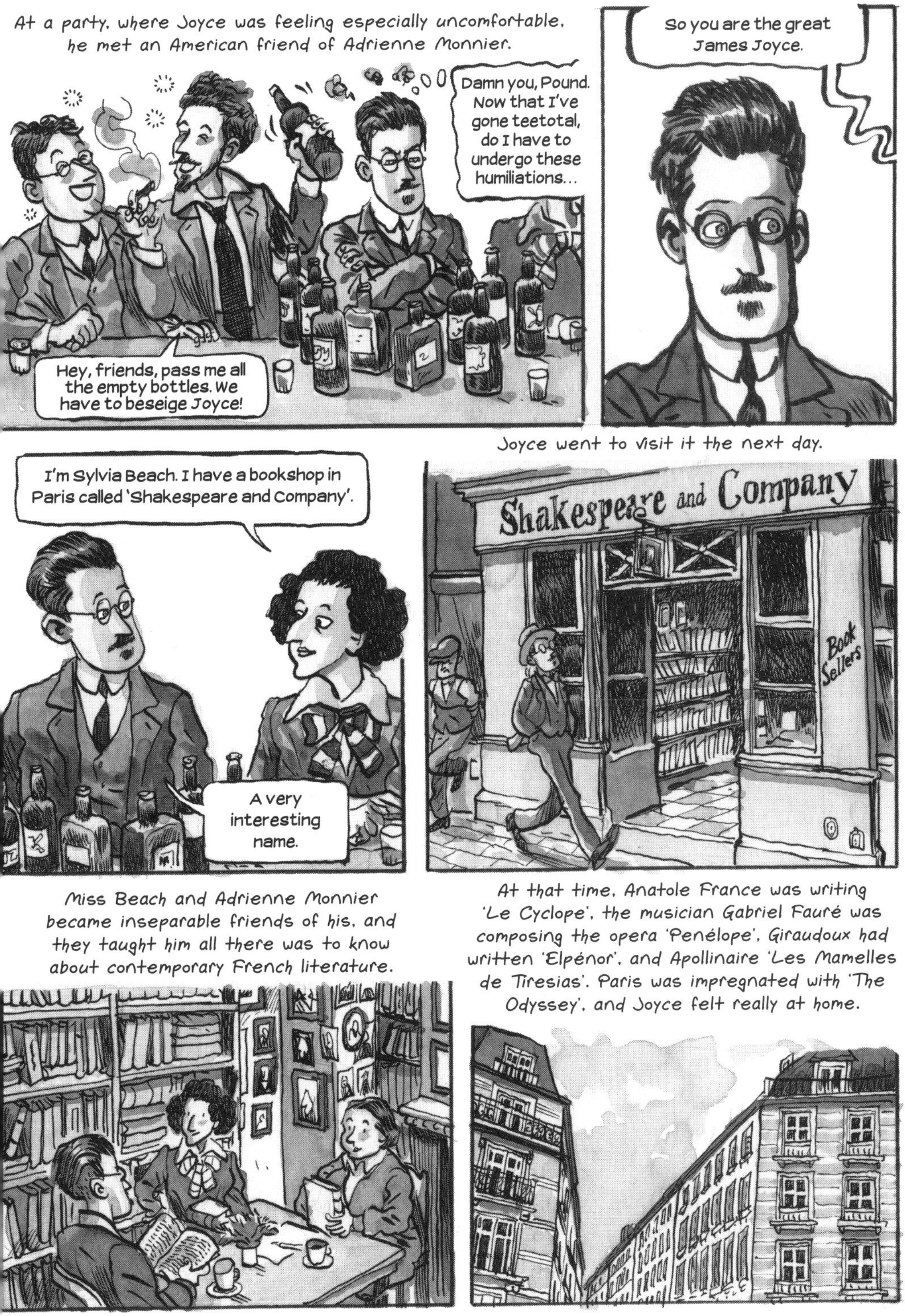

At a party, where Joyce was feeling especially uncomfortable, he met an American friend of Adrienne Monnier.
Hey, friends, pass me all the empty bottles. We have to beseige Joyce!
Damn you, Pound. Now that I've gone teetotal, do I have to undergo these humiliations...
So you are the great James Joyce.
I'm Sylvia Beach. I have a bookshop in Paris called 'Shakespeare and Company'.
A very interesting name.
Joyce went to visit it the next day.
Shakespeare and Company
Book Sellers
Miss Beach and Adrienne Monnier became inseparable friends of his, and they taught him all there was to know about contemporary French literature.
At that time, Anatole France was writing 'Le Cyclope', the musician Gabriel Fauré was composing the opera 'Penélope', Giraudoux had written 'Elpénor', and Apollinaire 'Les Mamelles de Tiresias'. Paris was impregnated with 'The Odyssey', and Joyce felt really at home.

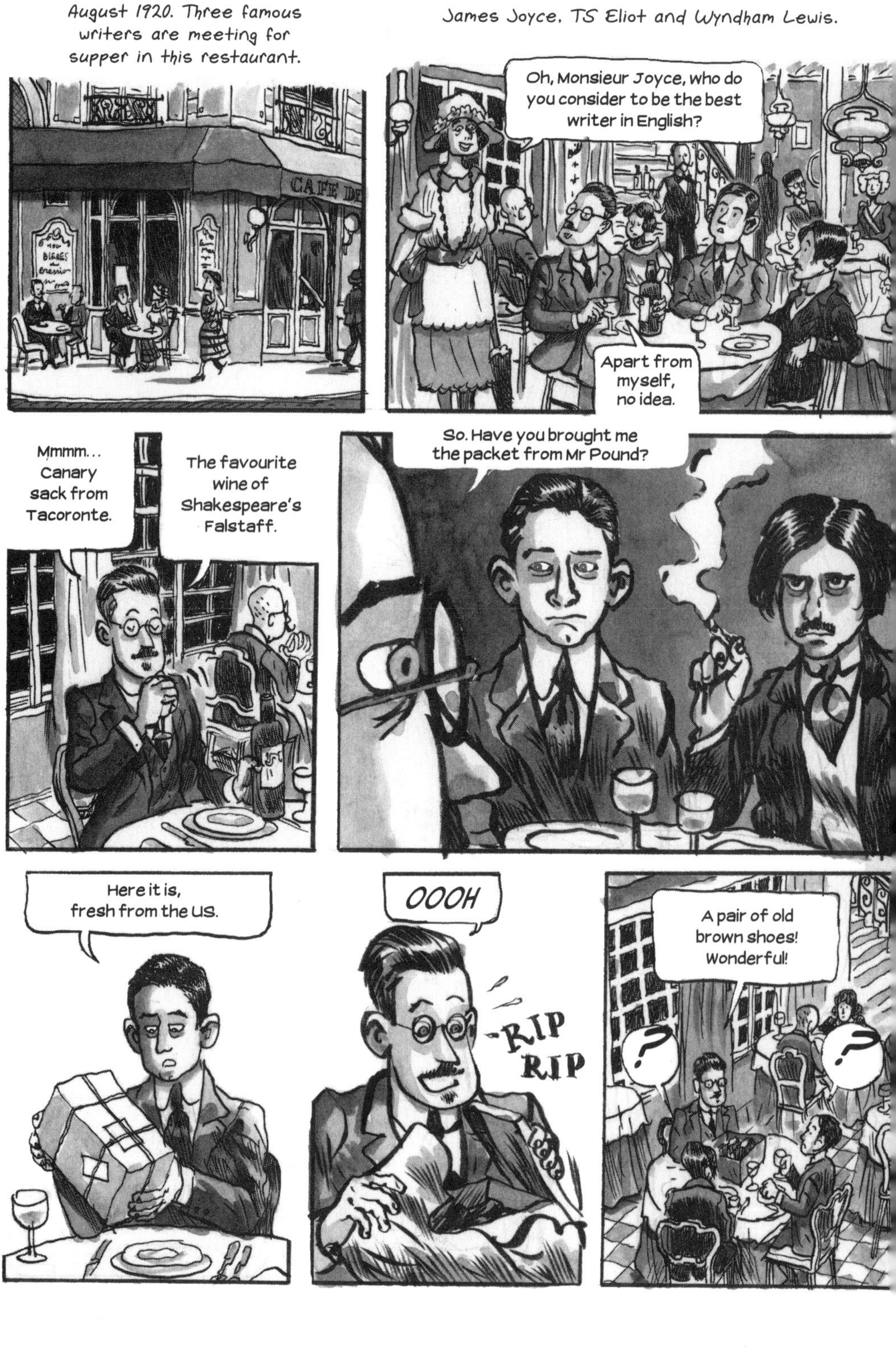
August 1920. Three famous writers are meeting for supper in this restaurant.
CAFE DE
James Joyce, TS Eliot and Wyndham Lewis.
Oh, Monsieur Joyce, who do you consider to be the best writer in English?
Apart from myself, no idea.
Mmmm... Canary sack from Tacoronte.
The favourite wine of Shakespeare's Falstaff.
So. Have you brought me the packet from Mr Pound?
Here it is, fresh from the US.
OOOH
RIP RIP
A pair of old brown shoes! Wonderful!

In spite of his busy life in Paris, Joyce missed his old Zürich friend, Frank Budgen. Budgen couldn't make up his mind to visit Paris, so Joyce wrote him an ironic letter, saying something like this:

'My dear Budgen:

Travelling is easy, you just need to get into a train carriage, which is usually behind the engine. Open the door and get in carefully with your luggage. Someone with a cap will come by and give you a piece of cardboard in exchange for money. If you look at this, you'll see a word printed on it: PARIS. Well, this is the name of the station where I live. Sit down before the train starts to move, and that's it.
If you follow my instructions, God willing, we'll meet again shortly.

Yours ever,

J.J.'

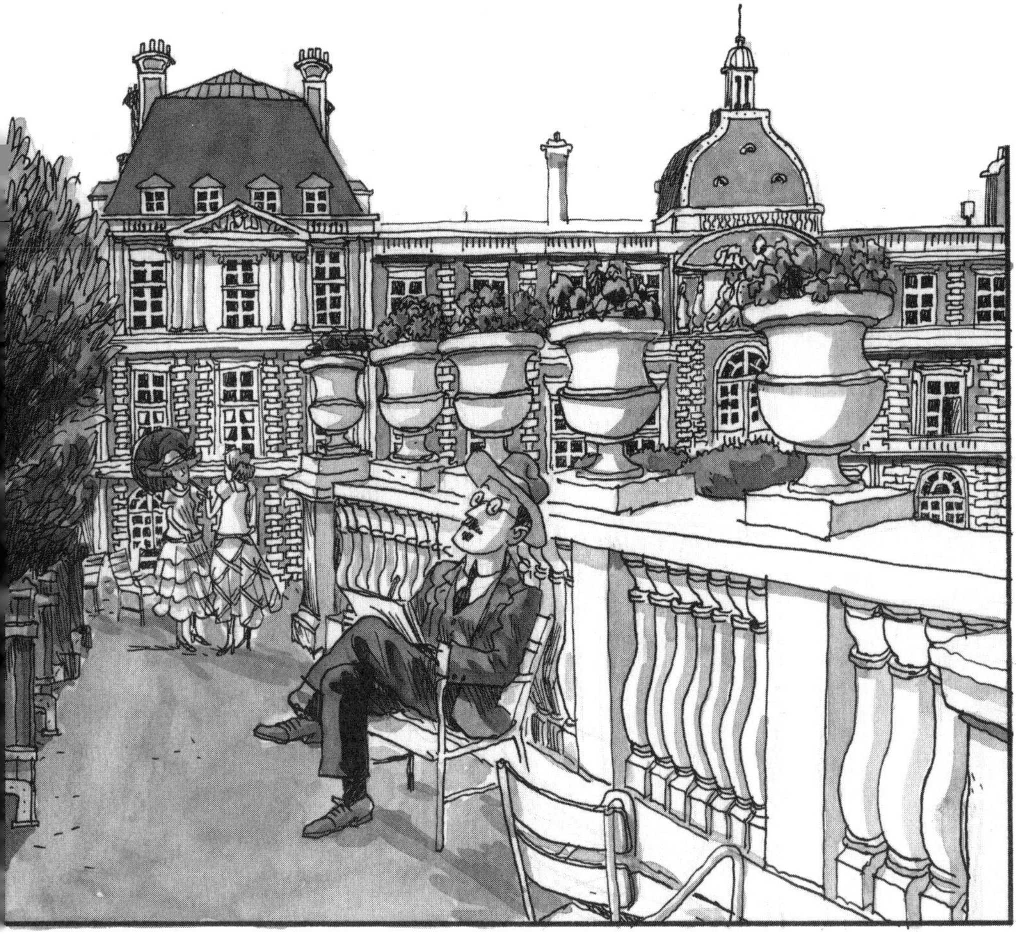

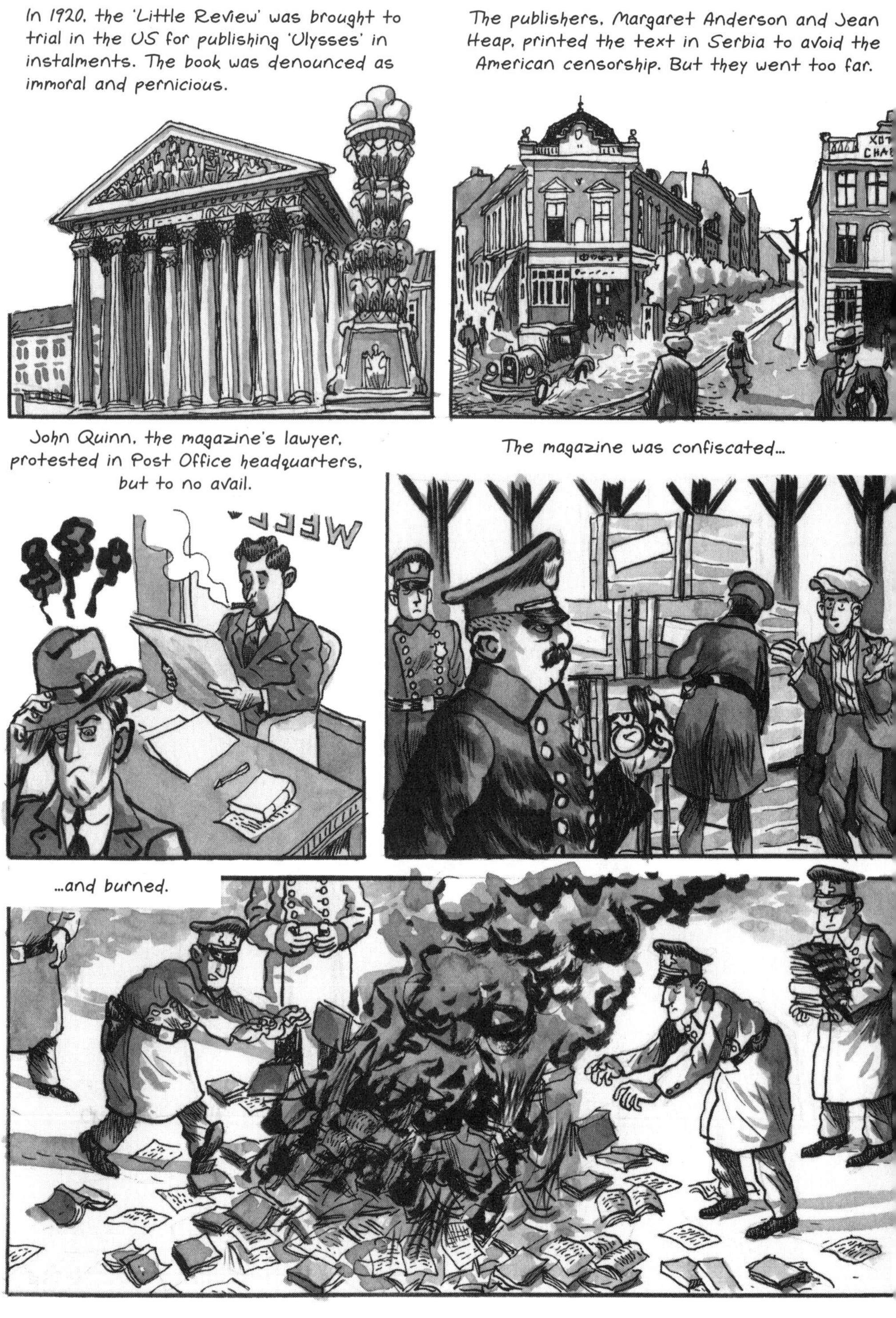
In 1920, the 'Little Review' was brought to trial in the US for publishing 'Ulysses' in instalments. The book was denounced as immoral and pernicious.
The publishers, Margaret Anderson and Jean Heap, printed the text in Serbia to avoid the American censorship. But they went too far.
John Quinn, the magazine's lawyer, protested in Post Office headquarters, but to no avail.
The magazine was confiscated...
...and burned.

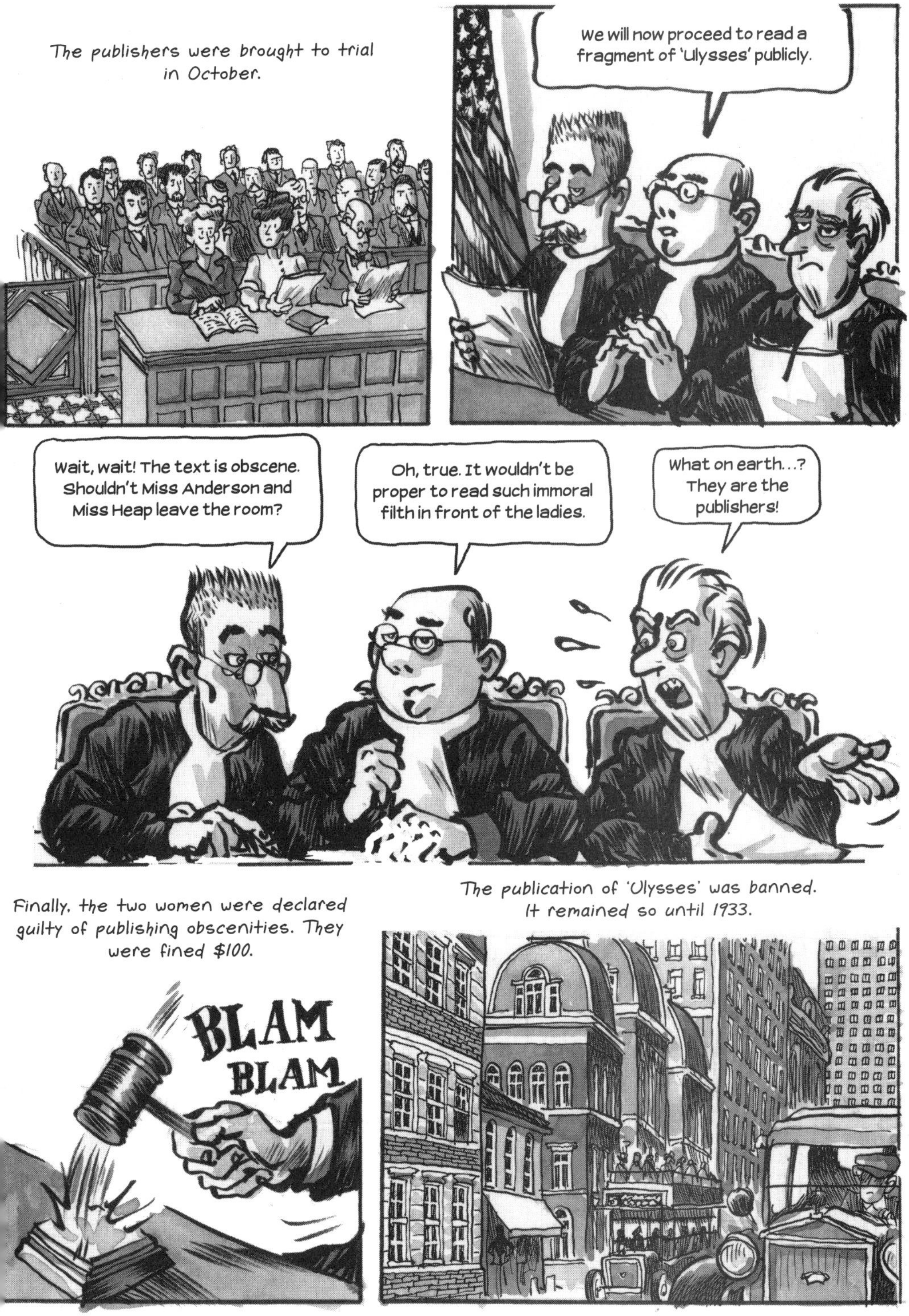
The publishers were brought to trial in October.
We will now proceed to read a fragment of 'Ulysses' publicly.
Wait, wait! The text is obscene. Shouldn't Miss Anderson and Miss Heap leave the room?
Oh, true. It wouldn't be proper to read such immoral filth in front of the ladies.
What on earth...? They are the publishers!
Finally, the two women were declared guilty of publishing obscenities. They were fined $100.
BLAM
BLAM
The publication of 'Ulysses' was banned. It remained so until 1933.

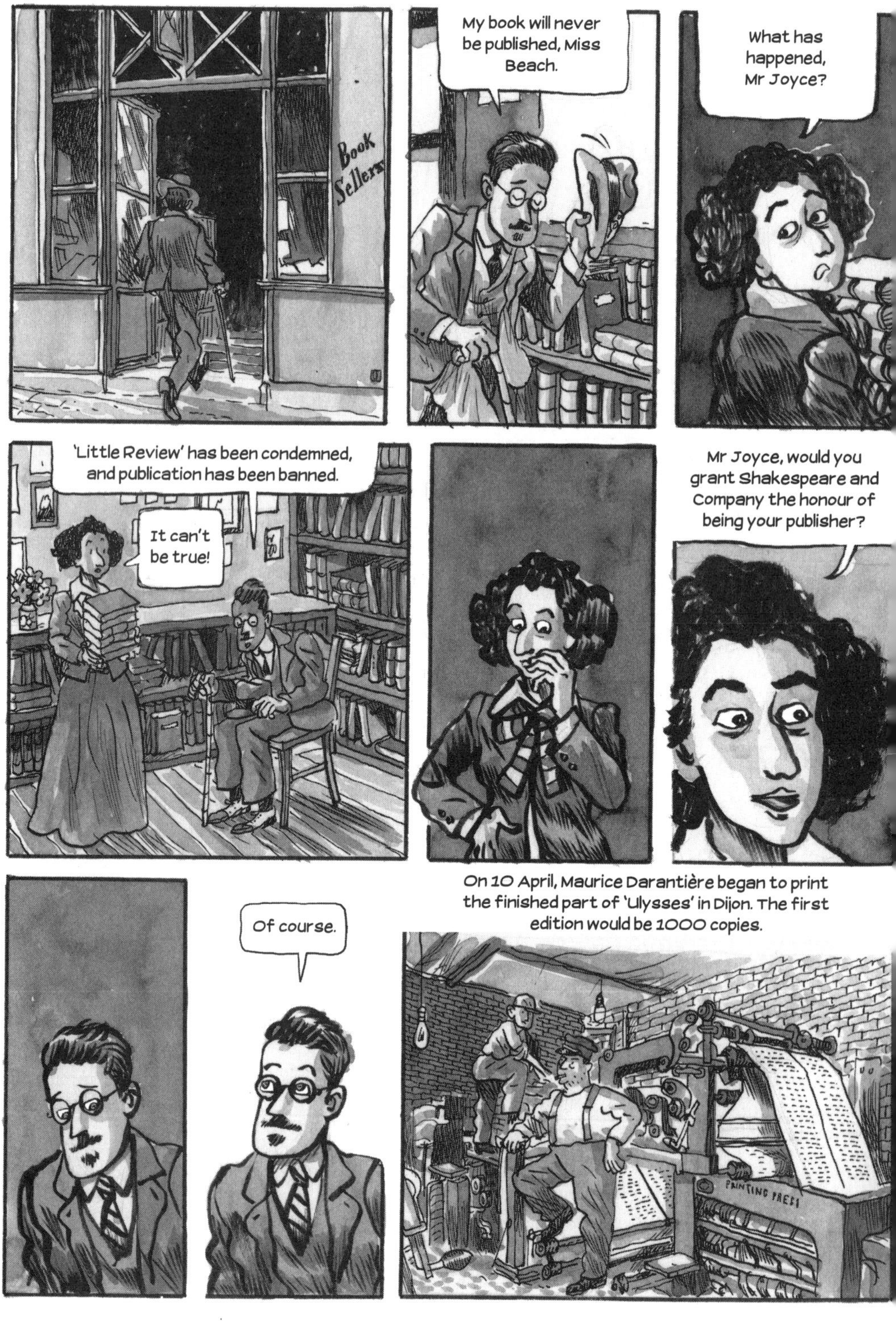

Book Sellers
My book will never be published, Miss Beach.
What has happened, Mr Joyce?
'Little Review' has been condemned, and publication has been banned.
It can't be true!
Mr Joyce, would you grant Shakespeare and Company the honour of being your publisher?
Of course.
On 10 April, Maurice Darantière began to print the finished part of 'Ulysses' in Dijon. The first edition would be 1000 copies.
PRINTING PRESS

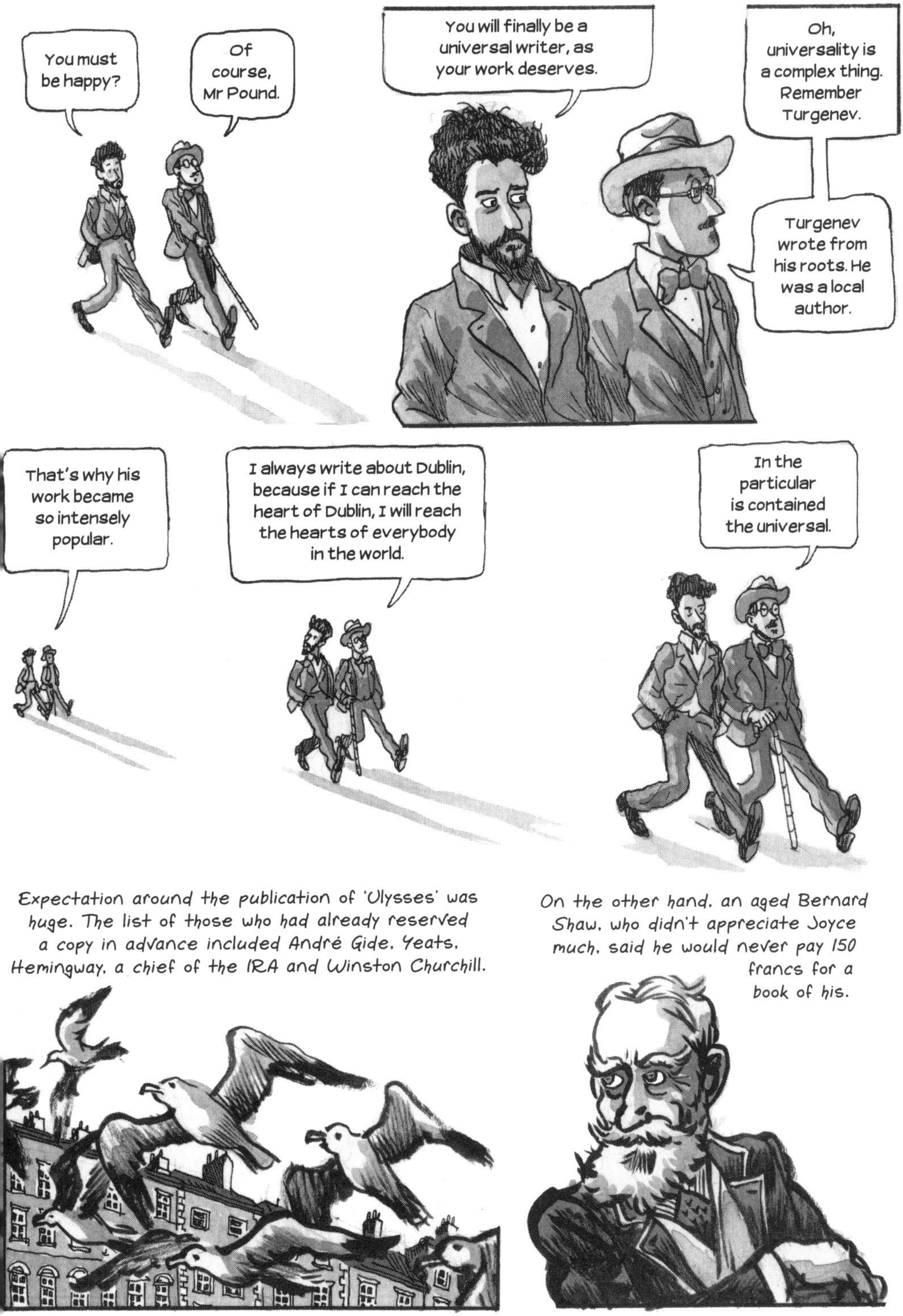
You must be happy?
Of course, Mr Pound.
You will finally be a universal writer, as your work deserves.
Oh, universality is a complex thing. Remember Turgenev.
Turgenev wrote from his roots. He was a local author.
That's why his work became so intensely popular.
I always write about Dublin, because if I can reach the heart of Dublin, I will reach the hearts of everybody in the world.
In the particular is contained the universal.
Expectation around the publication of 'Ulysses' was huge. The list of those who had already reserved a copy in advance included André Gide, Yeats, Hemingway, a chief of the IRA and Winston Churchill.
On the other hand, an aged Bernard Shaw, who didn't appreciate Joyce much, said he would never pay 150 francs for a book of his.

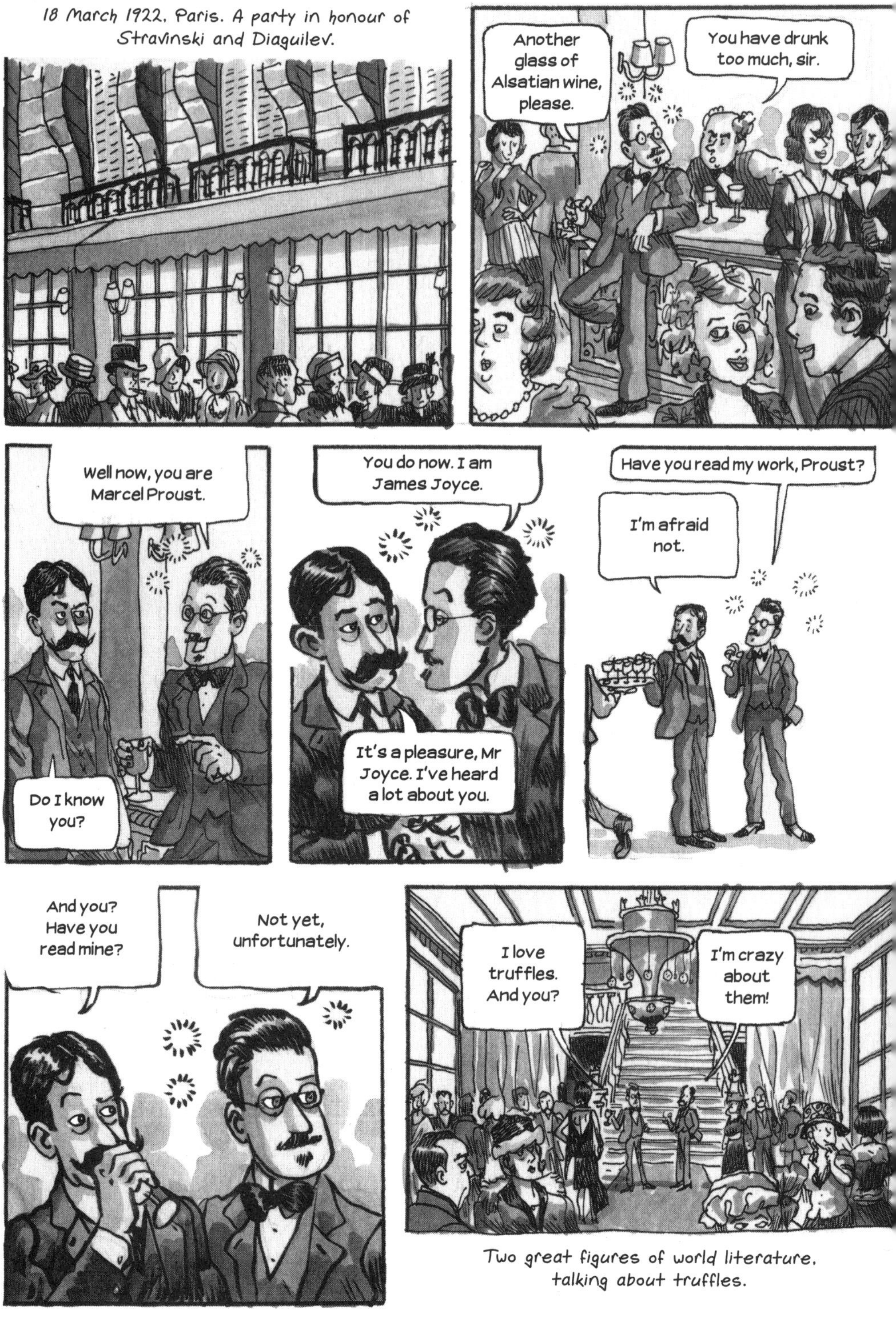
18 March 1922. Paris. A party in honour of Stravinski and Diaguilev.
Another glass of Alsatian wine, please.
You have drunk too much, sir.
Well now, you are Marcel Proust.
Do I know you?
You do now. I am James Joyce.
It's a pleasure, Mr Joyce. I've heard a lot about you.
Have you read my work, Proust?
I'm afraid not.
And you? Have you read mine?
Not yet, unfortunately.
I love truffles. And you?
I'm crazy about them!
Two great figures of world literature, talking about truffles.

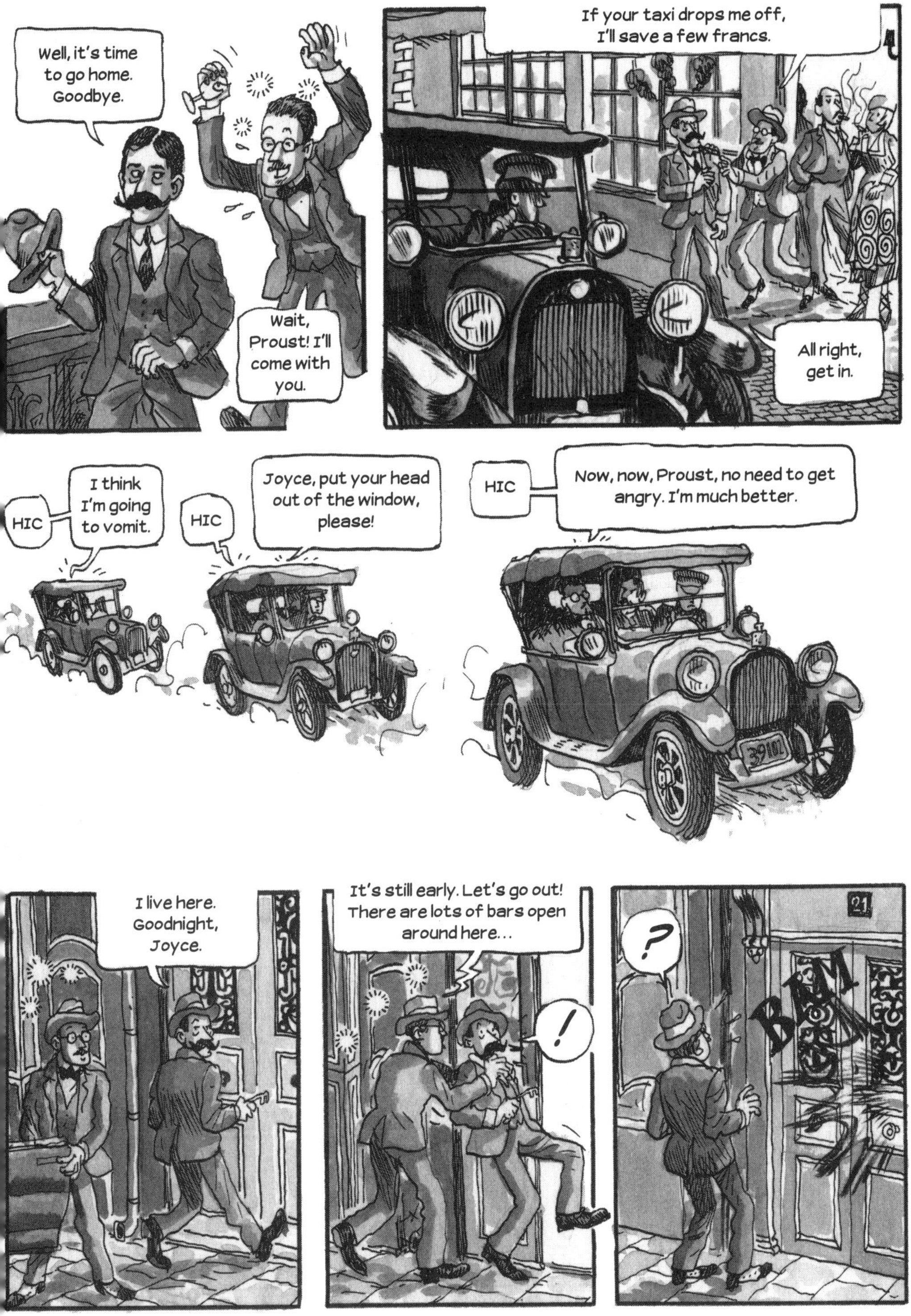
Well, it's time to go home. Goodbye.
Wait, Proust! I'll come with you.
If your taxi drops me off, I'll save a few francs.
All right, get in.
HIC
I think I'm going to vomit.
HIC
Joyce, put your head out of the window, please!
HIC
Now, now, Proust, no need to get angry. I'm much better.
I live here. Goodnight, Joyce.
It's still early. Let's go out! There are lots of bars open around here...
!
?
BAM
21

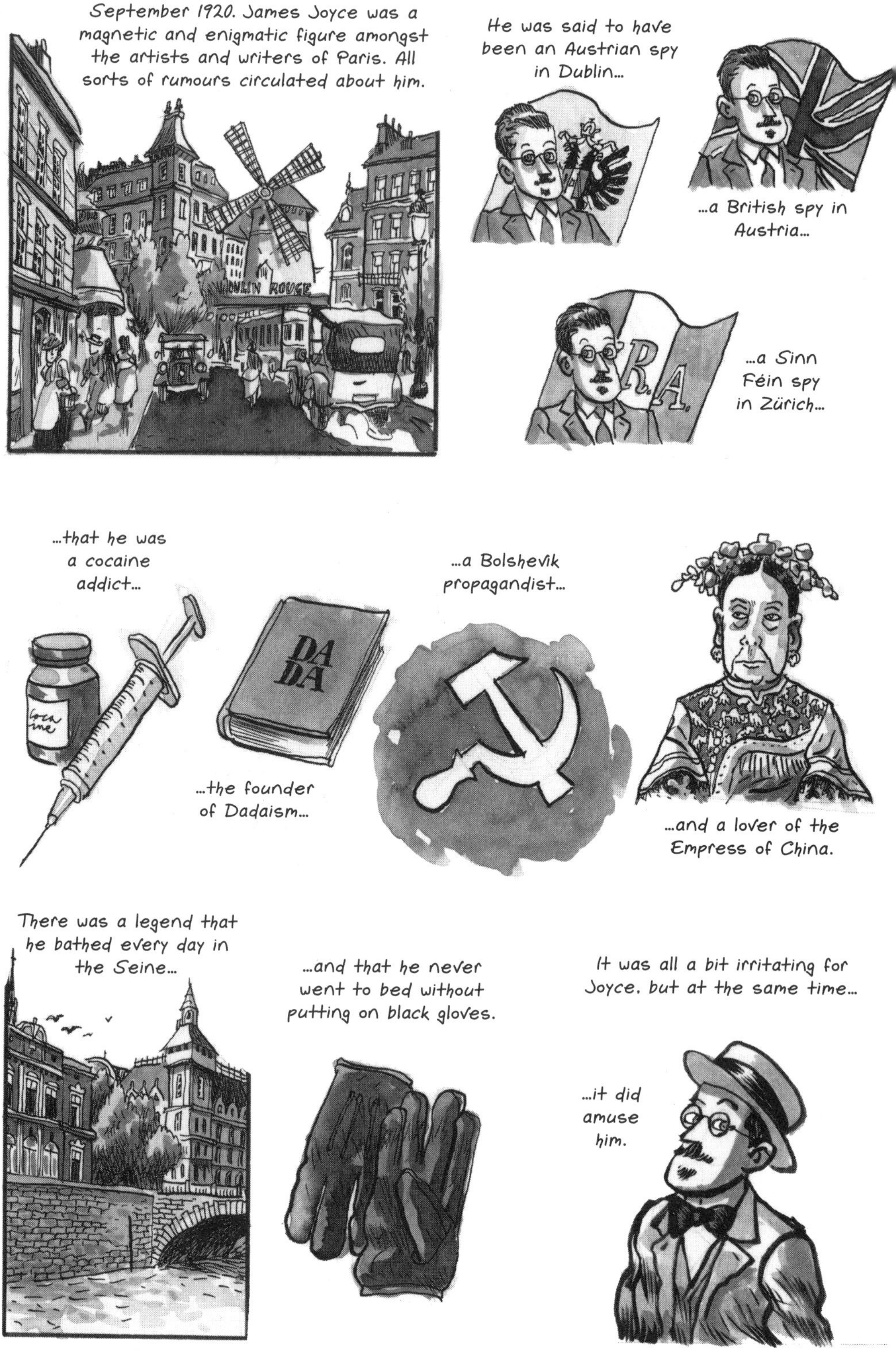
September 1920. James Joyce was a magnetic and enigmatic figure amongst the artists and writers of Paris. All sorts of rumours circulated about him.
MOULIN ROUGE
He was said to have been an Austrian spy in Dublin...
...a British spy in Austria...
R. A.
...a Sinn Féin spy in Zürich...
...that he was a cocaine addict...
Cocaine
DA DA
...the founder of Dadaism...
...a Bolshevik propagandist...
...and a lover of the Empress of China.
There was a legend that he bathed every day in the Seine...
...and that he never went to bed without putting on black gloves.
It was all a bit irritating for Joyce, but at the same time...
...it did amuse him.

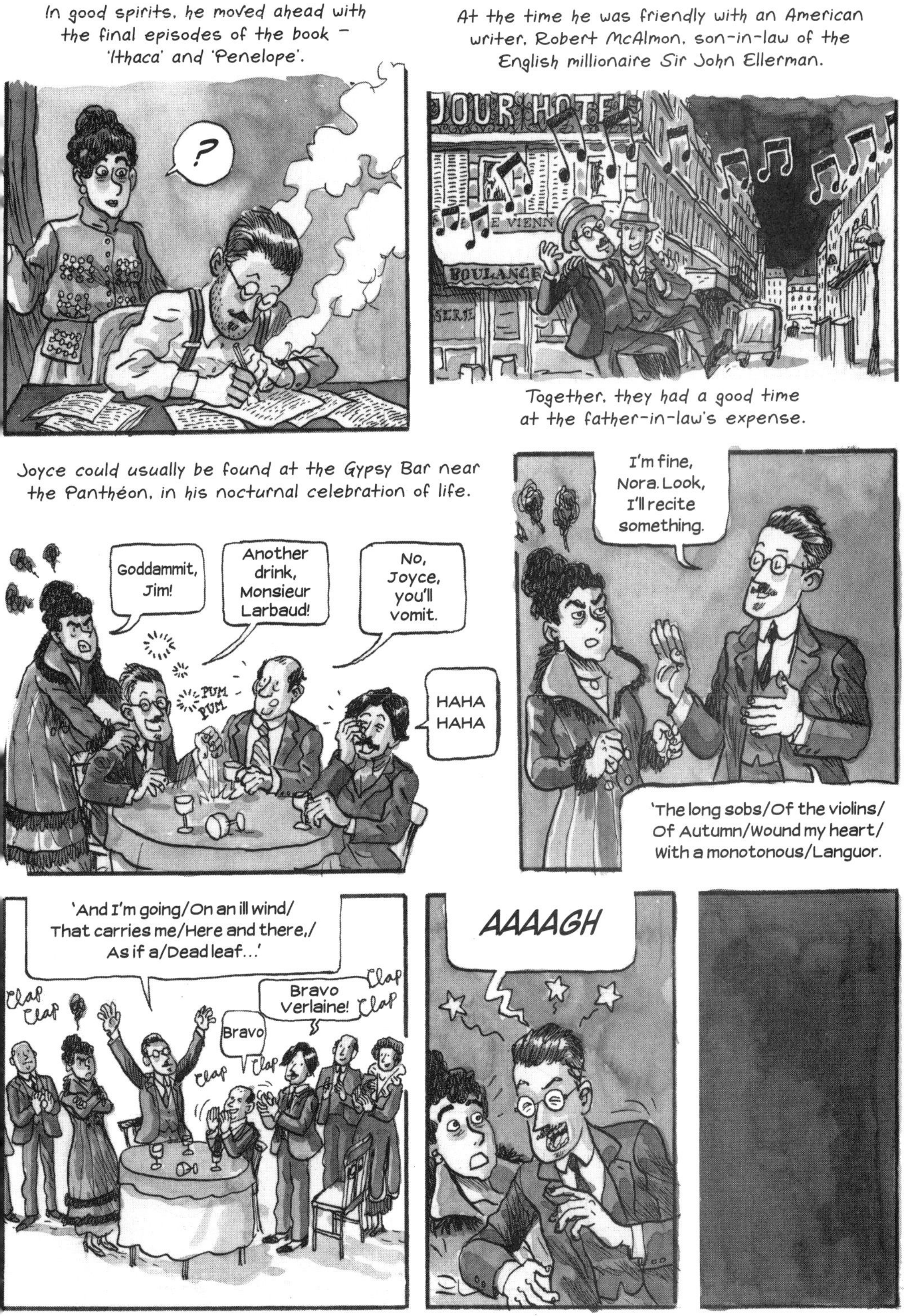
In good spirits, he moved ahead with the final episodes of the book – 'Ithaca' and 'Penelope'.
?
At the time he was friendly with an American writer, Robert McAlmon, son-in-law of the English millionaire Sir John Ellerman.
JOUR HOTEL
E VIENN
BOULANGE
Together, they had a good time at the father-in-law's expense.
Joyce could usually be found at the Gypsy Bar near the Panthéon, in his nocturnal celebration of life.
Goddammit, Jim!
Another drink, Monsieur Larbaud!
No, Joyce, you'll vomit.
PUM PUM
HAHA HAHA
I'm fine, Nora. Look, I'll recite something.
'The long sobs/Of the violins/Of Autumn/Wound my heart/With a monotonous/Languor.
'And I'm going/On an ill wind/That carries me/Here and there,/As if a/Dead leaf...'
Clap Clap
Bravo
Bravo Verlaine!
Clap Clap
Clap
Clap
AAAAGH

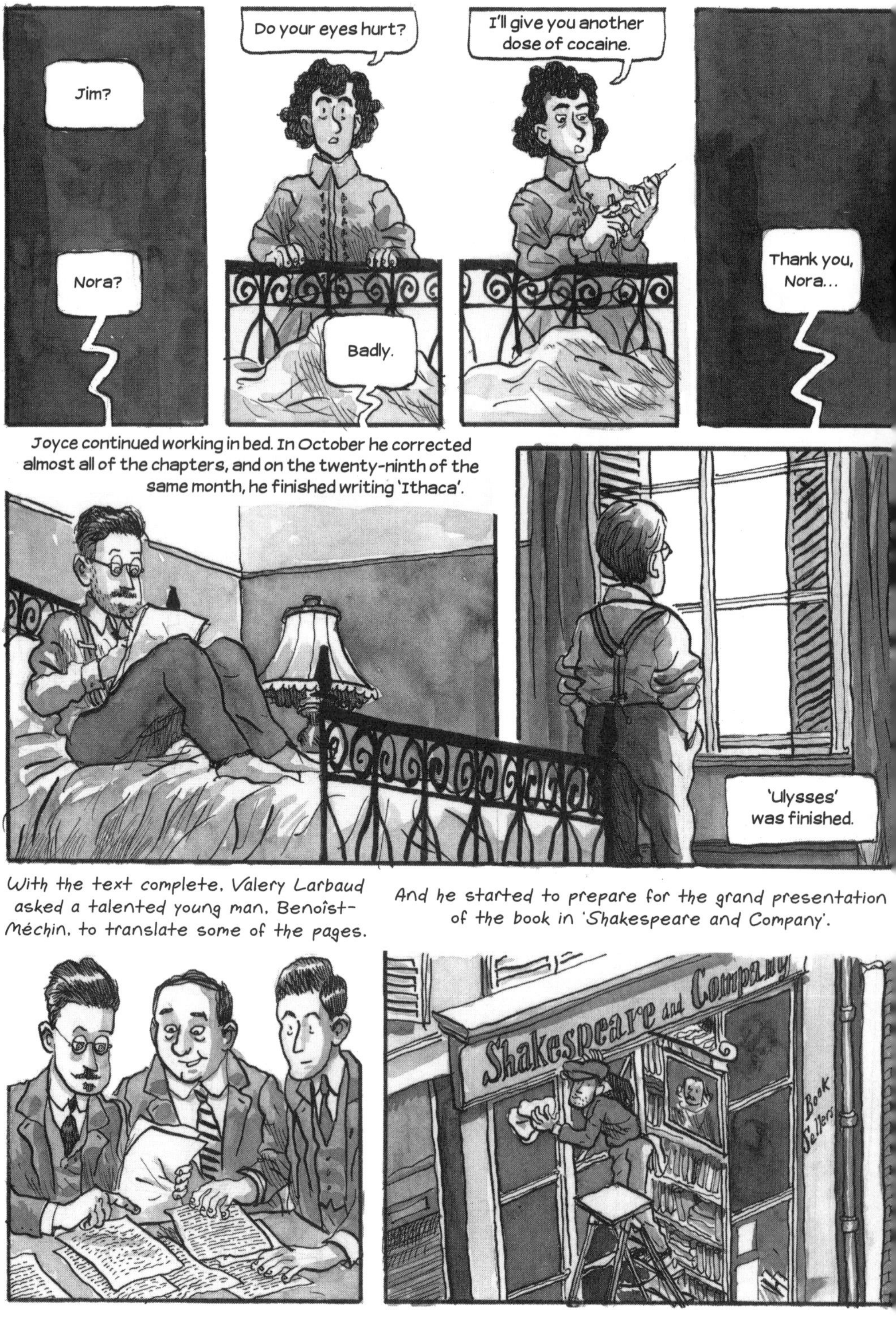

Jim?
Nora?
Do your eyes hurt?
Badly.
I'll give you another dose of cocaine.
Thank you, Nora...
Joyce continued working in bed. In October he corrected almost all of the chapters, and on the twenty-ninth of the same month, he finished writing 'Ithaca'.
'Ulysses' was finished.
With the text complete, Valery Larbaud asked a talented young man, Benoîst-Méchin, to translate some of the pages.
And he started to prepare for the grand presentation of the book in 'Shakespeare and Company'.
Shakespeare and Company
Book Sellers

On 7 December, almost 250 people squeezed into Sylvia Beach's bookshop.

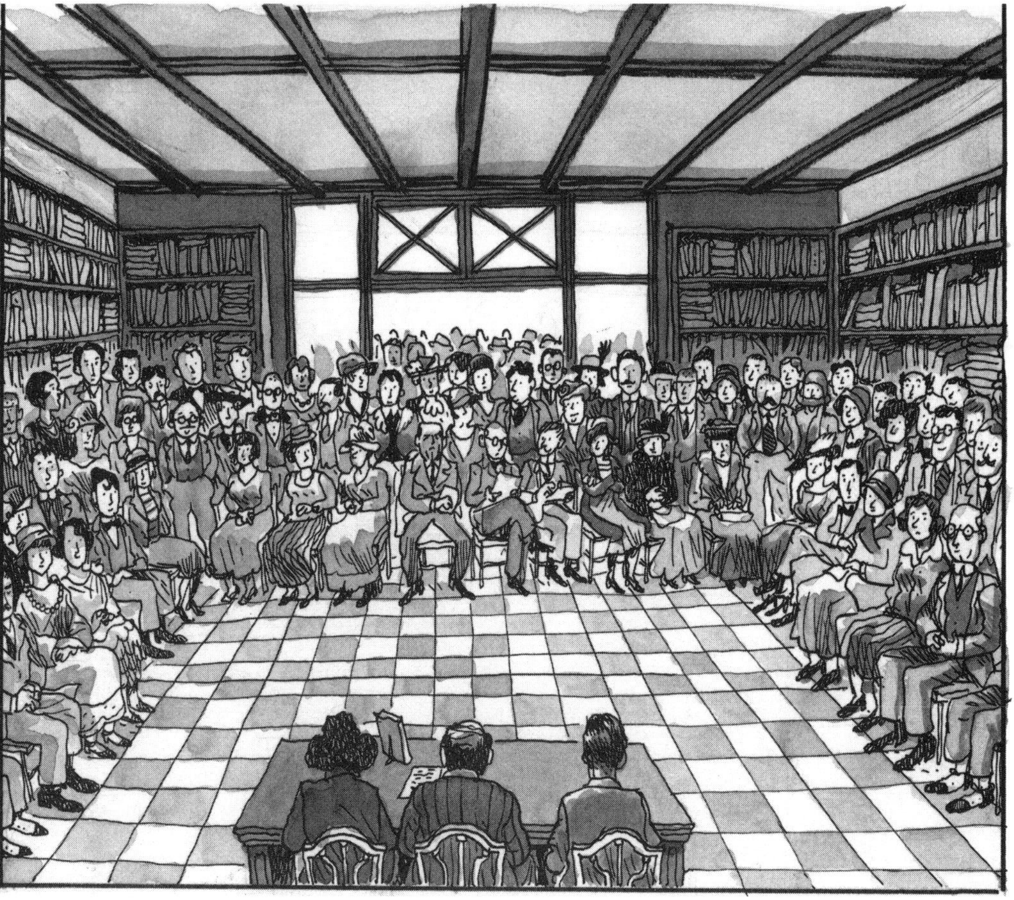

Larbaud spoke of Joyce's work, and of the complexity of 'Ulysses'...

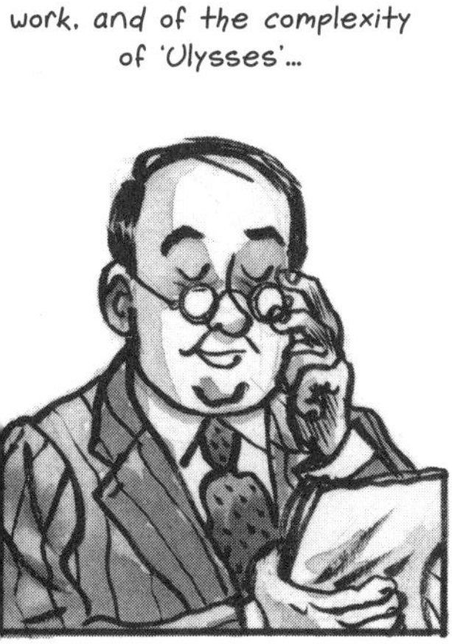

An actor recited some fragments from the book...

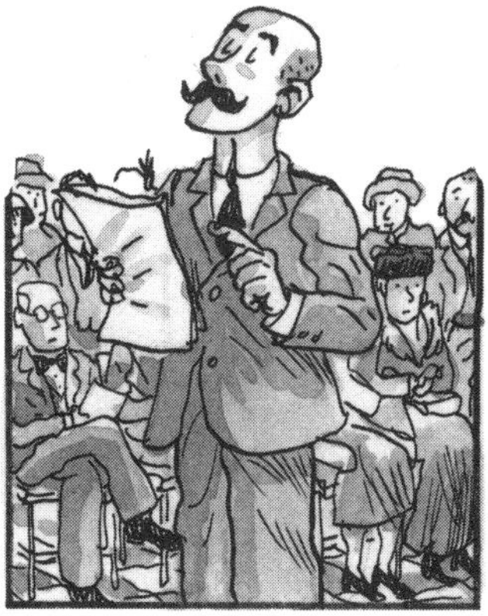

...and finally, confused and blushing, Joyce received the enthusiastic applause.

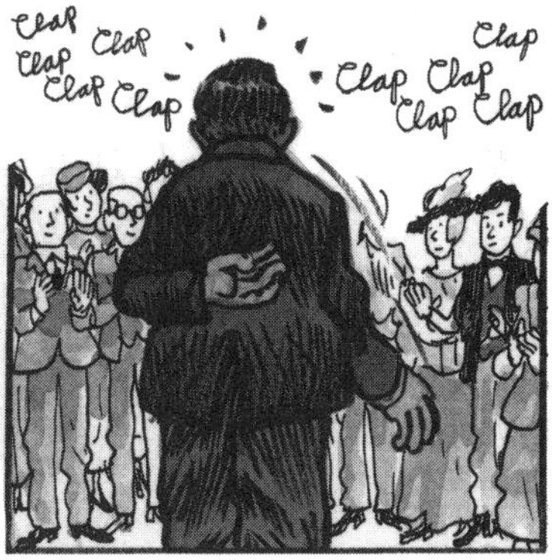
Clap Clap Clap Clap Clap
Clap Clap Clap Clap Clap

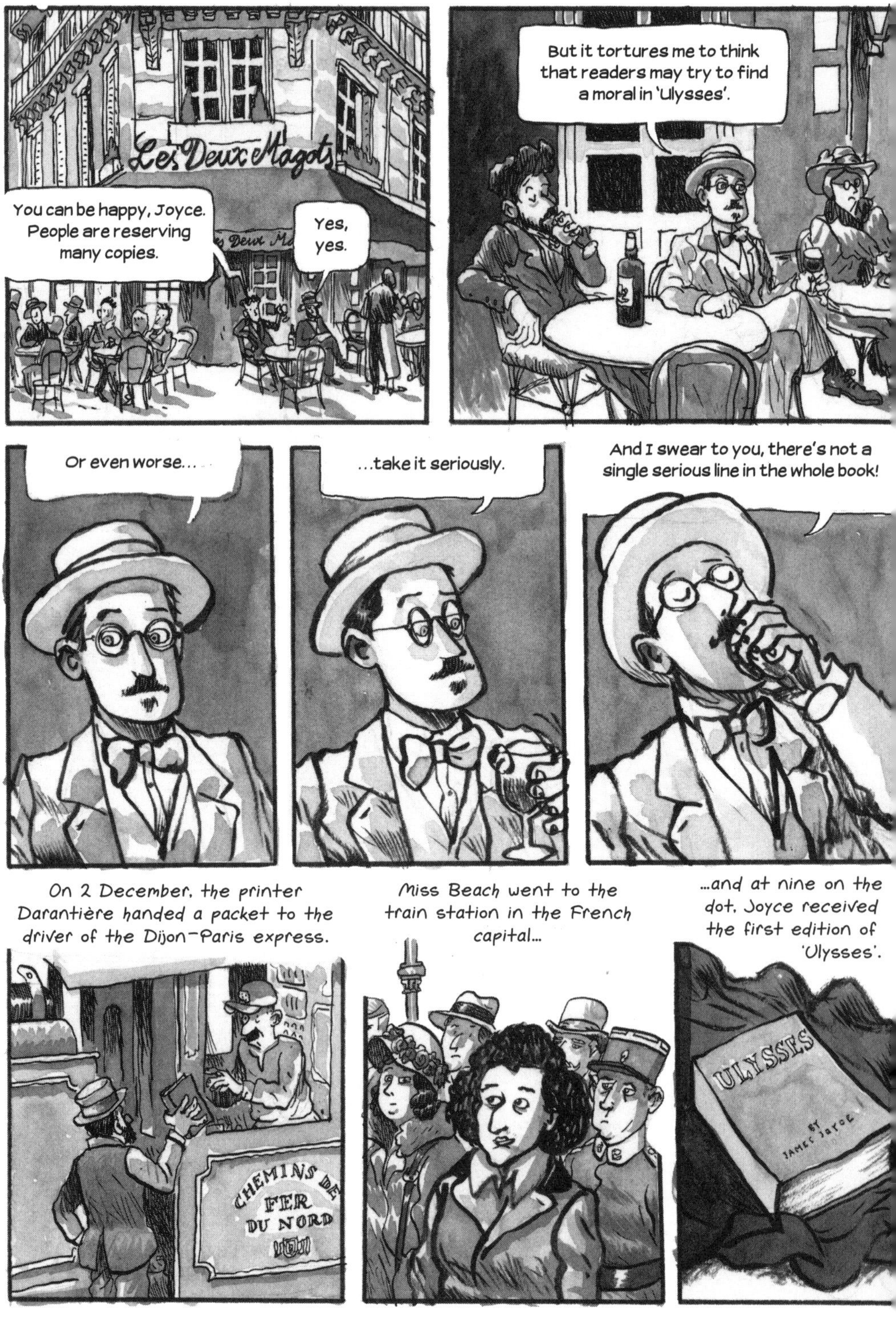
Les Deux Magots
You can be happy, Joyce. People are reserving many copies.
Yes, yes.
But it tortures me to think that readers may try to find a moral in 'Ulysses'.
Or even worse...
...take it seriously.
And I swear to you, there's not a single serious line in the whole book!
On 2 December, the printer Darantière handed a packet to the driver of the Dijon-Paris express.
CHEMINS DE FER DU NORD
Miss Beach went to the train station in the French capital...
...and at nine on the dot, Joyce received the first edition of 'Ulysses'.
ULYSSES
BY JAMES JOYCE

'Ulysses' was soon used amongst the cultural élite to stand out. Reading it became a sign of distinction and snobbery.

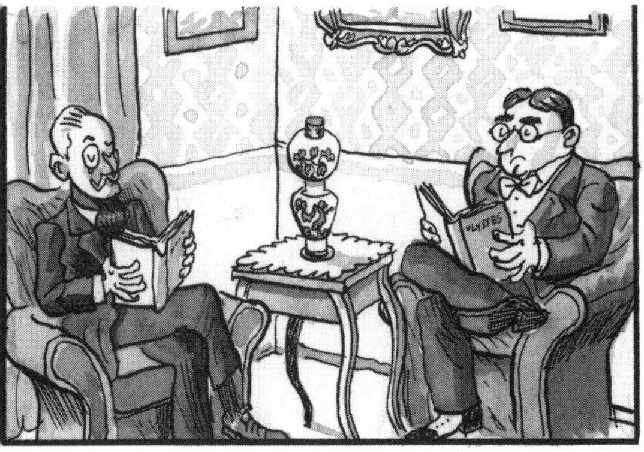
ULYSSES

It was thought to be a complex, cryptic book, requiring detailed study to reveal its parallels with the 'Odyssey'. Since no one else dared to face such a task, the writer TS Eliot decided to take it on.

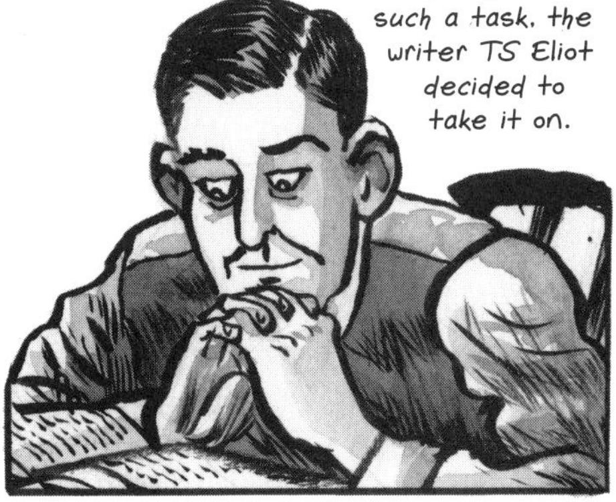

Obviously, the praise was not unanimous. Virginia Woolf said it was 'the book of a self-taught working man... a queasy undergraduate scratching his pimples'.

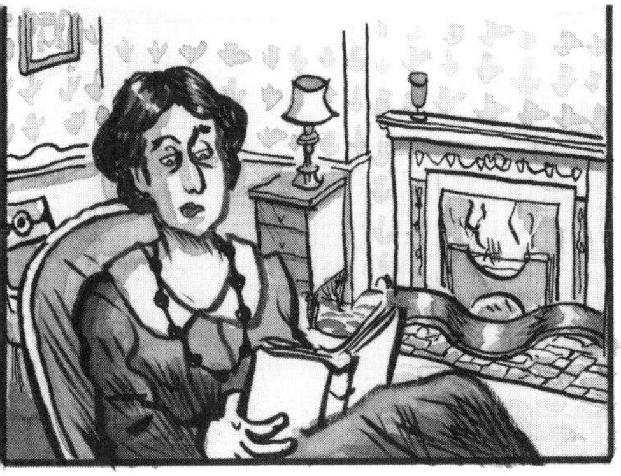

Gertrude Stein was furious to find herself stripped of her halo as 'the great experimentalist'.

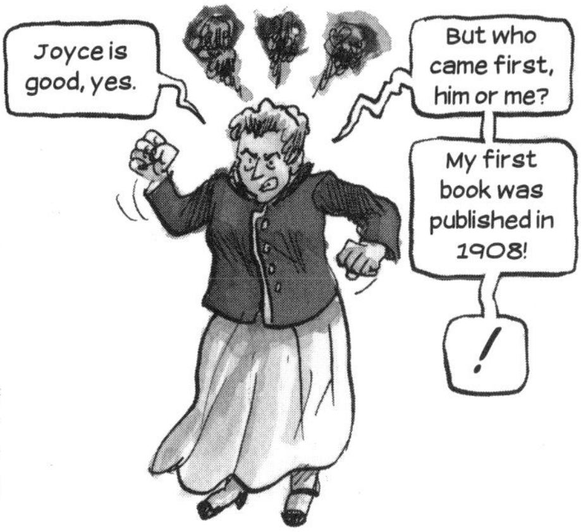
Joyce is good, yes.
But who came first, him or me?
My first book was published in 1908!
!

Ernest Hemingway adored 'Ulysses', and didn't hide the fact.

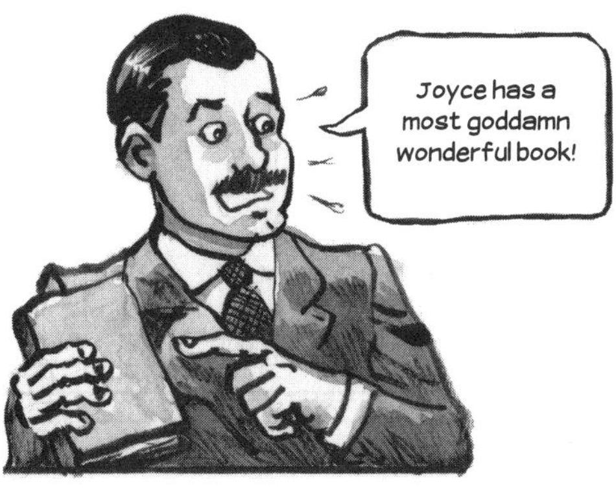
Joyce has a most goddamn wonderful book!

George Moore detested it, and said so publicly.

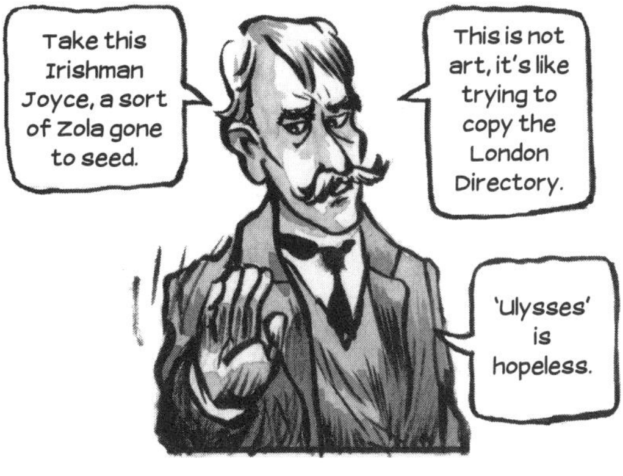
Take this Irishman Joyce, a sort of Zola gone to seed.
This is not art, it's like trying to copy the London Directory.
'Ulysses' is hopeless.

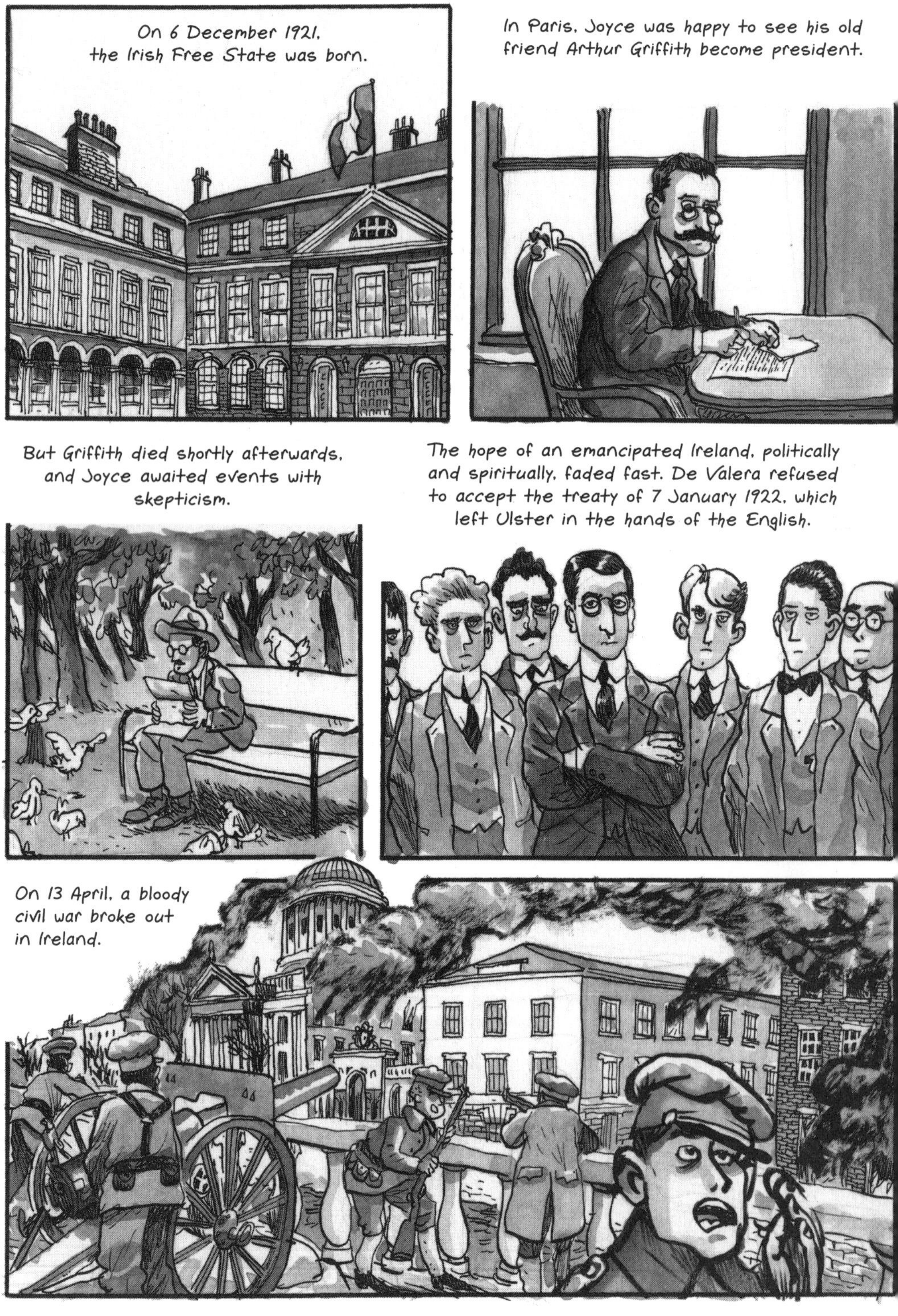
On 6 December 1921, the Irish Free State was born.
In Paris, Joyce was happy to see his old friend Arthur Griffith become president.
But Griffith died shortly afterwards, and Joyce awaited events with skepticism.
The hope of an emancipated Ireland, politically and spiritually, faded fast. De Valera refused to accept the treaty of 7 January 1922, which left Ulster in the hands of the English.
On 13 April, a bloody civil war broke out in Ireland.

Unaware of the unfolding events, Nora Joyce was on a visit to Galway with Giorgio and Lucia. She had travelled against James' wishes.

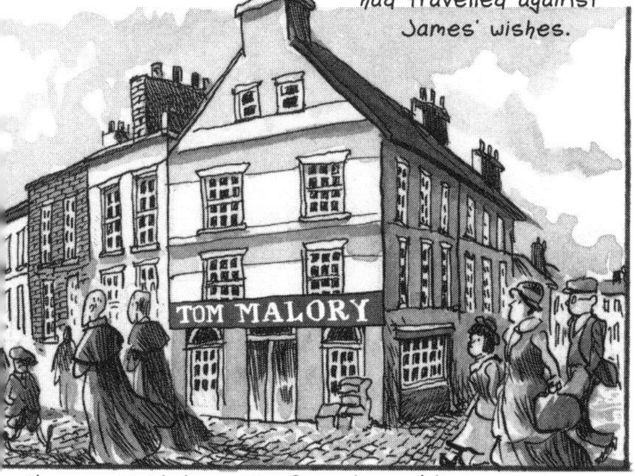
TOM MALORY

Meanwhile, Joyce was in Paris, on the verge of collapse, worried about the dangerous situation in Ireland.

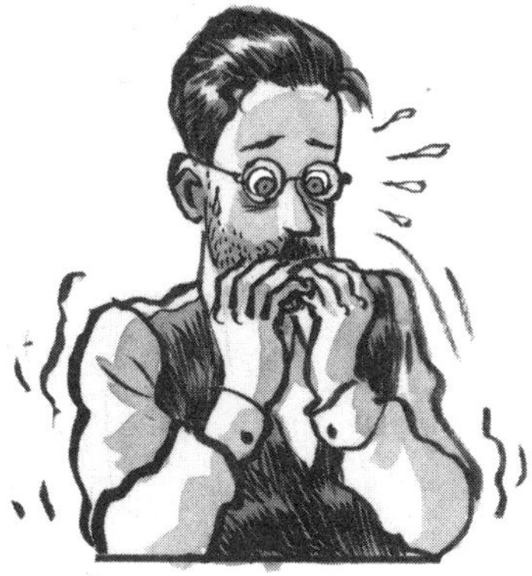

He was right to worry. One day, soldiers burst into Nora's bedroom to shoot at some RA snipers on the other side of the street.

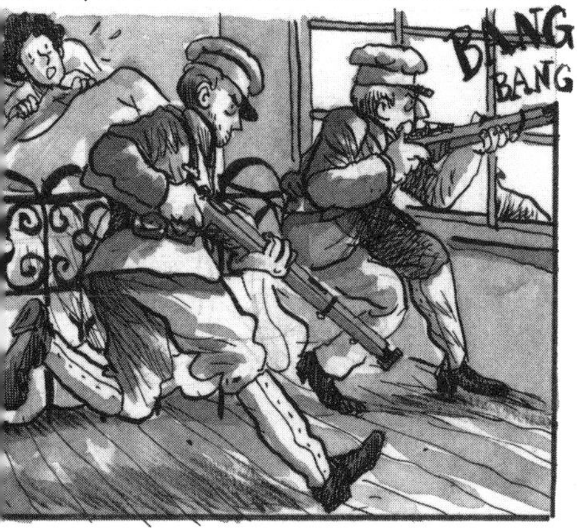
BANG
BANG

On their return journey, the train to Dublin was riddled with bullets by troops from both sides.

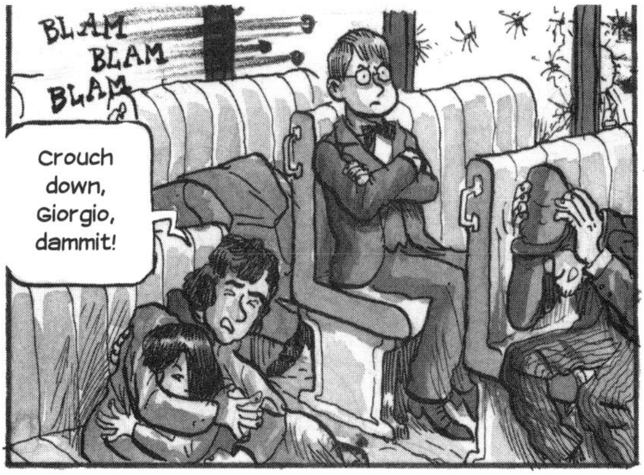
BLAM
BLAM
BLAM
Crouch down, Giorgio, dammit!

The family were reunited in Paris, safe and sound, but Joyce was deeply affected by it all.

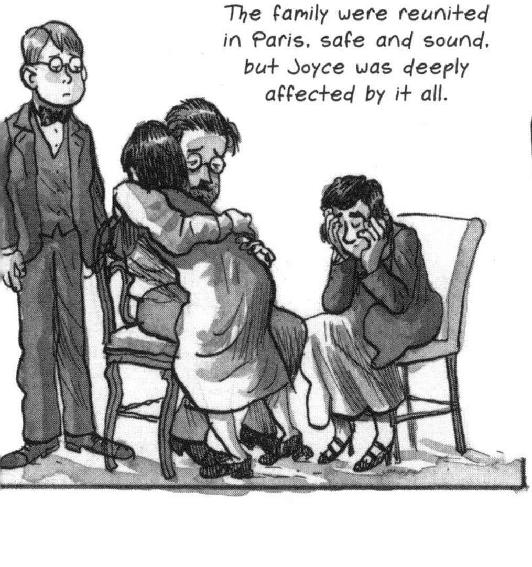

When the Irish Prime Minister, Desmond Fitzgerald, visited him to say that Ireland would nominate him for the Nobel Prize for Literature, he was not in the mood.

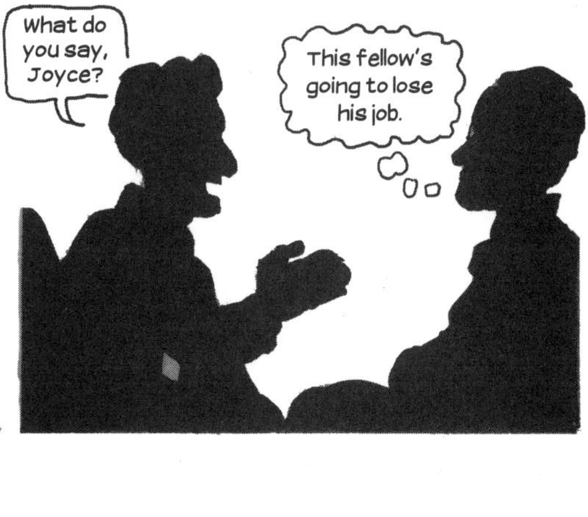
What do you say, Joyce?
This fellow's going to lose his job.

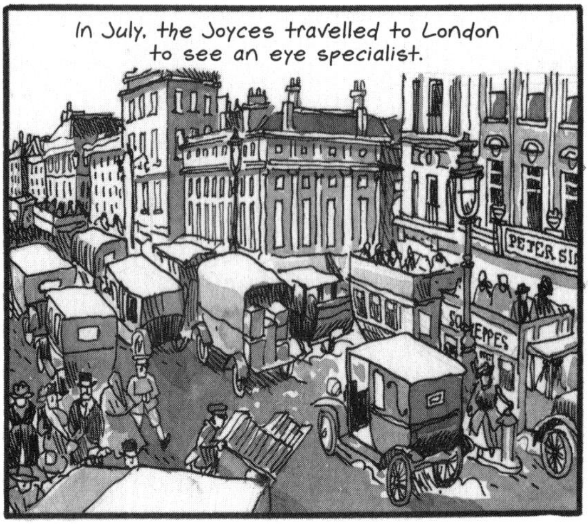
In July, the Joyces travelled to London to see an eye specialist.
PETER SI
SCHWEPPES

The diagnosis was not very hopeful: the liquid in the left eye could not be removed any more. The attacks of glaucoma would continue.

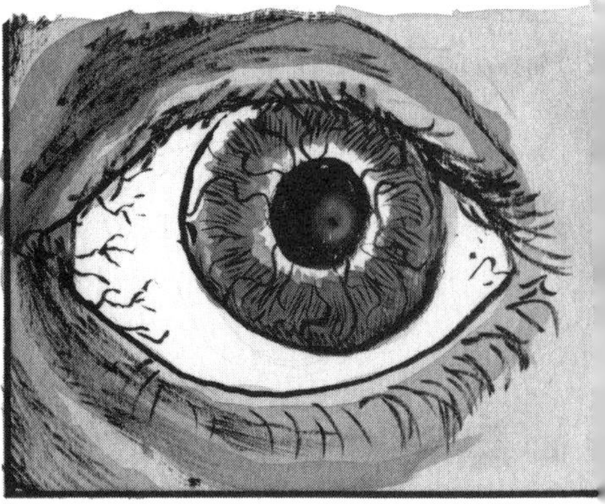

In France, Joyce was subjected to a very painful treatment, with leeches to extract blood from the eye, and a solution of dionine.

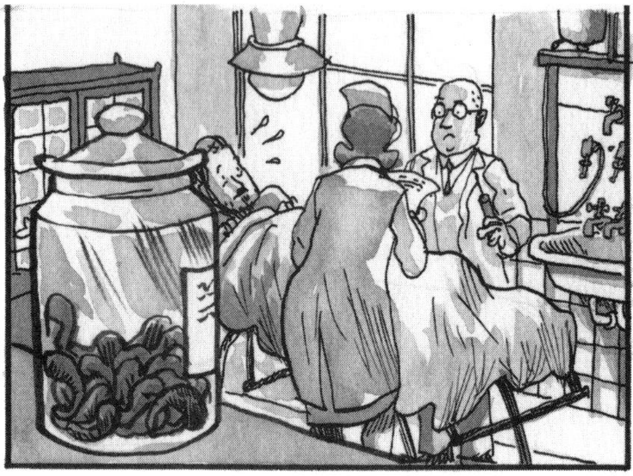

But Joyce reached his limit when the doctor told him he would have to exchange white wine for red.

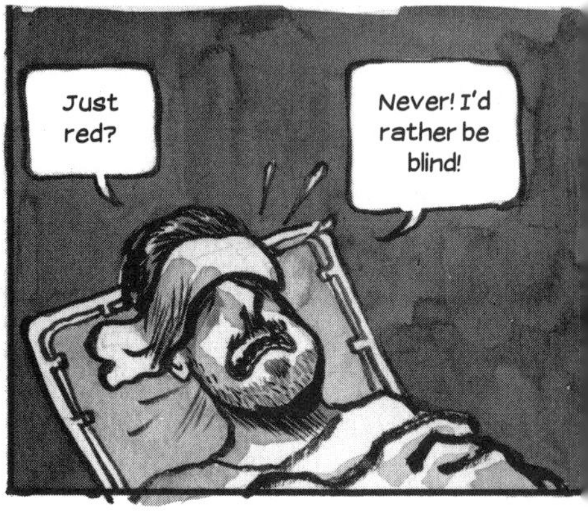
Just red?
Never! I'd rather be blind!

His bad health couldn't compete with the success of his prose. The second edition of 'Ulysses' was published on 12 October, and sold out in four days.

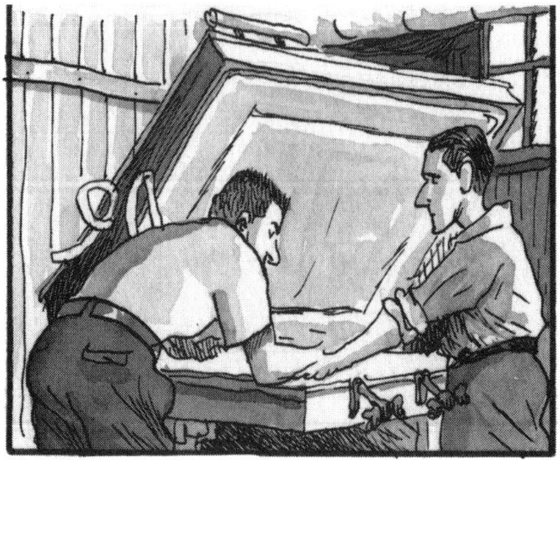

By then, Joyce had forgotten about the book. He was busy giving shape to his next book in his head.

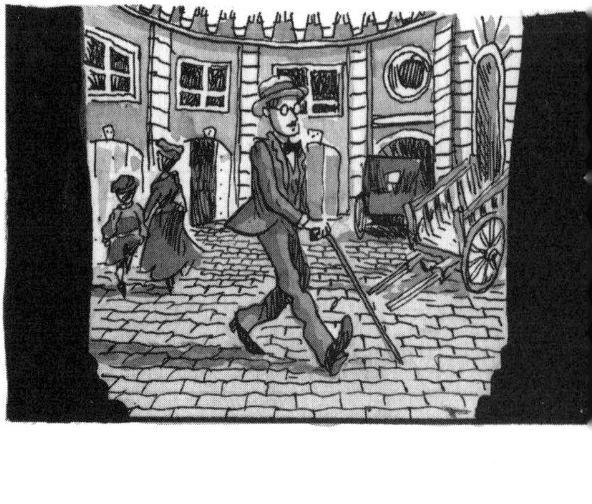

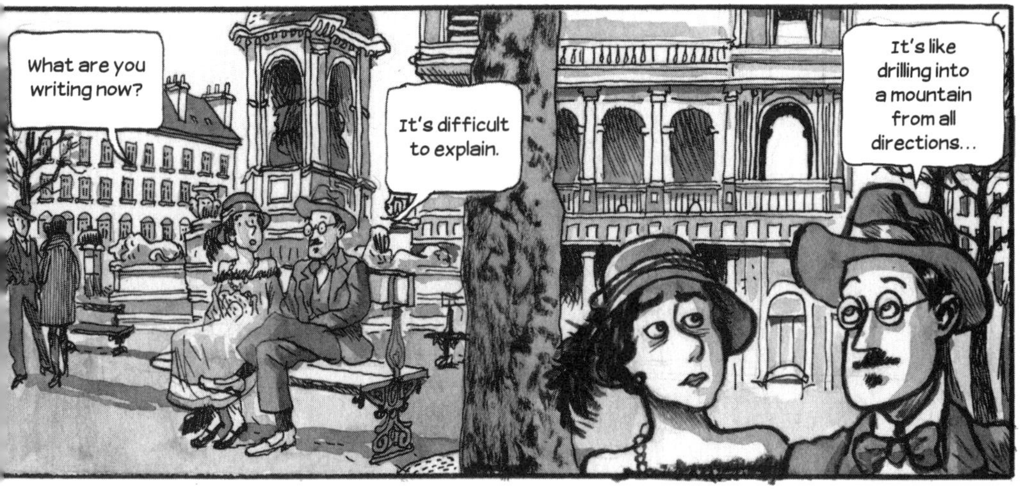
What are you writing now?
It's difficult to explain.
It's like drilling into a mountain from all directions...

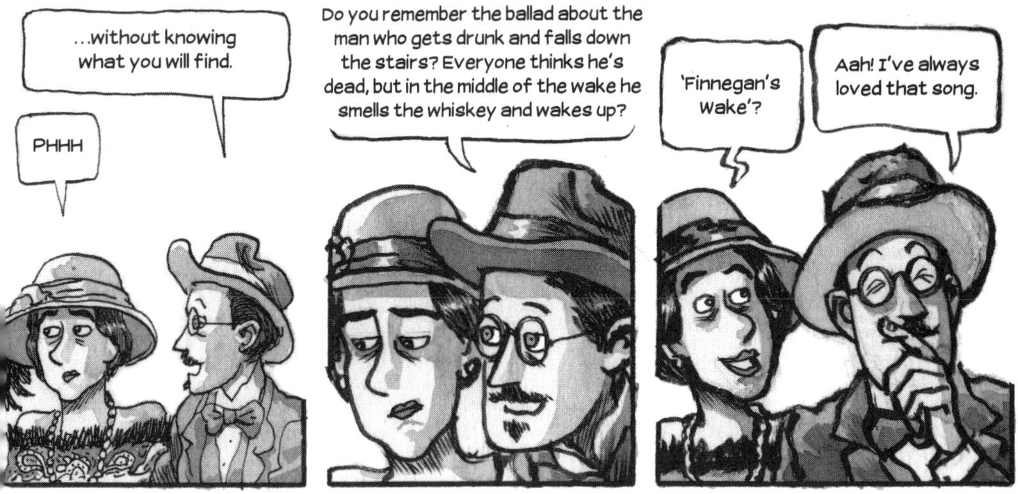
...without knowing what you will find.
PHHH
Do you remember the ballad about the man who gets drunk and falls down the stairs? Everyone thinks he's dead, but in the middle of the wake he smells the whiskey and wakes up?
'Finnegan's Wake'?
Aah! I've always loved that song.

On 11 March 1923, Miss Weaver received a premonitory letter from Joyce.

'I've started my new work. I use double folio paper and write in enormous letters, so I can read it afterwards. As the Italians say, the wolf loses its hair but not its sight.'

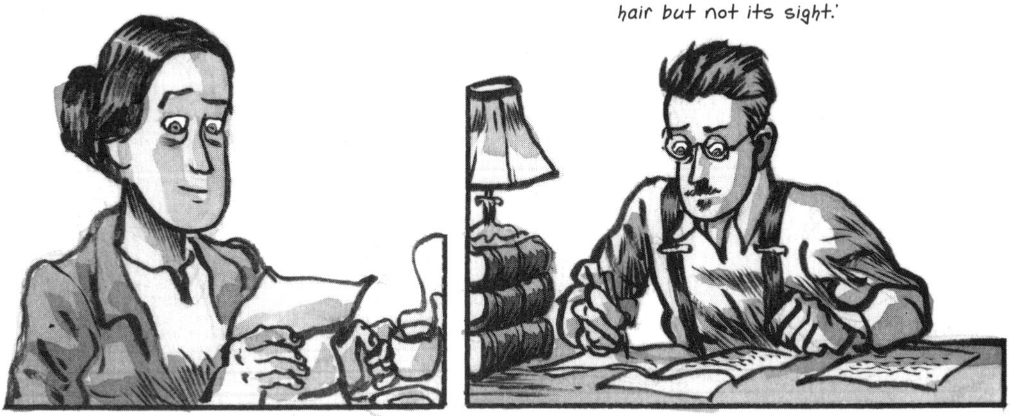

In October 1923, there was a memorable gathering in Paris: Joyce, the laywer John Quinn, Ezra Pound, Ford Madox Ford and Ernest Hemingway were all there together.

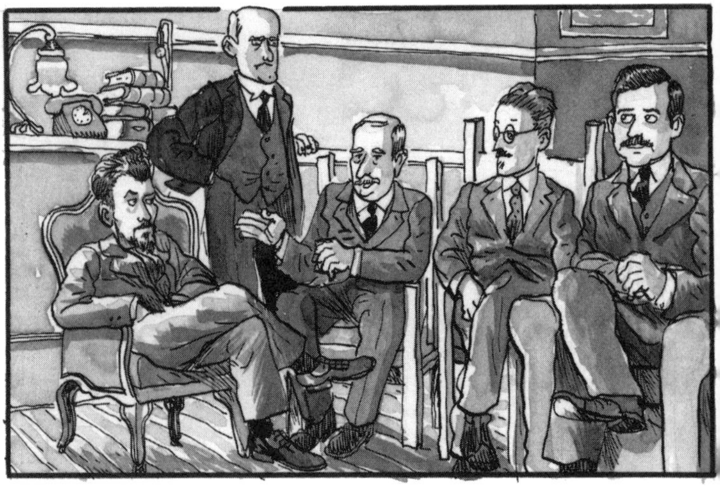

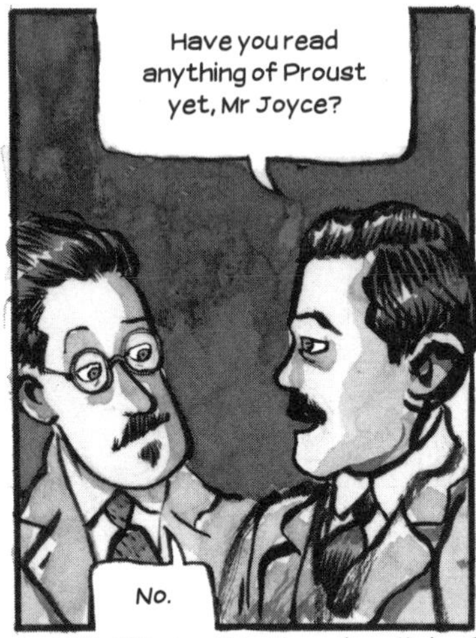
Have you read anything of Proust yet, Mr Joyce?
No.

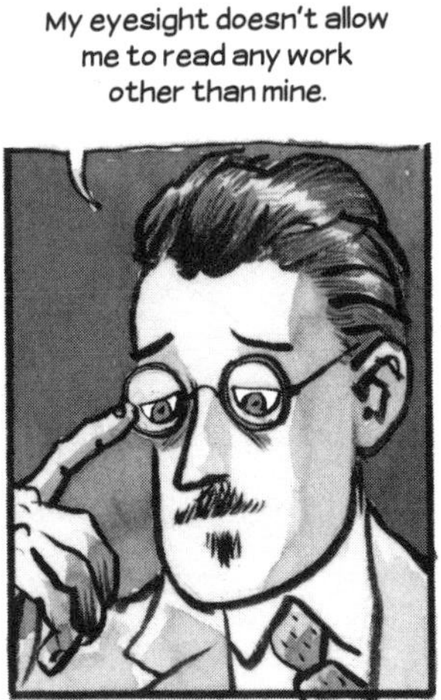
My eyesight doesn't allow me to read any work other than mine.

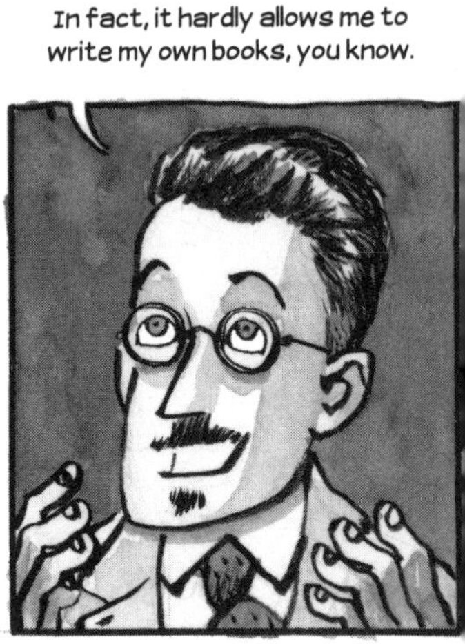
In fact, it hardly allows me to write my own books, you know.

In 1924, Ettore Schmitz, alias Italo Svevo, wrote 'Zeno's Conscience'. The book wasn't well received and, discouraged, the author got in contact with Joyce once more.

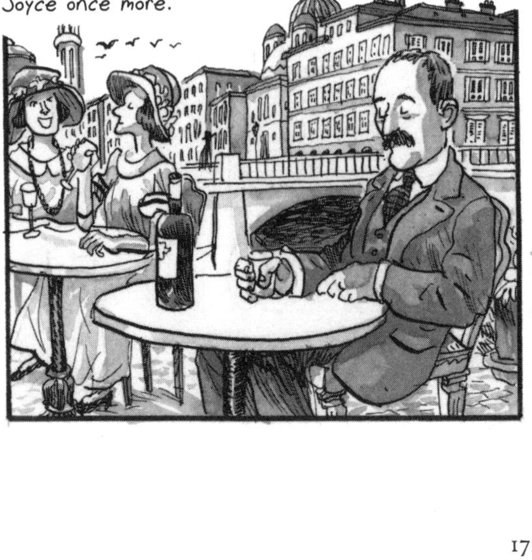

Joyce responded energetically to this cry for help from his old friend in Trieste.

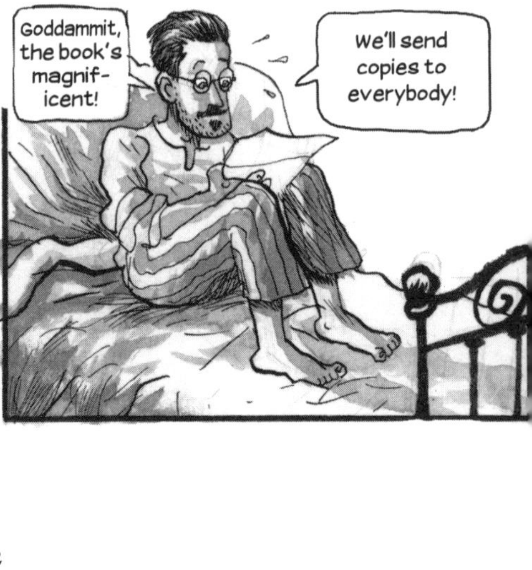
Goddammit, the book's magnif-icent!
We'll send copies to everybody!

Valery Larbaud joined the campaign, and wrote articles about it in the famous 'Nouvelle Revue Française' and 'Commerce'.

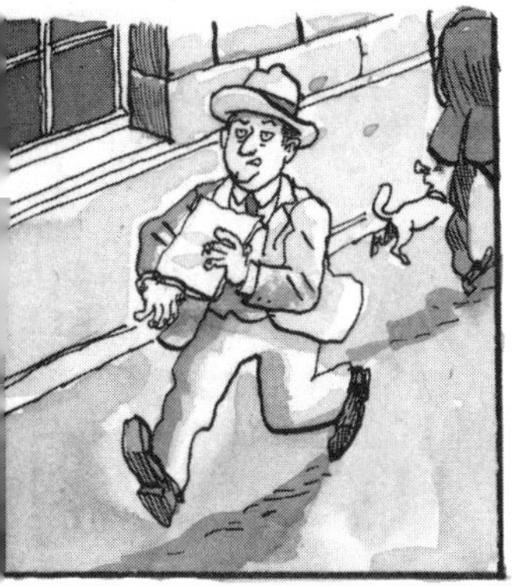

Adrienne Monnier did the same, and devoted a whole issue of 'Le Navire d'Argent' to Italo Svevo.

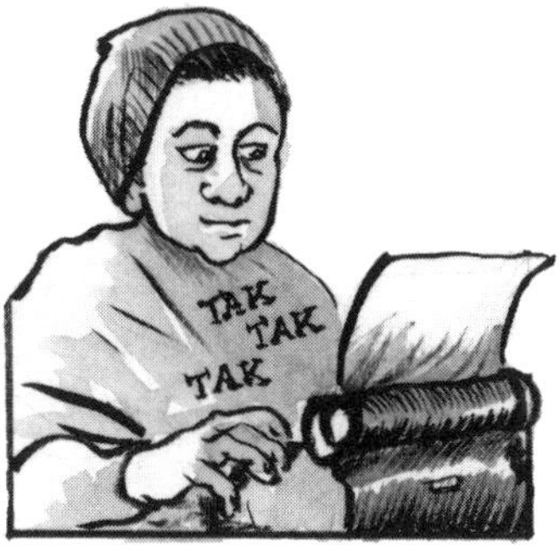
TAK
TAK
TAK

Joyce had resuscitated Schmitz.

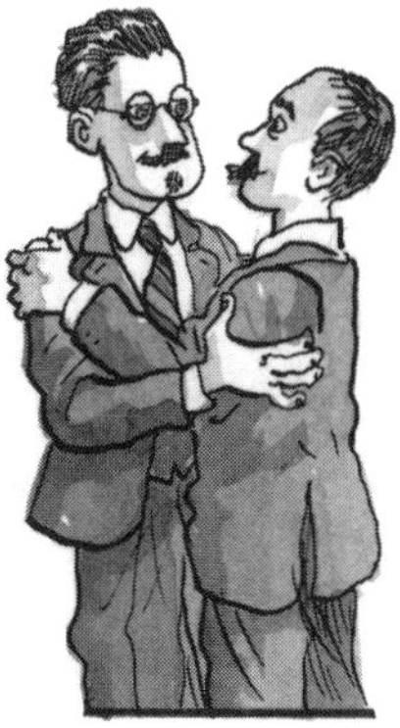

Meanwhile, Joyce carried on working on his latest book. It started to appear in instalments in 'The Transatlantic Review' in 1924.

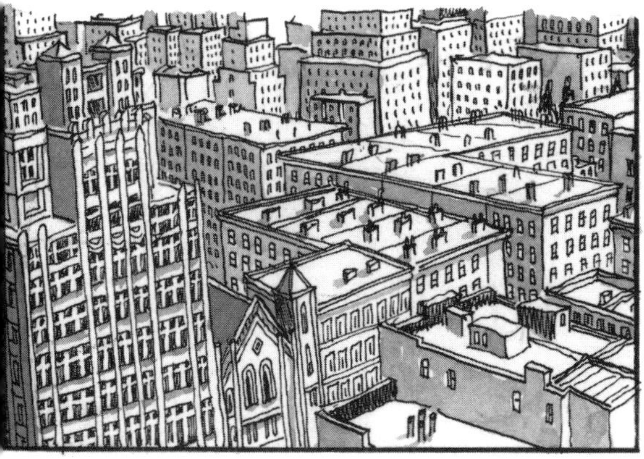

Curiously, it still had no title: Joyce simply called it 'Work in Progress'.

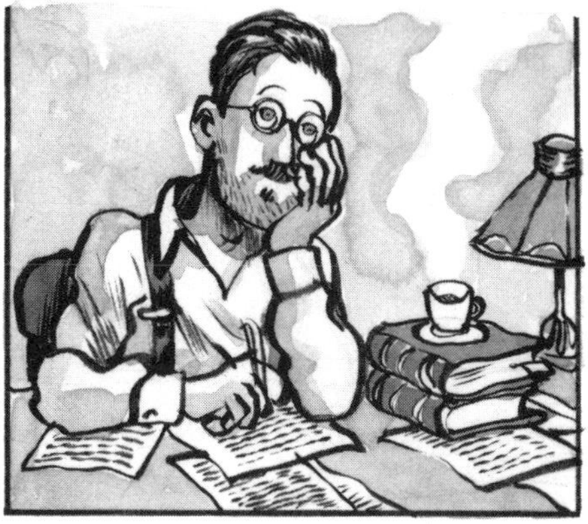

In fact, the book kept this provisional title until it was completed.

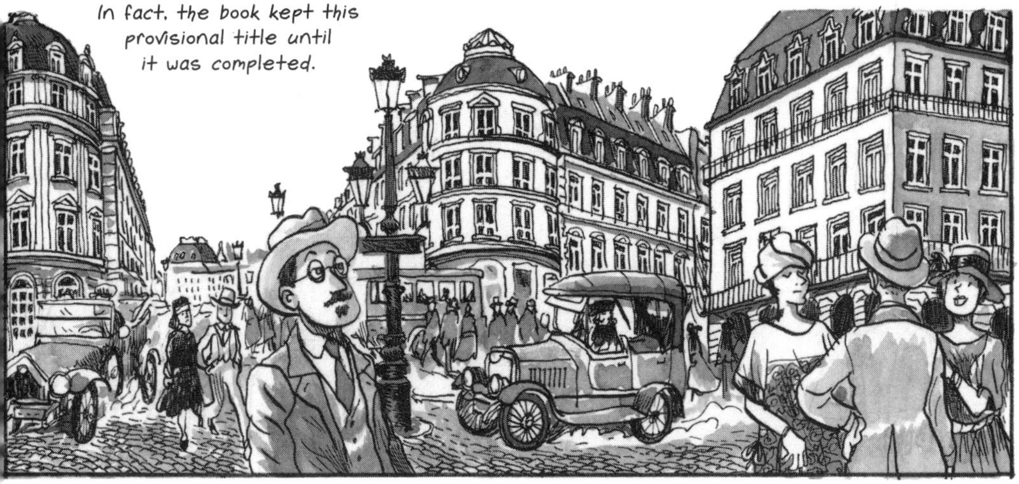

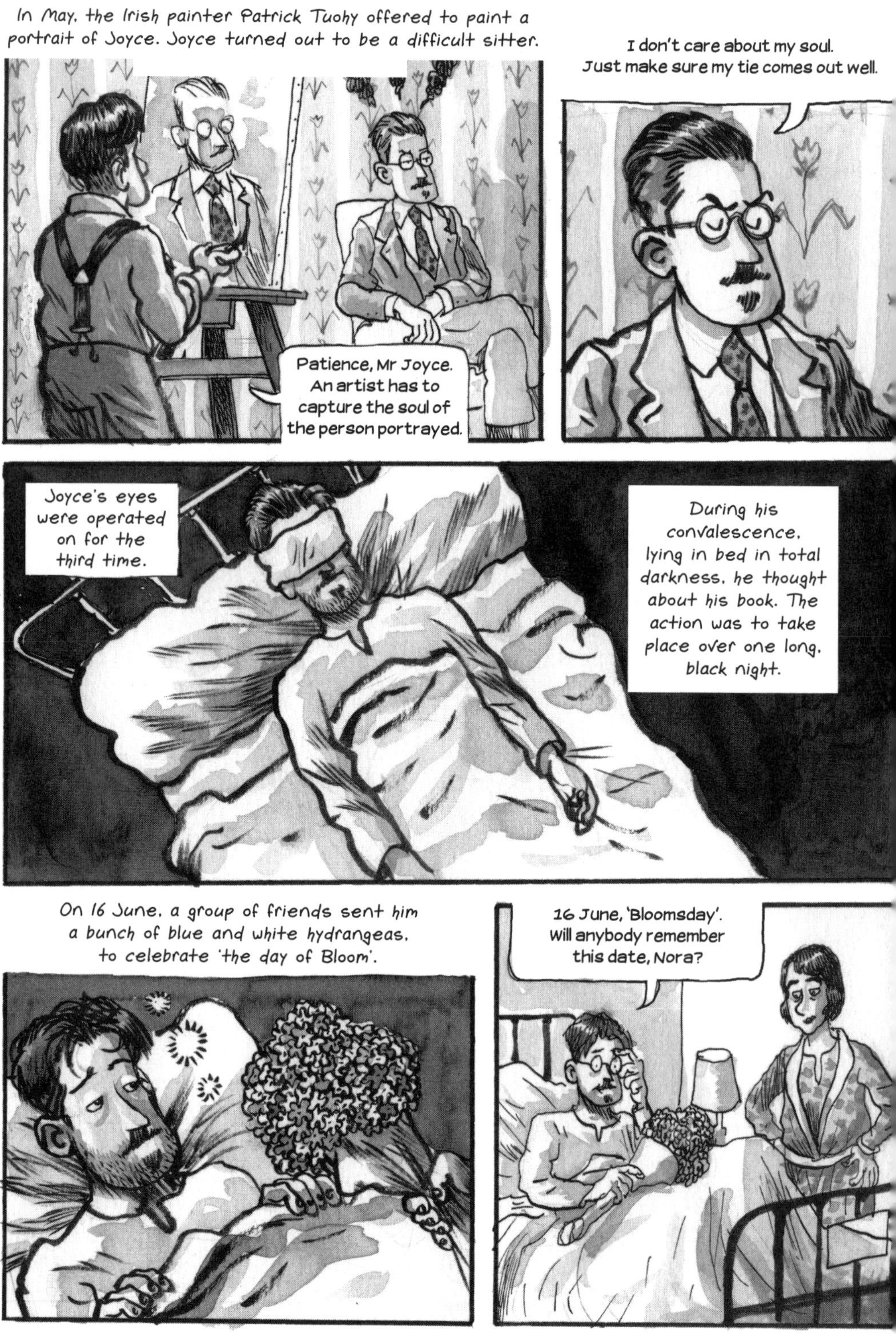

In May, the Irish painter Patrick Tuohy offered to paint a portrait of Joyce. Joyce turned out to be a difficult sitter.
Patience, Mr Joyce. An artist has to capture the soul of the person portrayed.
I don't care about my soul. Just make sure my tie comes out well.
Joyce's eyes were operated on for the third time.
During his convalescence, lying in bed in total darkness, he thought about his book. The action was to take place over one long, black night.
On 16 June, a group of friends sent him a bunch of blue and white hydrangeas, to celebrate 'the day of Bloom'.
16 June, 'Bloomsday'. Will anybody remember this date, Nora?

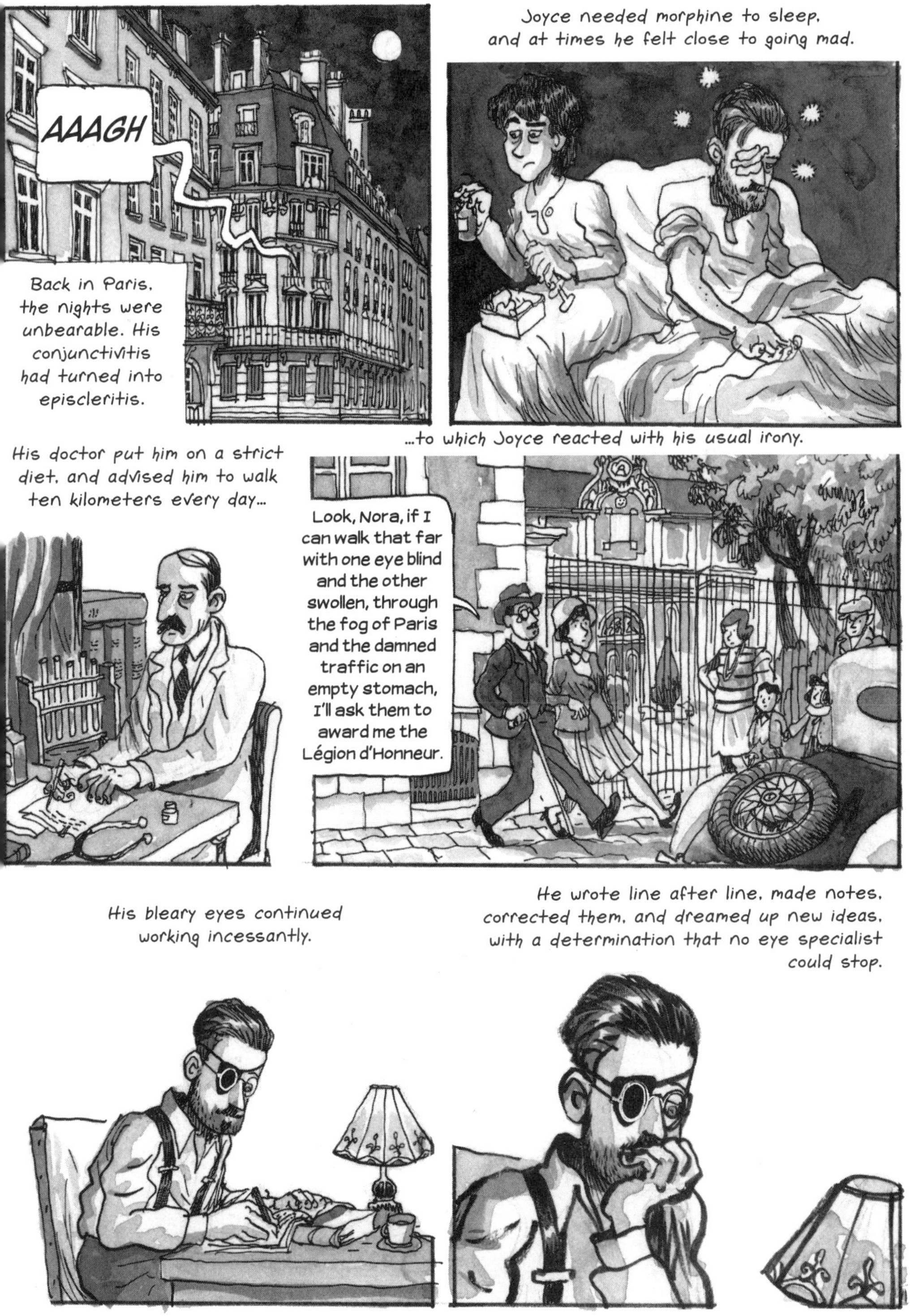
AAAGH
Back in Paris, the nights were unbearable. His conjunctivitis had turned into episcleritis.
Joyce needed morphine to sleep, and at times he felt close to going mad.
His doctor put him on a strict diet, and advised him to walk ten kilometers every day...
...to which Joyce reacted with his usual irony.
Look, Nora, if I can walk that far with one eye blind and the other swollen, through the fog of Paris and the damned traffic on an empty stomach, I'll ask them to award me the Légion d'Honneur.
His bleary eyes continued working incessantly.
He wrote line after line, made notes, corrected them, and dreamed up new ideas, with a determination that no eye specialist could stop.

From the very start, the new book, which experimented with language in every possible way, was a source of bafflement to all.

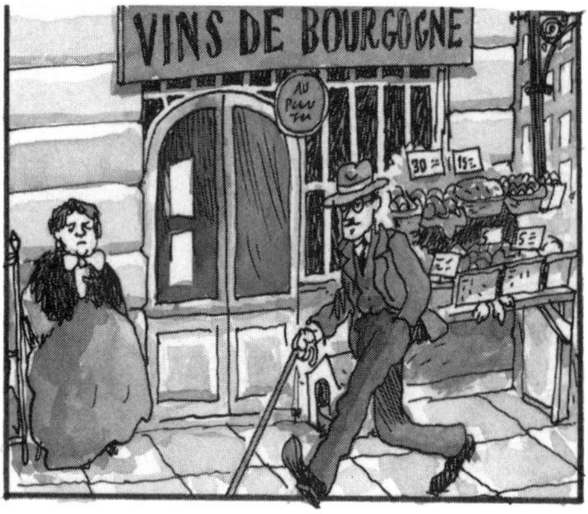
VINS DE BOURGOGNE

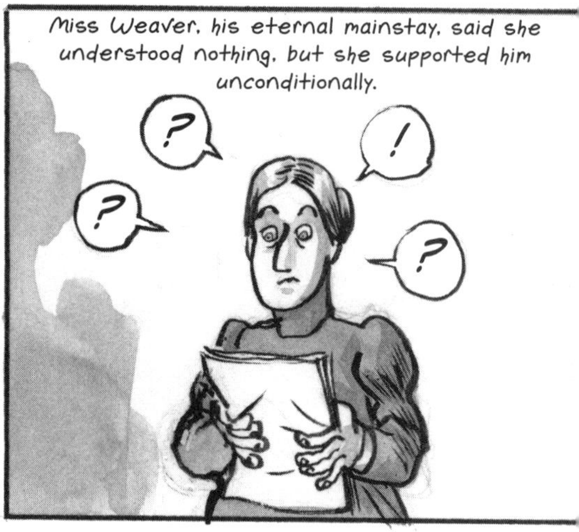
Miss Weaver, his eternal mainstay, said she understood nothing, but she supported him unconditionally.
?
?
!
?

Ezra Pound could make no sense of Joyce's new book either.

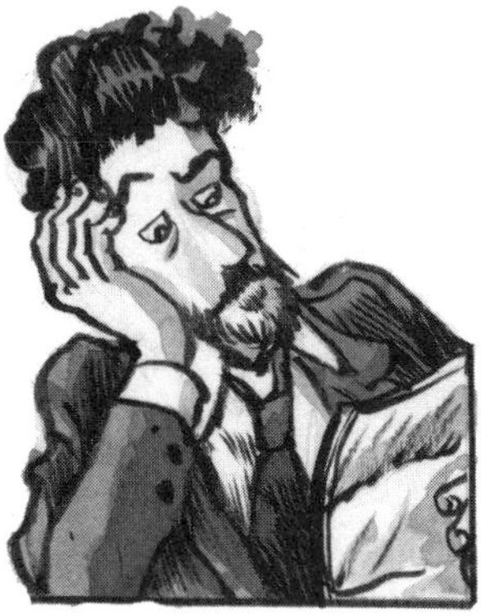

'Dear Jim: to me, all this chaos could be a divine vision, or a formula to cure gonorrhea. I understand nothing.'

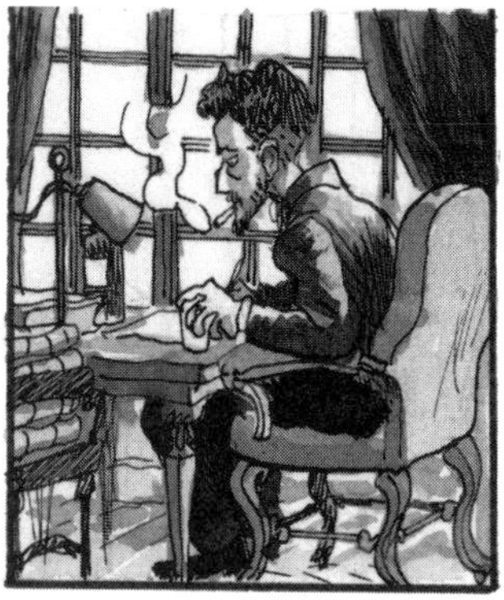

'So the only thing I can say is, good luck'.

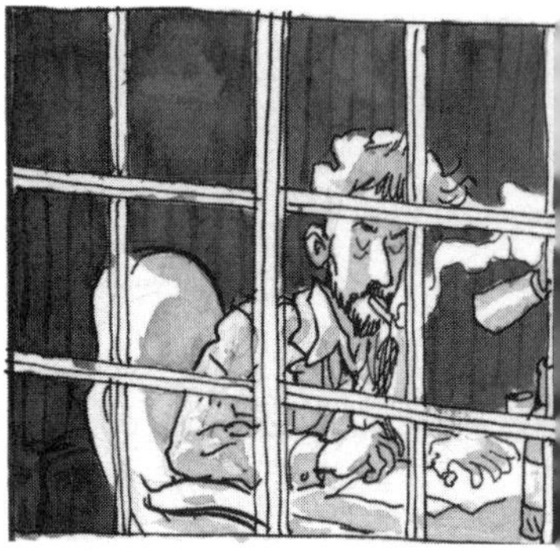

Ezra Pound had started to distance himself from Joyce.

While 'Work in Progress' was being written in Europe, a pirate edition of 'Ulysses' was printed and distributed in New York by a printer called Roth.

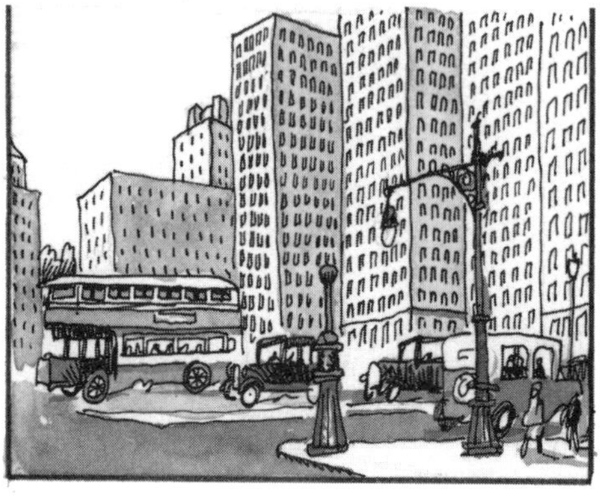

Joyce's American lawyers went to court, and there was an international outcry against Roth.

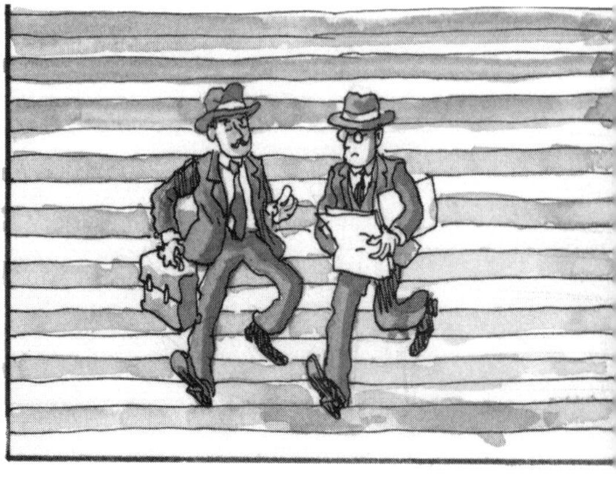

...manifesto against the piracy of 'Ulysses' was quickly signed by Robert Bridges, Einstein, Duhamel, Gide, Gómez de la Serna, Pirandello, Russell, Symons, Unamuno, HG Wells, and many others.

Strangely, Ezra Pound refused to sign, thus increasing the breach between them.

Bah! Joyce just wants publicity for himself.

Roth's presses went on working until October, despite the signatures and protests.

But in December, the New York High Court gave judgement in Joyce's favour, and against Roth. Publication of the book would remain forbidden until 1933.

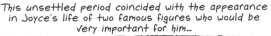

This unsettled period coincided with the appearance in Joyce's life of two famous figures who would be very important for him...

...Eugene and Marie Jolas.

Chapter VI

Work in Progress

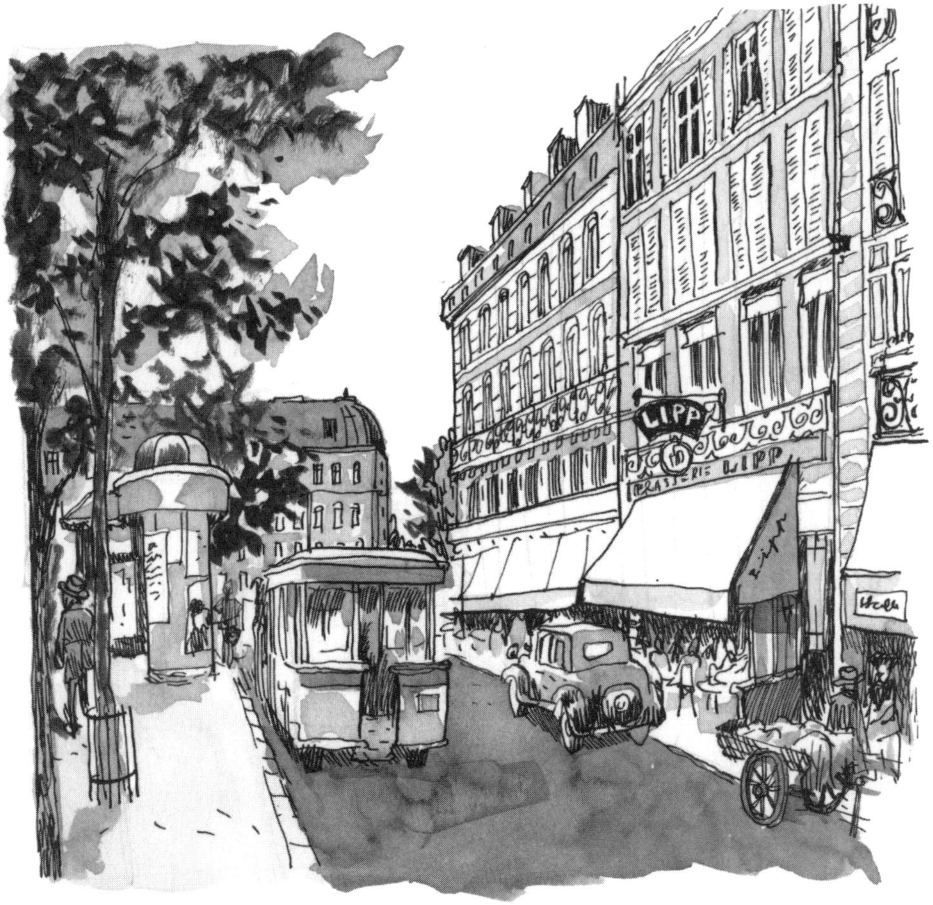
LIPP

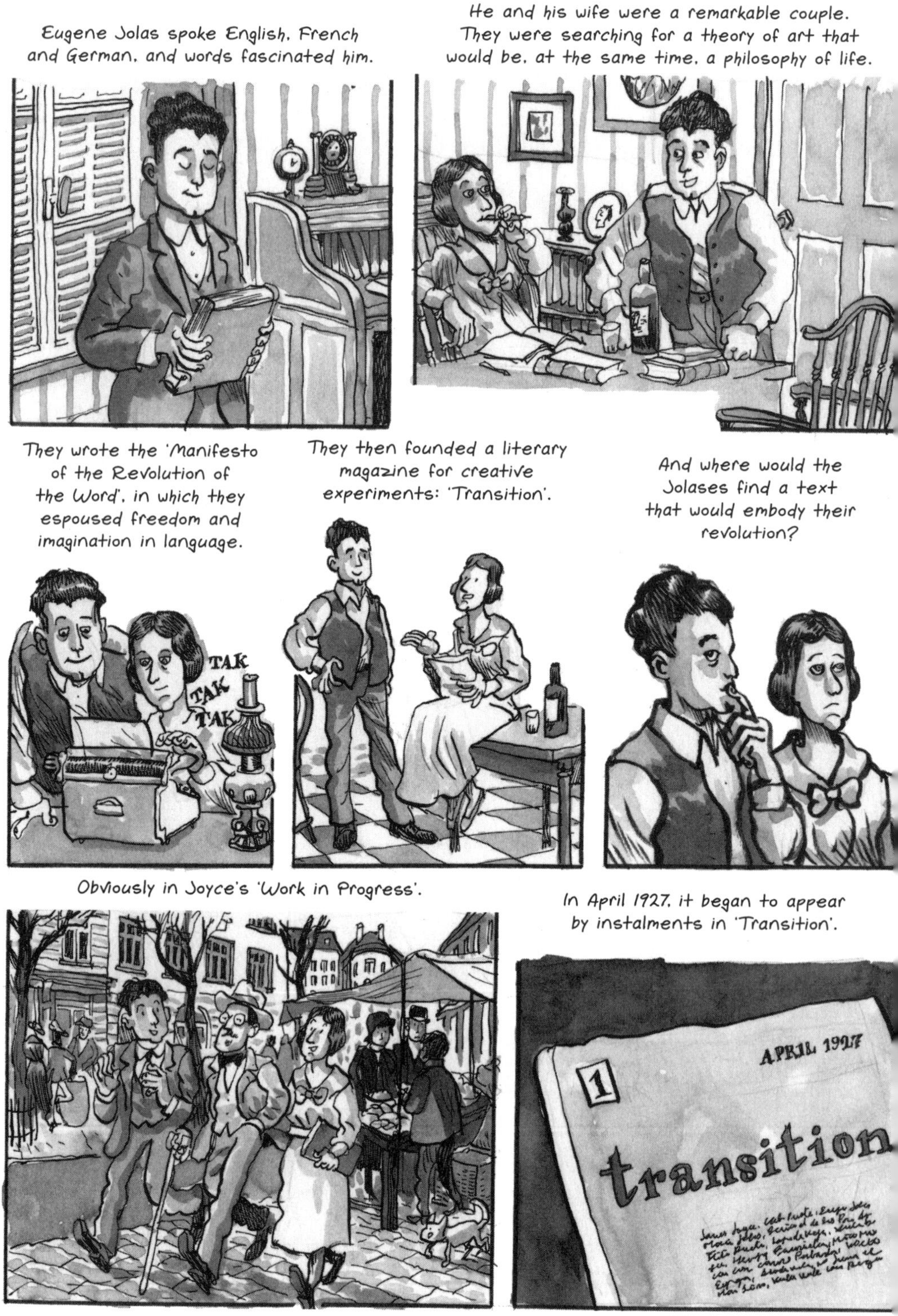
Eugene Jolas spoke English, French and German, and words fascinated him.
He and his wife were a remarkable couple. They were searching for a theory of art that would be, at the same time, a philosophy of life.
They wrote the 'Manifesto of the Revolution of the Word', in which they espoused freedom and imagination in language.
TAK
TAK
TAK
They then founded a literary magazine for creative experiments: 'Transition'.
And where would the Jolases find a text that would embody their revolution?
Obviously in Joyce's 'Work in Progress'.
In April 1927, it began to appear by instalments in 'Transition'.
APRIL 1927
1
transition

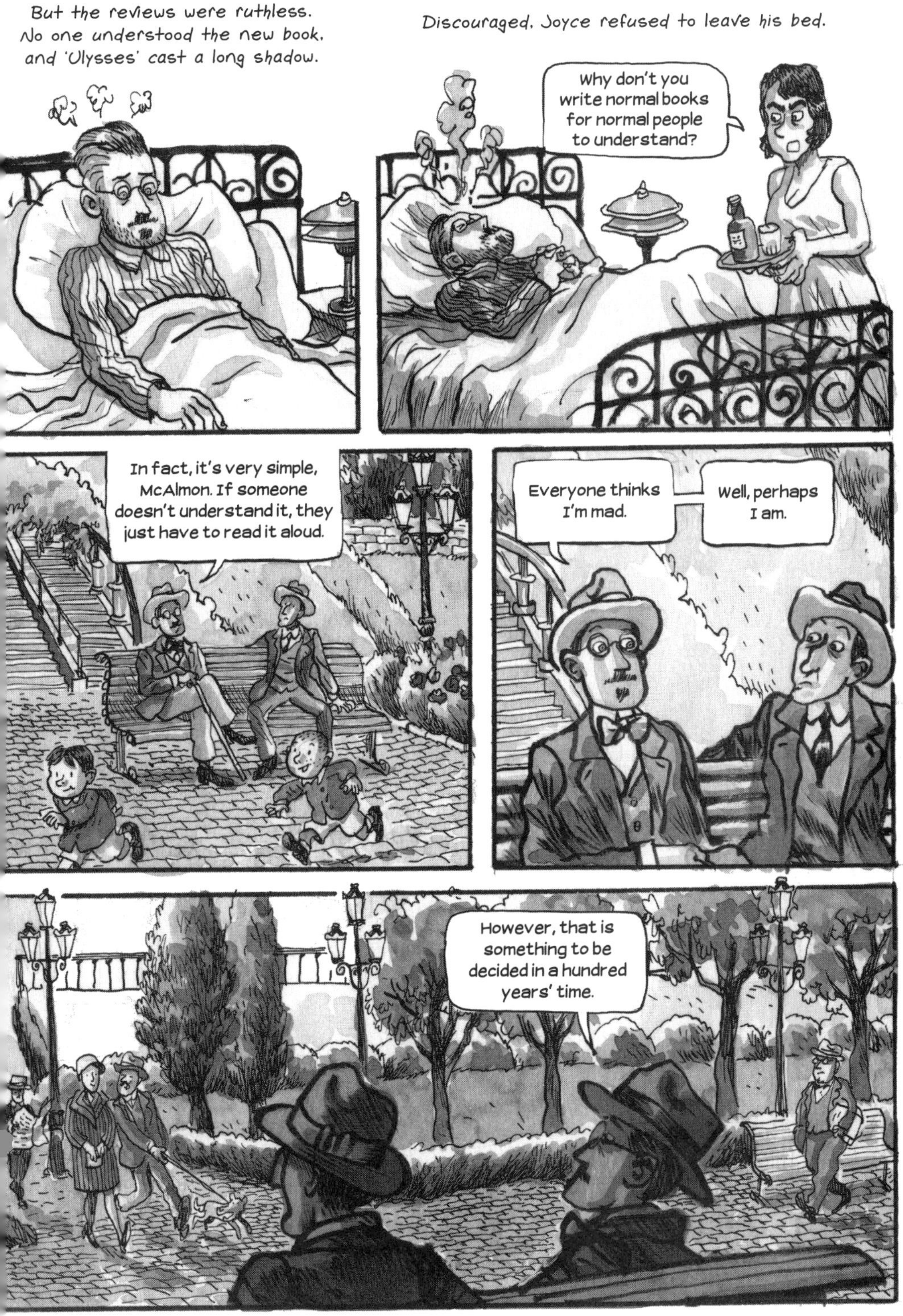
But the reviews were ruthless. No one understood the new book, and 'Ulysses' cast a long shadow.
Discouraged, Joyce refused to leave his bed.
Why don't you write normal books for normal people to understand?
In fact, it's very simple, McAlmon. If someone doesn't understand it, they just have to read it aloud.
Everyone thinks I'm mad.
Well, perhaps I am.
However, that is something to be decided in a hundred years' time.

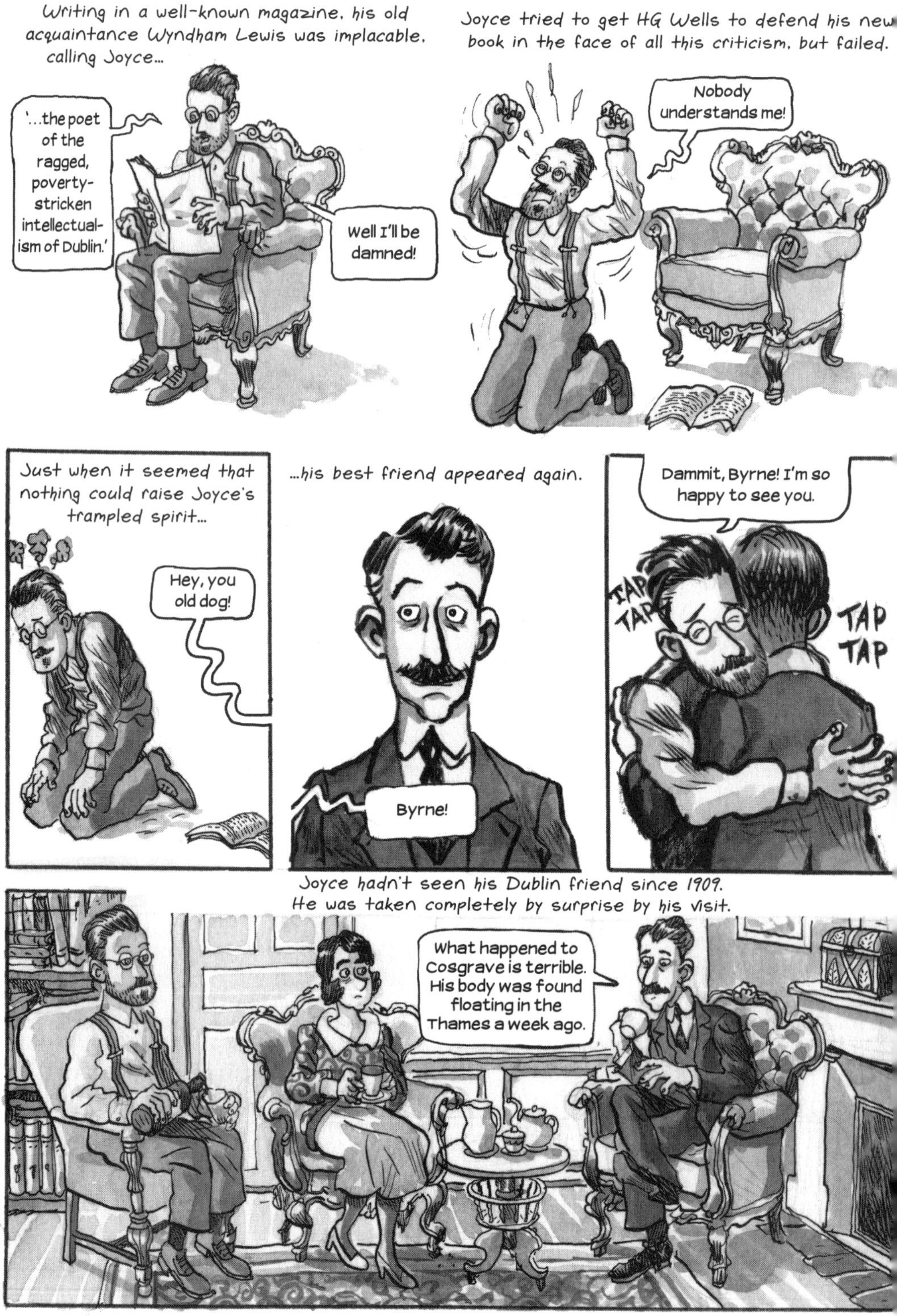
Writing in a well-known magazine, his old acquaintance Wyndham Lewis was implacable, calling Joyce...
'...the poet of the ragged, poverty-stricken intellectualism of Dublin.'
Well I'll be damned!
Joyce tried to get HG Wells to defend his new book in the face of all this criticism, but failed.
Nobody understands me!
Just when it seemed that nothing could raise Joyce's trampled spirit...
Hey, you old dog!
...his best friend appeared again.
Byrne!
Dammit, Byrne! I'm so happy to see you.
TAP TAP
TAP TAP
Joyce hadn't seen his Dublin friend since 1909. He was taken completely by surprise by his visit.
What happened to Cosgrave is terrible. His body was found floating in the Thames a week ago.

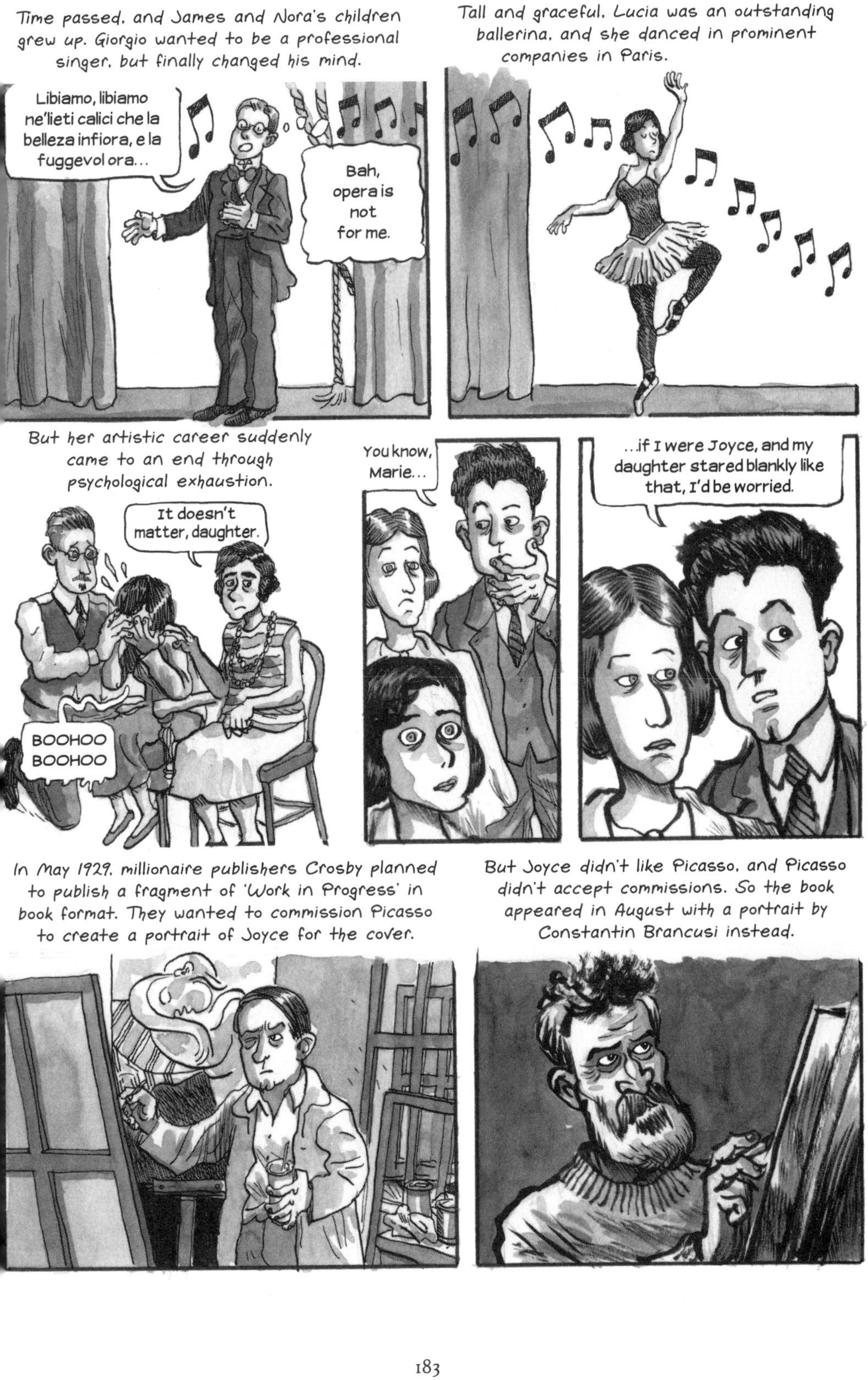

Time passed, and James and Nora's children grew up. Giorgio wanted to be a professional singer, but finally changed his mind.
Libiamo, libiamo ne'lieti calici che la belleza infiora, e la fuggevol ora...
Bah, opera is not for me.
Tall and graceful, Lucia was an outstanding ballerina, and she danced in prominent companies in Paris.
But her artistic career suddenly came to an end through psychological exhaustion.
It doesn't matter, daughter.
BOOHOO BOOHOO
You know, Marie...
...if I were Joyce, and my daughter stared blankly like that, I'd be worried.
In May 1929, millionaire publishers Crosby planned to publish a fragment of 'Work in Progress' in book format. They wanted to commission Picasso to create a portrait of Joyce for the cover.
But Joyce didn't like Picasso, and Picasso didn't accept commissions. So the book appeared in August with a portrait by Constantin Brancusi instead.

On 27 June, a bus full of literary figures was on its way back from the Hotel Leopold in Versailles. They had been celebrating a 'Ulysses Lunch', a banquet in honour of Joyce's book.

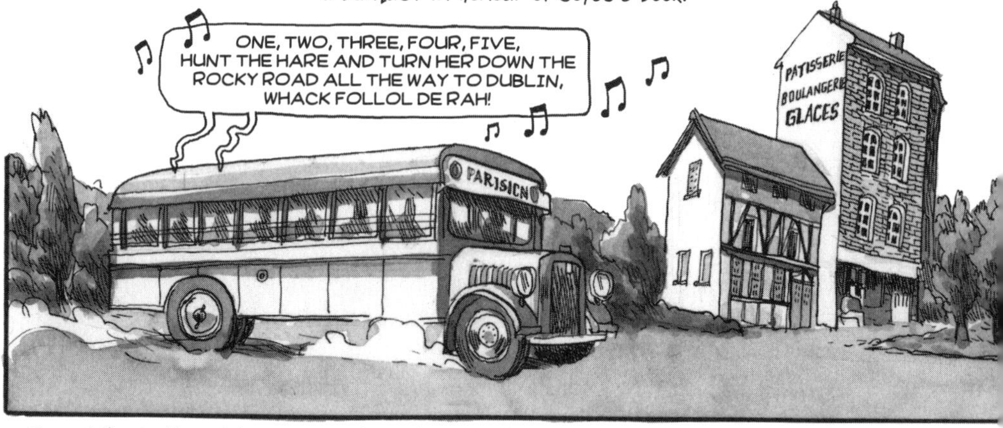
ONE, TWO, THREE, FOUR, FIVE, HUNT THE HARE AND TURN HER DOWN THE ROCKY ROAD ALL THE WAY TO DUBLIN, WHACK FOLLOL DE RAH!
PARISIEN
PATISSERIE
BOULANGERIE
GLACES

Samuel Beckett and Joyce were tipsy from the lunch, and wanted to continue the party.

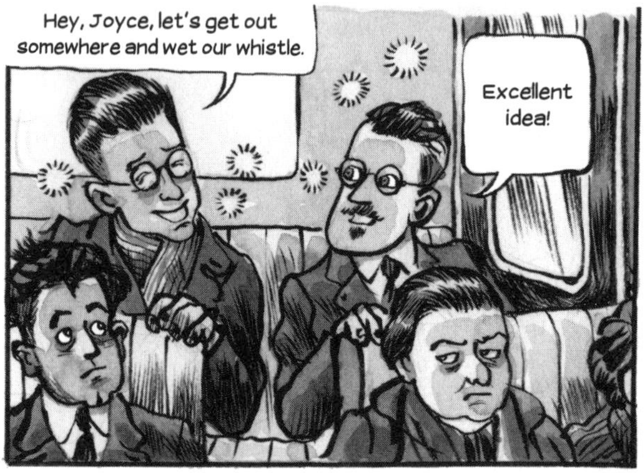
Hey, Joyce, let's get out somewhere and wet our whistle.
Excellent idea!

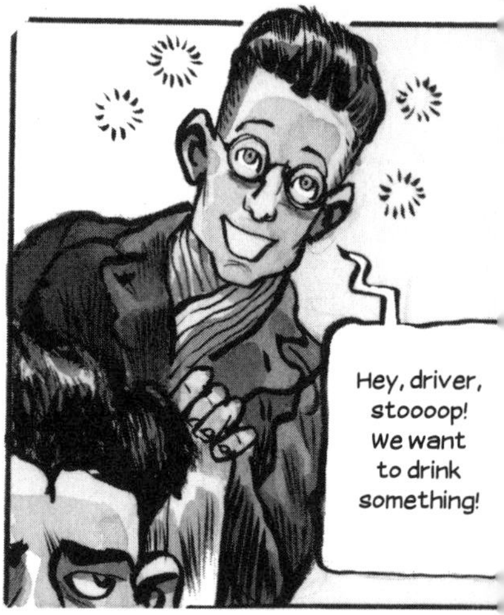
Hey, driver, stoooop! We want to drink something!

Finally, Adrienne Monnier's patience came to an end, and...

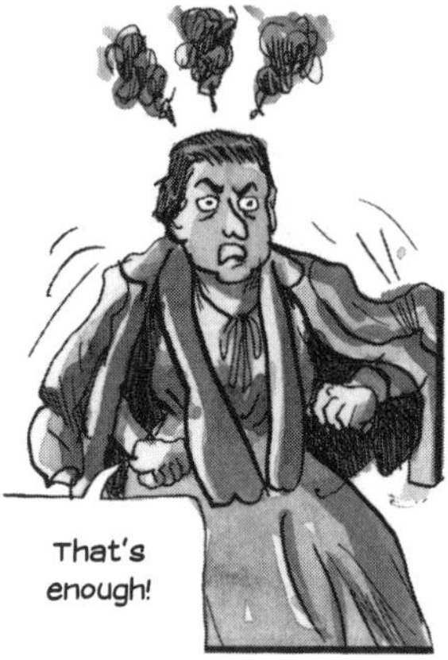
That's enough!

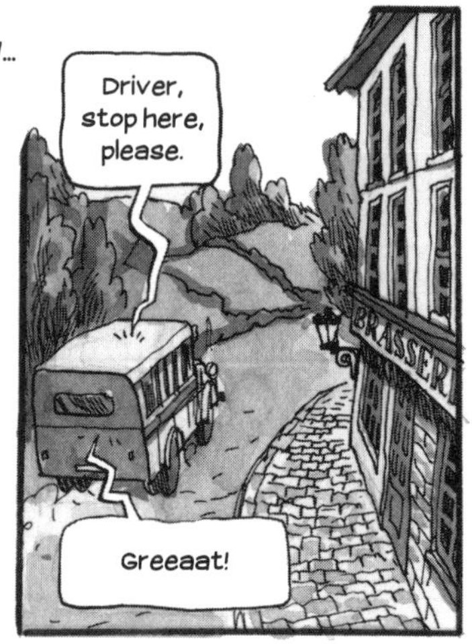
Driver, stop here, please.
Greeaat!
BRASSERI

...Beckett was dumped outside a roadside inn.

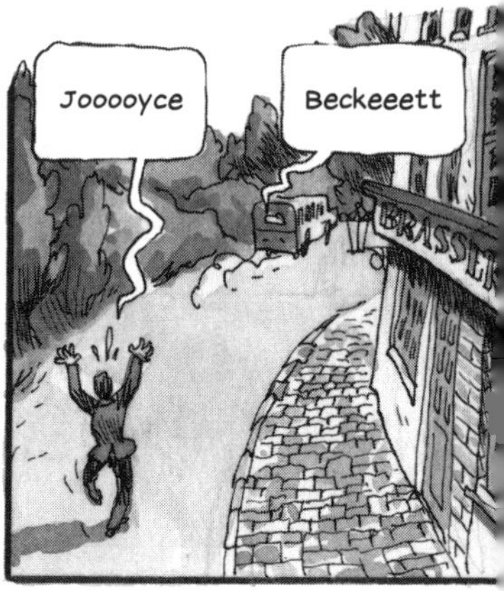
Jooooyce
Beckeeett

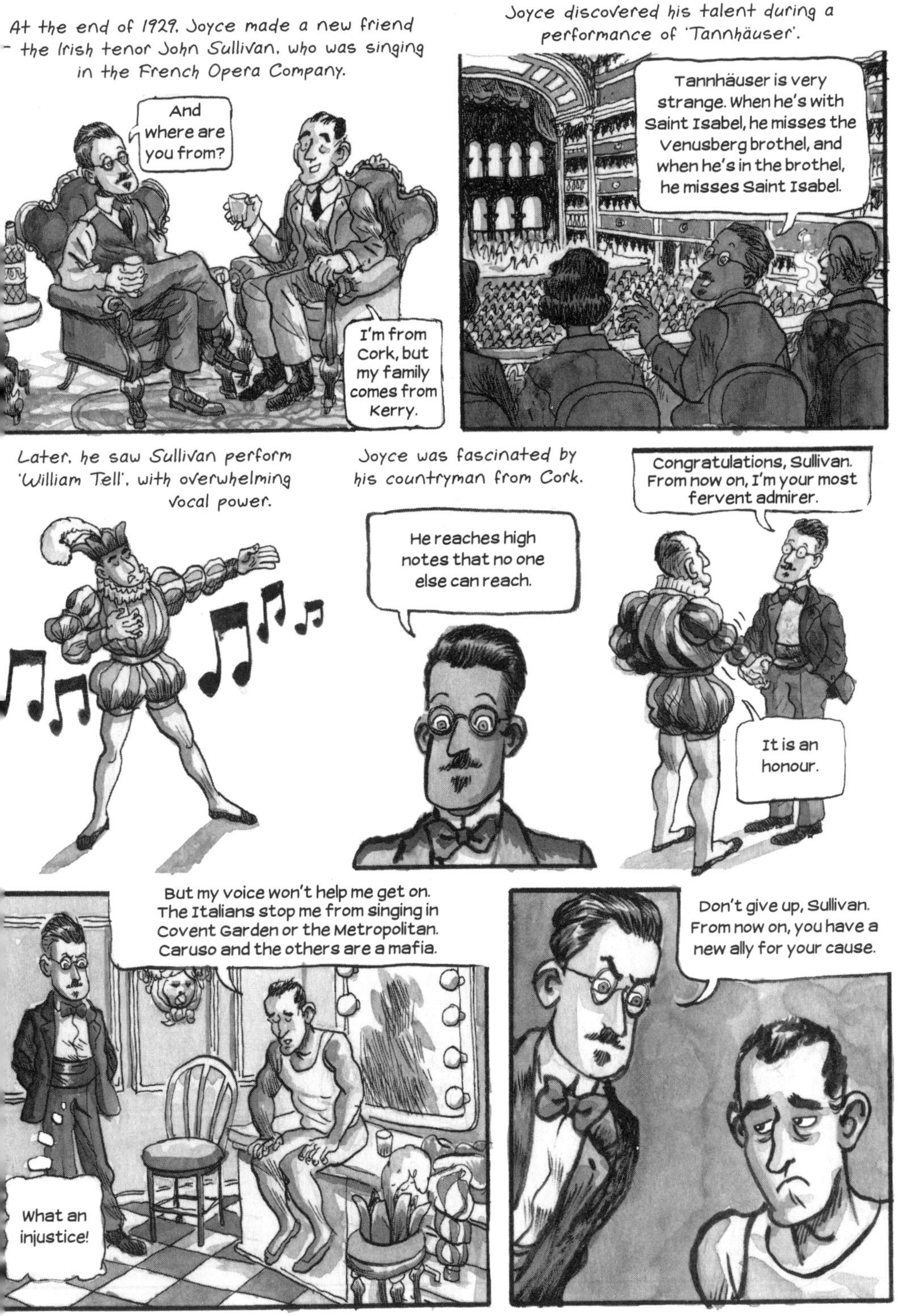

At the end of 1929, Joyce made a new friend – the Irish tenor John Sullivan, who was singing in the French Opera Company.
And where are you from?
I'm from Cork, but my family comes from Kerry.
Joyce discovered his talent during a performance of 'Tannhäuser'.
Tannhäuser is very strange. When he's with Saint Isabel, he misses the Venusberg brothel, and when he's in the brothel, he misses Saint Isabel.
Later, he saw Sullivan perform 'William Tell', with overwhelming vocal power.
Joyce was fascinated by his countryman from Cork.
He reaches high notes that no one else can reach.
Congratulations, Sullivan. From now on, I'm your most fervent admirer.
It is an honour.
But my voice won't help me get on. The Italians stop me from singing in Covent Garden or the Metropolitan. Caruso and the others are a mafia.
What an injustice!
Don't give up, Sullivan. From now on, you have a new ally for your cause.

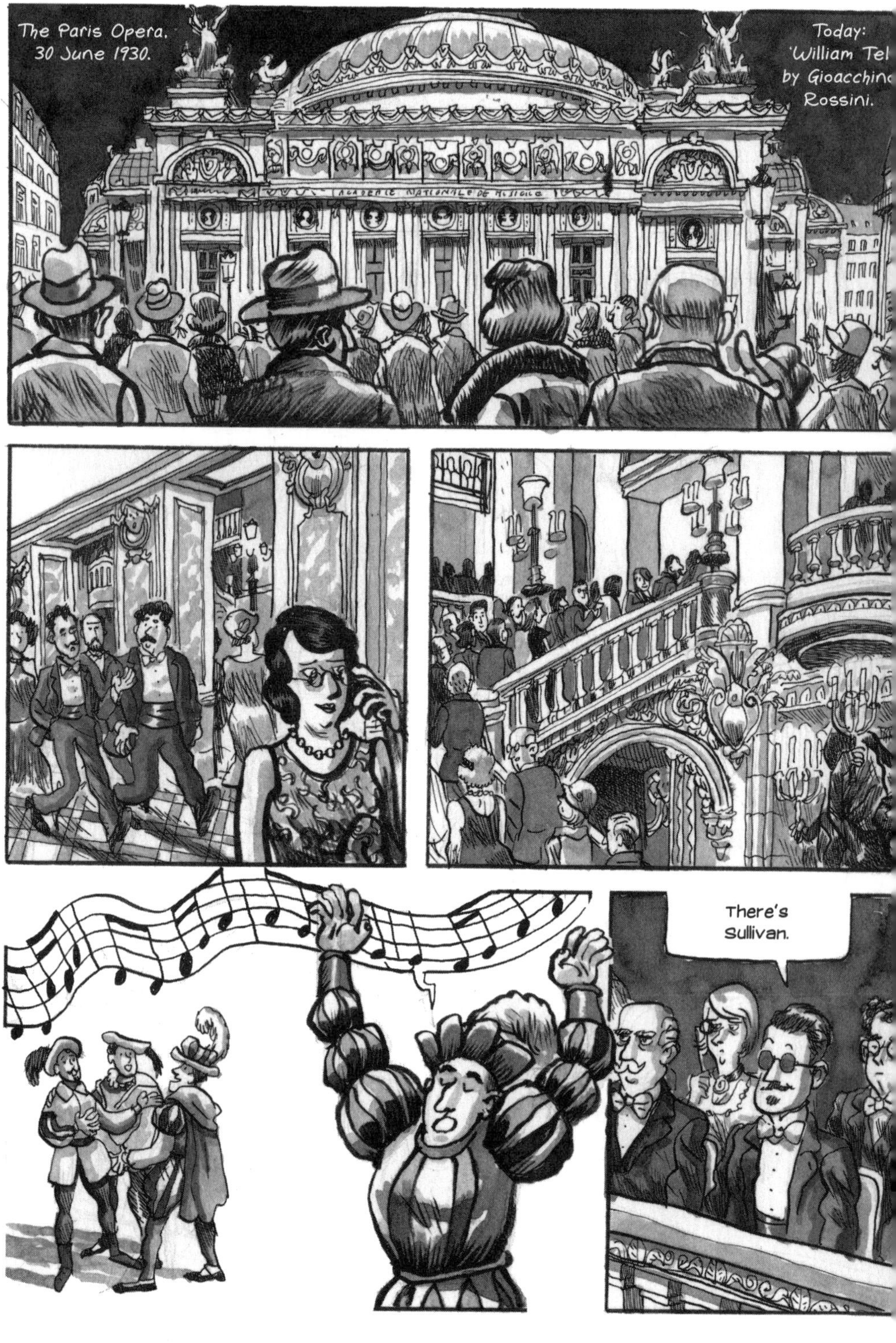
The Paris Opera.
30 June 1930.
Today:
'William Tel
by Gioacchin
Rossini.
There's
Sullivan.

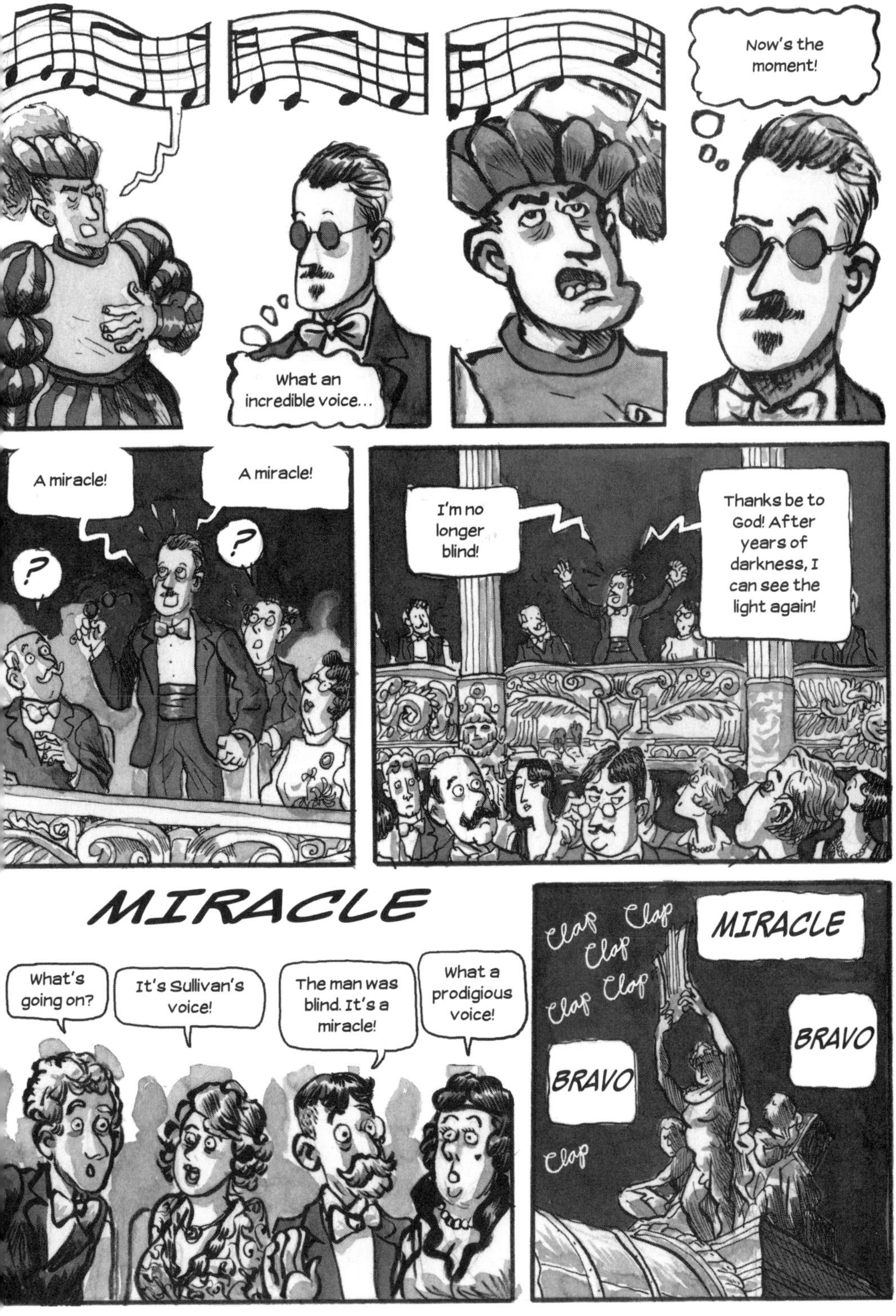
Now's the moment!
What an incredible voice...
A miracle!
A miracle!
I'm no longer blind!
Thanks be to God! After years of darkness, I can see the light again!
MIRACLE
What's going on?
It's Sullivan's voice!
The man was blind. It's a miracle!
What a prodigious voice!
Clap Clap Clap
Clap Clap
MIRACLE
BRAVO
BRAVO
Clap

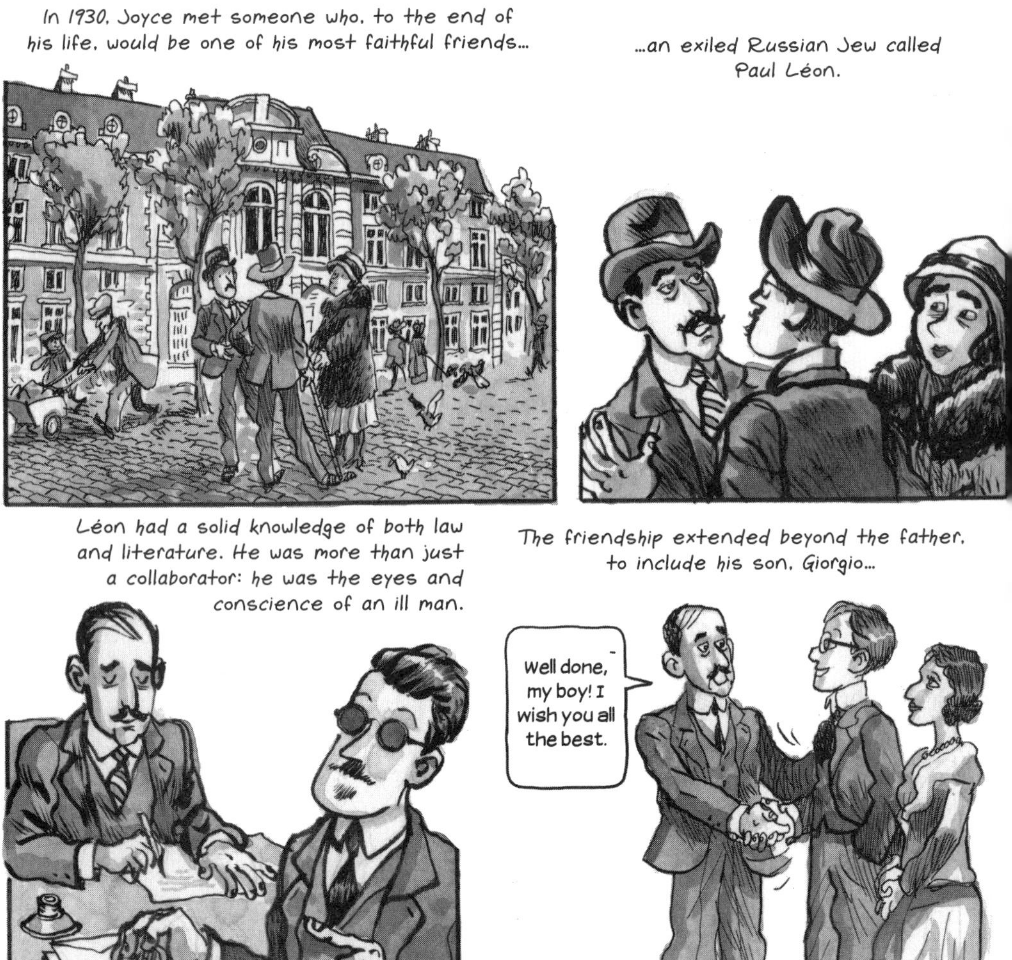
In 1930, Joyce met someone who, to the end of his life, would be one of his most faithful friends...
...an exiled Russian Jew called Paul Léon.
Léon had a solid knowledge of both law and literature. He was more than just a collaborator: he was the eyes and conscience of an ill man.
The friendship extended beyond the father, to include his son, Giorgio...
Well done, my boy! I wish you all the best.
...for which reason, on 10 December 1930, the Léons attended the marriage of Joyce's son to Helen Fleischmann, an American girl.

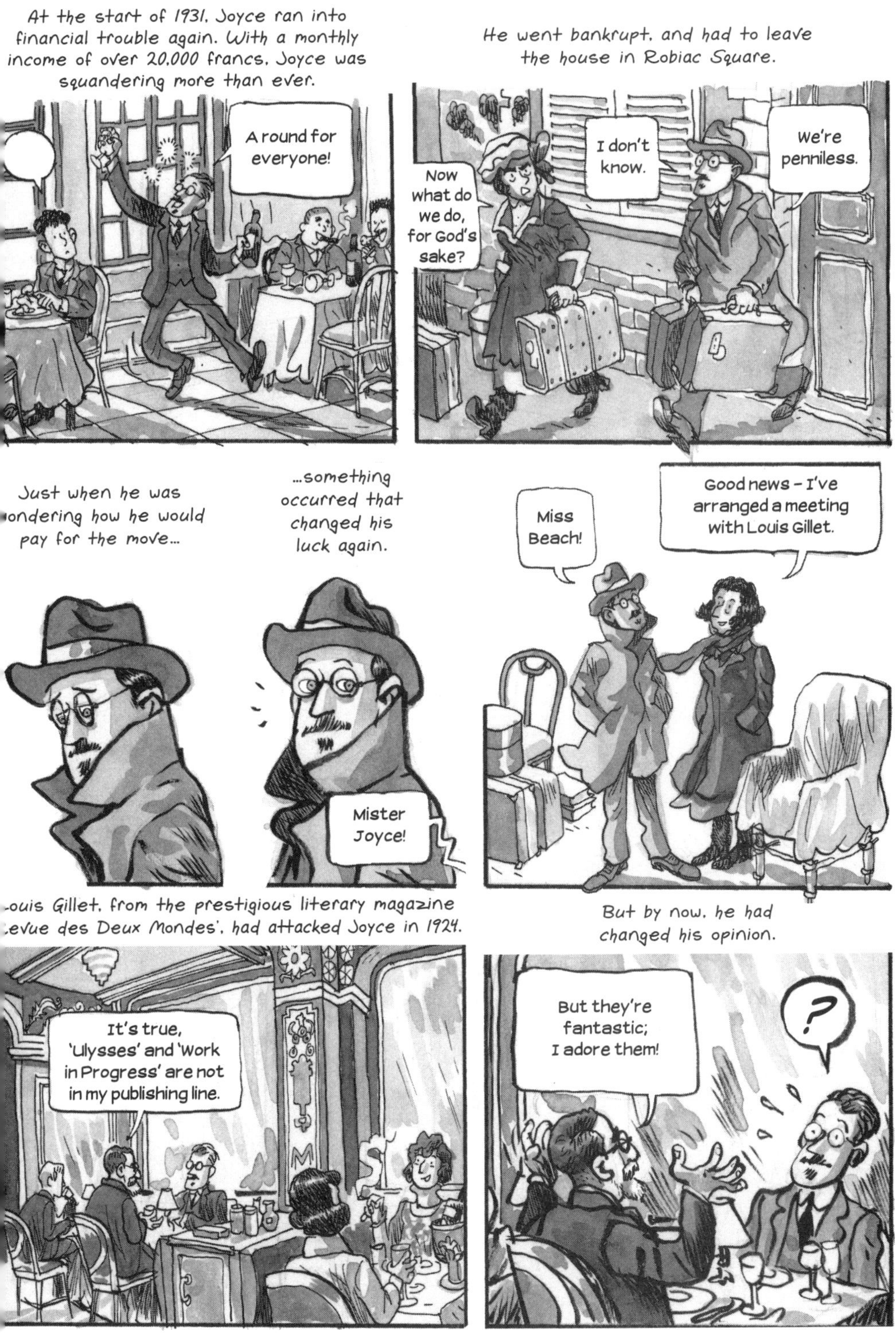
At the start of 1931, Joyce ran into financial trouble again. With a monthly income of over 20,000 francs, Joyce was squandering more than ever.
A round for everyone!
He went bankrupt, and had to leave the house in Robiac Square.
Now what do we do, for God's sake?
I don't know.
We're penniless.
Just when he was
ondering how he would pay for the move...
...something occurred that changed his luck again.
Mister Joyce!
Miss Beach!
Good news – I've arranged a meeting with Louis Gillet.
ouis Gillet, from the prestigious literary magazine
evue des Deux Mondes', had attacked Joyce in 1924.
It's true, 'Ulysses' and 'Work in Progress' are not in my publishing line.
But by now, he had changed his opinion.
But they're fantastic; I adore them!
?

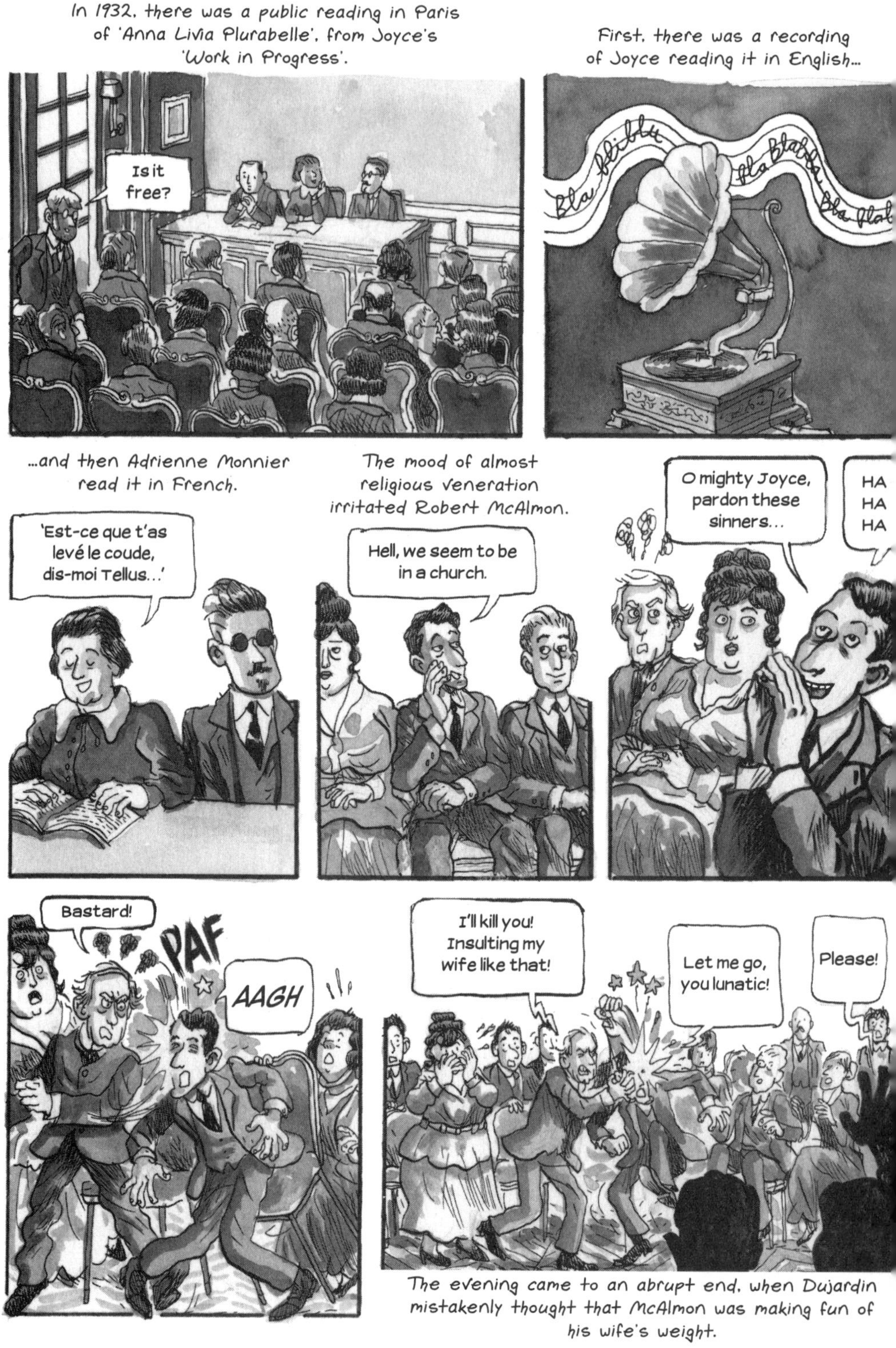
In 1932, there was a public reading in Paris of 'Anna Livia Plurabelle', from Joyce's 'Work in Progress'.
Is it free?
First, there was a recording of Joyce reading it in English...
...and then Adrienne Monnier read it in French.
'Est-ce que t'as levé le coude, dis-moi Tellus...'
The mood of almost religious veneration irritated Robert McAlmon.
Hell, we seem to be in a church.
O mighty Joyce, pardon these sinners...
HA HA HA
Bastard!
PAF
AAGH
I'll kill you! Insulting my wife like that!
Let me go, you lunatic!
Please!
The evening came to an abrupt end, when Dujardin mistakenly thought that McAlmon was making fun of his wife's weight.

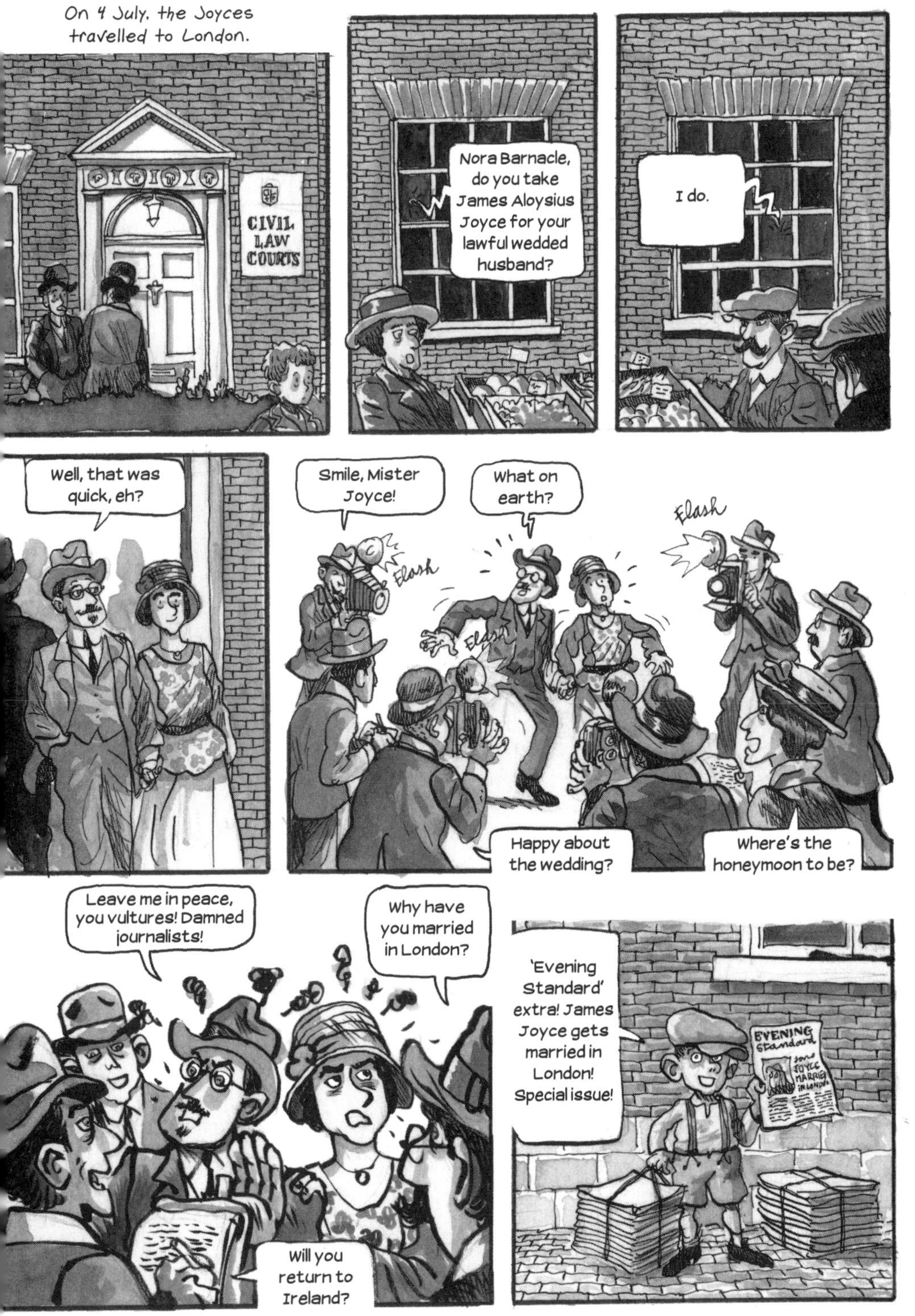
On 4 July, the Joyces travelled to London.
CIVIL LAW COURTS
Nora Barnacle, do you take James Aloysius Joyce for your lawful wedded husband?
I do.
Well, that was quick, eh?
Smile, Mister Joyce!
What on earth?
Flash
Flash
Flash
Happy about the wedding?
Where's the honeymoon to be?
Leave me in peace, you vultures! Damned journalists!
Why have you married in London?
Will you return to Ireland?
'Evening Standard' extra! James Joyce gets married in London! Special issue!
EVENING Standard

By 1932, the prohibitionist mood in America towards 'Ulysses' had changed.

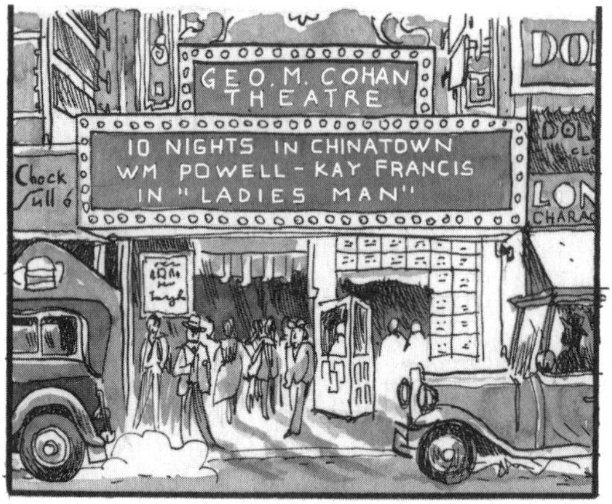
GEO. M. COHAN THEATRE
10 NIGHTS IN CHINATOWN
WM POWELL - KAY FRANCIS
IN "LADIES MAN"

Random House bought the rights for 'Ulysses' in March. The court case was pending, but the publishers were optimistic.

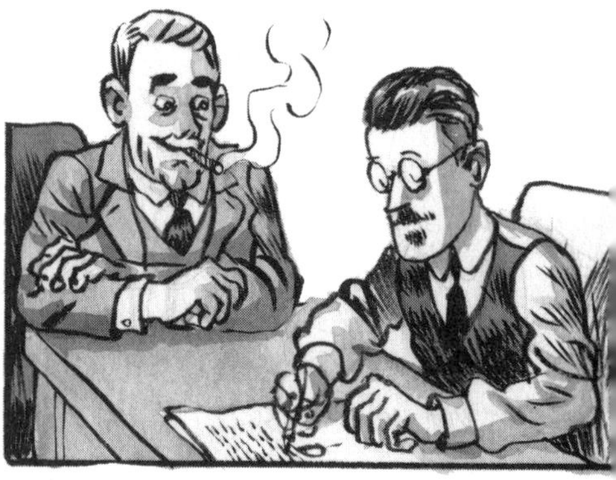

Meanwhile, a religious magazine in the US called 'Catholic World' published a polemical article, attacking Joyce and his work.

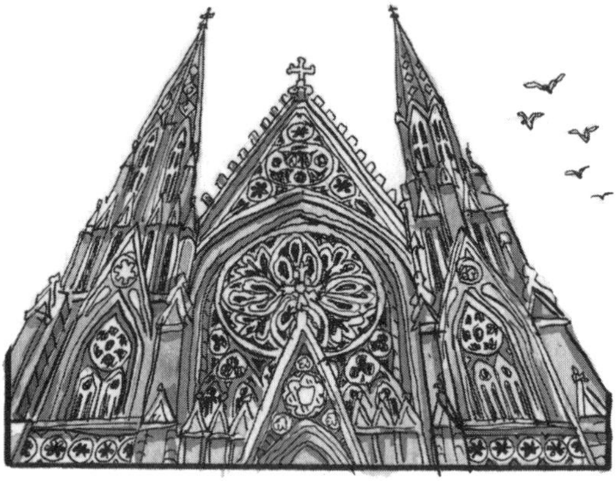

Worst of all, the author of the article was Michael Lennon, a Dublin judge and one-time friend of the Joyce family.

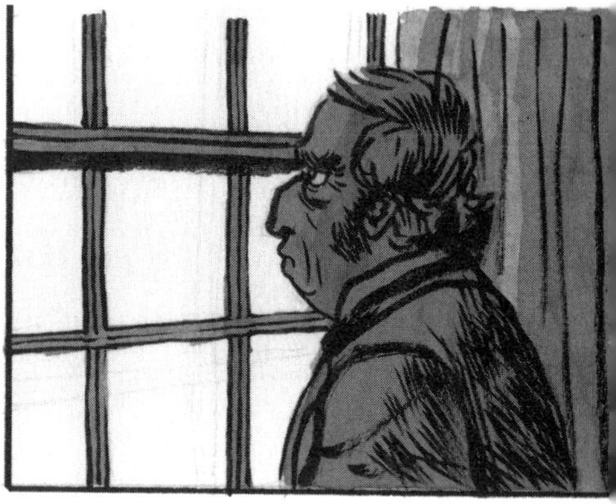

These problems were totally forgotten when his father was admitted to Drumcondra Hospital.

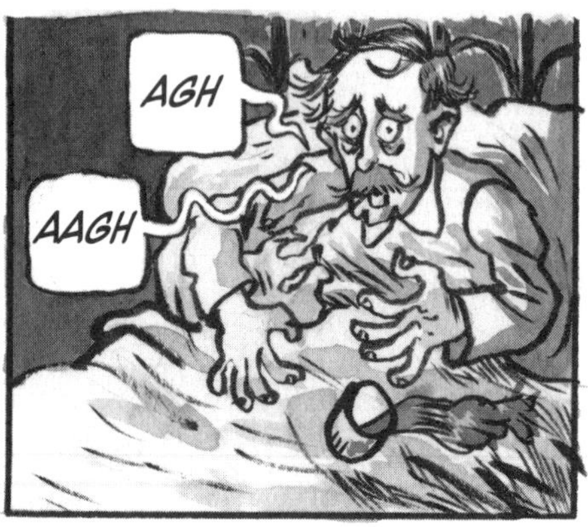
AGH
AAGH

On 29 December, John Joyce died.

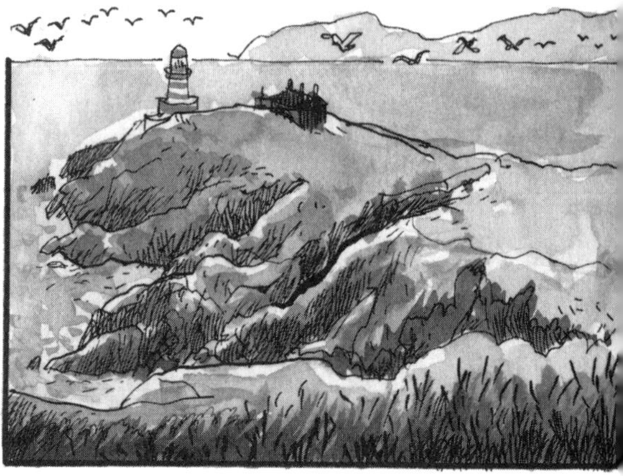

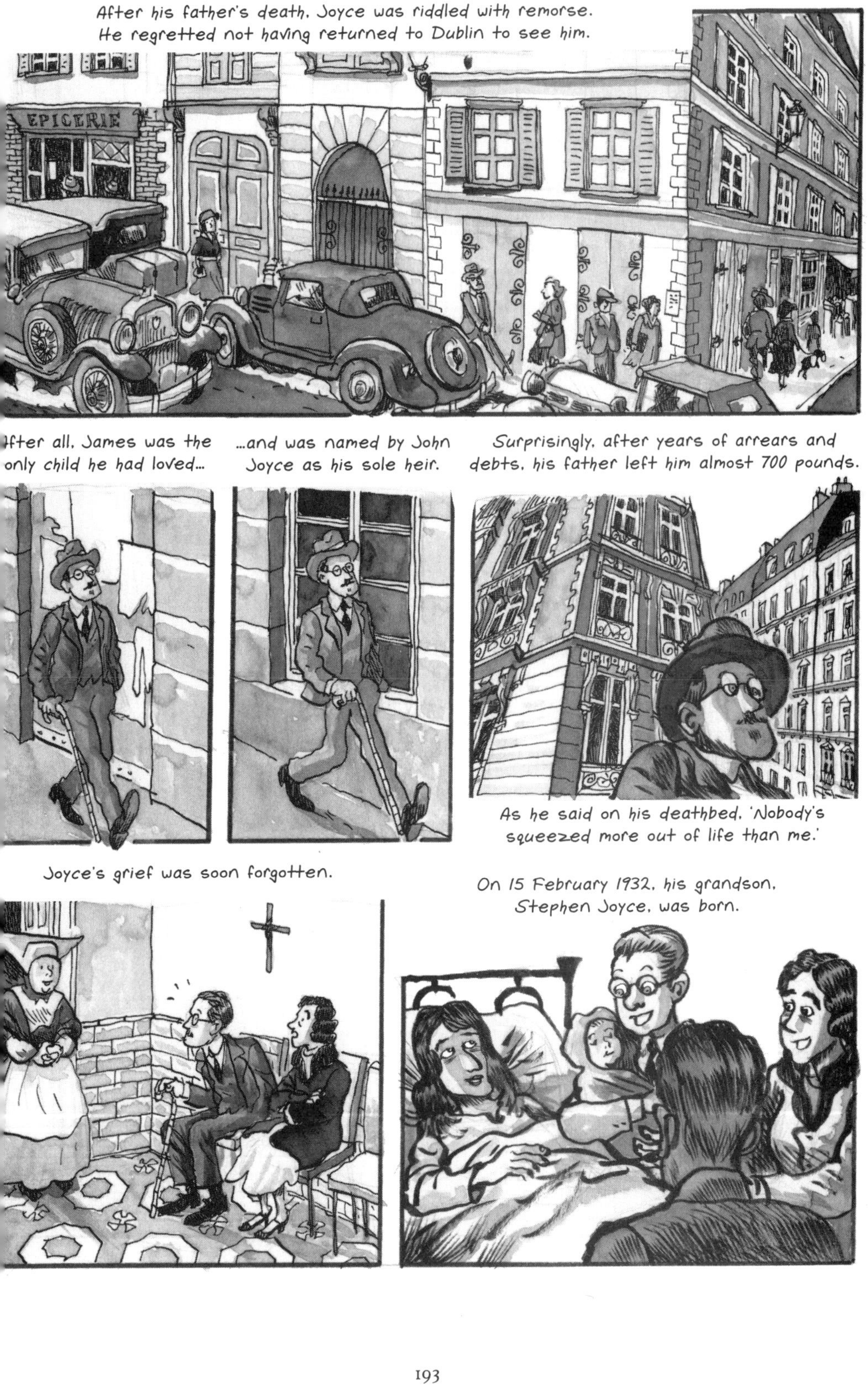
After his father's death, Joyce was riddled with remorse. He regretted not having returned to Dublin to see him.
EPICERIE
After all, James was the only child he had loved...
...and was named by John Joyce as his sole heir.
Surprisingly, after years of arrears and debts, his father left him almost 700 pounds.
As he said on his deathbed, 'Nobody's squeezed more out of life than me.'
Joyce's grief was soon forgotten.
On 15 February 1932, his grandson, Stephen Joyce, was born.

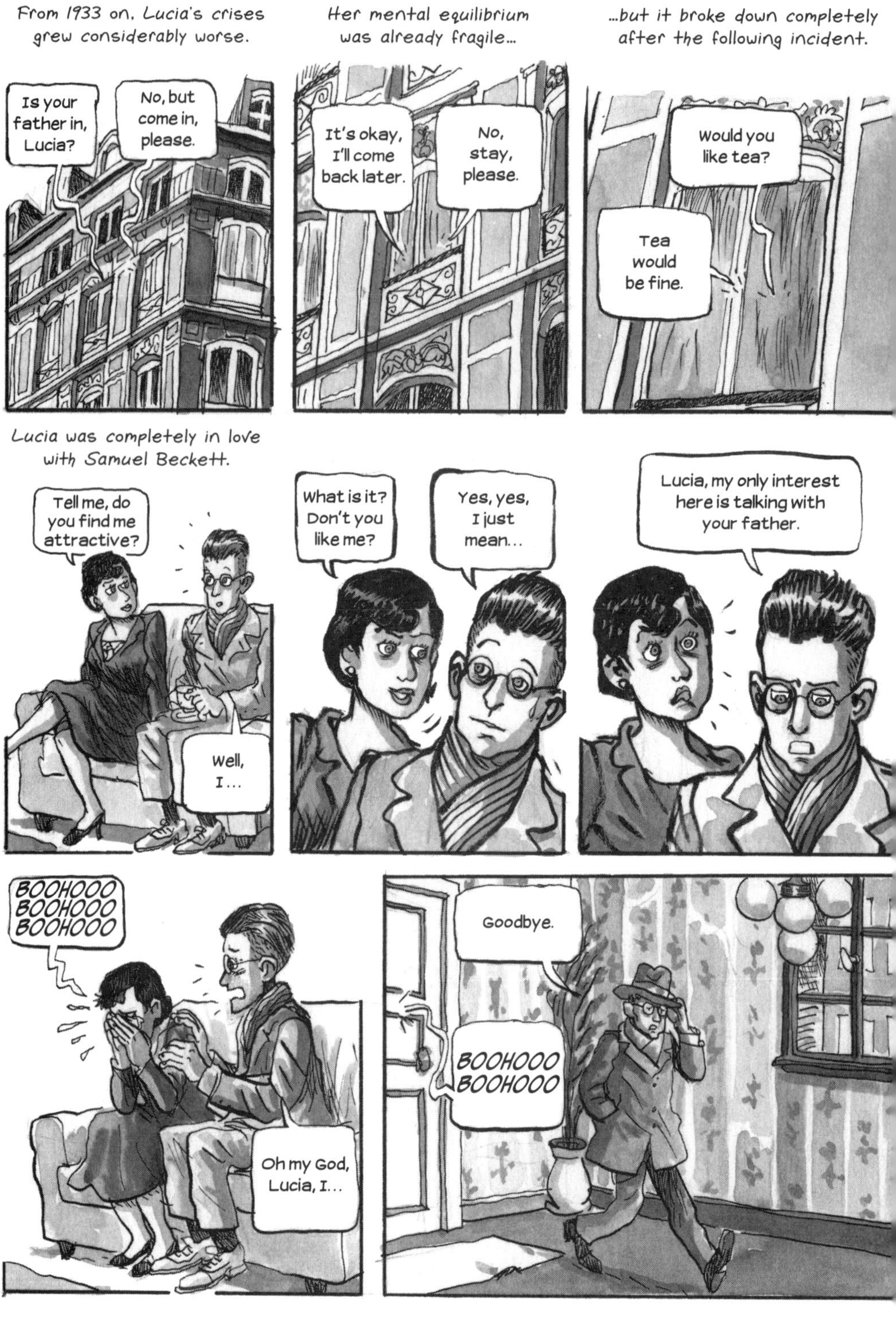
From 1933 on, Lucia's crises grew considerably worse.
Is your father in, Lucia?
No, but come in, please.
Her mental equilibrium was already fragile...
It's okay, I'll come back later.
No, stay, please.
...but it broke down completely after the following incident.
Would you like tea?
Tea would be fine.
Lucia was completely in love with Samuel Beckett.
Tell me, do you find me attractive?
Well, I...
What is it? Don't you like me?
Yes, yes, I just mean...
Lucia, my only interest here is talking with your father.
BOOHOOO BOOHOOO BOOHOOO
Oh my God, Lucia, I...
Goodbye.
BOOHOOO BOOHOOO

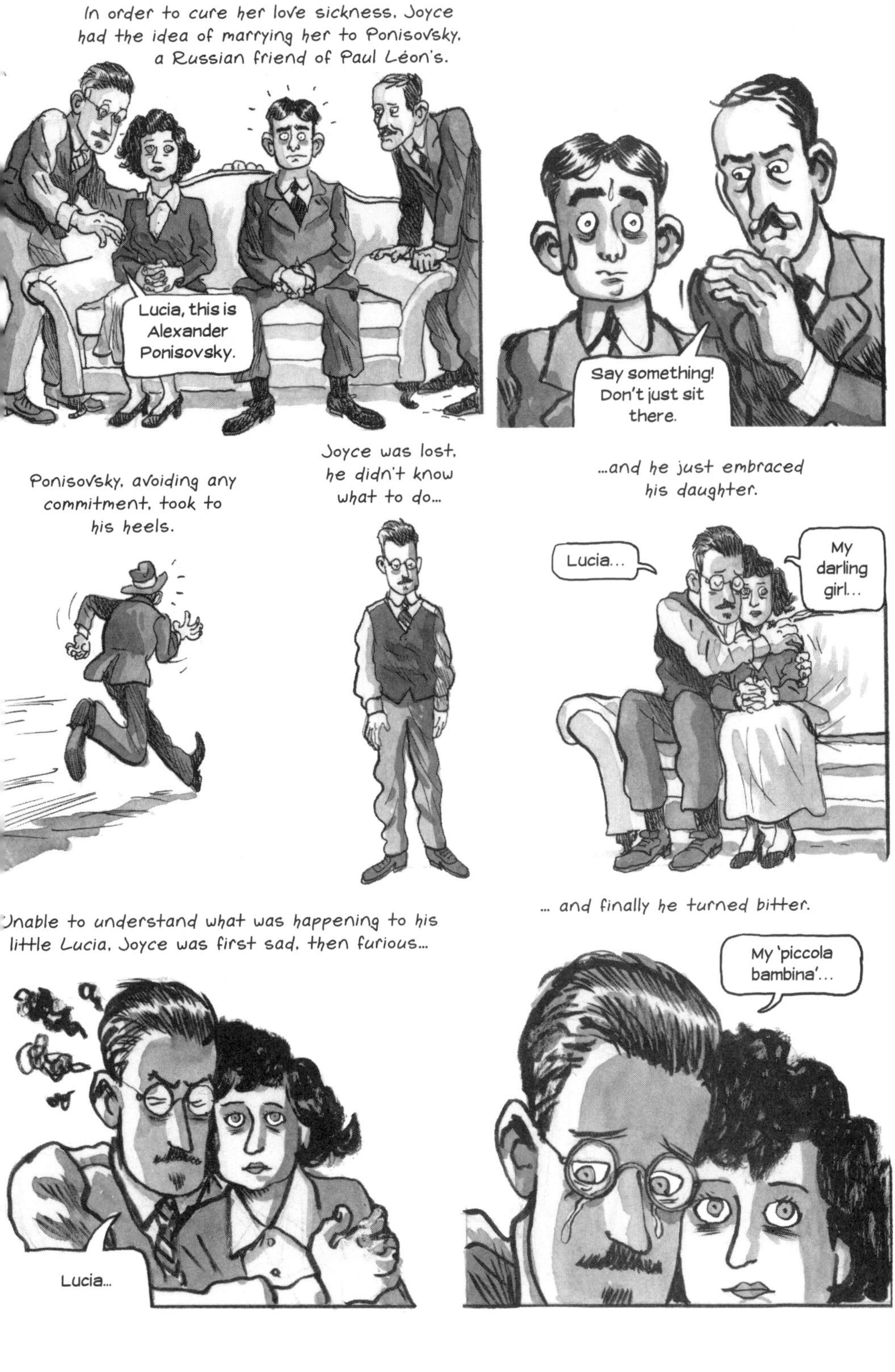
In order to cure her love sickness, Joyce had the idea of marrying her to Ponisovsky, a Russian friend of Paul Léon's.
Lucia, this is Alexander Ponisovsky.
Say something! Don't just sit there.
Ponisovsky, avoiding any commitment, took to his heels.
Joyce was lost, he didn't know what to do...
...and he just embraced his daughter.
Lucia...
My darling girl...
Unable to understand what was happening to his little Lucia, Joyce was first sad, then furious...
Lucia...
... and finally he turned bitter.
My 'piccola bambina'...

In 1932, the relationship between Joyce, Miss Beach and Adrienne Monnier had cooled a lot.

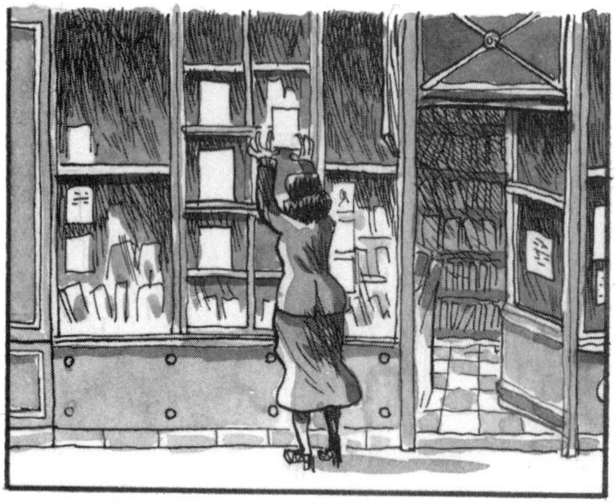

With the economic crisis, Miss Beach was unable to take on new challenges, and she handed over the publishing rights of 'Ulysses' to Odyssey Press, a major publishing house.

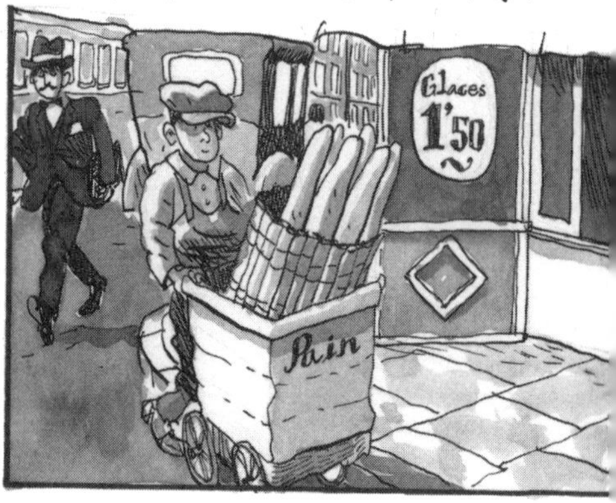

Glaces 1'50
Pain

Exhausted after seeing 'Ulysses' through to the end, she then had to suffer Joyce's indifference towards her in the last stage of their friendship.

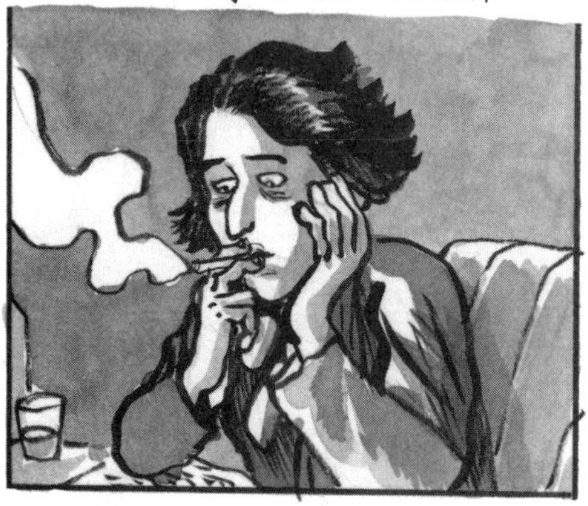

It was unfair, selfish behavior, which the author himself publicly acknowledged.

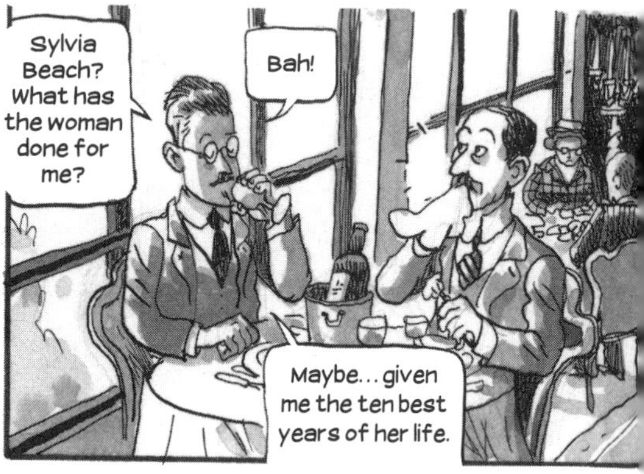

Sylvia Beach? What has the woman done for me?
Bah!
Maybe... given me the ten best years of her life.

By then, Joyce was already thought of as a genius. Warner Brothers tried, unsuccessfully, to buy the film rights for 'Ulysses'...

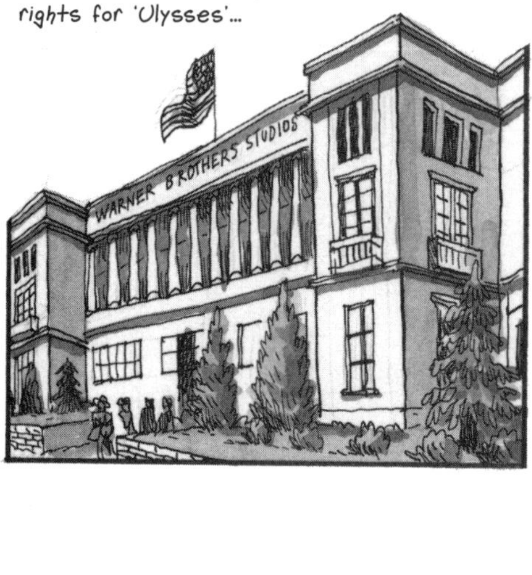

WARNER BROTHERS STUDIOS

...and the author received a visit from Sergei Eisenstein to examine the possibilities of adapting it for the screen.

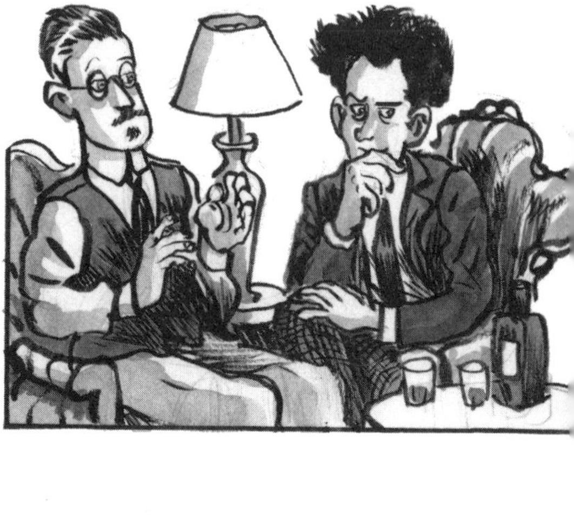

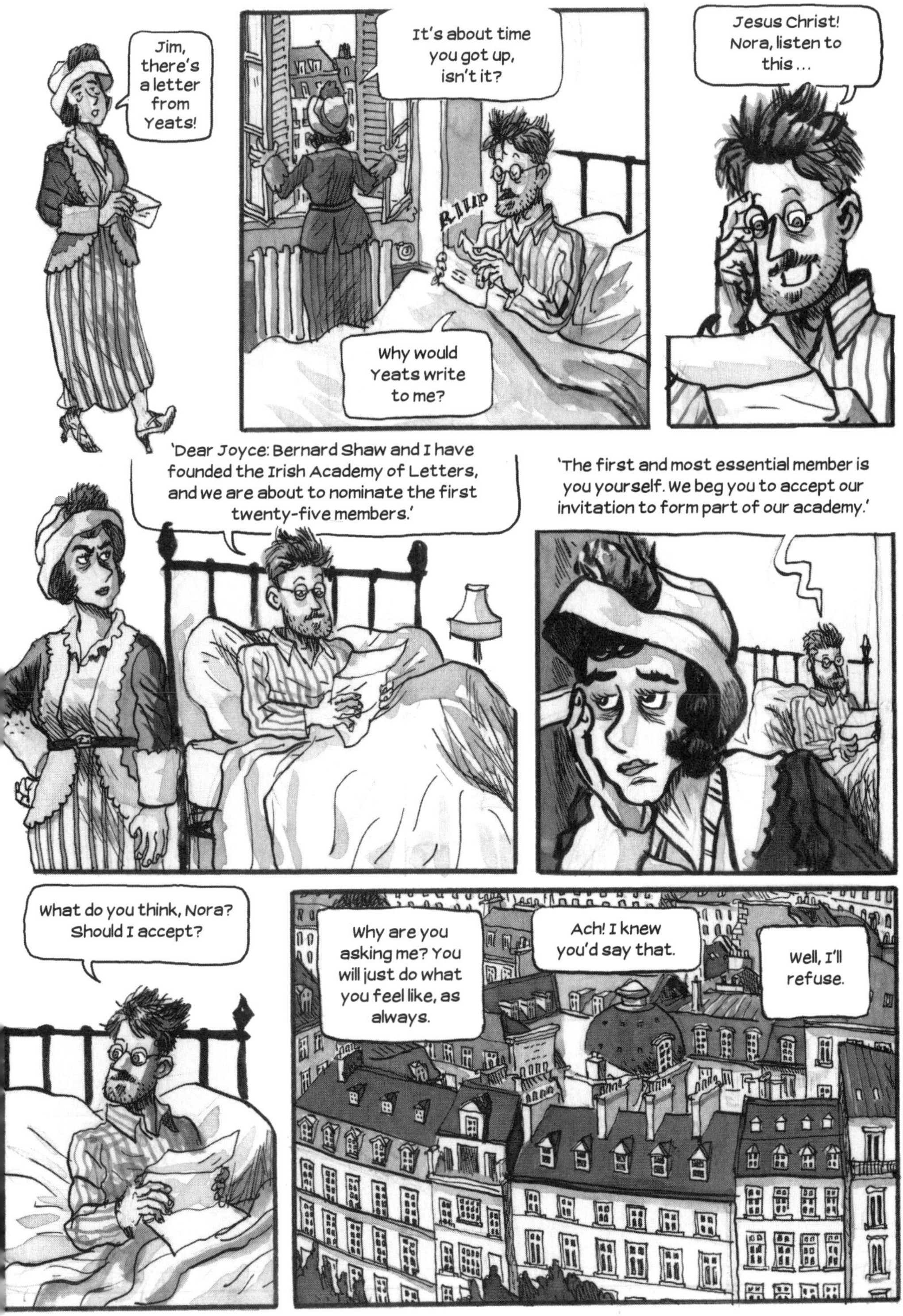
Jim, there's a letter from Yeats!
It's about time you got up, isn't it?
RIIIP
Why would Yeats write to me?
Jesus Christ! Nora, listen to this ...
'Dear Joyce: Bernard Shaw and I have founded the Irish Academy of Letters, and we are about to nominate the first twenty-five members.'
'The first and most essential member is you yourself. We beg you to accept our invitation to form part of our academy.'
What do you think, Nora? Should I accept?
Why are you asking me? You will just do what you feel like, as always.
Ach! I knew you'd say that.
Well, I'll refuse.

To keep Lucia busy, Joyce gave her educational activities such as designing letter types or illustrations for his books.

Lucia lived in a parallel world. She lied constantly, and became more and more enclosed within herself.

Absurd remedies recommended by incompetent doctors, such as drinking sea water, only worsened her condition.

Joyce suffered greatly for his daughter.

But he refused to accept the truth.

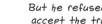

Well, she'll get over it.

He found Lucia's obvious schizophrenia unbearable, and blamed the rest of the world instead.

I've never been understood!

And they don't understand Lucia either, because she has my genius!

Lucia's illness caused her father insomnia and nervous disorders...

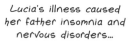

I can't sleep...

...and severe alcoholism.

I need a drink

In July, Lucia had a violent attack of hysteria in a Zürich train station.

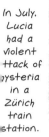

Leave me alone! Don't touch me, you monsters! You want to kill me! You want to kill me!

At the end of the month, she was admitted to Doctor Forel's mental hospital in Nyon.

The outbursts of violence gave way to a state of almost permanent sleepiness. Lucia was obsessed with imaginary conflicts between her parents.

But Dr Forel's aggressive treatment, based on mental suggestion and persuasion, terrified her.

After six days, Joyce took her away from there.

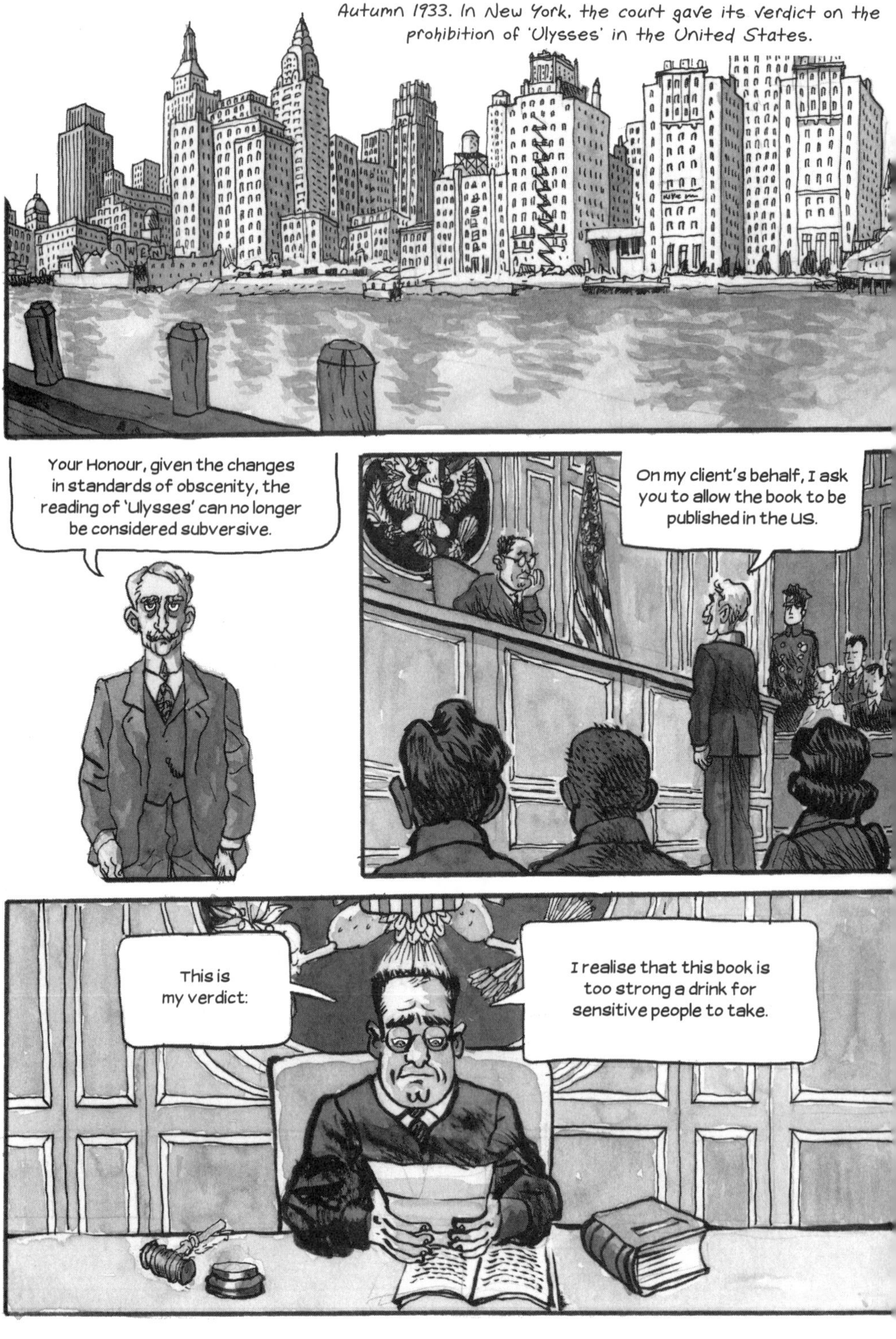
Autumn 1933. In New York, the court gave its verdict on the prohibition of 'Ulysses' in the United States.
Your Honour, given the changes in standards of obscenity, the reading of 'Ulysses' can no longer be considered subversive.
On my client's behalf, I ask you to allow the book to be published in the US.
This is my verdict:
I realise that this book is too strong a drink for sensitive people to take.

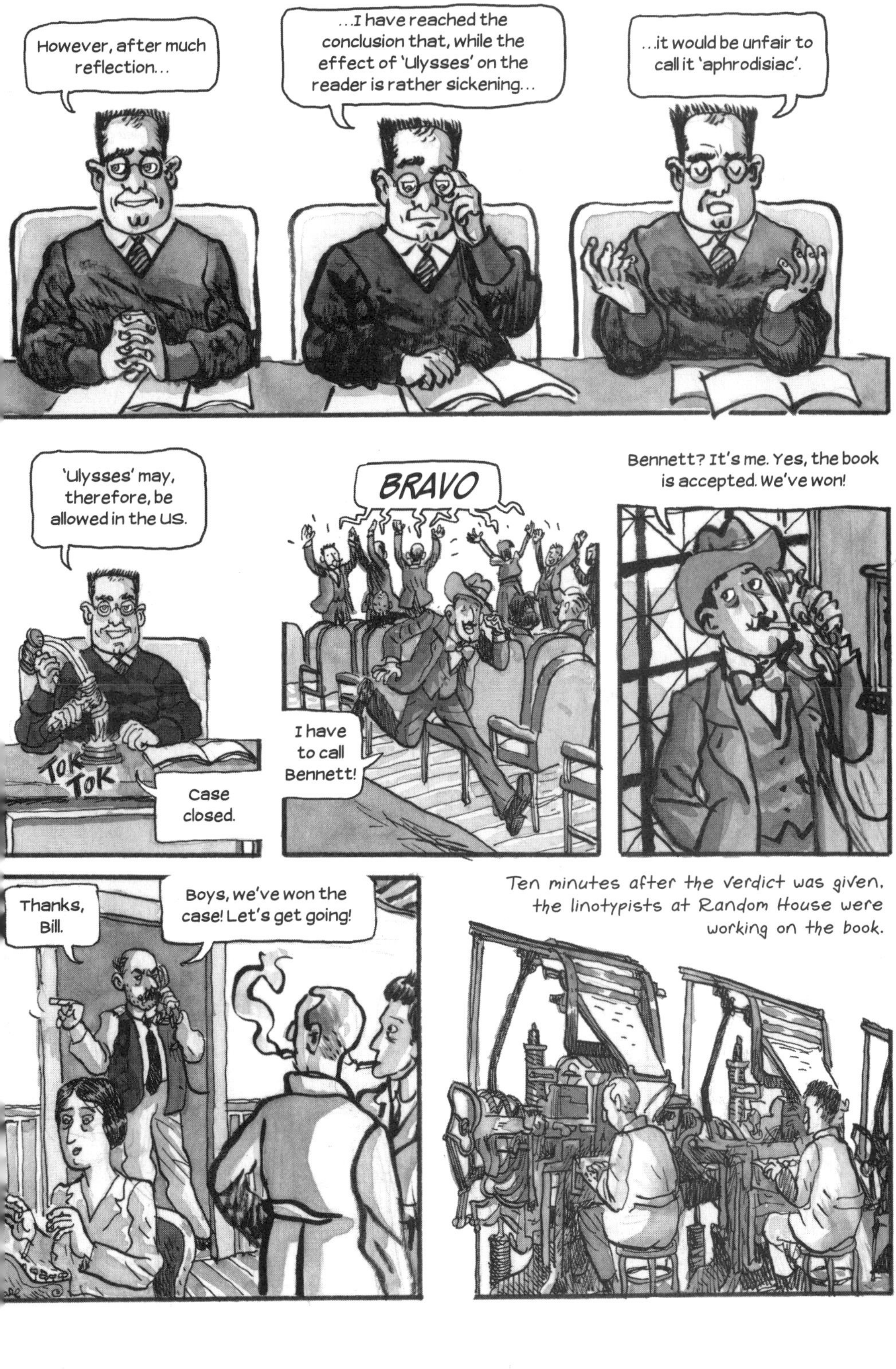
However, after much reflection...
...I have reached the conclusion that, while the effect of 'Ulysses' on the reader is rather sickening...
...it would be unfair to call it 'aphrodisiac'.
'Ulysses' may, therefore, be allowed in the US.
TOK TOK
Case closed.
BRAVO
I have to call Bennett!
Bennett? It's me. Yes, the book is accepted. We've won!
Thanks, Bill.
Boys, we've won the case! Let's get going!
Ten minutes after the verdict was given, the linotypists at Random House were working on the book.

On 2 February 1934, after hitting her mother during her birthday party, Lucia was admitted again to the Nyon hospital.

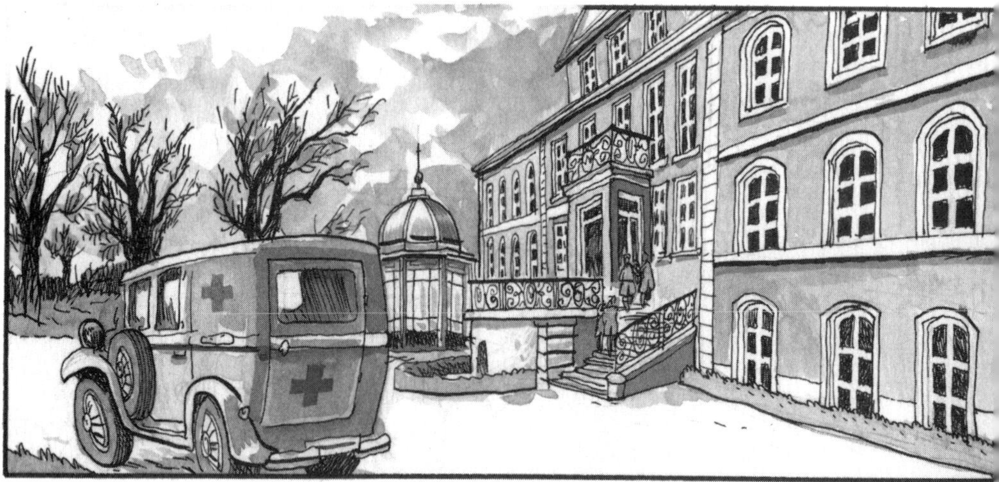

Lucia was completely apathetic.

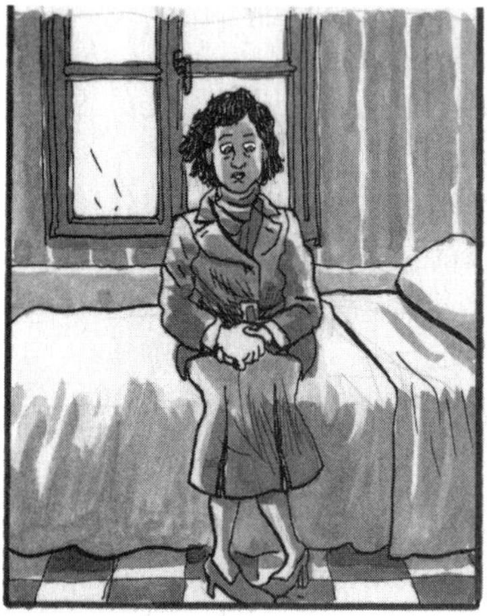

Joyce's hopes for an improvement disappeared after she suffered a 'pseudohallucinatory mental dissociation', and ran away from the centre.

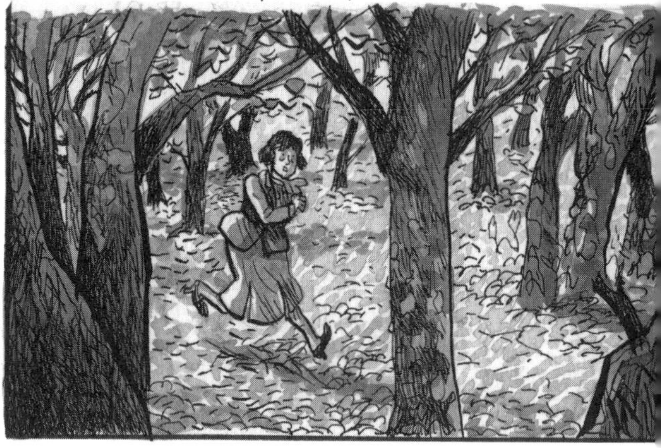

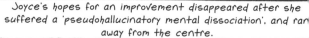

She was found by a farmer, sleeping in a mountain refuge near the frontier.

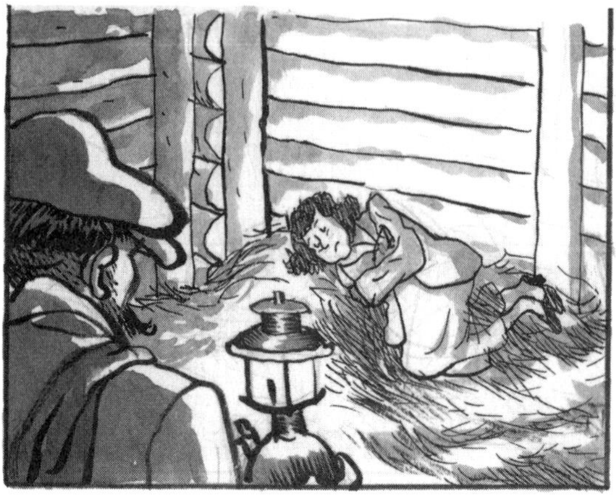

Joyce was still determined to save his daughter, but Lucia went from bad to worse.

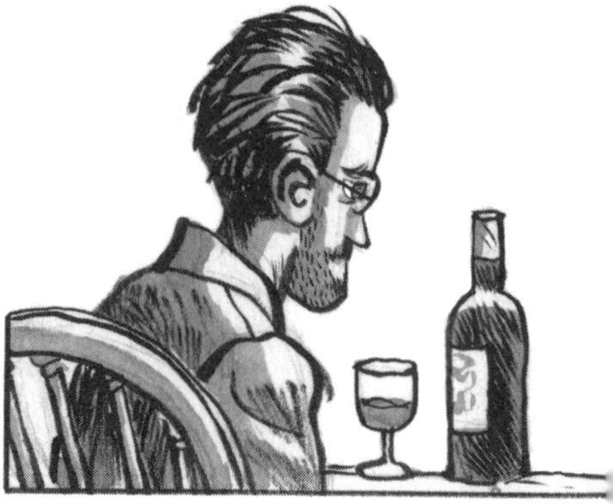

Joyce retired for a rest to Spa in Belgium. It was the time of the 'Anschluss'. and the rise of Nazism worried him.

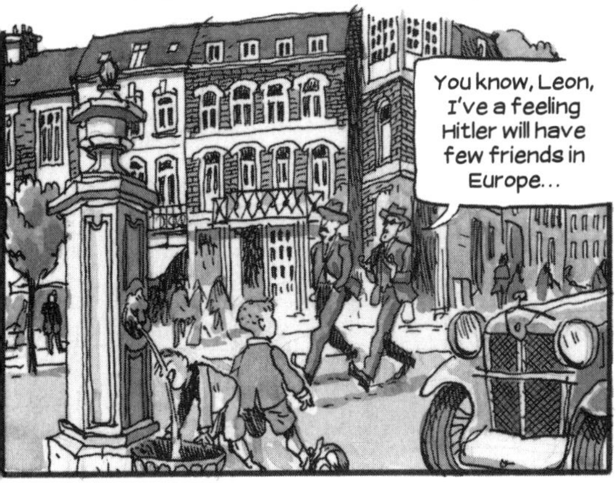
You know, Leon, I've a feeling Hitler will have few friends in Europe...

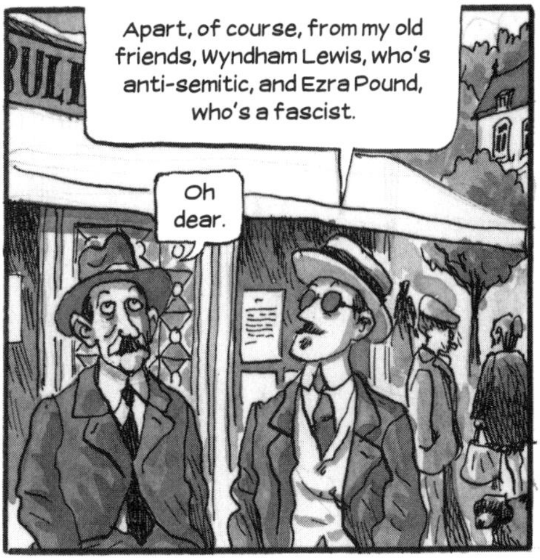
Apart, of course, from my old friends, Wyndham Lewis, who's anti-semitic, and Ezra Pound, who's a fascist.
Oh dear.

A special edition of 'Ulysses' was to be published in the US by the 'Limited Editions Club'. The French artist Matisse was commissioned to do the illustrations.

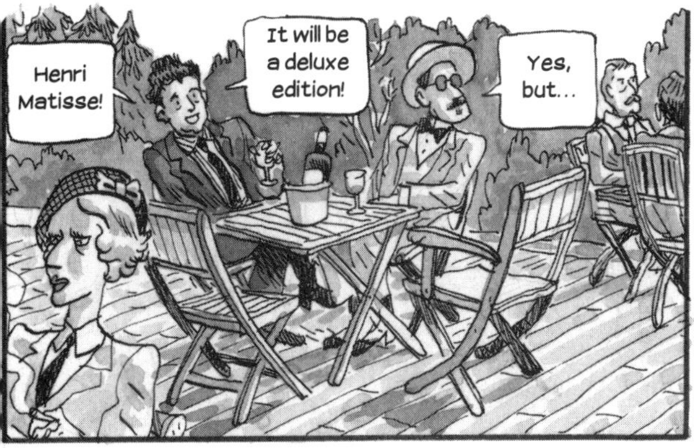
Henri Matisse!
It will be a deluxe edition!
Yes, but...

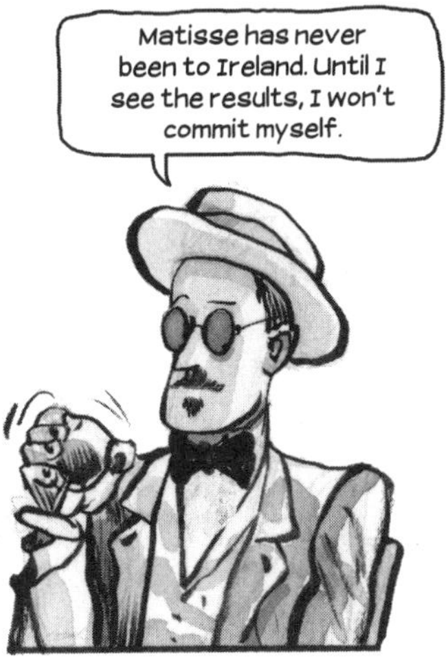
Matisse has never been to Ireland. Until I see the results, I won't commit myself.

Matisse had finished the illustrations by the end of 1934. Joyce was not happy.

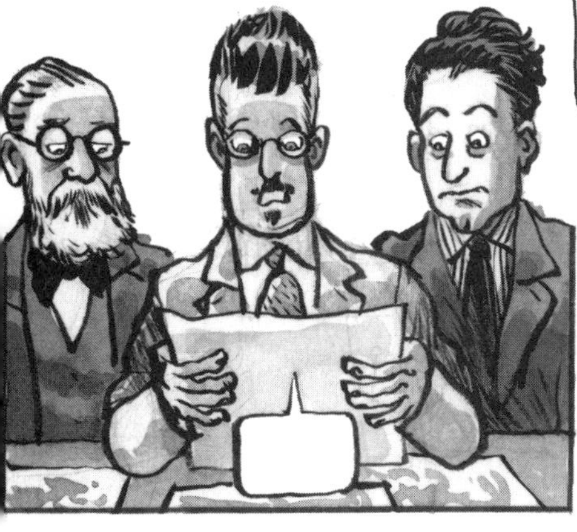

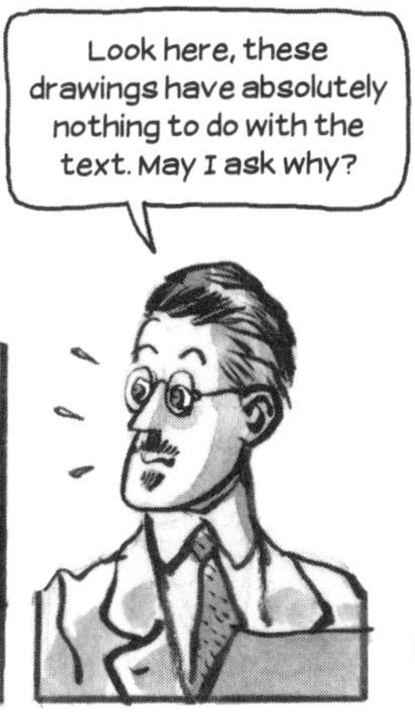
Look here, these drawings have absolutely nothing to do with the text. May I ask why?

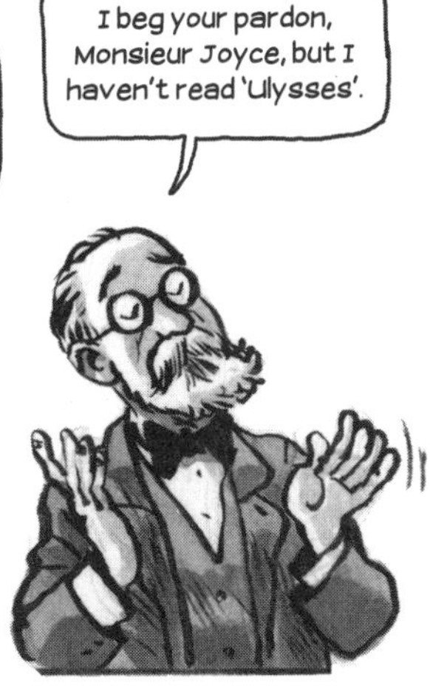
I beg your pardon, Monsieur Joyce, but I haven't read 'Ulysses'.

On 28 September, Lucia was moved to a private clinic in Küsnacht.

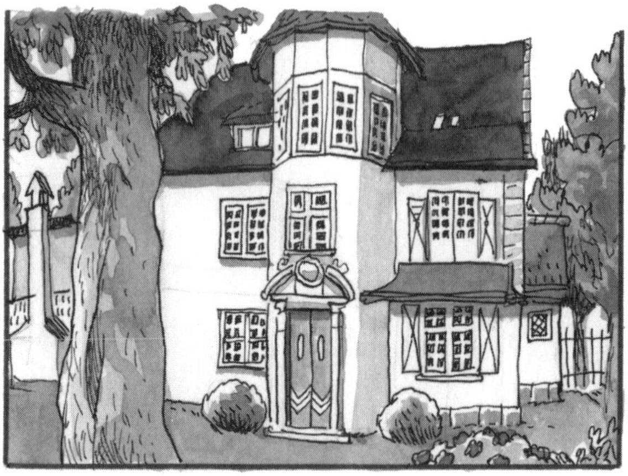

In desperation, Joyce sought help from someone he detested deeply:

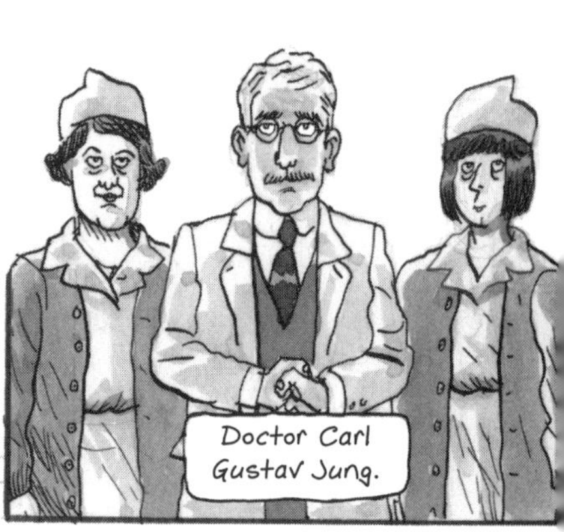
Doctor Carl Gustav Jung.

Lucia conversed animatedly with Jung, and she seemed happier. But it was just an illusion.

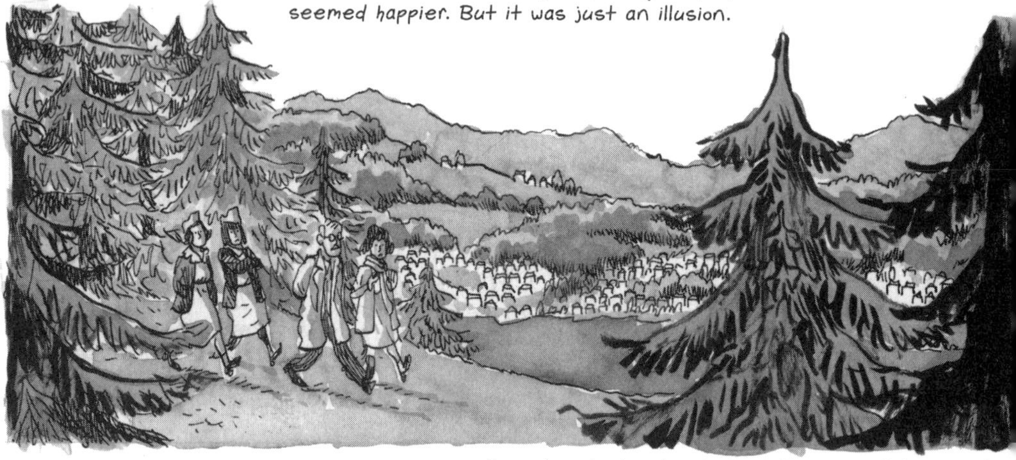

After some initial success, Jung lost control over her.

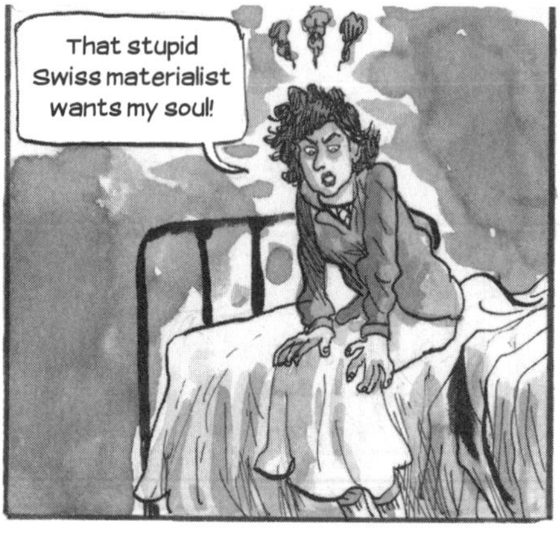
That stupid Swiss materialist wants my soul!

According to Jung's study of the case, father and daughter shared ideas, fixations and language. They were like two people at the bottom of a river, but while Joyce was able to swim, Lucia sank deeper and deeper.

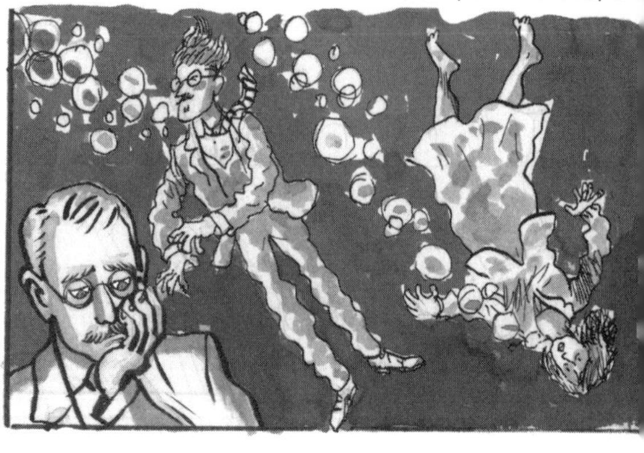

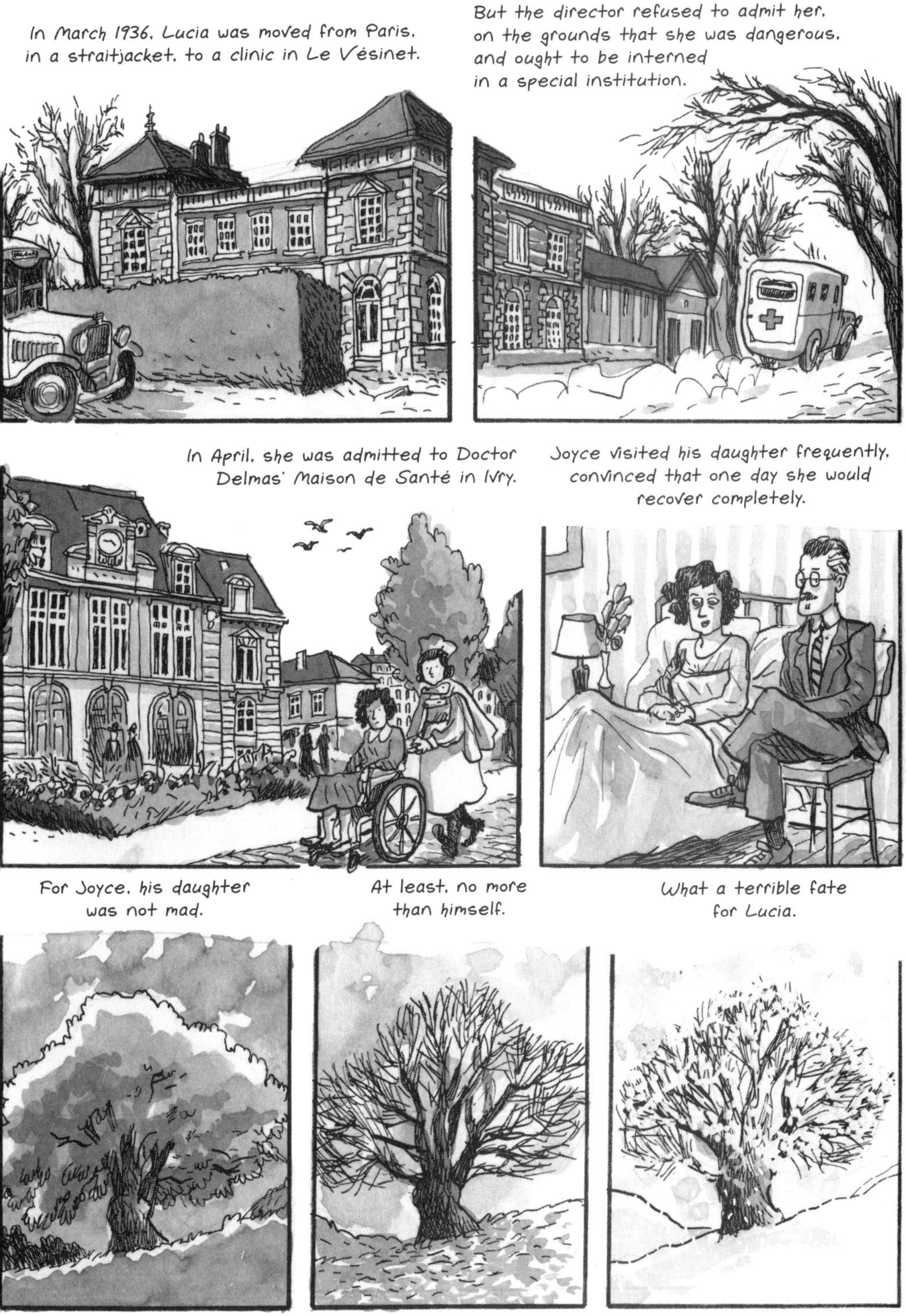
In March 1936, Lucia was moved from Paris, in a straitjacket, to a clinic in Le Vésinet.
But the director refused to admit her, on the grounds that she was dangerous, and ought to be interned in a special institution.
In April, she was admitted to Doctor Delmas' Maison de Santé in Ivry.
Joyce visited his daughter frequently, convinced that one day she would recover completely.
For Joyce, his daughter was not mad.
At least, no more than himself.
What a terrible fate for Lucia.

In April 1936, the pre-war climate in Europe was becoming clear. An Italian teacher was expelled from Malta, accused of espionage.

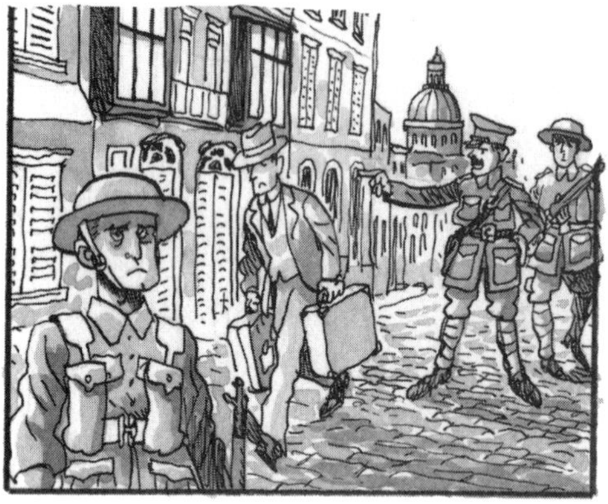

To return the affront, Mussolini expelled an English teacher from Italy.

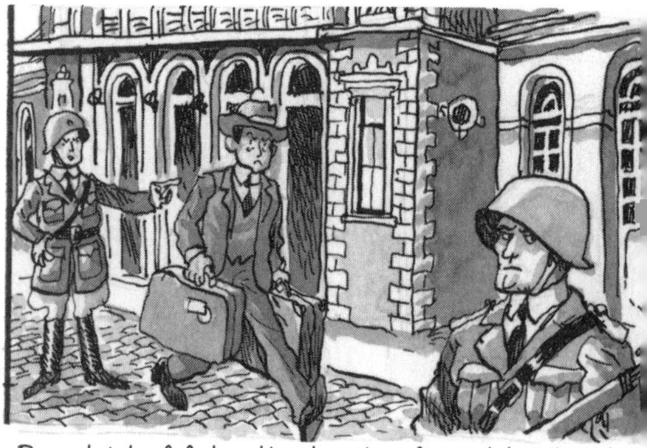

By a trick of fate, the teacher forced to abandon Trieste, accused of espionage, was Stanislaus Joyce

France wasn't immune to political agitation: militants on the left and the right threatened the fragile balance in Léon Blum's government.

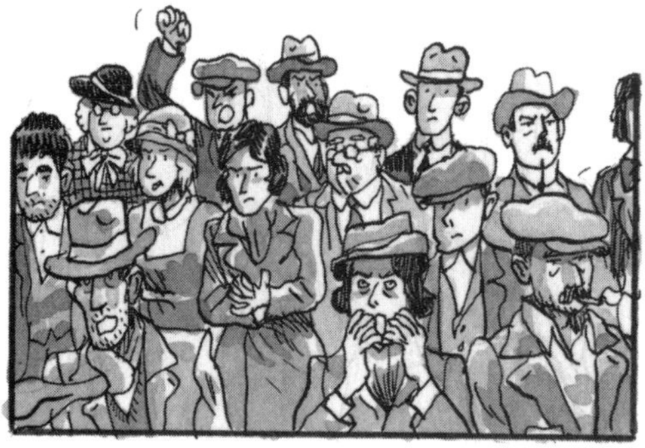

Here we have a young left-wing student, Armand 'Petit-Jean', a passionate admirer of Joyce.

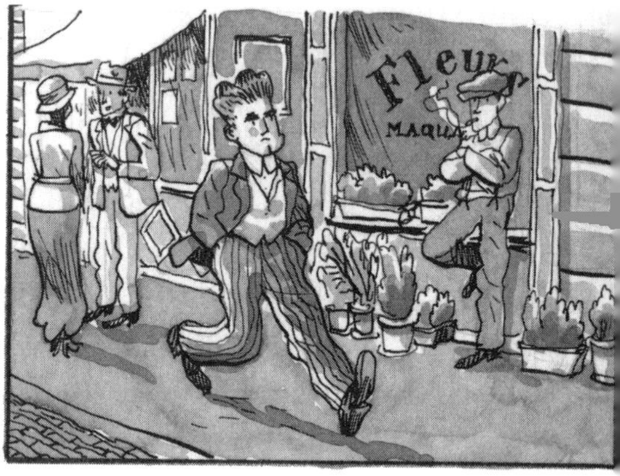

And here we have an illustrious communist, André Gide.

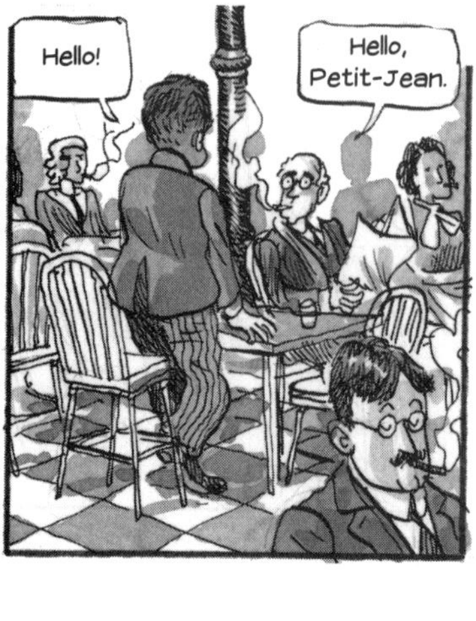
Hello!
Hello, Petit-Jean.

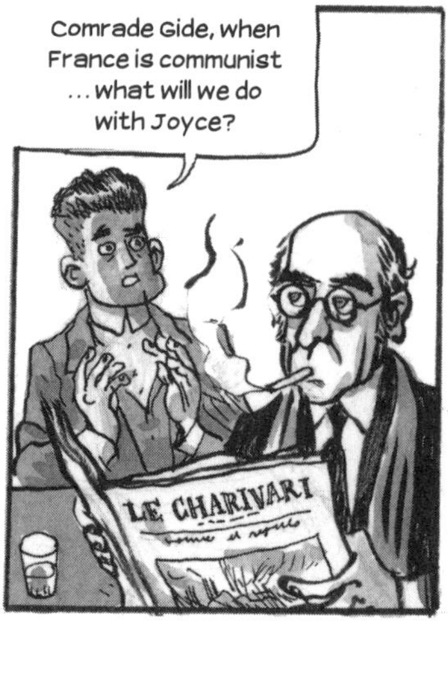
Comrade Gide, when France is communist ...what will we do with Joyce?
LE CHARIVARI

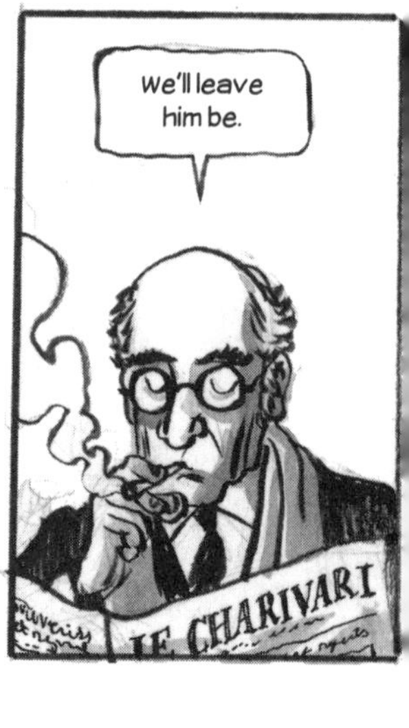
We'll leave him be.
LE CHARIVARI

Joyce continued working on his book, and reduced his social life.

He never visited Sylvia Beach's bookshop again, and saw her only on rare occasions.

His social circle was limited to old friends from the 'twenties.

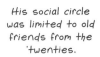

However, he sometimes met new people. In 1937, he received the architect Le Corbusier.

I am a passionate admirer of your work.

Thanks, thanks.

But let's not talk about books.

What do you think of my budgerigars?

?

This is Pierre and Pipo.

It's incredible the way the man talks of birds!

Strange as it might seem, talking about literature bored Joyce.

It is obvious that Zola didn't intend 'Germinal' as a political novel. His intention was simply to show pity for the deadened working class, condemned by its own ignorance...

Hmph! Let's get out of here, Beckett.

If that idiot had at least talked about turnips...

Turnips are interesting.

207

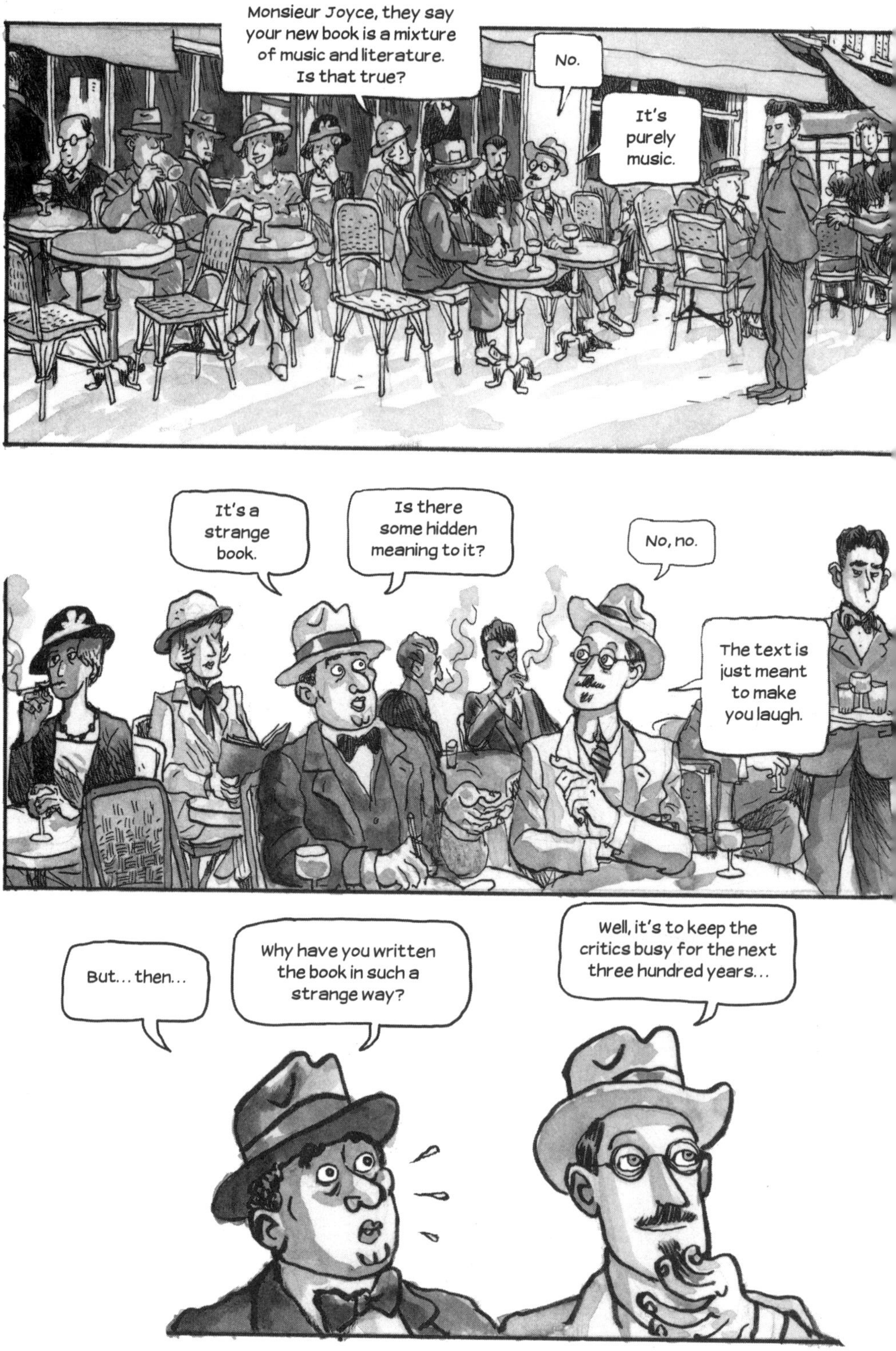

Monsieur Joyce, they say your new book is a mixture of music and literature. Is that true?
No.
It's purely music.
It's a strange book.
Is there some hidden meaning to it?
No, no.
The text is just meant to make you laugh.
But... then...
Why have you written the book in such a strange way?
Well, it's to keep the critics busy for the next three hundred years...

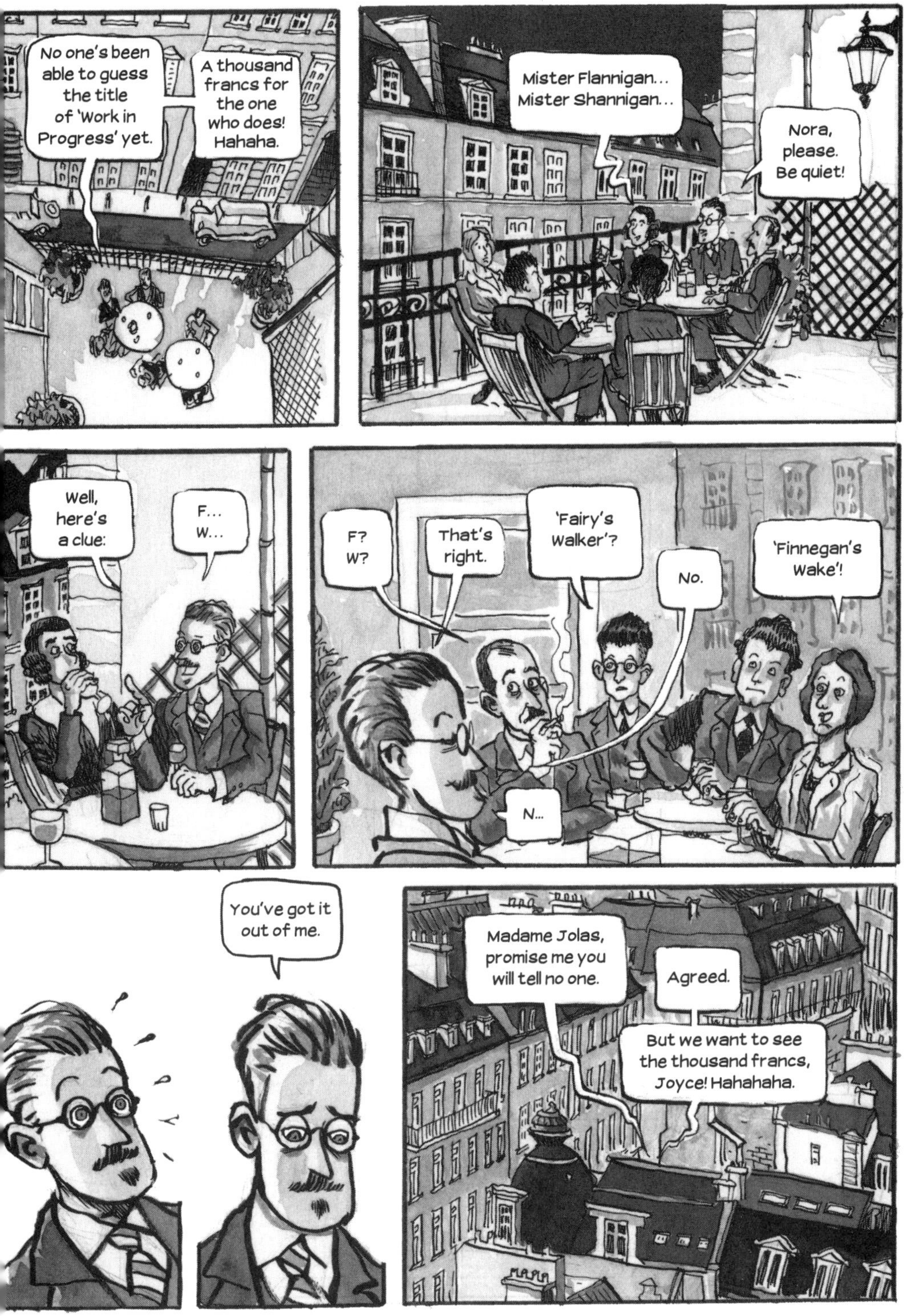
No one's been able to guess the title of 'Work in Progress' yet.
A thousand francs for the one who does! Hahaha.
Mister Flannigan... Mister Shannigan...
Nora, please. Be quiet!
Well, here's a clue:
F... W...
F? W?
That's right.
'Fairy's Walker'?
No.
'Finnegan's Wake'!
N...
You've got it out of me.
Madame Jolas, promise me you will tell no one.
Agreed.
But we want to see the thousand francs, Joyce! Hahahaha.

In 1937, Joyce just wanted to focus on his work, but the political situation got in the way.

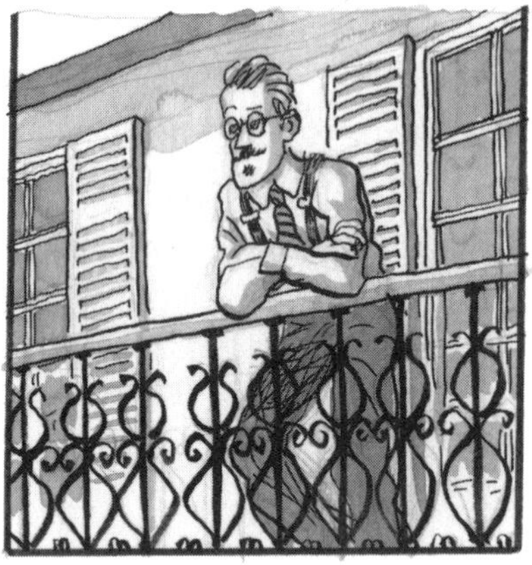

Translations of his works into Italian and German were cancelled. The Russians were also suspicious of him. Joyce took it lightly.

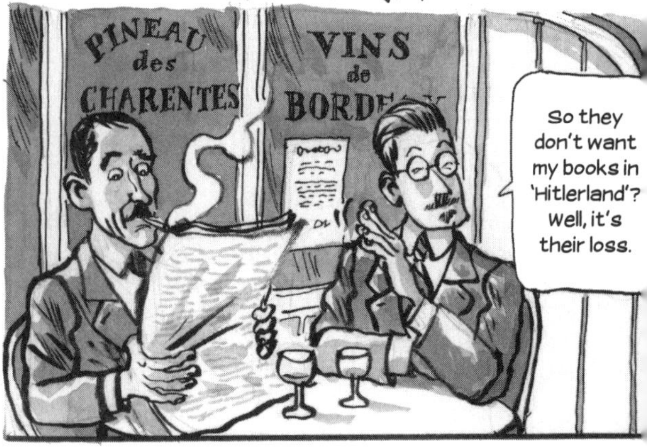
PINEAU des CHARENTES
VINS de
So they don't want my books in 'Hitlerland'? Well, it's their loss.

Joyce, who had been accused of disparaging the Jews in 'Ulysses', now showed that he couldn't turn a blind eye to what was happening.

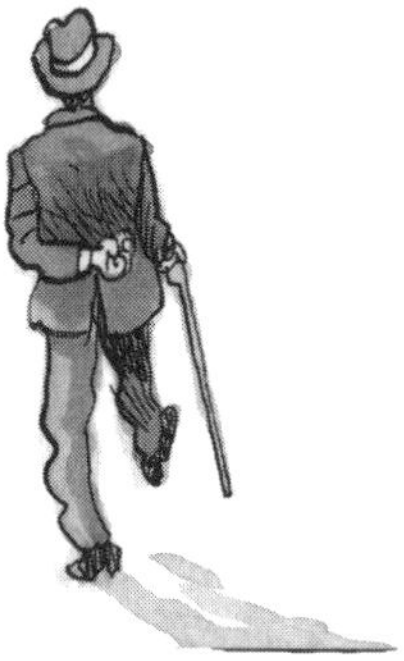

In 1938, he helped his friend Hermann Broch escape to England from annexed Vienna.

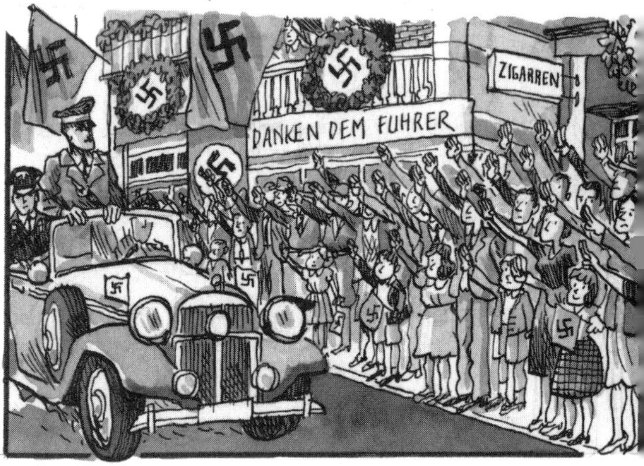
ZIGARREN
DANKEN DEM FUHRER

Thanks to Joyce, the son of his friend Charlotte Sauermann, and a nephew of another friend, Edmund Brauchbar, fled from Germany.

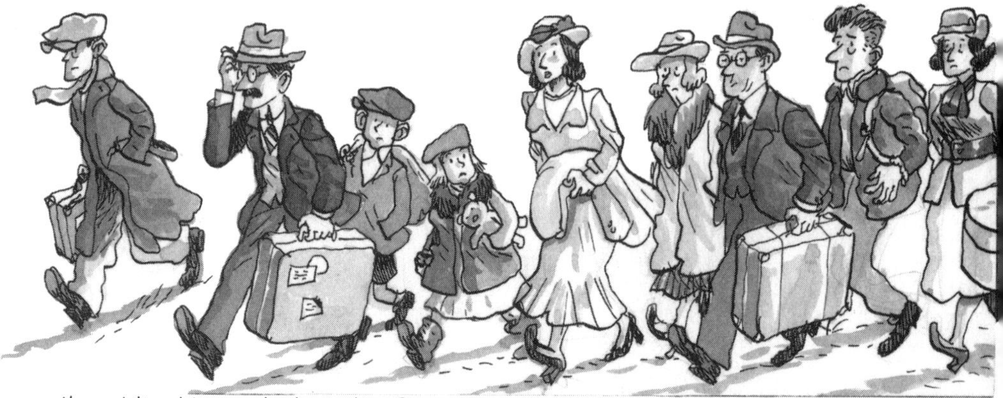

He mobilised his contacts in the French Ministry for Foreign Affairs, as well as Padraic Colum and the Irish Ministry of Justice, to get visas for sixteen more fugitives.

In September, with war threatening, James and Nora went to La Baule, to await the arrival of Lucia and other patients from the Maison de Santé.

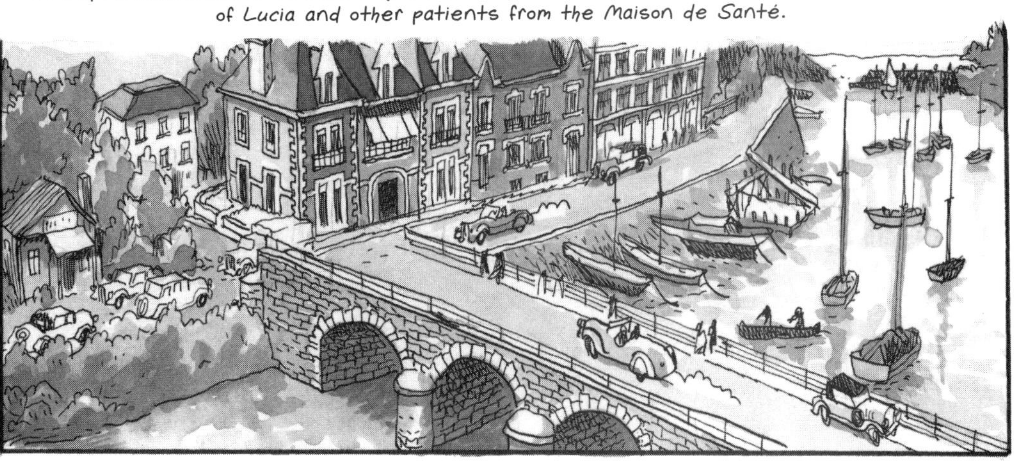

But the journey was cancelled, and the wait was in vain.

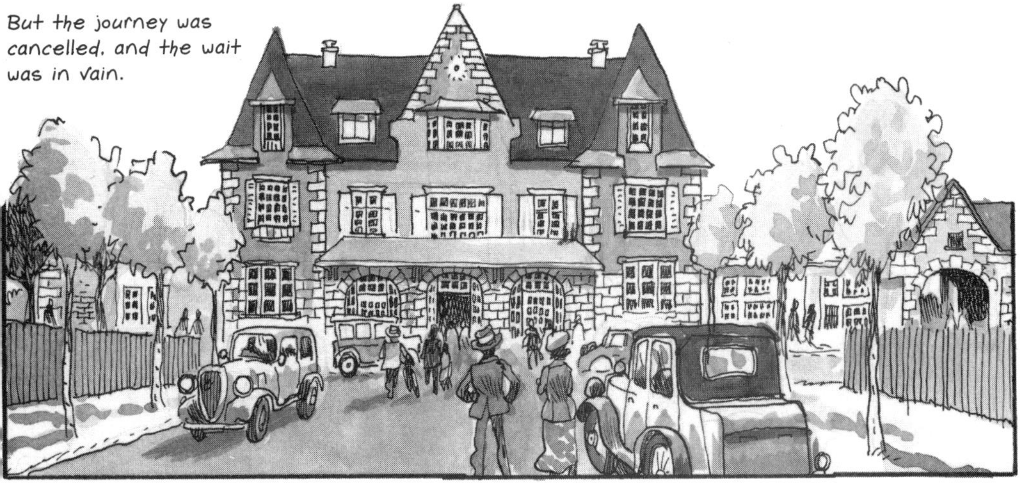

On 30 September, the Treaty of Munich was signed. Chamberlain, the British Prime Minister, flaunted his 'victory'.

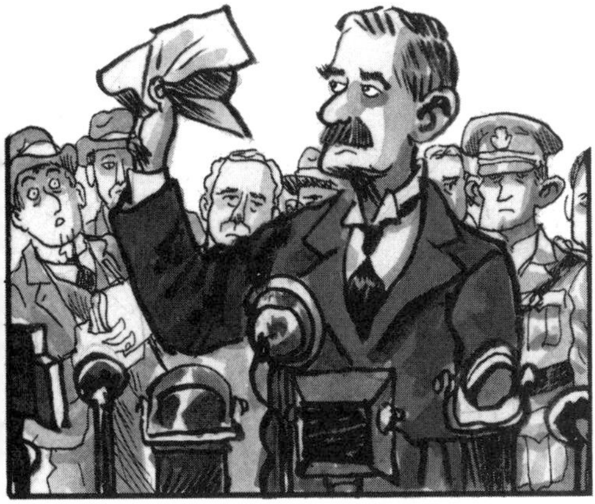

Joyce was not convinced.

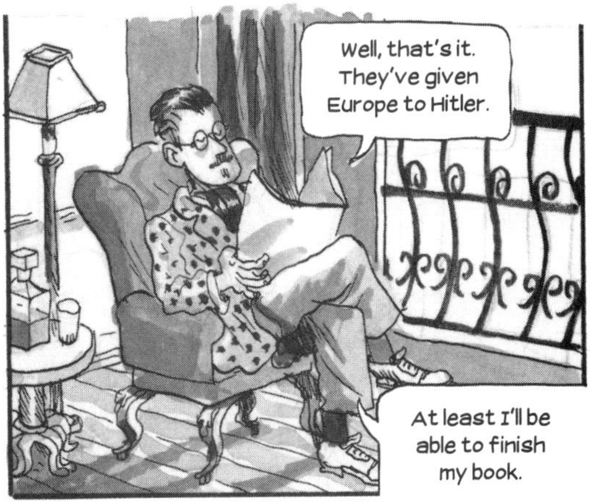

Well, that's it. They've given Europe to Hitler.
At least I'll be able to finish my book.

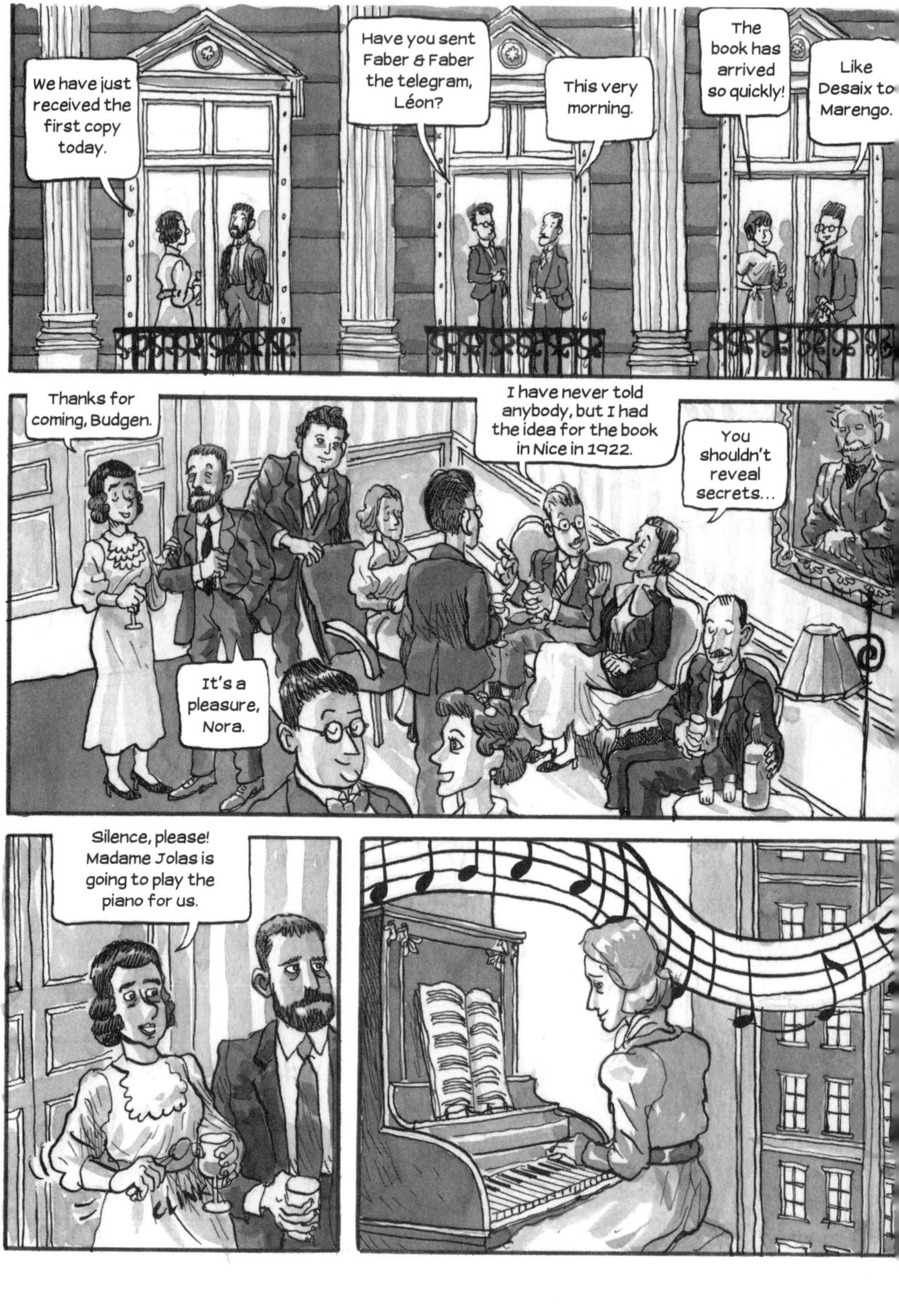
We have just received the first copy today.
Have you sent Faber & Faber the telegram, Léon?
This very morning.
The book has arrived so quickly!
Like Desaix to Marengo.
Thanks for coming, Budgen.
It's a pleasure, Nora.
I have never told anybody, but I had the idea for the book in Nice in 1922.
You shouldn't reveal secrets…
Silence, please! Madame Jolas is going to play the piano for us.
CLINK

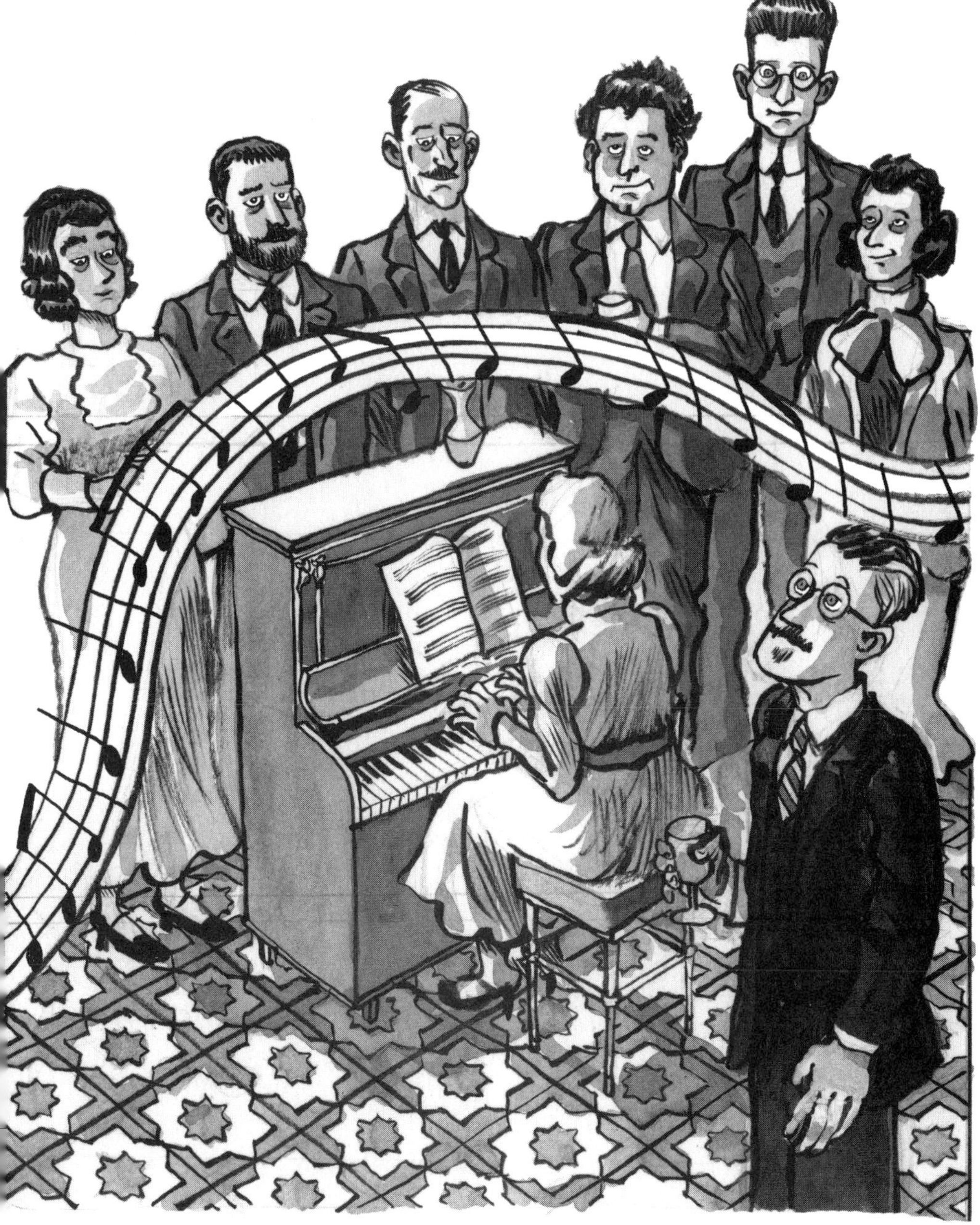

So, accompanied by music and Swiss wine, Joyce brought his last book to its conclusion, and embarked on the final stage of his life.
In the midst of darkness and gloom, this celebrator of life and inventor of jokes imposed his comic vision over the sadness and the misery of the times.

Chapter VII
The Last Journey

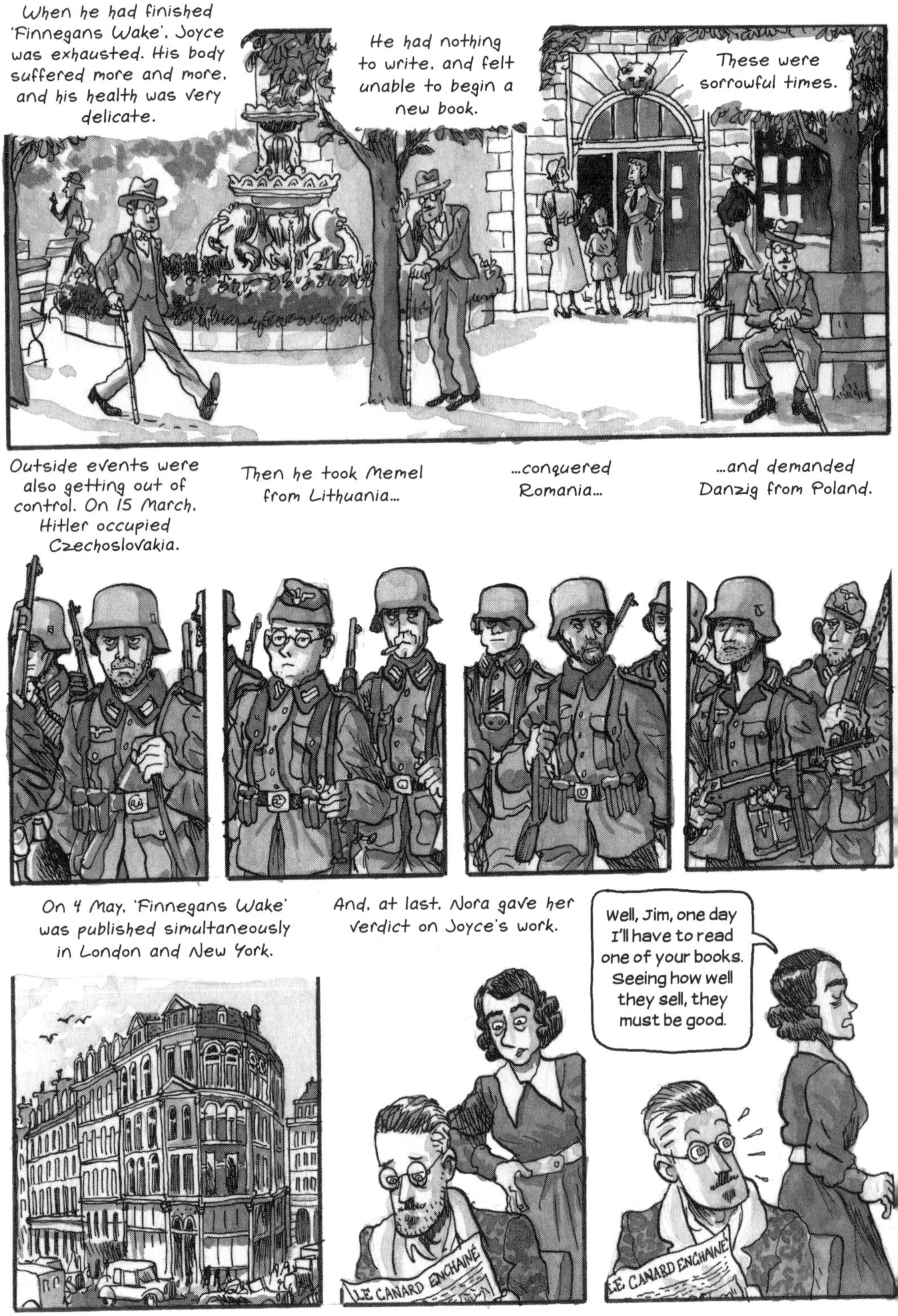
When he had finished 'Finnegans Wake', Joyce was exhausted. His body suffered more and more, and his health was very delicate.
He had nothing to write, and felt unable to begin a new book.
These were sorrowful times.
Outside events were also getting out of control. On 15 March, Hitler occupied Czechoslovakia.
Then he took Memel from Lithuania...
...conquered Romania...
...and demanded Danzig from Poland.
On 4 May, 'Finnegans Wake' was published simultaneously in London and New York.
And, at last, Nora gave her verdict on Joyce's work.
LE CANARD ENCHAINÉ
Well, Jim, one day I'll have to read one of your books. Seeing how well they sell, they must be good.
LE CANARD ENCHAINÉ

On 7 May 1937, Joyce read a surprising article in the English newspaper 'The Observer'.

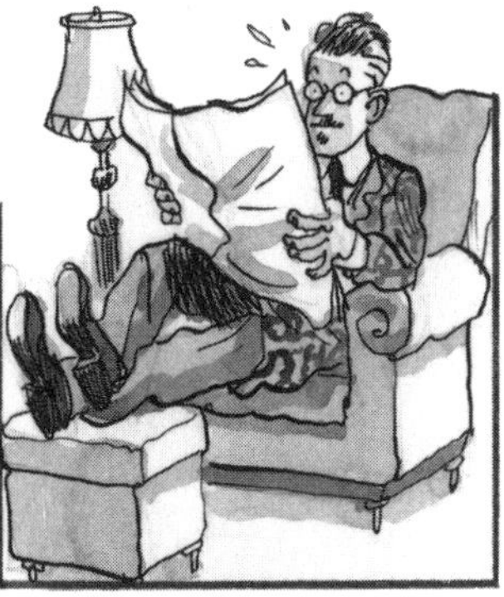

The article said that 'Finnegans Wake' was 'the most colossal leg-pull in literature', and recognised the 'indomitable spirit' of Joyce's humour.

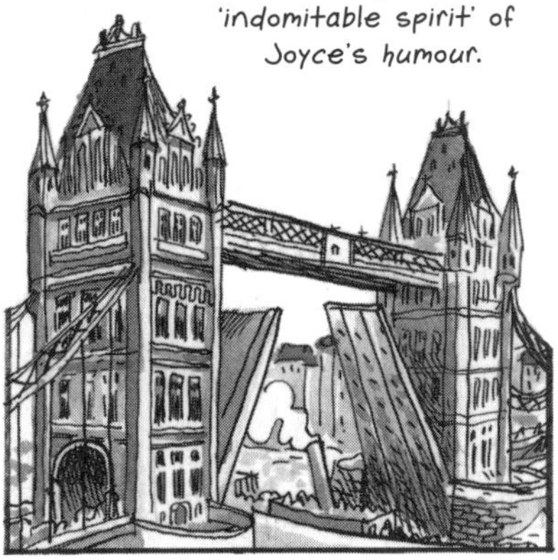

The author of the article was Oliver Gogarty, his old friend from Dublin.

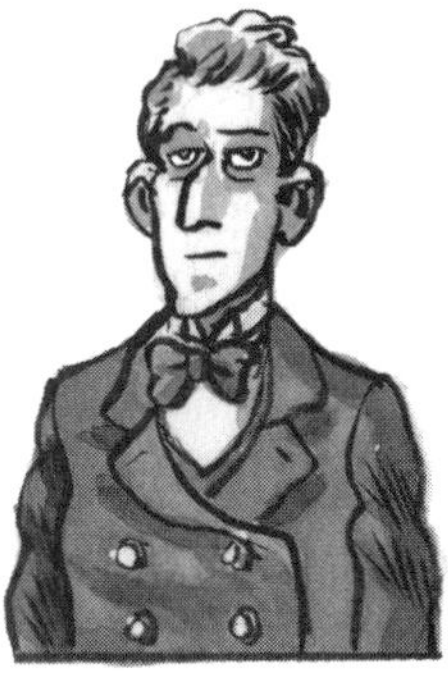

At last the patients of the Maison de Santé, including Lucia, were transferred urgently to La Baule.

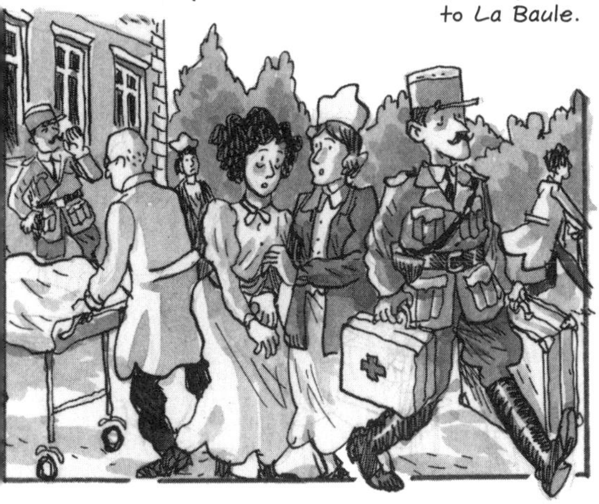

On 28 August, Joyce and Nora followed their daughter.

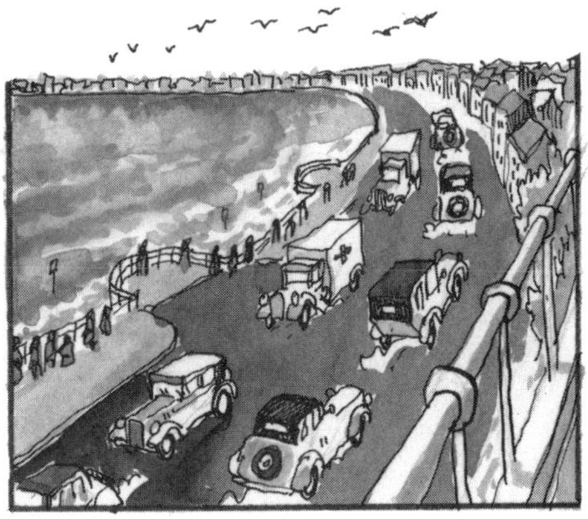

The tourist resort where the patients were rehoused was filling up with refugees and soldiers. Pre-war tension was growing.

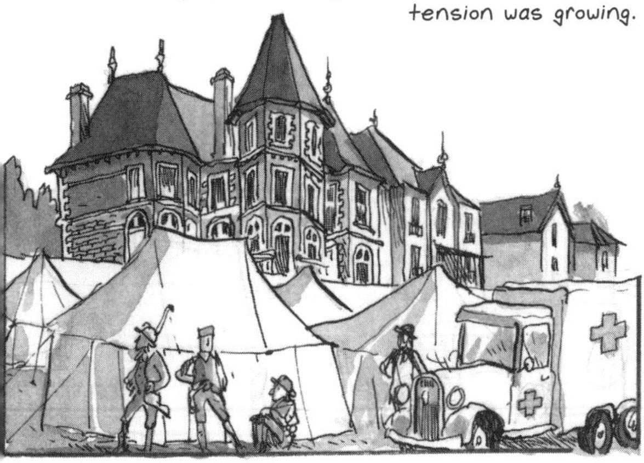

The depressed Joyce made friends with a British doctor, with whom he frequented the local cafés.

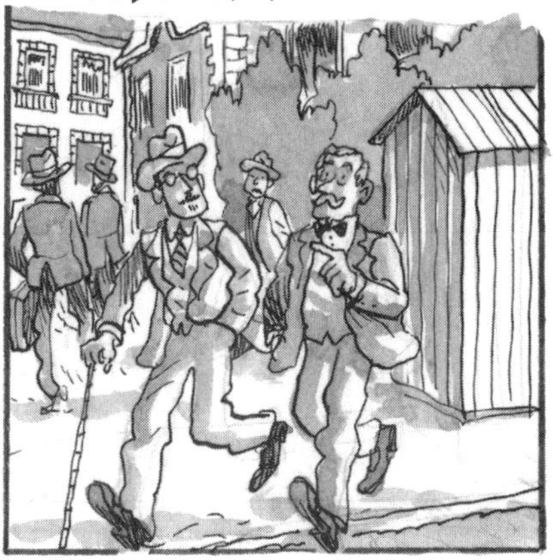

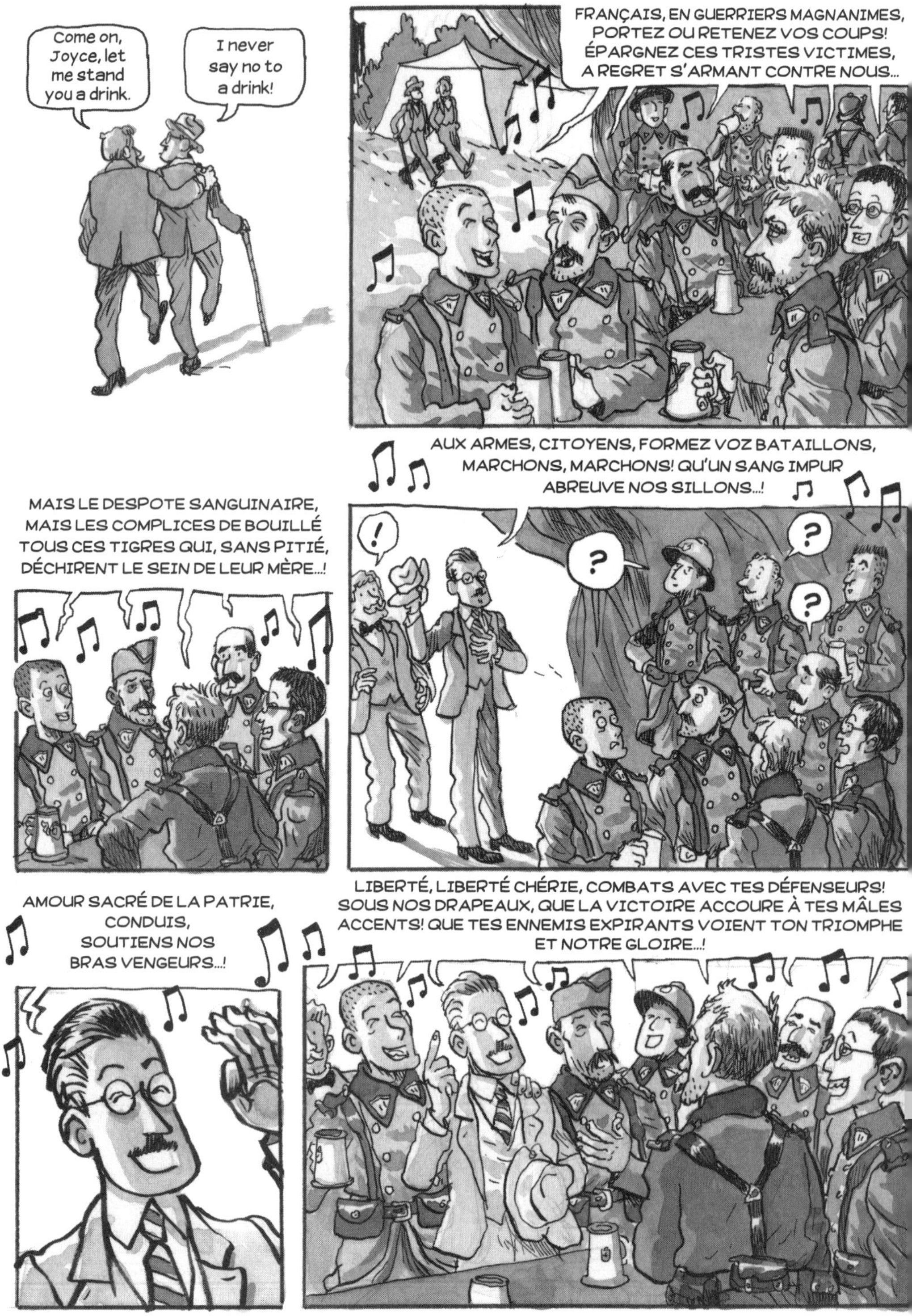

Come on, Joyce, let me stand you a drink.
I never say no to a drink!
FRANÇAIS, EN GUERRIERS MAGNANIMES, PORTEZ OU RETENEZ VOS COUPS! ÉPARGNEZ CES TRISTES VICTIMES, A REGRET S'ARMANT CONTRE NOUS...
MAIS LE DESPOTE SANGUINAIRE, MAIS LES COMPLICES DE BOUILLÉ TOUS CES TIGRES QUI, SANS PITIÉ, DÉCHIRENT LE SEIN DE LEUR MÈRE...!
AUX ARMES, CITOYENS, FORMEZ VOZ BATAILLONS, MARCHONS, MARCHONS! QU'UN SANG IMPUR ABREUVE NOS SILLONS...!
!
?
?
?
AMOUR SACRÉ DE LA PATRIE, CONDUIS, SOUTIENS NOS BRAS VENGEURS...!
LIBERTÉ, LIBERTÉ CHÉRIE, COMBATS AVEC TES DÉFENSEURS! SOUS NOS DRAPEAUX, QUE LA VICTOIRE ACCOURE À TES MÂLES ACCENTS! QUE TES ENNEMIS EXPIRANTS VOIENT TON TRIOMPHE ET NOTRE GLOIRE...!

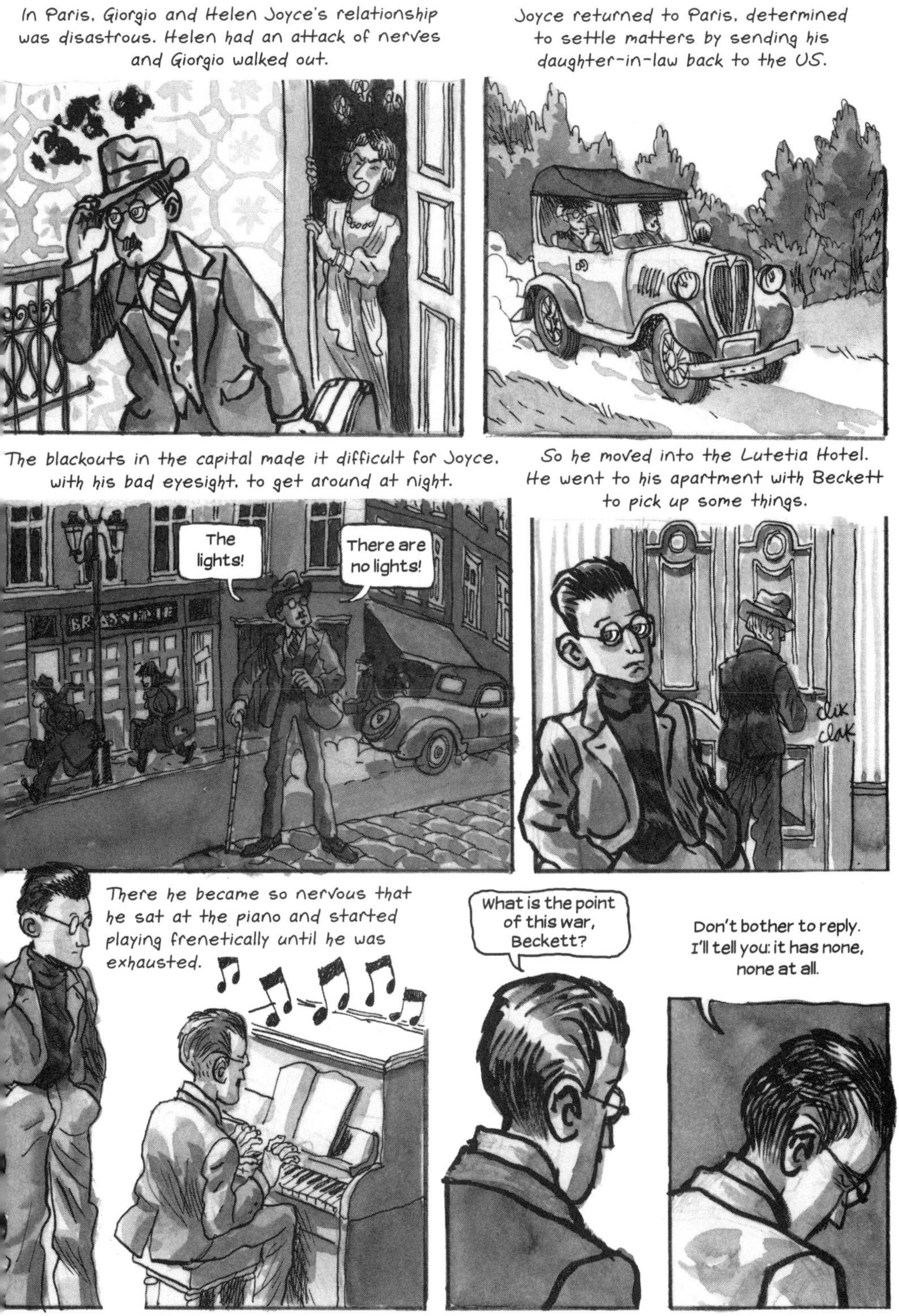
In Paris, Giorgio and Helen Joyce's relationship was disastrous. Helen had an attack of nerves and Giorgio walked out.
Joyce returned to Paris, determined to settle matters by sending his daughter-in-law back to the US.
The blackouts in the capital made it difficult for Joyce, with his bad eyesight, to get around at night.
The lights!
There are no lights!
So he moved into the Lutetia Hotel. He went to his apartment with Beckett to pick up some things.
clik
clak
There he became so nervous that he sat at the piano and started playing frenetically until he was exhausted.
What is the point of this war, Beckett?
Don't bother to reply. I'll tell you: it has none, none at all.

As far as Giorgio's marriage was concerned, Joyce was irrational. He blamed everything on Helen and wouldn't listen to reason.

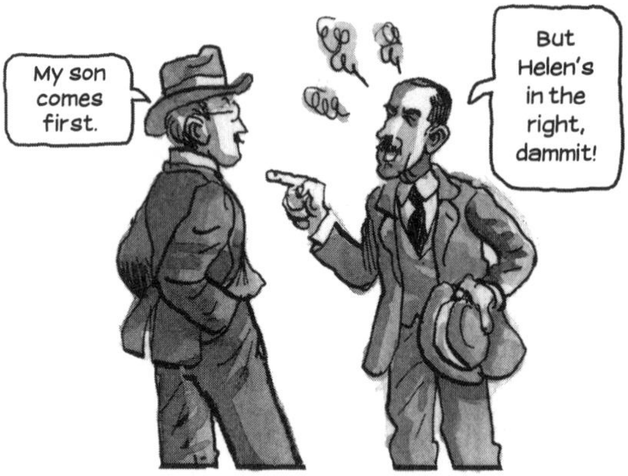
My son comes first.
But Helen's in the right, dammit!

His obstinacy even led him to break off his friendship with Paul Léon.

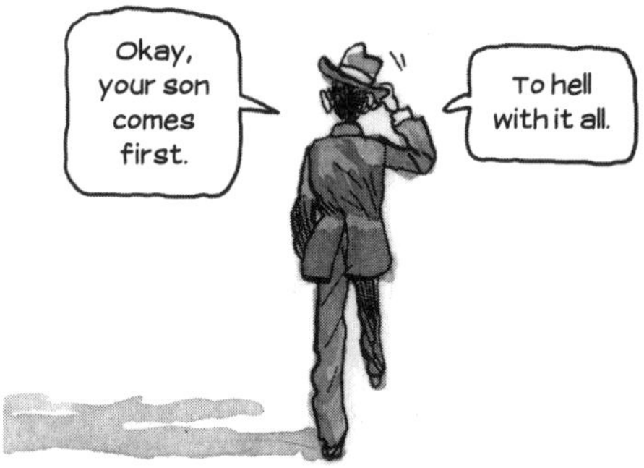
Okay, your son comes first.
To hell with it all.

On 24 December, the Joyces arrived in the small village of Saint Gérand-le-Puy, fleeing from the chaos of Paris.

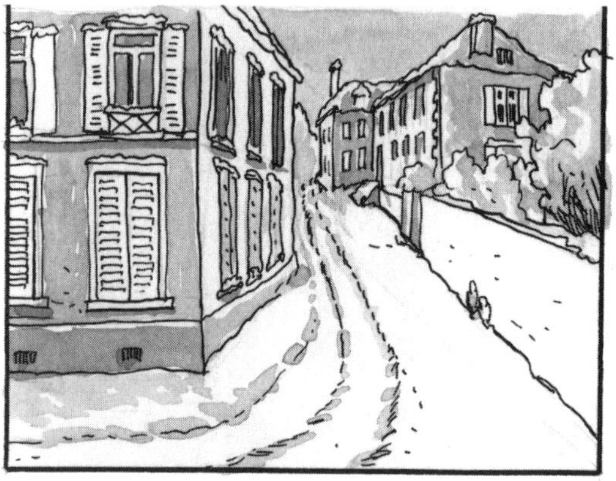

Joyce spent his days sleeping and walking. He was bored.

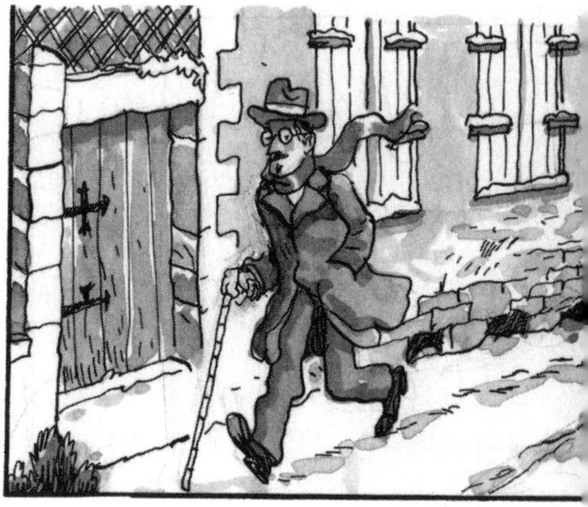

Sundays were the best. In the morning, with his grandson Stephen sitting on his bed, he smoked a 'Parisienne', and told stories.

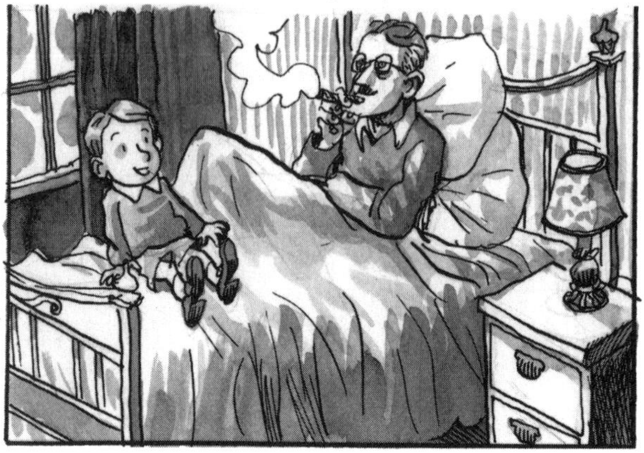

Stories of Ulysses.

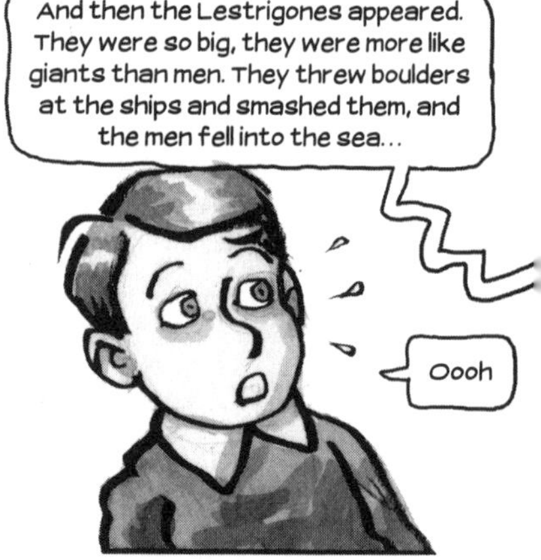
And then the Lestrigones appeared. They were so big, they were more like giants than men. They threw boulders at the ships and smashed them, and the men fell into the sea...
Oooh

On 9 April, Germany invaded Denmark and Norway. Then Belgium and Holland. And in May, they attacked France. By the twenty-eighth, Belgium had surrendered, and in June Italy entered the war.

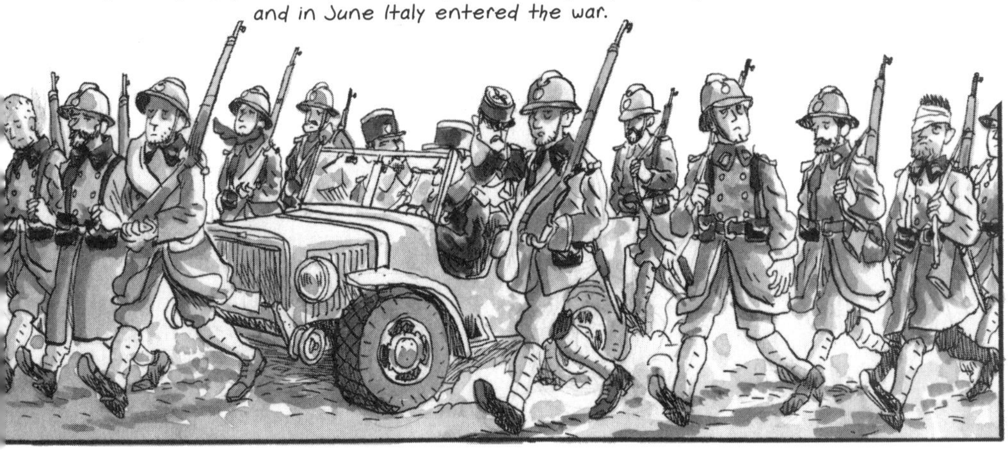

Paris fell on 14 June.

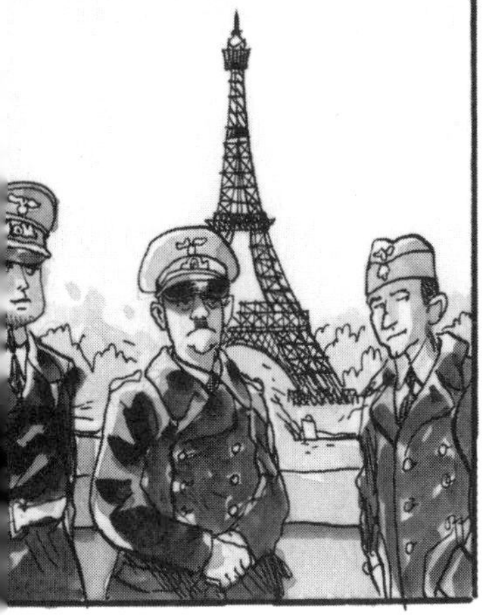

On 26 June, Giorgio reached St Gérand, escaping miraculously from the German occupation.

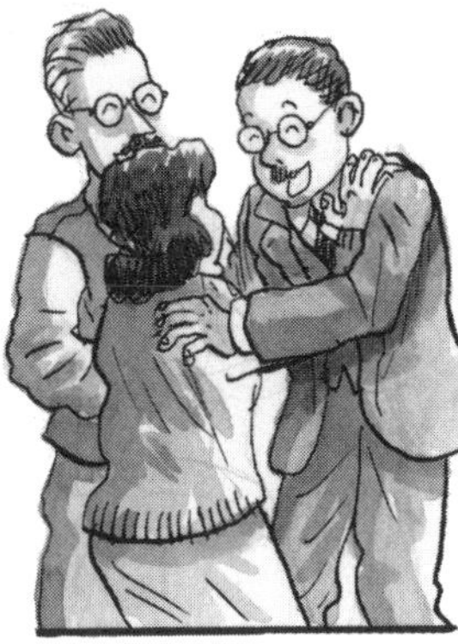

On the very same day, Paul Léon appeared in the village.

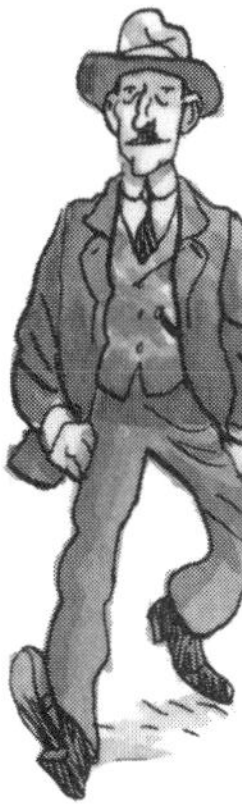

The two old friends had time to talk and become reconciled.

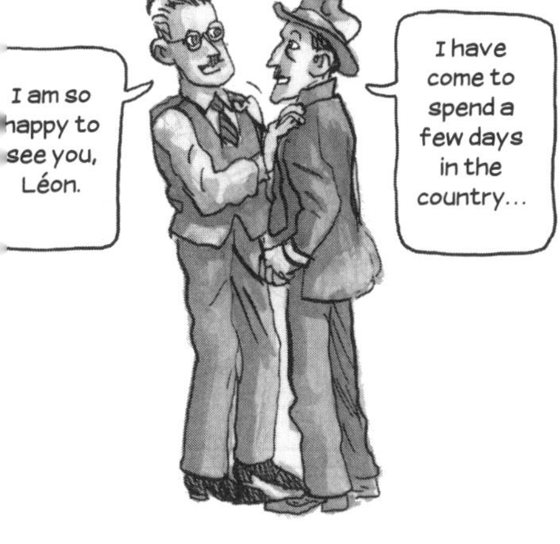
I am so happy to see you, Léon.
I have come to spend a few days in the country...

Afterwards, Léon returned to Paris. He was arrested by the Nazis and interned in a nearby prison. He was executed in 1942, because he was Jewish.

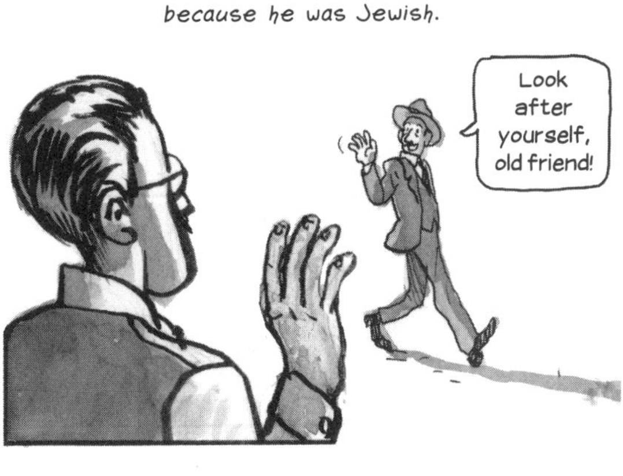
Look after yourself, old friend!

On 14 December, James, Nora, Giorgio and Stephen took a tra
in Saint-Germain-des-Fosses to Genevr

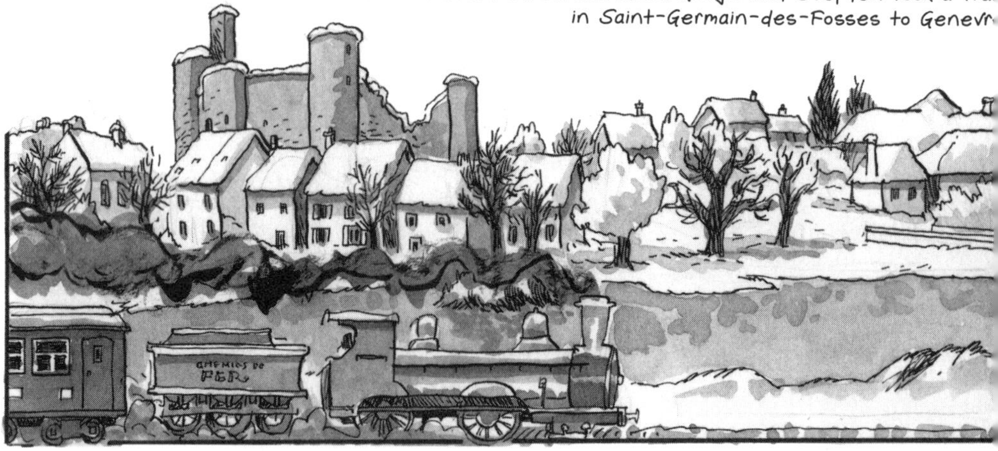

On the seventeenth, the Joyce family reached the Central Station in Zürich.

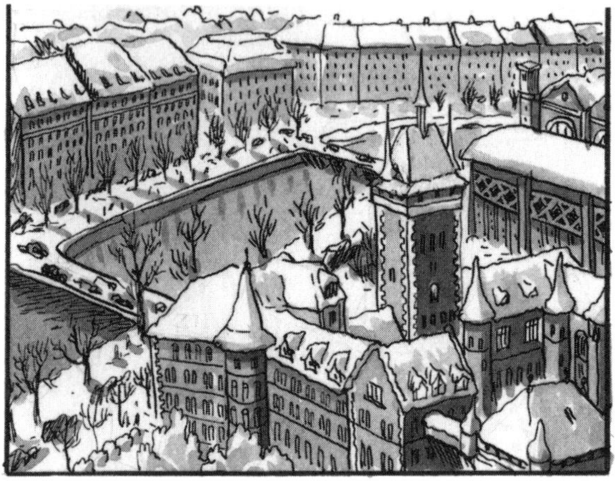

Joyce returned to the city which had welcomed him thirty-six years before, but now he was broken and ill.

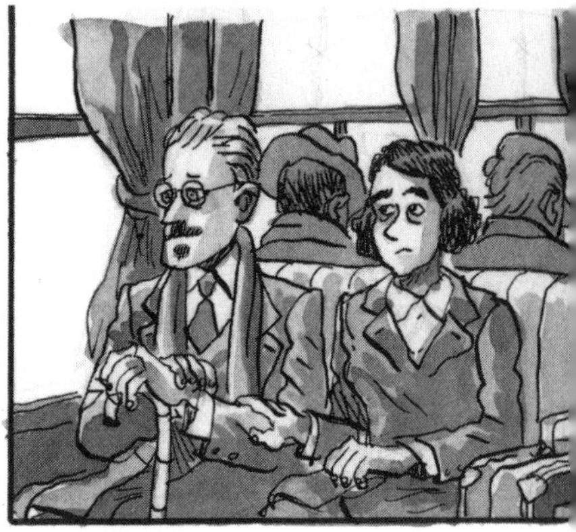

Too wise now to be arrogant, he had exhausted all his energy. He spent the afternoons with his grandson Stephen, as he played in the snow.

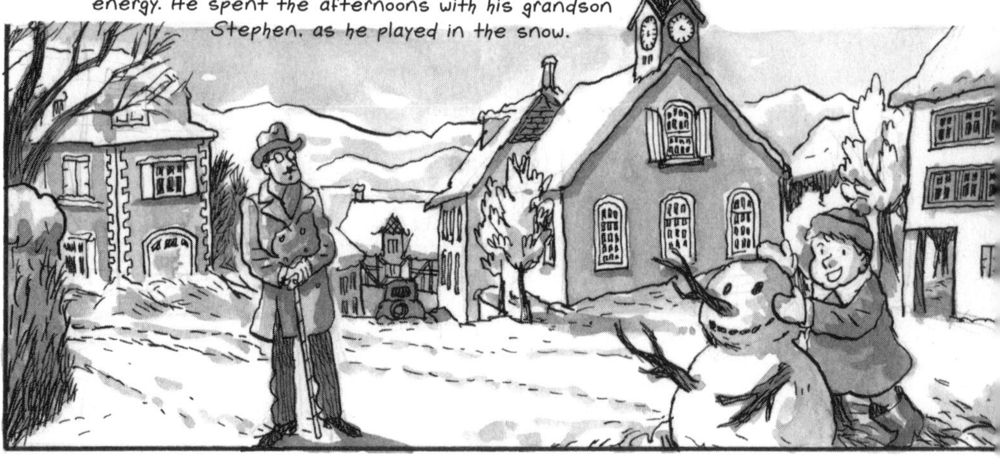

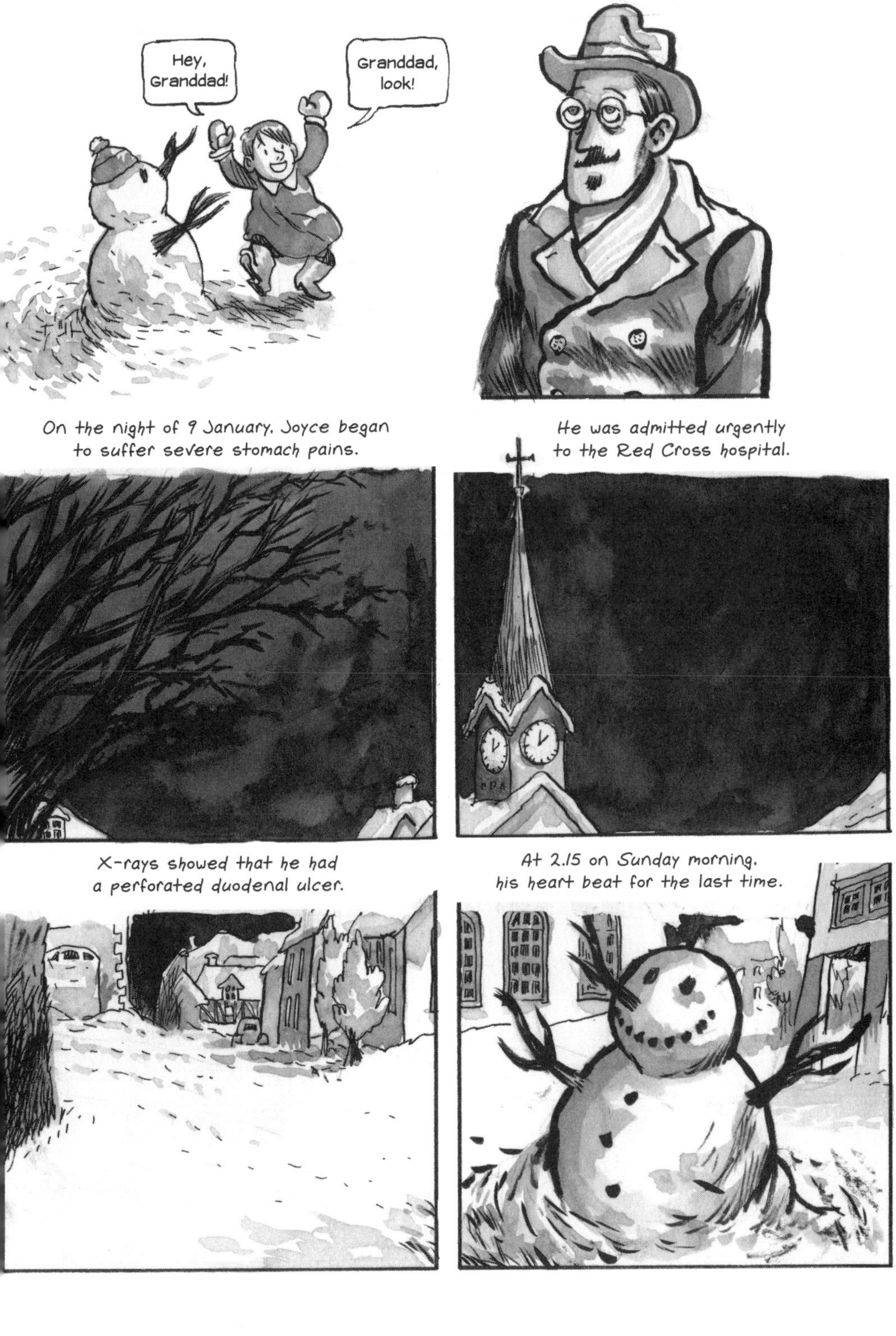
Hey, Granddad!
Granddad, look!
On the night of 9 January, Joyce began to suffer severe stomach pains.
He was admitted urgently to the Red Cross hospital.
X-rays showed that he had a perforated duodenal ulcer.
At 2.15 on Sunday morning, his heart beat for the last time.

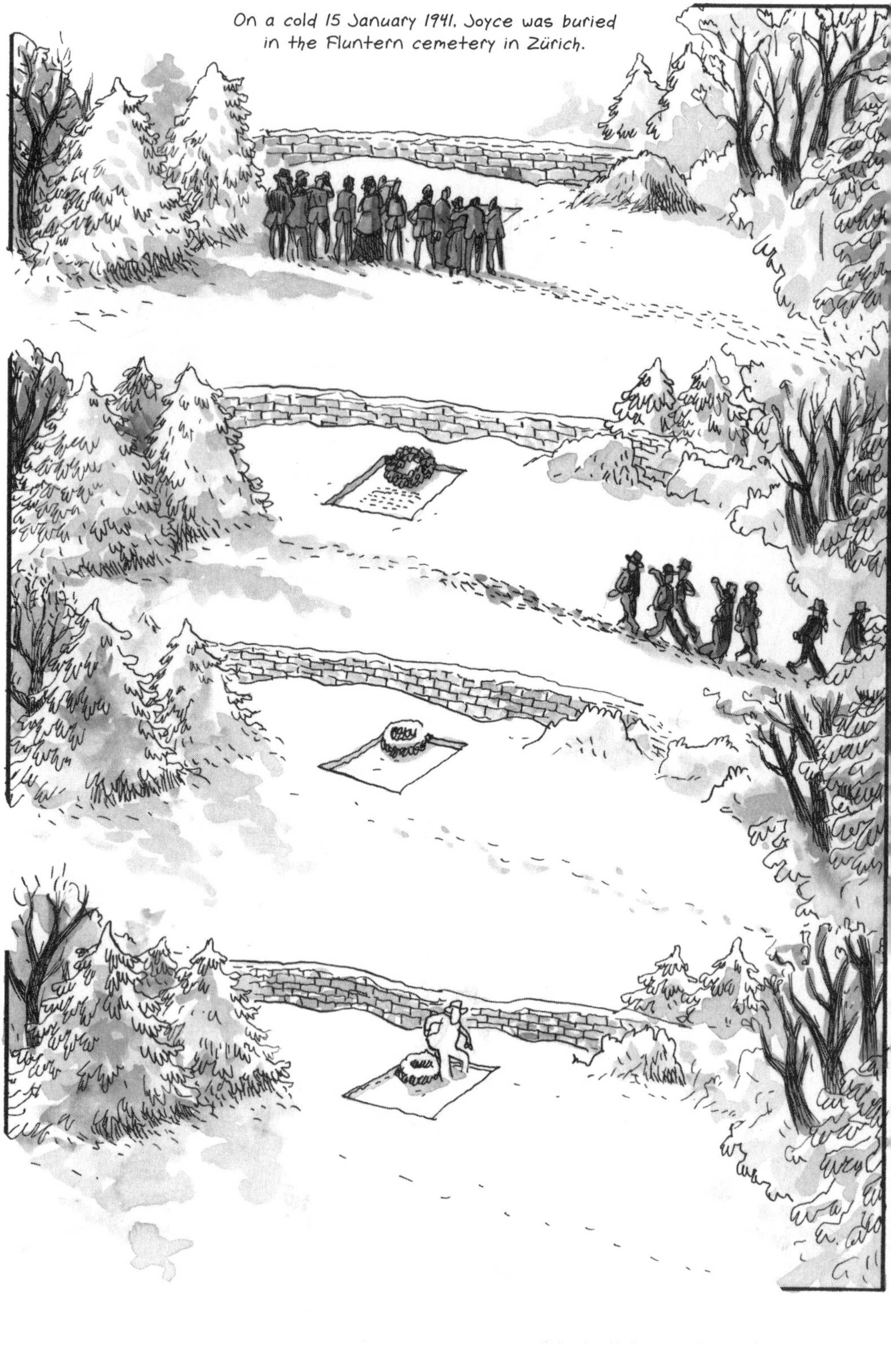
On a cold 15 January 1941, Joyce was buried
in the Fluntern cemetery in Zürich.

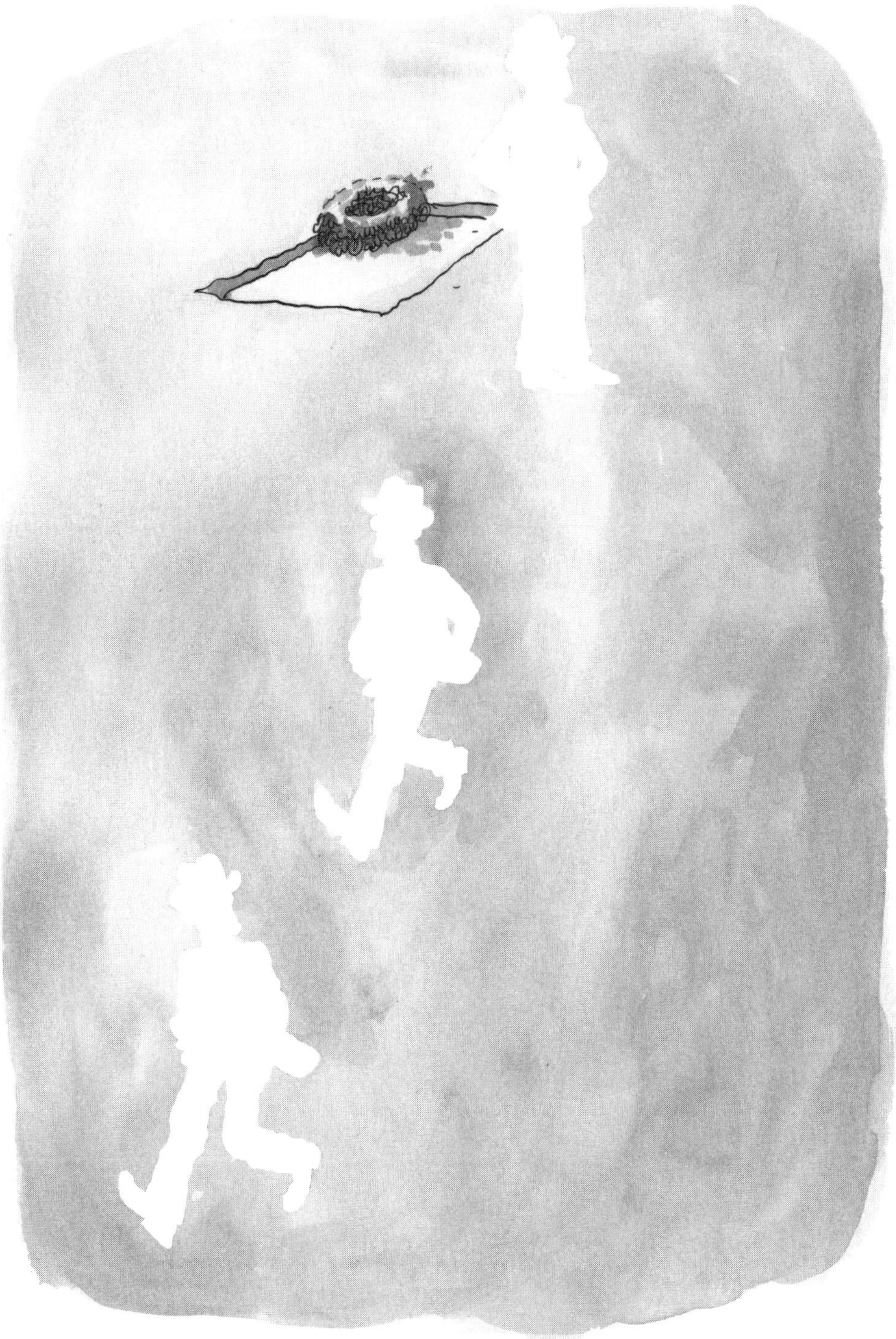

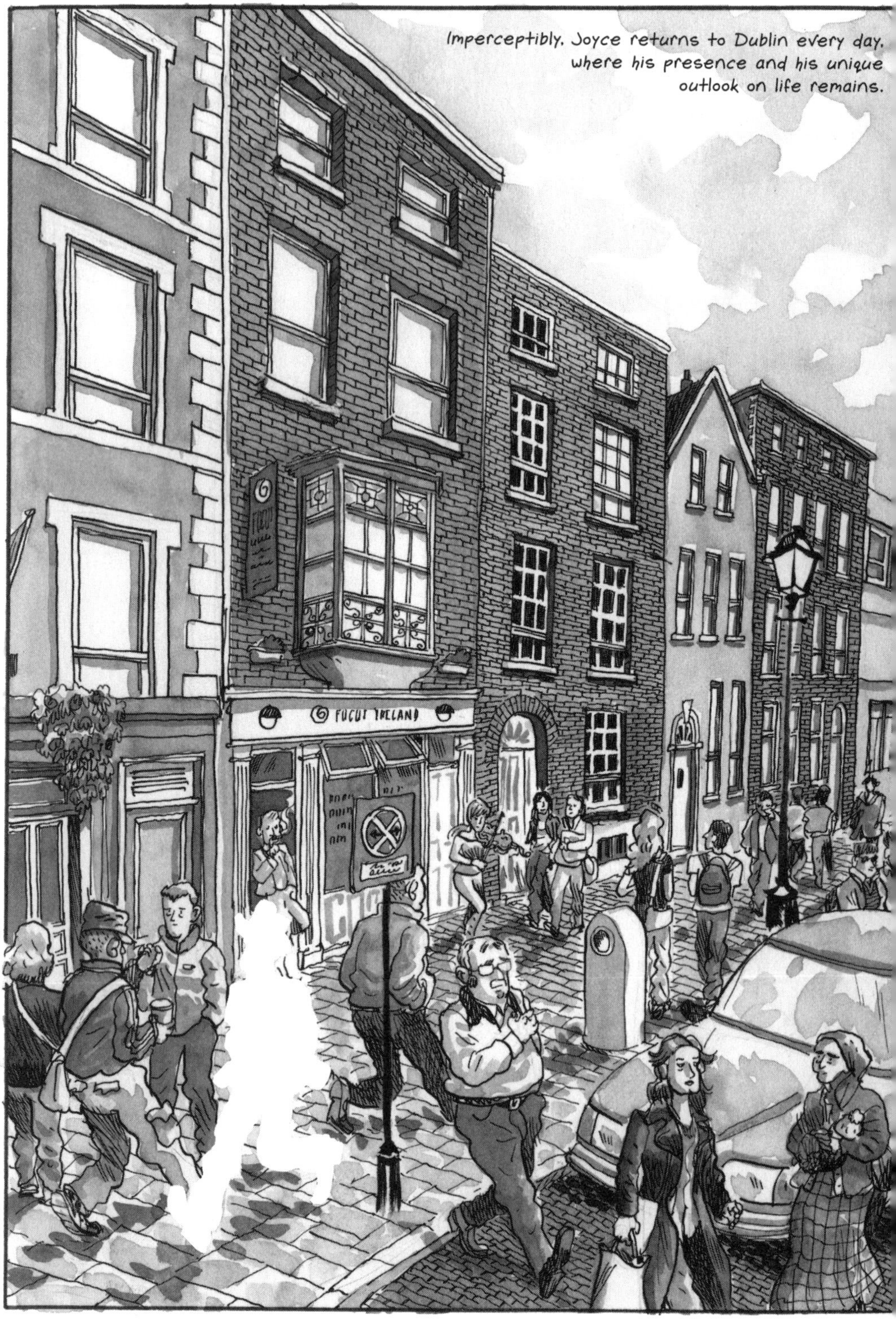
Imperceptibly, Joyce returns to Dublin every day, where his presence and his unique outlook on life remains.

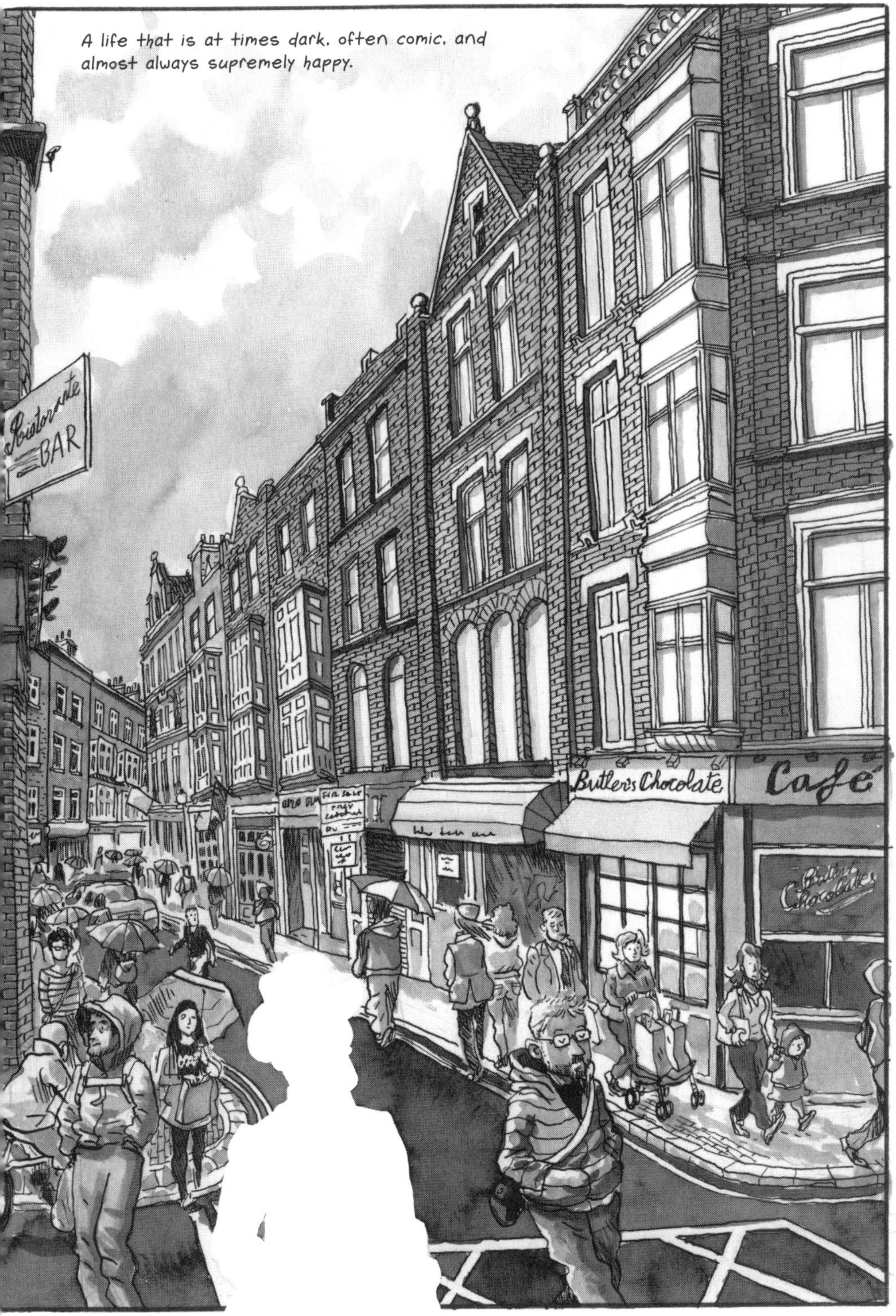
A life that is at times dark, often comic, and almost always supremely happy.
BAR
Butler's Chocolate
Café

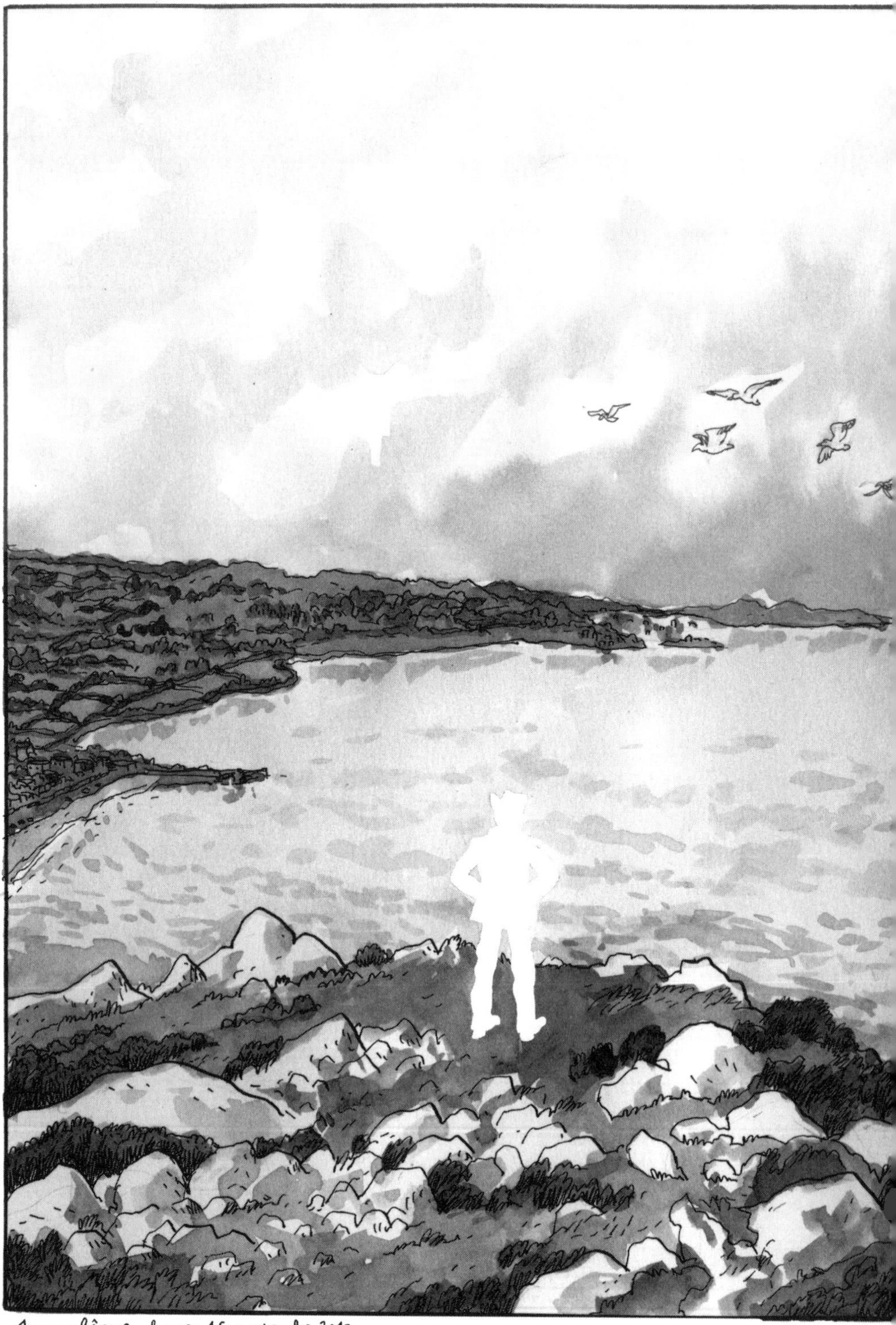

Angoulême, lunes 15 noviembre 2010

alfonso zapi

Dedication

To Michael, and to O'Brien Press.
Thanks for helping me to travel to his island
in the original language of Joyce.

Bibliography

James Joyce
Richard Ellmann
(Anagrama, 2002)

Joyce para principiantes
David Norris & Carl Flint
(Lectorum, 2007)

James Joyce's Ireland
David Pierce
(Yale University Press, 1992)

Faithful Departed
Kieran Hickey
(The Lilliput Press, 2004)

Alfonso Zapico, born in Blimea, Asturias, is a storyteller and freelance illustrator. He works on educational projects with the Principado de Asturias, as well as creating illustrations and design work for numerous advertising agencies, publishers and various institutions. He also creates illustrations for newspapers in Asturias.

His first published work was a historical comic book, *La Guerra del Profesor Bertenev,* which came out in the Franco-Flemish market (Paquet, 2006; Dolmen, 2009). His graphic novel *Café Budapest* (Astiberri, 2008; Timof, 2010) took the desolation of Budapest in 1947 as its starting point, and this was Zapico's first work to be published in Spain; the work was taken as a reflection of the chaos and barbarism of modernday Palestine.

Zapico's work has been published in comics in Spain, France, Belgium, Switzerland, Canada and Poland. He was awarded the Josep Toutain Prize at the Barcelona Comic Festival in 2010, and the Spanish National Comic Prize for *Dublinés,* his graphic biography of James Joyce.

He currently resides in France.

Previous publications include:

Café Budapest

La Guerra del Profesor Bertene

La Ruta Joyce

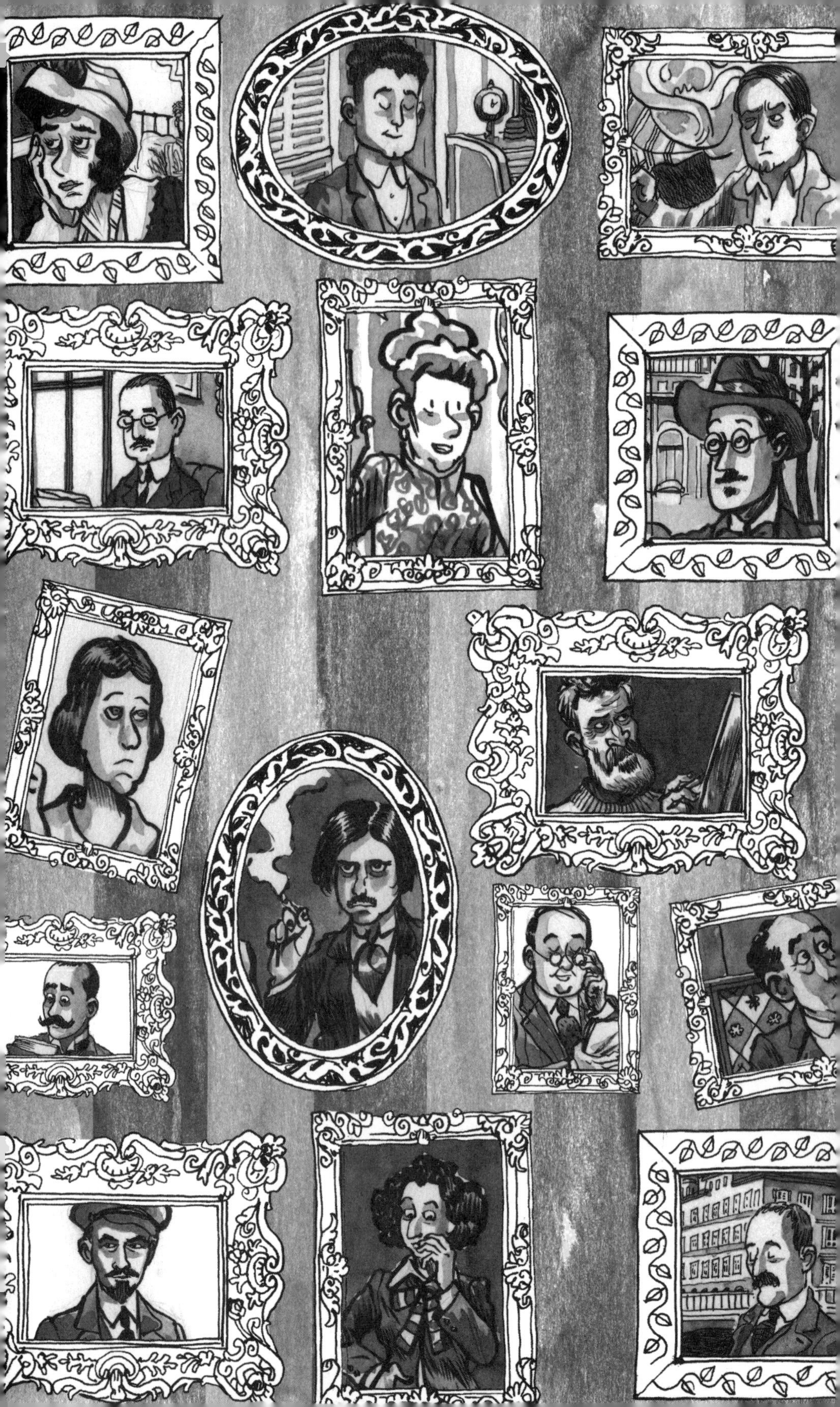

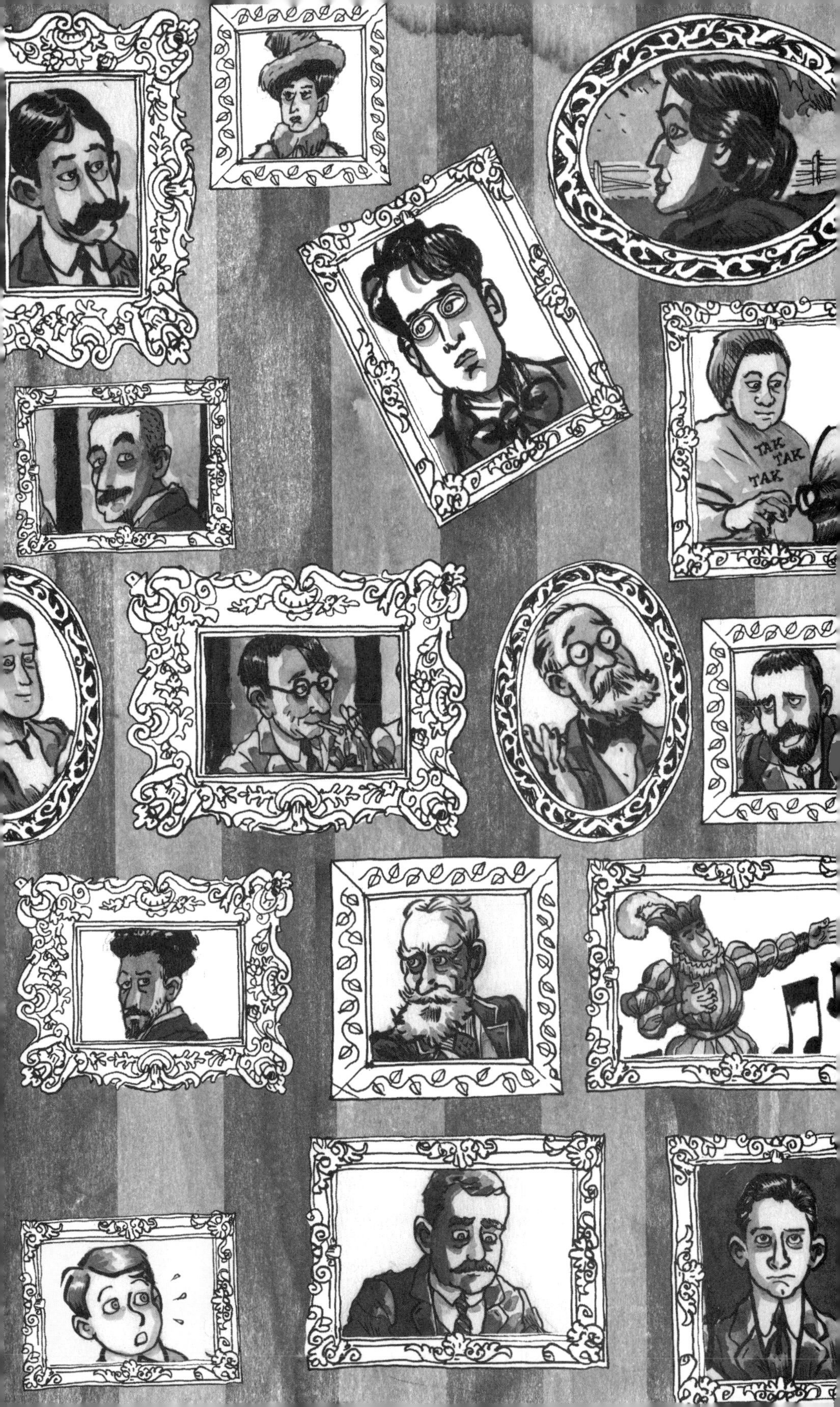
TAK
TAK
TAK